Namibia

Deanna Swaney

D1392091

LONELY PLANET PUBLICATIONS
Melbourne • Oakland • London • Paris

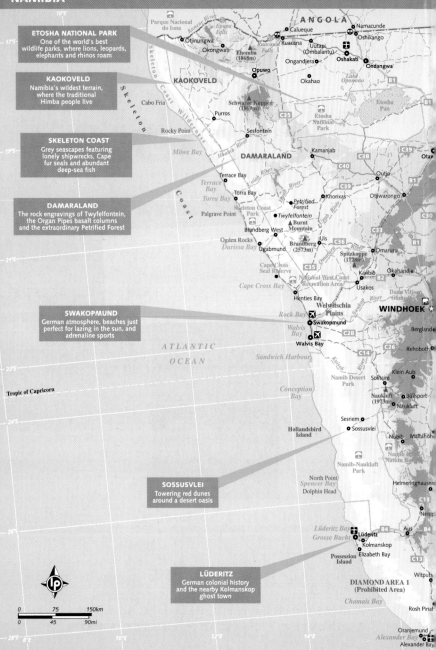

NAMIBIA

ETOSHA NATIONAL PARK
One of the world's best wildlife parks, where lions, leopards, elephants and rhinos roam

KAOKOVELD
Namibia's wildest terrain, where the traditional Himba people live

SKELETON COAST
Grey seascapes featuring lonely shipwrecks, Cape fur seals and abundant deep-sea fish

DAMARALAND
The rock engravings of Twyfelfontein, the Organ Pipes basalt columns and the extraordinary Petrified Forest

SWAKOPMUND
German atmosphere, beaches just perfect for lazing in the sun, and adrenaline sports

SOSSUSVLEI
Towering red dunes around a desert oasis

LÜDERITZ
German colonial history and the nearby Kolmanskop ghost town

ANGOLA

Parque Nacional do Iona
Kunene River
Epupa Falls
Otjinungwa
Okongwati
Calueque
Namacunde
Ruacana
Oshikango
Iuutapi (Ombalantu)
Oshakati
Ondangwa
Thomba (1868m)
Ruacana Falls
Ongandjera
Okahao
Lake Oponono
Opuwo
Okahao
B1
Cabo Fria
KAOKOVELD
Schwarze Kuppen (1360m)
Etosha Pan
Etosha National Park
B1
Purros
Okahao
C35
Rocky Point
Sesfontein
Mowe Bay
Kamanjab
C39
Otav
Terrace Bay
DAMARALAND
C40
Outjo
B1
Terrace Bay
Torra Bay
Khorixas
C39
Otjiwarongo
C30
Torra Bay
Skeleton Coast Park
Petrified Forest
Palgrave Point
Twyfelfontein
Burnt Mountain
C33
Brandberg West
Uis
C36
Ogden Rocks
Durissa Bay
Ugabmund
Brandberg (2573m)
Spitzkoppe (1728m)
Omaruru
B1
Cape Cross Seal Reserve
C35
Karibib
Okahandja
B2
Cape Cross Bay
National West Coast Recreation Area
Usakos
Dam Viljoen
Henties Bay
Welwitschia Plains
WINDHOEK
Rock Bay
Swakopmund
Bergland
Walvis Bay
C28
ATLANTIC OCEAN
Walvis Bay
C14
Rehoboth
Sandwich Harbour
C26
Namib Desert Park
Klein Aub
Conception Bay
Solitaire
Nauklüft (1973m)
Büllsport
Naukluft
Tropic of Capricorn
Sesriem
Sossusvlei
Hollandsbird Island
Nubib
Maltahöh
Namib-Naukluft Park
Namib Nature Re
North Point
Spencer Bay
Dolphin Head
Helmeringhausen
C13
Neisip
Lüderitz Bay
Grosse Bucht
Lüderitz
Aus
B4
Kolmanskop
Possession Island
Elizabeth Bay
C13
Witputs
DIAMOND AREA 1 (Prohibited Area)
Chamais Bay
Rosh Pinal
Oranjemund
Alexander Bay
Alexander Bay
Cliff Point

0 75 150km
0 45 90mi

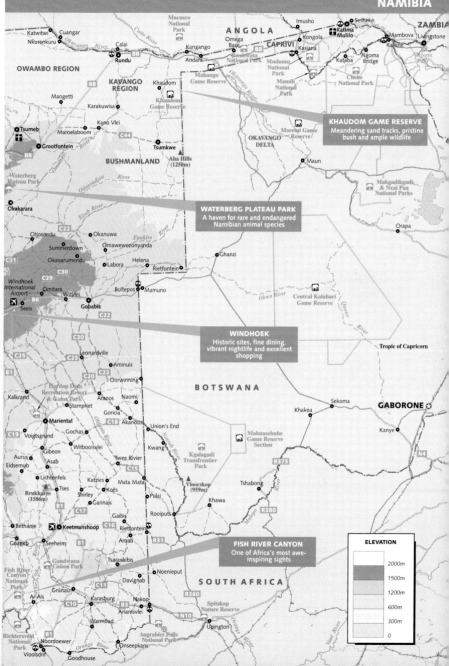

Namibia
1st edition – January 2002

Published by
Lonely Planet Publications Pty Ltd ABN 36 005 607 983
90 Maribyrnong St, Footscray, Victoria 3011, Australia

Lonely Planet offices
Australia Locked Bag 1, Footscray, Victoria 3011
USA 150 Linden St, Oakland, CA 94607
UK 10a Spring Place, London NW5 3BH
France 1 rue du Dahomey, 75011 Paris

Photographs
Many of the images in this guide are available for licensing from
Lonely Planet Images.
email: lpi@lonelyplanet.com.au
Web site: www.lonelyplanetimages.com

Front cover photograph
A Himba baby being carried on its mother's back (Adrien Vadrot)

Wildlife Guide title page photograph
Cheetah (Dennis Jones)

ISBN 1 74059 042 2

Printed by SNP SPrint (M) Sdn Bhd
Printed in Malaysia

Contents – Text

2 Contents – Text

Contents – Maps

The Author

Deanna Swaney

After completing university studies, Deanna made a shoestring circuit of Europe and has been addicted to travel ever since. Despite an erstwhile career in computer programming, she managed intermittent forays away from the corporate bustle of midtown Anchorage, Alaska, and at first opportunity made a break for South America, where she wrote Lonely Planet's guide to Bolivia. Subsequent travels steered her through a course of paradise destinations and resulted in six more first editions of Lonely Planet travel guides: *Tonga*; *Samoa*; *Iceland, Greenland & the Faroe Islands*; *Zimbabwe, Botswana & Namibia*; *Norway* and *The Arctic*. She has also coauthored the *Brazil* and *Mauritius, Réunion & Seychelles* guidebooks, updated *Madagascar & Comoros* and *Russia, Ukraine & Belarus*, and contributed to shoestring guides to *Africa*, *South America* and *Scandinavia*.

FROM DEANNA

Thanks to Aulden and Rachael Harlech-Jones and Crazy Kudu Mike Godfrey and Hannah.

Similarly, I'm indebted to Frenus, Sybille and Rafael Rorich at Alternative Space in Swakopmund; Dom at Enyandi Tours; Willie, for expert guiding services in the Kaokoveld; Val and Wynand Peypers at n'Kwasi Lodge, Rundu; Rob and Marianne Lowe at Zebra River; Dave at Wilderness Safaris; Louis and Riëtte Fourie, for their boundless hospitality in Keetmanshoop and Fish River; Detlef and Sandra at Oak Lodge in Cape Town; Genene Park at Access Car Hire, Cape Town; Herman and Louise at Wolwedans; Jackie at Chameleon Safaris; Liz and Allan at Wild Dog Safaris; Sam McConnell for help with Bushmanland; Willem and Piet Swiegers at Klein Aus; and Dr Fred Peterson, North Carolina, for careful checking of the Health section. Kudos also to Jackey, Bernard, Aulden and Rachael, for assistance with language information.

Also helpful were M Theart at Ngandu in Rundu; Kate, Philippa, John, Christine, Joey, Alyssa, Rolf, Vita, Diane, Chris, Shadrech, Festus and the whole Wild Bunch/staff at the Skeleton Coast Wilderness Lodge; Marion Schelke in Lüderitz; Samuel Egger and Mr Einstein in Swakopmund; Ernst at Büllsport; and Patrick at Campfire Safaris. Happy future travels to Ward Hulbert and Gina Holloman.

Thanks to Fred and Jennifer Peterson (North Carolina); Nancy Keller (Forestville); Zehava Bakeman (Tarzana & the universe); Pete and Christine (Austria); Resi and Jean (Netherlands); Keith and Holly Hawkings (Anchorage); Dean, Kim, Lauren, Jennifer and Earl Swaney and Cyndee Snyder (Fresno); Rodney, Heather, Bradley and 'forthcoming' Leacock (Colorado Springs); and Dave Dault, who holds the fort back home.

This Book

The first edition of *Zimbabwe, Botswana & Namibia* was written by Deanna Swaney and Myra Shackley. Deanna subsequently updated the next two editions. This book was based on the Namibia chapter of *Zimbabwe, Botswana & Namibia*, with Deanna Swaney expanding and updating the text.

From the Publisher

This first edition of *Namibia* was produced in Lonely Planet's Melbourne office. Justin Flynn coordinated the editing, with a great deal of editing and proofing help from Susan Holtham, Jenny Mullaly, Nancy Ianni and Shelley Muir. The mapping and design were coordinated by Shahara Ahmed, with assistance from Sarah Sloane, Jody Whiteoak, Maree Styles, Anna Judd, Hunor Csutoros, Yvonne Bischofberger and Huw Fowles.

Sean Pywell compiled the Wildlife Guide, based on text by Luke Hunter and Andy MacColl. Thanks to Emma Koch for compiling the Language chapter, Hunor Csutoros for the climate charts and David Else for his part in the Excursion to Victoria Falls chapter. Jenny Jones designed the cover and Mark Germanchis helped out with all things Quark. Thanks to Annie Horner and Brett Pascoe from Lonely Planet Images for organising the photographs and Martin Harris for drawing the chapter end illustration.

Kudos to Hilary Ericksen, Katie Butterworth and Adriana Mammarella for their assistance in checking artwork, and to Kerryn Burgess, John Hinman and Rodney Zandbergs for helping with last-minute corrections. Finally, thanks to our 'seniors', Kim Hutchins and Vince Patton, for their hard work, early mornings and late nights.

THANKS
Many thanks to the travellers who used the last edition of *Zimbabwe, Botswana & Namibia* and wrote to us with helpful hints, advice and interesting anecdotes. Your names appear on pages 324 & 325 of this book.

Foreword

ABOUT LONELY PLANET GUIDEBOOKS

The story begins with a classic travel adventure: Tony and Maureen Wheeler's 1972 journey across Europe and Asia to Australia. Useful information about the overland trail did not exist at that time, so Tony and Maureen published the first Lonely Planet guidebook to meet a growing need.

From a kitchen table, then from a tiny office in Melbourne (Australia), Lonely Planet has become the largest independent travel publisher in the world, an international company with offices in Melbourne, Oakland (USA), London (UK) and Paris (France).

Today Lonely Planet guidebooks cover the globe. There is an ever-growing list of books and there's information in a variety of forms and media. Some things haven't changed. The main aim is still to help make it possible for adventurous travellers to get out there – to explore and better understand the world.

At Lonely Planet we believe travellers can make a positive contribution to the countries they visit – if they respect their host communities and spend their money wisely. Since 1986 a percentage of the income from each book has been donated to aid projects and human rights campaigns.

Updates Lonely Planet thoroughly updates each guidebook as often as possible. This usually means there are around two years between editions, although for more unusual or more stable destinations the gap can be longer. Check the imprint page (following the colour map at the beginning of the book) for publication dates.

Between editions up-to-date information is available in two free newsletters – the paper *Planet Talk* and email *Comet* (to subscribe, contact any Lonely Planet office) – and on our Web site at www.lonelyplanet.com. The *Upgrades* section of the Web site covers a number of important and volatile destinations and is regularly updated by Lonely Planet authors. *Scoop* covers news and current affairs relevant to travellers. And, lastly, the *Thorn Tree* bulletin board and *Postcards* section of the site carry unverified, but fascinating, reports from travellers.

Correspondence The process of creating new editions begins with the letters, postcards and emails received from travellers. This correspondence often includes suggestions, criticisms and comments about the current editions. Interesting excerpts are immediately passed on via newsletters and the Web site, and everything goes to our authors to be verified when they're researching on the road. We're keen to get more feedback from organisations or individuals who represent communities visited by travellers.

Lonely Planet gathers information for everyone who's curious about the planet – and especially for those who explore it first-hand. Through guidebooks, phrasebooks, activity guides, maps, literature, newsletters, image library, TV series and Web site we act as an information exchange for a worldwide community of travellers.

6

Research Authors aim to gather sufficient practical information to enable travellers to make informed choices and to make the mechanics of a journey run smoothly. They also research historical and cultural background to help enrich the travel experience and allow travellers to understand and respond appropriately to cultural and environmental issues.

Authors don't stay in every hotel because that would mean spending a couple of months in each medium-sized city and, no, they don't eat at every restaurant because that would mean stretching belts beyond capacity. They do visit hotels and restaurants to check standards and prices, but feedback based on readers' direct experiences can be very helpful.

Many of our authors work undercover, others aren't so secretive. None of them accept freebies in exchange for positive write-ups. And none of our guidebooks contain any advertising.

Production Authors submit their manuscripts and maps to offices in Australia, USA, UK or France. Editors and cartographers – all are experienced travellers themselves – then begin the process of assembling the pieces. When the book finally hits the shops, some things are already out of date, we start getting feedback from readers and the process begins again …

WARNING & REQUEST

Things change – prices go up, schedules change, good places go bad and bad places go bankrupt – nothing stays the same. So, if you find things better or worse, recently opened or long since closed, please tell us and help make the next edition even more accurate and useful. We genuinely value all the feedback we receive. A well-travelled team reads and acknowledges every letter, postcard and email and ensures that every morsel of information finds its way to the appropriate authors, editors and cartographers for verification.

Everyone who writes to us will find their name listed in the next edition of the appropriate guidebook. They will also receive the latest issue of *Planet Talk*, our quarterly printed newsletter, or *Comet*, our monthly email newsletter. Subscriptions to both newsletters are free. The very best contributions will be rewarded with a free guidebook.

We may edit, reproduce and incorporate your comments in all Lonely Planet products, such as guidebooks, Web sites and digital products, so let us know if you don't want your comments reproduced or your name acknowledged.

Send all correspondence to the Lonely Planet office closest to you:

Australia: Locked Bag 1, Footscray, Victoria 3122
USA: 150 Linden St, Oakland, CA 94607
UK: 10a Spring Place, London NW5 3BH
France: 1 rue du Dahomey, 75011 Paris

Or email us at: talk2us@lonelyplanet.com.au

For news, views and updates see our Web site: www.lonelyplanet.com

HOW TO USE A LONELY PLANET GUIDEBOOK

The best way to use a Lonely Planet guidebook is any way you choose. At Lonely Planet we believe the most memorable travel experiences are often those that are unexpected, and the finest discoveries are those you make yourself. Guidebooks are not intended to be used as if they provide a detailed set of infallible instructions!

Contents All Lonely Planet guidebooks follow roughly the same format. The Facts about the Destination chapters or sections give background information ranging from history to weather. Facts for the Visitor gives practical information on issues like visas and health. Getting There & Away gives a brief starting point for researching travel to and from the destination. Getting Around gives an overview of the transport options when you arrive.

The peculiar demands of each destination determine how subsequent chapters are broken up, but some things remain constant. We always start with background, then proceed to sights, places to stay, places to eat, entertainment, getting there and away, and getting around information – in that order.

Heading Hierarchy Lonely Planet headings are used in a strict hierarchical structure that can be visualised as a set of Russian dolls. Each heading (and its following text) is encompassed by any preceding heading that is higher on the hierarchical ladder.

Entry Points We do not assume guidebooks will be read from beginning to end, but that people will dip into them. The traditional entry points are the list of contents and the index. In addition, however, some books have a complete list of maps and an index map illustrating map coverage.

There may also be a colour map that shows highlights. These highlights are dealt with in greater detail in the Facts for the Visitor chapter, along with planning questions and suggested itineraries. Each chapter covering a geographical region usually begins with a locator map and another list of highlights. Once you find something of interest in a list of highlights, turn to the index.

Maps Maps play a crucial role in Lonely Planet guidebooks and include a huge amount of information. A legend is printed on the back page. We seek to have complete consistency between maps and text, and to have every important place in the text captured on a map. Map key numbers usually start in the top left corner.

Although inclusion in a guidebook usually implies a recommendation we cannot list every good place. Exclusion does not necessarily imply criticism. In fact there are a number of reasons why we might exclude a place – sometimes it is simply inappropriate to encourage an influx of travellers.

Introduction

'As humans journey beyond 2000 and deeper into space, the distant dream of visiting new worlds is no longer a nebulous haze. But until a holiday on Mars is a reality, it is good to know there are places on earth that offer you the thrill of space exploration. Venture into the unknown. Visit Namibia.'

Namibia Holiday & Travel, 2001

And it's true. There are places in Namibia where you can stand on an expansive shore-line and not even a blade of grass interrupts the foggy greyness; walk down a country highway with nothing to shelter you but the big sky; venture into a dunefield and enter the realms of fantasy; or gaze across plains of uniformly spaced sunburnt rock and witness a scene that could have been beamed back by the Mars Challenger space craft.

But of course, Namibia's character also takes on other dimensions. Wedged between

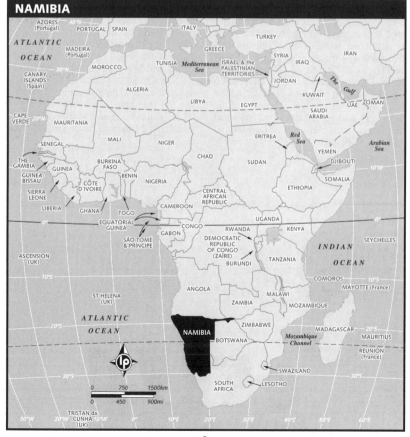

the vast Kalahari and the chilly South Atlantic, this forward-looking country of already-independent people gained its independence in 1990 and continues to present practically unlimited potential and promise. Rich in natural resources and unquestionably spectacular beauty, it has also inherited a solid, modern infrastructure and a diversity of cultures: Herero, Himba, San, Nama, Kavango, Owambo, Tswana, Afrikaner, German, Portuguese, Asian and others.

It's safe to say that Namibia's attractions are unparalleled anywhere. Well known only in Southern Africa, the country's European and African cities and villages, its friendly, educated people and its nearly unlimited elbow room are now being discovered by outsiders. Along the central coast stretches the Namib Desert with its vast dune seas and the surprising oasis of Sossusvlei. In the south, the immense Fish River Canyon dominates the stark landscape. The north features a diverse range of landscapes, from the lonely beaches of the Skeleton Coast and the desert expanses and traditional communal lands of Damaraland and the Kaokoveld to the more-densely populated palm veld of the Owambo country and the forests and wetlands of the Kavango and Caprivi regions.

Beyond Etosha National Park and its phenomenal wildlife, Namibia also hosts a whimsical array of floral and faunal oddities. Where else, for example, would you find a 'dead' plant that has lived for 1200 years, fields of apparently lifeless lichen that can be resurrected with a droplet of water, or lonely beaches shared by hyenas, gemsboks, flamingoes, penguins and sea lions.

Nearly every sort of visitor is accommodated. While the public transport system is an obvious weak link, car hire remains inexpensive and the country brims with camping grounds, backpacker lodges and reasonably priced hotels. At the other end of the spectrum, those who can splash out a bit will find some of the world's most beautifully designed and best-situated lodges, which are considerably better value than similar places in some neighbouring countries. Wherever you fall, one thing is certain: there's a good chance you'll fall in love with this country. In fact, leaving may well be the greatest travel challenge you'll face.

Facts about Namibia

HISTORY
Southern African Prehistory

Southern Africa's human history extends back through the millennia to the first rumblings of humanity on the planet and has an archaeological record dating back to the world's earliest human inhabitants. In geological time, the last two million years or so comprise the Pleistocene era – the last ice age – and, although no ice reached Southern Africa, its effects were apparent in a series of climatic shifts, which set the stage for human evolution.

Continuing controversy among scholars makes it difficult to determine who evolved into whom, but most accept that the earliest human-like creatures were upright-walking hominids, who became established nearly four million years ago in the savannas of Southern and East Africa. At least one advanced variety of these small creatures eventually developed rudimentary tool-making abilities around 1.3 million years ago, allowing them to hunt rather than just scavenge for food. This, combined with a series of climatic changes in the region (alternating wet and dry trends lasting thousands of years each), preceded an increase in brain size, changes in body form and a growing population.

During the next clearly identifiable stage came the human-like *Homo erectus* or 'man who stands upright', whose camps and stone tools are found scattered throughout the region. One archaeological site in the Namib Desert provides evidence that these early people were hunting the ancestors of present-day elephants and butchering their remains with stone hand-axes as early as 750,000 years ago. The tools of the era were large and clumsy, but by 150,000 years ago, people were using lighter stone points, projectile heads, knives, saws and other finer tools that were useful for various hunting-and-gathering activities.

By the Southern African middle Stone Age, which lasted until 20,000 years ago,

the Boskop people, the primary human group in Southern Africa, had progressed into an organised hunting-and-gathering society. These people are the presumed ancestors of the present-day San (also known as Bushmen, although there is some controversy over the use of this name nowadays). Use of fire was universal, tools – made from wood and animal products as well as stone – had become more sophisticated, and natural pigments were being used for personal adornment. Artefacts from middle-Stone-Age sites in the Namib Desert suggest that certain nomadic groups hunted only particular species.

Between 20,000 and 30,000 years ago, tools became smaller and better designed and this greatly increased hunting efficiency and allowed time for further innovation and artistic pursuits. This stage is known as the 'microlithic revolution' because it was characterised by small-flake working of microliths, or small stones. From around 8000 BC, the hunting-and-gathering people of the late Stone Age began producing pottery and occupied rock shelters and caves throughout the Southern Africa region.

The artistic traditions and material crafts of these people are evidenced by their use of pigments. Although pigments had been used for body ornamentation for thousands of years, they now found their way into rock paintings. Whether the San or some other group were responsible for the paintings remains a matter of dispute. Although the artistic tradition in Southern Africa chronologically and stylistically coincides with that of Europe, the spreading Sahara probably precluded any contact between the cultures and there's no substantial evidence supporting a theory of mutual influence.

Khoisan & Bantu Origins

The archaeological connection between the late-Stone-Age people and the first Khoisan arrivals isn't clear, but it is generally accepted that the earliest historically recognisable inhabitants of Southern Africa were San, a nomadic people organised into extended family groups who were able to adapt to the severe terrain.

During the early Iron Age, between 2300 and 2400 years ago, rudimentary farming techniques appeared on the plateaus of south-central Africa. Whether the earliest farmers were Khoisan who'd settled into a stationary existence or migrants fleeing the advancing deserts of Northern Africa remains in question, but the latter is the favoured hypothesis. The arrival of these farmers in Southern Africa marked the beginning of tribal society in the region. These people, commonly called Bantu, would more accurately be called Bantu-speaking, as the word actually refers to their language group. It has become a term of convenience to describe the black African peoples but the grouping is as ill-defined as American or Oriental. In fact, the Bantu-speaking ethnic group is made up of many subgroups or tribes, each with its own language and traditional culture.

These groups arrived in sporadic southward waves over many hundreds of years. They generally moved slowly – perhaps only from one valley or fertile area to the next in an entire generation, but, as they pressed southward, dominant groups subsumed or displaced others.

The first agriculturalists and iron workers of definite Bantu-speaking origin in Southern Africa belonged to the Gokomere culture. They settled the temperate savanna and cooler uplands of Zimbabwe and were the first occupants of the Great Zimbabwe site, in the south-eastern part of modern-day Zimbabwe, where a well-sheltered valley presented an obvious and inviting natural fortification.

Between AD 500 and 1000, the Gokomere and subsequent groups developed gold-mining techniques and produced progressively finer-quality ceramics, jewellery, soapstone carvings and textiles. Cattle ranching became the mainstay of the community and earlier hunting-and-gathering San groups either retreated to the west or were enslaved and/or absorbed by the Bantu speakers; this process continues to the present day.

Precolonial Namibian History

It's generally accepted that Namibia's earliest inhabitants were San, a nomadic people who had adapted to severe natural conditions. Among the traditional San, population densities were very low and extended family groups moved about in search of edible wild plants and game. These San communities probably came under pressure from Khoi-Khoi (also known by the now-unpopular Afrikaans term, 'Hottentot') groups, the ancestors of the modern Nama, with whom they share a language group. The Khoi-Khoi were organised loosely into tribes and raised livestock rather than employing hunting techniques. They probably entered the area from the south, gradually displacing the San, and remained the dominant group there until around 1500. They were probably also responsible for the first pottery in the region.

Around AD 1600, the Herero people, who were Bantu-speaking pastoralists, arrived in Namibia from the Zambezi Valley and occupied the north and west of the country, where they came into conflict with the Khoi-Khoi over the best grazing lands and water sources. (It is thought that the present-day Nama are descended from early Khoi-Khoi, who resisted the Herero.) Eventually, nearly all the indigenous Namibian groups submitted to the Herero, who displaced not only the San and Khoi-Khoi, but also the Damara, whose origins are unclear.

By the late 19th century, a new Bantu group, the Owambo – who were probably descended from people who'd migrated from eastern Africa more than 500 years earlier – had settled in the north along the Okavango and Kunene Rivers.

European Exploration & Incursion

Due to its barren, inhospitable coastline, Namibia was largely ignored by the European maritime nations until relatively recently. The first European visitors were

15th-century Portuguese mariners in search of a route to the Indies. In 1486, Captain Diego Cão sailed as far south as Cape Cross, where he erected a limestone *padrão* (a tribute to his royal patron, João II) to mark the big event. The cross also served as a navigational aid for subsequent explorers.

Bartolomeu Dias travelled to the site of present-day Lüderitz while en route to the Cape of Good Hope on Christmas Day 1487; the event is marked by another cross, on Diaz Point.

In the early 17th century, Dutch sailors from the Cape colonies explored the formidable desert coast of Namibia, but no formal settlements were established. In 1750, the Dutch elephant hunter Jacobus Coetsee became the first European to cross the Orange River into Namibia. He was followed by a series of traders, hunters and missionaries, and the Namibian interior was gradually opened up to Europeans. In 1878, the Cape Colony government put the Namibian ports of Angra Pequena and Walvis Bay under Dutch protection, fearing incursions by the British, Americans and French.

The first real European settlers, however, were missionaries, and by the early 19th century mission stations had been founded at Bethanie, Windhoek, Rehoboth, Keetmanshoop, and various other sites. In 1844, the German Rhenish Missionary Society, under Dr Hugo Hahn, began working among the Herero, but with limited success. More successful were the Finnish Lutherans who arrived in the north in 1870 and established missions among the Owambo.

By 1843, the rich coastal guano deposits of the southern Namib Desert were attracting attention. In 1867, the guano islands were annexed by the British, who took over Walvis Bay in 1878. The Brits also mediated the largely inconclusive Khoisan-Herero wars during this period.

Colonial Era

In 1883, Adolf Lüderitz negotiated the purchase of Angra Pequena and its surroundings from Nama chief, Joseph Fredericks, then petitioned the German chancellor Otto von Bismarck to place the region under German 'protection'. The chancellor, who was occupied with European issues, preferred to leave the African colonial scene to the British, French and Belgians. 'My map of Africa is here in Europe', he said. 'Here is Russia and here is France and here we are in the middle. That is my map of Africa.' But strong domestic lobbying – and the warning that Britain had designs on Lüderitz – forced him to concede and grant protectorate status. Years later, during the last-minute European scramble for colonies and territorial disputes between Britain and Germany, Lüderitz persuaded the chancellor to annex the entire country.

Initially, however, German interests were minimal, and between 1885 and 1890 the colonial administration amounted to three public administrators based at Otjimbingwe village, 55km south of present-day Karibib. Germany's Namibian interests were first served through a colonial company (along the lines of the British East India Company in India prior to the Raj), but this organisation couldn't maintain law and order.

In the 1880s, due to renewed fighting between the Nama and Herero, the German government dispatched Curt von François and 23 soldiers to restrict the supply of arms from British-administered Walvis Bay. However, this seemingly innocuous peacekeeping regiment evolved into the more powerful Schutztruppe, which constructed forts around the country to aid its efforts to put down opposition.

At this stage, Namibia became a fully fledged protectorate, known as German South-West Africa. The first German farmers arrived in 1892 to take up expropriated land on the Central Plateau, and were soon followed by merchants and other settlers. In the late 1890s, the Germans, the Portuguese in Angola and the British in Bechuanaland agreed on Namibia's boundaries.

This generated bitterness among local people, who resented the foreigners' laws, taxes and takeover of water rights and communal lands. In 1904, the paramount chief of the Herero invited his Nama, Baster and Owambo counterparts to join forces with him to resist the growing German presence.

This was an unlikely alliance between traditional enemies, especially considering that warring between the Herero and Nama had been a catalyst for increased involvement by the colonial powers, but by 1905, the Germans had been driven all the way back to Windhoek.

However, German Schutztruppe brought in reinforcements and eventually suppressed the rebellions, wiping out 60,000 Herero (which represented 75% of the Herero nation). At this stage, the Nama, under Hendrik Witbooi, took up their cause and launched a large-scale rebellion, but after defeat at the Battle of Vaalgras, on 29 October 1905, Witbooi died of his wounds.

The war ended in 1908, when the German forces defeated remaining guerrilla forces in the south. By 1910, the remaining Herero had fled to the inhospitable country east of Windhoek – some as far as Botswana – where many suffered from hunger and starvation. Survivors were eventually shifted to their allocated 'homeland', the four-part Hereroland district in the barren western Kalahari.

Meanwhile, in the south, diamonds had been discovered at Grasplatz, east of Lüderitz, by a South African labourer, Zacharias Lewala. Despite the assessment of De Beers that the find probably wouldn't amount to much, prospectors flooded in to stake their claims. By 1910, the German authorities had branded the entire area between Lüderitz and the Orange River a *Sperrgebiet* (closed area), chucked out the prospectors and granted exclusive rights to Deutsche Diamanten Gesellschaft.

The colonial era lasted until WWI, by which time the German Reich had dismantled the Herero tribal structures and taken over all Khoi-Khoi and Herero lands. As more colonial immigrants arrived from Europe, the best lands were parcelled into an extensive network of white farms.

The more fortunate Owambo, in the north, managed to avoid conquest until after the start of WWI, when they were overrun by Portuguese forces fighting on the side of the Allies. In 1914, at the beginning of WWI, Britain pressured South Africa into invading Namibia. The South Africans, under the command of Prime Minister Louis Botha and General Jan Smuts, pushed northwards, forcing the outnumbered Schutztruppe to retreat. In May 1915, the Germans faced their final defeat at Khorab near Tsumeb, and a week later a South African administration was set up in Windhoek.

By 1920, many German farms had been sold to Afrikaans-speaking settlers and the German diamond-mining interests in the south were handed over to the South Africa–based Consolidated Diamond Mines (CDM), which retains the concession to the present day.

South African Occupation

Under the Treaty of Versailles in 1919, Germany was required to renounce all its colonial claims, and in 1921 the League of Nations granted South Africa a formal mandate to administer Namibia as part of the Union, but not to prepare it for eventual independence. However, after a brief rebellion in 1924, the mixed-race Basters at Rehoboth were granted some measure of autonomy, and the following year the territorial constitution was amended to permit whites to set up a territorial legislature.

The mandate was renewed by the UN following WWII. However, South Africa was more interested in annexing South-West Africa as a full province in the Union and decided to scrap the terms of the mandate and rewrite the constitution. In response, the International Court of Justice determined that South Africa had overstepped its boundaries and ruled that the mandate would remain. The UN set up the Committee on South-West Africa to enforce the original terms and, in 1956, decided that South African control must somehow be terminated.

Undeterred, the South African government tightened its grip on the territory, and in 1949 granted the white population parliamentary representation in Pretoria. The bulk of Namibia's viable farmland was parcelled into some 6000 farms for white settlers and the other ethnic groups were relegated to newly demarcated 'tribal homelands'. The official intent was ostensibly to 'channel economic development into predominantly poor rural areas', but it was all too obvious that it was, in fact, simply a convenient way of retaining the majority of the country for white settlement and ranching.

As a result, a prominent line of demarcation appeared between the predominantly white ranching lands in the central and southern parts of the country, and the poorer but better-watered tribal areas to the north. Perhaps the only positive result of this effective imposition of tribal boundaries was the prevention of territorial squabbles between previously mobile groups now forced to live under the same political entity. This arrangement was retained until Namibian independence in 1990, and to some extent, continues up to the present day.

Independence

Throughout the 1950s, despite mounting pressure from the UN, South Africa refused to release its grip on Namibia. This intransigence was based on its fears of having yet another antagonistic government on its doorstep and of losing the income that it derived from the mining operations there. Namibia is rich in minerals such as uranium, copper, lead and zinc and is the world's foremost source of gem diamonds. These were all mined by South African and Western multinational companies under a generous taxation scheme that enabled them to export up to one-third of their profits every year.

Forced labour had been the lot of most Namibians since the German annexation, and was one of the main factors that led to mass demonstrations and the increasingly nationalist sentiments in the late 1950s. Several political parties were formed and strikes were organised, not only among workers in Namibia but also among contract labourers working in South Africa. Among the parties was the Owamboland People's Congress, founded in Cape Town under the leadership of Samuel Daniel Shafiishuna Nujoma and Adimba Herman Toivo ja Toivo.

In 1959, the party's name was changed to the Owamboland People's Organisation and Nujoma took the issue of South African occupation to the UN in New York. By 1960, his party had gathered the support of several others and they eventually coalesced into the South-West African People's Organization, or Swapo, with its headquarters in Dar es Salaam (Tanzania). Troops were sent to Egypt for military training and the organisation prepared for war.

In 1966, Swapo took the issue of South African occupation to the International Court of Justice. The court upheld South Africa's right to govern South-West Africa, but the UN General Assembly voted to terminate South Africa's mandate and replace it with a Council for South-West Africa (renamed the Commission for Namibia in 1973) to administer the territory.

In response, on 26 August 1966 (now called Heroes' Day), Swapo launched its campaign of guerrilla warfare at Ongulumbashe in the Owambo region of northern Namibia. The next year, one of Swapo's founders, Toivo ja Toivo, was convicted of terrorism and imprisoned in South Africa, where he would remain until 1984; Nujoma stayed in Tanzania. In 1972, the UN finally declared the South African occupation of South-West Africa officially illegal and called for a withdrawal, and the UN secretary Kurt Waldheim proclaimed Swapo the legitimate representative of the Namibian people.

In response, the South African government fired on demonstrators and arrested thousands of activists. While all this was going on, events were coming to a head in neighbouring Angola, culminating in its independence from Portugal in 1975, and the ascendancy of the Marxist-oriented Popular Movement for the Liberation of Angola (MPLA). This was anathema to South Africa, which, in an attempt to smash the MPLA, launched an invasion of Angola in support of the National Union for the Total Independence of Angola (UNITA) forces, which controlled southern Angola at the time. The attempt failed, and by March 1976 the troops had been withdrawn, although incursions continued well into the 1980s.

Back in Namibia, the Democratic Turnhalle Alliance (DTA; named after Turnhalle, the site of its meetings) was officially established in 1975. Formed from a combination of ethnic parties and white political interests, it turned out to be a toothless debating chamber that spent much of its time in litigation with the South African government over the scope of its responsibilities.

Meanwhile, in the late 1970s, the Swapo ranks were split when two officials of the government in exile, Solomon Mifima and Andreas Shipanga, called for long-overdue party elections. In response, the party's president, Sam Nujoma, had them imprisoned in Zambia with hundreds of their followers. Civil rights activists in Europe managed to have them freed, and they now head a minority party, Swapo-Democrats, or Swapo-D.

In 1983, after the DTA indicated it would accommodate Swapo, it was dissolved and replaced by yet another administration, known as the Multi-Party Conference. This turned out to be even less successful than the DTA and quickly disappeared, allowing control of Namibia to pass back to the South African–appointed administrator-general, Mr Justice Steyn, who was given the power to rule by proclamation.

The failure of these attempts to effect an internal solution did not deter South Africa, which refused to negotiate on a program for Namibian independence supervised by the UN until the estimated 19,000 Cuban troops were removed from neighbouring Angola. In response, Swapo intensified its guerrilla campaign. As a result, movement in the north became severely restricted.

In the end, however, it may not have been the activities of Swapo alone or international sanctions that forced the South Africans to the negotiating table. The white Namibian population itself was growing tired of the war and the economy was suffering badly. South Africa's internal problems also had a significant effect. By 1985, the war was costing some R480 million (around US$250 million) per year and conscription was widespread. Mineral exports, which once provided around 88% of the country's gross domestic product (GDP), had plummeted to just 27% by 1984. This was due mainly to falling world demand and depressed prices, but fraud and corruption were also significant factors.

By 1988, the stage was set for negotiations on the country's future. Under the watch of the UN, the USA and the USSR, a deal struck between Cuba, Angola, South Africa and Swapo provided for the withdrawal of Cuban troops from Angola and South African troops from Namibia. It also stipulated that the transition to Namibian independence would formally begin on 1 April 1989, and would be followed by UN-monitored elections held in November 1989 on the basis of universal suffrage. Although minor score-settling and unrest among some Swapo troops threatened to derail the whole process, the plan went ahead and in September, Nujoma returned from his 30-year exile. In the elections, Swapo garnered a clear majority of the votes but the numbers were insufficient to give it the sole mandate to write the new constitution.

Following negotiations between the various parties and international advisers, including the USA, France, Germany and the USSR, a constitution was drafted. This provided incentive for co-operation between the executive and legislative bodies and included an impressive bill of rights, covering provisions for protection of the environment, the rights of families and children, freedom of religion, speech and the press, and a host of other matters. It was adopted in February 1990 and independence was granted a month later, on 21 March, under Nujoma's presidency. His policies are based on a national reconciliation program to heal the wounds left by 25 years of armed struggle and a reconstruction program based on the retention of a mixed economy and partnership with the private sector.

Post-Independence Developments

In the elections of December 1994, President Nujoma and his Swapo party were re-elected with a 68% landslide victory over rival Mishake Muyongo and his DTA party. There was a great deal of concern, however, when the president was re-elected in 1999 (with 76.8% of the vote), after having changed the constitution to allow himself a third presidential term. In 2001, he was already mooting the possibility of another constitutional change, which would allow him a fourth term of office. He has also spoken out openly against homosexuality in Namibia and proclaimed opposition to the current role of Christian churches in Namibia. These developments have set off alarm bells among large sectors of the population, raising widespread concern about the future stability of the country's political processes and constitutional law.

Other political problems include episodes in the Caprivi region of north-eastern Namibia. On 2 August 1999, rebels – mainly members of Namibia's Lozi minority led by Mishake Muyongo, a former vice-president of Swapo and a long-time proponent of Caprivian independence – attempted to seize Katima Mulilo by attacking the Mpacha airport, as well as the television and police stations. However, the poorly trained perpetrators, who were dissatisfied with rule by the Owambo majority, failed to capture any of their intended targets. After only a few hours, they were summarily put down by the Namibian Defence Force (NDF), who then set about arresting anyone who appeared to be a separatist sympathiser.

The government reacted swiftly, closing the Caprivi's land borders with Zambia and Botswana for over a month, and dispatching a contingent of the Special Field Force (SFF). This unit, comprised of former freedom fighters, set about intimidating and torturing suspected rebel sympathisers, and zealously enforcing a 6pm-to-6am curfew which remained until early September 1999. During this period, motorists were intimidated at roadblocks, several innocent bystanders were killed or injured, and tourism in the region ground to a halt. Meanwhile, the rebel leadership escaped to Denmark (required by international agreement to provide asylum). Although a minority of locals quietly support Caprivian independence, further unrest over this matter seems unlikely.

In December 1999, however, the Caprivi again hit the headlines when Namibia committed NDF support to the Angolan government in its civil war against Unita rebels. As a result, fighting spilled over into the region, especially around the Omega military post. When a family of French tourists was robbed and murdered while driving along the Caprivi Strip's Golden Hwy between Kongola and Divundu (whether by Unita rebels or local criminals), the issue exploded in the international press, causing prospective visitors to Namibia to cancel their holidays. (Bizarrely, the US State Department and the British Home Office totally confused Namibia's troubled stretch of the Okavango River with Botswana's Okavango Delta, and as a result, tourist numbers in Botswana also plummeted.)

Since the Caprivi troubles began, there have been sporadic reports of fighting, attacks on civilians, and land-mine detonations in the region, and traffic has been conducted along the Golden Hwy in twice-daily military convoys. The whole situation has been aggravated by political strife in Zimbabwe, which slashed the number of visitors heading to or from Victoria Falls; tourist numbers still haven't recovered and it remains to be seen whether tourism will recover anytime in the near future.

GEOGRAPHY

Arid Namibia enjoys a wide variety of geographical and geological features. Broadly speaking, its topography can be divided into four main sections: the Namib Desert and the coastal plains; the eastward-sloping Central Plateau; the Kalahari sands along the Botswana and South African borders; and the densely wooded bushveld of the Kavango and Caprivi regions.

The Namib Desert, the world's oldest arid region, has existed for over 80 million years. It extends along the country's entire Atlantic coast and has an annual rainfall of between 15mm and 100mm. The Namib owes its existence to the cold Benguela Current, which flows northwards from the Antarctic. This current brings with it cold air, which is heavier than warm air and can carry much less moisture. When this cold air meets the warmer land, the little moisture it contains immediately condenses into a blanket of fog over the coast. This moisture sustains lichens and specialised plants that form the lowest echelons of the desert food chain and sustain the unique Namib flora and fauna that have adapted specifically to the hostile conditions.

Namib landscapes range from the mountainous red dunes in the south to the interior plains and flat-topped, steep-sided and isolated mountains (inselbergs) of the centre. The Skeleton Coast region in the north is known for bare scorched dunes.

Moving east, the altitude increases and the coastal dunes gradually give way to gravel plains. The width of these coastal plains varies from 25km in the northern Kaokoveld to almost 300km at Lüderitz in the south. In Damaraland, the coastal plain is punctuated by dramatic mountains and inselbergs, some of volcanic origin. These are honeycombed with caves and rock shelters, which provided homes for early humans. The Brandberg and Erongo Moun-

tains north of Karibib are both well-known examples.

The Namib Desert itself is scored by a number of rivers, which rise in the Central Plateau but are often dry. Some, like the ephemeral Tsauchab, once reached the sea but now end in calcrete pans. Others flow only during the summer rainy season, but at some former stage carried huge volumes of water and carved out dramatic canyons like the Fish River and Kuiseb Canyons.

East of the coastal plains, the terrain becomes more rugged and climbs steeply through rugged canyons to the savanna grasslands of the Central Plateau. This plateau is bisected by fossil river courses and is covered largely in thorn scrub. Still further east, the land slopes gently away to the sandy fossil valleys and dunes that characterise the western Kalahari.

Namibia's north-eastern strip, along the Angolan border from the Owambo country through to Kavango and Caprivi, is charac-

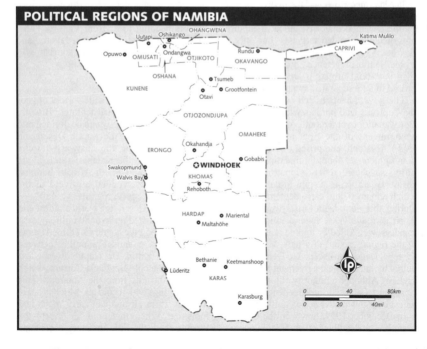

POLITICAL REGIONS OF NAMIBIA

terised by the well-watered bushveld. It's bounded by the great rivers – the Kunene, Okavango, Kwando/Mashi/Linyanti/Chobe and Zambezi – which flow year-round and provide water for most of Namibia's human population.

Politically, Namibia is now divided into 13 regions, which replace the old ethnically based regions demarcated by the colonial powers. However, only slowly are Namibians becoming familiar with these new regions and beginning to refer to them in common usage.

CLIMATE

Although it's predominantly a desert country, Namibia enjoys regional climatic variations corresponding to its geographical subdivisions. The most arid conditions are found in the Central Namib, which typically enjoys clear and windy weather. The region is cooled in the summer by cold onshore winds derived from the South Atlantic anticyclone pressure system.

The upwelling Benguela Current and onshore winds produce a steep temperature gradient between the sea and land. When the cold, moist sea breeze meets the dry desert heat, the result is instantaneous condensation and fog. In the desert, summer daytime temperatures climb to over 40°C, but they can fall to below freezing at night. Fog is common on the coast, generally developing during the night and often lasting well into the morning up to 20km inland.

In the winter, the Namib region is warmed by east winds, which reach their peak between June and August. As they descend from the Central Plateau, they heat up and dry out. Especially around Swakopmund and Walvis Bay, they often create miserable conditions as they whip up clouds of swirling sand that block out the sun and penetrate everything with coarse grit.

On the Central Plateau the low winter humidity and gentle breezes make for a pleasant and comfortable climate, but during summer, temperatures and humidity climb to uncomfortable levels. The area averages between 200mm and 400mm of precipitation annually, nearly all of which falls during this

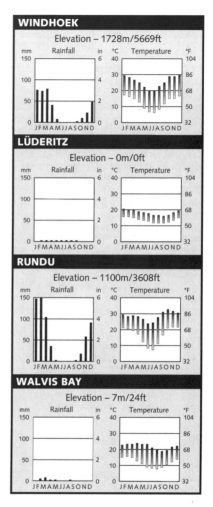

period. East of the Central Plateau, the rainfall decreases, and along the Botswana and South African borders this creates the near-desert conditions of the Kalahari.

Heading north, however, rainfall steadily increases, reaching its maximum of over 600mm per year along the Okavango River, which enjoys a subtropical climate. The northern and interior regions experience two rainy seasons. The 'little rains' fall between

October and December, while the main stormy period normally lasts from January to April.

ECOLOGY & ENVIRONMENT

With a small human population spread over a large land area, Namibia is in better environmental shape than most African countries, but challenges remain. The Ministry of Environment & Tourism (MET) is largely a holdover from pre-independence days and, as a result, its policies strongly reflect those of its South African counterpart.

Although changes are currently afoot, the country still lacks coherent environmental guidelines. Key environmental issues in Namibia include water schemes and water quality, uneven population distribution, bush and wildlife management, trophy-hunting policies, attitudes of farmers and villagers towards wildlife, conservation methods and ecotourism issues.

As yet, local people have seen few benefits from wildlife-oriented tourism and encroachment on protected areas continues to affect local ecosystems. Many ranchers in the southern part of the country view wildlife as a nuisance, while people in the more densely populated north see wildlife reserves as potential settlement areas and wildlife itself as a food resource and a threat to crops and human life. For more on species under pressure see Fauna later in this chapter.

Tourism & the Environment

It's hoped that international tourism will provide incentive to conserve wildlife species by attracting foreign money – and what better way than promising to bring to life the nature documentaries that enthral people all over the world? Enter the tourist industry, which has taken Namibia by storm and literally changed the face of the land and the direction of national policy.

Although tourism can be an environmental saviour in some instances, it's also a major environmental issue (it is one of the largest global industries), and is impossible to ignore. Significantly, when a destination cannot cope with its tourist numbers, the natural and social environments can end up seriously damaged.

This brings up the 'ecotourism' label, which is popularly slapped on any activity with an environmental connection (however vague), often simply because it's outdoors. The idea is to make it all feel nice and wholesome; even the more specific 'eco-friendly tourism' is now overused – and often inappropriately. This is mainly because activities such as camping, wildlife-viewing and sightseeing trips to remote or fragile areas can be *more* environmentally or culturally harmful than a conventional hotel holiday in a specifically developed resort. (A leading British environmentalist, perhaps surprisingly, reckons that the controversial Sun City complex in South Africa is one of the world's prime examples of ecotourism: 'a purpose-built resort complex, creating 4500 local jobs, and putting wildlife back onto a degraded piece of useless veld'.)

Those who wish to support truly eco-friendly operators will have to ignore any outward claims and ask specifically what they operators are doing to protect or support the plants, animals and people of Namibia.

While many folks in the Namibian government see tourism as the remedy for all the country's woes, common sense dictates that real benefits from tourism will only be realised if a balance is struck between growth in tourist numbers, environmental conservation and local participation. That is, development must be sustainable and the ordinary people must benefit from it.

To that end, several local NGOs have formulated conservation projects. An especially successful one is the Save the Rhino Trust (SRT), which promotes conservation education and public sponsorship of individual animals to provide local people with alternative sources of income. It also sponsors a lovely community camp site in the National West Coast Recreation Area where visitors will have a decent chance of seeing rare desert elephants and rhinos outside of any national park.

In addition, income is generated by the creation of jobs for hunting guides, rangers, tour guides and various posts in the hotels, lodges and camps, as well as craftspeople and artists who create all manner of wonderful items to be purchased by visitors.

Water & Power Issues

Other major environmental issues in Namibia involve projects designed to provide water and power resources for the country's growing industrial and human needs. Two major ones – which have now been placed on hold indefinitely – include a proposed dam and hydroelectric plant on the Kunene River in the Kaokoveld and the pipeline from the Okavango River to provide water for Windhoek. It's hoped that water conservation will continue to be an issue in Namibia, despite the extremely heavy rains of 2000 and 2001, which filled the dams and provided a water surplus – and flooding – through much of the country.

FLORA

Because Namibia is mostly arid, much of the flora is typical African dryland vegetation: scrub brush and succulents, such as euphorbia. Along the coastal plain around Swakopmund are the world's most extensive and diverse fields of lichen; they remain dormant during dry periods, but with the addition of water, they burst into colourful bloom (see the boxed text 'Lichen Fields' in the North-Western Namibia chapter).

Most of the country is covered by tree-dotted, scrub savanna grasses of the genera *Stipagrostis*, *Eragrostis* and *Aristida*. In the south, the grass is interrupted by ephemeral watercourses lined with tamarisks, buffalo thorn and camelthorn. Unique floral oddities here include the *kokerboom* (quiver tree), a species of aloe that grows only in southern Namibia.

In the sandy plains of south-eastern Namibia, raisin bushes *(Grewia)* and candlethorn grow among the scrubby trees, while hillsides are blanketed with green-flowered *Aloe viridiflora* and camphor bush.

The eastern fringes of Namib-Naukluft Park are dominated by semidesert scrub savanna vegetation, including some rare aloe species *(Aloe karasbergensis* and *Aloe sladeniana)*. On the gravel plains east of the Skeleton Coast grows the bizarre *Welwitschia mirabilis*, a slow-growing ground-hugging conifer that lives for more than 1000 years. This is surely one of the world's most unusual plants (see the boxed text 'Welwitschias' in the Central Namib Desert chapter).

In areas with higher rainfall, the characteristic grass savanna gives way to acacia woodlands, and Etosha National Park enjoys two distinct environments: the wooded savanna in the east and thorn-scrub savanna in the west. The higher rainfall of Caprivi and Kavango sustains extensive mopane woodland and the riverine areas support scattered wetland vegetation, grasslands and stands of acacias. The area around Katima Mulilo is dominated by mixed subtropical woodland containing copalwood, Zambezi teak and leadwood, among other hardwood species.

FAUNA

Etosha, Namibia's largest and best-known wildlife park, contains a variety of antelope species, as well as other African ungulates (hoofed animals), carnivores and pachyderms (large, thick-skinned mammals). Other major wildlife parks – Khaudom, Bwabwata, Mudumu, Mamili and Hardap Dam – may pale by comparison, but they do present a surprising range of species in a dwindling habitat.

Unprotected Damaraland, in Namibia's north-west, is home to numerous antelope species and other ungulates, and also harbours desert rhinos, elephants and other specially adapted subspecies. Hikers in the Naukluft and other desert ranges may catch sight of the elusive Hartmann's mountain zebra, and along the desert coasts you can see jackass penguins, flamingoes, Cape fur seals and perhaps even the legendary brown hyena, or *Strandwolf*.

For information on large mammals, see the special colour Wildlife Guide. For more on species under pressure see Ecology & Environment earlier in this chapter. The communities that inhabit Namibia's dunes are further covered in the special section

'The Namib Dunes'. The following information on endangered species covers non-mammalian creatures endemic to Namibia.

Endangered Species

Overfishing and the 1993–94 outbreak of 'red tide' along the Skeleton Coast have decimated the sea lion population, both through starvation and commercially inspired culling. Also, the poaching of desert rhinos, elephants and other Damaraland species has caused their numbers to decrease, and the desert lion, which once roamed the Skeleton Coast, is now considered extinct.

The stability of other endangered species, such as the lichen fields, the welwitschia plant, the Damara tern, the Cape vulture, and numerous lesser-known species, has been compromised by human activities (including tourism and recreation) in formerly remote areas. As yet, efforts to change local attitudes have met with limited success.

Rhinos Although white rhinos were wiped out in Namibia prior to 1900, they've now been reintroduced into Waterberg Plateau Park and Etosha National Park and are doing relatively well. A small population of black rhinos still inhabits the plains of Damaraland. Namibia was a pioneer in using dehorning to protect its rhinos, but, sadly, dehorned female rhinos in Namibia were unable to protect their young from attack by hyenas. During the drought of 1993, when other wildlife was scarce, all calves of dehorned females were lost. The rate of rhino loss to poachers is approximately 5% annually, and growing.

The nongovernmental Save the Rhino Trust (SRT; ☎ 061-222281, fax 223077), PO Box 22691, Windhoek, has been formed to promote conservation education.

Lions The country is also facing a dramatic decrease in its lion population. From a high of 700 animals in 1980, the number has now

The Ivory Debate

A major issue in Southern Africa is elephant conservation, and both arguments have an emotional following. Foreign interests generally hold that elephant herds should be preserved for their own sake or for aesthetic reasons; the local sentiment maintains elephants must justify their existence on long-term economic grounds – 'sustainable utilisation' – for the benefit of local people or for the country as a whole. In fact, the same arguments can be applied to other wildlife resources.

Since the 1970s various factors have led to a massive increase in elephant poaching in many parts of Africa. By the late 1980s the price of 1kg of ivory (US$300) was three times the *annual* income of over 60% of Africa's population. Naturally, the temptation to poach was great, although the real money was made not by poachers – often villagers who were paid a pittance for the valuable tusks – but by the dealers, who acted with the full knowledge (and support) of senior government figures. In East Africa and in some Southern African countries – notably in Zambia – elephant populations were reduced by up to 90% in about 15 years. But in other Southern African countries where parks and reserves are well managed – mainly Zimbabwe, South Africa, Botswana and Namibia – elephant populations were relatively unaffected.

In 1990, following a massive campaign by conservation organisations, a world body called the Convention on International Trade in Endangered Species (Cites) internationally banned the import and export of ivory. It also increased funding for antipoaching measures.

Although elephant populations recovered in some ravaged areas, Southern African populations continued to grow, and another problem surfaced. Elephants eat huge quantities of foliage but in the past, herds would eat their fill then migrate to another area, allowing time for the vegetation to regenerate. However, an increasing human population pressed elephants into smaller and smaller areas – mostly around national parks – and the herds were forced to eat everything available. In many places, the bush began to look as if an atom bomb had hit.

decreased to between 320 and 340. Of these, nearly 85% are confined to Etosha National Park and Khaudom Game Reserve. One problem is that game reserve fences are penetrable to lions, and once the lions have left protected areas, it's only a matter of time before they're shot by ranchers to protect cattle. The good news is that Etosha's lions are free of two of the most serious causes of disease found in other parks: Feline Immunodeficiency Virus (the feline form of HIV) and Canine Distemper Virus (which has killed 30% of the lions in Tanzania's Serengeti National Park).

Trophy Hunting Many foreign hunters are willing to pay handsomely for big game trophies (a leopard, for example, will fetch US$2000, while an elephant provides many times that amount) and farmers and ranchers frequently complain about the ravages of wildlife on their stock. As a result, the Namibia Professional Hunting Association

(Napha) and the MET have set up regulatory statutes on hunting (which comprises 5% of the country's revenue from wildlife). The idea is to provide farmers with financial incentives to protect free-ranging wildlife. Management strategies include encouraging hunting of older animals, evaluating the condition of trophies and setting bag limits in accordance with population fluctuations. Because both the government and private sectors have a stake in the success of this endeavour, it's very likely to succeed, at least as far as their economic objectives are concerned.

In addition, quite a few (enormous) private farms are set aside for hunting. The owners stock these farms with wildlife bred by suppliers – mainly in South Africa – and turn it loose into the farm environment. Not only do the hefty hunting fees bring a great deal of money into the country, this also ensures that more and more land reverts to wildlife.

The Ivory Debate

In some places, park authorities are currently facing elephant overpopulation. While Botswana has the most serious problem, some parts of Namibia's Caprivi region are suffering from the spillover from Botswana. Solutions include relocation (where animals are taken to other areas) and a pioneering contraception project, in which breeding cows are injected with the equivalent of the contraceptive pill. The alternative is to cull herds, sometimes in large numbers; this seems a bizarre paradox, but illustrates the seriousness of the problem, and at present the other options remain experimental and limited in their effect.

Culling also brought about a boon in legal ivory, which could have historically been sold to raise funds for elephant management. However, the Cites ban stopped that, and with the renewed culling programs, some Southern African countries called for the trade to be legalised again, in order to provide funds for conservation projects. They argued that in this way, the elephant would again become a valuable resource and provide local governments and people with the incentive to ensure its survival.

In March 1999, Botswana, Namibia, South Africa and Zimbabwe were permitted by Cites to resume strictly controlled ivory exports. Despite these measures, opponents of the trade warned that elephant poaching would increase in other parts of Africa, as poached ivory could now be laundered through the legal trade. Sure enough, 1999 saw an increase in poaching all over Africa – from Kenya to Gabon – and in late 1999, a Zimbabwean newspaper reported that 84 elephants were poached that year. Opponents of the trade protested loudly, but the Zimbabwean government, for one, dismissed the surge by attributing it to animal rights campaigners attempting to sabotage the trade. Either way, it is still too early to say if the resumed trade will have overall financial benefits in Southern Africa. The ban came under review again in mid-2000, and efforts by Botswana, Namibia, South Africa and Zimbabwe to expand the ivory trade were unsuccessful.

Although community-based hunting concessions have appeared in the Bushmanland area, these still aren't widespread.

Reptiles

Namibia's reptile extraordinaire is the Nile crocodile. Female crocodiles lay up to 80 eggs at a time, depositing them in sandy areas above the high-water line. After three months' incubation in the hot sand, the young emerge. Newly hatched crocodiles are avocado-green in colour and, like avocados, darken to nearly black as they age.

Other reptiles to watch for – but which shouldn't inspire bush paranoia – are snakes. The dry lands of Namibia boast more than 70 species of snake, including three species of spitting cobra. It is actually the African puff adder that causes the most problems for humans, since it inhabits dry, sandy, and otherwise harmless-looking riverbeds. Horned adders and sand snakes inhabit the gravel plains of the Namib, and the sidewinder adder lives in the Namib dune sea. Other venomous snakes include the slender green vine snake; both the green and black mamba; the very dangerous zebra snake; and the boomslang (Afrikaans for 'tree snake'), a slender 2m aquamarine affair with black-tipped scales.

Lizards are ubiquitous in Southern Africa, from the bathroom ceiling to the kitchen sink. The largest of these is the leguaan or water monitor, a docile creature that reaches over 2m in length, swims and spends a lot of time laying around water holes, probably dreaming of becoming a crocodile. A smaller version, the savanna leguaan, inhabits kopjes (small hills) and drier areas. Also present in large numbers are geckos, chameleons, legless lizards, rock-plated lizards and a host of others.

The Namib Desert supports a wide range of lizards, including a large vegetarian species, *Angolosaurus skoogi*. The sand-diving lizard, *Aprosaura achietae*, is known for its 'thermal dance'. To get some relief from the heat of the sand, it lifts its legs in turn as if following a dance routine. The unusual bug-eyed palmato gecko inhabits the high dunes and there's a species of chameleon.

Insects & Arachnids

Although Southern Africa doesn't enjoy the profusion of bug life found in countries further north, a few interesting specimens buzz, creep, and crawl around the place. Over 500 species of colourful butterflies – including the African monarch, the commodore, and the citrus swallowtail – are resident, as well as many fly-by-night moths.

Some of the more interesting buggy types include the large and rarely noticed stick insects, the similarly large (and frighteningly hairy) baboon spider and the ubiquitous and leggy shongololo (millipede), which can be up to 30cm long.

Common insects such as ants, stink bugs, grasshoppers, mopane worms and locusts sometimes find their way into frying pans for snack and protein supplements.

Nuisance insects include malarial Anopheles mosquitoes, which are profuse in northeastern Namibia; and the tsetse fly, which carries sleeping sickness and is found along the Caprivi Strip. There are also various stinging insects, such as the striped hornet, an evil-looking variety of house wasp. In the gravel plains of the Namib Desert, you'll also encounter such nuisance insects as ticks, which favour the shade of thorn trees and areas where there are lots of grazing animals.

The Namib Desert has several wonderful species of spider. The tarantula-like 'white lady of the dunes' is a white hairy affair that is attracted to light. It does a dance, of sorts, raising each of its eight hairy feet in turn. There is also a rare false spider known as a solifluge or sun spider. You can see its circulatory system through its light-coloured translucent outer skeleton. Much of the time, however, it remains buried in the sand.

The Namib dunes are also known for their extraordinary variety of *tenebrionid* (known locally as 'toktokkie') beetles, which come in all shapes and sizes. They've adapted well to their desert environment and most of their moisture is derived from fog.

Birds

Although Southern Africa offers an adequate sampling of LBJs (Little Brown

MANFRED GOTTSCHALK

LUKE HUNTER

PETER PTSCHELINZEW

DENNIS JONES

Namibia supports a rich variety of desert flora, including the hoodia **(top left)**, moringa **(top right)** and the flowering welwitschia plant **(middle left)**, though not everything survives the desert's extreme conditions.

LUKE HUNTER

JULIET COOMBE

ADRIEN VADROT

Namibia offers some of Africa's best wildlife-watching opportunities: Large numbers of Burchell's zebras roam Etosha National Park **(top)**; flamingoes are attracted to the lagoons around Walvis Bay **(middle)**; and Cape Cross is a breeding ground for thousands of lazy Cape fur seals **(bottom)**.

Jobs), it is also home to an array of colourful and exotic birdlife.

The coastal wildfowl reserves support an especially wide range of birdlife: white pelicans, grebes, herons, flamingoes, cormorants, ducks and hundreds of other wetland birds. The sheer number of birds, which survive on the fish stocks nurtured by the cold Benguela Current, has contributed to the country's lucrative guano industry. Near Walvis Bay, artificial offshore islands have been constructed to stimulate production. Further south, around Lüderitz, flamingoes and jackass penguins share the same desert shoreline.

The canyons and riverbeds slicing across the Central Namib are home to nine species of raptor, as well as the hoopoe, the unusual red-eyed bulbul and a small bird known as the familiar chat. Around the western edge of the Central Plateau you may see the colourful sunbirds or emerald cuckoos. Throughout the desert regions, you'll see the intriguing social weaver, which builds an enormous nest that's the avian equivalent of a 10-storey block of flats. Central Namibia also boasts bird species found nowhere else, such as the Namaqua sand-grouse and Grey's lark.

The well-watered areas of the far north support an entirely different range of birdlife, including such colourful species as lilac-breasted rollers, pygmy geese (actually a duck) and white-fronted, carmine and little bee-eaters. Other wetland species include the African jacanas, snakebirds, ibis, hoopoes, storks, egrets, parrots, shrikes, kingfishers, hornbills, great white herons and purple and green-backed herons. Birds of prey include Pel's fishing owl, goshawks, several species of vultures, and both bateleurs and African fish eagles.

Fish

Due to its usual drought conditions, Namibia has only a few freshwater fish species. However, the South Atlantic waters support a large number of fish species (and anglers). The most popular game fish along the Skeleton Coast is the delicious kabeljou, which can grow up to 2m long. For information on commercial fish species see Fishing under Economy later in this chapter.

NATIONAL PARKS, RESERVES & CONSERVANCIES

Despite its usually harsh climate, Namibia's landscapes are among the world's most magical, and the country boasts some of Africa's finest national parks. These range from the open bush of the central and northern areas, where wildlife is relatively plentiful, to spectacular Fish River Canyon and the barren and inhospitable coastal strip with its huge sand dunes. Even here, many species – including elephants, giraffes, zebras and other large herbivores – are desert-adapted. Sadly, the population of desert lions, which once prowled the coastal areas, has been wiped out by herders and poachers.

Bwabwata National Park This recently created park (although it is still technically unofficial) consolidates several Caprivi conservation areas (the West Caprivi Triangle, Buffalo area, the former Mahango Game Reserve, and the Popa Falls Rest Camp) into a single entity. While poaching and population growth have taken their toll in the Triangle and Buffalo regions, Mahango is rich in wildlife, especially in the dry season. The nearby Popa Falls rest camp provides pleasant riverside accommodation.

Daan Viljoen Game Park This small park is situated in Windhoek's backyard, and is popular with weekend visitors, who use it for picnics and weekend camping trips. In addition to its popular wildlife-drive circuit, several lovely hiking tracks take in its wilder areas.

Etosha National Park Namibia's best-known park is Etosha, a huge area of semi-arid savanna grassland and thorn scrub surrounding a calcrete pan. Etosha Pan contains water only a few days each year, but during this time it attracts immense herds of wildlife and flocks of flamingoes and other birds. During the dry season (May to September), the water holes support huge herds of gemsboks, springboks, wildebeests and zebras, as well as predators and elephants.

Fish River Canyon Park Claims that Fish River Canyon is second only to the USA's Grand Canyon in size are exaggerated, but it's still an impressive sight. It's also a great hiking venue, and the hot springs resort of Ai-Ais, at its southern end, offer a popular and relaxing getaway.

Hardap Dam Game Reserve This small reserve near Mariental includes both a recreation area

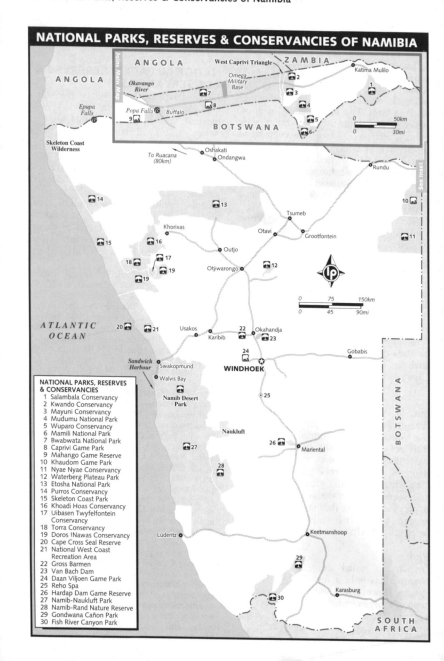

NATIONAL PARKS, RESERVES & CONSERVANCIES OF NAMIBIA

NATIONAL PARKS, RESERVES
& CONSERVANCIES
1 Salambala Conservancy
2 Kwando Conservancy
3 Mayuni Conservancy
4 Mudumu National Park
5 Wuparo Conservancy
6 Mamili National Park
7 Bwabwata National Park
8 Caprivi Game Park
9 Mahango Game Reserve
10 Khaudom Game Park
11 Nyae Nyae Conservancy
12 Waterberg Plateau Park
13 Etosha National Park
14 Purros Conservancy
15 Skeleton Coast Park
16 Khoadi Hoas Conservancy
17 Uibasen Twyfelfontein
     Conservancy
18 Torra Conservancy
19 Doros !Nawas Conservancy
20 Cape Cross Seal Reserve
21 National West Coast
     Recreation Area
22 Gross Barmen
23 Van Bach Dam
24 Daan Viljoen Game Park
25 Reho Spa
26 Hardap Dam Game Reserve
27 Namib-Naukluft Park
28 Namib-Rand Nature Reserve
29 Gondwana Cañon Park
30 Fish River Canyon Park

surrounding an artificial lake and a pleasant wildlife reserve.

Khaudom Game Reserve This surprising park in the western Kalahari is difficult to reach, but the wildlife viewing can approach that of Etosha. The bushveld landscape is crossed by a network of *omiramba* (fossil valleys).

Mamili National Park Remote Mamili, in the vast Linyanti Marshes of the Caprivi Strip, is often referred to as a mini Okavango Delta. The wetland landscape and the wildlife-viewing opportunities certainly justify the comparison.

Mudumu National Park Mudumu takes in the alluring wetlands of the Linyanti river system and surrounding wildlife areas. It has been ravaged by poaching and wildfire, and has suffered damage by cattle, but is one of Namibia's loveliest landscapes and has excellent bird-watching venues.

Namib-Naukluft Park Namibia's largest national park takes in much of the Namib Desert, as well as the surrounding gravel plains and the Naukluft Massif, a mountainous area with dramatic scenery and superb hiking trails that is also a refuge for Hartmann's mountain zebras. At Sossusvlei you can visit the archetypal Namib dunefield, where dunes rise 300m above the plains. Sandwich Harbour, south of Walvis Bay, is a well-known bird sanctuary.

Skeleton Coast Park The wild, foggy Skeleton Coast has long been a graveyard for ships and their crews, who were unable to survive the harsh desert conditions. Only the stretch between the Ugab River and Terrace Bay is open to the general public, while the remote northern area, the Skeleton Coast Wilderness, is open only to clients of the concessionaire, Wilderness Safaris Namibia (see Organised Tours in the Getting Around chapter).

Waterberg Plateau Park This lovely table mountain is a repository for the reintroduction of endangered wildlife. Attractions include a comfortable rest camp, superb views, and wonderful walking tracks.

Visiting the National Parks

Access to most wildlife-oriented parks is limited to closed vehicles only – no bicycles or motorcycles are allowed – so visitors need their own transport, a safari company or a good lift. For most parks, a 2WD vehicle is sufficient, but for Mamili National Park, Khaudom Game Reserve and parts of Bwabwata National Park, you need a 4WD.

National park and rest camp accommodation may be booked through the semiprivate Namibia Wildlife Resorts (NWR) offices in Windhoek, Swakopmund, Lüderitz and elsewhere, while park entry permits are available on arrival at park entrances.

Namib-Naukluft Park entry permits are available after hours from Hans Kriess Garage and petrol station in Swakopmund and from CWB petrol station in Walvis Bay.

Transit permits to drive between Ugabmund and Springbokwater in the Skeleton Coast Park are available at the park gates.

Reservations for Etosha, the Skeleton Coast Park and the Sesriem and Naukluft Mountains areas of Namib-Naukluft Park are officially handled only in Windhoek. Having said that, if pre-booking is impossible (eg, if you're pulling into a national park area on a whim), there's a good chance you'll find something available on the spot at the last minute, but have a contingency plan in case things don't work out.

For more information, contact Namibia Wildlife Resorts (NWR; ☎ 061-256446, fax 256715, **e** nwr@mweb.com.na, **w** www .namibiawildliferesorts.com), Private Bag 13378, Windhoek. For reservations see Tourist Offices under Information in the Windhoek chapter. For information on accommodation rates see NWR Camps, Rest Camps & Resorts under Accommodation in the Facts for the Visitor chapter.

Bookings may be made by phone up to 11 months in advance, while written applications are taken up to 18 months in advance. To independently pre-book by post, fax or email, you'll need to specify the type of accommodation required, the number of adults, the ages of any accompanying children, and the dates you wish to stay (along with alternative dates, if possible). The confirmation and invoice will be sent by post. Fees must be paid before the indicated due date. Full payment (by direct bank transfer – apparently they haven't yet heard of credit cards, but they may well figure it out in the near future) is necessary before the booking will be confirmed. Changes to the booking may be made without penalties up to 10 days before the first day of occupancy.

An easier way to book – and to pay by credit card – is to book through a Windhoek travel agency; see Organised Tours in the Getting Around chapter or Travel Agencies under Information in the Windhoek chapter.

Conservancies & Private Game Reserves

A new concept in Namibia is the conservancy, an amalgamation of private farms or an area of communal land where farmers and/or local residents agree to combine resources for the benefit of wildlife. There are currently 10 conservancies, with three more slated for the near future.

Another sort of protected area is the private game reserve, of which there are now 182 in Namibia. The largest of these, by far, are the 200,000-hectare NamibRand Nature Reserve, adjoining the Namib-Naukluft Park, and the 102,000-hectare Gondwana Cañon Park, bordering Fish River Canyon Park. In both, concessionaires provide accommodation and activities for visitors. Most of the smaller game reserves are either private game farms or hunting farms, which sustain endemic animal species rather than livestock.

Firewood

Firewood – normally split camelthorn acacia – is available for around US$2 per bundle at national park rest camps, most private camping grounds and general stores. Gathering of firewood and lighting open fires are prohibited in national parks, but even outside the parks wilderness hikers are advised to carry a fuel stove and avoid lighting open fires, which can scar the landscape and may get out of control in the typically dry conditions. If you must gather your own firewood, note that it's technically illegal in Namibia to use anything but mopane or acacia; burning or even carrying any other sort of wood will incur a fine, even outside national parks.

Warning: DO NOT burn dried branches of euphorbia, as the plant contains a deadly toxin and it can be fatal to inhale the smoke or eat food cooked on a fire containing it. If you're in doubt about any wood you've collected, leave it out of the fire.

GOVERNMENT & POLITICS

Namibia is an independent republic with three separate branches of government. The president, who has strong executive powers, is elected by popular ballot for a maximum of three five-year terms (in 1999, this was changed from two terms, to accommodate President Sam Nujoma's bid for a third term). The two-chamber national parliament makes up the legislative branch. One part, the National Assembly or lower house, consists of 78 members who are elected by popular vote every five years. The upper house, the 26-member National Council, is purely an advisory body and is comprised of two popularly elected representatives from each of Namibia's 13 regions, who serve six-year terms.

Any constitutional amendment requires a two-thirds majority vote of the National Assembly. In the case of an irreconcilable dispute between the executive and legislative branches, the president has the power to dismiss the entire assembly. However, in such an event, the president must also stand for re-election.

The judiciary, which is independent of the executive and legislative branches, is presided over by a chief justice.

All the national government functions are directed from the national capital, Windhoek. The country is divided into 13 regions, each with its own regional government, which in turn are subdivided into municipalities.

Since independence on 21 March 1990, Namibia has been governed by the socialist-oriented Swapo party. Headed by Executive President Samuel Daniel Shafiishuna (Sam) Nujoma (of Owambo heritage) and Prime Minister Hage Gottfried Geingob (Damara heritage), Swapo took 57% of the vote in the first national election.

Swapo again swept the elections in 1994, and in December 1999, it won 76.8% of the vote and 55 seats in the national assembly. The largest opposition group, Mr Ben Ulenga's social democratic Congress of Democrats, took 9.9% of the vote, winning seven assembly seats. Mishake Muyongo's conservative Democratic Turnhalle Alliance (DTA) – a coalition of 11 parties with little in common but an opposition to Swapo's Owambo-centred position – took 9.5% of the vote and seven assembly seats (over 80% less than it took in the 1990 election). The centrist United Democratic Front (UDF) captured two assembly seats and the Christian conservative Monitor Action Group (MAG) won one seat, while the conservative Democratic Coalition of Namibia (DCN) lost its only seat.

Extremist minority parties, such as the Herstigte Nasionale Party, which advocates apartheid, still exist but are politically powerless. The Action Front for the Retention of the Turnhalle Principles (Actur), a white-dominated party to the right of the DTA, lacks any seats in the assembly, but does retain some political influence.

Despite its former Marxist affiliations, Swapo isn't generally inclined towards political extremism, but instead it takes a pragmatic view regarding the domestic economy and international relations, and has adhered to a policy of national reconciliation. However, the tensions endure between the various races and tribes, and although the per-capita GDP of US$3700 is high by African standards, the statistic masks the inequalities between population groups. In the end, 5% of the population controls 72% of the economy.

The government openly admits that its main problem is a lack of discipline over fiscal spending. In the past, there were attempts to encourage investment and lower personal taxes, but the 1998–99 budget made expenditure a priority over investment and increased the tax burden on Namibian workers from 28.9% to 30.5% of the GDP. Funding for roads and welfare is being cut while spending on government personnel and cosy retirement packages for officials has increased in the name of 'affirmative action'.

Other hot political issues include the uncontrolled spread of HIV and AIDS, official disapproval of homosexuality (sodomy is illegal in Namibia), and freedom of speech and the freedom of the press regarding reports on governmental corruption. Significantly, the press has been gagged by legislation that strictly prohibits any dialogue on parliamentary issues before they're discussed in parliament.

ECONOMY

The Namibian economy is dominated by mining (diamonds, uranium and various ores), fishing, tourism, and meat, milk and wool production, as well as subsistence-level agriculture. By African standards, Namibia is already a prosperous country. It does suffer some disadvantages – sporadic water shortages, a lack of local fuel sources, vast distances and a widely scattered population – but its GDP is at least twice the African average and its population remains small and diverse. Currently, over 80% of the country's food and manufactured goods are imported from South Africa, creating a degree of economic dependence. The development of the economy rests on its ability to attract foreign investment, and develop (via education and training) its own human resources to exploit the country's vast resource potential.

Mining

Namibia's mining income is the fourth largest in Africa and the 17th largest in the world, mainly thanks to both the world's richest diamond fields and its largest uranium mine. The diamonds are extracted mostly by strip-mining the alluvial sand and gravel of the famed Sperrgebiet between Lüderitz and the Orange River. The major player is Consolidated Diamond Mines (CDM), one of Namibia's largest employers, which scours through 20 million tonnes of earth per year, for a yield of 200kg (one million carats) of diamonds. The Rössing uranium mine, near Swakopmund, produces more than 60 million tonnes of ore annually.

Of Namibia's other mineral deposits, which include lithium, germanium, silver, vanadium, tin, copper, lead, zinc and tantalum, 70% are extracted by the Tsumeb Corporation Ltd, which operates in the phenomenally rich environs of Tsumeb, Grootfontein and Otavi in North Central Namibia. Other major mining areas include Uis, with dwindling deposits of tin; Rosh Pinah, near the Orange River, which produces zinc, lead and silver; and Karibib, with quartz, lithium and beryllium.

A current source of controversy is the offshore Kudu gas field in south-western Namibia. The feasibility of development and a pipeline to the Cape region is now being assessed, but any real action is still many years off.

Herding & Agriculture

Around 16% of Namibia's active labour force is involved in commercial herding, but over 70% of the people depend on agriculture to some extent. Most farmers are engaged in subsistence agriculture in the heavily populated communal areas of the north, particularly the Owambo country, Kavango and Caprivi. However, over 80% of the agricultural yield is derived from commercial herding in the central and southern parts of the country.

The industry is dominated by farmers of German or Afrikaner heritage who are involved in raising stock, especially cattle and sheep. This occupation is dogged by water shortages, but most farms are generally well managed and sufficiently large to support stock numbers. A new trend is game ranching, and many farmers now augment their herds with gemsboks, springboks, kudus, zebras and ostriches for meat and hides – as well as for tourism and hunting.

In the drier areas of the south and Kalahari regions, the emphasis is on karakul sheep, which resemble scraggy goats but are well suited to the conditions and produce high-quality meat and wool. Karakul wool once formed the basis of an expanding weaving industry and the export market for luxury leather and skin goods was once dominated by karakul. However, in recent years the bottom has dropped out of the market and it remains to be seen whether a recovery is on the cards.

There is also a limited amount of commercial crop farming, mainly around Otavi, Grootfontein and Tsumeb, with maize as the principal crop. Thanks to irrigation from Hardap Dam, Mariental has a growing agricultural base, and around Omaruru, citrus is the particular speciality.

Fishing

The Namibian coastal waters are considered some of the world's richest, mainly thanks to the cold offshore Benguela Current, which flows northwards from the Antarctic. It's exceptionally rich in plankton, which accounts for the abundance of anchovies, pilchards, mackerels and other whitefish. But the limited offshore fishing rights have caused problems, and there is resentment that such countries as Spain and Russia have legal access to offshore fish stocks. Namibia has now declared a 200-nautical-mile exclusive economic zone to make Namibian fisheries competitive.

Each year, the waters off Lüderitz yield varying numbers of crayfish (rock lobsters), most for export to Japan in the form of frozen lobster meat. The fleet, which is comprised of 20 ships, operates from the Orange River mouth to Hottentot Bay, 75km north of Lüderitz. Strict seasons and size limits protect from overfishing. In all, the industry employs around 1000 people.

Lüderitz' port produces and processes tinned fish, fishmeal and fish oil. However, the current decline in the fishing industry has meant that of the 11 fish-processing plants that were active in Walvis Bay and Lüderitz 20 years ago, fewer than half survive. Oysters are cultivated and marketed around Swakopmund, Walvis Bay and Lüderitz.

Manufacturing

Accounting for less than 5% of Namibia's gross national product (GNP), manufacturing in Namibia is mostly comprised of meat processing, and goods and materials for the mining industry. Currently, most manufactured goods must be imported from South Africa.

It is vital that Namibia develops its manufacturing sector, but progress has been thwarted by the high cost of raw materials, the shortage of skilled labour and training, and a measure of political uncertainty. Currently, Namibia continues to court overseas investment for manufacturing projects, and to a large extent its success will determine Namibia's economic future.

Tourism

Since independence in 1990, Namibia has gone from a war-torn backwater known only to South African hunters, anglers and holiday-makers to a popular, chic and trendy destination for overseas visitors. Immediately following independence, the number of South African tourists dropped off sharply, then began to climb again. The country is also a big draw for German tourists, which isn't surprising since travel articles often describe the country as being 'more German than Germany'. That isn't exactly true, but in Windhoek, Swakopmund and Lüderitz, you'd be forgiven for making such an assertion.

As in Botswana, Namibia's official policy is to develop a high-cost, low-volume tourist base comprised primarily of comparatively wealthy Europeans, Australasians and North Americans. However, Namibia's national park fees are still the region's most affordable, and mid-range and top-end facilities are still considerably better value for foreigners than those in either Botswana or Zimbabwe. (Note, however, that although Namibians receive a 50% discount on national parks entry and accommodation, park visits remain out of reach for most Namibian citizens and residents.)

Strife in neighbouring Zimbabwe and the ongoing problems in the Caprivi region have affected tourist numbers. This is especially true in northern Namibia, where the tourism industry is currently suffering its lowest numbers since independence.

Retail

The expanding retail sector is flourishing, with a growing number of shopping venues in Windhoek and Swakopmund. However, many people depend upon small market and street-trading stalls. In the Owambo areas and other parts of the north, supply and distribution of goods is handled by small *cuca* shops (bush shops) spaced intermittently along the main routes.

POPULATION & PEOPLE

Namibia has an estimated 1,727,000 people, which, at approximately two people per square kilometre, represents one of Africa's lowest population densities, but its annual growth rate of over 3% is one of the world's highest. This number comprises 11 major ethnic groups, ranging from pastoralists and hunter-gatherers to rural farmers and town-dwellers (see the special section 'Peoples of Namibia'). These include Owambo (650,000 people), Kavango (120,000), Herero/Himba (100,000), Damara (100,000), Caprivian (80,000), Afrikaner (65,000), Nama (60,000), Baster (35,000), German (20,000), San (19,000) and Tswana (8000).

Although this ethnic diversity is overlain with Western cultural influences, since independence there have been efforts to emphasise the history and traditions of each group. About 75% of the people inhabit rural areas, but urban drift in search of work or higher wages has resulted in increased homelessness, unemployment and crime in the capital and other towns.

EDUCATION

During the German colonial era and the South African mandate, education for the masses took a low priority on the government agenda. As a result, there was a vast disparity between the educational performance of whites, who normally paid to attend private schools, and other ethnic groups. Less than 75% of Namibian children completed five years of schooling, only 8% attended secondary school and less than 1% went on to higher education or professional training. As a result, at the time of independence there was a severe shortage of qualified teachers, and furthermore they received very poor salaries. Despite government-subsidised teacher training colleges in both the Owambo areas and Windhoek, very few black Namibians had sufficient educational background to enter teacher training.

Nowadays, education is technically compulsory for all children. Swapo policy has designated English as the official language of instruction. (However, in some primary schools, classes may also be conducted in Afrikaans or Bantu languages, and some private schools still stick with German.) In the first four years of independence, 832 classrooms were constructed, expatriate teachers were brought in, high-quality instructional materials were purchased and enrolment increased by 21%. Between 1991 and 1993, secondary-school pass rates jumped from 38% to 51%. Nearly 75% of the population has received, or is receiving, at least a primary school education.

Another primary emphasis is on the need to 'catch up' and achieve full literacy. To that end, the government has established over 700 literacy centres around the country to provide basic reading and writing instruction for children and adults alike.

Namibia has three institutes of higher education: the University of Namibia, which began instruction in March 1993 and offers degree-level courses in arts, economics, education and medicine; the Technikon, a polytechnic school that emphasises career-oriented courses in business, agriculture, ecology, nursing and secretarial studies; and the College for Out-of-School Training, which provides theoretical and practical courses in crafts and nursing.

Many Namibians leave the country to attend university in South Africa (at Stellenbosch, Witwatersrand or Cape Town) or to study in Europe on UN or Commonwealth scholarships.

ARTS

Namibia is still developing a literary tradition but its musical, visual and architectural arts are now established. The country also enjoys a wealth of amateur material arts: carvings, basketry, tapestry, and simple but resourcefully designed toys, clothing and household implements.

Dance

Each group in Namibia has its own dances, but common threads run through most of them. First, all dances are intended to express social values, to some extent, and many dances reflect the environment in which they're performed.

Dances of the Ju/hoansi !Kung men (a San group in north-eastern Namibia) tend to mimic the animals they hunt, such as the eland, giraffe and elephant, or involve other elements that are important to them. For example, the 'melon dance' involves tossing and catching a tsama melon according to a fixed rhythm. The Himba dance *ondjongo* must be performed by a cattle owner and involves representing care and ownership.

Similarly, dances of people in more arid regions tend to be more subdued than those in well-watered areas, in order to conserve precious water and energy. Two Herero dances, the *outjina* (for women) and *omuhiva* (for men) are performed using a plank, known as an *otjipirangi*, strapped to one foot. As the dancers stamp their feet, the wood delivers a hollow, rhythmic sound, taking the place of drums (which can't be constructed due to a lack of sufficiently large trees in most Herero areas).

Dancing styles also follow set patterns, and in most cases attempt to reflect both power and youth (regardless of the age of the dancers). This is achieved by absorption of the energy that flows from the accompanying percussion instruments, and by turning the body itself into a percussion instrument. In some cases, dancers themselves make use of musical instruments – including anything from axes, blades, rattles and shakers – which may be shaken in the hands or are strapped onto the feet, arms or hips.

Forceful performances are valued, especially in dramatic dances, such as the popular *oudano*. However, one of the most significant elements of Namibian dance is 'coolness'; that is, an obvious composure, unity, smoothness and lack of visible emotion. While the body actively performs the dance – stamping, gyrating and even exaggerating movements – the face reveals only a calm comfort. In Mbukushu dancing, in the Caprivi, the eyes remain fixed on the earth; in the Oorlam *wals* (waltz), partners look fixedly past each other, despite the fact that their feet are executing rapid and complicated steps.

Specific dances are also used for various rituals, including rites of passage, political events, social gatherings and spiritual ceremonies. The Ju/hoansi male initiation dance, the *tcòcmà*, for example, may not even be viewed by women. In the Kavango and Caprivi region, dances performed by traditional healers require the dancer to constantly shake rattles held in both hands. Most festive dances, such as the animated Kavango *epera* and *dipera*, have roles for both men and women, but are performed in lines with the genders separated.

Music

Namibia's earliest musicians were the San, whose music probably emulated the sounds made by their animal neighbours and was sung to accompany dances and storytelling. The early Nama, who had a more developed musical technique, used drums, flutes and basic stringed instruments, also to accompany dances. Some of these were adopted and adapted by the later-arriving Bantu, who added marimbas, gourd rattles and animal-horn trumpets to the range. Nowadays, drums, marimbas and rattles are still popular, and it isn't unusual to see dancers wearing belts of soft-drink (soda) cans filled with pebbles to provide rhythmic accompaniment to their steps (see Dance earlier).

A prominent European contribution to Namibian music is the choir. Early in the colonial period, missionaries established religious choral groups among local people, and both school and church choirs still perform regularly. Namibia's most renowned ensemble is the Cantare Audire Choir, which was started by Windhoek music teacher Ernst von Biljon. It is composed of Namibians of all races and performs both African and European religious, classical and traditional compositions for audiences around the world. Naturally, the German colonists also introduced their traditional 'oom-pah-pah' bands, which feature mainly at WIKA (Windhoek Karnival) and at other German-oriented festivals.

Literature

Literature is fairly new to Namibia, and apart from several German colonial novels – most importantly Gustav Frenssen's *Peter Moor's Journey to Southwest Africa* (original 1905, English translation 1908) – and some Afrikaans writing, few noteworthy works emerged during the South African occupation. The best-known work from that period is Henno Martin's *The Sheltering Desert* (1956, English edition 1957), which records two years spent by the geologist author and his friend Hermann Korn avoiding internment as prisoners of war during WWII.

Only with the independence struggle did an indigenous literature begin to take root. Unfortunately, Namibian literature isn't widely distributed either in Namibia or abroad. For the undaunted, the following suggestions may help provide an introduction to the country.

One of contemporary Namibia's most significant writers is Joseph Diescho, whose first novel, *Born of the Sun*, was published in 1988, when he was living in the USA. To date, this refreshingly unpretentious work remains the most renowned Namibian effort. As with most African literature, it's largely autobiographical, describing the protagonist's early life in a tribal village, his coming of age and his first contact with Christianity. It then follows his path through the South African mines and his ultimate political awakening. Diescho's second novel, *Troubled Waters* (1993), which is a bit wooden and didactic, focuses on a white South African protagonist who is sent to Namibia on military duty and develops a political conscience.

Another significant Namibian voice is David Jasper Utley, whose first publication was a book of short stories entitled *Allsorts* (1991). These brief tales are remarkable for their incorporation of magical realism, including time travel. The stories also depart from the common African themes of gender issues and racial reconciliation. More recently, Utley has published *Ngoma* and *Click*, both Namibian detective stories.

Kapoche Victor's short *On the Run* (1994) is a political thriller set in pre-independence Namibia. Its main characters are four protesters, all A-level students, running from the South African police. In the first novel, *Meekulu's Homecoming*, by Kaleni Hiyalwa, the protagonist is a young girl called Kutya who does her growing up during Namibia's liberation war.

A new and increasingly apparent branch of Namibian work comes from women writers. *A New Initiation Song* (1994) is a collection of poetry and short fiction published by the Sister Namibia collective. This volume's seven sections cover memories of girlhood, body images, and heterosexual and lesbian relationships. Among the best works are those of Liz Frank and Elizabeth !Khaxas. The most outstanding short stories include, Uerieta, by Jane Katjavivi, which describes a white woman's coming to terms with African life, and, When the Rains Came, by Marialena van Tonder, in which a farm couple narrowly survives a drought. One contributor, Nepeti Nicanor, along with Marjorie Orford, also edited another volume, *Coming on Strong* (1996). Those who read German will appreciate the works of Giselher Hoffmann, which address historical and current Namibian issues. His first novel, *Im Bunde der Dritte* (Three's Company, 1984),
is about poaching. *Die Erstgeboren* (The Firstborn, 1991) is told from the perspective of a San group that finds itself pitted against German settlers. Similarly, the Nama-Herero conflict of the late 19th century is described from the Nama perspective in *Die Schweigenden Feuer* (The Silent Fires, 1994). It's also concerned with the impact of Western civilisation on indigenous cultures.

In addition, there are several novels set in the country written by non-Namibians. Wilbur Smith's *The Burning Shore* takes place during and after WWI. Its female protagonist is shipwrecked on the Skeleton Coast and survives by adapting to indigenous life with a San couple. The protagonist of Immo Vogel's intelligent German novel *Namutoni* is a young German immigrant who finds himself caught in a struggle between black freedom fighters, black workers, Afrikaners, German farmers and German racists, and has to take sides.

Ancient Rock Art

Many visitors to Southern Africa seek out examples of ancient rock paintings and engravings. There's a lot of speculation about their origins, but no reliable way of dating them without destroying them. Thanks to deposits left around major sites and the scenes depicted, it's surmised that the artists were nomadic hunter-gatherers, without knowledge of agriculture or pottery. For that reason, the works have summarily been attributed to the early San people.

As would be expected, most rock painting reflected people's relationship with nature. Some were stylised representations but the majority faithfully and skilfully portray the people and animals of the region: hunters, giraffes, elephants, rhinos, lions, antelopes and so on, in red, yellow, brown and ochre.

Common themes include the roles of men and women, hunting scenes and natural medicine. The natural medicine theme includes examples of trance dancing and spiritual healing using the San life force, known as *nxum*, which was invoked to control aspects of the natural world, including climate and disease. All these things still feature in San tradition.

It has been speculated that, as with similar cave art found in Europe, the animal paintings were intended to ensure an abundance of those animals. However, this concept hasn't been noted in any present-day African culture, and there's no evidence of ancient ties with Europe. Furthermore, few of the animals portrayed served as food for the ancient San.

Although the earliest works have long faded, flaked and eroded into oblivion, the dry climate and their normal location in sheltered granite overhangs have preserved many of the more recent ones. Anthropological studies have used the content, skill level and superposition of the paintings to identify three distinct stages.

The earliest paintings seem to reflect a period of gentle nomadism during which people were occupied primarily with the hunt. Later works, which revealed great artistic improvement, suggest peaceful incursions by outside groups, perhaps Bantu, San or Khoi-Khoi.

For further information on Namibian literature, check university libraries for Dorian Haarhoff's *The Wild South-West: Frontier Myths & Metaphors in Literature Set in Namibia, 1760–1988* (1991). See also Books in the Facts for the Visitor chapter.

Architecture

The most obvious architectural contribution in Namibia was made by the German colonial settlers, who attempted to re-create late-19th-century Germany in Namibia. In deference to the warmer African climate, however, they added such features as shaded verandas, to provide cool outdoor living space. The best examples may be seen in Lüderitz, Swakopmund and Windhoek, but German style is also evident in central and southern Namibia.

The most ornate and monumental structures, including the train station and old prison in Swakopmund, were done in an architectural style known as Wilhelminischer Stil. Jugendstil (Art Nouveau) influences are most in evidence in Lüderitz and in Windhoek's Christuskirche. See the special section 'Windhoek Walking Tour' in the Windhoek chapter.

Visual Arts

Most of Namibia's renowned modern painters and photographers are of European origin and concentrate largely on the country's colourful landscapes, bewitching light, native wildlife and, more recently, its diverse peoples. Well-known names include François de Mecker, Axel Eriksson, Fritz Krampe and Adolph Jentsch. The well-known colonial landscape artists Carl Ossman and Ernst Vollbehr are exhibited in Germany.

Non-European Namibians, who have concentrated on three-dimensional and material arts, have been developing their own traditions. Township art, which develops sober

Ancient Rock Art

The final stage indicates a decline in the standard of the paintings; either a loss of interest or a loss of facility with the genre, or imitation of earlier works by more recently arrived peoples. For the archaeologist, there are considerable difficulties in relating the paintings to the cultural sequences preserved in soil layers of caves and rock shelters, but recent advances in radiocarbon dating are beginning to shed some light.

The red pigments were ground mainly from iron oxides, which were powdered and mixed with animal fat to form an adhesive paste. The whites came from silica, powdered quartz and white clays and were by nature less adhesive than the red pigments. For that reason, white paintings survive only in sheltered locations, such as well-protected caves. Both pigments were applied to the rock using sticks, the artist's fingers and brushes made from animal hair.

The most poignant thing about rock art is that it remains in the spot where it was created. Unlike in a museum, sensitive viewers may catch a glimpse of the inspiration that went into the paintings. In Namibia, you'll find examples of the genre in rock overhangs all over the country, but the most renowned sites are at Twyfelfontein, Spitzkoppe and the Brandberg, all in northwestern Namibia.

Most ancient rock art dates back at least 6000 years to the early Stone Age.

themes in an expressive, colourful and generally light-hearted manner, first appeared in the townships of South Africa during the apartheid years. Over the past decade, it has taken hold in Namibia and is developing into a popular art form. Names to keep an eye on include Tembo Masala and Joseph Madisia.

Cinema

Although Namibia's bizarre desert landscapes are appearing in an increasing number of films and nearly everyone has seen foreign car, airline and insurance commercials filmed at the dunes at Sossusvlei, Namibia's own film industry is still in its infancy.

The most notable Namibian film that has been seen internationally is *Sophia's Homecoming*, which tells the story of an Owambo woman who, to support her family, goes to work as a domestic in Windhoek. She is away for 12 years, during which time her husband Naftali finds a job and takes up with her sister Selna. During Sophia's absence, Selna takes over the affections of not only Naftali, but also of Sophia's children. When Sophia pressures her sister to leave the family, Naftali confesses that he prefers Selna, who is pregnant with his child. Ironically, in an attempt to shift her direction, Sophia returns to Windhoek and attempts to build a new life for herself and her three children.

Theatre

Namibian theatre has yet to develop its potential, but one work has gained international acclaim. The play *Mogomotsitang*, or 'Who Will Comfort Me', by Lucky Peters, tells the tale of a Tswana-Namibian who lives a traditional Tswana lifestyle as his ancestors did. The story follows the protagonist, who struggles to support his children after the death of his wife. The work has won the National Drama Award and has played in Europe (in the Tswana language).

SOCIETY & CONDUCT

Short of public nudity or open vocal criticism of the government, there aren't really any unforgivable faux pas that must be avoided (by foreigners, anyway). However,

in most places, any open displays of affection are frowned upon and show insensitivity to local sentiments.

Greetings

A few straightforward courtesies may greatly improve a foreigner's chances of acceptance by the local community, especially in rural areas. In Namibia, pleasantries are taken quite seriously, and it's essential to greet or say goodbye to someone entering or leaving a room. Learn the local words for hello and goodbye and use them unsparingly.

Emphasis is also placed on handshakes. The African handshake consists of three parts: the normal Western handshake, followed by the linking of bent fingers while touching the ends of upward-pointing thumbs, and then a repeat of the conventional handshake.

Status

As in most traditional societies, the achievement of old age is an accomplishment worthy of respect and elders are treated with deference – their word should not be questioned and they should be accorded utmost courtesy. Teachers, doctors and other professionals often receive similar treatment.

Likewise, people holding positions of authority – immigration officers, government officials, police, village chiefs and so on – should be dealt with pragmatically. Officials in Namibia are not as sensitive as those in most neighbouring countries and are normally refreshingly open and friendly. However, if you do cross them or strike a nerve, all that may change. It is one thing to stand up for your rights, but blowing a fuse, undermining an official's judgment or authority, or insulting an ego may only serve to waste time, tie you up in red tape and inspire closer scrutiny of future travellers.

At the other end of the spectrum, children rate very low on the social scale. They are expected to do as they're told without complaint and defer to adults in all situations. For example, it is considered very rude for a child to occupy a seat in a bus if adults are standing. Foreigners are normally exempted. Similarly, Southern Africa is largely still a man's country and a black man will not normally give up his seat to a woman, never mind that she is carrying a baby and luggage and minding two toddlers. It makes one wonder what they must think of the local whites and other Westerners who habitually do.

Visiting Settlements

When visiting rural settlements, it's a good idea to request to see the chief to announce your presence and ask permission before setting up camp or wandering through a village. You will rarely be refused permission. Women should dress and behave modestly, especially in the presence of chiefs or other highly esteemed persons.

Visitors should also ask permission before drawing water from community boreholes. If you do draw water at a community tap or borehole, avoid letting it spill on the ground, especially in desert areas, where it's as precious as gold. If you wish to wash your body or your clothing, fill a container with water and carry it elsewhere.

Lone travellers may be looked upon with suspicion: women because they should be at home rearing families, and men because, in many areas, foreigners are potentially spies for right-wing factions. It may help to carry photographs of your family or evidence of a nonespionage-related profession.

Food Etiquette

Most travellers will have the opportunity to share an African meal sometime during their stay and will normally be given royal treatment and a seat of honour. Although concessions are sometimes made for foreigners, table manners are probably different from what you're accustomed to. The African staple, maize or sorghum meal, is the centre of nearly every meal. It is normally taken with the right hand from a communal pot, rolled into balls, dipped in some sort of relish – meat gravy or vegetables – and eaten. As in most societies, it is considered impolite to scoff food, or to hoard it or be stingy with it. If you do, your host may feel that he or she hasn't provided enough. Similarly, if you can't finish your food, don't worry; the host will be pleased that you have been satisfied.

Often, containers of water or home-brew beer may be passed around from person to person. However, it is not customary to share coffee, tea or bottled soft drinks.

Gifts

Finally, if you do visit a remote community, please tread lightly and leave as little lasting evidence of your visit as possible. In most traditional Namibian societies, it isn't considered impolite to ask others for items you may desire. If you're besieged with requests, it's perfectly acceptable to refuse without causing offence. If you start feeling guilty about your relative wealth and hand out all your earthly belongings, you may be regarded as very silly indeed. As for gift-giving, reciprocation of kindness is one thing but superficial altruism is another. Indiscriminate distribution of gifts from outside, however well-intentioned, tends to create a taste for items not locally available, erodes well-established values, robs people of their pride and in extreme cases, creates villages of dependent beggars.

On the other hand, when you're offered a gift, don't feel guilty about accepting it; to refuse it would bring shame on the giver. To receive a gift politely, accept it with both hands and perhaps bow slightly. If you're receiving some minor thing you've asked for, such as a salt shaker or a pen, or getting back change at a shop, receive it with your right hand while touching your left hand to your right elbow; this is the equivalent of saying thanks. Spoken thanks aren't common and local people tend to think Westerners say thank you too often and too casually, so don't be upset if you aren't verbally thanked for a gift.

RELIGION

At least 75% of Namibians profess Christianity, and German Lutheranism is the dominant sect in most of the country. As a result of early missionary activity and Portuguese influence from Angola, there is also a substantial Roman Catholic population, mainly in the central and northern areas.

Most non-Christian Namibians – mainly Himba, San and some Herero – live in the north and continue to follow animist traditions. In general, their beliefs are characterised by ancestor-veneration, and most practitioners believe that deceased ancestors continue to interact with mortals and serve as messengers between their descendants and the gods.

LANGUAGE
Indigenous Languages
As a first language, most Namibians speak either a Bantu dialect – which would include Owambo, Kavango, Herero and Caprivian languages – or one of several Khoisan languages, including Khoi-Khoi (Nama), Damara or a San dialect.

The Bantu language group includes eight dialects from Owambo; Kwanyama and Ndonga are the official Owambo languages. The Kavango has four separate dialects: Kwangali, Mbunza, Sambiyu and Geiriku, of which Kwangali is the most widely used. In the Caprivi, the most widely spoken language is Rotsi (or Lozi), which originally came from Barotseland in Zambia. Herero (not surprisingly) speak Herero, which is a rolling, melodious language, rich in colourful words. Most Namibian place names beginning with an 'O' – eg, Okahandja, Omaruru and Otjiwarongo – are derived from the Herero language.

Khoisan dialects are characterised by 'click' elements, which make them difficult to learn, and only a few foreigners ever get the hang of them. Clicks are made by compressing the tongue against different parts of the mouth to produce different sounds. Names that include an exclamation mark are of Khoisan origin and should be rendered as a sideways click sound, similar to the sound one would make when encouraging a horse, but with a hollow tone (like the sound made when pulling a cork from a bottle). The other three clicks are formed by quickly drawing the tongue away from the front teeth, which is represented as /; clicking a tutting disapproval, represented as //; and a sharp pop formed by drawing the tongue from the roof of the mouth, which is represented more or less as a vertical line with two crossbars.

The first English-Ju/hoansi dictionary (Ju/hoansi is the dialect spoken by most Namibian San) was compiled in 1992 by the late Patrick Dickens, and published by Florida State University in the USA.

Many native Khoisan speakers also speak at least one Bantu and one European language, normally Afrikaans. The language of the Damara, who are actually of Bantu origin, is also a Khoisan dialect and is closely related to Nama.

European Languages
When the new constitution was drawn up at the time of independence, the official language of Namibia was designated as English. Although that may seem odd when English is the native tongue of only about 2% of the population, it was decided that using English would put all ethnic groups at an equal disadvantage. Furthermore, it was recognised that the adoption of the language of international business would appeal to both tourists and investors. Since independence, Namibia's educational system has used an English-language curriculum, but only in the Caprivi region is English the officially preferred language for communication between ethnic groups.

Having said that, the most widely used lingua franca is Afrikaans, which is technically a dialect of Dutch. While it's often dismissed as the language of apartheid, it's the first language of more than 100,000 Namibians of diverse ethnic backgrounds. Most Namibian Nama and Basters use Afrikaans as a first language, and Namibians of Owambo, Damara, Herero/Himba and other ethnic backgrounds use it to communicate among themselves. Written Afrikaans may be decipherable to Dutch and/or English speakers, but even native Dutch-speakers may require some effort to master the spoken language.

Thanks to Namibia's colonial past, German is widely spoken, and around Swakopmund, it's the main lingua franca used by all ethnic groups. In the Kavango region and parts of the Caprivi, Portuguese also figures prominently as a common language.

PEOPLES OF NAMIBIA

Although Namibia is one of the world's least densely populated countries, its rich mix of ethnic and tribal backgrounds provides a wealth of social and cultural diversity. The indigenous peoples of Namibia, the Khoisan (comprised of San hunter-gatherers and Nama pastoralists), have inhabited the region from time immemorial. They were followed by Bantu herders, with the first Europeans trickling in during the 17th century. This special section outlines the background and cultural trends of each major population group.

Owambo

The 650,000-strong Owambo make up the largest population group and, not surprisingly, most of the ruling Swapo party. The Owambo live mainly in the north and are subdivided into 12 distinct tribal groups. Four of these occupy the Kunene region of southern Angola, while the other eight comprise the Owambo groups in Namibia. The most numerous group is the Kwanyama, which makes up 35% of Namibia's Owambo population and dominates the Namibian government. The next largest groups are the Ndonga, with 30%, and the Kwambi, with

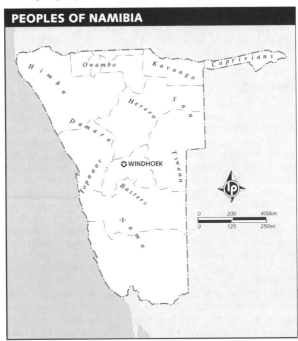

PEOPLES OF NAMIBIA

Inset: The San people were the region's earliest inhabitants. (Photo by Deanna Swaney)

12%, while the remaining five groups each make up from 1% to 8% of the total.

Historically, each of these tribes was headed by an all-powerful hereditary king who had below him a council of headmen. However, thanks to changes brought about by Christianity and German and South African colonial influences, most of these tribes now operate under a council of chiefs or headmen. Other changes have included a gradual shift from a predominantly matrilineal to a patrilineal system of inheritance.

The allocation of land is handled by the appropriate chief or headman of each tribal group. Land may not be owned, sold or inherited and when a tenant dies, the authorities will decide whether it is passed on in the same family or is allotted to someone else.

In rural Owambo areas, each family has its own immaculate kraal or *eumbo*, which is very much like a small village enclosed within a stockade-like fence.

Housing in these villages is in either round or square thatched huts, and there's always an area reserved for large round storage containers made of woven bark and chinked with mud. These hold mainly *mahango* or millet, which is used to make a delicious beer. In the centre of each eumbo is the family's *omulilo gwoshilongo* (sacred fire), a log of mopane that is kept burning around the clock. The eumbo is surrounded by the family lands, which are used for agriculture, including grazing cattle.

Recently, large numbers of Owambo have migrated southwards to Windhoek or to the larger towns in the north to work as labourers, craftspeople and professionals.

Kavango

The 120,000 Kavango are divided into five distinct subgroups: the Mbukushu, the Sambiyu, the Kwangari, the Mbunza and the Geiriku. Since the 1970s, their numbers have been swelling rapidly, thanks mainly to immigrants and refugees from warring Angola. As with other groups in northern Namibia, large numbers of Kavango, particularly young men, are migrating southwards in search of employment on farms, in mines and around urban areas.

Most rural Kavango live on the level, wooded flood plains of the north-east, south of the Okavango River, where they make a living from fishing, herding livestock and subsistence farming of millet, maize and sorghum. They're also known as highly skilled woodcarvers and some of their works are sold along the Kavango roadsides and in tourist shops around the country. Although most carvers regard their work as merely a commercial endeavour, there are several competent artists.

Kavango society is organised according to matrilineal succession, which governs inheritance, marriage, family matters and traditional religious rites. However, the tribe is governed by hereditary male chiefs, whose relatives and appointees, along with representatives from each clan, constitute the lower echelons of tribal government.

Herero

Namibia's 100,000 Herero, who are mainly herders, occupy several regions of the country and are divided into several subgroups. The largest band includes the Tjimba and Ndamuranda groups in Kaokoland, the Maherero around Okahandja, and the Zeraua, who are centred on Omaruru. The Himba of Kaokoland are also a Herero subgroup (see Himba following) and the Mbandero occupy the colonially demarcated territory formerly known as Hereroland, around Gobabis in eastern Namibia.

From the early part of this century, the Herero have established various organisations, including chiefs' councils, to assert their nationalism, handle defence and oversee tribal affairs. One of these chiefs was Hosea Katjikururume Kutako, who became a national hero for his many direct petitions to the UN for help in securing Namibia's independence.

The Herero were originally part of the early Bantu migrations southwards from central Africa and their traditions assert that their origins were in the Great Rift Valley of East Africa. They arrived in present-day Namibia in the mid-16th century, and after a 200-year sojourn in Kaokoland they moved southwards to occupy the Swakop Valley and the Central Plateau. Until the colonial period, they remained as seminomadic pastoralists in this relatively rich grassland, herding and grazing cattle and sheep.

However, bloody clashes with the northwards, migrating Nama and German colonial troops and settlers led to violent uprisings. As a result, approximately 75% of the country's Herero population was wiped out and the remainder were dispersed around the country.

Large numbers of Herero also fled into neighbouring Botswana, where they settled down to a life of subsistence agriculture, growing grains and pulses and raising sheep, cattle and fowl. Now that Namibia is independent, many Herero would like to return to their roots, but the Botswana government has made it clear that anyone who returns to Namibia must leave behind both their herds and their money. In some cases, families have been split; some family members have gone to Namibia while others have remained behind to look after the family wealth.

For most rural Herero people in Namibia, cattle are the most prized possessions. Tribal hierarchy divides responsibilities for inheritance between *eendag* (matrilineal) and

MITCH REARDON

Right: A Herero mother with a calfskin baby backpack

oruzo (patrilineal) lines of descent, to which each person belongs. Mothers pass down material possessions, including cattle, while fathers handle religious and political instruction, rites and authority, and possessions that are considered sacred.

The characteristic Herero women's dress is derived from Victorian-era German missionaries who took exception to what they considered a lack of modesty among local women. It consists of an immaculate crinoline of enormous proportions worn over a series of petticoats, with a horn-shaped hat or headdress.

Himba

The distinctive Himba (or Ovahimba, which means 'Those Who Ask for Things') of the Kaokoveld are actually descended from a group of Herero herders who were displaced by Nama warriors in the 19th century. They fled to the remote north-west and continued their semi-nomadic lifestyle, raising sheep, goats and some cattle.

The Himba still eschew the modern world, and the missionary 'modesty police' never managed to persuade Himba women not to go topless. As a result, they maintain their lovely and distinctive traditional dress of multilayered goat-leather miniskirts and their ochre-and-mud-encrusted iron, leather and shell jewellery.

They use a natural herbal perfume known as *otjizumba*, and their skin is smeared with a mixture of butter, ash and ochre (known locally as *otjize*). This is ostensibly to keep it youthful-looking and it must work, as even elderly Himba women have beautifully smooth skin. They also plaster their plaited hair with the same mixture, and the effect is truly stunning.

DAVID WALL

MITCH REARDON

Left: The traditional headdresses of these Himba women signify that they are married.

Damara

The Damara, who number around 100,000, share a language group, but presumably no ethnic kinship with the Nama, with whom they've historically had major conflicts.

The Damara have presented researchers with one of Africa's greatest anthropological mysteries: how did a group of hunter-gatherers of Bantu origin wind up in Southern Africa speaking a Khoisan dialect? Their resemblance to some Bantu of West Africa has led some anthropologists to believe they were among the first people to migrate into Namibia from the north. However it happened, it's tempting to conclude that the Damara have occupied the region far longer than their other Bantu neighbours, and perhaps that early trade with the Nama and San caused them to adopt Khoisan as a lingua franca. Whether such a thing ever happened, however, is still a matter of speculation, and no conclusive evidence is available.

What is known is that prior to the 1870s, the Damara occupied much of central Namibia from around the site of Rehoboth westwards to the Swakop and Kuiseb Rivers and north to present-day Outjo and Khorixas. When the Herero and Nama began expanding their domains into traditional Damara lands, large numbers of Damara were displaced, killed or captured and enslaved. Between the 1870s and the early 20th century, the Rhenish Missionary Society persuaded the Herero chiefs and the colonial authorities to cede bits of territory to create a Damara homeland.

When Europeans first arrived in the region, the Damara were described as seminomadic gardeners, pastoralists and hunter-gatherers, who also maintained small-scale mining, smelting and trading operations. However, with colonial encouragement, they settled down to relatively sedentary subsistence herding and agriculture. In the 1960s, the South African administration purchased for the Damara over 4.5 million hectares of marginal European-owned ranchland in the desolate expanses of present-day Damaraland. Unfortunately, the soil in this region is generally poor, most of the land is communally owned and it lacks the good grazing that prevails in central and southern Namibia. Most Damara work in urban areas and on European farms, and only about one-third of them actually occupy Damaraland.

Europeans & Coloureds

Namibia's 85,000 Europeans are mostly of Afrikaner (65,000) and German (20,000) heritage and are concentrated in urban, central and southern Namibia.

The first Europeans, in the form of Portuguese sailors, arrived in the 15th century, but no-one settled until 1760. After 1780 came the traders, hunters and missionaries. Today, the Europeans are involved mainly in ranching, commerce, manufacturing and administration.

People of mixed European and African descent, known as coloureds, number 52,000 and live mainly in Windhoek and other urban areas.

Caprivians

In the extreme north-east, along the fertile Zambezi and Kwando river-banks, live the 80,000 Caprivians, comprising five main tribal groups: the Lozi, Mafwe, Subia, Yei and Mbukushu. Most Caprivians derive their livelihood from fishing, subsistence farming and herding cattle.

Until the late 19th century, the Caprivi was under the control of the Lozi kings and today, the lingua franca of the various Caprivian tribes is known as Rotse, which is a derivative of the Lozi language still spoken in parts of Zambia and Angola.

San

The 37,000 San people – 19,000 of whom remain in Namibia – were the region's earliest inhabitants, and still inhabit the north-eastern areas of the country. They are divided into three groups: the Naro of the Gobabis area; the !Xukwe and Hei//kom of western Bushmanland, Kavango and Caprivi; and the Ju/hoansi (or !Kung) in eastern Bushmanland, particularly around the town of Tsumkwe. However, it has been over a decade since any Namibian San followed an entirely traditional lifestyle, and many now work as servants and farm hands in Kavango and Caprivi.

We know a great deal about the traditional life of the San because they are one of the most heavily studied peoples in the history of anthropology. An important stimulus for this research was the idea that they were one of the world's last original hunter-gatherer societies. Scholars treated them as if they had lived in complete isolation, and this belief soon took hold among the general public. In fact, however, they have interacted and traded with other peoples for centuries.

Historically, the San have generally lived as hunter-gatherers or foragers. The women were skilled at finding the fruits, nuts and roots that

Left: The San were one of the last of the hunter-gatherer societies.

JOHN BORTHWICK

provided most of the daily diet. The meat that was hunted by the men – mostly various species of antelope – was a treat and was the most valued food. Some researchers have suggested that the San lived in a state of 'primitive affluence'. That is, they had to work only a short time each day to satisfy all their basic needs. At certain times and locations this might have been true, but during some seasons and conditions life could be harsh, for their desert environment was above all very unpredictable.

Mostly, the San lived in nomadic groups of between 25 and 35 people. Each group comprised several families. They had their own land-division system; groups had well-defined territories, which could measure up to 1000 sq km. During part of the year, the whole group camped together at a water hole; then in the wet season they'd scatter over the country. They had no political hierarchy or chiefs, and decisions were reached by group consensus; both men and women had a say.

However, not all the San lived by hunting and gathering alone. In the early 19th century, the San were responsible for one of the most extensive precolonial trade networks, which extended across the Kalahari.

The San people today are, by modern standards, unequivocally impoverished. However, some are finding new lifestyles such as learning to farm or keeping small numbers of cattle and goats on what land remains for them. Nevertheless, many still hunt when they have the opportunity. A group of such farmers in Namibia have joined together to form the Nyae Nyae Farmers' Co-operative (NNFC), which is supported by the Ju/hoansi Bushmen Development Foundation in Namibia. In 1991, at the Namibian National Land Conference, the minister for land stated that the San system of land-holding would be recognised by the government.

In the past, the flexibility of their society helped the San people to evade conquest and control. But, at the same time, it made it exceedingly difficult for them to organise themselves to form pressure groups and claim and defend their rights. However, through organisations such as the NNFC in Namibia, the Nyae Nyae Conservancy (which oversees tourism in Bushmanland) and The First People of the Kalahari in Botswana, some things, at least, are improving. The first signs of hope were the two regional conferences on Development for Africa's San Peoples (in 1992 and 1993), in which San delegations from both Namibia and Botswana were present and made their needs known.

Nama

Another Khoisan group is the Nama, who are variously known as the Bergdama, Oorlam, Khoi-Khoi or Hottentots (although this last designation is now out of favour). There are around 60,000 Nama in Namibia. As do the San, most Nama have a light skin colour, a slight frame and small bones, but on average they are a bit taller. They normally have high cheekbones, flattish noses and beautiful almond-shaped eyes, narrowed by an Oriental-like fold of skin on the upper eyelid.

MITCH REARDON

The Nama's origins were in the southern Cape, where they were known as Hottentots. However, during the early days of European settlement in the Cape, they were either exterminated or pushed northwards by land-hungry colonial farmers. They eventually came to rest in Namaqualand, around the Orange River, where they lived as seminomadic pastoralists until the mid-19th century, when their leader, Jan Jonker Afrikaner, led them to the area of present-day Windhoek.

On Namibia's Central Plateau, they came into conflict with the Herero, who already occupied that area, and the two groups fought a series of bloody wars. Eventually, the German government confined them to several separate reserves.

Today, the Nama occupy the region colonially designated as Namaland, which stretches roughly from Mariental southwards to Keetmanshoop. Many Nama have adopted Western dress and Christianity, and now work in towns or on commercial farms. They're especially known for their extraordinary musical and literary abilities; their traditional music, folk tales, proverbs and praise poetry have been handed down through the generations to form a basis for their culture today.

Topnaar

The Topnaar (or Aonin), who are technically a branch of the Nama, mainly occupy the western central Namib, in and around Walvis Bay. However, unlike the Nama, who historically had a tradition of communal land ownership, the Topnaar passed their lands down through family lines.

Today, the Topnaar are perhaps the most marginalised group in Namibia. Historically, they were utterly dependent upon the !nara melon, a thorny desert plant that derives its water by sending a tap root deep into the earth. This plant was the Topnaar's only source of income and the primary element in their diet, which was supplemented by hunting. Now, however, their hunting grounds are tied up in Namib-Naukluft Park – and therefore off limits to hunting – and the melon is under threat due to depleted water tables, which are being tapped to supply Walvis Bay's industrial needs.

As a result, many Topnaar have migrated into Walvis Bay and settled in the township of Narraville, from where they commute to fish-canning factories. Others live around the perimeter in cardboard boxes

Top: The Nama people's physical characteristics include high cheekbones.

and make their living scrounging other groups' cast-offs. In the Topnaar community south-east of Walvis Bay, a primary school and hostel have been provided, but few students ever go on to secondary school, which would require a move into Narraville.

Those that remain in the desert eke out a living growing !nara melons and raising stock, mainly goats.

Basters

The 35,000 Basters are descended mainly from intermixing between the Nama and Dutch farmers in the Cape Colony. From early on, they strongly professed Calvinist Christianity. In the late 1860s, when they came under pressure from the Boer settlers in the Cape, they fled north of the Orange River and established the settlement of Rehoboth. Although their name is derived from 'bastards', this fiercely independent group of people still uses it proudly because it stresses their mixed heritage. Most Basters still live around Rehoboth and either follow an urban lifestyle or raise cattle, sheep and/or goats.

Tswana

Namibia's 8000 Tswana make up the country's smallest ethnic group. They're related to the Tswana of South Africa and Botswana and live mainly in the eastern areas of the country, around Aminuis and Epukiro.

Right: The Tswana people number only 8000 and make up Namibia's smallest ethnic group.

BOTH PHOTOGRAPHS BY ERIC L WHEATER

Facts for the Visitor

HIGHLIGHTS

Namibia is a large and sparsely populated country. Superimposed on a rich diversity of African cultures is a modern and efficient infrastructure recalling the German and South African colonial legacies. Where else in the world could you eat *Sachertorte* (a popular German-style cake) on the edge of the desert, watching flamingoes flying overhead?

Namibia is packed with fabulous sights, sounds, experiences and wonderful accommodation options. Although most visitors discover their own highlights, the boxed text below covers some tried and true attractions.

Highlights of Namibia

Windhoek Namibia's Big Smoke is a clean, attractive capital city that occupies a lovely setting amid arid aloe-covered mountains. The centre blends turn-of-the-century German colonial buildings with unusually coloured, postmodernist architecture – in fact, much of it appears to be sweet and edible! Other attractions in the area include Daan Viljoen Game Reserve and Arnhem Cave.

Etosha National Park This park surrounds a vast ephemeral pan, and the surrounding bushveld is dotted with water holes that attract wildlife. Namutoni, one of the three rest camps, revolves around the striking 'Beau Geste' German colonial fort.

Waterberg Plateau Park This small and lovely park with far-ranging views is a repository for endangered species such as white rhinos. You can hike or join wildlife drives on the plateau.

Caprivi National Parks The Caprivi Strip, the corridor of land stretching eastwards towards Zimbabwe and Zambia, has the new Bwabwata National Park, as well as Mudumu and Mamili National Parks, where you can experience Namibia's most verdant environments.

Khaudom Game Reserve This wild and hard-to-reach park is an unexpected surprise. It's packed with wildlife and you're likely to have the whole place to yourself. Access is by 4WD only.

Skeleton Coast Characterised by an ethereal, fog-bound coastline, this has long been a graveyard for ships and their stranded crews. Don't miss the colony of Cape fur seals at Cape Cross.

Damaraland The vast spaces of Damaraland support many desert species – outside any artificially protected reserve – and many natural attractions: the imposing Spitzkoppe; Brandberg massif with its rock paintings; the rock engravings of Twyfelfontein; and the Petrified Forest and Organ Pipes.

Namib Desert Namibia's signature image is its intriguing 'dune sea', and Sossusvlei, its best-known attraction, is on nearly everyone's itinerary. The northern part of the Namib is flatter and more stony, dotted with lighter-coloured dunes that march across the landscape before the wind.

Swakopmund The coastal holiday resort of Swakopmund is Namibia's most German town, with colonial architecture, European bakeries, coffee shops, beer gardens and seafood restaurants. Nearby sites of interest include Welwitschia Drive and the Walvis Bay lagoon.

Fish River Canyon The immense Fish River Canyon, 161km long, up to 27km wide and 550m deep, ranks as one of Africa's most spectacular natural wonders. It's great for hiking or luxuriating in the hot springs at Ai-Ais. As a base of operations, you can choose between the Fish River Canyon National Park, the Fish River Lodge or the Gondwana Cañon Park.

Lüderitz The arid southern Namib Desert is characterised by wide expanses and extraordinary pastel colours, and Lüderitz is the northern anchor of the diamond-rich Sperrgebiet. Other major draws are Lüderitz Peninsula and Kolmanskop ghost town, which is steadily being swallowed by the dunes.

Safari Lodges For the finest settings and most pleasantly imaginative architecture – if you aren't on a strict budget – you may want to consider Wolwedans Dune Lodge or Sossusvlei Mountain Lodge in the NamibRand Nature Reserve (Central Namib Desert), Mowani Lodge (north-western Namibia), Twyfelfontein Country Lodge (north-western Namibia), Lianshulu Lodge (northern Namibia) and Skeleton Coast Wilderness Camp (north-western Namibia).

SUGGESTED ITINERARIES

Independent travellers who want to spend their time rewardingly may want to consider the following suggestions.

One week Spend two days exploring Windhoek (with side trips to either Daan Viljoen Game Reserve or Arnhem Cave), a day or two in Swakopmund (with side trips to Walvis Bay, Cape Cross or Welwitschia Drive), and then spend a couple of days in either Etosha National Park or Sossusvlei.

Two weeks See Windhoek, Swakopmund, Etosha National Park and Sossusvlei, plus the Waterberg Plateau and Twyfelfontein; this is the ideal length of time for a classic 10-day budget safari, which will typically include all these sites. If you're on a less restrictive budget, a Namibian travel agency can cobble together a more upmarket version of these safaris.

Three weeks To the above, add one or two of the following: time exploring or adrenaline-tripping around Swakopmund; several nights at private lodges in the Namib-Naukluft region; Lüderitz and Fish River Canyon; a hike through the Naukluft or Fish River Canyon areas; a comprehensive Damaraland tour (Twyfelfontein, Petrified Forest, Brandberg, Spitzkoppe, Sesfontein etc); or a basic Kaokoveld tour (taking in Opuwo, at least one traditional village and perhaps Epupa Falls).

One month Everything listed under two weeks, plus more time in Damaraland, an excursion through Kaokoveld and a visit to Lüderitz and Fish River Canyon.

Two months All options listed under one month, with more time in the Kaokoveld, plus an excursion to the Skeleton Coast (budget permitting); a cultural circuit through the Owambo country, Bushmanland, the Kavango region and/or the Caprivi Strip; and perhaps a more thorough exploration of the Namib-Naukluft or Fish River Canyon areas (including hikes).

PLANNING
When to Go

Most of Namibia enjoys a minimum of 300 days of sunshine a year, and in the winter dry season (May to October) you can expect clear, warm and sunny days and cold, clear nights, often with temperatures falling below freezing. Generally, the mountainous and semi-arid Central Plateau (including Windhoek) is a bit cooler than the rest of the country. While the Kalahari region of eastern Namibia is mostly hotter than the Central Plateau, it also receives less rain.

There are two rainy seasons, the 'little rains' from October to December and the main rainy period, which lasts from January to April. The latter is characterised by brief showers and occasional thunderstorms that clean the air and settle. January temperatures in Windhoek can soar to 40°C, and from December to March, Namib-Naukluft Park and Etosha National Park become hot and uncomfortable. From January to March, the north-eastern rivers may flood, making some roads either impassable or hard to negotiate.

Note that some resort areas, such as the hot springs oasis of Ai-Ais, close in the summer. Others, such as Swakopmund, are booked solid over Christmas and Easter and during school holidays.

What Kind of Trip

Your style of travel depends largely on your budget, available time and preparedness for unknowns. In Namibia, as in most places, low-budget travel requires sacrificing the security of structure and allowing time to accommodate uncertainties.

For budget travellers, Namibia especially lends itself to low-cost organised tours – not only for young, elderly or inexperienced travellers, but also for backpackers. Not only do these tours minimise hassles and uncertainties, but they allow visitors to enjoy the best of Namibia without having to sort out complicated transport options. Hitching is possible but difficult, and public transport is scarce – especially to sites of interest – and requires more time and patience than most travellers want to expend.

Independent 'fly-drive' tours are popular, and any good travel agency can organise self-drive itineraries between wilderness lodges, guest farms, guesthouses or camping grounds. Namibian agencies are more familiar with available options than those outside the country. At the other end of the spectrum is a host of upmarket tour options which will take you into Namibia's wildest country, but prepare to pay for their luxury offerings.

For suggestions for all budgets, see Organised Tours in the Getting Around chapter.

Maps

Government survey topographical sheets and aerial photos are available from the Office of the Surveyor General (☎ 061-245055, fax 249802) on Robert Mugabe Ave, Windhoek. However outdated when it comes to roads and settlements, many of these beautiful and colourful maps – most of which date from the South African mandate – are suitable for framing. The 1:250,000 series maps cost US$3.50 and the 1:50,000 maps are US$2.50. When originals aren't available, you can purchase black-and-white photocopies for a discounted rate.

The Ministry of Environment & Tourism (MET) produces the official *Republic of Namibia Tourist Road Map 1998* (1:2,000,000) tourist map, which shows major routes and sites of interest. It's distributed free at tourist offices, hotels and travel agencies. The reverse side has detailed maps of Windhoek, Swakopmund and Walvis Bay.

Shell Roadmap – Namibia (US$1.50) is a good reference for remote routes and includes a good Windhoek city map, but the Caprivi Strip is only a small-scale inset. Shell publishes *Kaokoland-Kunene Region Tourist Map*, which depicts most major routes and tracks in north-western Namibia. It's sold at bookshops and tourist offices for US$2.50. Another petrol company, BP Namibia (PO Box 3594, Windhoek), produces a 1:2,500,000 map, with insets for most towns, including Oshakati, Ondangwa and Otjiwarongo. It's sold for US$3 at some bookshops and petrol stations.

The Macmillan *Namibia Travellers' Map*, at 1:2,400,000, looks very nice, with clear print and colour-graded altitude representation, but minor back routes aren't depicted. The reverse side has maps of Windhoek, Swakopmund, Lüderitz, Walvis Bay, Etosha National Park and Namib-Naukluft Park.

The Automobile Association Travel Service (☎ 061-224201, fax 222446), Carl List Building, on the corner of Independence Ave and Peter Müller St in Windhoek, has produced *Namibia*, a 1:2,500,000 map. It does include most back roads and settlements, but the Kaokoveld and Bushmanland are largely blank. On the reverse side is a series of thumbnail town plans. To pick up these maps, you must be a member of an Automobile Association affiliate.

Another good map, at 1:1,250,000, is *Namibia*, produced by the Ray Maphouse World Mapping Project (W www.123buch .de). It's sold for US$3 at Namibian bookshops and tourist offices, and also through the Internet. However, we were disappointed to find some surprises (eg, a fictitious bridge between Katima Mulilo in Namibia and Sesheke in Zambia). Alternatively, pick up the excellent 1:1,400,000 *Contimap Namibia*, which is published by 4WD-oriented mapmaker International Motoring Productions (☎ 27-21-785 5752, e andrew@4xforum .co.za), PO Box 1000, Sun Valley 7975, South Africa. It sells for around US$10 at Namibian and South African bookshops.

In the USA, Maplink (☎ 805-692 6777, fax 805-692 6787, e custserv@maplink .com, W www.maplink.com), 30 S La Patera Lane, Unit 5, Santa Barbara, CA 93117, is an excellent and exhaustive source for maps of Namibia. A similarly extensive selection of maps is available in the UK from Stanfords (☎ 020-7836 1321), 12–14 Long Acre, London WC2E 9LP.

What to Bring

When preparing for a trip, your packing will depend on your budget, itinerary, mode of travel, time of visit and length of stay. Travelling as light as possible is always a good idea if you want to enjoy the trip, however, you may find you will have to bring certain items from home.

Bags The type of luggage you should carry will depend largely upon your style of travel. Those on pre-arranged tours who are staying in finer hotels and using taxis around town will get by with traditional suitcases or shoulder bags. For independent travellers, a backpack – or a pack that zips into a suitcase – is probably the most practical and useful carry-all. The most important factors to consider are comfort, strength, weight and manageability.

Essentials As always, the most important advice is to travel light, and only take items that are indispensable. The following checklist outlines items that will probably be used often enough to justify their weight.

- first-aid kit (see Health later in this chapter)
- antimalarial tablets (for northern Namibia)
- travel alarm clock
- small calculator
- camera, if desired, and film (it's generally cheaper in Europe, North America or Australasia than in Southern Africa)
- small torch (flashlight) and extra batteries
- water bottle – aluminium or plastic
- water-purification tablets (if you'll be drinking surface water)
- Swiss army–type pocket knife with bottle opener, corkscrew, scissors etc
- spare glasses or contact lenses and a copy of your optical prescription
- towel
- flip-flops (thongs)
- clothesline – 2m to 3m of cord is useful for all sorts of things
- sewing kit
- writing implements
- contraceptives
- any prescription medications you normally take

Clothing Without going overboard, it's wise to prepare for Namibia's typically sunny days and chilly nights, as well as the odd rainy day (especially between December and April). A good rule is to bring two sleeveless shirts, two pairs of shorts, a long-sleeved shirt, long trousers, a nicer dress or casual suit (for nights out in Windhoek or elsewhere), a pair of sneakers and a pair of sandals or flip-flops. For winter evenings, you'll need a long-sleeved jacket or sweatshirt; summer visitors, on the other hand, may well need a lightweight waterproof jacket.

Hiking & Camping Gear Hikers and bushwalkers will need a good pair of hiking boots, as well as a warm sleeping bag (especially for winter nights – this will also be handy in hostels). Those who camp will need a lightweight tent. Given Namibia's early darkness, especially in winter, you may also want to bring a light source, such as a camping lantern or candle lantern.

Bushwalkers will appreciate a lightweight stove, preferably one that will run on unleaded petrol or paraffin (kerosene), since white gas (Shellite/Coleman fuel) isn't readily available. Note that you may not carry stove fuel or butane cartridges on aircraft.

RESPONSIBLE TOURISM

Visitors who stay in the bush – especially at upmarket tourist lodges – should realise that their experience of Namibia's wilderness is quite different from that of the people who call the area home. For tourists, electricity is typically provided by solar cells and water comes from boreholes (or in some cases, is trucked in from elsewhere). To limit your impact and keep environmentally sensitive costs to a minimum, place all waste materials in receptacles, keep your showers short and be sure to switch off the lights when you're away from your room.

Similarly, hikers and campers in remote areas should either cook on well-established *braaivleis* (a special stand used for grilling meat), normally in vehicle-accessible sites with access to allowable firewood (see the boxed text 'Firewood' in the Facts about Namibia chapter), or cook on a camping stove and use only unleaded petrol or paraffin. The following points outline some things you can do to limit negative effects on the area (see the boxed text 'Minimum-Impact Camping' later in this chapter as well as 'Visiting a Fragile Environment' in the North-Western Namibia chapter).

Guidelines for Responsible Tourism

Here are some guidelines for travellers wishing to minimise negative impacts:

- Avoid establishments that clearly consume limited resources at the expense of local residents.
- Support Namibian enterprise. Use locally owned hotels and restaurants. Employ local guides. Support craftspeople by buying locally made souvenirs, but avoid items made from natural material – wood, skin, ivory etc – unless they come from a sustainable source.
- Recognise land rights. In Namibia, communal lands are open to all – including visitors – but outsiders should recognise the interests of those

who subsist on these lands and behave as you would as a guest on private lands at home.
- Ask permission before taking close-up photos of people; if you don't speak the language, a smile and gesture will be understood and appreciated.
- Please don't give money, sweets and pens to children, as it encourages begging and demeans the child. A donation to a recognised project – a health centre or school – is a more constructive and meaningful way to help local communities.
- Respect for local etiquette earns you respect. Politeness is a virtue everywhere, but remember that different cultures have different ideas about what's polite. In some places, skimpy or tight-fitting clothing may be considered inappropriate, as are public displays of affection.
- Learn something about Namibia's history and current affairs; this will help you understand its idiosyncrasies and help to avoid misunderstanding or frustration.
- Be patient, friendly and sensitive, and remember that you're a guest.

TOURIST OFFICES
Local Tourist Offices
Windhoek has both city and national tourist offices, and Karibib, Usakos, Okahandja, Gobabis, Keetmanshoop, Lüderitz, Swakopmund, Grootfontein and Tsumeb all have private or municipal tourist information offices.

Look for the useful publication *Welcome to Namibia – Tourist Accommodation & Info Guide*, which is distributed free by Namibia Tourism (☎ 061-284 2360, fax 284 2364, e tourism@mweb.com.na, W www .tourism.com.na), Ground floor, Continental Building, 272 Independence Ave, Private Bag 13346, Windhoek. Also useful is the incredible glossy production *Namibia Holiday & Travel* (☎ 061-225665, fax 220410, e nht@mac.com.na, W www.holi daytravel.com.na), PO Box 21593, Windhoek, which provides background information in addition to travel listings.

Both of these are published annually and are available at tourist offices, as well as some hotels and guesthouses.

Tourist Offices Abroad
Namibian tourist offices abroad include:

Germany
Namibia Verkehrsbüro (☎ 069-1337 3620, fax 1337 3615, e info@namibiatourism.com)

42–44 Schillerstrasse, D60313 Frankfurt-am-Main
W www.namibia-tourism.com
South Africa
Johannesburg: Namibia Tourism (☎ 011-784 8025, fax 784 8340, e namtour@citec.co.za) 11 Alice Lane, 3rd floor, East Wing, Standard Bank Bldg, PO Box 78946, Sandton 2146
Cape Town: (☎ 021-419 3190, fax 421 5840, e info@ct.namtour.com.na) Ground floor, Main Tower, Standard Bank Centre, Adderley St, PO Box 739, Cape Town 8000
UK
Namibia Tourism (☎ 020-7636 2924, fax 7636 2969, e info@namibiatourism.co.uk) 6 Chandos St, London W1M 0LQ
W www.namibiatourism.co.uk
USA
Kartagener Associates (☎ 212-465 0619, fax 868 1654) 12 W 37th St, New York, NY 10018
W www.tourism.com.na

VISAS & DOCUMENTS
All visitors require a passport from their home country that is valid for at least six months after their intended departure date from Namibia. You may also be asked for an onward plane, bus or rail ticket (note, however, that checks are rarely made). Nationals of the following countries do not need visas to visit Namibia: Angola, Australia, Botswana, Brazil, Canada, EU countries, Iceland, Japan, Kenya, Mozambique, New Zealand, Norway, Russia, Singapore, South Africa, Switzerland, Tanzania, the USA, Zambia, Zimbabwe and most Commonwealth countries. Citizens of most Eastern European countries do require visas.

Tourists are granted an initial 90 days, which may be extended at the Ministry of Home Affairs (☎ 061-292 2111, fax 292 2185, e mlusepani@mha.gov.na), on the corner of Kasino St and Independence Ave, Private Bag 13200, Windhoek. For the best results, be there when it opens at 8am, submit your application at the 3rd-floor offices (as opposed to the desk on the ground floor) and make an effort to be polite.

Travel Insurance
In general, all travellers need a travel insurance policy, which will provide some sense of security in the case of a medical emer-

gency or the loss or theft of money or belongings. Travel health insurance policies can usually be extended to include baggage, flight departure insurance and a range of other options. It's sensible to buy your policy as early as possible; if you wait too long, you may not be covered for delays caused by industrial action.

Finding a good-value policy may require some shopping around. Long-term or frequent travellers can generally find an annual policy for under US$200, but they're normally written by general business insurance companies rather than those specialising in travel. However, they may exclude or limit coverage in the USA (where health care costs are extremely high) and may offer very limited baggage protection. Always read the fine print.

Claims on your travel insurance must be accompanied by proof of the value of any items lost or stolen (purchase receipts are the best, so if you buy a new camera for your trip, for example, hang onto the receipt). In the case of medical claims, you'll need detailed medical reports and receipts for amounts paid. If you're claiming on a trip cancelled by circumstances beyond your control (illness, airline bankruptcy, industrial action etc), you'll have to produce all flight tickets purchased, tour agency receipts and itinerary and proof of whatever glitch caused your trip to be cancelled.

If you book an organised tour, the company will probably encourage you to purchase its travel insurance policy, which may or may not be a good deal. Bear in mind that some unscrupulous companies – particularly in Europe – manage to keep their tour prices low and appealing by requiring overpriced travel insurance as part of the package.

Other Documents
In nearly all cases, your home driving licence will allow you to drive in Namibia for up to 90 days. Hostel cards are of little use in Namibia, but student cards score a 15% discount on Intercape Mainliner buses and occasionally receive discounts on museum admissions. Seniors over 60, with proof of age, also receive a 15% discount on Inter-

Visas for Onward Travel

Windhoek is a good place to pick up visas for several countries; for contact details, see Embassies & Consulates in Namibia later in this chapter.

Angola Visas are readily available only to Namibian citizens and residents. Others must apply in their home country – as most travel to Angola is for business purposes, this is normally handled by one's employer. However, nonbusiness travellers may be granted visas – it's just a matter of turning up at the consulate and presenting a good case.

Kenya UK citizens need a visa, which costs US$50 and takes two days to process. Multientry visas costs US$100 and can take up to six weeks to issue. Citizens of the USA and Australia can enter Kenya for 30 days without a visa; longer stays require a visa which is issued in two days and costs US$53.

Zambia Visas are required by USA, Australian and British citizens. In Windhoek, they take a day to process and cost US$59/94 for single /double-entry visas, and US$188 for a multientry visa. Visas are available at the border for considerably less (normally US$25 for US citizens and UK£45 for British subjects). However, they're free if you're 'introduced' to Zambia by a Zambian company (such as a hotel, backpacker hostel or tour company) and placed on their border 'manifest' 48 hours before your arrival in the country.

Zimbabwe Australians, New Zealanders and US citizens need a visa, which can be processed at the border (US$30/45 for single /double entry). However, you can also secure a visa in advance for the same rates; multientry visas cost US$55 and aren't available at the border.

cape Mainliner and good discounts (as much as 50%) on domestic Air Namibia fares.

Copies
When it comes to passports, identification and other valuable documents, prepare for the worst. Even if your passport is registered

with your embassy, keep separate records of your passport number and issue date, and photocopies of the pages with the passport number, name, photograph, place of issue and expiration date.

Also make copies of visas, birth certificate, travellers cheque receipt slips, health and travel insurance policies and addresses, personal contact addresses, credit card numbers (with emergency loss numbers) and airline tickets, and keep them separate from your passport and money. Most hotels have safes, but only those in finer hotels are likely to be truly safe. Keep one copy with you, one copy inside your luggage and, if applicable, deposit another with a travelling companion. As a hedge against disaster, slip US$100 or so into an unlikely place for an emergency.

EMBASSIES & CONSULATES
Namibian Embassies & Consulates

If you need a visa and your country doesn't have a Namibian diplomatic mission, fax or post your passport details and requested length of stay to the Ministry of Home Affairs (☎ 061-292 2111, fax 292 2185, ⓔ mlus epani@mha.gov.na), Private Bag 13200, Windhoek, and hope for the best. Visas may sometimes be issued at Windhoek international airport, but not at land borders.

Angola (☎ 02-395483, fax 333923) 95 Rua dos Coqueiros, PO Box 953, Luanda

Belgium (☎ 02-771 1410, fax 771 9681) 454 Ave de Tervueren, 1150 Brussels

France (☎ 01 44 17 32 65, fax 01 44 17 32 73) 80 Ave Foch, Square de l'Avenue Foch, F-75116 Paris

Germany (☎ 0228-346021, fax 346025) Mainzerstrasse 47, D-53179 Bonn

South Africa (☎ 012-344 5922, fax 342 3565) Tulbach Park, Eikendal Flat Suite 2, 1234 Church St, Colbyn, Pretoria, PO Box 29806, Sunnyside 0132

UK (☎ 020-7636 6244, fax 7637 5694) 6 Chandos St, London W1M 0LQ

USA (☎ 202-986 0540, fax 986 0443) 1605 New Hampshire Ave NW, Washington, DC 20009

Zambia (☎ 01-252 250, fax 252 497) 6968 Kabanga Rd & Addis Ababa Dr, Rhodes Park, Lusaka

Zimbabwe (☎ 14-304856, fax 304855) 31A Lincoln Rd, Avondale, Harare

---

Your Own Embassy

As a tourist, it's important to realise what your country's embassy can and can't do. Don't expect help, especially if your trouble is remotely your own fault. You are bound by the laws of Namibia, and your embassy won't be too sympathetic if you end up in jail, even if the infraction in question is legal in your home country. In genuine emergencies it may well lend some assistance, but only if other channels have been exhausted. For example, if your money and documents are stolen, it might assist with getting a new passport, but a loan for onward travel is out of the question.

On the positive side, if you are going to remote or politically volatile areas (such as the Caprivi Strip), you might consider registering with your embassy, so that it knows where you are. Note that some embassies post useful warning notices about potential dangers and problems but – especially in the case of the UK and the USA – these can get a bit hysterical.

Embassies & Consulates in Namibia

Since Namibian independence, numerous countries have established diplomatic missions. All the following addresses are in Windhoek (☎ code 061) and opening hours are weekdays only.

Angola (☎ 227535, fax 221498) Angola House, 3 Dr Agostinho Neto St, Ausspannplatz, Private Bag 12020. Open 9am to 1pm.

Botswana (☎ 221941, fax 236034) 101 Nelson Mandela Dr, PO Box 20359. Open 8am to 12.30pm.

European Union (EU; ☎ 220099) 4th floor Sanlam Centre

France (☎ 229022, fax 231436) 1 Goethe St, PO Box 20484. Open 9am to 12.30pm and 1.30pm to 5pm.

Germany (☎ 223100, fax 222981) 6th floor, Sanlam Centre, 152 Independence Ave, PO Box 231. Open 9am to 12.30pm.

Kenya (☎ 226836, fax 221409) 5th floor, Kenya House, 134 Robert Mugabe Ave, PO Box 2889. Open 9am to 12.30pm and 2pm to 5pm.

Malawi (☎ 221391, fax 227056) 56 Bismarck St, Windhoek West, PO Box 23547. Open 8am to noon and 2pm to 5pm.

South Africa (☎ 2057111, fax 224140) RSA House, Corner of Jan Jonker St & Nelson Mandela Dr, Klein Windhoek, PO Box 23100. Open 8.15am to 12.15pm.

UK (☎ 223022, fax 228895) 116A Robert Mugabe Ave, PO Box 22202. Open 9am to noon.

USA (☎ 221601, fax 229792) 14 Lossen St, Ausspannplatz, Private Bag 12029. Open 8am to noon Monday, Wednesday and Friday.

Zambia (☎ 237610, fax 228162) Corner of Sam Nujoma Drive & Mandume Ndemufeyo Ave, PO Box 22882. Open 8am to 1pm and 2pm to 4pm.

Zimbabwe (☎ 228134, fax 226859) Gamsberg Bldg, Corner of Independence Ave & Grimm St, PO Box 23056. Open 9am to 12.30pm and 2pm to 3pm.

CUSTOMS

Most items from elsewhere in the Southern African Customs Union – Botswana, South Africa, Lesotho or Swaziland – may be imported duty free. From elsewhere, visitors can import duty free 400 cigarettes or 250g of tobacco, 2L of wine, 1L of spirits and 250ml of eau de Cologne. There are no limits on currency import, but entry and departure forms ask how much you intend to spend or have spent in the country.

Firearms require a temporary import permit and must be declared at the time of entry; automobiles may not be sold in Namibia without payment of duty. For pets, you need a health certificate and full veterinary documentation; note that pets aren't permitted in national parks or reserves.

MONEY

Currency

The Namibian dollar (N$) equals 100 cents, and in Namibia it's pegged to the South African rand (in South Africa, it fetches only about R0.70). The rand is also legal tender here at a rate of 1:1. This can be confusing, given that there are three sets of coins and notes in use: old South African, new South African and Namibian.

To complicate matters, the three coins of the same denomination are all different sizes. It takes a while to get the hang of it. Namibian dollar notes, which all bear portraits of Nama leader Hendrik Witbooi, come in denominations of N$10, N$20, N$50, N$100 and N$200, and coins in values of 5, 10, 20 and 50 cents, and N$1 and N$5.

Exchange Rates

At the time of going to print, the Namibian dollar had the following values against other currencies:

country	unit		Namibian dollar
Australia	A$1	=	4.41
Canada	C$1	=	5.34
Euro zone	€1	=	7.56
Japan	¥100	=	6.84
New Zealand	NZ$1	=	3.62
South Africa	R1	=	1.00
UK	UK£1	=	11.89
USA	US$1	=	8.24
Zimbabwe	Z$10	=	0.14

Exchanging Money

Major foreign currencies may be exchanged at any bank, but travellers cheques normally fetch a better rate than cash. When changing money, you may be given either South African rand or Namibian dollars; if you'll need to change any leftover currency outside Namibia, the rand is a better choice.

If you're changing travellers cheques, shop around for the bank offering the lowest commission. Currently, some banks charge as much as US$6.50 per transaction. Travellers cheques may also be exchanged for US dollars cash – if the cash is available – but banks charge a hefty 7% commission. There is no currency black market, so beware of street changers offering unrealistic rates; they could be passing counterfeit notes or setting you up for a robbery.

Credit Cards

Credit cards are accepted in most shops, restaurants and hotels (but not petrol stations), and credit-card cash advances are available from automatic teller machines (ATMs) such as BOB, which is operated by First National Bank. You'll find BOB machines and other ATMs in main towns.

Credit-card cash advances are available at foreign-exchange desks in most major banks, but set aside at least an hour or two to complete the rather tedious transaction.

If your credit card is lost or stolen, contact the company immediately: American Express (☎ 061-249037); Diners Club (☎ 061-294 2143); MasterCard (☎ 061-294 2143, 24-hour 080-002 8000); Visa (☎ 061-299 2213, 24-hour 027-11-352 5432).

Costs

If you're camping or staying in backpacker hostels, cooking your own meals and hitching or using local minibuses, you'll get by on as little as US$15 per day. Unfortunately, to get around the country on this sort of budget would prove both frustrating and time-consuming, since hitching opportunities aren't great and minibus routes are limited to the main highways.

A plausible mid-range budget, which would include B&B or double accommodation in backpacker hostels, public transport and one restaurant meal daily, would be around US$50 to US$80 per person (if accommodation costs are shared between two). In the upper range, accommodation at hotels, meals in restaurants and escorted tours will cost upwards of US$300 per person per day. Your best option may be to pre-book a fly-drive or organised tour package overseas rather than making arrangements on the spot.

To reach the most interesting parts of Namibia, you'll have to take an organised tour or hire a vehicle (see the Getting Around chapter). Car hire may be expensive for budget travellers, but if you can muster a group of four people and share costs, you can squeak by on an additional US$20 to US$50 per day – that's assuming a daily average of around 200km in a 2WD/4WD vehicle with the least-expensive agency, including petrol, tax and insurance. The plus side of a 4WD is that many vehicles are equipped with camping gear, which would decrease the price of accommodation.

Tipping & Bargaining

Tipping is welcomed everywhere but is expected only in upmarket tourist restaurants. Some of these add a service charge as a matter of course, obviating any tipping expectations. In any case, don't leave more than 5% to 10% of the bill. As a rule, taxi drivers aren't tipped, but it is customary to give N$1 or so to petrol-station attendants who clean your windows and/or check the oil and water. Note that tipping is officially prohibited in national parks and reserves.

At safari lodges, it's customary to tip any personal guides directly (assuming they merit a tip) and also to leave a tip with the proprietor, to be divided among all the staff; this means that behind-the-scenes staff also receive something.

On upmarket safaris, it's best to tip all staff directly, with the guide receiving the most (generally around US$5 to US$8 per day), followed by the driver (US$2 to US$3 per day) and any cooks or other camp hands (US$1 to US$2 per day). On budget safaris, tips should reflect a good balance between the price of the safari and the quality of the service.

Bargaining is only acceptable when purchasing handicrafts and arts directly from the producer or artist, but in remote areas, prices asked normally represent close to the market value. The exception is crafts imported from Zimbabwe, which are generally sold at large craft markets for inflated prices that are always negotiable. Shop prices aren't usually open to bargaining, although you may be able to wrangle discounts on bulk purchases or very expensive curios or artwork.

Taxes & Refunds

A Value Added Tax (VAT) of 15.5% is applied to most purchases, including meals and accommodation. Tourists buying such luxury items as leather and jewellery for export may be exempt from this tax if they can produce a valid passport and airline tickets.

POST & COMMUNICATIONS
Post

Domestic post generally moves slowly; it can take up to six weeks for a letter to travel from Lüderitz to Katima Mulilo, for example. Overseas airmail post is normally more efficient, and is limited only by the time it takes the letter to get from where it's posted to Windhoek. Poste restante works best in Windhoek (Poste Restante, GPO, Windhoek,

ADRIEN VADROT

DAVID ELSE

DEANNA SWANEY

DAVID ELSE

Traditional Namibian housing: a thatched hut of the Herero people **(top)**; semipermanent San dwellings **(middle left and bottom)**; and an Owambo *kraal* (family homestead) decorated with traditional water carriers **(middle right)**

MANFRED GOTTSCHALK

DEANNA SWANEY

The Namibian landscape features much more than sand and desert: The tranquil waters of the Kunene River **(top)** eventually become the majestic Epupa Falls; and the 1728m-high Spitzkoppe **(bottom)** is regarded as the most recognisable landmark in Namibia.

Namibia). Photo identification is required to collect mail.

All post offices sell current issues of Namibia's lovely pictorial and commemorative stamps. Stamp enthusiasts will probably want to visit the philatelic bureau upstairs in the GPO in Windhoek.

Telephone

Telephone area codes in Namibia are being greatly simplified, as large areas with many different codes are being consolidated into just a few three-digit codes. When phoning long-distance within Namibia, dial the regional area code, including the leading zero, followed by the six-digit (or, in rare cases, seven-digit) number. To phone some rural areas, you must dial the code and ask the exchange operator for the desired number; in a very few cases, a farmline (party line) code replaces the standard area code.

When phoning Namibia from abroad, dial the international access code (usually 00, but 011 from the USA), followed by the country code (☎ 264), the area code without the leading zero, and finally, the required number. To phone out of Namibia, dial 00 followed by the desired country code, area code (if applicable) and the number. Currently, international calls cost around US$3.50 per minute to any foreign country.

Telecom Namibia phonecards are sold at post offices and some retail shops; public telephone boxes are available at most post offices. In addition, cellphones (mobile phones) are gaining popularity and cellular services are available up to 10km or 20km from major towns. Most Namibian cellphone numbers begin with 081, which is followed by a seven-digit number.

There's only one slim telephone directory for the entire country, but it conveniently lists most people's private and work addresses and has a separate section for government departments. The *Yellow Pages* also covers the whole country.

Email & Internet Access

Both email and Internet access are available at a growing number of backpacker hostels, Internet cafes and hotels in larger towns, and also at several tourist offices and remote lodges. Plan on spending US$3 to US$6 per hour online.

DIGITAL RESOURCES

Lonely Planet's Web site (W www.lonely planet.com) has several pages of information on Namibia, plus the travellers dialogue site, the Thorn Tree.

For excellent background, a range of options and efficient bookings, check out the Cardboard Box Travel Shop site (W www .namibian.org), which is Namibia's best budget- and adventure-travel agency. Another useful trip-planning site is GorpTravel (W www.gorp.com), with links to adventure outfits featuring Namibia.

An especially useful Web site is Horizon (W www.horizon.fr/Namibia.html), with links in English and French to useful peripheral sites, tourist services, booking information and news snippets. Another good tourism site with useful links is W www.natron.net/etour.htm. For up-to-date news from Namibia, log on to the *Namibian* newspaper's Web site at W www .namibian.com.na.

Namibia Tourism's Web site (W www .tourism.com.na) provides a wide range of travel information and the Namibia Wildlife Resorts (NWR) Web site (W www.namibia wildliferesorts.com) includes guidelines on booking national parks, permits, and accommodation. Information from the glossy publication *Namibia Holiday & Travel* is also available on the Internet (W www .holidaytravel.com.na).

Telephone & Current Adaptors

If you're carrying a laptop computer with you and you need to access the Internet during your travels, you'll more than likely need an adaptor plug for your telephone linkup, as each country has its own configuration. You may also need a plug adaptor – even if your system automatically switches between 110/220 mains. One recommended source of information and plugs is Tele-Adapt (W www.teleadapt.com), a company which has office locations in the UK, USA and Australia.

BOOKS

Thanks to its unique history, cultures and environments, Namibia is the subject of a growing number of books in English – as well as German and Afrikaans – and most Namibian bookshops have a section dealing with Namibian and African topics. Few such books, however, are distributed in other countries; you'll have the most luck with specialist travel bookshops in the UK or the USA.

Windhoek and Swakopmund both have decent bookshops with separate sections for works in Afrikaans and German, but most books are in English. In smaller towns, a stationery shop, supermarket or general store may stock a selection of pulp paperbacks.

See also Literature under Arts in the Facts about Namibia chapter for more local titles and travellers' accounts of Namibia.

Lonely Planet

For coverage of the entire region, take a look at Lonely Planet's *Southern Africa, Africa on a shoestring* and the *Southern Africa Road Atlas*. For travel beyond Namibia, you may also want to check out Lonely Planet's *South Africa, Lesotho & Swaziland; Mozambique; Malawi; Tanzania; Kenya; Ethiopia, Eritrea & Djibouti*; and the forthcoming *Zimbabwe, Botswana* and *Zambia* books.

Guidebooks

Hiking Trails of Southern Africa by Willie & Sandra Olivier. This book covers major hiking and backpacking routes in South Africa and Namibia. It's distributed internationally.

Guide to Namibian Game Parks by Willie & Sandra Olivier. This book has the lowdown on the national parks, wildlife reserves and other conservation areas, with useful maps and advice on wildlife viewing. It's available locally.

Travel & Personal Accounts

Horns of Darkness – Rhinos on the Edge by Carol Cunningham & Joel Berger. This book describes a journey through the Namibian wilds to find and protect the country's remaining desert rhino.

The Place of Stunted Ironwood Trees: A Year in the Lives of the Cattle-Herding Himba of Namibia by David P Crandall. This sensitive study recounts the author's year-long observations in Himba country.

The Harmless People by Elizabeth Marshall Thomas. Before she started writing historical fiction, this author spent several years with the San people in north-western Botswana and north-eastern Namibia. This is a personal take on her experiences there.

The Sheltering Desert by Henno Martin. This Namibian classic recounts the adventures of German geologists Henno Martin and Hermann Korn, who spent two years in the Namib Desert avoiding Allied forces during WWII.

History & Politics

The Colonising Camera by Wolfram Hartmann (ed) et al. An illustrated history of Namibia.

To Free Namibia: The Life of the First President of Namibia by Sam Nujoma. This is the president's autobiography.

Herero Heroes: A Socio-Political History of the Herero of Namibia, 1890–1923 by JB Gewald. This book blends oral and written sources to recount the tragic and fascinating history of Namibia's Herero people.

Namibia – The Struggle for Liberation by Alfred T Moleah. This account of Swapo's independence struggle describes the situation before success was certain.

Namibia's Liberation Struggle: The Two-Edged Sword by Colin Leys. This is another take on the long war that ended in Namibia's independence in 1990.

The Scramble for Africa – White Man's Conquest of the Dark Continent from 1876 to 1942 by Thomas Pakenham. This book details the colonial history of Africa in well written and entertaining prose. It was one of the first studies to tell both sides of the story and has become established as the standard work on the topic.

The History of Southern Africa by Kevin Shillington. This provides an overall historical discussion of Botswana, Namibia, South Africa, Lesotho and Swaziland in textbook form. It objectively and sensitively covers prehistory as well as black African and colonial history.

General

The Burning Shore by Wilbur Smith. This entertaining tale is probably the best novel set in Namibia.

Nisa: The Life and Words of a !Kung Woman photographed by Marjorie Shostak. This simple and rather naive work provides insight into the lifestyles of the Namibian San. There's also a sequel, *Return to Nisa*.

Peoples of Namibia by JS Malan. This informative book, available in Namibia, describes the country's various cultures.

Namibia – Fascination of Geology – A Travel Handbook by Nicole Grünert. This is the best book on Namibia's incredible geology; it's available in Namibia.

Journey through Namibia by Mohamed Amin, Duncan Willetts & Tahir Shah. This is a good collection of stunning photos, but the text does have some problems.

Kaokoveld – The Last Wilderness by Anthony Hall-Martin, J du P Bothma & Clive Walker. This compilation of beguiling photos is breathtaking and will have you heading for northwestern Namibia.

Skeleton Coast by Amy Schoemann. This photographic essay is also worth a look.

The Namib – Natural History of an Ancient Desert by Mary Seely. This is a useful handbook written by the director of the Desert Research Unit in the Namib Desert Park.

Field Guides

In the UK, an excellent source of wildlife and nature titles is Subbuteo Natural History Books Ltd (☎ 01352-756551, fax 756004, ✉ sales@subbooks.demon.co.uk), Pistyll Farm, Nercwys, near Mold, Flintshire CH7 4EW. International mail orders are welcome. In the USA, try the Adventurous Traveler Bookstore (☎ 800-282 3963) or Nature Co (☎ 800-227 1114). In Australia, check out Andrew Isles (☎ 03-9510 5750), 115 Greville St, Prahran 3181, Victoria.

Namib Flora: Swakopmund to the Giant Welwitschia via Goanikontes by Patricia Craven & Christine Marais. This book is excellent for plant identification around the northern Namib-Naukluft Park.

The Birds of Daan Viljoen Park and *The Birds of Etosha National Park* by RAC Jensen & CF Clinning. Both books identify many endemic Namibian species.

Robert's Birds of Southern Africa by Gordon Lindsay. This is a bird-watching requisite, but it's not a featherweight volume.

Ian Sinclair's Field Guide to the Birds of Southern Africa by Ian Sinclair. This comprehensive work has all colour plates of all avian species in the region.

Illustrated Guide to the Birds of Southern Africa by Ian Sinclair. This guide concentrates on commonly observed species.

Newman's Birds of Southern Africa by Kenneth Newman. A comprehensive work on the region's avifauna; all species are identified in colour or black-and-white illustrations.

Field Guide to the Mammals of Southern Africa by Chris & Tilde Stuart. This is a well illustrated field guide to just about every furry thing you're likely to encounter in this part of the world.

Southern, Central & East African Mammals. Field Guide to Mammals of Africa Including Madagascar by Haltenorth & Diller. This is a good portable choice with lots of colour plates.

Field Guide to the Snakes and Other Reptiles of Southern Africa by Bill Branch. This is the one to consult if you want to know what it is that's slithering underfoot – and whether or not it's dangerous.

South African Frogs by Neville Passmore & Vincent Carruthers. This has all the answers for 'frogophiles'. It concentrates on South Africa, but includes most species found north of the border.

The Field Guide to the Butterflies of Southern Africa by Igor Migdoll. This book isn't totally comprehensive, but you probably won't encounter a butterfly that isn't included here.

Flowers of Southern Africa by Auriol Batten. Less a field guide than a large-format celebration of major flowering species, illustrated with colourful paintings.

Trees of Southern Africa by K Coates. This book provides the most thorough coverage of Southern Africa's arboreal richness, illustrated with colour photos and paintings.

Medicinal Plants of South Africa provides background on regional medicinal plants. It's available from Briza Publications (☎ 27-12-329 3896, fax 329 4525), PO Box 56569, Arcadia 0007, South Africa.

NEWSPAPERS & MAGAZINES

Most of Namibia's English-language newspapers are based in Windhoek: the *Namibian* (the most popular), published weekdays; the *Windhoek Observer*, published on Saturday; and the government-owned *New Era*. The *Namib Times*, published in Walvis Bay, is published twice-weekly. The two main German-language newspapers are *Allgemeine Zeitung* and *Namibia Nachrichten*.

While Namibia ostensibly enjoys freedom of the press, no Namibian paper is known for its coverage of international events or mastery of journalistic conventions, and none takes an avant-garde stance on political issues. The readily available

South African daily papers are marginally better sources of world news, and some European newspapers, including the London dailies and various large German papers, as well as the *International Herald Tribune* and *Washington Post*, are available in Windhoek and Swakopmund, together with such news magazines as *Der Spiegel*, the *Economist*, *Time* and *Newsweek*.

The monthly English-language *Namibia Review* follows national political, cultural and economic issues; contact Namibia Review (☎ 061-222246, fax 224937), Ministry of Information & Broadcasting, Private Bag 11334, Windhoek. The newsletter *Namibia Holiday & Travel* (☎ 061-225665, fax 220410, e tnn@iafrica.com.na), PO Box 21593, Windhoek, keeps interested parties up-to-date with Namibia's latest tourist industry information.

For travel-, culture- and arts-related articles and advertising, see Air Namibia's inflight magazine *Flamingo*. It's available by subscription from Flamingo (☎ 27-11-315 1771, fax 315 2072, e tapubs@iafrica.com), PO Box 30177, Kyalami 1684, South Africa.

Getaway is South Africa's largest, most-popular travel magazine, and most issues contain articles on Namibia. The contact details are Getaway (☎ 27-21-531 0404, fax 531 7303), PO Box 596, Howard Place 7450, South Africa. You may also enjoy *Out There*, a bimonthly publication that features adventure activities in Africa and beyond. Contact Out There (☎ 27-11-497 2711, fax 834 6246, e outthere@tml.co.za), PO Box 1138, Johannesburg 2000, South Africa.

The award-winning semimonthly *Africa Geographic* examines issues all over the continent, with an emphasis on Southern Africa. Foreign subscriptions cost R105, US$32 or UK£21 annually; contact Subscriptions, Africa Geographic (☎ 27-21-686 9001, fax 686 4500, e wildmags@iafrica .com, W www.africamag.co.za), 14 College Rd, Rondebosch 7700, PO Box 44223, Claremont 7735, Cape Town, South Africa.

RADIO & TV

The Namibian Broadcasting Corporation (NBC) operates nine radio stations broadcasting on different wavebands in 12 languages; the best pop station is Radio Wave, at 96.7FM in Windhoek.

The NBC broadcasts government-vetted television programs in English and Afrikaans from 4pm to 11pm Monday to Friday and later on Friday and Saturday. On Sunday, Christian programming is broadcast from 11am to 1pm and other programming from 3pm. News is broadcast at 10pm nightly.

Most top-end hotels and lodges with televisions provide access to satellite-supported DSTV, which broadcasts NBC and a cocktail of cable channels: MNET (a movie and entertainment package), CNN, ESPN, MTV, BBC World, Sky, Supersport, SABC, SATV, NatGeo, Disney and Discovery, among other channels.

PHOTOGRAPHY & VIDEO
Film & Equipment

Photographers will probably want to bring their equipment from home, as it can be expensive in Namibia. Video cartridges and both print and slide film are sold in photo shops in Windhoek and Swakopmund, and at some upmarket lodges. However, they're all generally cheaper in Europe, North America and Australasia, and local shops may not have your preferred brand.

Useful accessories would include a small flash, a cable release, a polarising filter, a lens-cleaning kit (fluid, tissue and aerosol), and silica-gel packs to protect against humidity. Also, remember to take spare batteries for cameras and flash units and make sure your equipment is insured. If you're using a video camera, you'll normally find 12V plugs in vehicles (cigarette lighters) and in hotels where you can recharge batteries. Heat, humidity, fine sand and sunlight can spoil equipment, so take precautions.

Technical Tips

Many find 100 ASA adequate for most situations, but for morning or evening shots at longer focal lengths (ie, 300mm to 500mm), 200 or 400 ASA allows greater flexibility. For transparencies, you'll generally have the best results with Fujichrome Sensia 100, Provia 100, Velvia 50 or Kodachrome 64.

On sunny days, the best times for photos are the first two hours after sunrise and the last two before sunset, when the shadows are the least harsh and colours are strongest (due to colour-enhancing rays cast by a low sun). At other times, colours may be washed out by harsh sunlight and glare, although you can counter this with a polarising (UV) filter. If you're shooting on sand or near water, always adjust for glare and keep your photographic equipment away from salt water and sand.

When photographing outdoors, take light readings on the subject and not the brilliant African background or your shots will be underexposed.

Restrictions

Officials in Namibia aren't as sensitive about photography as in some other African countries, but it still isn't a good idea to photograph borders, airports, communications equipment or military installations without first asking permission from any uniformed personnel that might be present.

Photographing Animals

To score some excellent wildlife shots effortlessly, a good lightweight 35mm SLR camera, a UV filter, and a 70mm to 300mm zoom or a minimum 300mm fixed-length telephoto lens should do the trick. If your subject is nothing but a speck in the distance, however, resist wasting film on it but keep the camera ready – anything can happen at any time. Unless you're an experienced photographer, you may want to carry a 'point-and-shoot' automatic camera rather than a manual camera; once you've adjusted the aperture, exposure and focus, your subject could be long gone.

Photographing People

The quest for that perfect 'people shot' will prove a photographer's greatest challenge. While many Africans enjoy being photographed, others do not; people could be superstitious about your camera, suspicious of your motives, or simply interested in whatever economic advantage they can gain from your desire to photograph them. The main point is that you must respect the wishes of the locals, however photogenic or colourful, who may be camera-shy for whatever reason. If you can't get a candid shot, make sure you ask permission and don't insist or snap a picture anyway if permission is denied.

Often, people will allow you to photograph them provided you give them a photo for themselves, a real treasure in rural Africa. Understandably, people are sometimes disappointed not to see the photograph immediately materialise. If you don't carry a Polaroid camera, take their address and make it clear that you'll send the photo by post once it's processed. Never promise to send a copy and then fail to do so.

When photographing people, particularly dark-skinned people, remember to take the light reading from the subject's face and not the background.

TIME

In the summer months (October to April), Namibia is two hours ahead of GMT/UTC. Therefore, if it's noon in Southern Africa, it's 10am in London, 5am in New York, 2am in Los Angeles and 8pm in Sydney. In the winter (April to October), Namibia turns its clocks back one hour, making it only one hour ahead of GMT/UTC and one hour behind South African time.

ELECTRICITY

Namibia generates electricity at 220V AC, 15 amps, and uses either two- or three-pin round plugs. If you don't have the right adaptor, you can always buy a plug locally and connect it yourself. Note that a voltage adaptor is needed for US appliances.

WEIGHTS & MEASURES

Namibia uses the metric system. To convert between metric and imperial units, refer to the conversion chart on the inside back cover of this book.

LAUNDRY

Nearly all hotels have some sort of laundry service – normally it's an employee who washes clothing by hand – and most small towns have a laundry. Washing facilities are often provided at government camp sites and resorts. Dry-cleaners are found in major towns and charge about US$2 per piece. However, self-service laundrettes are scarce outside Windhoek and Swakopmund.

HEALTH

In theory, Namibia's public health care system provides free or very inexpensive health services for all Namibian citizens. In practice, however, public clinics are desperately understaffed and underfunded, and nearly everyone who can afford it opts for private health care, which is of a relatively high standard and also quite affordable. If you'd rather not wait in a queue all day to see a doctor, you'll want to go the same route. The best hospitals are in Windhoek.

Pharmacies, even in the poorer areas of the far north, are generally well stocked and you'll have few problems finding any well-known prescription medicine. Dental treatment is probably best handled in Windhoek, Swakopmund or Walvis Bay.

Many doctors recommend malaria prophylactics for travel in the Caprivi and Kavango regions, the Owambo country and some northern areas of Kunene province, particularly around Epupa Falls.

In general, travel health depends on your predeparture preparations, your daily health care while travelling and how you handle problems that develop. While potential dangers can seem frightening, in reality few travellers in Namibia experience anything more serious than an upset stomach.

Predeparture Planning

Immunisations It's wise to seek medical advice at least six weeks before travelling to Southern Africa, and discuss with your doctor the range of vaccinations that are available (for more details about the diseases themselves, see later in this section). Also, plan ahead for getting your vaccinations. Some of them require more than one injection, while others shouldn't be given simultaneously.

Be aware that children and pregnant women are more prone to disease, and the effects can be more serious. Note that some vaccinations aren't recommended during pregnancy or for people with allergies.

Once you've had the vaccinations, carry an International Health Card which documents all the vaccinations you've had, especially yellow fever, as it is obligatory for entry into Namibia if you are coming from infected areas.

Cholera The current cholera vaccine isn't very effective and has many side effects, so it is not generally recommended for travellers.

Diphtheria & Tetanus Vaccinations for these two diseases are usually combined and are recommended for everyone. After an initial course of three injections (usually given in childhood), boosters are necessary every 10 years.

Hepatitis A Vaccinations provide long-term immunity (possibly more than 10 years) after an initial injection and a booster at six to 12 months. Alternatively, an injection of gamma globulin can provide short-term protection against hepatitis A – two to six months, depending on the dose given. It is not a vaccine, but a ready-made antibody collected from blood donations. It is reasonably effective and, unlike the vaccine, it is protective immediately, but because it is a blood product, there are current concerns about its long-term safety. A combined vaccine for hepatitis A and hepatitis B is also available. Three injections over six months are required. The first two provide good protection against hepatitis A.

Hepatitis B Consider a vaccination against hepatitis B if you're going on a long trip or visit-

Everyday Health

Normal body temperature is up to 37°C (98.6°F); more than 2°C (4°F) higher indicates a high fever. The normal adult pulse rate is 60 to 100 per minute (children 80 to 100, babies 100 to 140). As a general rule the pulse increases about 20 beats per minute for each 1°C (2°F) rise in fever.

Respiration (breathing) rate is an indicator of illness. Count the number of breaths per minute: Between 12 and 20 is normal for adults and older children (up to 30 for younger children, 40 for babies). People with a high fever or serious respiratory illness breathe more quickly than normal. More than 40 shallow breaths a minute may indicate pneumonia.

ing countries where there are high levels of hepatitis B infection, where blood transfusions may not be adequately screened or where sexual contact or needle sharing is a possibility. Vaccination involves two or three vaccinations; some doctors recommend a booster at 12 months. More rapid courses are available if necessary.

Malaria Although a vaccine against malaria may be developed in the near future, there's currently no vaccine against this dangerous disease. While antimalarial drugs do not prevent infection, they do kill nonimmune malaria parasites while they're reproducing and significantly reduce the risk of serious illness or death. Expert advice should be sought, as there are many factors to consider, including the area to be visited, the risk of exposure to malarial mosquitoes, the side effects of medication, your medical history and your age or reproductive status. At the very least, travellers to malarial areas of Namibia will probably want to carry a treatment dose of medication to use if symptoms occur. Seek medical advice before travel.

Meningococcal Meningitis Vaccination is recommended for certain parts of Africa. A single injection gives good protection against the major epidemic forms of the disease for three years. Protection may be less effective in children under two years.

Polio Everyone should keep up to date with this vaccination, normally given in childhood. A booster every 10 years maintains immunity.

Rabies Vaccination should be considered if you will spend a month or longer in Southern Africa, where rabies is common, especially if you're cycling, handling animals, caving or travelling to remote areas. It is also recommended for children (who may not report a bite). Pre-travel rabies vaccination involves having three injections over 21 to 28 days. If someone who has been vaccinated is bitten or scratched by an animal, they will require two booster injections of vaccine; those not vaccinated require more.

Tuberculosis The risk of tuberculosis (TB) to travellers is usually very low, unless you will be living with local people in high risk areas. Vaccination against TB (known as BCG) is recommended for children and young adults spending more than three months in these areas, but the response is variable. In fact, BCG provides more consistent resistance to Hansen's disease (leprosy) than it does against TB.

Typhoid Vaccination against typhoid may be required if you are travelling for more than two weeks. It is now available either as an injection or as capsules to be taken orally.

Yellow Fever A yellow fever vaccine is now the only vaccine that is a legal requirement for entry

Medical Kit Check List

Following is a list of items you should consider including in your medical kit – consult your pharmacist for brands available in your country.

☐ **Aspirin or paracetamol (acetaminophen in the USA)** – for pain or fever

☐ **Antihistamine** – for allergies, eg, hay fever; to ease the itch from insect bites or stings; and to prevent motion sickness

☐ **Cold and flu tablets, throat lozenges and nasal decongestant**

☐ **Multivitamins** – consider for long trips, when dietary vitamin intake may be inadequate

☐ **Antibiotics** – consider including these if you're travelling well off the beaten track; see your doctor, as they must be prescribed, and carry the prescription with you

☐ **Loperamide or diphenoxylate** –'blockers' for diarrhoea

☐ **Prochlorperazine or metaclopramide** – for nausea and vomiting

☐ **Rehydration mixture** – to prevent dehydration, which may occur, for example, during bouts of diarrhoea; particularly important when travelling with children

☐ **Insect repellent, sunscreen, lip balm and eye drops**

☐ **Calamine lotion, sting-relief spray or aloe vera** – to ease irritation from sunburn and insect bites or stings

☐ **Antifungal cream or powder** – for fungal skin infections and thrush

☐ **Antiseptic (such as povidone-iodine)** – for cuts and grazes

☐ **Bandages, Band-Aids (plasters) and other wound dressings**

☐ **Water purification tablets or iodine**

☐ **Scissors, tweezers and a thermometer** – note that mercury thermometers are prohibited by airlines

☐ **Sterile kit** – in case you need injections in a country with medical hygiene problems; discuss with your doctor

into certain countries, usually only enforced when coming from an infected area. Vaccination is recommended for travel in areas where the disease is endemic (including parts of Africa). To get the vaccination you may have to go to a special health centre.

Health Insurance Make sure you have adequate health insurance. See Travel Insurance under Visas & Documents earlier in this chapter.

Travel Health Guides Long-term travellers, or those travelling in remote areas, may want to carry a more detailed health guide. Such guides include:

CDC's Complete Guide to Healthy Travel, Open Road Publishing, 1997. The US Centers for Disease Control & Prevention's recommendations for international travel.

Staying Healthy in Asia, Africa & Latin America by Dirk Schroeder, Moon Publications, 1994. Probably the best all-round guide to carry; it's detailed and well organised.

Travellers' Health by Dr Richard Dawood, Oxford University Press, 1995. This guide is comprehensive, easy to read, authoritative and highly recommended, although it's rather large to lug around.

Where There Is No Doctor by David Werner, Macmillan, 1994. This is a very detailed guide intended for people, such as volunteers, working in small villages.

Healthy Travel Africa by Isabelle Young, Lonely Planet Publications, 2000. This handy pocket-size guide is packed with useful information about pre-trip planning, emergency first aid, immunisation and diseases and what to do if you get sick on the road.

There are also a number of excellent travel health sites on the Internet. The Lonely Planet home page has links at W www.lonelyplanet.com/weblinks/wlheal.htm to the World Health Organization and the US Centers for Disease Control & Prevention.

Other Preparations Make sure you're healthy before you leave home, and visit the dentist to take care of any dental problems. If you wear glasses or contacts, take a spare pair and your prescription.

If you require a particular medication, take an adequate supply for your entire trip, as it may not be available locally. Also, make sure the packaging includes the generic name, which will help immeasurably in finding emergency replacements for lost or stolen prescriptions. You should also carry a legible prescription or letter from your doctor showing you legally use the medication.

If you're going on safari or visiting remote lodges, remember to alert the operator to any medical conditions that may present problems: diabetes, epilepsy, a heart condition, food restrictions, bee-sting allergy or the like. It probably won't stop you going, but it could make matters easier if the guide knows of your condition before (and if) you do run into problems.

Basic Rules

Food An old adage advises: 'If you can cook it, boil it or peel it, you can eat it...otherwise forget it'. Vegetables and fruit should be washed with purified water or peeled where possible. Beware of ice cream that might have been melted and refrozen; if there's any doubt (eg, a recent power cut), avoid it. Undercooked meat, particularly mince (hamburgers etc), should be avoided, as should shellfish such as mussels, oysters and clams (unless they're served in a reputable restaurant). Note that steaming does not render questionable shellfish safe for consumption.

If a takeaway or food stall looks clean and well run and the vendor also looks clean and healthy, then the food is probably safe. In general, places full of travellers or locals will be fine, because the food in busy takeaways is cooked and eaten quickly and is probably not reheated.

Water Although Namibian tap water and most mountain water is generally drinkable, it's wise to err on the side of caution. If you're not sure the water is safe, assume the worst. Reputable brands of bottled water or soft drinks (sodas) are generally fine, but only use water from containers with a seal. Take care with fruit juice, particularly if water may have been added. Milk should be treated with suspicion as it is often unpasteurised, though boiled milk and UHT milk are fine if kept hygienically. Tea or coffee should also be OK, since the water will have been boiled.

Water Purification If you don't want to rely on bottled water, you can purify water

Nutrition

If your diet is poor or limited in variety, if you're travelling hard and fast and therefore missing meals or if you simply lose your appetite, you can soon start to lose weight and place your health at risk.

Make sure your diet is well balanced. Cooked eggs, tofu, beans, lentils and nuts are all safe ways to get protein. Fruit you can peel (bananas, oranges or mandarins, for example) is usually safe and a good source of vitamins. Melons can harbour bacteria in their flesh and are best avoided. Try to eat plenty of grains (including rice) and bread. Remember that although food is generally safer if it is cooked well, overcooked food loses much of its nutritional value. If your diet isn't well balanced or if your food intake is insufficient, it's a good idea to take vitamin and iron pills.

In hot climates make sure you drink enough – don't rely on feeling thirsty to indicate when you should drink. Not needing to urinate or voiding small amounts of very dark yellow urine is a danger sign. Always carry a water bottle with you on long trips. Excessive sweating can lead to loss of salt and therefore muscle cramping. Salt tablets are not a good idea as a preventative, but in places where salt is not used much, adding salt to food can help.

---

for drinking. The simplest method is to boil it for about eight minutes.

You may also want to consider carrying a water filter, especially if you'll be visiting other African countries further north. Total filters remove all parasites, bacteria and viruses, but they're often expensive (costs need to be weighed against the price of bottled water). Simple filters (which can even be a nylon mesh bag) filter out dirt and larger foreign bodies, allowing chemical solutions to work much more effectively. When buying a filter, it's important to read the specifications and know what it removes from the water and what it doesn't. Remember also that a poorly maintained filter can be a breeding ground for germs.

However, simple filtering doesn't kill all dangerous organisms, so if you cannot boil water it should be treated chemically. Chlorine tablets will kill many pathogens, but not some parasites like giardia and amoebas. Iodine is more effective in purifying water and is available in tablet form. Follow the directions carefully and remember that too much iodine can be harmful.

Medical Problems & Treatment

Self-diagnosis and treatment can be risky, so the best course is to seek medical help. An embassy, consulate or top-end hotel can usually recommend a good local doctor or clinic. Although we do provide drug dosages in this section, correct diagnosis is vital, and

they are for emergency use only. In this section we have used generic names (rather than trade names) for medications – check with a pharmacist for brands available locally.

Note that antibiotics should ideally be administered only under medical supervision; take only the recommended dose at the prescribed intervals and use the entire course, even if the illness seems to be cured sooner. Stop immediately if there are any serious reactions and don't use the antibiotic at all if there's any chance it's not the correct one. Be aware of any allergies you may have (many people are allergic to commonly prescribed antibiotics, such as sulphates or penicillin), and carry this information (eg, on a bracelet) when travelling.

Environmental Hazards

Heat Exhaustion Dehydration and salt deficiency can cause heat exhaustion, so carry a water bottle on hikes and long journeys. Take time to acclimatise to high temperatures and drink sufficient liquids – don't rely on feeling thirsty to indicate when you should drink. Danger signs are dark yellow urine or failure to urinate regularly.

Salt deficiency is characterised by fatigue, lethargy, headaches, giddiness and muscle cramps; salt tablets may help, but adding extra salt to your food is better (and safer).

Heatstroke This serious, occasionally fatal condition can occur if the body's heat-regulating mechanism breaks down and the body temperature rises to dangerous levels. Long, continuous periods of exposure to high temperatures and insufficient fluids can leave you vulnerable to heatstroke. The symptoms are: feeling unwell, not sweating very much (or at all) and a high body temperature (39° to 41°C or 102° to 106°F). Where sweating has ceased, the skin becomes flushed and red. Severe, throbbing headaches and lack of coordination will also occur, and the sufferer may be confused or aggressive, eventually becoming delirious or convulsive. Hospitalisation is essential, but in the interim get the sufferer out of the sun, remove their clothing, cover them with a wet sheet or towel and then fan continually. Give fluids if they are conscious.

Hypothermia Cold, wet conditions can be as dangerous as extreme heat, and hikers in mountain regions, especially in the winter or during wet periods, may be at risk from hypothermia. This condition occurs when the body loses heat faster than it can produce it and the core temperature of the body falls. Even if the air temperature is above freezing, a combination of wind, wet clothing, fatigue and hunger can make a person susceptible to this problem.

To avoid hypothermia it is best to dress in layers; silk, wool and some 'thermal' artificial fibres are all good insulating materials. It's helpful to wear a hat because a lot of heat is lost through the head, and wear a strong, waterproof outer layer. It may also be useful to carry a 'space blanket' for emergencies.

Symptoms of hypothermia include exhaustion, numb skin (particularly toes and fingers), shivering, slurred speech, irrational or violent behaviour, lethargy, stumbling, dizzy spells, muscle cramps and violent bursts of energy. Irrationality may take the form of sufferers claiming they are warm and trying to take off their clothes.

To treat mild hypothermia, first get the victim out of the wind and rain, replace wet clothing with dry warm clothes and administer hot liquids – not alcohol – and some high-energy, easily digestible food. Do not rub the skin; instead, allow the victim to slowly warm themself. This should be enough to treat the early stages of hypothermia. The early recognition and treatment of mild hypothermia is the only way to prevent severe hypothermia, which is a critical condition.

Jet Lag A product of rapid, long-distance east-west travel, jet lag occurs because many of the functions of the human body (such as temperature, pulse rate and emptying of the bladder and bowels) are regulated by internal 24-hour cycles which are disrupted by passage between time zones. As a result, the body needs time to adjust to the 'new time' of the destination. Affected travellers may experience fatigue, disorientation, insomnia, anxiety, impaired concentration and loss of appetite. These effects will usually diminish within three days of arrival, but to minimise the impact:

- Rest for a couple of days prior to departure.
- Select flight schedules that minimise sleep deprivation; arriving late in the day means you can go to sleep soon after you arrive. For very long flights, try to organise a stopover.
- Avoid excessive eating (which bloats the stomach) and alcohol (which causes dehydration) during the flight. Instead, drink water or uncarbonated, nonalcoholic drinks.
- Avoid smoking.
- Make yourself comfortable by wearing loose-fitting clothes and perhaps bringing an eye mask and ear plugs to help you sleep.
- Try to sleep at the appropriate time for the time zone of your destination.

Motion Sickness Eating lightly before and during a trip will reduce the chances of motion sickness. If you are prone to motion sickness, try to find a place that minimises movement – near the wing on aircraft; on lower decks and close to midship on boats; or near the centre on buses. Fresh air usually helps; reading and cigarette smoke don't. Antisickness preparations, which can cause drowsiness, have to be taken before the trip commences. Ginger (available in capsule form) and peppermint (including mint-flavoured sweets) are natural preventatives.

Prickly Heat Excessive perspiration trapped under the skin causes an itchy rash called prickly heat. It usually strikes people who have arrived in a hot climate. Keeping cool, bathing often, drying the skin and using a mild talcum or prickly heat powder or resorting to air-conditioning may help.

Sunburn Even through clouds, sunburn comes on surprisingly quickly. Use a good strong sunscreen, a hat, and a barrier cream for your nose and lips. Protect your eyes with good quality sunglasses, particularly if you will be near water, sand or snow. Calamine lotion or an after-sun preparation will relieve a mild sunburn.

Infectious Diseases

Diarrhoea Simple things like a change of water, food or climate can all cause a mild bout of diarrhoea, but a few rushed toilet trips with no other symptoms is not indicative of a major problem.

Dehydration is the main danger, particularly for children or elderly travellers, as dehydration can occur quite quickly. In all cases, the first concern should be to replace fluids that have been lost by drinking small amounts at regular and frequent intervals. Weak black tea with a little sugar, soda water, or soft drinks (sodas) allowed to go flat and diluted with 50% water are all good. If you have severe diarrhoea a rehydrating solution will replace lost minerals and salts.

Commercially available oral rehydration solutions (ORS) are very useful; add them to boiled or bottled water. In an emergency, make up a solution of six teaspoons of sugar, a half teaspoon of salt and 1L of clean water. You need to drink at least the same volume of fluid that you are losing in bowel movements and vomiting. Urine is the best guide to the adequacy of replacement – if you have small amounts of concentrated urine, you need to drink more. Stick to a bland diet as you recover.

Gut-paralysing drugs such as loperamide or diphenoxylate (imodium or lomotil) can be used to relieve the symptoms, but don't actually cure the problem and should *never* be taken if there's fever or a bloody stool. Otherwise, use them only if you do not have access to toilets (eg, if you must travel) and note that they aren't recommended for children under 12 years of age.

Diarrhoea with blood or mucus (dysentery); diarrhoea with fever; profuse, watery diarrhoea; persistent diarrhoea; or severe diarrhoea that doesn't improve after 48 hours all suggest a more serious underlying cause. In these situations, a stool test may be necessary to diagnose the guilty bug. Avoid gut-paralysing drugs and seek medical help urgently.

If medical help isn't available, the recommended drugs for bacterial diarrhoea (the most likely cause of severe travellers diarrhoea) are norfloxacin 400mg twice daily for three days or ciprofloxacin 500mg twice daily for three days. Note, however, that these are not recommended for children or pregnant women. The drug of choice for children would be a five-day course of co-trimoxazole with dosage dependent on weight. Pregnant women may often take ampicillin or amoxycillin, but only under medical direction.

Other causes of persistent diarrhoea include giardiasis and amoebic dysentery. The former is caused by a common parasite, called *Giardia lamblia*, which enters the body via the faecal-oral route. Symptoms include stomach cramps, nausea, a bloated stomach, watery, foul-smelling diarrhoea and frequent gas. Symptoms can appear several weeks after you have been exposed to the parasite, but may disappear after a few days and then return; this cycle can continue for several weeks. Amoebic dysentery, caused by ingestion of the protozoan *Entamoeba histolytica*, is characterised by a gradual onset of low-grade diarrhoea, often with blood and mucus.

Cramping, abdominal pain and vomiting are less typical than with other causes of diarrhoea, and may not be associated with fever. However, the condition will persist until treated and can recur and cause other, more serious health problems. If you suspect either giardiasis or amoebic dysentery, seek medical advice. If this isn't possible, the recommended treatment is a 2g single dose of tinidazole or 250mg of metronidazole three times daily for five to 10 days.

Hepatitis A common disease, hepatitis is a general term for inflammation of the liver. It's caused by several different viruses. Although they differ in the way they're transmitted, symptoms are usually fairly similar: fever, chills, headache, fatigue, feelings of weakness and aches and pains, followed by loss of appetite, nausea, vomiting, abdominal pain, dark urine, light-coloured faeces, jaundiced skin and yellowed eyes.

Hepatitis A is transmitted by contaminated food and drinking water. If you suspect Hepatitis A, seek medical advice, rest, drink lots of fluids, eat lightly and avoid alcohol and fatty foods. Hepatitis E is transmitted in the same way, but can be especially serious in pregnant women.

Hepatitis B is spread through contact with infected blood, blood products or body fluids – mainly through sexual contact, unsterilised needles and blood transfusions, or contact with blood via small breaks in the skin. Shaving or tattooing with contaminated equipment may also transmit the disease. Early symptoms may be more severe than type A and the disease can lead to long-term problems; victims may become long-term carriers, and may eventually suffer chronic liver damage or liver cancer. Hepatitis C and D are spread in the same way and can also lead to long-term complications.

Vaccines are available against hepatitis A and B, but not for other strains. To prevent contact with hepatitis of any strain, follow basic rules about food and water (hepatitis A and E) and avoiding risk situations (hepatitis B, C and D). Those who have had hepatitis should avoid alcohol and other toxins for some time after the illness, as the liver needs time to recover.

HIV & AIDS Infection with the human immunodeficiency virus (HIV) could lead to acquired immune deficiency syndrome (AIDS), which is a fatal disease. Any exposure to blood, blood products or body fluids puts you at risk. The disease is often transmitted through sexual contact – and Southern Africa has one of the highest populations of HIV/AIDS sufferers in the world (see the boxed text 'AIDS in Southern Africa' later in this chapter). Be prudent in your choice of sexual partners, and insist on using condoms, especially in new or short-term relationships.

The disease can also be spread via dirty needles – vaccinations, acupuncture, tattooing and body piercing are as dangerous as intravenous drug use. Any needle you use must be sterile and if you need a transfusion or blood test, make sure the needle and syringe is unwrapped in front of you. If you're likely to need such treatment, be sure to carry a medical kit with safely-wrapped needles and syringes to be used in such emergencies.

HIV/AIDS can also be spread through infected blood transfusions, and although Namibia currently screens all blood donations for HIV, many other African countries fail to do so.

Intestinal Worms Most common in rural, tropical areas, intestinal worms cause a range of infections. Some (eg, tapeworms) may be ingested on food such as undercooked meat, and some (eg, hookworms) enter through your skin. Infestations may not show up for some time, and although they are generally not serious, if left untreated some can cause severe health problems later. Consider having a stool test when you return home to check for these and determine the appropriate treatment.

Meningococcal Meningitis This serious disease can be fatal, and sub-Saharan Africa suffers recurring epidemics. Early symptoms include fever, severe headache, sensitivity to light and stiffness in the neck, which inhibits nodding. There may also be purple patches on the skin. Urgent medical treatment is warranted, as death can occur within a few hours of the onset of symptoms. Treatment will usually include intravenous administration of penicillin and/ or injections of chloramphenicol.

Bilharzia Also known as schistosomiasis, this disease is transmitted by minute worms, which infect freshwater snails found in rivers, streams, lakes and dams. When the worms are discharged in the water, they enter through the skin of swimmers and attach themselves to the intestines and bladder. There are few people who experience serious symptoms immediately after infection – it's the long-term damage that is potentially more harmful.

The first symptom may be a general feeling of being unwell, or a tingling and sometimes a light rash around the area where the worms entered. Weeks later a high fever may develop. Once the disease is established, abdominal pain and blood in the urine are other signs. However, it's also possible that symptoms won't appear until the disease is well established (several months to years after initial exposure), and damage to internal organs is irreversible.

The best way to avoid bilharzia is to stay out of fresh water where the worms may be present. Places with the highest risk are shallow or stagnant, reed-lined areas near villages, but even deep water can be infected (fast-running streams and rivers are normally safe). If you're forced to wade across a stream or dam, dry off quickly afterwards, and dry your clothes.

If you swim in still waters anywhere in Namibia – especially in the north – it's probably wise to have a blood test when you get home. However, few overseas physicians have even heard of this disease, so you may have to direct them to literature on it. Note also that the test will not show positive for two weeks to three months after exposure and may occasionally show negative even if you are carrying the disease. If you're in any doubt after the first test, have another test a few weeks later. If you have bilharzia, the cure is a simple single dose of tablets, such as Biltricide (which is readily available in local pharmacies).

Sexually Transmitted Infections HIV/AIDS and hepatitis B can be transmitted through sexual contact – for details, see the relevant sections. Other sexually transmitted infections (STIs) include gonorrhoea, herpes and syphilis. Common symptoms are sores, blisters or rashes around the genitals, and discharges or pain when urinating. In some STIs, such as wart virus or chlamydia, symptoms may be less marked or not observed at all, especially in women. Chlamydia infection can cause infertility in men and women before any symptoms have been noticed. Syphilis symptoms eventually disappear completely but the disease continues and can cause severe problems in later years. While abstinence from sexual contact is the only 100% effective prevention, using condoms is also effective. The different STIs each require specific antibiotics for treatment. There is no known cure for HIV or herpes.

Typhoid This dangerous gut infection is caused by contaminated water and food. In its early stages sufferers may feel they have a bad cold or flu, as early symptoms are a headache, body aches and a fever that rises a little each day until it is around 40°C (104°F) or more. The pulse is often slow relative to the degree of fever present – unlike a normal fever where the pulse increases. There may also be vomiting, abdominal pain, diarrhoea or constipation. In the second week the high fever and slow pulse continue and a few pink spots may appear on the body; trembling, delirium, weakness, weight loss and dehydration may occur. Complications such as pneumonia, perforated bowel or meningitis may occur. If you contract this disease, medical help is essential.

Fungal Infections These infections occur more commonly in hot weather and are usually found on the scalp, between the toes (athlete's foot) or fingers, in the groin and on the body (ringworm). You get ringworm (which is a fungal infection, not a worm) from infected animals or other people. Moisture encourages these infections.

To prevent fungal infections wear loose, comfortable clothes, avoid artificial fibres, wash frequently and dry yourself carefully. If you do get an infection, wash the infected area at least daily with a disinfectant or medicated soap and water, and rinse and dry well. Apply an antifungal cream or powder such as tolnaftate. Try to expose the infected area to air or sunlight as much as possible and wash all towels and underwear in hot water, change them often and let them dry in the sun.

Insect-Borne Diseases

Malaria This serious and potentially fatal disease is spread by mosquito bites. If you are travelling in endemic areas, it is extremely important to avoid mosquito bites and to take tablets to prevent this disease. Symptoms range from fever, chills and sweating, headache, diarrhoea, abdominal pains and joint pains to loss of interest in day-to-day life and a vague feeling of ill-health. If malaria is suspected, it's essential to seek medical help early, as delays can allow the disease to progress rapidly into more serious and potentially fatal levels.

If medical care is not available, malaria tablets can be used for treatment. There is a variety of medications such as mefloquine, Fansidar and Malarone. You should seek medical advice, before you travel, on the right medication and dosage for you.

Malaria is best prevented by observing the following precautions:

• Wear long trousers and long-sleeved shirts, ideally light-coloured and treated with a repellent such as Permethrin.
• Use mosquito repellents containing the compound DEET on exposed areas of skin (prolonged overuse of DEET may be harmful, especially to children, but the use of DEET is considered preferable to being bitten by disease-transmitting mosquitoes).
• Avoid perfumes or aftershave, which may attract mosquitoes.
• Sleep under a mosquito net – ideally impregnated with repellent (such as Permethrin); it is well worth carrying your own.

Dengue Fever Known locally as 'Congo Fever', this viral and potentially deadly disease is transmitted by mosquitoes and is fast becoming one of the top public health problems in the tropical world. Unlike the malaria mosquito, the mosquito that transmits the dengue virus (*Aedes aegypti*) is most active during the day, and is found mainly in urban areas, in and around human dwellings.

Signs and symptoms of dengue fever include a sudden onset of high fever, headache, joint and muscle pains (hence its old name, 'breakbone fever') and nausea and vomiting. A rash of small red spots (which is in fact capillary haemorrhaging) sometimes appears three to four days after the onset of fever. In the early phase of illness, dengue may be mistaken for other infectious diseases, including malaria and influenza. Minor bleeding such as nose bleeds may occur in the course of the illness.

The illness can progress to the potentially fatal dengue haemorrhagic fever (DHF), characterised by heavy bleeding, which is thought to be a result of second infection due to a different strain (there are four major strains) and usually affects residents of the country rather than travellers. Recovery even from simple dengue fever may be prolonged, with tiredness lasting for several weeks.

If you suspect dengue fever, seek medical attention as soon as possible; a blood test can exclude malaria (which has similar symptoms) and indicate the correct diagnosis. Unfortunately, there's no specific treatment for dengue fever, which can only be treated symptomatically. To facilitate the immune system's ability to fight the infection, avoid aspirin, as it increases the risk of haemorrhaging – and progression of the disease to haemorrhagic fever.

The best prevention is to avoid mosquito bites at all times by covering up, using mosquito nets and insect repellents containing the compound DEET (see the precautions discussed under Malaria earlier).

Cuts, Stings & Bites

Cuts Wash well and treat any cut with an antiseptic such as povidone-iodine. Where possible avoid bandages and sticking plasters, which can keep wounds moist. Note if you're diving that stone and coral cuts are notoriously slow to heal, and that small pieces of stone or coral can become embedded in the wound if it is not adequately cleaned.

Stings Bee and wasp stings are usually painful rather than dangerous. Calamine lotion or a sting-relief spray will give relief and ice packs will reduce the pain and swelling. However, in people who are allergic to these stings, severe breathing difficulties may occur and require urgent medical care. If you have a known allergy to bee or wasp stings, discuss your travel plans with your doctor, who may suggest you carry medication that can be self-administered in the event of a sting.

Scorpions often shelter in shadowy places. Their stings are notoriously painful – and potentially dangerous – so look carefully before you put on your clothing or stick your feet into your hiking boots!

When diving, avoid contact with jellyfish, which may have stinging tentacles – fortunately, most Namibian jellyfish are more painful than life-threatening. If you do have a jellyfish encounter, douse it in vinegar, which will de-activate any stingers that haven't yet 'fired'. Calamine lotion, antihistamines and analgesics may reduce the reaction and relieve the pain. Various other sea creatures can deliver a dangerous bite or sting – always seek local advice.

Bedbugs & Lice You may be bitten by bedbugs if you're using budget hotels, as they tend to lurk particularly in dirty mattresses and bedding, evidenced by spots of blood. Bedbugs leave itchy bites in neat rows. Calamine lotion or a sting relief spray may help.

Lice cause itching and discomfort. They make themselves at home in your hair (head lice), your clothing (body lice) or in your pubic hair (crabs). You catch lice through direct contact with infected people or by sharing combs, clothing and the like. Powder or shampoo treatment will kill the lice, and infected clothing should then be washed in very hot, soapy water and left in the sun to dry.

Ticks Bites from ticks can cause skin infections and other more serious diseases. You should always check all over your body if you have been walking through a potentially tick-infested area – especially long grass where cattle or other animals graze. If a tick is found attached, press down around the tick's head with tweezers, grab the head and gently pull upwards. Avoid pulling the rear of the body as this may squeeze the tick's gut contents through the attached mouth parts into the skin, increasing the risk of infection and disease. Smearing chemicals on the tick will not make it let go and is not recommended.

Snake Bites To minimise your chances of being bitten, always wear boots, socks and long trousers when walking through undergrowth where snakes may be present. Don't put your hands into holes and crevices, and be careful when collecting firewood.

Snake bites do not cause instantaneous death, and antivenenes are usually available. Immediately wrap the bitten limb tightly, as you would for a sprained ankle, and then attach a splint to immobilise it. Keep the victim still and immediately seek medical help. Tourniquets and sucking out the poison are now comprehensively discredited.

Less Common Diseases

The following diseases pose a small risk to travellers, and so are only mentioned in passing. Seek medical advice if you think you may have any of these diseases.

Cholera This is the worst of the watery diarrhoeas and urgent medical help should be sought. Outbreaks of cholera are generally widely reported, so you can avoid problem areas. Fluid replacement is the most vital treatment – the risk of dehydration is severe as you may lose up to 20L of fluids a day. If there is a delay in getting to hospital, then begin taking tetracycline. The adult dose is 250mg four times daily. It is not recommended for children under nine years nor for pregnant women. Tetracycline may help shorten the illness, but adequate fluids are required to save lives.

Filariasis This is a mosquito-transmitted parasitic infection found in many parts of Africa. Possible symptoms include fever, pain and swelling of the lymph glands; inflammation of lymph drainage areas; swelling of a limb or the scrotum; skin rashes; and blindness. Treatment is available to eliminate the parasites from the body, but some of the damage already caused may not be reversible. Medical advice should be obtained promptly if the infection is suspected.

Leishmaniasis This is a group of parasitic diseases transmitted by sandflies, which are found in many parts of Africa. Cutaneous leishmaniasis affects the skin tissue causing ulceration and disfigurement, and visceral leishmaniasis affects the internal organs. Seek medical advice, as laboratory testing is required for diagnosis and treatment. Avoiding sandfly bites is the best precaution. Bites are usually painless, itchy and another reason to cover up and apply repellent.

Rabies This fatal viral infection is found in many countries, including those of Southern Africa. Many animals can be infected (such as dogs, cats, bats and monkeys) and it is their saliva that is infectious. Any bite, scratch or even lick from an animal should be cleaned immediately and thoroughly. Scrub with soap and running water, and then apply alcohol or iodine solution. Medical help should be sought promptly to receive a course of injections to prevent the onset of symptoms and death.

Sleeping Sickness In parts of tropical Africa, tsetse flies can carry trypanosomiasis, or sleeping sickness. The tsetse fly is about twice the size of a housefly and recognisable by the scissorlike way it folds its wings when at rest. Only a small proportion of tsetse flies carry the disease, but it is a serious disease that can be fatal without treatment. No protection is available except avoiding the tsetse fly bites. The flies are attracted to large moving objects such as safari buses, to perfume and aftershave and to colours such as dark blue. Swelling at the site of the bite, five or more days later, is the first sign of infection; this is followed within two to three weeks by fever.

Tetanus This disease is caused by a germ that lives in soil and in the faeces of some animals. It enters the body via breaks in the skin. The first symptom may be discomfort in swallowing, or stiffening of the jaw and neck; this is followed by painful convulsions of the jaw and whole body. The disease can be fatal. It is prevented by vaccination.

Tuberculosis This is a bacterial infection usually transmitted from person to person by coughing; it may also be transmitted through consumption of unpasteurised milk. Milk that has been boiled is safe to drink, and the souring of milk to make yogurt or cheese also kills the bacilli. Travellers are usually not at great risk, as close household contact with the infected person is usually required before the disease is passed on. You may need to have a TB test before you travel as this can help diagnose the disease later if you become ill.

Typhus This disease is spread by ticks, mites or lice. It begins with fever, chills, headache and muscle pains followed a few days later by a body rash. There is often a large painful sore at the site of the bite and nearby lymph nodes are swollen and painful. Typhus can be treated under medical supervision. Seek local advice on areas where ticks pose a danger and always check your skin carefully for ticks after walking in a danger area such as a tropical forest. An insect repellent can help, and walkers in tick-infested areas should consider having their boots and trousers impregnated with benzyl benzoate and dibutylphthalate.

Yellow Fever This viral disease is endemic throughout Central African countries and is transmitted by mosquitoes – another good reason to protect yourself against mosquito bites. The initial symptoms are fever, headache, abdominal pain and vomiting. If you think you have the disease, seek medical care urgently and drink lots of fluids.

Women's Health
Gynaecological Problems Antibiotic use, synthetic underwear, sweating and contra-

AIDS in Southern Africa

The 11th World AIDS Conference was held in Zambia in September 1999, but despite all the earnest discussions aimed at curtailing the risks, AIDS is an increasingly pertinent issue throughout Africa. AIDS is acquired more quickly and is more easily transmitted in Africa than it is in the West, due to a lack of nutrition, a high incidence of venereal disease, limited awareness of risks and fewer precautions against infection. While Namibia has done a relatively good job of educating its populace about HIV risks, officials in some neighbouring countries remain in denial and some even blame the scourge on racially motivated 'outside conspiracies'.

Perhaps the most tragic factor is that AIDS tends to strike adults of a productive age, and in Southern Africa, it's particularly rife among those who are educated and have relatively high earnings or mobility. Thus, male teachers, truck drivers, and civil servants (and their stay-at-home wives) are at greater risk than those with a more stationary lifestyle.

Despite the fact that Africa has been plagued by wars, famines, natural disasters and political unrest, AIDS remains the greatest problem it has ever faced, and the statistics are shocking. Since the mid-1990s, AIDS has been the leading cause of death in Africa. Across the continent over 30 million people will die of AIDS by 2020, and 90% of AIDS sufferers worldwide are of African origin.

As far as Namibia is concerned, here are the frightening statistics: 19.5% of the population is infected with HIV, and a total of 18,000 adults and children die of the disease each year. A total of 57% (and growing) of this number are women who have been infected by their husbands. The current number of AIDS orphans is 67,000. Only 50% of Namibians use condoms during sex (this may seem high by African standards, but even this degree of compliance with 'safe sex' directives has not halted the spread of the disease). In 1996, the national life expectancy was 59/66 years for men/women; in 2000, it was 52/53 years.

Neighbouring countries also suffer. In Zimbabwe, 25% of the population is HIV positive; each year, the death toll approaches 190,000, leaving at least 900,000 AIDS orphans. In Malawi and Zambia, the infection rates are 800,000 and 870,000 people respectively. Botswana's 36% HIV infection rate is one of the highest on the continent, and the sparsely populated country loses 24,000 people each year. Even in prosperous South Africa, 250,000 people die of AIDS annually, and every day, 1500 more become infected. Currently, AIDS orphans in South Africa number at least 450,000.

AIDS continues to decimate the ability of African countries to function in the modern world. Treating sufferers places a great burden on under-funded health services, while the increasing number of AIDS orphans decreases public morale while increasing strain on the state and on extended families. Although a few Western programs now provide affordable AIDS-resistant drugs, there's not yet any effective cure for the disease, and it will probably be many years before the benefits of these programs become visible in the statistics.

To learn more about AIDS in Namibia, or to offer help, contact one of the following, all in Windhoek: AIDS Care Trust (☎ 061-259590, fax 218673, e aidscare@iafrica.com.na), Catholic AIDS Action (☎ 061-225265, e nbc@iafrica.com.na) or Lifeline/Childline (☎ 061-232221, e llinenam@mweb.com.na).

ceptive pills can lead to fungal vaginal infections, especially when travelling in hot climates. Thrush or vaginal candidiasis is characterised by a rash, itch and discharge. Nystatin, miconazole or clotrimazole pessaries are the usual treatment, but some women use a traditional remedy involving vinegar or lemon-juice douches, or yogurt.

Maintaining good personal hygiene and wearing loose-fitting clothes and cotton underwear may help prevent these infections.

Symptoms of sexually transmitted vaginal infections include a smelly discharge, painful intercourse and sometimes a burning sensation when urinating. Medical attention should be sought and male sexual partners must also be treated (see also Sexually Transmitted Infections earlier). Apart from abstinence, condoms offer the best protection from such problems.

Pregnancy Women planning to travel during pregnancy should consult their doctor, mainly because some recommended vaccinations are not advisable and several diseases endemic to Africa (eg, malaria) may present more serious consequences for pregnant women (including miscarriage or the birth of a stillborn child).

Miscarriage, which may lead to severe internal bleeding, occurs during the first three months of pregnancy. The last three months should also be spent within reasonable distance of good medical care, as a child born as early as 24 weeks stands a chance of survival, but only in a good modern hospital.

Pregnant women should avoid all unnecessary medication, although vaccinations and malarial prophylactics should still be taken where necessary, and personal medical consultation with your doctor is absolutely essential. Additional care should be taken to prevent illness and particular attention should be paid to diet and nutrition; under all circumstances, avoid alcohol and nicotine.

Each airline has its own policy, but many won't allow women to fly after their 36th week of pregnancy. Before booking, verify the policies of each airline involved.

Tampons & Sanitary Napkins Tampons and sanitary napkins from Europe or South Africa are sold in pharmacies and supermarkets in Windhoek and other major towns. They may also be available from shops at hotels and upmarket safari lodges.

WOMEN TRAVELLERS

Generally, women travellers reckon Southern Africa is one of the few places in the developing world where it is possible for women to meet and communicate with local men – of any race – without automatically being misconstrued. When it comes to evening entertainment, however, the region is very much a conservative, traditional male-dominated society and women may come up against a few glass walls and ceilings. Many bars are men only (by either policy or convention), but even in places which welcome women, you may be more comfortable with a male companion. Note that accepting a drink from a local man is usually construed as a come-on (as it is in much of the world).

Although unwanted interest is normally unpleasant, real harm or rape is very unlikely in Africa. If you're alone in an uneasy situation, act prudish; stick your nose in a book or invent an imaginary husband who will be arriving shortly. If you're travelling with a male companion, one of the best ways to avoid unwanted interest is to introduce him as your husband.

Solo female travellers will have few serious security problems, but common sense is still in order. By day, it's generally safe for women to walk around any Namibian town, although in recent years, muggings and rapes have increased in Windhoek. Don't walk through isolated areas alone at any time of day, and at night, especially in Windhoek, always take a taxi. In townships, seek local advice regarding areas to avoid.

In Windhoek and other urban areas, wearing shorts and sleeveless dresses or shirts is fine, and even in villages Western dress is becoming more popular. However, if you're visiting former tribal areas or mission stations, wear knee-length skirts or loose trousers. Beach wear is fine on the beach in Swakopmund or for lounging around pools but isn't really appropriate elsewhere.

For women hitching, Namibia is safer than Europe and considerably safer than North America (the greatest danger is from drunken drivers). There are still risks, however, which can be lessened by hitching with a male companion, or at least in pairs.

GAY & LESBIAN TRAVELLERS

In traditional African societies, homosexual relationships are normally considered a cultural taboo. As a result, Namibia is quite conservative in its attitudes towards gays and lesbians. In fact, President Sam Nujoma recently launched a vocal crusade against homosexuality, and has recommended that all foreign gays and lesbians be either deported or excluded from entry into the country. In one well-publicised quote, the president stated:

In Namibia, we don't allow lesbianism or homosexuality…We will combat this with vigour…Police are ordered to arrest you and deport you and imprison you…Those who are practicing homosexuality in Namibia are destroying the nation. Homosexuals must be condemned and rejected in our society.

While the president seems to deny that homosexuality exists locally, Namibia does in fact have a substantial gay community – especially among younger men. In April 2001, hundreds of local gays and lesbians staged a protest march in Windhoek, denouncing the official policy. Namibian lesbians (and other women's interests) are represented by the organisation Sister Namibia (☎ 230618, ℮ sister@windhoek .org.na), 163 Nelson Mandela Ave, Eros, PO Box 40092, Windhoek.

The bottom line is that sensitivity and discretion are highly recommended, and that open displays of affection, whatever your orientation, are inappropriate here.

DISABLED TRAVELLERS

Although Africa has more disabled people per capita than the West, there are very few special facilities and people with limited mobility will not have an easy time in Namibia. While some official buildings may have ramps and lifts, they're not generally places that foreigners visit, and safari lodges that are accessible to disabled people are often beyond the budget of most travellers.

All is not lost, however, and with an able-bodied travelling companion, wheelchair travellers will manage here. This is mainly because Namibia has some advantages over other parts of the developing world: Footpaths and public areas are often surfaced with tar or concrete, rather than with sand, mud or gravel; many buildings (including safari lodges and national park cabins) are single-storey; car hire is easy and hire cars

can be taken into neighbouring countries; and assistance is usually available on internal and regional flights.

In addition, most safari companies – including budget operators – are happy to 'make a plan' to accommodate travellers with special needs, and it never hurts to ask.

Organisations

In the USA, Mobility International (☎ 541-343 1284, fax 343 6812), PO Box 1076, Eugene OR 97440, advises disabled travellers on mobility issues. It primarily runs educational exchange programs, including African travel. For assistance and advice specific to individual needs, disabled travellers in the USA can contact Society for the Advancement of Travel for the Handicapped (☎ 212-447 7284, fax 725 8253), 347 Fifth Ave, Suite 610, New York, NY 10016. A one-year subscription to its quarterly magazine, *Access to Travel*, costs US$13.

In the UK, a useful contact is the Royal Association for Disability & Rehabilitation (☎ 020-7242 3882), 25 Mortimer St, London W1N 8AB. Take a look at its Web site at Ⓦ www.acess-able.com.

SENIOR TRAVELLERS

Namibia is an excellent destination for senior travellers. While few hotels or tour companies offer senior discounts, Intercape Mainliner buses offer 15% discounts and Air Namibia provides discounted domestic fares – often up to 50% – for travellers over 60 years of age.

Many seniors (especially South Africans) tour Namibia independently, and there is a thriving caravan scene. Older people from other countries will have few problems travelling around Namibia on fly-drive holidays.

Alternatively, a host of package tours is available. While the higher-priced tours will provide a bit of luxury and require little physical effort, lots of more adventurous and relatively fit seniors have thoroughly enjoyed budget participation safaris.

Organisations

Some organisations in the USA may be able to provide advice for senior travellers. The

American Association of Retired Persons (AARP; ☎ 800-424 3410 toll free, W www .aarp.org), 601 E St NW, Washington, DC 20049, is an advocacy group for residents of the USA over 50 years of age and a good source of travel bargains. Nonresidents can get yearly memberships for US$10. Grand Circle Travel (☎ 617-350 7500, ☎ 800-350 7500 toll free), 347 Congress St, Boston, MA 02210, offers escorted tours and travel information and also distributes the free booklet *Going Abroad: 101 Tips for Mature Travelers*.

TRAVEL WITH CHILDREN

Namibia presents few problems specific to children, and it's relatively safe, health-wise, largely due to its dry climate and relatively good medical services. In addition, foreigners who visit Namibia with children are usually treated with great kindness, and a widespread local affection for the younger set opens up all sorts of social interaction for travelling families.

While there are few attractions or facilities designed specifically for kids, Namibian food and lodging are mostly quite familiar and manageable. On the downside, distances between sites of interest can be long, especially on public transport, so parents may well need to provide supplemental entertainment (toys, books, games, a Nintendo Game-Boy etc).

Namibia also especially lends itself to family travel by camper van and the attractions – such as the wildlife of Etosha National Park, or the world's biggest sandbox at Sossusvlei – may well provide entertainment enough for young people. However, it's still wise to alternate adult activities (museums, galleries, shopping and tours) with things the kids will enjoy. Older children may especially appreciate horse riding and sandboarding around Swakopmund; looking for interesting rocks (and Namibia has some truly incredible rocks!); beachcombing along the Skeleton Coast; or running and rolling in the dunes at Lüderitz, Sossusvlei, Swakopmund and elsewhere along the coast.

In tourist hotels and lodges, family rooms and chalets are normally available for only slightly more than doubles; these normally consist of one double bed and two single beds (typically placed in a separate room or a loft). Otherwise, it's normally easy to arrange more beds in a standard adult double for a minimal extra charge. On public transport, however, children are expected to pay for their seats unless they spend the entire journey on the laps of their parents.

For travel with very young children, it's useful to carry a baby-backpack, but note that prams/strollers can be quite cumbersome. Older children will normally enjoy having their own small backpacks to carry favourite toys or teddies, books, crayons and paper. For more advice and anecdotes, see Lonely Planet's *Travel with Children*.

USEFUL ORGANISATIONS

In Namibia's post-independence governmental reorganisation, the ministries for tourism and wildlife were combined into the Ministry of Environment & Tourism (MET), which in turn handed over responsibility for tourism in the national parks to the semiprivate Namibia Wildlife Resorts (NWR). For information and contact details, see National Parks, Reserves & Conservancies in the Facts about Namibia chapter.

The Namibia Community Based Tourism Association (Nacobta; ☎ 061-250558, fax 222647, e nacobta@iafrica.com.na), 18 Liliencron St, PO Box 86099, Windhoek, supports community-based tourism projects and publishes a list of community camps, crafts projects and tours.

For highway information, contact the Automobile Association of Namibia (☎ 061-224201, fax 222446), 15 Carl List House, Independence Ave, PO Box 61, Windhoek.

DANGERS & ANNOYANCES
Theft

Theft isn't rife in Namibia, but Windhoek, Swakopmund, Tsumeb and Grootfontein have increasing problems with petty theft and muggings, so it's sensible to conceal your valuables, not leave anything in your car, and avoid walking alone at night.

Theft from camp sites is also a problem, particularly near urban areas. Locking up your tent may help, but anything left un-attended, even in a vehicle, is still at risk.

Wildlife & Vegetation

The Kavango region and the Caprivi Strip have lots of mosquitoes, so it's important to take antimalarial precautions. Bilharzia is present in the Kunene, Okavango and Kwando river systems, and bathing isn't recommended. The tsetse fly, present in the eastern Caprivi, is especially active at dusk. Most northern rivers also sustain hippo and crocodile populations that pose dangers to swimmers, anglers and canoeists.

Do not burn dried branches of euphorbia species, as these plants contain a deadly toxin; it can be fatal to inhale the smoke or eat food cooked on a fire containing it. If you're in doubt about any wood you've col-lected, leave it out of the fire.

The Sperrgebiet

En route to Lüderitz from the east, keep well clear of the Sperrgebiet, the prohibited diamond area. Well-armed patrols can be overly zealous and aren't interested in ask-ing questions. The area begins immediately south of the A4 Lüderitz-Keetmanshoop road and continues to just west of Aus, where the off-limits boundary turns south towards the Orange River.

LEGAL MATTERS

Police, military and veterinary officials are generally polite and on their best behaviour. However, during a national threat (such as the recent attempted coup in the Caprivi re-gion), they can get quite aggressive and should be either avoided or treated with ut-most deference.

BUSINESS HOURS

Normal business hours are from 8am to 1pm and 2.30pm to 5pm Monday to Friday. In the winter, when it gets dark early, some shops open at 7.30am and close at around 4pm. Lunch-time closing is almost univer-sal. Most city and town shops open from 8am to 1pm on Saturday. Banks, govern-ment departments and tourist offices also keep these hours, but some petrol stations,

especially along highways, are open 24 hours. In outlying areas, however, it may be hard to find fuel after hours or on Sunday.

PUBLIC HOLIDAYS & SPECIAL EVENTS

Resort areas are busiest over both Namibian and South African school holidays, which normally occur from mid-December to mid-January, around Easter, from late July to early August, and for two weeks in mid-October. Banks, government offices and most shops are closed on the following pub-lic holidays; when a public holiday falls on a Sunday, the following day also becomes a holiday.

New Year's Day 1 January
Good Friday March or April
Easter Sunday March or April
Easter Monday March or April
Independence Day 21 March
Ascension Day April or May
Workers' Day 1 May
Cassinga Day 4 May
Africa Day 25 May
Heroes' Day 26 August
Human Rights Day 10 December
Christmas 25 December
Family/Boxing Day 26 December

A major event to watch for is Maherero Day, on the weekend nearest 26 August, when the Red Flag Herero people gather in traditional dress at Okahandja for a memor-ial service to the chiefs killed in the Khoi-Khoi and German wars. A similar event, also at Okahandja, is staged by the Mban-deru or Green Flag Herero on the weekend nearest 11 June. On the weekend nearest 10 October, the White Flag Herero gather in Omaruru to honour their chief, Zeraua.

Major social events, mainly among the European community, include the follow-ing: the Windhoek Karnival (WIKA) in late April/early May; the Küska (Küste Karni-val) at Swakopmund in late August/early September; the Windhoek Agricultural, Commercial and Industrial Show in late September; and the Windhoek Oktoberfest in late October.

ACTIVITIES
Hiking

Hiking is a highlight in Namibia, and a growing number of private ranches have established wonderful hiking routes for their guests. Some of the finest ones include Klein-Aus Vista, near Aus; Namibgrens Rest Camp, in the Khomas Hochland; Eningu Clay House Lodge, near Dordabis; Palmwag Lodge and Kavita Lion Lodge, in Damaraland; Büllsport, Zebra River Lodge and Tsauchab River Camping, all near the Namib-Naukluft Park; and Fish River Lodge, south of Keetmanshoop.

You'll also find superb routes in several national parks. Multiday walks are available at Waterberg Plateau (US$13/27 unguided/guided), the four- or eight-day Naukluft (US$13), the Ugab River (US$27), Daan Viljoen (US$9) or Fish River Canyon (US$13), but departures are limited, so book as far in advance as possible.

Hiking groups on national park routes must consist of at least three but no more than 10 people, and each hiker needs a doctor's certificate of fitness (forms are available from the Windhoek NWR office) issued no more than 40 days before the start of the hike. This requirement may be waived if you can convince them you've completed 16 marathons and just scaled Everest, but don't count on it.

This system is a remnant of South African rule in Namibia. As cumbersome as it may seem to hikers and backpackers from other parts of the world, who are accustomed to strapping on a pack and taking off, it does protect the environment from

Desert Hiking

While Namibia offers a host of hiking and backpacking opportunities, the conditions are quite different from those to which most visitors are accustomed. However, it's important to note that hiking isn't recommended during the heat of the summer months, when temperatures can exceed 40°C. In national parks, summer hiking is officially forbidden, and most hiking trails are closed from November or December to April or May.

In Namibia, a main issue is water, and in the desert heat, hikers should carry 4L per person per day (an excellent way to carry water is in 2L plastic Coke bottles, which are available everywhere in Namibia). The most effective way to conserve water isn't necessarily to drink sparingly, as this tends to psychologically focus attention on water availability, and may lead to an unhealthy hysteria. Before setting off in the morning (assuming that water is available at your overnight stop), flood your body's cells with water. That is, drink more water than you feel you can possibly hold. After a few hours, when you grow thirsty, do the same again from the supply you're carrying. Believe it or not, with this method you'll actually use less water and feel less thirsty than if you drink sparingly all day long.

Another major concern is the desert sun, which can be brutal. Wear light-coloured and lightweight clothing; use a good sunscreen (at least UV Protection Factor 30); and never set off without a hat that shelters your neck and face from the direct sun.

If the heat is a major problem, it's best to rise before the sun and hike until the heat becomes oppressive. You may then want to rest through the heat of the middle of the day and begin again after about 3pm. (Note, however, that summer thunderstorms often brew up at around this time and may continue into the night.) During warmer months, it may also be worthwhile timing your hike with the full moon, which will allow you to hike at night.

Because many trails follow canyons and riverbeds, it's also important to keep a watch on the weather. Rainy periods can render normally dry kloofs and streambeds impassable, and rivers with large catchment areas can quickly become raging – and uncrossable – torrents of muddy water, boulders and downed trees. Never camp in canyons or dry riverbeds, and always keep to higher ground whenever there's a risk of flash flooding.

unrestrained tourism. It also ensures that you'll have the trail to yourself – you'll certainly never see another group.

Sandboarding

A growing craze is sandboarding, which is commercially available in Swakopmund and Walvis Bay. You can choose between sled-style sandboarding, in which you lay on a masonite board and slide down the dunes at very high speeds, or the stand-up version, in which you schuss down on a snowboard. See under Swakopmund in the Central Namib Desert chapter.

Fishing

Namibia draws anglers from all over Southern Africa, and rightfully so. The Benguela Current along the Skeleton Coast is one of the world's most prolific, bringing kabeljou, steenbras, galjoen, blacktails and copper sharks close to shore. Favoured spots include the various beaches north of Swakopmund, as well as more isolated spots further north.

In the dams, especially Hardap and Von Bach, you can expect to catch tilapia, carp, yellowfish, mullet and barbel. Fly-fishing is possible in the Chobe and Zambezi Rivers in the Caprivi region; here you'll find barbel, bream, pike and Africa's famed fighting tiger fish, which can grow up to 9kg.

4WD Trails

One of the most popular activities with locals in Southern Africa is to travel through the bush in 4WD vehicle. Traditionally, 4WD trips were limited to rugged wilderness tracks through the Kaokoveld, Damaraland and Bushmanland, but recently an increasing number of 4WD trails have been established for 4WD enthusiasts. Participants are required to pre-book up to a year ahead. They must pay a daily fee and are obligated to travel a certain distance each day and stay at prespecified camp sites.

Among the most popular routes are Isabis Trail in the Khomas Hochland, Naukluft 4x4 Route in the Naukluft Mountains and the recently established Topnaar and Coastways routes on the desert coast. Major routes are found in the relevant chapters.

For maps and further suggestions, pick up Jan Joubert's 4WD booklet, which is sold for around US$15 at Cymot Greensport in Windhoek (see Camping Gear in the Windhoek chapter).

Other Activities

Around Swakopmund, operators offer horse riding, camel riding, quadbiking, deep-sea fishing, sea kayaking, bird-watching, parasailing and skydiving. For information see Activities under Swakopmund in the Central Namib Desert chapter.

Rock climbing is popular on the red rocks of Damaraland – particularly the Spitzkoppe and the Brandberg – but participants need their own gear and transport. For more information on these sites, see the North-Western Namibia chapter.

Both canoeing and rafting are gaining popularity, and several agencies offer good-value descents through the spectacular canyons of the Orange River, along the South African border (see The Far South section in the Southern Namibia chapter). White-water rafting on the Kunene River is available through the inexpensive Kunene River Lodge at Swartbooi's Drift, and also through several more upmarket operators (see the North-Western Namibia chapter).

WORK

The chances of a foreigner legitimately scoring a long-term Namibian work or residence permit aren't terribly good but, some people are successful. Currently, the official policy is to accept only wealthy overseas investors starting up a business in the country or those who can provide skills and expertise (and cash) not available locally. If you are offered a job, you (or better, your prospective employer) must secure a temporary work permit from the Ministry of Home Affairs (☎ 061-292 2111, fax 292 2185, e mlusepani@mha.gov.na), Private Bag 13200, Windhoek.

While it's often possible to get a three-month work permit with the help of your prospective employer, extending a three-month permit or securing a one-year work permit will be a monumental, bureaucratic headache. If you've accomplished the impossible and secured a one-year work permit, look forward to jumping through the same hoops twice more to extend those permits before you can even apply for permanent residence. Once you've applied for permanent status – if you haven't yet gone mad – your application may remain in review for five years or more. Note that marrying a Namibian citizen does not guarantee a permanent residence permit.

Direct investment or business inquiries to the Investment Centre, Ministry of Trade & Industry (☎ 061-283 7111), 3rd floor, Government Offices, Private Bag 13340, Windhoek. Normally, investors are required to have a Namibian partner who holds a controlling interest in the business.

A few overseas volunteer organisations – including Voluntary Service Overseas (VSO), Peace Corps and others – have programs in Namibia. However, volunteers are discouraged from selecting their own postings (Peace Corps doesn't allow it at all), so your chances of winding up in Namibia may well depend on the luck of the draw.

ACCOMMODATION

Namibia has an exhaustive array of hotels, rest camps, camping grounds, caravan parks, guest farms, backpacker hostels, B&Bs, guesthouses and safari lodges. Most places are very good, and while this book mentions most of those that are highly recommended, it would take a much larger volume to list everything.

Hotels and most other establishments are graded using a star system; awards are based on regular inspections carried out by the Hospitality Association of Namibia (HAN). While these can be ridiculously fussy (even towel racks must meet specific criteria), the result is a T-grading, which indicates that they're geared towards foreigners. Hotels with restaurants also get a Y rating: YY means it only has a restaurant licence, while YYY indicates full alcohol licensing.

Some Namibian establishments – mainly lower-budget and backpacker places – include in their rates only a place to sleep. Others advertise themselves as 'bed & breakfast' and provide either a buffet continental or English breakfast. Safari lodges and farmhouse accommodation options typically provide either a half-board or full-board program. The former would include breakfast and a set dinner, while the latter also provides lunch: either a set lunch or a buffet-style spread.

The following publications, which are free from tourist offices, contain exhaustive accommodation listings: *Southern African Where to Stay*, *Welcome to Namibia – Tourist Accommodation & Info Guide* and the *Namibia B&B Guide*. HAN also publishes a map showing the locations of most lodges and guest farms.

The accommodation rates listed in this section are 'rack rates' for overseas bookings, and include the standard 15.5% VAT; in many cases, you'll get better rates when booking from within Namibia.

Camping

Most towns have caravan parks with bungalows or rondavels, as well as a pool, restaurant and shop. Prices are normally per site, with a maximum of eight people and two vehicles per site; there's normally an additional charge per vehicle. In addition, a growing number of private rest camps with well-appointed facilities is springing up in rural areas and along major tourist routes.

For information on camping in national parks, see NWR Camps, Rest Camps & Resorts later in this chapter. To camp on private land, you'll need to secure permission from the landowner. On communal land – unless you're well away from human habitation – it's a courtesy to make your presence known to the leaders in the nearest community.

Hostels

In Windhoek, Swakopmund, Lüderitz and other places, you'll find private backpacker hostels, which provide inexpensive dorm accommodation, shared ablutions and cooking facilities. Most offer a very agreeable atmosphere and are popular with budget travellers. Prices per night range from US$5 to US$10 per person. Some also offer private doubles which cost around US$20.

Minimum-Impact Camping

Wild campers will help to preserve Namibia's beauty and foster goodwill by heeding the following guidelines:

- The number-one rule should always be to carry out your rubbish, unless it can be burned completely. Do not leave cans or silver foil (including the inner lining from drinks and soup packets) in the fireplace. Some hikers bury rubbish, but this is generally a no-no, as animals may smell the food and dig it up, or it may be exposed by soil erosion during rain. Carrying out a few empty tins and packets should be no problem – it's got to be much lighter than when you carried it in.
- Select a well-drained camp site and, especially if it's raining, use a plastic or other waterproof groundsheet to prevent having to dig trenches, which just leads to more erosion.
- In some areas you have to camp at designated areas. In others you can camp where you like, but along popular tracks and trails, try to set up camp in established sites.
- Carry away all your rubbish, including cigarette butts. Biodegradable items may be buried but anything with food residue should be carried out, lest it be dug up and scattered by animals.
- Use toilet facilities if they are available. Otherwise, select a site at least 50m from water sources and bury wastes at least several inches deep. If possible, burn the used toilet paper or carry it in plastic bags until it can be burnt properly.
- Use only biodegradable soap products (you'll probably have to carry them from home) and use natural temperature water where possible. When washing up with hot water, avoid pollution and damage to vegetation either by letting the water cool to outdoor temperature before pouring it out or dumping it in a gravelly place away from natural water sources and vegetation.
- Wash dishes and brush your teeth well away from watercourses.
- When building a fire, try to select an established site and keep fires as small as possible. Use only fallen dead wood and when you're finished, make sure ashes are cool and buried before leaving the site. (See also the boxed text 'Firewood' in the Facts about Namibia chapter.)

B&Bs

B&B establishments are also mushrooming all around the country. These are typically private homes where the homeowner lets out extra rooms to guests and, as you can imagine, standards vary. Although they're known as B&Bs, some don't provide breakfast at all, so it pays to ask when booking. For listings, pick up the *Namibia B&B Guide* or contact the B&B Association of Namibia (☎ 064-464195), PO Box 1930, Swakopmund.

Hotels

Hotels in Namibia are much like hotels from anywhere else, ranging from flea-pits to palaces.

The Namibian hotel classification system rates everything from small guesthouses to four-star hotels. One-star hotels must have a specific ratio of rooms with private and shared facilities. They tend to be quite simple, but most are locally owned and managed, and do provide clean, comfortable accommodation with adequate beds and towels. Rates range from around US$20 to US$30 for a double room, including breakfast. They always have a small dining room and bar, but few offer frills, such as air-conditioning.

Hotels with two- and three-star ratings are generally more comfortable and are often used by local businesspeople. Rates start at around US$30 for a double and climb to US$90 for the more elegant places.

Currently, there is only a handful of four-star hotels, but more are planned. For a four-star rating, a hotel needs to be an air-conditioned palace with a salon, valet service and a range of ancillary services for business and diplomatic travellers.

Any hotel that appends the word *garni* does not have a restaurant and is only equipped to handle simple breakfasts.

NWR Camps, Rest Camps & Resorts

NWR offers reasonable value at its rest camps and resorts, but note that prices are steadily climbing – especially for camping – while the upkeep doesn't necessarily keep apace.

In most units, camp sites cost from US$8 for an undeveloped wilderness site to US$21 in a rest camp with a pool, shop, restaurant, kiosk and well maintained ablutions blocks. These rates are good for two people, one vehicle and one tent or caravan; for each additional adult/child (up to a maximum of eight people) you'll have to pay US$2/1.

NWR also offers other possibilities. All accommodation is self-catering, but most resorts also have a restaurant and shop. Prices are determined by the number of rooms and beds and the degree of luxury. Linen, towels and soap are normally provided, but only a few options provide cutlery, crockery and cooking facilities. For example, a four-bed flat with kitchen facilities, toilet and hot shower is around US$45; a four-bed hut with shared facilities and a cooking area is US$35; and two-/five-bed bungalows with kitchens, toilets and showers cost US$33/45. Etosha National Park accommodation costs about 20% more, while the dearest option is the eight-bed luxury hut at Terrace Bay at Skeleton Coast Park, where you'll pay US$267.

Namibian citizens and residents receive a 50% discount on park entry fees but not on vehicle fees or park accommodation. National parks accommodation may be occupied from noon on the day of arrival to 10am on the day of departure. During school holidays, visitors are limited to three nights at each camp in Etosha National Park and Namib-Naukluft Park, and 10 nights at all other camps. Pets aren't permitted in any of the rest camps, but kennels are available at the gates of Daan Viljoen Game Park, Von Bach Dam, Gross Barmen, Ai-Ais and Hardap Dam.

For booking information, see National Parks, Reserves & Conservancies in the Facts about Namibia chapter.

Guest Farms

Many private farms are turning to tourism, and they provide insight into the rural white lifestyle in Namibia. Many have designated blocks of land as wildlife reserves and offer excellent wildlife viewing; many also serve as hunting reserves. The emphasis is on personal service, and often there's even a measure of quaint rural luxury. With so many springing up, it's impossible to mention them all, but the most outstanding ones are described in the relevant chapters.

Advance bookings are essential. You may also want to ascertain whether and when hunting is permitted; some farms have a set 'hunting season' but are open for photography and wildlife viewing at other times. Also note that many farmers keep wild animals in zoo-like enclosures, which seems curious when you consider that most farms are attached to wildlife ranches that could only be called vast.

Safari Lodges

In recent years, a new crop of safari lodges has sprouted all around Namibia, and there now seems to be a lodge behind every tree. Most of these are set on large private ranches or in concession areas. They range from affordable family-run places with standard meals or self-catering options to luxurious – and often creative – accommodation with superb international cuisine.

While there are some very expensive options, Namibian safari lodges are generally more affordable than comparable places in Zimbabwe or Botswana, yet more expensive than those in South Africa. Fortunately, with a few exceptions, multitier pricing has not yet taken hold, so foreigners are not gouged.

FOOD
European Cuisine

Outside of Windhoek and Swakopmund, Namibia is short of gourmet pretences. Most hotels serve three meals, but menus are almost always meat-orientated and rarely very creative.

For a great treat, try one of the German-style *Konditoreien* (cake shops), where you

Traditional Namibian Foods

Each Namibian tribal group has its own pantry of preferred foods. For example, the staple for the Owambo people of the north is mealie pap, or cornmeal porridge. The second grain favoured in Owamboland is *mahango* (millet), which is made into a porridge, a soup or an alcoholic beverage known as *oshikundu*. Both mealie and mahango are typically eaten with fish, goat, lamb or beef stew cooked in a *potjie*, a three-legged black pot. Pumpkins, peppers and onions also feature prominently in the Owambo diet.

The spiny *!nara* melon or *Acanthosicyos horrida* (the exclamation point is pronounced as a glottal click) is found in the lower reaches of the Kuiseb, and is popular with the Nama people, who make them into flour and cakes. Alternatively, the melons are mashed or fermented to yield a sweet beer. The roots are thought to have medicinal properties.

The Herero subsisted mainly on milk products such as curds and butter and, while they still enjoy these staples to some extent, the Herero diet now revolves around mealie, meat and black beans.

The traditional diet of the San consists mainly of desert plants – wild fruits, nuts, berries and tubers – as well as birds' eggs (especially ostrich eggs), lizards, locusts and game hunted with small, poison-tipped arrows.

For a rundown of Namibia's 'bush tucker', look for the book *People's Plants – A Guide to the Useful Plants of Southern Africa* by Ben-Erik van Wyk & Nigle Gericke.

can pig out on *apfelstrudel* (apple strudel), Sachertorte (a rich chocolate cake with apricot jam in it), *Schwartzwälder Kirschtorte* (Black Forest cake) and other delicious pastries and cakes. Several places in Windhoek and Swakopmund are national institutions, and other towns also have pleasant cafes and small coffee shops. You may also want to try Afrikaners' sticky-sweet *koeksesters* (small doughnuts dripping with honey) and *melktart*.

Cooked breakfasts include bacon and *boerewors* (farmer's sausage), and don't be surprised to find something bizarre – curried kidneys, for example – alongside your eggs. Some people still eat beef for breakfast.

Small hotels normally provide a cooked breakfast with cereal and toast, and most big hotels and lodges include a buffet breakfast in the room price. In addition to the usual English breakfast constituents, they may also include such delights as smoked kingklip (kippers), porridge and a range of German breads, cold meats, cereals and fruit. If you take full advantage of what's on offer, you may not have to eat again for the rest of the day.

One of the cheapest lunch options is a takeaway snack. Takeaway favourites among Namibians include fish and chips, pies (especially chicken and mushroom, pepper steak, steak and kidney, Cornish pasties, spinach and cheese etc), and *Brötchen*, or 'little bread' – sandwiches on a German-style bread roll.

Evening meals feature meat – normally beef or game – and carnivores will enjoy the typically high-quality cuts served in restaurants. A huge beef fillet steak or a kudu cutlet will set you back about US$8. Fish and seafood are best represented by kingklip, kabeljou and several types of shellfish. These are available all over Namibia, but are best at finer restaurants in Windhoek, Swakopmund and Lüderitz, where they'll normally be fresh from the sea.

Chicken is also very popular and is scoffed by the masses at numerous greasy fast-food joints. Of these, Nando's, with its fiery Portuguese-Angolan peri-peri sauce, is the hands-down best.

Fruit & Vegetables

Namibia's small fruit and vegetable crops ripen during the winter season, roughly from May to September. At other times, fresh fruit and vegetables must be imported from South Africa and are quite expensive, so Namibians aren't great connoisseurs of fresh produce and vegetarianism hasn't really caught on. As a result, chips are the most popular potato incarnation and green vegetables are served sparingly and often from a tin or the deep freeze.

Among the most popular fresh vegetables are the small and delicious gem squash; pumpkin; and butternut squash, which resembles a gourd. In season, Namibian oranges are delicious; in the Kavango region, papayas are picked with a 6m pole and a basket to catch them, and are served with a squeeze of lemon or lime.

For longer road trips, you can buy fruit in bulk at Windhoek supermarkets, at the open market in Tal St or at one of the wholesalers in the North Windhoek Industrial Estate. It's also sold at roadside stalls in northern Namibia and occasionally elsewhere.

Self-Catering

All major towns have at least one supermarket selling basic necessities, and several in Windhoek and Swakopmund are as well-appointed as those you would find at home. Because groceries become more expensive the further you move from Windhoek, it's wise to stock up before heading out on a tour. Petrol stations along major routes sell an increasing range of grocery items and many towns also have corner shops – often Portuguese-run, hence their generic name, 'Portuguese markets' – which sell everything from groceries and animal feed to paraffin lamps and spit-roasted chicken.

You'll find the best variety of meat and sausage, or *wors*, at the *slagtery* (butcher shop). *Biltong* (dried meat in strips or shavings), either beef or *wildsbiltong* (normally kudu or ostrich), comes in several shapes and sizes. Excellent choices include the spicy chili bites and *peri-peri biltong*. A similar concoction is *droewors*, or dry sausage, which is quite fatty and takes more fortitude to fully appreciate. There is also a range of German salami and smoked meats, as well as an utterly solid 15cm variety known as *Landjäger*. It's normally gnawed like a bone, but it's cheap, tasty and lasts a long time.

Cheese is expensive and there's little variety; edam and mozzarella are the most popular varieties. Campers may want to buy tinned feta, which lasts longer than plastic-wrapped cheeses.

DRINKS
Nonalcoholic Drinks

Tap water is safe to drink but in some places it may emerge rather salty or brackish, especially around the desert areas and in Etosha National Park. Bottled water is expensive and is available in 1L or 2L containers. Packaged fruit juices provide an alternative; the best are the local Ceres juices and South African Liquifruit.

Every takeaway place serves coffee and tea – including a distinctively flavoured (some would say insipid) herbal tea known as *rooibos* (red bush), which reputedly has therapeutic properties. Both Windhoek and Swakopmund have several particularly fine coffee shops. Unfortunately, some places – including upmarket lodges – still serve coffee blended with chicory, which is definitely an acquired taste.

Alcoholic Drinks

You'll always find a pleasant place for a drink. Nearly all Namibian hotels have an attached bar and some larger hotels feature a beer garden with table service. Many serve food as well as drink, but some open only in the evening. The bars in smaller, inexpensive hotels, however, are less sophisticated, and away from the cities and tourist lodges, you'll find plenty of beer and booze, but no cocktails or mixed drinks. Many cafes also serve wine and beer. On Sunday outside of licensing hours, alcoholic drinks are available only at hotel bars.

Alcohol isn't sold in supermarkets, and must be purchased from a *drankwinkel* (bottle store); standard opening hours are 8am to 6pm Monday to Friday and 8.30am to 1pm Saturday.

Beer Namibia's dry heat means big sales for Namibia Breweries. The most popular drop is the light and refreshing Windhoek Lager (4% alcohol volume), but the brewery also produces Tafel Lager (4%), the stronger and more bitter Windhoek Export (4.5%) and the slightly rough Windhoek Special (5.3%). Windhoek Light (2%) and DAS Pilsener (3%) are both drunk as soft drinks (DAS is often called 'breakfast beer'!), and in winter, Namibia Breweries also brews up a 7% stout known as Urbock. Its main competitor is Swakopmund's Hansa, which produces both standard and export-strength beer.

Both big Namibian breweries produce their beer in accordance with the *Reinheitsgebot*, the German purity law, which stipulates that the product can contain nothing but malted barley, hops and water.

South African beers like Lion, Castle and Black Label are also widely available.

Beer is typically packaged in cans and bottles of varying sizes from a 375ml *dumpi* (equivalent to the Australian stubby) to a 'large' 500ml bottle. A dumpi costs from US$0.75 to US$1.25 in a beer garden; drankwinkels charge US$10 or so for a tray (slab) of 24 bottles or cans.

Wine You'll find a range of excellent South African wines. Most drankwinkels stock everything from 750ml bottles to large 1L to 5L boxes and economy-size 1L or 2L jars. South African red wines definitely have the edge; among the best are the Cabernet and Pinot varieties grown in the Stellenbosch region of Western Cape Province. Nederberg Winery produces particularly good inexpensive wines, which are available in both 250ml and 750ml bottles. If you're into casks (boxed wines), the best is Overmeer red, which costs around US$10 for 5L.

Namibia also has its own winery, the Kristall Kellerei, 3km east of Omaruru. Here it produces cabernet (the best), colombard (also good), prickly-pear-cactus schnapps (a good blast) and grappa (a rough, powerful blast). If you're not into blasts, its mineral water is also nice.

Liqueur An excellent speciality liqueur is Amarula Cream, which is distilled in South Africa from the marula fruit. It tastes a bit like Bailey's Irish Cream – but is arguably better – and is best chilled, served over ice, or with coffee.

Traditional Brews In the rural Owambo areas, people socialise in tiny makeshift

Keeping Cool

When you're camping in the wilderness without a cooler (Esky), an excellent means of cooling a beer or soft drink (soda) without refrigeration is to soak a sock in water, place the cans or bottles inside and tie it from a branch – or even the side mirrors on your vehicle. The contents are cooled as heat is drawn away from the liquid to provide energy for evaporation – and it really works.

bars, enjoying such inexpensive local brews as *oshikundu* (an excellent beer made from mahango, or millet), *mataku* (watermelon wine), *tambo* (fermented millet and sugar) or *mushokolo* (a beer made from a small local seed) and *walende*, which is distilled from the *makalani* palm and tastes similar to vodka. All of these concoctions, except walende, are brewed in the morning and drunk the same day, and they're all dirt-cheap, costing less than US$0.20 per glass.

ENTERTAINMENT

Naturally, Namibia's entertainment capital is Windhoek, with a range of bars, discos and nightclubs to suit every taste. The capital also offers cinemas, theatre productions, concerts and sporting events. The beach resort of Swakopmund, with its several discos and a light-hearted atmosphere, is a favourite haunt with Namibia's more affluent youth.

In northern Namibia, the local social scene is dominated by the hundreds of *cuca* shops (small bush shops selling beer), bush bars, bottle stores and roadside discos and nightclubs. At the bush bars, you can sometimes partake of popular traditional brews, along with a bit of relaxation and conversation. Especially in the Owambo areas, both men and women eagerly participate in these sessions.

SPECTATOR SPORTS

Football is far and away Namibia's most popular sport, and the national team, the Brave Warriors, enjoys a huge following. While the supporters' enthusiasm and commitment are unquestionable, the team's on-field performance quite often falls short of expectations. The high point to date was the team's qualification – and first-round elimination – from the African Cup of Nations in Burkina Faso in 1998.

Namibia's most spirited sporting (and social) events surround visits of South Africa's national team, whether it be for friendlies or qualifiers for the African Cup or World Cup. At such times, Namibia grinds to a standstill as people flock to Windhoek's Independence Stadium or head for the nearest cuca shop to watch the match on TV. The Brave Warriors have a superb record in Windhoek against their South African neighbours, and after the final whistle – whatever the outcome – huge parties erupt spontaneously all over the country. Check the *Namibian* for advertising and ticket information for upcoming sporting events.

Other major spectator sports include boxing, cricket, rugby, athletics and netball. In boxing, Harry Simon has been crowned WBO junior middleweight champion. Track and field star Frankie Fredericks (see the boxed text) has excelled in sprinting for over a decade, winning both Olympic and World Championship medals in both the 100m and 200m events. Inspired by Fredericks' success, a new generation of sprinters may well produce another world-class Namibian athlete.

Lack of regular international rugby and the fact that the South African provinces snap up all the country's promising rugby talent has left the local rugby scene in disarray. Although Namibia's national rugby team qualified for the World Cup in the UK in 1999, it failed to win any matches. However, many Namibians expect their cricket team to qualify for the 2003 World Cup in South Africa, and it is hoped Windhoek might host one of the tournament matches.

SHOPPING
Namibia's range of inexpensive souvenirs includes all sorts of things, from kitsch African curios and 'airport art' to superb Owambo basketry and Kavango woodcarvings. Most of the items sold along Post Street Mall in Windhoek are cheap curios imported from Zimbabwe. Along the highway between Rundu and Grootfontein, roadside stalls sell locally produced items, from woven mats, baskets and simple pot-

Frankie Fredericks

If Windhoek has a favourite son, it's sprinting sensation Frankie Fredericks, who is probably the greatest role model for Namibian youth and aspiring athletes. Fredericks, who was born in 1968 in Katutura, began as a backstreet football player. He was eventually offered a place on the South African professional team, the Kaizer Chiefs, but refused because he preferred track-and-field events.

Frankie credits his success to his mum, Riekie Fredericks, who financially supported his efforts at school and on the athletics track by working long hours as a seamstress. Her contribution was augmented by a Rössing Corporation scholarship that gave Frankie the opportunity to attend university in the USA and concentrate on his athletic training. Their efforts have apparently paid off, as Frankie Fredericks is now Africa's fastest sprinter, and won the silver medal for both the 100m and 200m sprinting events in the 1992 and 1996 Olympics in Barcelona and Atlanta. He consistently runs the 100m dash in under 10 seconds, but during the Sydney Olympics in 2000, he was sidelined by an injury.

For much of the year, Fredericks trains in the USA, at his alma mater Brigham Young University in Provo, Utah (where he earned a degree in computer science and a Masters of Business Administration), but he frequently returns to Windhoek, where a street has been named in his honour. He is also the patron of a charitable organisation in Katutura that promotes excellence for low-income youth. One of the secrets of his success, Fredericks claims, is that his religious convictions prevent him from touching drugs or alcohol.

tery jars to the appealing woven mats and wooden aeroplanes and helicopters that are a Kavango speciality. In Rundu and other areas of the north-east, you'll find distinctive San material arts – bows and arrows, ostrich-egg beads, leather pouches and jewellery made from seeds and nuts.

The pastel colours of the Namib provide inspiration for a number of local artists, and lots of galleries feature local paintings and sculpture. Also, some lovely items are produced in conjunction with the karakul wool industry, such as rugs, wall hangings and textiles, which may be made to order. The best rug and carpet weaveries are found in Dordabis, Swakopmund and Lüderitz.

Windhoek is the centre of the upmarket leather industry, and there you'll find high-quality products, from belts and handbags to beautiful made-to-measure leather jackets. Beware, however, of items made from crocodile or other protected species, and note that those comfortable shoes known as *Swakopmunders* are made from kudu leather. Several shops have now stopped selling them.

Minerals and gemstones are popular purchases, either in raw form or cut and polished as jewellery, sculptures or carvings. Malachite, amethyst, chalcedony, aquamarine, tourmaline, jasper and rose quartz are among the most beautiful. Chess sets and other art objects are made from marble quarried near Karibib. For fine work, see Kristall Galerie in Swakopmund, Henckert Tourist Centre in Karibib or House of Gems near the corner of Stübel and John Meinert Sts in Windhoek.

Namibian postage stamps are also interesting and collectable. See the Namibia Post Philatelic Services (☎ 061-201 3107, fax 259467, ⓔ philately@nampost.com.na,

Ekipa

For an interesting cultural memento, you may want to look for an *ekipa*, a traditional medallion historically worn by Owambo women as a sign of wealth and status. They were worn on leather straps hung from the waist and were originally made from elephant ivory or hippopotamus tooth but later were carved from bone, wood or vegetable ivory (the fruit of the makalani palm). Early ekipa were buried in urine-soaked earth to achieve the necessary yellowed effect, and were decorated with geometric designs. Although they're no longer produced by the Owambo, both expensive originals and artistic renditions are available in a few shops in Windhoek and Swakopmund.

ⓦ www.nampost.com.na) at the main post office in Windhoek.

If you're interested in something that appears to be exotic or resembles an artefact, ask about its provenance. Any antiquity must have an export/import permit and the dealer must have a licence to sell antiquities.

Buying souvenirs derived from protected wild species – cheetahs, leopards, elephants or (heaven forbid) rhinos – isn't necessary or ethically defensible. In Windhoek and other places, you'll see lots of ivory pieces and jewellery for sale, but anything imported from Hong Kong is of dubious origin and should be avoided. The only legitimate stuff is clearly marked as culled ivory from Namibian national parks. Still, it's probably better to avoid ivory altogether and stop fuelling the trade that makes poaching (and culling) profitable.

Getting There & Away

AIR

Namibia isn't exactly a hub of international travel, nor is it an obvious transit point along the major international routes – and air fares to or from Europe, North America and Australasia certainly reflect that. However, bargain fares to Johannesburg (Jo'burg) and Cape Town are popping up on several airlines, and from either place, it's fairly easy to travel overland or find decent short-haul flights to Windhoek.

Most international flights into Namibia land at Windhoek's Chief Hosea Kutako International Airport, 42km east of the capital city. Shorter-haul international flights may also use Windhoek's in-town Eros airport.

Buying Tickets

Your plane ticket will probably be the most expensive item in your budget, and there is likely to be a multitude of airlines and travel agencies hoping to separate you from your money. Start looking early – some of the cheapest tickets must be purchased months in advance and popular flights sell out early. Speak with recent travellers, look at the ads in newspapers and magazines (not forgetting the press of the African community in your home country), consult reference books and watch for special offers. Then phone around travel agencies for bargains. (Airlines supply information on routes and timetables, but often don't supply the cheapest tickets.) Find out the fare, route, duration of the journey and any restrictions on the ticket. Then sit back and decide which is best.

You may discover that those incredibly good deals are 'fully booked, but we have another one that costs a bit more...'. Or the flight is on an airline notorious for its poor safety standards and leaves you mid-journey in the world's least favourite airport for 14 hours. Or they may claim only to have the last two seats available for that country for the whole of July, which they will hold for a maximum of two hours. Don't panic – keep ringing around.

Use the fares quoted in this book as a guide only. They are approximate and based on the rates advertised by travel agencies at the time of going to print. (Note that quoted air fares don't necessarily constitute a recommendation for the carrier.)

Bucket Shop Tickets At certain times of the year and/or on certain sectors, many airlines fly with empty seats. This isn't profitable and it's more cost-effective for them to fly full even if that means selling drastically discounted tickets. This is done by offloading them onto 'bucket shops', travel agencies that specialise in discounted fares. The agencies, in turn, sell them to the public at reduced prices. As you can imagine, there's lots of scope in this business for less-than-straightforward dealings. Many bucket shops are reputable organisations, but there will always be the odd fly-by-night operator that sets up shop, takes your money and then either disappears or issues an invalid or unusable ticket. Be sure to check what you're buying before handing over the dough.

Buying Tickets Online Purchasing tickets online is a growing trend. Many airlines now have their own Web sites that allow you to book and purchase tickets with a credit card. There are also Web sites specialising in discounted tickets, including the following:

W www.lowestfare.com
W www.travelocity.com
W www.cheaptickets.com
W www.1800airfare.com
W www.previewtravel.com
W travel.yahoo.com
W www.priceline.com

In most cases, you can choose between electronic tickets, which are issued at the time of check-in at the airport, and paper tickets, which will be delivered by post or courier at an additional cost.

There are glitches, however. On Priceline, for example, you're effectively limited to routings of three or fewer legs, so if you're travelling to Africa from Asia or South America – or even smaller centres in North America, Europe or Australasia – you can forget it. With Priceline, you bid on available tickets and can sometimes score very good deals.

Travelocity does well with domestic US routes, but has less success with international itineraries, especially to relatively obscure destinations (such as Namibia).

With Lowestfare, weird things .can happen such as an itinerary to one city with the return leg departing from a city of the same name in another country. Check your itinerary very carefully and question any oddities.

The Yahoo site is good because it doesn't require online registration.

Travel Seasons Fortunately, Namibia's low season partially coincides with the best times to visit. Low-season fares from Europe and North America are typically applicable from April to June, while high season is between July and September. The rest of the year, with the exception of Christmas, which is also considered high season, falls into the shoulder-season category.

Travellers with Special Needs

If you have special needs – you're vegetarian, diabetic, halaal, kosher or allergic to peanuts; travelling in a wheelchair; using a guide dog; taking the baby; terrified of flying, or whatever – let the airline staff know in advance so they can make arrangements. Remind them when you reconfirm your booking (at least 72 hours before departure) and again when you check in at the airport.

Children aged under two travel for 10% of the full fare – or free on some airlines – as long as they don't occupy a seat. They don't get a baggage allowance in this case. 'Skycots', baby food and nappies (diapers) are normally provided by the airline if requested in advance. Children aged two to 14 can usually occupy a seat for half to two-thirds of the full fare, and are allowed a standard baggage allowance.

Departure Tax

Namibia imposes different departure taxes for different destinations. To Zimbabwe, Botswana and Zambia, it's US$12, to South Africa N$167.50 (US$23) and elsewhere N$231 (US$31). These are paid at the time of ticket purchase, so there's nothing to pay at the airport.

The USA

For bargains, check the Sunday travel sections in major newspapers, such as the *New York Times*, *Chicago Tribune*, *Los Angeles Times* or *San Francisco Examiner* or *Chronicle*. While the articles are rarely very imaginative (they tend to focus on popular destinations and expensive package tours), they are normally accompanied by ads revealing the lowest fares for the week.

Competition between carriers and governmental interference mean that USA fare structures are subject to numerous restrictions and regulations. This is especially true of discounted tickets. Anything cheaper than the standard tourist or economy fare – such as an APEX fare – must be purchased

Air Travel Glossary

Alliances Many of the world's leading airlines are now intimately involved with each other, sharing everything from reservations systems and check-in to aircraft and frequent-flyer schemes. Opponents say that alliances restrict competition. Whatever the arguments, there is no doubt that big alliances are the way of the future.

Courier Fares Businesses often need to send urgent documents or freight securely and quickly. Courier companies hire people to accompany the package through customs and, in return, offer a discount ticket which is sometimes a bargain. However, you may have to surrender all your baggage allowance and take only carry-on luggage.

Fares Airlines traditionally offer-1st class (coded F), business-class (coded J) and economy-class (coded Y) tickets. These days there are so many promotional and discounted fares available that few passengers pay full fare.

Lost Tickets If you lose your airline ticket, an airline will usually treat it like a travellers cheque and, after inquiries, issue you with another one. Legally, however, an airline is entitled to treat it like cash and if you lose it then it's gone forever. Take very good care of your tickets.

Onward Tickets An entry requirement for many countries is that you have a ticket out of the country. If you're unsure of your next move, the easiest solution is to buy the cheapest onward ticket to a neighbouring country or a ticket from a reliable airline which can later be refunded if you do not use it.

Open-Jaw Tickets These are return tickets where you fly out to one place but return from another. If available, this can save you backtracking to your arrival point.

Overbooking Since every flight has some passengers who fail to show up, airlines often book more passengers than they have seats. Usually excess passengers make up for the no-shows, but occasionally somebody gets 'bumped' onto the next available flight. Guess who it is most likely to be? The passengers who check in late. If you do get 'bumped', you are normally offered some form of compensation.

Reconfirmation Some airlines require you to reconfirm your flight at least 72 hours prior to departure. Check your travel documents to see if this is the case

Restrictions Discounted tickets often have various restrictions on them – such as needing to be paid for in advance and incurring a penalty to be altered or cancelled. Others are restrictions on the minimum and maximum period you must be away.

Round-the-World (RTW) Tickets RTW tickets give you a limited period (usually a year) in which to circumnavigate the globe. You can go anywhere the carrying airlines go, as long as you don't backtrack. The number of stopovers or total number of separate flights is decided before you set off and they usually cost a bit more than a basic return flight.

Ticketless Travel Airlines are gradually waking up to the realisation that paper tickets are unnecessary encumbrances. On simple one-way or return trips, reservations details can be held on computer and the passenger merely shows ID to claim their seat.

Transferred Tickets Airline tickets cannot be transferred from one person to another. Travellers sometimes try to sell the return half of their ticket, but officials can ask you to prove that you are the person named on the ticket. On an international flight, tickets are compared with passports.

at least 14 days – and sometimes as much as 30 days – prior to departure. Whatever you do, don't wait until the last minute in hopes of scoring a standby fare; those days are long gone, and late purchase almost always results in a fare two or three times the APEX fare.

In the USA, you won't find tickets with open return dates, and penalties of up to 50% (but more often US$75 to US$150 per change) are imposed if you change the return booking. Departure and return dates must be booked in advance and tickets are normally subject to minimum and maximum stay requirements: usually seven days and three to six months, respectively. Note that it's often cheaper to purchase a return ticket and trash the return portion than to pay the one-way fare.

Delta Air Lines and South African Airways (SAA) now offer nonstop flights from Atlanta to Cape Town and Jo'burg, and SAA also has a nonstop flight from New York to Jo'burg (at the time of writing it's the world's longest commercial flight, at around 15 hours). When booked through a savvy travel agency, either of these flights costs US$1050/1300 return in low/high season. From Los Angeles, via New York, you'll pay around US$1500/1900. To continue on to Windhoek, add around US$200.

Otherwise, the main link to Southern Africa is London, accessible via direct flights from most major US cities, but good offers are also available via Amsterdam, Frankfurt, Zürich and even Rome. To Cape Town or Jo'burg from New York via Europe, plan on paying US$1000 to US$1500.

Discount Travel Agencies North America doesn't have the bucket shop traditions of Europe and Asia, therefore ticket availability and restrictions should be weighed against standard APEX or economy (coach) fares.

The student travel bureaus – STA Travel or Council Travel – are also worth a go but you may need proof of student status and, in some cases, be under 26 years of age to qualify for some discounted fares.

North Americans won't get the great deals that are available in London and elsewhere, but discount agencies watch out for the best air fares.

Adventure Travel Network
(☎ 800-467 4595, 415-247 1800, e info@ atntravel.com) 785 Market St, Suite 1710, San Francisco, CA 94012. These folks offer especially good fares from the USA's west coast, starting at US$1299/1639 return to Cape Town in low/high season.
w www.atntravel.com

Cheap Tickets, Inc
(☎ 800-377 1000) As the name suggests, this telephone-only outlet comes up with discounted air fares.

Council Travel
(☎ 800-226 8624) This network has offices all over the USA.

Educational Travel Center
(☎ 800-747 5551) 438 N Frances St, Madison, WI 53703

High Adventure Travel
(☎ 800-428 8735, 415-912 5600, fax 912 5606, e travel@airtreks.com) 442 Post St, 4th floor, San Francisco, CA 94102. This company specialises in round-the-world travel – itineraries including Southern Africa start at around US$2000.
w www.airtreks.com

Last Minute Travel Services
(☎ 800-527 8646)

Premier Tours & Travel
This company specialises in Africa (see Organised Tours later in this chapter).

Skylink
(☎ 800-247 6659) 265 Madison Ave, 5th floor, New York, NY 10014

Spector Travel
(☎ 800-879 2374, fax 338 0110, e africa@ spectortravel.com) 31 St James Ave, Boston, MA 02116. This company combines tours with discounted air fares.
w www.spectortravel.com

STA Travel
nationwide: (☎ 800-777 0112)
Los Angeles: (☎ 310-824 1574) 920 Westwood Blvd, Los Angeles, CA 90024
New York: (☎ 212-627 3111) 10 Downing St, New York, NY 10014
San Francisco: (☎ 415-391 8407) 36 Geary St, San Francisco, CA 94108
w www.statravel.com

Uni Travel
(☎ 314-569 2501, fax 569 2503, e resdept@un itravel.com) 11737 Administration Dr, Suite 120, St Louis, MO 63146
w www.flightsforless.com

Canada

Canadians will typically find the best deals starting with a hop to New York or Atlanta, as fares from Toronto and Vancouver are generally higher than from the USA. To connect with the nonstop flights from New York to Jo'burg, you will have to pay US$1691 from Toronto and US$1964 from Vancouver.

Alternatively, you can fly via London or another European city. At the time of writing, Lufthansa Airlines charged US$1803 return between Toronto and Jo'burg, via Frankfurt; from Vancouver, it was US$2161. For other possibilities, see The USA earlier in this chapter.

Discount Travel Agencies For travel-agency ads, see travel sections in the Toronto *Globe and Mail* and other major papers.

Flight Centre (☎ 604-739 9539, fax 739 9521) 3030 Granville St, Vancouver, BC V6H 3J8. These folks offer excellent customer service.
W www.flightcentre.com

Travel CUTS (☎ 800-954 2666, 416-979 2406) 187 College St, Toronto, Ontario M5T 1P7. This budget travel agency has offices all over Canada; for a complete listing, phone the toll-free number or see the Web site.
W www.travelcuts.com

Australia & New Zealand

When it comes to Southern Africa, Australians and New Zealanders are conveniently located in the southern hemisphere, but are at a disadvantage when it comes to routings and cheap deals.

The cheapest options normally include routings via Jo'burg. Qantas Airways and SAA both fly between Sydney and Jo'burg for as little as A$1550 return, if you stay less than 30 days. To stay longer than 30 days, you'll pay around A$2800. There are no direct flights from New Zealand to Southern Africa; Kiwis must first get to Sydney; the lowest fare at the time of writing was NZ$3700, via Sydney. Note that one-way flights may also be available as part of a round-the-world package.

For the latest deals, look in the Saturday editions of the *Sydney Morning Herald*, the *Age* in Melbourne or the *New Zealand Herald* in Auckland.

Discount Travel Agencies Two well-known agencies for cheap fares are STA Travel and Flight Centre.

STA Travel
Australia: (☎ 03-9349 2411, nationwide ☎ 131 776) 224 Faraday St, Carlton, Melbourne. STA has offices in all major cities and on many uni campuses nationwide.
W www.statravel.com.au
New Zealand: (☎ 09-309 0458) Main office 10 High St, Auckland. STA has other offices in Auckland as well as in Hamilton, Palmerston North, Wellington, Christchurch and Dunedin.
Flight Centre
Australia: (nationwide ☎ 131 600) Central office, 82 Elizabeth St, Sydney. This company has offices throughout Australia.
W www.flightcentre.com.au
New Zealand: (☎ 09-309 6171) Flight Centre has a large central office at National Bank Towers, on the corner of Queen and Darby Sts, Auckland, and many branches throughout the country.
W www.statravel.co.nz

In addition, the following agencies specialise in Africa travel:

Africa Travel Company (☎ 02-9264 7661) Level 1, 69 Liverpool St, Sydney 2000, NSW
Africa Travel Shop (☎ 09-520 2000) 21 Remuera Rd, Newmarket, Auckland 3
African Wildlife Safaris (☎ 03-9696 2899, fax 9696 4937, ℮ office@africasafaris.com.au) 1/259 Coventry St, South Melbourne 3205, Victoria. Cobbles together custom tours to Namibia and the entire region. The focus is on wildlife safaris.

The UK & Ireland

London has bucket shops by the dozen, and a number of reputable discount travel agencies. To get an idea of what's available, seek deals well before your intended departure. You'll find the latest deals listed in the travel sections of the Saturday and Sunday editions of London newspapers. Prices for discounted flights between London and Jo'burg start at around UK£600 return – bargain hunters may well find much lower prices.

However, don't take fares advertised by travel agencies as gospel. To comply with advertising laws in the UK, companies must be able to offer *some* tickets at the cheapest quoted price, but they may only have one or two of them per week. If you're not one of the lucky ones, you may be looking at higher fares. The key is to start searching early.

Your options include taking a direct flight to Windhoek on Air Namibia, although you may find better deals flying to Harare, Jo'burg or Cape Town on whatever bargain basement airline is currently operating. In the past, this typically meant travelling on Aeroflot via Moscow or Balkan Airlines via Sofia; now airlines that are more reputable are offering good deals, but to get them, you have to use a savvy travel agency and be shopping around at the right time.

SAA has daily flights between London and Jo'burg with frequent connections to Windhoek. Air Namibia operates direct flights to Chief Hosea Kutako International Airport in Windhoek from London, via Frankfurt, several times weekly; the flight duration is about 10 hours. Similarly, LTU International Airways' (Germany) Munich-Windhoek flight has connections from London's Stansted Airport.

UK Travel Publications The following publications will provide guidance for prospective travellers, and most are happy to post copies to overseas clients who may want to study current offers before deciding on a course of action. In London, some of these are available free on street corners and at London Underground stations:

Globe (BCM Roving, London WC1N 3XX) This newsletter, published for members of the Globetrotters' Club, covers obscure destinations and can help in finding travelling companions.

Star & SA Times (☎ 020-7405 6148, fax 7405 6290, e satimes@atlas.co.uk) Tower House, Sovereign Park, Market Harborough, Leics LE16 9EF. Published mainly for South African visitors and expats in London, this paper contains a lot of good travel advertising.

Time Out (☎ 020-7836 4411) Tower House, Southampton St, London WC2E 7HD. London's weekly entertainment guide also contains travel information and advertising, and is available at bookstores, newsagencies and newsstands. Subscribe through Time Out Subs, Unit 8, Grove Ash, Bletchley, Milton Keynes MK1 1BZ.

TNT Magazine (☎ 020-7937 3985) 52 Earls Court Rd, London W8. Available free at most London Underground stations and on street corners around Earls Court and Kensington, *TNT* caters to Aussies and Kiwis working in the UK, so it's full of travel advertising.

Trailfinder (☎ 020-7603 1515, fax 7938 3305) 42-8 Earls Court Rd, London W8 6EJ. This quarterly magazine is free in London, but mail subscribers pay UK£6 in the UK and Ireland and UK£10 or the equivalent for four issues elsewhere. The affiliated travel agency, Trailfinder, can organise ticketing, as well as jabs, antimalarials, visas and travel publications.

Wanderlust (☎ 01753-620426, fax 620474) PO Box 1832, Windsor, Berks SL4 6YP. This excellent travel magazine includes articles, advertising, fare and package tour information, guidebook reviews and pointers for both independent and tour-group travellers. It's available by subscription worldwide.

Discount Travel Agencies Make sure the agency you select belongs to some sort of traveller-protection scheme, such as the Association of British Travel Agents (ABTA). If you have paid for your flight to an ABTA-registered agency that subsequently folds, ABTA guarantees a refund or an alternative. The following are good places to begin your price comparisons:

Bridge the World
(☎ 0870-444 7474, fax 020-7813 3350, e sales@bridgetheworld.com) 47 Chalk Farm Rd, London NW1 8AN, or 4 Regent Place, Regent St, London W1R 5F
W www.b-t-w.co.uk

Flynow.com
London: (☎ 020-7835 2000, e sales@flynow .com), 125 Gloucester Rd, London SW7 4SF
Manchester: (☎ 0161-721 4000, fax 721 4202) 597 Cheetham Hill Rd, Manchester M8 5EJ
W www.flynow.com

STA Travel
(☎ 020-7581 4132, 0870-160 0599) 86 Old Brompton Rd, London SW7 3LQ
W www.statravel.co.uk

Trailfinders
(☎ 020-7938 3939) 194 Kensington High St, London W8 7RG
W www.trailfinders.co.uk

Travel Mood
(☎ 020-7258 0280, fax 7258 0180, e sales@ travelmood.co.uk) 214 Edgware Rd, London W2 1DH
W www.travelmood.com

USIT Now
  (☎ 01-602 1600, fax 679 2124) 19–21 Aston
  Quay, O'Connell Bridge, Dublin 2
  W www.usitnow.ei

Continental Europe

From continental Europe, the easiest options are Air Namibia's nonstop flights from Frankfurt or Munich to and from Windhoek (US$550 to US$850 return). LTU International Airways has low-/high-season return air fares between Munich (with connections to London's Stansted Airport) and Windhoek for around UK£520/600, although time restrictions do apply. Alternatively, most major European carriers fly to Jo'burg, Cape Town and/or Harare; from any of these places, it's easy to find connecting flights to Windhoek.

There are bucket shops by the dozen in Paris, Amsterdam, Brussels, Frankfurt and other places.

Many travel agencies in Europe have ties with STA Travel, where you'll find cheap tickets that may be altered once without incurring any extra charge. STA and other discount outlets in major transport hubs include the following:

Alternativ Tours (☎ 030-881 2089, fax 883
  5514, e info@alternativtours.de) Wilmersdor-
  ferstrasse 94, Berlin, Germany
  W www.alternative-tours.de
CTS (☎ 06-687 2672) Corso Vittoria Emanuele
  11, 297 Rome, Italy
  W www.cts.it
International Student & Youth Travel Service
  (☎ 01-3233 7676) Nikis 11, 10557 Athens,
  Greece
Kilroy Travels (☎ 030-310 0040, e germany
  .sales@kilroytravels.de) Hardenbergstrasse 9,
  D-10623 Berlin, Germany
  W www.kilroytravels.com
Malibu Travel (☎ 020-638 6059, e malfares@
  etn.nl) Damrak 30, Amsterdam, The Netherlands
NBBS (☎ 020-624 0989) Rokin 38, Amsterdam,
  The Netherlands
SSR (☎ 01-261 2954) Leonhardstrasse 5–10,
  CH-8001 Zürich, Switzerland
  W www.ssr.ch
STA Travel (☎ 069-703035, e frankfurt.uni@
  statravel.de) Bokenheimer Landstrasse 133,
  D-60325 Frankfurt, Germany
  W www.statravel.de

Voyages Wasteels (☎ 08 36 68 22 06, 01 43 25
  38 20, e parisstmichel@wasteels.fr) Blvd St-
  Michel, F-75005 Paris, France. This agency
  has 66 offices all over the country.
  W www.voyages-wasteels.fr

Africa

SAA has frequent flights between South African cities and Windhoek for around US$200 return. It operates daily flights between Jo'burg, Cape Town and Windhoek's Chief Hosea Kutako International Airport.

Air Namibia flies from Windhoek to Harare, Zimbabwe (US$400); Maun, Botswana (US$250); and Victoria Falls, Zimbabwe (US$276). Air Namibia has daily flights from Windhoek's Eros Airport to and from Alexander Bay, the airport for Oranjemund. A one-way fare between Windhoek and Jo'burg or Cape Town costs around US$220 to US$250.

Air Zimbabwe and Air Namibia both fly between Harare and Windhoek, as well as to and from South Africa. To fly between Windhoek and other African cities – Gaborone (Botswana), Nairobi (Kenya), Cairo (Egypt), cities in West Africa, and other places – you'll probably have to pass through Jo'burg.

There are few travel agencies in Africa selling discounted tickets, although there are some in Nairobi, Jo'burg and Cape Town.

Asia

The only reasonable way to travel between southern or South-East Asia and Africa is to fly. From Delhi (India), the cheapest fare to Jo'burg is US$1168. From Bangkok (Thailand), there are several options, the easiest (and at the time of writing the cheapest!) of which is SAA's nonstop flight to Jo'burg, which starts at US$1286 return.

Discount Travel Agencies Coming from South-East Asia, the best possible departure point is Bangkok, which has bucket shops galore. There are also several discount agencies in major Indian cities. Recommended agencies include the following.

Cozy Travels (☎ 331 2873) BMC House, 1N
  Connaught Place, Delhi

Tan's Travel (☎ 332 1490) 72 Janpath, Delhi
Transway International (☎ 262 6066, e transkam
.etn@smt.sprintrpg.ems.vsnl.net.in) Pantaky
House, 8 Maruti Cross Lane, Mumbai (Bombay). This discount travel agency is renowned.
Travellers' Express Club, 20 Mirza Ghalib St,
Kolkata (Calcutta)

LAND

Describing how to reach Namibia overland
in your own vehicle is beyond the scope of
this book, but thanks to the Southern African
Customs Union, you can drive through
Botswana, Lesotho, Namibia, South Africa
and Swaziland with a minimum of ado, and
with the proper paperwork – a Blue Book
sheet detailing the vehicle's particulars and
proof of insurance and current registration –
you can secure temporary import permits for
Malawi, Mozambique, Zimbabwe and Zambia. To travel further north requires a carnet
de passage, which can amount to heavy expenditure and serious consideration.

In late 2000, Namibia implemented a
road tax, known as a Cross-Border Charge
(CBC), for foreign-registered vehicles entering the country (motorcycles don't have
to pay). Passenger vehicles carrying fewer
than 25 passengers are charged N$70
(US$9.50) per entry. Keep the receipt, because you may be asked to produce it at police roadblocks.

Border Crossings

There are border control posts between
Namibia and Botswana at Ngoma Bridge
(open 6am to 6pm), Buitepos/Mamuno
(8am to 7pm), Mahango/Mohembo (sunrise
to sunset) and Mpalila Island/Kasane (7am
to 12.30pm and 1.45pm to 5pm).

The only border crossing between Namibia and Zambia is at Wenela ferry (6am to
6pm), 4km west of Katima Mulilo (see Zambia later for more information).

Traffic between South Africa and Namibia
can cross at Velloorsdrift-Onseepkans/
Pofadder (24 hours), Karasburg/Noenieput
(6am to 5pm), Nakop/Ariamsvlei (24 hours),
Aroab/Rietfontein (24 hours), Klein
Menasse-Aroab/Rietfontein (6am to 10pm)
or Noordoewer/Vioolsdrif (24 hours – this is
the main highway between Windhoek and

Cape Town). There's no public access between Alexander Bay and Oranjemund (6am
to 10pm) without permission from the diamond company CDM.

There are three border crossings between
Namibia and Angola (mainly for commercial vehicles), all of which are open from
6am to 6pm: Ruacana/Koaleck/Concor,
Mahenene, and Oshikango/Santa Clara/Namacunda. There's also a small crossing over
the Okavango River at Rundu/Calai.

Angola

To enter Namibia overland, you'll need an
Angolan visa permitting overland entry.
Namibians may be granted visas, but travellers of other nationalities normally must
enter Angola by air. At Ruacana Falls, you
can enter the border area temporarily without
a visa by signing in at the border crossing.
It's also possible to cross for the day between
Oshikango and Santa Clara without a visa.

Botswana

The Trans-Kalahari Hwy from Windhoek to
Botswana, via Gobabis, crosses the border
at Buitepos/Mamuno. A weekly Trans-Namib Star Line bus leaves Gobabis at 9am
Friday, arrives at the Buitepos border at
12.30pm, then continues on to Ghanzi, in
Botswana (where you'll find at least one or
two daily buses to Maun). This bus costs
US$7 and links nicely with Trans-Namib's
Thursday overnight train from Windhoek to
Gobabis.

You can also cross between Namibia and
Botswana via the Caprivi Strip at either
Ngoma Bridge or Mohembo. Sparse traffic
makes hitching unreliable, but you'll eventually find a lift. The crossing between
Mpalila Island and Kasane is mainly used
by guests of tourist lodges on the island.

A convenient way to travel between
Windhoek and Maun is the Audi Camp
Shuttle, which leaves Windhoek at 7.30am
Wednesday and arrives in Maun around
4pm. From Maun, it leaves at the same
time on Monday. The trip costs US$50 per
person. This may also be done as a return
trip, including an inexpensive Audi Camp
safari in Botswana's Okavango Delta.

Unfortunately, passengers on the Intercape Mainliner between Windhoek and Victoria Falls may not disembark in Botswana.

South Africa

Bus The Intercape Mainliner (☎ 061-227847) service from Windhoek to Cape Town (US$51) runs four times weekly. Travelling between Jo'burg and Windhoek (US$64) involves a connection in Upington; the service also runs four times weekly. Students and seniors receive a 15% discount.

In South Africa, book through the offices in Cape Town (☎ 021-386 4400) or Jo'burg (☎ 011-333 5231). In Windhoek, the office is on Gallilei St.

Train The only rail service still operating connects Keetmanshoop with Upington, South Africa. It departs Keetmanshoop at 8.50am Wednesday and Saturday and from Upington at 5am Sunday and Thursday. In Namibia, these trains connect with services to and from Windhoek. In South Africa, they connect with services to and from Jo'burg and Cape Town.

Car & Motorcycle You can drive to Namibia along good tarred roads from South Africa, either from Cape Town in the south, crossing the border at Noordoewer, or from Jo'burg in the east, in which case the border crossing is at Nakop.

Hitching You'll find that hitching is easiest with trucks but most drivers will want payment, so agree on a price before climbing aboard. After bargaining, the standard rate is around US$1.50 per 100km.

Zambia

The only crossing between Namibia and Zambia is via the Zambezi pontoon ferry at Wenela/Sesheke. From Sesheke, one daily bus (sometimes more) chugs down the terribly potholed road to Livingstone (US$8.50), five hours away. From Livingstone, buses to Sesheke leave anytime after 6am from Muramba bus station, 1km from the centre. If you're heading for Namibia, check whether your bus continues to the border; if not, you'll have to walk or hitch the remaining 5km to the border crossing.

The pontoon ferry over the Zambezi between Wenela in Namibia and Sesheke in Zambia costs US$12 per vehicle; pedestrians ride free. It's about 4km from Katima Mulilo (Namibia), and 5km from Sesheke (Zambia). If you don't want to wait for the ferry, you can opt for the small private boats that carry passengers across the river for a negotiable fee – usually between US$0.50 and US$1.50. The Zambian border crossing is 500m from the ferry crossing and the Namibian border crossing is 1km away.

A bridge is planned in the next few years, but don't hold your breath. (An alternative route involves crossing into Botswana at Ngoma Bridge, transiting Chobe National Park, and then using the Kazungula ferry into Zambia).

Zimbabwe

There's no direct border crossing between Namibia and Zimbabwe: To get there you must take the Chobe National Park transit route from Ngoma Bridge through northern Botswana to Kasane/Kazungula, and from there to Victoria Falls.

At present, the only public transport between Namibia and Zimbabwe is the weekly Intercape Mainliner, which travels between Windhoek and Victoria Falls (US$56) via Grootfontein, Rundu and Katima Mulilo. It departs Windhoek at 8pm Friday and arrives in Victoria Falls at 4pm Saturday. In the other direction, it leaves at 9am Sunday and arrives in Windhoek at 3.30am Monday. Although this bus passes through Botswana en route, it's not possible to disembark there.

ORGANISED TOURS

Literally hundreds of tour and safari companies now organise package tours to Namibia. With packages, it always pays to shop around for deals. Especially in Europe, it's becoming increasingly popular to look for late bookings, which may be advertised in travel sections of weekend newspapers, or even at special late bookings counters in some international airports. If you prefer a more independent approach, you can pre-book flights and hotels for the first few nights, then join tours locally (see Organised Tours in the Getting Around chapter).

While it would be impractical to include a comprehensive rundown of package operators, the following list will provide some idea of the range available, and includes some of the more creative and offbeat offerings. Most of these can be booked through your travel agency.

Australia

Adventure World (☎ 02-9956 7766, fax 9956 7707, e info@adventureworld.com.au) 73 Walker St, North Sydney, NSW 2060. Organises tours, safaris, car hire and hotel packages all over Southern Africa.

w www.adventureworld.com.au

African Wildlife Safaris (☎ 03-9696 2899, fax 9696 4937, e office@africansafaris.com.au) Level 1, 259 Coventry St, South Melbourne, Vic 3205. This is a specialist in safaris mainly to Southern Africa.

Peregrine Travel (☎ 03-9663 8611, fax 9663 8618, e simon.cameron@peregrine.net.au) Level 2, 258 Lonsdale St, Melbourne, Vic 3000. This Africa specialist cobbles together safaris for all budgets. A six-day camping safari to Sossusvlei and Swakopmund is A$755 and a two-week circuit through the highlights is A$3635, both from Windhoek.

w www.peregrine.net.au\

South Africa

Wayfarer Adventures (☎ 021-470792, fax 474675) 4 Norwich Ave, Observatory, Cape Town 7925. Wayfarer offers wilderness adventure travel throughout Southern Africa, including Land Rover tours around Namibia.

Which Way? (☎ 021-845 7400, fax 845 7401, e whichway@iafrica.com) 21 Chilwan Crescent, Helderberg Industrial Park, Strand 7140, PO Box 2600, Somerset West 7129, Western Cape. This popular local overland company does 'mobile party' camping safaris throughout Southern Africa, including several Namibian itineraries.

Wilderness Safaris (☎ 011-807 1800, fax 807 2110, e enquiry@wilderness.co.za) 3 Autumn St, PO Box 4219, Rivonia. This company offers a range of tours in Zimbabwe, Botswana, Namibia and other African countries. In addition to the standard luxury lodge-based tours in remote areas, it offers fly-in safaris and activity-based trips.

w www.wilderness-safaris.com

Continental Europe

Compañia Africana de Veiajes Cèsar Cañaveras (☎ 91-519 6778, fax 519 3301, e african adeviajes@ctv.es) C/ Mantuano 56, Madrid 28002. This company specialises in tours through Etosha National Park and around northern Namibia.

Makila Voyages (☎ 01 42 96 80 00, fax 01 42 96 18 05) 4 Place de Volois, F-75001 Paris. This upmarket company organises tours and safaris all over East and Southern Africa.

UK

Discover the World (☎ 01737-218800, fax 362341) 29 Nork Way, Bamstead, Surrey SM7 1PB. This company operates exclusive wildlife-oriented tours to various sites throughout the world, including a two-week excursion through Namibia.

Explore Worldwide Ltd (☎ 01252-319448, 760000, fax 760001) 1 Frederick St, Aldershot, Hampshire GU11 1LQ. Explore's organised group tours through Zimbabwe, Botswana and Namibia focus on hands-on adventure and activities.

w www.exploreworldwide.com

In the Saddle (☎ 01256-851665, fax 851667, e namibia@inthesaddle.com or ponyboy@ inthesaddle.com) Baaughurst Rd, Ramsdell, Tadley, Hampshire RG26 5SH. This company appeals specifically to horse aficionados. In Namibia, it organises several riding adventures, including the renowned nine-day Desert Trail from the Khomas Hochland to Swakopmund (US$2288).

w www.inthesaddle.com

Naturetrek (☎ 01962-733051, fax 736426, e info@naturetrek.co.uk) Cheriton Mill, Cheriton, Alresford, Hampshire SO24 9RB. This company's aim is to get you to where the animals are. It offers specialised wildlife-viewing itineraries in Namibia, as well as other areas of Southern Africa.

w www.naturetrek.co.uk

Temple World (☎ 020-8940 4114, fax 8332 2456) 13 The Avenue, Kew, Richmond, Surrey TW9 2AL. This very sophisticated and recommended company organises middle- to upper-range tours to the best of Namibia.

USA

Adventure Center (☎ 800-227 8747, 510-654 1879, fax 654 4200, e lp@adventurecenter .com) 1311 63rd St, Suite 200, Emeryville, CA 94608. This travel specialist organises adventure tours worldwide, and is the US agency for several overland operators, including Guerba,

Dragoman and Karibu.

W www.adventurecenter.com

Africa Adventure Company (☎ 800-882 9453, 954-491 8877, fax 491 9060, e noltingaac@aol.com) 5353 N Federal Hwy, Suite 300, Fort Lauderdale, FL 33308. These top safari specialists can organise any sort of Namibia tour.

W www.africa-adventure.com

Africa Travel Center, Explorers Travel Group (☎ 800-631 5650, 732-542 9006, fax 542 9420, e explorers@monmouth.com) One Main St, Suite 304, Eatontown, NJ 07724. This is a travel and resource centre for prospective Africa travellers. It organises flights, hotels, overland tours, safaris, custom tours, visas and insurance.

Born Free Safaris (☎ 800-372 3274, fax 818-753 1460, e bornfreesafaris@att.net) 12504 Riverside Dr, North Hollywood, CA 91607. Offering safaris, trekking cultural tours and flights.

W www.bornfreesafaris.com

Bushtracks (☎ 800-995 8689, 650-326 8689, fax 463 0925, e info@bushtracks.com) 845 Oak Grove Ave, Suite 204, PO Box 4163, Menlo Park, CA 94025. This is a US sales agency for Wilderness Safaris; one-week lodge-based safaris to Sossusvlei, Damaraland and Etosha are US$3500; four days on the Skeleton Coast is US$2800 and 12-day regional itineraries start at US$6710.

W www.bushtracks.com

Global Adventures (☎/fax 303-791 9959, e mikem@globaladventures.com) 8762 South Mourning Dove Lane, Highlands Ranch, CO 80126. Organises adventure tours in Zimbabwe, Botswana, Namibia and other parts of Africa. Its first contact with clients normally includes a questionnaire, which will ascertain individual interests.

W www.globaladventures.com

Premier Tours & Travel (☎ 215-893 9966, fax 893 0357, e info@premiertours.com) 217 S 20th St, Philadelphia, PA 19103. Premier organises inexpensive participation camping safaris all over Southern Africa. For example, a 12-day circuit around Namibia costs US$920, plus discounted air fare.

W www.premiertours.com

Voyagers (☎ 800-633 0299, e explore@voyagers.com) PO Box 915, Ithaca, NY. Voyagers offers photographic and wildlife-viewing safaris.

W www.voyagers.com

Wilderness Travel (☎ 800-358 8530, e info@wildernesstravel.com) 801 Alston Way, Berkeley, CA 94710. This company offers guided group tours with an emphasis on down-to-earth touring, including hikes, treks and other hands-on pursuits.

Overland Companies

Although overlanding across Africa all the way from Europe or the Middle East has now become quite difficult due to the various 'roadblocks' imposed by unrest, overland operators still take up the challenge. Some begin in Morocco and head down through Mauritania, Mali, Niger and onwards as far as possible. Others take the easier option and begin in Kenya.

While these trips are popular, they're designed mainly for inexperienced travellers who feel uncomfortable striking out on their own or for those who prefer guaranteed social interaction to the uncertainties of the road. If you have the slightest inclination towards independence or would feel confined travelling with the same group of 25 or so people for most of the trip (although quite a few normally drop out along the way), think twice before booking an overland trip.

Increasingly, many overland companies are opting for shorter hauls and some also provide transport – a sort of backpackers bus and transfer service. Independent travellers may join overland trucks for around US$20 per day, plus food kitty contributions. Just visit an overland truck stop and ask the driver if there's space available. This is a particularly useful way to transfer quickly between Nairobi and Southern Africa.

There are now literally dozens of overland companies, and every day, new ones pop up while others fade away. For information and recommendations on the latest offerings, attend travel fairs, check ads in adventure-travel magazines, ask around discounted travel agencies and visit backpacker hostels (where these companies invariably leave stacks of brochures).

Getting Around

AIR
Domestic Air Services
Air Namibia services domestic routes mainly from Eros Airport in Windhoek, although a few domestic flights use Windhoek's Chief Hosea Kutako International Airport. There are regular flights to and from Tsumeb; Rundu and Katima Mulilo; Lüderitz and Alexander Bay (South Africa); and Swakopmund and Oshakati/Ondangwa. Passengers are allowed a baggage limit of 20kg; additional weight is US$2 per kilogram.

Air Namibia Offices
Air Namibia has the following offices:

Katima Mulilo (☎ 0677-3191, fax 2191)
Lüderitz (☎ 063-202850, fax 202845)
Ondangwa (☎ 065-240655, fax 240656)
Oshakati (☎ 065-220567, fax 220568)
Swakopmund (☎ 064-405123, fax 402196)
Tsumeb (☎ 067-220520, fax 220821)
Walvis Bay (☎ 064-202938, fax 202928)
Windhoek central reservations (☎ 061-299 63333, fax 221382, e creservations@air namibia.com.na); Chief Hosea Kutako International (☎ 062-540315, fax 540367); Eros Airport (☎ 061-238220, fax 236460); Gustav Voigts Centre (☎ 061-229630, fax 228763) Independence Ave

Air Charter
Namibia has a few air charter operations.

Atlantic Aviation (☎ 064-404749, fax 405832, e aviation@natron.net) 5 Roon St, Swakopmund, PO Box 465
w www.natron.net/tour/aviation
Bush Pilots Namibia (☎ 061-248316, fax 225083, e bushpilo@iafrica.com.na)
w www.bushpilots.com
COMAV (☎ 061-227512, fax 245612, e comav@mweb.com.na)
w resafrica.net/comav/
Desert Air (☎ 061-228101, fax 254345, e deserta@iafrica.com.na) PO Box 11624, Windhoek

Sample prices (including the return to base – with or without passengers) from Eros Air-port for up to five passengers are as follows: Victoria Falls US$1550; Etosha National Park (Mokuti Lodge) US$630; Sesriem US$510 (via Swakopmund US$700); Swakopmund US$440.

BUS
Namibia's bus services aren't extensive. Luxury services are limited to the Intercape Mainliner (☎ 061-227847, e info@inter cape.co.za), which has scheduled services between Windhoek, Cape Town, Johannesburg (Jo'burg), Swakopmund, Walvis Bay, Grootfontein, Rundu, Katima Mulilo and Victoria Falls. You're allowed only two items of baggage, which must not exceed a total of 30kg. Fares include meals.

The rail service, Trans-Namib, has an expanding system of Star Line buses that not only replace defunct rail services, but also service places that have never been connected by rail. Services go to Lüderitz, Bethanie, Gochas, Buitepos, Ghanzi (Botswana), Helmeringhausen, Outjo, Kamanjab, Khorixas, Henties Bay, Grootfontein, Oshakati, Rundu, and a route across the Central Namib between Mariental and Walvis Bay.

MINIBUS
There are also local minibuses, which depart when full and follow main routes around the country. Fares work out at around US$0.03 per kilometre, plus US$2 per large piece of luggage. From Windhoek's Rhino Park petrol station, they depart for Swakopmund, Walvis Bay, Tsumeb, Grootfontein, Keetmanshoop, Ondangwa, Oshakati, Kavango and Caprivi. There are additional services from Windhoek on Friday afternoons, especially on the route north to the Oshakati and Ondangwa in the Owambo region; extra southbound services operate from Oshakati and Ondangwa on Sunday afternoons.

TRAIN
Trans-Namib Railways connects most of the major towns, but trains are slow – as one

reader remarked, moving 'at the pace of an energetic donkey cart'. In addition, passenger and freight cars are mixed on the same train, and trains tend to stop at every post.

On the other hand, rail travel isn't popular and services are rarely fully booked. Trains carry economy and business class seats but, although most services operate overnight, sleepers are no longer available. Book at train stations or through the Windhoek Booking Office (☎ 061-298 2032). Tickets must be collected before 4pm on the day of departure. They're fully refundable up to 48 hours before departure, and 50% thereafter.

Windhoek is Namibia's rail hub, with services south to Keetmanshoop and Upington (South Africa), north to Tsumeb, west to Swakopmund and Walvis Bay and east to Gobabis. Regular fares (which are quoted in this book) are valid from Thursday to Monday; on Tuesday and Wednesday, fares are 33% lower, while at peak periods, such as holidays, they're 33% more.

Tourist Trains

There are also two 'tourist trains'. The relatively plush 'rail cruise' aboard the *Desert Express* (☎ 061-298 2600, fax 298 2601, ℮ dx@transnamib.com.na, ⓦ www.trans namib.com.na/dx), Windhoek Railway Station, Private Bag 13204, Windhoek, provides a luxurious overnight trip between Windhoek and Swakopmund twice weekly in either direction. Singles/doubles cost US$236/355, including dinner.

The *Shongololo Dune Express* (☎ South Africa 27-21-556 0372, fax 557 1034, ℮ info@shongo.co.za, ⓦ www.shongo .co.za), which journeys between Cape Town and Tsumeb, via Aus, Mariental, Swakopmund and Otjiwarongo, does 15-day trips taking in Namibia's main sites. The one-way fare, all-inclusive, is US$2470/4580 in single/double compartments.

CAR & MOTORCYCLE
Road Rules & Conditions

The easiest way to get around Namibia is by road, and an excellent system of tarred roads runs the length of the country from the South

African border at Noordoewer to Ngoma Bridge on the Botswana border and Ruacana in the north-west. Similarly, tarred spur roads connect the main north-south routes to Buitepos, Lüderitz, Swakopmund and Walvis Bay. Elsewhere, towns and most sites of interest are accessible on good gravel roads. Most C-numbered highways are well maintained and passable to all vehicles, and D-numbered roads, although a bit rougher, are mostly (but not always) passable to 2WD vehicles. In the Kaokoveld, however, most D-numbered roads can only be negotiated with a 4WD.

As in the rest of Southern Africa, vehicles keep to the left. The general speed limit of 120km/h applies on open roads; in built-up areas it's 60km/h. Drivers and front-seat passengers must use seat belts. At the time of research, petrol cost around US$0.70 per litre.

Foreigners can drive in Namibia on their home driving licence for up to 90 days, and most (if not all) car hire companies will accept foreign driving licences for car hire.

Note that motorcycles aren't permitted in the national parks, with the exception of the main highway routes through Namib-Naukluft Park.

If you're looking to purchase a 4WD in Namibia, a good point of contact is Dion Barnard at the Klein Windhoek petrol station (☎ 061-224352) in Windhoek.

In addition to its fantastic system of tarred roads, Namibia has everything from high-speed gravel roads to badly maintained main routes, farm roads, bush tracks, sand tracks and challenging 4WD routes. Driving under these conditions requires special techniques, appropriate vehicle preparation, a bit of practice and a heavy dose of caution.

Gravel Roads Many of Namibia's roads – even major routes – have unsealed gravel surfaces, and while some are very well maintained, others are rutted, potholed, corrugated and unevenly surfaced. For drivers, this can be at best tricky and at worst, treacherous. In fact, the price of car hire relates directly to the number of cars rolled by foreigners who are not used to driving on gravel roads. The following points may help:

- Restrict your speed to a maximum of 100km/h.
- Maximise your control by keeping both hands on the steering wheel.
- Follow ruts made by other vehicles.
- If the road is corrugated, gradually increase your speed until you find the correct speed – it'll be obvious when the rattling stops.
- Be especially careful on bends; slow right down before attempting the turn.
- If you have a tyre blowout, DO NOT hit the brakes or you'll lose control and the car may roll. Instead, steer straight ahead as best you can and let the car slow itself down before you attempt to bring it to a complete stop.
- You don't meet other cars very often, but when you do, it's like dust clouds passing in the night. When a vehicle approaches from the opposite direction, reduce your speed and keep as far left as possible. On remote roads, it's customary to wave at the other driver as you pass.
- Keep your tyre pressure slightly lower than you would when driving on tarred roads.
- Try to avoid travelling at night when dust and distance may create confusing mirages.
- In rainy weather, gravel roads can turn to quagmires and desert washes may fill with water. If you're uncertain about the water depth in a wash, get out to check the depth (unless it's a raging torrent, of course!) and only cross when it's safe for the type of vehicle you're driving.
- Be on the lookout for animals. Kudus, in particular, often bound onto the road unexpectedly, resulting in an unpleasant meeting.
- Avoid swerving sharply or braking suddenly on a gravel road or you risk losing control of the vehicle. If the rear wheels begin to skid, steer gently into the direction of the skid until you regain control. If the front wheels skid, take a firm hand on the wheel and steer in the opposite direction of the skid.
- Dust permeates everything on gravel roads; wrap your food, clothing and camera equipment in dust-proof plastic or keep them in sealed containers. To minimise dust inside the vehicle, pressurise the interior by closing the windows and turning on the fan.
- In dusty conditions, switch on your headlights so you can be more easily seen.
- Overtaking (passing) can be extremely dangerous because your view may be obscured by flying dust kicked up by the car ahead. Try to gain the attention of the driver in front by flashing your high-beam lights, which will indicate that you want to overtake (this isn't considered obnoxious in Namibia). If someone behind you flashes their lights, move as far to the left of the road as possible.

Wilderness Routes Especially in Bushmanland, the Kaokoveld and parts of Damaraland, there is a network of 4WD routes that will prove both exciting and challenging for adventurous drivers. If you want to get right out into the wildest parts of Namibia, the following information will help to keep you, and your vehicle, out of trouble:

- For rough road conditions, you'll need a robust, high-clearance vehicle, but you'll only have to engage the 4WD when driving in sand or mud, or over boulder-sized rocks.
- In especially rocky conditions, have someone get out and direct the driver over the route of least resistance.
- At river crossings, always check the water depth and bottom conditions before starting across. It may take a bit of exploring to find the best route. It will be obvious that sand, stones and gravel are preferable to mud and muck.
- Make sure your vehicle is in good running order before you start. Carry tools, spares and equipment, including towrope, torch (flashlight), shovel, fan belts, vehicle fluids, spark plugs, wire, jump leads, fuses, hoses, a good jack and a wooden plank to act as a base in sand. A second spare tyre is highly advised, and even a third if you've got room. You could also carry tyre levers, spare tubes and repair kit, but mending punctures in the bush is much harder than the manuals imply, and should be avoided if possible. A pump *is* useful though, and a winch would also be an asset. And of course you'll need the expertise to handle and install all this stuff.
- Wrap tools and heavy objects in blankets or padding. Pack supplies that are likely to be pitched around in strong plastic or metal containers and strap everything down tightly on the roof or in the back. Keep breakable items with you in the cabin. Once you're off the tar, dust permeates everything – so tightly wrap food, clothing and camera equipment in strong dust-proof containers.
- When calculating fuel requirements, estimate your intended distance and then double it to allow for getting lost and emergencies. For serious off-roading, remember to allow for petrol consumption up to four times higher than in normal conditions – it will probably be less than this, but it can be frighteningly high on sandy tracks.
- In indestructible containers, carry at least 5L of water per person per day – allowing for delays and breakdowns. Extra petrol should be carried in strong, leak-proof jerry cans.

ROAD DISTANCES (km)

	Gobabis	Grootfontein	Kalkfeld	Kamanjab	Karasburg	Keetmanshoop	Lüderitz	Mariental	Noordoewer	Okahandja	Ondangwa	Otjiwarongo	Rehoboth	Ruacana	Rundu	Swakopmund	Tsumeb	Usakos	Walvis Bay	Windhoek
Gobabis	---																			
Grootfontein	657	---																		
Kalkfeld	516	275	---																	
Kamanjab	668	425	286	---																
Karasburg	895	1142	1001	1153	---															
Keetmanshoop	687	934	749	945	208	---														
Lüderitz	1021	1268	1015	1279	471	334	---													
Mariental	466	713	572	724	429	221	555	---												
Noordoewer	991	1238	1097	1249	147	304	609	525	---											
Okahandja	276	381	240	392	761	553	889	332	857	---										
Ondangwa	878	307	496	646	1363	1155	1489	934	1459	602	---									
Otjiwarongo	450	207	68	218	935	727	1061	506	1031	174	428	---								
Rehoboth	292	539	398	550	603	395	729	174	699	158	760	332	---							
Ruacana	1065	494	683	272	1550	342	1676	1121	1646	789	187	615	876	---						
Rundu	905	248	523	645	1390	182	1516	961	1486	629	555	455	787	742	---					
Swakopmund	563	578	303	412	1048	840	731	619	1144	287	799	371	445	684	826	---				
Tsumeb	631	60	249	399	1116	907	1242	687	1241	355	247	181	513	434	308	552	---			
Usakos	418	523	158	444	903	695	1029	474	999	142	654	226	300	716	681	175	407	---		
Walvis Bay	594	690	334	443	1079	814	938	650	1175	318	831	403	476	715	947	31	673	206	---	
Windhoek	205	452	311	463	690	482	816	261	786	71	673	245	87	860	700	356	426	211	389	---

- Take the best maps, plus a GPS or compass that you know how to use. Take readings periodically to make sure you're still travelling in the right direction. To get an accurate compass reading, stand at least 3m from the vehicle. A good source of GPS co-ordinates in Namibia is the 4WD booklet by Jan Joubert, which is available from Cymot Greensport in Windhoek.

Bush Tracks Maps rarely show bush tracks, whose ever-changing routes can confound drivers. Some provide access to remote cattle posts or small villages and then disappear, often to re-emerge somewhere else. Some never re-emerge, leaving you stranded.

- Take care driving through high grass – seeds can block radiators and cause overheating. Dry grass next to the exhaust pipe can also catch fire. Stop regularly and remove plant material from the grille or exhaust.

Sand In sandy conditions you may be following a faint track – often just the tyre marks of previous vehicles – or driving across completely bare wilderness. Either way, driving is easier if the air is cool (usually mornings), as the sand is more compact at these times.

- Tyre pressure should be low – around half that for normal road conditions. To prevent bogging or stalling, move as quickly as is safely possible and keep the revs up, but avoid sudden acceleration. Shift down a gear before you reach deep sandy patches, not when you're in them.
- Allow the vehicle to wander along the path of least resistance when negotiating a straight course through rutted sand. Anticipate corners and turn the wheel slightly earlier than you would on a solid surface – this will allow the vehicle to slide smoothly around.

Rental

Car rental is the easiest way of seeing Namibia. If you're on a tight budget, this can be expensive, but if you can muster a group to share costs it can still work out cheaper than joining an organised tour. However, be warned that Namibia suffers from a chronic shortage of rental cars, so book well in advance.

For a compact car, the least-expensive companies charge US$40 to US$60 per day (the longer the hire period, the lower the daily rate) with unlimited kilometres.

Most companies include insurance and unlimited kilometres in their standard rates, but some require a minimum rental period before they allow unlimited kilometres. Note that some internationally known companies, such as Avis and Budget, charge amenable daily rates but only allow 200 free kilometres per day. If one company's rates seem quite a bit higher than another's, check whether it includes VAT, which would otherwise add 15.5% to the quoted figure. Most companies also require a N$1000 (about US$155) deposit and won't hire to anyone under the age of 25 (although some go as low as 21).

It's cheaper to hire a car in South Africa and drive it into Namibia, but you need permission from the rental agency and paperwork to cross the borders. Drivers entering Namibia in a foreign-registered vehicle must pay a N$70 road tax at the border (see Land in the Getting There & Away chapter).

To drive a Namibian-registered hire car into a neighbouring country, you must have a police permit. To enter South Africa, Botswana or elsewhere in the Southern African Customs Union, you need a Blue Book sheet outlining the vehicle's particulars, such as the engine's serial number. If you're continuing to Zimbabwe, request proof of insurance (including the company name) and all the paperwork to get a Zimbabwean temporary import permit (bizarrely, the Zimbabwean form is entitled 'Permit for Temporary Export of Aircraft' – no joking!).

Some large agencies use travellers to return vehicles to Cape Town for the cost of petrol. However, you're limited to 24 hours for the 1700km journey from Windhoek.

Hiring a 4WD vehicle opens up remote parts of the country, but it can get expensive and the excess can be as much as US$2500. A good choice is Triple Three Car Hire, with offices in Swakopmund and Walvis Bay, which charges US$55 per day with insurance and unlimited kilometres for a min-

To Go or Not To Go?

A dangerous traffic quirk in Namibia concerns the use and significance of indicator lights. When a car comes up behind a slow vehicle, wanting to overtake, the driver of the slower vehicle will often flash one indicator to let the other driver know whether or not it's safe to go. Logically, the left indicator would mean 'go' (that is, it 'may' potentially be turning right and the way is clear) and the right would mean 'don't go' (it 'may' potentially be turning right, indicating that the way is not clear). Unfortunately, quite a few confused drivers get this backwards, creating a potentially disastrous situation for a trusting driver in the vehicle behind. The moral is: Ignore the well-intentioned signals and never overtake unless you can see that the road ahead is completely clear.

imum of three days. Camping Car Hire, in Windhoek, charges US$77 per day, including insurance, VAT and unlimited kilometres, with a minimum 14-day rental.

Rental Agencies The following agencies offer car and/or 4WD hire; many of these can also equip the vehicles with all the safari gear you'll need:

Auto Garage Car Hire (☎ 061-226681, 081-124 0574, fax 224718, e autogarage@ yahoo.com) PO Box 5166, Windhoek

Avis Car Hire (☎ 061-233166, fax 223072) Hotel Safari, PO Box 2057, Aviation Rd, Windhoek; (☎ 064-402527, fax 405881) Swakopmund Hotel, Swakopmund; (☎ 067-220520, fax 220821) Safari Centre, Jordaan St, Tsumeb; (☎ 064-207527, fax 209150) Rooikop Airport, Walvis Bay
w www.avis.com

Budget Car Hire (☎ 061-228720, 081-128 7200, fax 227665) 72 Mandume Ndemufayo, Windhoek; (☎ 064-204128, 081-128 6900, fax 202931) Protea Lodge, corner of 10th Rd & Sam Nujoma Dr, Walvis Bay
w www.budget.co.za

Camping Car Hire (☎ 061-237756, fax 237757, e carhire@iwwn.com.na) 36 Joule St, Southern Industrial Area, Windhoek, PO Box 5526
w www.namibiaweb.com/cch

Car-Hire Warnings

Don't let an unscrupulous agency try to use your deposit for unauthorised extras. Be sure to verify what sort of repairs will be your responsibility; your liability should be limited to tyres and windows. Also ask whether you'll be charged for a 'valet' (cleaning the car) after the hire period.

If you don't have an unlimited-kilometres deal and are paying by credit card, insist on a copy of the contract so you'll know the charge for any excess kilometres. If you're paying a cash deposit and want to return the car just before you fly out, ensure that it will be repaid in foreign currency.

Note that you may not carry more than three people in the cheapest Group A car; groups of four must hire a Group B car. If you ignore this regulation and roll the car, your insurance will be void, leaving you liable for the vehicle's full (former) value. This caveat cannot be stressed enough (as some unfortunate travellers will attest).

If you do have a bad experience, or you want more information about a specific company, contact the Car Rental Association of Namibia (Caran; ☎ 061-233451, fax 224 551), PO Box 20274, Windhoek.

Elena Travel Services & Car Hire (☎ 061-244443, 081-124 6286, fax 244558, e elena@namibweb.com)
w www.namibweb.com
Imperial Car Rental (☎ 067-220728, fax 220916, e tnn@iafrica.com.na) Travel North Namibia, 1551 Omeg Allee, Tsumeb
Into Namibia Car & 4x4 Hire (☎ 061-253591, 081-128 8899, fax 253593, e admin@ intonam.com.na) 76 Sam Nujoma Dr, PO Box 31551, Klein Windhoek
w www.iwwn.com.na/intonam
Namibia Car Hire (☎ 061-255700, 081-128 8442, fax 255701, e c@rhire.com) Outeniqua St 13, PO Box 1307, Windhoek
w www.namibia-car-hire.com
Savanna Car Rental (☎ 061-229272, 081-127 6060, fax 223292, e scr@iafrica .com.na) 57 John Meinert St, PO Box 5180, Windhoek
w www.natron.net/tours/savanna
Triple Three Car Hire (☎ 064-403190, 081-127 3331, fax 403191) 28 Kaiser Wilhelm St, Swakopmund; (☎ 064-200333, 081-127 3331,

e oliver@iafrica.con.na) 12th Rd 42, Walvis Bay
w www.333.com.na

HITCHING

Although hitching is possible in Namibia, it's illegal in national parks, and even main highways receive relatively little traffic. For example, hitching through the Caprivi is especially slow – and currently not recommended. On a positive note, it isn't unusual to get a lift of 1000km in the same car. Truck drivers generally expect to be paid, so agree on a price beforehand; the standard charge is US$1.50 per 100km.

Lifts wanted and offered are advertised daily on Windhoek radio (☎ 061-291311) and at Cardboard Box Backpackers in Windhoek. At the Namibia Wildlife Resorts office, also in Windhoek, there's a notice board with shared car hire and lifts offered and wanted.

Note that hitching is never entirely safe in any country; if you decide to hitch, understand that you are taking a small but potentially serious risk. Travel in pairs and let someone know where you're planning to go.

LOCAL TRANSPORT
Bus
In Windhoek, a few cheap local buses connect the city centre with outlying townships, but they're rapidly being phased out in favour of the more convenient share taxis.

Taxi
In Windhoek, the main taxi stand is at Grab-a-Phone bus terminal (☎ 061-237070). It's better, however, to stop a taxi on the street, pick up a share taxi at Wernhil Park Centre, or simply order one by telephone (see Getting Around in the Windhoek chapter). If you need a taxi in the wee hours, you'll need to book it beforehand.

The standard share taxi fare within Windhoek is approximately US$0.60, including to Khomasdal and Katutura. Note, however, that they operate like buses and follow standard routes, so you have to know which ones are going your way.

Individual taxis, especially if you order one by phone, may charge anywhere from

US$2 to US$5, and drivers may think up all sorts of add-on charges if they think you're an ignorant tourist. This is especially true for anyone arriving at the Grab-a-Phone bus terminal on the airport bus.

Only in Windhoek are taxis common – no other place is big enough to warrant extensive services. To get a taxi from a provincial airport or train station, look for business cards attached to telephone boxes.

ORGANISED TOURS

Even if you normally spurn organised trips, independent travellers will find there's a good case for joining a tour in Namibia, as many highlights – the Skeleton Coast, Damaraland, the Kaokoveld, the Kunene Valley, Fish River Canyon and the wild Namib Desert – are off the public transport routes and in some cases, are difficult or inconvenient to reach by low-slung rental cars.

There are plenty of upmarket tours, which provide unforgettable adventures without sacrificing comfort, but you'll also find a range of exceptionally good-value camping tours that will show you the best of Namibia for budget prices.

Prominent tour companies include the following:

Afro Ventures (☎ 064-463812, fax 400216, e swp@afroventures.com) PO Box 1772, Swakopmund. Afro Ventures offers several Namibian highlights tours, focusing on fine lodges and 4WD tours. Its five- and seven-day Namib Desert tours explore the desert coast and dunes. It also runs the beautiful Sossusvlei Mountain Lodge.
W www.afroventures.com

Campfire Safaris (☎ 062-523946, 081-242 6116, e namibia@bigfoot.com) PO Box 4500, Rehoboth. This company offers combi tours through a range of Namibian highlights. From Windhoek, the three-day Sossusvlei and Etosha circuits cost US$130 each. A 10-day circuit through Waterberg, Etosha, Damaraland, Swakopmund and Sossusvlei is US$415 and a 10-day Southern Circuit through Keetmanshoop, Fish River Canyon, Lüderitz, Klein Aus Vista, Sossusvlei and Rehoboth is US$290. The booking agency is Cardboard Box Travel Shop.

Cardboard Box Travel Shop (☎ 061-256580, fax 256581, e namibia@bigfoot.com) PO Box 5142, Windhoek. This friendly, recommended

agency offers bookings (including last-minute options) for all budget safaris; lodge, safari, and transport bookings; national parks bookings; good advice; and other travel services.
W www.namibian.org

Chameleon Safaris (☎/fax 061-247668, e info@chameleon.com.na) 8 Voight St, PO Box 6017, Windhoek. This budget safari company is geared to backpackers and does a range of good-value safaris.
W www.chameleonsafaris.com

Charly's Desert Tours (☎ 064-404341, fax 404821, e charlydt@mweb.com.na) 11 Kaiser Wilhelm St, PO Box 1400, Swakopmund. A variety of reasonably priced day tours around Swakopmund, including geology tours, the Spitzkoppe, Welwitschia Drive, Cape Cross and Sandwich Harbour.

Crazy Kudu Safaris (☎ 061-222636, fax 255074, e namibia.safaris@crazykudu.com) 50 Van der Merwe St, Pioneers Park, PO Box 99031, Windhoek. One of Namibia's friendliest and most economical safari companies does 10-day all-inclusive 'Namibia Explorer' adventures through northern and central Namibian highlights (US$440); a six-day northern highlights tour (US$300); and a three-day Sossusvlei Express tour (US$140). There's also a Fish River Canyon extension and a Kaokoland tour (US$335). All departures are guaranteed. It also organises tailor-made safaris for the best possible price.
W www.crazykudu.com

Desert Adventure Safaris (☎/fax 064-404459, fax 404664, e dassaf@iafrica.com.na) 14A Kaiser Wilhelm St, PO Box 339, Swakopmund. This company operates inexpensive day tours around Swakopmund, the Spitzkoppe and Cape Cross, and longer tours to Damaraland and the Kaokoveld. Options include three days from Palmwag to Epupa Falls (US$808), three-/five-day Kaokoland safaris (US$720/1000) and a fly-in safari to Serra Cafema Camp on the Kunene River (US$1904).
W www.das.com.na

Desert Exec (☎ 061-257642, fax 240802, e sam@desert-exec.com) PO Box 26188. This Namibian equivalent of Outward Bound concentrates on two-week extreme adventures, including desert wilderness training, 4WD courses and long-distance dune trekking. It's only for the physically and mentally fit!

Eco-Marine Kayak Tours (☎/fax 064-203144, e jeannem@iafrica.com.na) PO Box 225, Walvis Bay. Jeanne Mientjes guides wonderful sea-kayaking trips around the beautiful Walvis Bay wetlands, as well as trips to Pelican Point and Bird Island.

Hata Angu Cultural Tours (☎ 081-251 5916, e in_a_nut_shell@hotmail.com) This motivated company runs recommended township tours in Mondesa; see Organised Tours under Swakopmund in the Central Namib Desert chapter.

Kaokohimba Safaris (☎/fax 061-222378, e kaokohimba@natron.net) PO Box 11580, Windhoek. Kaokohimba organises cultural tours through Kaokoveld and Damaraland, wildlife-viewing trips in Etosha National Park and hiking around northern Namibia. A highlight is Camp Syncro, in remote Marienflüss.
W www.natron.net/tour/kaoko/himbae.htm

Kunene Tours & Safaris (☎/fax 064-402779, e zandberg@iafrica.com.na) 3 Aukas St, PO Box 1648, Swakopmund. This company does camping trips from Swakopmund, including rhino tracking in Damaraland and Kaokoland.

Lüderitzbucht Tours & Safaris (☎ 063-202719, fax 202863) PO Box 76, Lüderitz. In addition to Kolmanskop tours, this company also runs trips to other recently opened parts of the Sperrgebiet (Diamond Area 1) such as Elizabeth Bay, Atlas Bay and the Bogenfels. Tours are available in English, German or Afrikaans.

Mola Mola Safaris (☎ 064-205511, fax 207593, e mola-mola@iafrica.com.na) PO Box 980, Walvis Bay. Mola Mola offers a range of tours from Walvis Bay (see Organised Tours under Walvis Bay in the Central Namib Desert chapter).
W www.mola-mola.com.na

Muramba Bushman Trails (☎ 067-220659, e bushman@natron.net) PO Box 689, Tsumeb. This recommended company, owned by Reinhard Friedrich, provides a unique introduction to the Heikum San people. See under Tsumeb in the North Central Namibia chapter.

Namib Sky (☎ 061-293233, fax 293241, e namibsky@mweb.com.na) PO Box 5197, Windhoek. For those who dream of looming over the dunes in a balloon, this company offers Namib Desert balloon flights for US$246 per person.

Okakambe Trails (☎ 064-402799, 081-124 6626) PO Box 1668, Swakopmund. This company offers rides on horseback along the Swakop River to a Moon Landscape.

Pleasure Flights (☎/fax 064-404500, e redbaron@iml-net.ocm.na) PO Box 537, Swakopmund. Pleasure Flights runs 'flightseeing' tours from Skeleton Coast down to Fish River Canyon. For a good price, you need a group of five people.
W www.pleasureflights.com.na

Ranch Hilton Reit Safaris (☎ 061-217940, 081-127 0248, fax 256300, e info@reitsafaris.com) PO Box 20706, Windhoek. Horse-riding safaris in the Namib, plus day tours.
W www.reitsafari.com

Skeleton Coast Fly-In Safaris (☎ 061-224248, fax 225713, e sksafari@mweb.com.na) PO Box 2195, Windhoek. This highly recommended operator runs all-inclusive four-day tours of the Skeleton Coast and Kunene River region for US$2585 per person; add Sossusvlei and it's US$2770. Five-day trips to the Skeleton Coast, the Kunene River, Etosha and Sossusvlei are US$3040. Add the NamibRand Nature Reserve and Lüderitz and the six-day trip is US$3575.
W www.orosovo.com/sksafari

Turnstone Tours (☎ 064-403123, fax 403290, e turn@iafrica.com.na) PO Box 307, Swakopmund. Camping tours around Swakopmund, including Sandwich Harbour and Damaraland.
W www.swk.namib.com/turn

Westcoast Angling Tours (☎ 064-402377, fax 402532) 9 Otavi St, PO Box 545, Swakopmund. This company specialises in fishing tours, from deep-sea fishing to rock and surf angling.

West Coast Safaris (☎/fax 061-256770, e wescoast@iafrica.com.na) Windhoek. Camping safaris, including: seven-day tours through Kaokoland for US$460, eight days in Kaokoland and Etosha for US$447, seven-day tours to Etosha, Damaraland and Waterberg for US$442, seven-day Bushmanland tours for US$442 and Damaraland tours for US$460.

Wild Dog Safaris (☎ 061-257642, fax 240802, e info@wilddog-safaris.com) 19 Johann Albrecht St, PO Box 26188, Windhoek. This friendly operation runs seven-day Northern Namibia Adventures and Southern Swings (US$340 each); the northern circuit takes in Etosha, Twyfelfontein, Brandberg, Cape Cross, and Swakopmund; the southern option includes Sossusvlei, Lüderitz, Klein Aus Vista, Fish River Canyon and the Kokerboom forests around Keetmanshoop. Other options include a three-day Etosha (Sundays) or four-day Sossusvlei (Wednesdays) tour for US$160 each, a 15-day excursion through the Namib, Kalahari and Okavango Delta (in Botswana) for US$1300, and a 12-day tour to Sossusvlei, Swakopmund, Damaraland, Etosha and the Waterberg for US$1800 (US$270 single supplement). Hiking tours are available on request.
W www.wilddog-safaris.com

Wilderness Safaris Namibia (☎ 061-274500, fax 239455, e info@nts.com.na) 8 Bismarck St, PO Box 6850, Windhoek. This company does camping safaris, rock-hounding/geology tours, Namib Desert tours and Etosha wildlife drives, as well as rafting trips on the Kunene. It also owns and operates several upmarket lodges throughout the country.
W www.wilderness-safaris.com

Windhoek

☎ 061 • pop 160,000 • elevation 1660m

Namibia's Central Highlands are dominated by its small, German-influenced capital, Windhoek. This isn't only Namibia's geographical heart, it's also the country's road and rail crossroads, as well as its commercial nerve centre. Set among low hills at an elevation of 1660m, the capital city enjoys dry, clean air, a healthy highland climate, and an optimistic outlook that sets an example for all of Africa.

Windhoek's population reflects the country's ethnic mix: On the streets, you'll see Owambo, Kavango, Herero, Damara and Caprivian people, together with Nama, San, coloureds and Europeans, all contributing to the hustle and bustle – but only during working hours. While Windhoek provides about as much action as Namibia has to offer, 'vibrant' probably isn't the best word to describe its surprisingly staid and orderly capital city.

Visitors can check off most of the sights in a couple of days – and of course get in a bit of shopping – but most people just use Windhoek as a staging post and launching point for exploring the wondrous hinterlands that are Namibia's main drawcard.

History

The city of Windhoek has existed for just over a century, but its history is as colourful as its population. During the German colonial occupation, the city became the headquarters for the German Schutztruppe, which was ostensibly charged with brokering peace between the warring Herero and Nama in exchange for whatever lands their efforts would gain for German occupation. For over 10 years at the turn of the 20th century, Windhoek served as the administrative capital of German South-West Africa.

In 1902, a narrow-gauge railway was built to connect Windhoek to the coast at Swakopmund, and the city experienced a sudden spurt of growth. During this period, Windhoek began to evolve into the business,

Highlights

Daan Viljoen Game Park p131

Windhoek p109
Central Windhoek pp120-1
Windhoek Walking Tour p113

Around Windhoek p130

- Wander down Post St Mall to see the Gibeon meteorites and shop for curios.

- Enjoy the African nightlife in half a dozen vibrant nightspots.

- Hike in beautiful Daan Viljoen Game Park.

- Enjoy a night out at one of the city's fine dining establishments.

- Visit Windhoek's collection of historical museums and colonial architecture.

- Explore Namibia's longest cave system at Arnhem Cave.

commercial and administrative centre of the country, although the modern city wasn't officially founded until 1965. Windhoek is now home to all Namibia's government ministries and functions, as well as most of the country's commercial concerns.

Orientation

Windhoek isn't a typical African city, but could nevertheless be considered interesting and even attractive. The city centre grid pattern is characterised by a blend of German colonial architecture and taffy-coloured modern buildings that look vaguely edible.

WINDHOEK

What's in a Name?

Windhoek's original settlement, in what is now Klein Windhoek, was called Aigams (originally /Ae//Gams) or 'Fire Waters' by the Nama, and Otjomuise, 'Smoky Place', by the Herero. These two names refer to the hot springs that attracted early tribal attention and settlement. On a visit in 1836, British prospector Sir James Alexander took the liberty of re-naming it Queen Adelaide's Bath, although it's fairly certain the monarch never did soak there. In 1942, for reasons known only to them, a pair of German missionaries named the settlement Elbersfeld, but in 1844, the rival Wesleyan mission decided a better name would be Concordiaville. Meanwhile, in 1840, Nama leader Jan Jonker Afrikaner and his followers arrived and began referring to it as Winterhoek, after the Cape Province farm where he was born. The modern name, which means 'Windy Corner', was probably corrupted from Winterhoek by the Germans sometime around the turn of the 20th century.

Central Windhoek is bisected by Independence Ave, where most shopping and administrative functions are concentrated. The shopping district is focused on the Post St pedestrian mall and the nearby Gustav Voigts Centre, Wernhil Park Centre and Levinson Arcade. Zoo Park, beside the main post office, provides a green lawn and shady lunch spots.

North along Independence Ave are the industrial expanses of Windhoek's Northern Industrial Area. To the west and north-west are the amenable high-density townships of Khomasdal and Katutura, as well as several pockets of serious poverty: Goreangab, Hakahana and Wanaheda. In other directions, middle-class suburbs sprawl across the hills, which encircle the city, affording impressive views. Immediately beyond the city limits, the wild country begins.

Maps Free city plans are available from the tourist offices. You can purchase topographic sheets of much of Namibia for US$3.50 each from the map section of the Office of the Surveyor General (☎ 245055, fax 249802), which is on the corner of Robert Mugabe Ave and Korn St. Photocopies of out-of-stock sheets cost US$3.20. See also Maps under Planning in the Facts for the Visitor chapter.

Information

Tourist Offices The friendly Windhoek Information & Publicity Office (☎ 290 2058, fax 290 2050) on Post St Mall answers questions and distributes local advertising, including *What's On in Windhoek*. There's also an information desk at the Grab-a-Phone bus terminal.

The national tourist office, Namibia Tourism (☎ 220640, 284 2360, fax 284 2364, e tourism@mweb.com.na, W www.tourism.com.na) Private Bag 13346, on Independence Ave, can provide information from all over the country.

Namibia Wildlife Resorts (NWR; ☎ 236 175, fax 224900, e reservations@mweb.com.na, W www.namibiawildliferesorts.com), Private Bag 13267, in the Oode Voorpost on the corner of John Meinert and Moltke Sts, books national park accommodation and hikes. It's open from 8am to 1pm Monday to Friday for bookings and payment and from 2pm to 3pm for bookings only.

The *Windhoek Advertiser* provides information about current events; the Arts Association of Namibia (☎ 231160) provides news on coming cultural events.

Immigration Office For visa extensions, information on work permits and other immigration matters, check with the Ministry of Home Affairs (☎ 292 2111, fax 292 2185, e mlusepani@mha.gov.na), near the corner of Independence Ave and Kasino St. It's open 8am to 1pm Monday to Friday.

Money Major banks and bureaus de change are concentrated around Independence Ave, and all will change foreign currency and travellers cheques and give credit card advances. American Express (AmEx) customers can exchange travellers cheques for free at the AmEx office on Post St Mall. Thomas Cook customers can change their

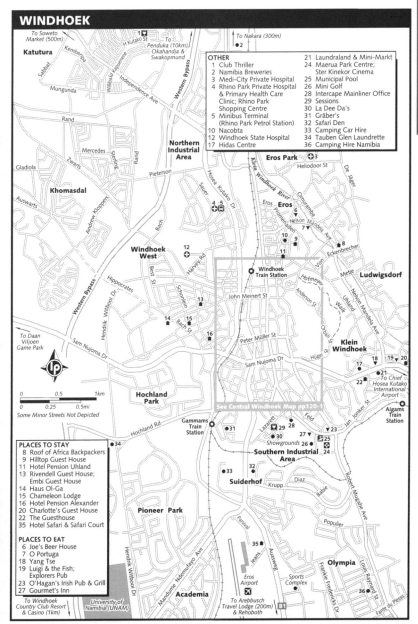

WINDHOEK

OTHER
1 Club Thriller
2 Namibia Breweries
3 Medi-City Private Hospital
4 Rhino Park Private Hospital
   & Primary Health Care
   Clinic; Rhino Park
   Shopping Centre
5 Minibus Terminal
   (Rhino Park Petrol Station)
10 Nacobta
12 Windhoek State Hospital
17 Hidas Centre

21 Laundraland & Mini-Markt
24 Maerua Park Centre;
   Ster Kinekor Cinema
25 Municipal Pool
26 Mini Golf
28 Intercape Mainliner Office
29 Sessions
30 La Dee Da's
31 Gräber's
32 Safari Den
33 Camping Car Hire
34 Tauben Glen Laundrette
36 Camping Hire Namibia

PLACES TO STAY
8 Roof of Africa Backpackers
9 Hilltop Guest House
11 Hotel Pension Uhland
13 Rivendell Guest House;
   Embi Guest House
14 Haus Ol-Ga
15 Chameleon Lodge
16 Hotel Pension Alexander
20 Charlotte's Guest House
22 The Guesthouse
35 Hotel Safari & Safari Court

PLACES TO EAT
6 Joe's Beer House
7 O Portuga
18 Yang Tse
19 Luigi & the Fish;
   Explorers Pub
23 O'Hagan's Irish Pub & Grill
27 Gourmet's Inn

travellers cheques free of charge at Thomas Cook, in the Levinson Arcade.

First National Bank's BOB and other ATM systems handle Visa, MasterCard and home ATM transactions, but like everyone else, they run short of cash at weekends.

Post & Communications The modern main post office on Independence Ave can readily handle overseas post. It also has telephone boxes in the lobby, and next door is the Telecommunications Office, where you can make international calls and send or receive faxes. You could try the expensive Grab-a-Phone (at the main bus terminal). Plenty of supermarkets and shops sell phonecards.

Internet access is available for US$3 per hour at the Internet cafe, opposite the post office; it's open during business hours and charges US$3 per hour. Club Internet, on Bülow St near John Meinert St, charges US$3 per hour and is open from 8am to 8pm Monday to Friday and 9am to 2pm Saturday. Most backpacker hostels also offer Internet and email services.

Travel Agencies Most travel agencies are clustered around the central area. The best is probably Cardboard Box Travel Shop (☎ 256580, fax 256581, e namibia@bigfoot.com, w www.namibian.org), attached to the backpacker hostel of the same name. This place can arrange both budget and upmarket bookings all over the country. Alternatively, try Trip Travel (☎ 236880, fax 225 430), in the Levinson Arcade, or Tourist Junction (☎ 231246, fax 231703, e info .ritztours@galileosa.co.za), 40 Peter Müller St. All of these provide travel information and will book accommodation, tours, car hire and air travel.

Bookshops The Windhoek Book Den (☎ 239976, e wbd@mweb.com.na), just off Post St Mall, is the best place to look for novels, European and African literature, and travel books.

Der Bucherkeller, on Peter Müller St, has novels, literature and travel books in German and English. The best place for books on African topics and politics is New Namibia Books (☎ 235796, e nnb@iafrica .com.na). A limited selection of books, maps and stationery can be found at the CNA Bookshops in the Gustav Voigts and Wernhil Park Centres.

Camping Gear Camping Hire Namibia (☎/fax 252995, e camping@natron.net), at 12 Louis Raymond St, hires camping equipment, but phone first. Dome tents cost from US$3 per day, sleeping bags are US$6, and cool boxes, jerry cans, gas cookers and camping showers are less than US$1 per day each; a full kitchen box is US$3.

Cymot Greensport (☎ 234131), 60 Mandume Ndemufayo Ave, is a good place to buy quality camping and cycling equipment or arrange vehicle outfitting.

Limited camping gear is also available at Le Trip, downstairs in the Wernhil Park Centre, and Trapper's Trading, beside Pie City in Post St Mall.

Safari Den (☎ 231932), 20 Bessemer St, stocks gear for serious 4WD expeditions. You could also try Gräber's (☎ 222732), at Bohr St, Southern Industrial Area.

Cultural Centres French travellers may want to drop by the Franco-Namibian Cultural Centre (☎ 225674, 222122, fax 224927) at 118 Robert Mugabe Ave, PO Box 11622. A main focus here is French-language courses for Namibians hoping to work as French-speaking tour guides or attend university in France. It also offers art courses, presents tasteful art exhibitions and screens French-language films.

For information on religious services, call the Hebrew Association (☎ 226491), the Council of Churches (☎ 218031) or the Islamic Centre (☎ 229672).

Laundry Self-service laundry is available at Tauben Glen (☎ 252115), at Village Square, and Laundraland (☎ 224912), near Mini-Markt in Klein Windhoek. You'll pay around US$2 per load to wash and about US$1.50 to dry. Most of the hotels, guesthouses and hostels also offer laundry services – these wonderful women will normally get your clothes sparkling clean for quite reasonable rates.

Medical Services A recommended physician, who accepts travellers, is Dr Algene Mouton (☎ 229628, fax 229634), in the M & Z Building on John Meinert St. She can also provide medical certificates for hikers.

A good clinic is Rhino Park Primary Health Care Clinic (☎ 230926). Recommended hospitals include the nearby Rhino Park Private Hospital (☎ 225434) and the Catholic Hospital (☎ 237237). The private hospital Medi-City (☎ 222687), on Heliodoor St in Eros, provides excellent care and service, but patients must pay up front.

Those who are short of cash but have time to wait – and nothing seriously wrong with them – can try the Windhoek State Hospital (☎ 303 9111) or the government clinic on Robert Mugabe Ave, near John Meinert St.

The Medi-Sun Pharmacy (☎ 235254) in the Wernhil Park Centre is open 8.30am to 6.30pm Monday to Friday, 8.30am to 1.30pm Saturday and 10am to 1pm Sunday.

Emergency Oddly enough, the all-purpose emergency number – officially known as 'Rescue 911' (probably from the TV program) – is in fact something completely different (see emergency below).

Ambulance/ Fire Brigade	☎ 211111
Crime report (24-hour phone service)	☎ 290 2239, 290 2018 (if your safety is threatened)
Emergency	☎ 222255, or from a cell phone ☎ 112
National police	☎ 10111 (if your safety is threatened)
Police	☎ 228328

Dangers & Annoyances By day, Windhoek is generally safe, but avoid going out alone at night and stay wary of newspaper-sellers, who may shove paper in your face as a distracting ruse. Be especially wary when walking with your luggage – especially on backstreets – as there has been a spate of muggings at knifepoint. Most importantly, don't use bum-bags or carry swanky camera or video totes – they're all prime targets.

The southern areas of Katutura township and the north-western suburbs of Goreangab, Wanaheda and Hakahana, where boredom and unemployment are rife, should be avoided unless you have a local contact and/or a specific reason to go there.

Although the rains have been good for several years, Windhoek often suffers drought conditions, so be frugal with water usage: Take short showers, flush toilets only when essential and don't leave taps running longer than necessary.

Never leave anything of value visible in your vehicle and don't be tempted to park a safari-packed private vehicle anywhere in Windhoek. The safest and most convenient parking is the underground lot beneath the Wernhil Park Centre, where you'll pay less than US$0.30 per hour.

Film & Photography A good range of film is available at the Express Foto Photo Lab, downstairs in the Wernhil Park Centre. It even sells Kodachrome, Sensia and Velvia slide film for relatively good rates.

Private Castles
Uphill from Robert Mugabe Ave are the three Windhoek 'castles' – **Schwerinsburg** (1913) on Schwerinsburg St, **Heinitzburg** (1914) on Heinitzburg St, and **Sanderburg** (1917) on Kastell St. Schwerinsburg and Sanderburg are now private homes (Schwerinsburg is the Italian ambassador's residence). Heinitzburg Castle, which was commissioned in 1914 by Count von Schwerin for his fiancee, Margarethe von Heinitz, now houses a hotel and a fine restaurant (see under Places to Stay – Top End later in this chapter).

The European **cemetery** just down the hill also merits a brief look.

South-West Brewery Building & Namibia Breweries
Formerly the home of Windhoek Lager, the old South-West Brewery building *(Tal St)* was where the company used to produce Namibia's favourite liquid. The building

[Continued on page 117]

WINDHOEK WALKING TOUR

This suggested walking tour begins at the Wernhil Park Centre, where there's a good safe car park, and heads east along Post St Mall.

Post St Mall & Gibeon Meteorite Exhibit The throbbing heart of the Windhoek shopping district is the bizarrely colourful Post St pedestrian mall, which might have been a set in the film *Dick Tracy*. It's lined with vendors selling curios, artwork, clothing and practically anything else that may be of interest to tourists.

In the centre of the mall is a display of meteorites from the Gibeon meteor shower, which deposited upwards of 21 tonnes of mostly ferrous extraterrestrial boulders around Gibeon, in southern Namibia (see the boxed text 'Beware of Falling Rock' in the Southern Namibia chapter).

Gathemann's Complex Along Independence Ave (just north of Post St Mall) are three colonial-era buildings, all designed by architect Willi Sander. The one furthest south was built in 1902 as the **Kronprinz Hotel** *(179 Independence Ave)*. In 1920, Heinrich Gathemann bought it and converted it into a private business, to adjoin **Gathemann House** *(181 Independence Ave)* next door, which he had built in 1913. The furthest north of the three is the **Erkrath Building** *(183 Independence Ave)*, dating from 1910 and originally a private home and business.

Zoo Park Formerly Hendrik Verwoerd Park, Zoo Park, on Independence Ave, served as a zoo until 1962. In the park is a column designed by Namibian sculptor Dörthe Berner, which commemorates a Stone-Age elephant hunt there some 5000 years ago. In 1962, the remains of two elephants and several quartz tools used to cut up the carcasses were unearthed. The fossils and tools were displayed *in situ* under glass, but in 1990 they were transferred to the State Museum.

The rather anachronous Kriegerdenkmal (war memorial), topped by a golden imperial eagle, was dedicated in 1987 to the memory of German Schutztruppe soldiers who died fighting the troops of Nama leader Hendrik Witbooi in the Nama wars of 1893–94.

Ludwig von Estorff House The Ludwig von Estorff House *(Cnr Neser & Peter Müller Sts)* was built in 1891 as a mess for military engineers and was named after the former Schutztruppe commander who lived there between campaigns from 1902 to 1910. It has also served as a residence for senior military officers, a hostel and a trade school, and now houses the **Estorff Reference Library** *(☎ 293 3021)*.

Kaiserliche Realschule Heading south along Robert Mugabe Ave, you'll have a good view over the city, and the road is lined with notable buildings. The first one on the right is the Kaiserliche Realschule *(Cnr Peter Müller St & Robert Mugabe Ave)*, Windhoek's first German primary school, which was built in 1907–08. It opened in 1909 with 74 students, but over the next few years enrolment increased and the building had to be enlarged. The curious turret with wooden slats,

Start

● Post St Mall & Gibeon Meteorite Exhibit

● Gathemann's Complex
● Kronprinz Hotel

● Gathemann House

● Erkrath Building

● Zoo Park

● Ludwig von Estorff House

● Estorff Reference Library
● Kaiserliche Realschule

which was part of the original building, was designed to provide ventilation. The building later housed Windhoek's first German high school, and after WWII an English middle school.

Alte Feste ●
(National
Museum of
Namibia)

Alte Feste (National Museum of Namibia) The whitewashed ramparts of Alte Feste, Windhoek's oldest surviving building, date from 1890–92. It originally served as the headquarters of the Schutztruppe, which arrived in 1889 under the command of Major Curt von François. Minor alterations made in 1901 didn't affect the overall character. Today it houses the historical section of the National Museum of Namibia (☎ 293 4437, Robert Mugabe Ave; admission free; open 9am-6pm Mon-Fri, 3pm-6pm Sat & Sun), which contains memorabilia and photos from the colonial period as well as indigenous artefacts. The highlight is the display on Namibia's independence struggle.

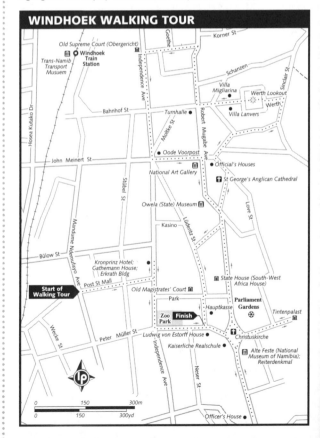

WINDHOEK WALKING TOUR

The railway engines and coaches outside formed one of the country's first narrow-gauge trains. The bronze statue is known as the **Reiterdenkmal** (rider's memorial), and commemorates Schutztruppe soldiers killed during the Herero-Nama wars of 1904–08. It was unveiled in 1912 on Kaiser Wilhelm II's birthday, 27 January.

● Reiterdenkmal

Officers' House A side trip will take you to the Officers' House, built in 1905–06 by the works division of the colonial administration to provide accommodation for senior officers. It's closed to the public, but you can visit the outbuildings, which include a six-horse stable and saddle room now used as garages.

● Officers' House

Christuskirche Windhoek's best-recognised landmark, the German Lutheran Christuskirche, stands on a traffic island at the top of Peter Müller St. This unusual building, which was constructed from local sandstone, was designed by architect Gottlieb Redecker in conflicting neo-Gothic and Art-Nouveau styles. The altarpiece, the *Resurrection of Lazarus*, is a copy of the renowned work by Rubens. The cornerstone was laid in 1907. To view the interior, pick up the key during business hours from the nearby church office on Peter Müller St.

● Christuskirche

Tintenpalast The road east from Alte Feste leads to the Tintenpalast, now the parliament building, which was designed by Gottlieb Redecker and built in 1912–13 as the administrative headquarters for German South-West Africa. The name means 'Ink Palace', in honour of all the ink spent on the typically excessive government paperwork it generated. It has also served as the nerve centre for all subsequent governments, including the present one.

● Tintenpalast

The building is remarkable mainly for its construction from indigenous materials. The surrounding gardens were laid out in the 1930s, and include an olive grove and a bowling green. In front, have a look at Namibia's first post-independence monument, a bronze-cast statue of the Herero chief, Hosea Kutako, who was best known for his vociferous opposition to the South African rule.

Short 45-minute tours are conducted on weekdays, except when the assembly is in session; reserve by phoning ☎ 288 5111.

State House (South-West Africa House) The site of the State House was once graced by the residence of the German colonial governor, but that was razed in 1958 and replaced by the present building, which became the home of the South African administrator and, from 1977, the administrator-general. After independence, it became the official residence of the Namibian president. All that remains of the original building is part of the old garden wall.

● State House (South-West Africa House)

St George's Anglican Cathedral The Anglican Cathedral of St George (*19 Love St*) has the distinction of being the smallest cathedral in Southern Africa.

● St George's Anglican Cathedral

On the grounds of the nearby St George's Diocesan School is the oddly constructed Mansard Building, once a private home but now belonging to the school. It's remarkable for its mansard (double-sloped) roof – the only one in Namibia – which is unsuited to the desert climate.

Officials' Houses On John Meinert St near Love St is a block of six Officials' Houses, which were built for government employees in 1908.

Werth Lookout & Villas The Werth Lookout affords a broad view over the city centre. Just below, near the end of upper Bahnhof St, are **Villa Migliarina** *(Werth St)* and **Villa Lanvers** *(Werth St)*. These private homes, which are closed to the public, were designed in 1907 by Otto Busch. A cylindrical tower on the Lanvers house lends it a castle-like appearance. Both homes are surrounded by lovely gardens, which are visible from the street but closed to the public.

Turnhalle The Turnhalle *(Cnr Bahnhof St & Robert Mugabe Ave)* was designed by Otto Busch and was built in 1909 as a practice hall for the Windhoek Gymnastic Club. In 1975, it was modernised and turned into a conference hall, and on 1 September of that year it was the venue for the first Constitutional Conference on Independence for South-West Africa, which subsequently – and more conveniently – came to be called the Turnhalle Conference. During the 1980s, it hosted several political summits and debates on the way to Namibian independence. It's now the site of meetings of the National Council.

Old Supreme Court (Obergericht) The Old Supreme Court *(Cnr Korner St & Robert Mugabe Ave)* is a gabled brick structure dating from 1908. It was a court from 1920 to 1930, when the legal system was changing from the German to the South African model. Cases were heard according to the most appropriate system for the circumstances.

Oode Voorpost The Oode Voorpost *(Cnr John Meinert & Moltke Sts)* is a classic 1902 building that originally held the colonial surveyors' offices. Early government maps were stored in a fireproof archive. It was restored in 1988 and now houses the Namibia Wildlife Resorts reservations office. The nearby bronze **kudu statue** *(Cnr Independence Ave & John Meinert St)* honours the many kudu that died from the 1896 rinderpest epidemic.

National Art Gallery The National Art Gallery *(☎ 240930, Cnr Robert Mugabe Ave & John Meinert St; admission free; open 8am-5pm Mon-Fri, 8am-1pm Sat)* contains a permanent collection of works reflecting Namibia's historical and natural heritage.

Owela (State) Museum & National Theatre of Namibia The other half of the National Museum of Namibia, about 600m from the main building, is known as Owela (State) Museum *(☎ 293 4358,*

4 Lüderitz St; admission US$1; open 9am-6pm Mon-Fri, 3pm-6pm Sat & Sun). Exhibits focus on Namibia's natural and cultural history.

Practically next door is the National Theatre of Namibia *(☎ 237966, 12 John Meinert St, ⓔ ntn@iafrica.com.na)*, built in 1960 by the Arts Association of Namibia. It's still Windhoek's major cultural centre.

Old Magistrates' Court Take a look at the Old Magistrates' Court *(Near cnr Lüderitz & Park Sts; open 8am-1pm & 2pm-5pm Mon-Fri, 8am-1pm Sat)*, which was built in 1897–98 as quarters for Carl Ludwig, the state architect. However, he never used the house and it was eventually drafted into service as the magistrates' court. The veranda on the south side provided a shady sitting area for people waiting for their cases to be called. The building now houses the Namibia Conservatorium.

● Old Magistrates' Court

Prior to the construction of Christuskirche (see Christuskirche earlier), the 1896 building opposite the Magistrates' Court served as Windhoek's German Lutheran church. It currently houses a nursery school.

Hauptkasse Diagonally opposite Christuskirche on Lüderitz St, Hauptkasse was built in 1898–99 and was the revenue office of the German colonial administration. It was extended in 1906 and 1909, and later used as a school hostel. It now houses the Ministry of Agriculture.

● Hauptkasse

Finish

Train Station & Trans-Namib Transport Museum
Windhoek's beautiful old Cape Dutch–style train station on Bahnhof St dates from 1912 and was expanded in 1929 by the South African administration. Across the driveway from the entrance is the German steam locomotive *Poor Old Joe*, which was shipped to Swakopmund in 1899 and reassembled for the run to Windhoek.

Upstairs is the small but worthwhile Trans-Namib Transport Museum *(☎ 298 2186; admission US$0.50; open 9am-noon & 2pm-4pm Mon-Fri)* outlining Namibian transport history, particularly that of the railway.

The **Owambo Campaign Memorial** at the entry to the station parking area was erected in 1919 to commemorate the 1917 British and South African campaign against the resistant chief Mandume, of the Kwanyama Owambo. When he ran out of firepower, the chief committed suicide rather than surrender.

Hofmeyer Walk
The Hofmeyer Walk walking track through Klein Windhoek Valley starts from either Sinclair or Uhland St and heads south through the bushland to finish at the point where Orban St becomes Anderson St. The walk takes about an hour at a leisurely pace and affords panoramic views over the city and a close-up look at the aloes *(Aloe littoralis)* that characterise the hillside vegetation. These cactus-like plants are at their best in winter, when their bright red flowers attract tiny sunbirds, mousebirds and bulbuls.

Hikers have recently been robbed along this route, so don't go alone, and avoid carrying valuables.

[Continued from page 111]

now houses the Warehouse Theatre (see Entertainment later in this chapter), which is now a well-known night spot, and the Namibia Crafts Centre (see Shopping later in this chapter).

The brewing operation has changed its name to Namibia Breweries *(☎ 320 4999)* and moved to the Northern Industrial Area, off Okahandja road. Worthwhile tours of the modern brewery are on Monday, Tuesday, Wednesday and Thursday by appointment.

Katutura

Unlike its South African counterparts, the township of Katutura is relatively safe by day if you stick to the northern areas and/or find a local who can act as a guide. An especially interesting spot is the informal Soweto Market, where traders sell just about anything imaginable.

A shared taxi from the Wernhil Park Centre to Katutura costs US$0.80 (N$5) per person.

Namibia Community Based Tourism Association (Nacobta; ☎ 250558) sponsors township tours with ***Katutura Face-to-Face Tours** (☎ 265446)*, but it still has quite a few bugs to work out, so don't get too excited until the operators actually turn up.

Activities

Windhoek has fine sporting facilities, including a municipal pool and minigolf course near the corner of Jan Jonker and Centaurus Sts. There's also an in-line skating rink here. Admission is US$1; it's open 7pm to 9pm Tuesday, 2pm to 7pm Friday and 2pm to 6pm Saturday. Equipment is available for hire.

Close by, the Maerua Park Centre has a popular Health and Racquet club that's open for day visits.

Major sporting events, including rugby, football, netball and track-and-field are held at Independence Stadium off the B1, about 2km south of town. See local papers for event announcements.

Katutura – A Permanent Place?

In 1912, during the days of the South African mandate – and apartheid – the Windhoek town council set aside two 'locations', which were open to settlement by black Africans who were working in the city: the Main Location, which was west of the centre, and Klein Windhoek, to the east. The following year, people were forcibly relocated to these areas, which effectively became communal areas of haphazard settlement. In the early 1930s, however, streets were laid out in the Main Location and the area was divided into regions set aside for each ethnic group. Each subdivision within these regions was referred to by the name of its assigned ethnic group (eg, Herero, Nama, Owambo, Damara, or whatever...), followed by a soulless numerical reference.

In the 1950s, the Windhoek municipal council – with encouragement from the South African government (which regarded Namibia as a province of South Africa) – decided to 'take back' Klein Windhoek and consolidate all 'location' residents into a single settlement north-west of the main city. However, there was strong opposition to the move, and in early December 1959, a group of Herero women launched a protest march and boycott against the city government. On 10 December, unrest escalated into a confrontation with the police, resulting in 11 deaths and 44 serious injuries. Frightened, the roughly 4000 residents of the Main Location submitted and moved to the new settlement, which was ultimately named 'Katutura', which is Herero for 'We Have No Permanent Place' but it can also be translated as 'The Place We Do Not Want To Settle'.

Today, in independent Namibia, Katutura is a vibrant Windhoek suburb – Namibia's Soweto – where poverty and affluence brush elbows. Sadly, Katutura's once-lovely independence murals along Independence Ave have been inexplicably removed, but the town council has extended municipal water, power and telephone services to most areas of Katutura and has also established the colourful and perpetually busy Soweto Market.

Organised Tours

Gourmet Tours (☎/fax 231281, 081-128 0338, PO Box 2148) These folks offer 3½-hour city tours, visiting most of the main central sites, passing through Katutura, and winding up for coffee at Heinitzburg Castle, for US$25. They also offer half-day trips to Düsternbrook (US$42; see under North of the City in the Around Windhoek section later in this chapter), Daan Viljoen Game Park (US$28), Auas Game Lodge (US$42) and Okapuka Game Ranch (US$39).

See under Katutura earlier for details on tours to Katutura township, and also under Organised Tours in the Getting Around chapter for details of tour operators and tours in Namibia.

Special Events

Windhoek's first big annual bash is the **Mbapira/Enjando Street Festival**, which is held in March around the city centre. It features colourful gatherings of dancers, musicians and people in ethnic dress. For information, contact the Windhoek Information & Publicity Office. **Independence Day** on 21 March is also usually celebrated in grand style, with a parade and sports events.

True to its partially Teutonic background, Windhoek stages an **Oktoberfest** towards the end of October, which beer lovers should not miss. The German-style **Windhoek Karnival (WIKA)** takes place in late April and features a week of events and balls. In late September/early October, the city holds the **Windhoek Agricultural, Commercial and Industrial Show**, on the showgrounds near the corner of Jan Jonker Ave and Centaurus St.

Places to Stay – Budget

Camping For other camping options see Daan Viljoen Game Park in the Around Windhoek section later in this chapter.

Arebbusch Travel Lodge (☎ 252255, fax 251670, e atl@iwwn.com.na, Auasweg, PO Box 554, Windhoek) Camping US$1 per car plus US$6.25 per person in a tent, caravan sites US$10 plus US$6.25 per person, double rooms US$50, 2-/5-bed chalets with bathroom US$46/60. This place on the road south is the nearest camping ground to town. Amenities include a bar, shop, laundrette, swimming pool and trampoline. Taxis from the centre cost around US$3.

Hostels There is a good range of hostels on offer for the budget-conscious traveller.

Cardboard Box Backpackers (☎ 228 994, fax 245587, e cardboardbox@big foot.com, W www.namibian.org, 15 Johann Albrecht St, PO Box 5142, Windhoek West) Camping US$3, dorm beds US$4.50-5.50, double campervan US$10, double rooms US$15 (pre-booking is essential for doubles). All rates include use of the cooking facilities and swimming pool. This lively, popular and long-established choice is just a 15-minute walk from the centre. There's a notice board for lifts and it's a great place to find groups for car hire and safaris; the on-site Cardboard Box Travel Shop (see Travel Agencies earlier in this chapter) can take care of all your travel arrangements. The owners and staff organise braais (barbecues), *potjies* (stew made in a three-legged iron pot over an open fire), pool parties (featuring both kinds of pool) and other events; there's also a great bar. Phone, fax, Internet and email services (US$3 per hour) are available.

Chameleon City Backpackers (☎/fax 244347, e info@chameleon.com.na, W www .chameleonbackpackers.com, 5 Voight St, PO Box 6107) Dorm beds US$5.50, permanent garden tents US$13, doubles/triples US$16/27. All rates include a self-catering breakfast and pick-up from Grab-a-Phone bus terminal. This appealing place creates a friendly, welcoming atmosphere and guests have access to the swimming pool, kitchen, video library and bar. Phone, fax, email and Internet services are also available.

Roof of Africa Backpackers (☎ 254708, 081-124 4930, fax 248048, e roofofaf @mweb.com.na, 124 Nelson Mandela Ave, PO Box 11745, Klein Windhoek) Camping US$3, dorm beds US$5.50, double tents US$16, doubles US$19-24. This quiet place makes a pleasant haven away from the centre, but it's still within a 30-minute walk north-east of the centre. Highlights include the outdoor bar, with its Hansa draught beer, and the frog pond, which is hopping with activity. Email and Internet services are available for US$3 per hour and car hire costs US$27 per day. A pick-up service from the Grab-a-Phone bus terminal costs US$0.80 for pre-booked guests.

Tramper's Haven (☎/fax 223669, 78 Bülow St, PO Box 20222) Dorm beds US$7.50, singles/doubles US$16/20. This very comfortable and ultra-clean Christian-oriented backpacker hostel provides a quiet setting within a 15-minute walk of the city centre. Sparkling kitchen facilities are available, as well as plenty of showers. There's no bar but you can buy soft drinks (sodas) and light beer; smoking cigarettes and drinking 'adult beverages' are allowed in the garden, but only married couples may use the doubles. Internet and email access is available next door at Club Internet.

Puccini House Backpackers (☎/fax 236355, e puccinis@ mweb.com.na, 4 Puccini St, PO Box 31396) Camping US$3.50, 4-/7-bed dorms US$6/5.50, singles/doubles US$10/ 16.50. Rates include bedding, a continental breakfast and pick-up from the Grab-a-Phone bus terminal. This is the nearest backpacker place to the city centre – it's a three-minute walk from the Wernhil Park Centre – but the neighbourhood, especially the Mozart St bridge, requires some vigilance. Phone for a pick-up rather than walking with all your luggage. The sauna costs US$3 per session.

Guesthouses The following options provide a comfortable alternative to the hostels.

Rivendell Guesthouse (☎ 250006, fax 250010, e rivendell@toothfairy.com, w www .rivendell-namibia.com, 40 Beethoven St, PO Box 5142) Doubles with shared bathroom US$16, small/large doubles with private bathroom US$20/24. This friendly, quiet and comfortable option may well be the best value for money in Windhoek. Rates include use of the inviting pool and while you're there, don't miss the cute wall paintings on the corner of Beethoven and Simpson Sts. You can get a continental breakfast here for US$2.

Embi Guest House (☎ 255556, fax 252128, e brianhj@iafrica.com.na, w www .maries.com.na, 176 Diaz St, PO Box 6406, Ausspannplatz) Singles/doubles B&B US$14/ 22. With four comfortable rooms, this is a quiet and amenable place to relax and enjoy Windhoek. Free town transfers are available in the morning and other amenities include braai facilities, swimming pool, off-road parking and guest lounge with fax, email and Internet access.

Chameleon Lodge (☎/fax 247668, e info@ chameleon.com.na, 22 Wagner St) Dorm beds US$7, doubles B&B without/with bathroom US$16/20. This new lodge – the former Chameleon Backpackers – occupies a quiet site in Windhoek West and is still home to the legendary dog Crash and a couple of friendly meerkats. Free pick-up is available from the Grab-a-Phone bus terminal and guests have access to the pool, kitchen, bar and video library, as well as email and Internet facilities.

The Guesthouse (☎ 255458, 29 Stein St, Klein Windhoek) Singles/doubles B&B US$23/31. This industrial-looking place provides basic accommodation west of the centre.

Haus Ol-Ga (☎ 235853, 91 Bach St, Windhoek West) Singles/doubles B&B US$20/30. The name of this German-oriented place is derived from the owners' names: Gesa Oldach and Erno Gauerke. It enjoys a nice, quiet garden atmosphere in Windhoek West. Add 10% to the cost if you are only staying one night.

Places to Stay – Mid-Range

Accommodation in this price bracket is also available at farms and lodges north of Windhoek (see North of the City in the Around Windhoek section).

Guesthouses All of the following have rooms with private facilities.

Hotel Pension Handke (☎ 234904, fax 225660, e pensionhandke@iafrica.com .na, 3 Rossini St, PO Box 20881) Singles/doubles B&B US$34/47, family rooms US$20 per person. This homely, family-oriented place offers good value within just a short walk of the city centre.

WINDHOEK

CENTRAL WINDHOEK

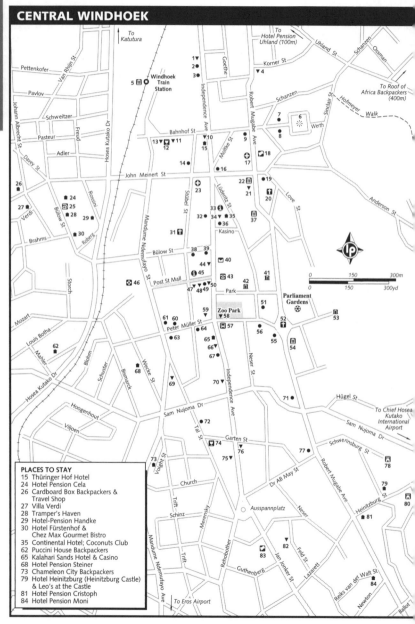

To
Katutura

Pettenkofer

Pavlov

Schweitzer

Pasteur

Adler

Johann Albrecht St

Davey St

Verdi

Brahms

Mozart

Louis Botha

Mahler

Hoogenhout

Viljoen

Van Rhijn St

Hosea Kutako Dr

Freud

Rossini

Robert

Bülow St

Mandume Ndemufayo St

Stübel St

Lüderitz St

Molke St

Robert Mugabe Ave

Schanzen

Uhland St

Sinclair

Hofmeyer

Schanzen

Osman

Love St

Anderson St

Storch

Blühm

Schuster

Bismarck

Wecke St

Neser St

Independence Ave

Tal St

Sam Nujoma Dr

Garten St

Voight St

Church

Trift

Schinz

Merensky

Rehobother

Mandume Ndemufayo Ave

To Eros Airport

Guthenberg

Trift

Ausspannplatz

Dr AB May St

Jan Jonker St

Feld St

Neser

Lazarett

Robert Mugabe Ave

Schwerinsburg St

Sam Nujoma Dr

Heinitzburg St

Reiks van der Walt St

Newton

Ballot St

To
Hotel Pension
Uhland (100m)

Korner St

Werth

Kasino

Bahnhof St

John Meinert St

Bülow St

Post St Mall

Peter Müller St

Park

Zoo Park

Parliament
Gardens

Hügel St

To Chief Hosea
Kutako
International
Airport

To Roof of
Africa Backpackers
(400m)

Walk

Windhoek
Train
Station

5

1▼
2●
3●

▼4

7
6
8

9

▼10
15

13▼ ▼11
12

14●

●16

17

18

22 ●19
▼
21

20

23

33 ●
32● 34▼ ▲35
●36
37

31

38 39
44▼
45
46
47 48 49 50

40

43

42

41

51

59
▼58
57

60
61
●63

64

65
66▼
67●

62

68

69

70▼

71●

52
53

56

55

54

72

74
▼
76

73
75▼

77●

78

79

80

81

82
83

84

0   150   300m
0   150   300yd

PLACES TO STAY
15 Thüringer Hof Hotel
24 Hotel Pension Cela
26 Cardboard Box Backpackers &
    Travel Shop
27 Villa Verdi
28 Tramper's Haven
29 Hotel-Pension Handke
30 Hotel Fürstenhof &
    Chez Max Gourmet Bistro
35 Continental Hotel; Coconuts Club
62 Puccini House Backpackers
65 Kalahari Sands Hotel & Casino
68 Hotel Pension Steiner
73 Chameleon City Backpackers
79 Hotel Heinitzburg (Heinitzburg Castle)
    & Leo's at the Castle
81 Hotel Pension Cristoph
84 Hotel Pension Moni

24
25
26
27
28
29
30

Hotel Pension Moni (☎ 228350, fax 227124, 🇪 pensionmoni@hgud.de, 7 Rieks van der Walt St, PO Box 2805) Singles/doubles B&B US$42.50/60. The bright and clean rooms at this recommended motel-style place south-east of the centre include phone, TV and use of the swimming pool. English and German are spoken.

Hotel Pension Alexander (☎/fax 240775, 🇪 hotelale@iafrica.con.na, 10 Beethoven St, PO Box 251121, Windhoek West) Singles/doubles B&B US$32/44. This personable German-run guesthouse offers a quiet suburban site just a 15-minute walk west from the city centre.

Hotel Pension Steiner (☎ 222898, fax 224234, 🇪 steiner@iafrica.com.na, 🇼 www.steiner.com.na, 11 Wecke St, PO Box 20481) Singles/doubles B&B US$36/56. This comfortable and spotless place has been recently renovated. Guests have access to the swimming pool, braai and lounge. Light lunches are available by pre-booking.

Hotel Pension Uhland (☎ 229859, fax 229108, 🇪 uhland@mweb.com.na, 147 Uhland St, PO Box 96284) Singles/doubles/triples B&B US$33/44/60. This friendly guesthouse is just a 10-minute walk north of the centre, and offers a swimming pool and secure parking. All rooms have private bathroom, TV, radio, phone and a minibar.

Hotel Pension Cristoph (☎ 240777, 081-129 6828, fax 248560, 🇪 cristoph@mweb.com.na, 33 Heinitzburg St, PO Box 6116, Ausspannplatz) Singles/doubles/triples US$35/48/62. At the foot of Windhoek's eastern hills, this pleasant German-oriented lodge offers a pool and satellite TV. The dining area decor is appealing.

Charlotte's Guest House (☎/fax 228846, 2A John Ludwig St, PO Box 4234, Klein Windhoek) Singles/doubles US$33/47. Charlotte provides pleasant rooms, tranquillity and healthy breakfasts. It's a bit out of the centre, but handy to the airport road.

Hotels All of the following rates include breakfast.

Thüringer Hof Hotel (☎ 226031, fax 232981, 🇪 thurhof@mweb.com.na, Independence Ave, PO Box 112) Singles/doubles

US$43/65, suites US$74/82. This business travellers hotel is at the upper end of mid-range in Windhoek; all rooms have air-con and DSTV satellite TV. It's well known for its shady and amenable beer garden.

Continental Hotel (☎ 237293, fax 231539, **e** contihtl@mweb.com.na, 5 Continental Arcade, Independence Ave, PO Box 977) Singles US$42-48, doubles US$54-60. This centrally located hotel lies on Windhoek's main street, just downhill from the post office. Rooms have DSTV and there's an attached bar, disco (see Coconuts Club under Entertainment later), sauna and workout room.

Hotel Safari & Safari Court (☎ 240240, fax 235652, **e** safari@safarihotel.com.na, **W** www.safarihotel.com.na, Aviation Rd, Eros Airport, PO Box 3900) Budget singles/doubles US$42/50, others US$51/60. These adjoining hotels near Eros Airport share leafy gardens, a shady beer garden, a large pool and a golf course next door.

Places to Stay – Top End
Guesthouses The following establishments offer some of the Windhoek's most comfortable accommodation.

Villa Verdi (☎ 221994, fax 222574, **e** villav@mweb.com.na, 4 Verdi St, PO Box 6784) Singles/doubles US$55/91. This unique Mediterranean-African hybrid also has a pool, bar and dining room, and the ethnically decorated rooms feature private bathrooms, phone and satellite TV. Fax and email services are available to guests.

Hotel Heinitzburg (☎ 249597, fax 249598, **e** heinitz@mweb.con.na, 22 Heinitzburg St, PO Box 458) Singles/doubles from US$86/127. This is Windhoek's royal B&B option at Heinitzburg Castle, and probably the best and most personable upmarket place in town. The comfortable rooms have TV and air-con, and the dining room offers excellent gourmet cuisine and an extensive wine dungeon.

Hilltop Guest House (☎ 249116, fax 247818, **e** hilltop@iafrica.com.na, 12 Lessing St, PO Box 4327) Singles/doubles US$67/100. This popular guesthouse, which is widely used by safari companies, enjoys

a nice hilltop view over the Klein Windhoek Valley. It features a pool and sun deck.

Hotels These places offer more luxury for those who can flash the cash.

Hotel Fürstenhof (☎ 237380, fax 228 751, **e** fuerst@iafrica.com.na, Bülow St) Singles/doubles in old wing US$53/69, in new wing US$67/91. All rates include breakfast, air-con and cable TV. This prominent hotel may seem large and impersonal, but it's just a 10-minute walk from the centre and offers good value for money. The dining room, which features seafood, French and German cuisine, is one of Windhoek's finest restaurants (see Chez Max Gourmet Bistro under Places to Eat later).

Kalahari Sands Hotel & Casino (☎ 222 300, fax 222260, Gustav Voigts Centre, 129 Independence Ave, PO Box 2254) Singles/doubles from US$87/97. Rates include a full English breakfast. This high-rise hotel in the heart of the city is a solid choice with international standards. All of the 187 rooms have DSTV, a phone, a minibar and coffee machines, but note that standards vary from room to room. The casino offers another angle and guests may also use the gym, sauna and rooftop pool.

Windhoek Country Club Resort & Casino (☎ 205 5911, fax 252797, **e** hr ccr@stocks.com.na, **W** www.legacyhotels .co.za, Western Bypass, PO Box 30777, Windhoek) Singles/doubles US$113/135, weekend B&B specials US$57/73. Constructed specifically for the 1995 Miss Universe pageant (Miss Namibia, Michelle McLean, who now has a street named for her, had won the pageant the previous year), this place offers a taste of Las Vegas in Windhoek. And yes, the fountains and green lawns seem as incongruous here as they do in the Nevada deserts.

Places to Eat
Fast Food & Takeaways For a bite to eat on the cheap or on the run try the following.

Steenbras (☎ 231445, Bahnhof St) Takeaway snacks & sit-down lunches US$1-3. This place, just a block off Independence Ave, does some of Windhoek's best takeaways, including memorable fish, chicken burgers and spicy chips.

Senato's (☎ 231792, Bahnhof St) Takeaways US$1-3. Senato's provides tempting competition to its next-door neighbour, Steenbras, with its burgers and other hot and cold sandwiches, as well as sausages, curry and rice and local dishes.

King Pies (☎ 248978, Levinson Arcade & 46 Independence Ave) Pies US$0.75-1. These two outlets serve up a variety of filled meat and vegetable pies, and offer super lunch deals: a large pie and a large soft drink (soda) for US$1.

Pie City (Post St Mall) Pies US$0.50-1. This place bakes up interesting pie combinations for people on the run, including curry and vegetarian choices. It also offers a US$1 lunch special.

Nando's (☎ 231792, 43 Bahnhof St, Cnr Independence Ave) Chicken combinations US$1-5, salads US$3. Open 9am-9pm daily. Always popular, Nando's serves up superb Portuguese-style peri-peri chicken, spicy rice, chips and other goodies. You can also buy bottles of Nando's delicious sauces, which come in extra hot, hot, medium and mild (spicy enough for most people!).

For something more familiar, you can fall back on the two *KFC* outlets *(Independence Ave & 67 Tal St).*

Cafes The following serve up a range of light and casual meals.

Le Bistro (☎ 228742, Post St Mall) Continental/English breakfasts US$2.50/3, basic lunches US$3-5. Open 7am-midnight Tues-Sun, breakfast available 7am-11am. This place is known for its breakfasts, pizzas, salads and kebabs. It's a bit of a fishbowl inside, but you can also opt for the sunny sidewalk seating right on Windhoek's most animated corner.

Central Café (☎ 222659, Levinson Arcade) Full breakfast US$4, lunch or dinner US$3-5. Open for lunch only Mon, for lunch & dinner Tues-Sat, 8am-midnight Sun. This pleasantly laid-back place is great for meals or just coffee. Lunch times get busy, but there's a takeaway window selling filled *brötchen* (bread rolls) and other fast snacks.

Café Schneider (☎ 226304, Levinson Arcade) Lunch or dinner US$3-5. This place is a less-busy alternative to Central Café.

Tim Sum (☎ 232312, Wernhil Park Centre) Sandwiches & mains US$2-4. Open lunch Mon-Sat. A recommended quick option, this friendly restaurant and coffee shop specialises in appealing vegetarian Chinese dishes, sandwiches, soup, salads and other healthy fare.

Grass Roots Café (☎ 243344) Light meals US$2.50-3. Open noon-8pm Tues-Sun. Between the National Theatre and the National Art Gallery, this place has amazing decor featuring papier-mâché, bottles, tins and razor wire. It serves light set lunches and dinners, as well as drinks and sweets, and you may even catch a live performance at the adjoining theatre.

Wecke & Voigts Coffee Bar (Wecke & Voigts Department Store, Gustav Voigts Centre) This is a good place for a lunchtime snack of *Wiener schnitzel* (crumbed fried veal) or brötchen.

Café Zoo (Zoo Park) Coffee & cake US$0.50-2. Open 8am-6pm daily. This new cafe provides a nice leafy afternoon break.

In's Wiener Coffee Shop (☎ 231082, Wernhil Park Centre) Coffee US$1, cake or pie US$1.50-2, lunch US$4.50. Open 11am-5pm Mon-Fri. Shoppers can stop by for nice hot coffee, sweet treats and light meals. However, it's normally quite busy and the service reflects the harried atmosphere.

Restaurants Namibia's multicultural capital provides a relatively wide range of culinary choices.

Zum Wirt (☎ 170179, 43 Independence Ave) Lunches US$3-6. Open daily. This restaurant and beer garden serves up both European and local standards.

Grand Canyon Spur (☎ 231003, 251 Independence Ave) Steaks, chicken, pork, fish & other mains US$4-5, salad bar US$2. Open 8am-10.30pm daily. Don't miss the salad bar and the renowned chocolate brownies, which are the highlights of this widespread South African chain. The varied menu features steak and such other standards as chicken, fish and attempts at

Mexican dishes. The balcony seating affords a shaded view over Independence Ave.

O'Hagan's Irish Pub & Grill (☎ *234677, Cnr Jan Jonker St & Robert Mugabe Ave*) Full dinner US$6-10. Open noon-11pm daily. This chain pub near Maerua Park Centre, south-east of the centre, features a range of popular international dishes, but specialises in steak and is best known for its well-attended sports bar.

Sardinia's (☎ *225600, 39 Independence Ave*) Pizza & pasta dishes US$3.50-5. Open lunch & dinner Wed-Mon. This rather loud and boisterous place is good for pizza and standard Italian fare, as well as great coffee and gelato.

Gathemann's (☎ *223853, 179 Independence Ave*) Lunch US$5-8, dinner US$7-10, US$15-20 with wine & a starter. Open noon-2pm & 6pm-late daily. This very nice lunch and dinner spot occupies a prominent colonial building overlooking Independence Ave. In the morning and afternoon, it does rich European-style gateaux and pastries, and downstairs, there's a good sandwich takeaway featuring brötchen. The focus is on German and other European food; the snails in garlic butter is a recommended starter.

Chez Max Gourmet Bistro (☎ *237380, Hotel Fürstenhof, Bülow St*) Starters US$3.50-8, soups US$3-4, mains US$10-15, desserts US$5. Open for lunch Mon-Fri, for dinner daily. Chef Jürgen Raith of Hotel Fürstenhof makes this one of Windhoek's finest dining spots. The French and German specialities include a wonderful range of beef, pork and fresh fish and seafood dishes, as well as imaginatively prepared springbok, oryx and ostrich.

Leo's at the Castle (☎ *249597, 22 Heinitzburg St*) Mains US$7-10. Open 7pm-10pm daily. A snack menu is available on the terrace here every afternoon. This slightly elegant spot, housed in Heinitzburg Castle (see Hotel Heinitzburg under Places to Stay – Top End earlier) overlooking Windhoek, specialises in gourmet cuisine and a large cellar of fine wines. It's perfect for a nice, romantic splash-out.

Homestead (☎ *221958, 53 Feld St, Near Ausspannplatz*) Starters US$1-4, salads US$5-8, mains US$8-12. Open for dinner Mon-Sat. Bookings are advised for this, Windhoek's most recommended restaurant. The menu features a range of starters, salads (including the renowned Homestead salad), pasta, vegetarian dishes, a variety of fresh fish, beef and chicken dishes, oryx, crocodile, fondues, and a hunters' grill featuring zebra. The herbs and vegetables come straight from the restaurant's own garden and the food is all served up in a pleasant outdoor setting. There's also an extensive selection of wines, liqueurs and cigars.

O Portuga (☎ *272900, 151 Nelson Mandela Ave*) Starters US$3-4, mains US$6-10. Open for dinner daily. This fully licensed restaurant is the best place for genuine Portuguese and Angolan dishes, including plenty of seafood options. It also offers a good selection of wines.

Joe's Beer House (☎ *254849, Green Market Square, 160 Nelson Mandela Ave*) Mains US$5-7. Open for dinner daily. Joe's is an extremely popular spot north of the centre for a large, meat-oriented evening meal in a crowded and very hectic atmosphere – and prolonged drinking thereafter. You need to reserve a table here.

China Grand Restaurant (☎ *225751, Kenya House, 68 Robert Mugabe Ave*) Mains US$4-8. Open 6pm-midnight daily. This is Windhoek's best Chinese option.

Yang Tse (☎ *234779, /Ae//Gams Shopping Centre, 106 Sam Nujoma Dr*) Mains US$3-5. This long-standing place in Klein Windhoek is a fairly good choice if you crave Chinese cuisine.

Windhoek Country Club Resort & Casino (☎ *205 5911, Western Bypass*) At this place, south of the centre, you can choose between two restaurants: ***Kokerboom***, which is a buffet option on the main floor, and ***Silas***, upstairs, which does varied Asian cuisine, including Chinese and Thai. Both are relatively upmarket.

La Dolce Vita (☎ *230141, Post St Mall*) Mains US$4-8. Open 8am-late daily. The fully licensed La Dolce Vita serves champagne breakfasts and top-quality Italian meals and pizza, but the portions and service are variable. You will find it at the

Kaiserkrone, which is an early hotel and social centre dating back to 1927.

Luigi & the Fish (☎ 256399, 320 Sam Nujoma Dr, Klein Windhoek) Starters US$2.50-4, fish dishes US$3-7.50, seafood US$6-10, vegetarian, beef or chicken dishes US$4-9. Open noon-3pm & 6pm-late daily. This popular and highly recommended place features reasonably priced seafood (fish, shellfish, seafood paella, calamari etc) as well as steaks, game, pasta, chicken, cajun dishes and vegetarian cuisine. The attached *Explorers Pub* is known for its extensive list of shooters, and the deck wobbles even before you've had your first drink. Both the restaurant and bar offer great outdoor seating.

La Marmite (☎ 248022, Independence Ave) Mains US$7-10. Open 6pm-10pm daily. Here you can sample wonderful North and West African cuisine, from Algerian, Senegalese, Ivoirian, Malagasy, Cameroonian and Nigerian dishes. This excellent restaurant deserves its growing popularity. Bookings are advisable.

Epata Africa (☎ 247178, Alte Feste, Robert Mugabe Ave) Mains US$4-10. Open breakfast, lunch & dinner daily. If you're open to new experiences and have time to accommodate the typically slow service, this place is worth a try. It conjures up specialities from Tunisia, Nigeria, Kenya, Ethiopia, Cameroon, Angola (the *camarão de coco*, shrimp with coconut, is excellent), Ghana (lots of palm oil!), and of course Namibia. Try the *omaungu* (mopane worms), which you can talk about for years to come.

Gourmet's Inn (☎ 232360, 195 Jan Jonker St) Mains US$7-15. Despite the fact that it boasts a minigolf course, this is a standard haunt of ambassadors, government ministers, dignitaries, VIPs and general power trippers. Reservations are essential and not easy to get.

Deliveries *Dial-a-Meal (☎ 220111)* Delivery charges US$1.50-2.50. If you're feeling lazy, Windhoek's remarkable Dial-a-Meal service delivers orders from a range of local restaurants for a nominal charge. Among the choices are Nando's, King Pies, Grand

Canyon Spur, O'Hagan's Irish Pub & Grill and even the Pioneerspark Drankwinkel.

Self-Catering Windhoek is a grocery paradise for self-caterers. The big names are *Pick & Pay* at the Wernhil Park Centre, the cheap and cheerful *Checkers* at Gustav Voigts Centre, and the attached *Wecke & Voigts*. The last one is a small, expensive department store that specialises in things Germanic and has an excellent food section in the basement, with a wide selection of local smoked meats and biltong (dried meat). It also makes good cakes, breads (especially Brötchen) and sandwiches.

The cheapest supermarket is the always crowded *Shoprite* on lower Independence Ave. The *Mini-Markt* in Klein Windhoek is larger than it sounds and is open from 7am to midnight seven days a week. The well-stocked *Hidas* supermarket in Klein Windhoek is the best place for foreign and ethnic ingredients. On weekdays, a small *market* on Mandume Ndemufayo Ave sells fruit and vegetables.

Entertainment
Pubs, Discos & Clubs Windhoek offers a good choice of lively night-time distractions.

Joe's Beer House (☎ 254849, Green Market Square, 160 Nelson Mandela Ave) is one of the liveliest pubs around, with a large beer garden, good food and service. Bookings are essential.

Explorers Pub (☎ 256399, 320 Sam Nujoma Dr) For a night of music, socialising, drinking and meeting trendy middle-class Namibians in the warm night air, go upstairs at Luigi & the Fish restaurant.

O'Hagan's Irish Pub & Grill (☎ 234677, Cnr Jan Jonker St & Robert Mugabe Ave) This chain Irish pub near the Maerua Park Centre offers mainstream music and continuous sports on a big-screen TV.

Club Thriller (Samuel Shikongo St, Katutura) Admission US$2.50. Once you're past the weapons search at the door, the music is Western and African and the atmosphere upbeat and relatively secure. Most people are there to have fun, and hassles are rare, but foreigners may have to fend off strangers

Gem Consciousness

The owner of House of Gems, Sid Pieters, is Namibia's foremost gem expert. In 1974, along the Namib coast, Pieters uncovered 45 crystals of jeremejevite, a sea-blue tourmaline containing boron – the rarest gem on earth. His discovery was only the second ever; the first was in Siberia in the mid-19th century. Another of his finds was the marvellously streaky *crocidolite pietersite* (named for Pieters himself), from near Outjo in North Central Namibia. Pietersite, a beautiful form of jasper shot through with asbestos fibres, is certainly one of the world's most beautiful and unusual minerals, and some believe that it has special energy- and consciousness-promoting qualities. Other New Age practitioners maintain that it holds the 'keys to the kingdom of heaven'; stare at it long enough and perhaps you'll agree.

asking for beer and cash. Peripherals include a snack bar, braais and pool tables. Don't carry valuables or wear jewellery and avoid walking around Katutura at night. Always take a taxi (US$0.70 from town).

Palm Groove (☎ 081-247 1651, *Independence Ave*) Open 5pm-2am Mon & Thur, 11pm-2am Tues, Wed & Fri, 1pm-2am Sat & Sun. This friendly and animated local drinking and dancing spot features African and techno-beat music. Meat-based African snacks and outdoor seating are available.

Coconuts Club (☎ 237293, *Continental Hotel, Independence Ave*) Admission US$1.50. Open 3pm-midnight Mon-Wed, 7pm-3am Thur-Sat. This bar and disco features mainly pop, African and rap music. There's a cool spot outside with pool tables and fruit machines.

Zum Wirt (☎ 234503, *101 Independence Ave*) Admission US$1.50 for live music Wed, Fri & Sat. Open 11am-2am daily. This German-style beer garden attracts a mixed crowd with a friendly bar for drinking and socialising and a separate area for dancing and live performances.

La Dee Da's (☎ 081-243 4432, *Ferry St near Patterson, Southern Industrial Area*)

Admission US$2/3 before/after midnight. Open 10.30pm-4am Thur-Sat and the night before a public holiday. This extremely popular mixed club, which is especially frequented by coloured Namibians, is home to Namibia's largest national flag (it's enormous!). Here you can dance to *kizomba* (a popular Angolan style of music), hip-hop, rave, traditional African, rock and commercial pop accompanied by all sorts of special effects. This mixed venue is also a good place to connect with the more sophisticated players in Windhoek's same-sex community.

Sessions (☎ 234849, *Lazarett St*) This three-in-one club offers several atmospheres, and is most popular with European-Namibians. *Sessions Rock & Blues bar* has a US$1.50 cover charge and is open for dancing from 9pm to 5am on Wednesday, Friday and Saturday. *Equinoxx* is a dance club with louder, heavier music and a cover charge of US$3 when there's live music. It's open from 10pm to 6am Friday and Saturday. *Corner Pocket Lounge*, open from 6pm to 1am Monday to Saturday, features billiards, burgers and beer.

Kudissanga (*Bahnhof St*) Admission US$3. Open 10.30pm-6am Wed, Fri & Sat and the night before public holidays. At this friendly club, which is especially popular with Angolan-Namibians, you'll dance to powerful kizomba music, as well as other African rhythms.

An interesting nightspot for those wishing to check out the local same-sex scene is *After Dark* (*Mercedes St, Khomasdal*); discretion and protection are the order of the day.

Cinemas & Theatre Whether you're after the big screen or a night of theatre, this city has a few established venues.

Warehouse Theatre (☎ 225059, *Old South-West Brewery Bldg, Tal St*) Admission US$3. This delightfully integrated club stages live African and European music and theatre productions, but it's only open when an event is scheduled.

Ster Kinekor (☎ 249267, *Maerua Park Centre, off Robert Mugabe Ave*) This place shows recent films and has half-price admission on Tuesday.

The New Space (☎ 206 3111, University of Namibia complex) New Space sometimes stages theatre productions.

Windhoek Conservatorium (☎ 293 3111, Peter Müller St) The conservatorium occasionally holds classical concerts.

National Theatre of Namibia (☎ 237 966, 12 John Meinert St, ℮ ntn@iafrica.com.na) Next to Grass Roots Café, the national theatre stages infrequent theatre presentations; for information see the Friday edition of *The Namibian*.

Theatre in the Park (Parliament Gardens) This outdoor venue stages two live shows each month and also promotes children's theatre and screens African films. For the latest schedules, see the Windhoek Information & Publicity Office on Post St Mall.

Grass Roots Theatre (☎ 243344) Grass Roots offers down-to-earth cultural performances, and is attached to a pleasant cafe. The bizarre decor features papier-mâché furniture.

Warehouse Theatre (☎ 225059, 48 Tal St) This place offers jazz and light music concerts, as well as serious dramatic performances (see Pubs, Discos & Clubs earlier in this section).

The *Franco-Namibian Cultural Centre* screens French films and hosts visiting art and theatre exhibitions. (See Cultural Centres under Information earlier for details.)

Shopping

Handicrafts stalls are a common sight in the main shopping areas; the stuff in Post St Mall is mostly brought in from Zimbabwe (where the same things cost much less). Better choices might be the locally made Herero dolls, sold in the Gustav Voigts Centre, or the baskets and woodcarvings sold around Zoo Park. Alternatively, save your money for the less expensive handicrafts sold by artists, craftspeople and cooperative shops in other parts of Namibia (especially the north).

Windhoek also has a thriving jewellery industry, based on locally mined gold, minerals and gemstones. You'll find them mainly in specialist shops where artisans work to order; some of the best pieces are done with malachite and tiger-eye agates.

Leather shops are good for inexpensive, high-quality belts and purses; locally farmed ostrich leather is quite expensive, while buffalo-hide belts start at US$25 and will last forever. Handbags cost from US$110 and briefcases are double that.

If you buy anything unwieldy, most reputable shops are happy to arrange shipping.

Handicrafts You may want to check out the following places.

Namibia Crafts Centre (☎ 222236, 40 Tal St) Open 9am-5.30pm Mon-Fri & 9am-1pm Sat. This place is an outlet for heaps of wonderful Namibian inspiration – leather work, basketry, pottery, jewellery, needlework, hand-painted textiles and other material arts – and the artist and origin of each piece is documented. The attached snack bar is well known for its coffee and healthy snacks.

House of Gems (☎ 225202, 131 Stübel St, ℮ scrap@iafrica.com.na) This is the place to go for the best deals on raw minerals and gemstones (see the boxed text 'Gem Consciousness').

Bushman Art (☎ 228828, 187 Independence Ave) If you aren't venturing into the Kalahari, check out Bushman Art. It's extremely upmarket, but even nonbuyers will enjoy the variety and beauty of the wares. It also sells Himba material arts.

Nakara (☎ 215003, fax 215531, 165 Independence Ave; Factory shop, 3 Solingen St, Northern Industrial Area) This boutique and its factory outlet are major distributors of leather goods, ostrich skin products, and karakul woollen carpets and fashions in Windhoek.

Yebo Gallery (Adjoining Parliament Gardens) Open 9am-5pm Mon-Fri. This is the public sales outlet for the John Muafangejo Art Centre, which is a training school for prospective local artists.

Penduka (☎/fax 257210, ℮ penduka@namibnet.com) Open 8am-5pm Mon-Sat. Penduka, which means 'wake up', operates a nonprofit women's needlework project at Goreangab Dam, 10km north-west of the centre. You can purchase needlework, baskets, carvings and fabric creations for fair prices and be assured that all proceeds go to the producers. To get there, take the Western Bypass north and turn left on Monte Cristo Rd, left on Otjomuise Rd, right on Eveline St and right again on Green Mountain Dam Rd. Then follow the signs to Goreangab Dam/Penduka. To be picked up from town call ☎ 081-129 4116.

Getting There & Away

Air Air Namibia operates flights daily between Chief Hosea Kutako International Airport (42km east of the city centre), Cape Town and Johannesburg (Jo'burg). There is also a twice-weekly flight to/from London and Frankfurt; several airlines offer other international services to/from Maun, Botswana (US$250); Harare, Zimbabwe (US$385); and Victoria Falls, Zimbabwe (US$276).

Domestic Air Namibia flights connect Eros Airport, immediately south of the city centre, with Katima Mulilo (US$132), Lüderitz (US$105), Ondangwa (US$89), Rundu (US$132), Swakopmund/Walvis Bay (US$83) and Tsumeb (US$85).

Coming from Windhoek, make sure the taxi driver knows which airport you are going to (ie, in-town Eros versus the more distant international airport).

Airlines with flights into and out of Windhoek include:

Air Namibia (☎ 299 6333, fax 221382,
  ⓔ creservations@airnamibia.com.na)
British Airways/Comair (☎ 248528, fax
  248529) Sanlam Centre, 154 Independence Ave
LTU International Airlines (Germany;
  ☎ 237480) 5 Macadam St
Lufthansa Airlines (☎ 226662) 3rd floor,
  Sanlam Centre
South African Airways (SAA; ☎ 237670) Carl
  List Bldg, corner of Independence Ave and
  Peter Müller St

Bus Intercape Mainliner uses the Grab-a-Phone bus terminal on Independence Ave. It operates on Monday, Wednesday, Friday and Sunday to and from Cape Town (US$51) and Jo'burg (US$64), via Upington (US$34) in South Africa. Fares to places en route from Windhoek are: Rehoboth (US$4, one hour), Mariental (US$16, three

hours), Keetmanshoop (US$24, five hours) and Grünau (US$27, seven hours). There are also daily buses to Walvis Bay (US$14) via Swakopmund (US$13, four hours); and Friday departures to Victoria Falls (US$56, 18 hours) via Okahandja (US$9, one hour), Otjiwarongo (US$16), Grootfontein (US$25), Rundu (US$34) and Katima Mulilo (US$48, 12 hours).

For long-distance travel, the most economical option is the local minibuses, which serve all the main routes from the Rhino Park petrol station. They depart when full – at least once daily – for Keetmanshoop, Swakopmund, Walvis Bay, Tsumeb, Grootfontein, Oshakati, Ondangwa, Rundu and Katima Mulilo. You'll pay around US$0.03 per kilometre and an additional US$2 per trip for each large piece of luggage.

Train The station booking office is open from 7.30am to 4pm Monday to Friday; note that all fares quoted here double at weekends. Overnight trains run daily, except Saturday, between Windhoek and Keetmanshoop, leaving at 7.10pm/6.25pm southbound/northbound. Weekday business-class fares and travelling times from Windhoek are: Rehoboth (US$3, 2¾ hours), Mariental (US$4, six hours) and Keetmanshoop (US$6, 11½ hours).

The northern-sector line connects Windhoek with Tsumeb (US$4, 16 hours) via Okahandja (US$1.50, 2¼ hours) and Otjiwarongo (US$5, 10½ hours). At Otjiwarongo, this train connects with buses to Outjo, Khorixas, Kamanjab and Henties Bay.

The other main lines connect Windhoek with Swakopmund (US$3.50, 3¾ hours) and Walvis Bay (US$3.50, five hours) daily, except Saturday; and Windhoek with Gobabis to the east (US$4.25, eight hours) on Tuesday, Thursday and Sunday, on a very slow overnight run.

See Train in the Getting Around chapter for information on the *Desert Express* to Swakopmund.

Car & Motorcycle Windhoek is literally the crossroads of Namibia – the point where the main north-south route (the B1) and east-west routes (B2 and B6) cross – and all approaches to the city are extremely scenic, passing through beautiful desert hills. Roads are clearly signposted and those travelling between northern and southern Namibia can avoid the city centre by taking the Western Bypass. For a list of car rental agencies, see under Car & Motorcycle in the Getting Around chapter.

Hitching Due to its location and traffic, hitching to or from Windhoek is easier than anywhere else in Namibia.

Getting Around
To/From the Airport The Intercape Mainliner airport shuttle (☎ 263211), which costs US$7, connects Chief Hosea Kutako International Airport with Eros Airport and the Grab-a-Phone bus terminal in the city centre. It leaves from town two hours and 10 minutes prior to international departures and from the international airport one hour after the arrival of an international flight. Taxis between the international airport and the city centre cost around US$20.

Taxi Share taxis run between their main taxi stand at the Wernhil Park Centre and follow set routes to and from parts of Windhoek West, Khomasdal and Katutura. Along these routes, they charge US$0.60 (N$5) per person and stop on the way to pick up any passengers. Any deviation from these routes will incur charges at the whim of the driver.

For personal taxi services, phone a radio taxi, which will charge US$2 to US$5 for trips around the city. Fares are either metered or per kilometre, but you may be able to negotiate a set fare per journey. Be warned that taxis from Grab-a-Phone often charge much more, and may also charge extra for luggage. For longer distances (eg, to Daan Viljoen Game Park), phone any of the following and negotiate a reasonable fare:

Express Radio Taxis	☎ 239739
F&P Radio Taxis	☎ 211116
Sunshine Radio Taxis	☎ 221029
Taxis Prime Radio	☎ 272307
Wind-Cheetah Radio Taxis	☎ 223098

Around Windhoek

The following places to stay and sites around Dordabis, are on the North Central Namibia map in the North Central Namibia chapter.

NORTH OF THE CITY
There are several very amenable places to stay in the hills both north and west of Windhoek.

Sundown Lodge (☎ *232566, fax 232541,* e *sundown@iafrica.com.na, D1474 Brakwater, PO Box 5378)* Singles/doubles B&B US$30/45. This refreshing out-of-town place provides a nice, rural atmosphere within 25km of Windhoek. Amenities include a pool and a cosy campfire beneath the stars.

Gästefarm Elisenheim (☎*/fax 264429,* e *awerner@mweb.com.na,* W *www.natron .net/tour/elisenheim, D1473 Brakwater, PO Box 3016)* Singles/doubles US$34/64. A full breakfast is US$7, other meals cost US$9. This place is closed from 15 December to 31 January. In the Eros Mountains, 15km from town, this German-style guest farm is owned by Andreas and Christina Werner. Rates include wildlife viewing and use of the pool. Take the Okahandja road 15km north of Windhoek, get off at Brakwater and follow the D1473 until it curves north. Turn east at the first opportunity and follow this road to the farm. Transfers are available for pre-booked guests.

Düsternbrook (☎ *232572, fax 257112,* e *dbrook@mweb.com.na, D1499 off the Okahandja road)* Camping with half/full board US$40/47, tented accommodation DB&B US$84/133, singles/doubles DB&B US$98/129, the Felsenhaus view suite B&B US$99/157. This scenic guest farm on a working cattle and wildlife ranch is best known for its leopard and cheetah populations, which are a popular attraction for Windhoek visitors. For the 2.30pm leopard feeding, including a wildlife drive, you'll pay US$18/30 without/with lunch beforehand; dinner afterwards costs US$5. The wildlife drive alone costs US$22 and horse riding is US$7 per

WINDHOEK

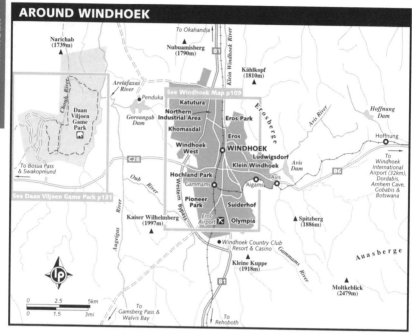

AROUND WINDHOEK

hour. Transfers from town cost US$20 for up to five people; on your own, follow the B1 for 30km north towards Okahandja and turn west onto the D1499. From there, it's 18km to the farm.

Eagle's Rock Lodge (☎ 234542, fax 257122, *e lodge@eaglesrock.com, w www .eaglesrock.com, D1958, PO Box 6176*) Single/double bungalows B&B US$55/86, full board US$64/108. This friendly lodge, surrounded by the rolling hills of Khomas Hochland, occupies a pleasant garden-like setting 38km from Windhoek; take the C28 (the Bosua Pass road) west and turn north on the D1958. The full-board meals are Mediterranean-oriented, but vegetarian meals are also available.

AVIS DAM

Just east of Windhoek on the road to the airport, Avis Dam offers bird-watching and quiet waterside hikes, but there's no public transport, except radio taxis.

DAAN VILJOEN GAME PARK

The Daan Viljoen Game Park *(admission US$3 per person, US$3 per vehicle; open to day visitors sunrise-6pm year-round)* is 25km west of Windhoek in the Khomas Hochland (see the Central Namib Desert chapter for more on this area). Various artefacts and stone structures discovered within this beautiful park reveal that the area has been inhabited for at least several centuries, and in fact, several Damara communities were forcibly relocated when the park was created in 1957.

Because there are no seriously dangerous animals, you can walk to your heart's content through lovely wildlife-rich desert hills and see gemsboks, kudus, mountain zebras, springboks, hartebeests and even elusive elands. Daan Viljoen is also known for its birdlife, and over 200 species have been recorded, including the rare green-backed heron and pin-tailed whydah; the park office sells a bird-identification booklet. Angling is also popular (a licence is required) and Augeigas Dam is stocked with barbels, kurpers and black bass.

Hiking
Daan Viljoen's hills are covered with open thorn-scrub vegetation that allows excellent wildlife viewing, and three walking tracks have been laid out.

The 3km **Wag 'n Bietjie (Wait-a-Bit) Trail** follows a dry riverbed from near the park office to Stengel Dam. The fabulous 9km **Rooibos Trail** crosses hills and ridges and affords great views of Windhoek.

The two-day, 34km Sweet-Thorn Trail circuits the beautiful eastern reaches of the park, and only the distant views of the city give away your proximity to Windhoek. One group of three to 12 people is allowed each day; it's US$9 per person, including accommodation in a simple shelter halfway along. Water is available at the mountain hut, but note the Augeigas River is polluted and is unsuitable for filtering. Advance bookings are required through NWR (see Tourist Offices under Information earlier) in Windhoek.

Places to Stay & Eat
Daan Viljoen Game Park camp site *(Off the C28, Bosua Pass Hwy)* Camp sites US$13 for 2 people plus US$2/1 for each additional adult/child, single/double self-catering huts US$26/35, luxury 4-bed self-catering suites US$67. This is the area's most popular camping ground, which curls around one side of Augeigas Dam. The ***restaurant***, 2km from the camping ground, is open 7.30am to 9am, noon to 2pm and 7pm to 10pm; there's also a kiosk selling drinks and refreshments.

The popularity of Daan Viljoen means that you're advised to pre-book accommodation, camp sites and picnic sites at NWR in Windhoek.

Getting There & Away
Take the C28 west from Windhoek; Daan Viljoen is clearly signposted off the Bosua Pass Hwy, about 18km from the city. You're welcome to walk in the park but no motorcycles are permitted. There's no public

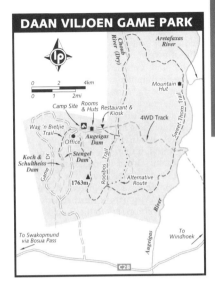

DAAN VILJOEN GAME PARK

transport to Daan Viljoen, but persistent hitchers will eventually get a lift.

DORDABIS & AROUND
☎ 062

The lonely ranching area around Dordabis is the heart of Namibia's karakul country, and supports several sheep farms and weaveries.

Farm Ibenstein Weavery *(☎ 573524, 4km down the C15 from Dordabis; open 8am-12.30pm & 2.30pm-5.30pm Mon-Fri, 8am-noon Sat)* is where visitors learn about spinning, dyeing and weaving – and may purchase the finished rugs and carpets.

Dorka Teppiche Weavery *(Peperkorrel Farm)* produces some of the finest original rugs and weavings you'll find anywhere and the manager Volker Berner's wife, Dörthe, creates progressive marble and soapstone sculpture (see Eningu Clay House Lodge under Places to Stay following for this place at the same farm).

Places to Stay
Eningu Clay House Lodge *(☎ 226979, fax 226999,* e *logufa@mweb.com.na,* w *http://natron.net/tour/eningu/main.html, Peperkorrel Farm)* Singles/doubles US$61 per

person with half-board & activities. Yes, the name sounds a lot like the title of a children's book and appropriately, this place is a bit of a fantasy. It was painstakingly designed and constructed by Volker and Stephanie Hümmer, whose efforts with sundried adobe have resulted in an appealing African-Amerindian architectural cross. It really is beautiful, and activities include wonderful hiking trails (with a mountain hut en route), wildlife viewing, archery, stargazing through their telescope and tours to the adjoining Dorka Teppiche and sculpture studio. To get there, follow the D1458 for 63km south-east of Chief Hosea Kutako International Airport and turn west on the D1471; travel for 1km to the Eningu gate.

Holiday Farm Scheidthof (☎/fax 573584, e discovaf@iafrica.com.na) Camping US$5 per person, farmhouse B&B US$40. This lovely 7400-hectare farm near Peperkorrel Farm offers a full complement of activities, but the highlights are a 32km hiking trail and two 4WD tracks (which may also be used for hiking). Turn south on the M51, east of the international airport, then east on the DR1506. The farm is 6km down this road.

Getting There & Away
Head east from Windhoek on the B6 and turn right onto the C23, 20km east of town. Dordabis is 66km down this road. At 7.30am on Friday, Star Line runs a bus from Windhoek to Dordabis (US$3). The bus returns at 4.45pm the same day.

ARNHEM CAVE
At 4.5km, Arnhem Cave is the longest cave system in Namibia. It was formed in a layer of limestone and dolomite, sandwiched between quartzite and shale, in the rippled Arnhem Hills synclines and anticlines (folds of stratified rock). The cave was dis-

covered in 1930 by farmer DN Bekker, and shortly thereafter, mining operations began extracting the deposits of bat guano, which were used as fertiliser.

Guided tours cost US$8, plus US$3.50 to hire helmets and torches. The route dives into darkness, beyond the reach of sunlight. Because it's dry, there are few stalagmites or stalactites, but it's possible you could see up to six bat species: the giant leaf-nosed bat *(Hipposideros commersoni)*, the leaf-nosed bat *(Hipposideros caffer)*, the long-fingered bat *(Miniopterus schreibersi)*, Geoffroy's horseshoe bat *(Rhinolophus clivosis)*, Denti's horseshoe bat *(Rhinolophus denti)* and the Egyptian slit-faced bat *(Nycteris thebalca)*. It's also inhabited by a variety of insects, worms, shrews and shrimps. The grand finale is the indescribable first view of the blue-cast natural light as you emerge from the depths.

Note that it gets extremely dusty, so wear old clothing and avoid wearing contact lenses. Tours must be booked in advance through Arnhem Cave Guest House.

Places to Stay
Arnhem Cave Guest House (☎/fax 573585, e arnhem@mweb.com.na) Camping US$7 per person, rooms B&B US$27 per person, double self-catering chalets US$84. This pleasant place offers an excellent overnight getaway from Windhoek, and lies within an hour's walk of Arnhem Cave, on the same farm. Meals are available by pre-booking.

Getting There & Away
The cave is on the private farm of Mr J Bekker. To get there, turn south 3km east of Chief Hosea Kutako International Airport on the D1458. After 66km, turn north-east on the D1506 and continue for 11km to the T-junction, where you turn south on the D180. The farm is 6km down this road.

North Central Namibia

For tourists, North Central Namibia is dominated by Etosha National Park, one of the world's pre-eminent wildlife areas, but the region is also replete with historical sites and lovely natural landscapes. The picturesque towns of Okahandja, Tsumeb and Grootfontein all merit a visit, and no-one will be disappointed with Waterberg Plateau Park, a lovely island in the sky, or the Erongo Mountains (Erongoberg), which form a dramatic backdrop along the route from Windhoek to Swakopmund.

In the north, the economy is carried by two major mining districts and vast, lonely cattle ranches, while Gobabis, the main settlement of the Namibian Kalahari, dominates the cattle country east of Windhoek.

See the North Central Namibia map for the many accommodation options throughout this chapter that are outside of towns and cities.

See the Around Windhoek section in the Windhoek chapter for more destinations both east and west of the capital.

OKAHANDJA
☎ 062

Okahandja, less than an hour's drive north of Windhoek, functions mainly as a highway service centre and crossroads between the B1 and the Swakopmund road (B2). It's also the administrative centre for the Herero people, who settled in this formerly Nama homeland in the early 19th century and thereby sparked a series of tribal wars.

History

Okahandja (Herero for 'Short Broad River') is named for its normally dry riverbed, which the Nama originally called Gei-Keis, the 'Broad Sand'. The first German visitor, missionary Heinrich Schmelen, arrived in 1827 and renamed it Schmelen's Hope, but the first missionaries, Heinrich Kleinschmidt and Carl Hahn, didn't begin their activities until 1843. In 1849, Friedrich Kolbe established a formal mission, but it

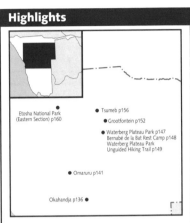

Highlights

Etosha National Park (Eastern Section) p160
Tsumeb p156
Grootfontein p152
Waterberg Plateau Park p147
Bernabé de la Bat Rest Camp p148
Waterberg Plateau Park
Unguided Hiking Trail p149
Omaruru p141
Okahandja p136

- Spend a few days on the wild side in Etosha National Park, one of the world's premier wildlife venues.

- Climb to Mountain View on the Waterberg Plateau for a view that will take your breath away.

- Learn about Namibia's Herero heritage at a festival in Okahandja.

- Visit the Tsumeb Mining Museum and see its impressive array of minerals.

- Look for dinosaurs – or at least their tracks – on Otjihaenamparero Farm near Kalkfeld.

was destroyed after only a few months by Nama forces under their highly charged leader, Jan Jonker Afrikaner, who had been commandeering Herero cattle and objected to German interference. A subsequent German mission lasted from 1870 to 1890, when it gave way to earnest German colonisation – and the founding of German Okahandja in 1894. During the 20th century, the town grew and developed into a main service centre and highway junction between Windhoek, Swakopmund and the north.

NORTH CENTRAL NAMIBIA

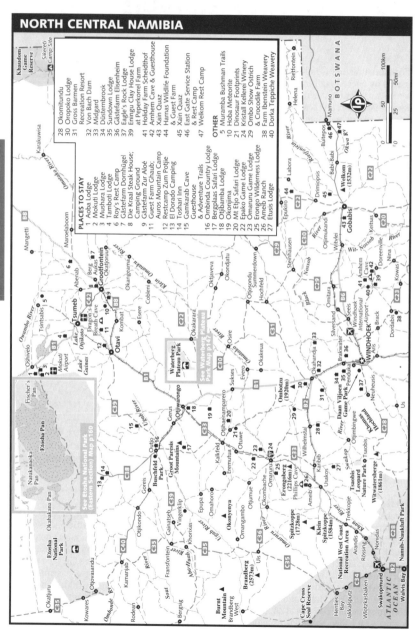

PLACES TO STAY

1 Aoba Lodge
2 Mokuti Lodge
3 Mushara Lodge
4 Tamboti Lodge
5 Roy's Rest Camp
6 Gästefarm Dornhügel
7 Gästefarm Eisenheim
8 Die Kraal Steak House; Camping Ground
9 Gästefarm Zur Aloé
10 Auros Mountain Camp
11 Guest Farm Ghaub; Restcamp Zum Potjie
12 El Dorado Camping
13 Toshari Inn
14 Gamkarab Cave Guesthouse
15 Ombinda Country Lodge & Adventure Trails
16 Bergplaas Safari Lodge
17 Otjibamba Lodge
18 Okonjima
19 Mt Etjo Safari Lodge
20 Epako Game Lodge
21 Omaruru Game Lodge
22 Erongo Wilderness Lodge
23 Ameib Ranch
24 Ongombo Estate
25 Omaruru Rest Camp
26 Ameib Ranch
27 Etusis Lodge

28 Okomitundu
30 Oropoko Lodge
31 Gross Barmen Recreation Resort
32 Von Bach Dam
33 Midgard
34 Düsternbrook
35 Sundown Lodge
36 Gästefarm Elsenheim
37 Eagle's Rock Lodge
39 Eningu Clay House Lodge at Pepperkorrel Farm
41 Holiday Farm Scheidthof
42 Arnhem Cave & Guesthouse
43 Xain Quaz
44 Hamas Wildlife Foundation & Guest Farm
45 Xain Quaz
46 East Gate Service Station & Rest Camp
47 Welkom Rest Camp

OTHER

5 Muramba Bushman Trails
10 Hoba Meteorite
21 Dinosaur Footprints
24 Kristall Kellerei Winery
29 Ombo Show Ostrich & Crocodile Farm
38 Farm Ibenstein Weavery
40 Dorka Teppiche Weavery

Cemeteries

In the churchyard of the 1876 Rhenish mission church, Friedenskirche, are the graves of several historical figures, including Willem Maharero. Opposite the church is another church, the Friedenskirche (Church of Peace) and three other notable graves: Nama leader Jan Jonker Afrikaner, who died in 1861; Clemens Kapuuo, a former Democratic Turnhalle Alliance (DTA) president, who was assassinated in Windhoek in 1978; and Hosea Kutako, the father of Namibian independence who, as president of the DTA, was the first leader to petition the UN against the South African occupation of Namibia.

East of Kerk St, near the swimming pool, is the **Herero Heroes Cemetery**. Among others buried here are Tjamuaha, who led the Herero against the Nama; Maherero, who led the people to Otjimbingwe in the face of Nama aggression; and Samuel Maherero, who led his people to Botswana after their defeat by the Germans at the Battle of the Waterberg. The cemetery is the starting point of the annual procession by the Red Flag Herero to pay respect to their leaders and – in the spirit of unity – to former enemy, Jan Jonker Afrikaner.

German Fort

A **town museum** (☎ 502700) is planned for the 1894 German fort, but this project has been ongoing for some time now with no visible progress. Phone before you attempt to make a visit.

Moordkoppie

The historical animosity between the Nama and Herero had its greatest expression at the **Battle of Moordkoppie** (Afrikaans for 'Murder Hill') on 23 August 1850, during which over 700 Herero under the command of chief Katjihene were massacred by Nama forces. Half of the victims were men; the rest were women and children, whose bodies were dismembered for the copper bangles on their arms and legs. The scene of this tragedy is a small rocky hill near the centre of town between the B2 and the railway line, 500m north of the Gross Barmen turn-off.

Ombo Show Ostrich & Crocodile Farm

At the Ombo Show Ostrich & Crocodile Farm (☎ 501176, on the D2110, 3km north of the town centre) you can feed ostriches, sit on one, watch them hatching and dancing and, of course, eat them. You can also see crocodiles lazing in the sun and watch locals making Herero dolls and Kavango woodcarvings. Tours cost US$3/1.50 per adult/child.

Von Bach Dam Recreation Resort

Thanks to the healthy rains in the last couple of years, this lovely green oasis offers excellent fishing prospects. Whether that lasts or not, even nonanglers can enjoy picnics, bird-watching or bushwalking. All visits must be pre-booked. Fishing licences may be purchased at the gate. This resort (☎ 501475, south of town off the B1; admission US$1.50 per person plus US$1.50 per vehicle) offers **camping** for US$10 for two people plus US$2 for each additional person up to a total of eight. Basic huts with shared ablutions cost US$13 and there is an extra US$10 charge for bedding.

Special Events

Okahandja's big event is **Maherero Day**, on the weekend nearest 26 August, when the Red Flag Herero people meet in traditional dress in memory of their fallen chiefs, killed in battles with the Nama and Germans. A similar event is held by the Mbanderu, or **Green Flag Herero**, on the weekend nearest 11 June.

Places to Stay

Villa Nina Guesthouse (☎/fax 502497, Peter Brand Way 327, ⓔ friedrich-doerr@ t-online.de, PO Box 1497) Singles/doubles B&B US$29/34; entire lodge US$54. This friendly and comfortable German-oriented place has a pool and self-catering facilities.

Sylvanette Guesthouse (☎ 501213, fax 501079, ⓔ sylvanet@iafrica.com.na, ⓦ www .triponline.net, 311 Hoogenhout St, PO Box 529) Singles/doubles B&B US$29/34. All seven rooms in this friendly little place have

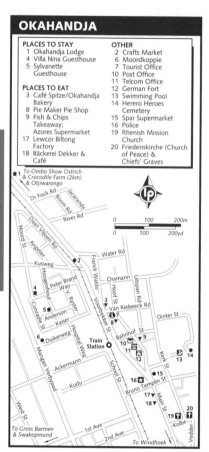

OKAHANDJA

PLACES TO STAY
1 Okahandja Lodge
4 Villa Nina Guesthouse
5 Sylvanette
   Guesthouse

PLACES TO EAT
3 Café Spitze/Okahandja
   Bakery
8 Pie Maker Pie Shop
9 Fish & Chips
   Takeaway;
   Azores Supermarket
17 Lewcor Biltong
   Factory
18 Bäckerei Dekker &
   Café

OTHER
2 Crafts Market
6 Moordkoppie
7 Tourist Office
10 Post Office
11 Telcom Office
12 German Fort
13 Swimming Pool
14 Herero Heroes
   Cemetery
15 Spar Supermarket
16 Police
19 Rhenish Mission
   Church
20 Friedenskirche (Church
   of Peace) &
   Chiefs' Graves

private bathrooms, and guests may use the pool and *braai* (barbecue) facilities. Transfers are available from Windhoek.

Okahandja Lodge (☎ 504299, fax 502551, e okalodge@africaonline.com.na, PO Box 1524) Camping US$5.50 per person, singles/doubles B&B US$54/94. This hotel and conference centre offers nice, cool rooms with thatched ceilings. The camp site is several hundred metres away; turn off at Pro-Thatch (Namibia's largest thatching company). The a la carte restaurant serves standard international fare for US$4-8; on

Sundays from noon to 2pm it offers a buffet lunch for US$8. It costs US$2 to use the swimming pool.

Several rural guest farms also stand out:

Okomitundu (☎ 503901, fax 503902, e okomitun@mweb.com.na, W www.oko mitundu.com, south of Wilhelmstal on the D1967, PO Box 285) Singles/doubles US$75/133 with full board and activities. Set amid 11,000 hectares of scenic rocky hills, Okomitundu offers walking safaris and wildlife drives, as well as horse riding, bird-watching and star-gazing through a good telescope.

Oropoko Lodge (☎ 503871, fax 503842, e oropoko@iafrica.com.na, W www.nam ibia-lodge.com, B2, 40km from Okhandja, PO Box 726) Singles/doubles US$70/ 104, including meals and activities. This large 35-room lodge, which is situated on an 11,000 hectare private reserve, offers wildlife drives, guided hikes, 4WD trips and other outdoor activities.

Midgard (☎ 503888, fax 503818, e mid gard@mweb.com.na, W www.namibsunho tels.com.na/midgard, D2102, PO Box 16, Windhoek) Singles/doubles B&B US$60/84. The words 'over the top' may well have been invented for this German-oriented lodge. Activities include a gym, bowling alley, tennis, volleyball, badminton and croquet courts, unusual swimming pools, open-air chess and even a serious children's playground – and then you can go hiking, horse riding, abseiling or driving around the farm. The restaurant serves vegetables lovingly grown from its own garden; lunch and dinner plans cost US$12.

Places to Eat

Café Spitze/Okahandja Bakery (☎ 502268, Van Riebeeck St) Sandwiches & light meals US$1.50-2. This is your best casual option, with a takeaway and pleasant little cafe.

Bäckerei Dekker & Café (☎ 501962, Main St) Meals & snacks US$1.50-3. This place serves full breakfasts, toasted sandwiches, healthy snacks, pies, light lunches and desserts. It's a popular stop with early morning travellers heading north from Windhoek.

Full meals are available at *Okahandja Lodge* (see Places to Stay earlier). For fast snacks, try *Pie Maker Pie Shop (Main St)* or *Fish & Chips* takeaway located in Azores supermarket.

Biltong (dried meat) fans will love the *Lewcor Biltong Factory*, which is Namibia's best; try the delicious *chili bites* (beef seasoned with *peri-peri*, a hot pepper sauce of Portuguese/Angolan origin).

Shopping
The two immense *craft markets* – one near the junction of the B1 and B2, the other about 1km out on the B1 towards Windhoek – are great for shopping and spirited bargaining. Note, however that few of the articles are made in Namibia, as Zimbabwean curios can be imported cheaply and provide greater profit margins.

Getting There & Away
Okahandja, 70km north of Windhoek on the B1, lies on the Intercape Mainliner and minibus routes to the north and west, and on the rail line between Windhoek and Tsumeb or Walvis Bay (via Swakopmund). For rail information, phone Trans-Namib (☎ 503315).

GROSS BARMEN RECREATION RESORT
Gross Barmen *(admission US$1.50 per person plus US$1.50 per vehicle)*, a former mission station, 26km south-west of Okahandja, is Namibia's most popular hotspring resort (the Herero name, Otjikango, means 'weak spring in the rocks'), with mineral baths, tennis courts, a restaurant, and naturally heated indoor and outdoor pools. It feels like a cross between an oasis and a health farm and most people come to swim or soak (use of the mineral springs and baths costs US$1.50), but there are also nice walks around the dam and hillsides. For bird-watchers, a path has been cut through the reedbeds, with benches where you can wait and see what flies in.

Note that even day visits must be booked in advance through Namibia Wildlife Resorts (NWR) in Windhoek (see under Information in that chapter).

Places to Stay & Eat
Camping/Bungalows (☎ 501091) Camping US$10 for 2 people plus US$2 for each additional person, 2-bed economy rooms/ bungalows US$20/21, 2-/5-bed bungalows US$23/34, 4-bed self-catering suites US$66. The site has a shop, bar, restaurant and petrol station. At the restaurant, hard-core carnivores can cash in all their hot water health chips and indulge in huge slabs of T-bone steak and inexpensive draught beer.

Getting There & Away
There's no public transport but on weekends, it may be possible to hitch from the highway turn-off south of Okahandja.

KARIBIB
☎ 064
The small ranching town of Karibib, 100km west of Okahandja, began as a station on the narrow gauge Windhoek-Swakopmund railway line. Early rail services travelled only by day, and Karibib's position halfway between Swakopmund and Windhoek made it an ideal overnight stop. At one stage during the colonial period it had six hotels.

Modern Karibib is best known for the **Navachab gold mine**, 5km south-west of town, which was discovered in 1985. Consolidated Diamond Mines in consortium with the Anglo-American Corporation developed the mine. It was operational by November 1989 and now produces more than 700,000 tonnes of ore each year, at a relatively low yield of 3g of gold per tonne.

Information
For tourist information, contact the helpful Wolfgang Henckert Tourist Centre (☎ 550 028, fax 550230, e henckert@iwwn.com .na), 38 Main St, PO Box 85. The Der Webervogel carpet weavery at the back of the building produces quality woollens and the attached shop sells Namibian gemstones – including the beautiful Karibib tourmaline – as well as minerals and curios. The office also distributes a brochure describing Karibib's historic buildings and can organise visits to the Palisandro marble quarry. It is open from 8am to 5.30pm daily.

Marmorwerke

The Palisandro marble (aragonite) quarries annually yield over 1200 tonnes of the hardest, highest-quality marble in the world. The marble is processed at the Marmorwerke (German for 'Marble Works'), west of the centre.

Historic Buildings

Most buildings along Karibib's main street have historical significance. Among them are the old **train station**, which dates from 1900; the **Rösemann & Kronewitter Building**, built in 1900 as the headquarters of an early German trading firm; the church-like **Haus Woll**, built of granite in the first decade of the 20th century; and the **Christuskirche**, built in 1910. It was the first church in Namibia to be constructed of marble.

Places to Stay

Hotel Erongoblick (☎ *550009, fax 550095, 24 Park St*) Singles/doubles with bathroom US$22/36, with shared bathroom US$16/24. Rates include breakfast. This hotel in the town centre occupies a well-refurbished boarding school. With a great pool and good restaurant (closed on Saturdays), it's a good mid-range option.

Irmi's Lodge (☎ *550081, fax 550240, Main St*) Singles/doubles US$29/39 with aircon and continental breakfast. English breakfast US$5. Cool and shady, this place at the eastern end of town has a restaurant (closed Monday) and swimming pool. A sign over the bar claims staff speak German, Italian, Afrikaans, English, Bavarian and Nonsense.

Etusis Lodge (☎ *550826, fax 223994,* e *etusis@natron.net,* w *www.natron.net/ tour/etusis, 36km south of Karibib, PO Box 5*) Single/double bungalows US$115/192, double luxury tents US$134. Rates include full board and activities. This well-appointed thatched complex occupies a 12,000 hectare ranch with wildlife and hiking trails in a landscape of acacia scrub, *sandveld* (sandy open grassland) and rocky mountains. Activities include guided hikes, horse riding and wildlife drives. To get there, drive 20km south on the C32, then follow the P1954 for 15km to the lodge.

Places to Eat & Drink

Springbok Cafe & Steakhouse (☎ *550094, Main St*) Lunch or dinner US$3-5. This place is locally popular for steak and other meat-based meals.

Western Restaurant (*Main St*) Lunch or dinner US$3-5. This little place is probably Karibib's best option for steaks and Namibian standards. There's also a recommended beer garden.

Karibib Bakery (*Main St*) Breakfast or lunch US$2.50-3.50. This is great for breakfast and real brewed coffee; it was constructed in 1913 as one of Karibib's first hotels.

Halfway Takeaway (☎ *550010, 3rd St*) Light meals US$1.50-3. A block off the main road, this place does chips, burgers and cool drinks.

Klippenberg Country Club (☎ *550300*) Mains US$3-5. This country club serves up steak and chips, goulash, spaghetti and other popular lunch and dinner options. You can also avail yourself of the pool, the tennis and squash courts and the golf course. Turn south at the post office.

Self-catering is available at the *I Graser Sentra Supermarket*.

You'll find a taste of local colour by having a beer at the historic and slightly rough *Pub 1913*.

Getting There & Away

Karibib is accessible by any bus between Windhoek and Swakopmund. The Intercape Mainliner from Windhoek (US$11, 2½ hours) stops at Irmi's Lodge.

Except on Sundays, trains between Windhoek and Swakopmund/Walvis Bay stop at Karibib at 2.20am eastbound and 12.40am westbound.

OTJIMBINGWE
☎ 064

One would never suspect that the forgotten village of Otjimbingwe, 55km south-east of Karibib on the D1953, was once the administrative capital of German South-West Africa. In Herero the name means 'Place of Refreshment', after the freshwater spring near the confluence of the Omusema and

Swakop Rivers. The presence of water and the fact that Otjimbingwe lay midway along the wagon route between Windhoek and Walvis Bay led Reichskommissar Heinrich Göring to declare it the colonial capital in the early 1880s.

History
Otjimbingwe was founded by Johannes Rath in 1849 as a Rhenish mission, but the church wasn't built until 1867. After copper was discovered in the mid-1850s, the Walvis Bay Mining Company (WBM) set up operations, and the quiet mission station turned into a rollicking, Wild West–style mining town in the mid-1880s. In the early 1880s the town became the administrative seat of German South-West Africa and, in 1888, the site of the country's first post office. However, when the capital was transferred to Windhoek in 1890, Otjimbingwe declined. The final blow came when it was bypassed by the Windhoek-Swakopmund railway in the early 20th century.

Historic Buildings
Have a look at the Rhenish church; the historic WBM trading store; the wind-driven generator used to power the Hälbich wagon factory; and the 1872 powder magazine, which was intended as a first line of defence against attack by the Nama.

Tsaobis Leopard Nature Park
Tsaobis Leopard Nature Park (☎ 550811, fax 550954, ⓔ tsaobis@iafrica.com.na) occupies 37,000 hectares of rugged rocky country along the southern bank of the Swakop River. It was here in 1889 that Major Curt von François constructed a fortified barracks for the Schutztruppe (German imperial army). In 1969, it was established as a nominal wildlife sanctuary and is now home to a handful of leopards, antelopes, mountain zebras, wild dogs, cheetahs and various other enclosed animals. The scenery and accommodation are wonderful but access is difficult without a vehicle.

Camping costs US$4 per person, with up to six people per site. Standard/luxury two-bed self-catering bungalows cost US$34/47.

Breakfast/lunch/dinner are available on request for US$7/3/8. Activities on this large and scenic property include a swimming pool and two 8km-long hiking trails. There are also wilderness wildlife drives, which cost US$10 to US$14.

The park is 35km west of Otjimbingwe, just west of the junction of the C32 and the D1976.

USAKOS
☎ 064

Usakos (Nama/Damara for 'Grasp by the Heel') was originally developed as a station on the narrow-gauge railway that linked the port of Walvis Bay with the mines of the Golden Triangle (Otavi, Tsumeb and Grootfontein). Its charming architecture still makes it one of Namibia's nicest small towns. In the first decade of the 20th century, its location was deemed ideal for the country's first railway workshops and Usakos became Namibia's railway capital. It held this position until 1960, when narrow gauge was replaced by standard gauge. At that time steam-powered locomotives gave way to diesel engines and the works yard was shifted to Windhoek.

The Namib i Tourist Information office is in the Shell petrol station.

Locomotive No 40
In honour of Usakos' railway past, Locomotive No 40 stands proudly in front of the train station. It was one of three Henschel heavy-duty locomotives built in 1912 by the firm of Henschel & Son in Kassel, Germany. (Its counterpart, Locomotive No 41, occupies a similar position at the station in Otjiwarongo.)

Places to Stay & Eat
Usakos Hotel (☎ 530259, fax 530267, 15 Bahnhof St, PO Box 318) Rooms US$16 per person B&B. This austere but historic place offers simple, anachronous accommodation. The wall of the bar is a veritable museum of beer labels.

Das Bahnmeister Guesthouse (☎ 530 554, Bahnhof St) Camping or dorm beds US$3.50 with linen, singles/doubles B&B

with TV and air-con US$17/20. This reno-
vated 1928 railway building also has a
small railway museum and a beer garden
where you can enjoy light pub meals.

Namib Wüste Farm Stall *(☎ 530283,
Plot 65)* Camping US$1.50 per person,
US$1.50 per vehicle and US$3 per caravan,
beds in the rail car US$13 per person B&B.
Meals are available on the patio, and it sells
home-made biltong and farm produce.

Khan Takeaways *(530517, Moltke St)*
For snacks you're limited to this place opposite the post office, which mainly does
fish and chips.

Bahnhof Hotel *(☎ 530444, fax 530765,
e jakes@hehe.com, W www.hop.to/namibia,
Theo Ben Gurirab St)* Singles/doubles B&B
US$24/34. This fully licensed hotel, restau-
rant and beer garden, beside the post office,
features rooms with private facilities, TV,
air-con and phones.

Getting There & Away
Usakos is situated on the bus, minibus and
railway routes between Windhoek and
Swakopmund/Walvis Bay. Except on Sunday, trains stop at 12.45am eastbound and at
1.55am westbound.

ERONGO MOUNTAINS (ERONGOBERG)
☎ 064
The volcanic Erongo Mountains, often referred to as the Erongoberg, rise as a 2216m
massif north of Karibib and Usakos. After
the original period of volcanism some 150
million years ago, the volcano collapsed on
its magma chamber, allowing the basin to
fill with slow-cooling igneous material. The
result is this hard granite-like core, which
withstood the erosion that washed away the
surrounding rock.

Things to See
The Erongo range is best known for its
caves and rock paintings, particularly the
50m-deep **Phillips Cave** on Ameib Ranch
(see Places to Stay following). This cave,
3km off the road, contains the famous
humpbacked white elephant painting. Superimposed on the elephant is a large hump-

backed antelope (an eland?) and around it
frolic ostriches and giraffes. The Ameib
paintings were brought to attention in the
book *Phillips Cave* by prehistorian Abbè
Breuil, but his speculations about their
Mediterranean origins have now been discounted. The site is open to day hikers via
Ameib Ranch.

The Ameib picnic site is backed up by
outcrops of stacked boulders, one of which,
the notable **Bull's Party**, resembles a circle
of gossiping bovines. Other formations that
are often photographed include one resem-
bling an **Elephant's Head** and another that
recalls a Herero woman in traditional dress,
standing with two children.

Day permits for Ameib Ranch cost US$3.

Places to Stay
Ameib Ranch *(☎ 530803, fax 530904,
e ameib@natron.net, W www.natron.net/
tour/ameib, PO Box 266, Usakos)* Camping
US$7 per person, US$36 B&B, half/full
board US$46/49. The name of this place at
the base of the Erongo foothills means
'Green Hill'. It started out in 1864 as a
Rhenish mission station and today it operates as an atmospheric guest farm and camp
site. Lodging is in the historic farmhouse;
rates include use of the pool and *lapa* (a circular area with a firepit, used for socialising). Farm tours and guided hikes to
Phillips Cave, Bull's Party or Elephant's
Head are US$3 per person. Transfers from
Usakos are provided free to pre-booked
guests, including campers.

Erongo Wilderness Lodge *(☎ 570537,
fax 570536, e eronwild@iafrica.com.na,
W www.erongowild.com.na or www.orus
ovo.com/erongo, PO Box 581, Omaruru)*
Luxury single/double tented bungalows
US$96/167, 'tree houses' on stilts from
US$84 per person. All rates include full
board and guided activities. This highly
acclaimed lodge combines spectacular
mountain scenery, wildlife viewing, bird-
watching and sensitive architecture to
create one of Namibia's nicest accommodation choices. There's also plenty of interesting country to explore here, including
'singing rocks' and several ancient rock

paintings. To get to the lodge, go to Omaruru, turn west on the D2315 (off the Karabib road 1km south of town) and continue 10km to the lodge.

Getting There & Away
North of Ameib, the D1935 skirts the Erongo Mountains before heading north into Damaraland. Alternatively, you can head east towards Omaruru on the D1937. This route virtually encircles the Erongo massif, and provides access to minor 4WD roads into the heart of the mountains. These roads will take you to some excellent wild bushwalking.

OMARURU
☎ 064
Omaruru's dry and dusty setting beside the shady Omaruru riverbed lends it a real outback feel. Its name means 'Bitter, Thick Milk' in Herero and refers to the milk produced by cattle that have grazed on bitterbush *(Pechuelloeschae leubnitziae)*. In dry periods, this hardy plant remains green and tasty long after other vegetation has become insipid.

Omaruru no longer has a tourist office, but the hotels provide tourist information.

History
Omaruru was founded in 1870 as a trading post and Rhenish mission station. Courtesy of the missionary zeal of Gottlieb Veihe, it was here that the New Testament and the liturgies were first translated into Herero.

As with so many central Namibian towns, the colonial occupation brought with it a German garrison and, consequently, local resistance. In January 1904, Omaruru was attacked by Herero forces under chief Manassa. German captain Victor Franke, who had been engaged in suppressing an uprising in southern Namibia, petitioned Governor Leutwein for permission to march north and relieve the besieged town. After a 20-day, 900km march, Franke arrived in Omaruru and led the cavalry charge which defeated the Herero attack.

For his efforts Franke received the highest German military honours and, in 1908, the grateful German residents of Omaruru erected the Franke Tower in his honour.

Franke Tower
Captain Franke's tower, which was declared a national monument in 1963, holds a historical plaque and affords a view over the

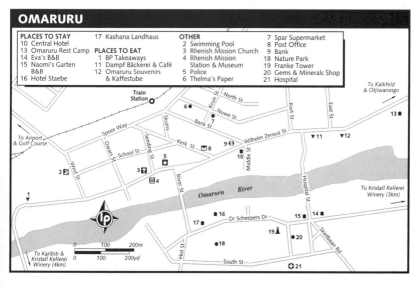

OMARURU

PLACES TO STAY	17 Kashana Landhaus	OTHER	7 Spar Supermarket
10 Central Hotel		2 Swimming Pool	8 Post Office
13 Omaruru Rest Camp	PLACES TO EAT	3 Rhenish Mission Church	9 Bank
14 Eva's B&B	1 BP Takeaways	4 Rhenish Mission	18 Nature Park
15 Naomi's Garten	11 Dampf Bäckerei & Café	Station & Museum	19 Franke Tower
B&B	12 Omaruru Souvenirs	5 Police	20 Gems & Minerals Shop
16 Hotel Staebe	& Kaffestube	6 Thelma's Paper	21 Hospital

town. It's normally locked; if you want to climb it, pick up a key at either the Central Hotel or Hotel Staebe (see Places to Stay).

Rhenish Mission Station & Museum

The Rhenish Mission Station & Museum *(Wilhelm Zeraua St; admission free)*, which was constructed in 1872 by missionary Gottlieb Viehe, now houses the town museum. Displays include 19th-century household and farming implements, an old drinks dispenser, and lots of historical photographs. Opposite is the cemetery where Herero chief Wilhelm Zeraua and several early German residents are buried. Pick up the museum keys from the Central Hotel.

Kristall Kellerei Winery

Kristall Kellerei Winery *(☎ 570083, fax 570593, 4km east of town on the D2328; open 10am-10pm Mon-Fri, 9am-2pm Sat)* is Namibia's only winery, growing not only red and white grapes to produce ruby cabernet, colombard, blanc de noir, sparkling wine and grappa (Italian schnapps), but also prickly pear cactus, which is the main ingredient in its cactus schnapps (definitely an acquired taste). In the afternoon you can enjoy light meals – cheese and cold meat platters, salads and schnitzels – while tasting the wines and other products; dinners are available by pre-booking. Don't miss the winery's wonderful mineral water – Namibia's best – which has been naturally filtered through Omaruru's sand formations.

Special Events

Each year on the weekend nearest 10 October, the White Flag Herero people hold a procession from the Ozonde suburb to the graveyard, opposite the mission station, where their chief Wilhelm Zeraua was buried after his defeat in the German-Herero wars.

Places to Stay

In Town Omaruru has quite a few accommodation options for its size.

Omaruru Rest Camp (☎ 570516, Wilhelm Zeraua St, PO Box 400) Camping US$4 per person, basic rooms US$18 per person B&B. This nice leafy spot provides a pleasant, quiet environment with good bird-watching. The restaurant and pub are available to guests.

Kashana Landhaus (☎/fax 570204, Dr Scheepers Drive) Camping US$4 per person. These shady and reedy riverside sites are wonderfully quiet and private. The oddly stranded fishing boat – occupying a prominent position – was once stolen in Walvis Bay; the owners retrieved it in neighbouring Angola.

Eva's B&B (☎/fax 470338, Dr Scheepers Drive) Singles/doubles B&B US$16/24. This little place is clean and friendly, but you'll need to speak German to communicate.

Naomi's Garten B&B (☎ 570142, 081-248 5557, fax 062-570165, Dr Scheepers Drive) Self-catering bungalow US$19 per person B&B. Naomi offers a comfortable four-bed bungalow with Himba decor and one bizarre semicircular bed.

Hotel Staebe (☎ 570035, fax 570450, ⓔ staebe@iafrica.com.na, Dr Scheepers Drive, PO Box 92) Singles/doubles/triples/ quads US$32/47/60/64, economy singles/ doubles US$29/42, all rates are B&B. This one-star German-run place occupies a nice green setting over the river from town.

Central Hotel (☎ 570030, fax 571100, ⓔ central@africaonline.com.na, Wilhelm Zeraua St) Single/double rooms or bungalows B&B US$30/43. This small and spartan place enjoys a central location and a friendly staff. At lunchtime, the dining room serves German-style set meals and there's an a la carte menu in the evenings.

Out of Town Omaruru is situated in the heart of guest-farm country, and there are also several worthwhile out-of-town lodges (see also Erongo Mountains (Erongoberg) earlier in this chapter).

Omaruru Game Lodge (☎ 570044, fax 570134, ⓔ omlodge@iafrica.com.na, ⓦ www .omaruru-game-lodge.com, 16km northeast of town, PO Box 208) Single/double rondavels B&B US$50/75, self-catering lodges US$23 per person. This lodge on the

Omaruru River offers a taste of the bush on a scenic, well-watered game farm with a variety of antelopes and other wildlife.

Epako Game Lodge (☎ *570551, fax 570553,* e *epako@iafrica.com.na,* w *www .etosha.com/epako-game-lodge.htm, C33, 22km north of town, PO Box 108)* Singles/ doubles US$116/160 with half board and one wildlife drive. This hillside lodge, on an 11,000 hectare game farm, offers wildlife viewing, bird-watching and fine dining.

Places to Eat

Omaruru is in a major fruit-growing area and people sell citrus fruits at roadside stalls from July to September. For main meals, you're pretty much limited to *Central Hotel* and *Hotel Staebe* (see Places to Stay).

Omaruru Souvenirs & Kaffestube (☎ *570230, Wilhelm Zeraua St)* This cosy cafe is housed in an historic building dating from 1907. From Monday to Friday you'll get good filter coffee, snacks and German baked goods in the beer garden, and on Friday it does full lunches from noon to 2pm.

For takeaways, fresh bread and ice cream, see *BP Takeaways*, on the main road west of town. You'll find groceries at *Spar Supermarket (Cnr Kruis & Nuwe Sts)* and baked goods are available at the superb *Dampf Bäckerei & Café (Wilhelm Zeraua St)*.

Shopping

You'll find Namibian gems and minerals at the small *gems & minerals shop* behind the Franke Tower. Alternatively, commemorate your visit to Omaruru by buying a few sheets of paper at *Thelma's Paper (Nuwe St)*, which is homemade from cattle, elephant and/or rhino dung.

Getting There & Away

Omaruru is 280km from Windhoek, but there are no bus services. With your own vehicle, the well maintained C33, which passes through Omaruru, provides the quickest route between Swakopmund and Etosha. Trains between Windhoek and Tsumeb or Walvis Bay (via Swakopmund) pass through Omaruru. For train information, phone Trans-Namib (☎ 570006).

KALKFELD
☎ 067

Around 200 million years ago Namibia was covered in a shallow sea, which gradually filled with wind-blown sand and eroded silt. Near the tiny town of Kalkfeld, these sandstone layers bear the evidence of a 25m dinosaur stroll which took place 170 million years ago. The prints were made in what was then soft clay by a three-toed dinosaur that walked on its hind legs – probably a forerunner of modern birds.

The tracks are 29km from Kalkfeld on Otjihaenamparero Farm, just off route D2414. The site was declared a national monument in 1951, but visits are still subject to the farmer's permission.

There's no accommodation in Kalkfeld, but nearby is the following option:

Mt Etjo Safari Lodge (☎ *304464, fax 304035, PO Box 81)* Standard singles/ doubles US$57/107, suites US$62/113, all with half board. The name of this place in the heart of a private nature reserve means 'Place of Refuge' and refers to the nearby table mountain. Its place in history was sealed in April 1989 when the Mt Etjo Peace Agreement was signed, ending Swapo's liberation struggle and setting the stage for Namibian independence the following March. Wildlife drives are available at an additional charge.

OUTJO
☎ 067

Bougainvillea-decked Outjo, established in 1880 by trader Tom Lambert, was never a mission station, but in the mid-1890s it did a short, uneventful stint as a German garrison town. Today, Outjo's environs boast citrus groves and, as with most of central Namibia, the economy revolves squarely around cattle-ranching. For visitors, Outjo is a convenient jumping-off point for trips into the Okaukuejo Rest Camp area of Etosha National Park.

You'll find basic tourist information in the small and informal Etosha i (☎/fax 313072), PO Box 380. It's housed in the curio shop on the main traffic circle. Email and Internet access are available during business hours at the Outjo Café-Bäckerei (see Places to Eat for contact details).

Naulila Monument

This monument commemorates the 19 October 1914 massacre of German soldiers and officials by the Portuguese near Fort Naulila on the Kunene River in Angola. It also commemorates soldiers killed on 18 December 1914, under Major Franke, who was sent to avenge the earlier losses.

Franke House Museum

The Franke House *(admission free; open 10am-12.30pm & 3pm-5pm Mon-Fri)*, originally called the Kliphuis or stone house, is one of Outjo's earliest buildings. It was constructed in 1899 by order of Major von Estorff as a residence for himself and subsequent German commanders. It was later occupied by Major (formerly Captain) Victor Franke, who gave it his name. It now houses the Franke House Museum (also known as Outjo Museum), with exhibits on political and natural history.

Windmill Tower

Outjo's old 9.5m stone windmill tower was constructed in 1900 to provide fresh water for German soldiers, their horses and the colonial hospital. It rises above the C39, immediately east of Outjo.

Gamkarab Cave

Gamkarab Cave, 50km north-east of Outjo, is replete with lovely stalagmites and stalactites, and the surrounding area has hiking trails, unusual vegetation and the world's only source of pietersite. For details see under Places to Stay following.

Places to Stay

In Town This town has a decent range of accommodation.

Outjo Backpackers (☎/fax 313470) Camping US$3 per person, dorm beds US$6.50, doubles US$14. This simple and friendly backpacker place is a great spot to hole up. Breakfast is available for US$2, and other meals on request for US$4.50 each. To get there, follow the road past the museum,

up the hill; Outjo Backpackers is just past the prominent water tower.

Buschfeld Park (☎ 313665, fax 313072, 2km from town on Etosha Rd, PO Box 380) Camping US$4, bungalows US$26 per person B&B. This well-located camp nestles beneath scenic Outjo Kopje, just north of town. Features include a restaurant and swimming pool.

Etosha Garten Hotel (☎ 313130, fax 313419, ⓔ egh@mweb.com.na, ⓦ www.etosha-garden-hotel.com, 6 Otavi St, PO Box 31) Singles/doubles/triples B&B US$29/52/66. This charming little place lays buried beneath acacia, jacaranda and bougainvillea; its restaurant is the best place to eat in town (see Places to Eat).

Hotel Onduri (☎ 313405, fax 313408, PO Box 14) Singles/doubles US$39/60. Outjo's typical town hotel has a restaurant, bar, pool table, swimming pool, and a beer garden set amid fragrant citrus trees.

Ombinda Country Lodge (☎ 313181, fax 313478, ⓔ discoveraf@iafrica.com.na, ⓦ www.discover-africa.com, Otjiwarongo Rd, PO Box 90538, Windhoek) Camping US$6 per person, single/double reed-and-thatch chalets B&B US$36/54. This pleasant hideaway is situated off the main road about 1km south of town.

Out of Town The following accommodation options provide a rural alternative.

Bergplaas Safari Lodge (☎ 313842, fax 061-224247, 40km south of Outjo on the D63, PO Box 60) Camping US$4, bed/B&B/half board US$22/26/30 per person. While the accommodation here is comfortable, the real draw of this 12,000 hectare spread is the opportunity to experience the bizarre Groot Paresis Mountains, which could easily qualify for national park status. The hiking trails here will take you through amazing granite domes to waterfalls and incongruous green hideaways.

Gamkarab Cave Guesthouse & Adventure Trails (☎ 313827, 313386, fax 313318, PO Box 197) Camping US$7 per person, simple self-catering accommodation US$10 per person. At this farm, 50km north-east of Outjo, Charles Dall offers cave tours

(US$5), horse riding (US$8.50 per hour), three-day horse tours (US$130) and hiking trails (US$8.50 per day). With your own equipment, you can also go cave diving in the underground lake (US$8.50). There are also camping tours to Mooeihoek Cave and the upper Ugab Canyon (US$80, with meals). Don't miss the showers, which are housed in the old charcoal ovens.

Places to Eat

Etosha Garten Hotel Beef or game dishes US$6-7. Here the Austrian chef creates wonderful dishes. How about zebra steak with blueberry-red wine sauce; oryx with yellow boletus mushrooms; rump of eland with dill, *roesti* (Swiss-style grated potatoes) and apple-horseradish; or roast kudu with red apple, cabbage, croquettes and blueberry pears? The salads, pastas and desserts are equally imaginative.

Outjo Café-Bäckerei (☎ 313055, Etosha St) Light meals US$2-3. Open 6.30am-5.30pm Mon-Fri, 7am-1pm Sat. This super little place serves chicken, Wiener schnitzel, burgers and other light meals; the bread and sweet treats are famous throughout the region.

Self-caterers headed for Etosha will find joy at *OK Supermarket (Otjiwarongo Rd)*.

Getting There & Away

A Star Line bus from Walvis Bay passes through Outjo on Friday at 11.15pm and continues to Otjiwarongo (US$3, one hour). From Otjiwarongo, it departs at 8am on Thursday, passing through Outjo at 9.30am, then continuing to Khorixas (US$3.50, three hours), Henties Bay (US$9, 7½ hours), Swakopmund (US$10, nine hours) and Walvis Bay (US$11.50, 9½ hours).

Hitchers see Outjo as a logical jumping-off point for Etosha's Andersson Gate, which is 105km away on the C38.

OTJIWARONGO
☎ 067

The roads between Windhoek, Swakopmund, Outjo/Etosha and the Golden Triangle (Otavi, Tsumeb and Grootfontein) converge at the agricultural and ranching centre of Otjiwarongo (Herero for 'the Pleasant Place'). In September and October, the town explodes with the vivid colours of blooming jacaranda and bougainvillea.

After the 1891 treaty between German missionaries and the Herero chief Kambazembi, a Rhenish mission station was established and a German military garrison arrived in 1904. The town was officially founded in 1906 with the arrival of the narrow-gauge railway from Swakopmund to the mines at Otavi and Tsumeb.

The tourist office (☎ 303658, e otjtc@iafrica.com.na) is situated opposite Hotel Hamburger Hof.

Locomotive No 41

At the train station stands Locomotive No 41, which was manufactured in 1912 by the Henschel company of Kassel, Germany, and was brought to Namibia to haul ore between the Tsumeb mines and the port at Swakopmund. It was retired from service in 1960 when the 0.6m narrow gauge was replaced with a 1.067m gauge.

Crocodile Ranch

One unusual attraction is Namibia's first crocodile ranch *(☎ 302121, Cnr Zingel & Hospital Sts; admission US$1.75; open 9am-4pm Mon-Fri, 11am-2pm Sat-Sun)*. This ranch produces skins for export to Asia and has a cafe serving snacks and light meals.

Places to Stay

In Town The following places to stay are among Otjiwarongo's best.

Acacia Caravan Park (☎ 302121, fax 302926, Hindenburg St) Camping US$5/7 per tent/caravan plus US$1.50 per person. The park is conveniently located beside the crocodile ranch, but security is poor and there have been reports of violent robbery.

Falkennest (☎/fax 302616, e otjbb@iafrica.com.na, W www.natron.net/tour/falkennest/main.html, 21 Industria Ave) Singles/doubles B&B US$16/27. This friendly B&B is a welcome mid-range option, and bird lovers will appreciate the colourful aviary. It has self-catering facilities and an outdoor braai area.

Out of Africa B&B *(☎ 303397, fax 304383, Near cnr Tuin St & Oosweg, PO Box 2122)* Singles/doubles B&B US$20/ 38. Set in a tropical garden, this place near the southern end of town offers a homely atmosphere, as well as a secluded pool, lapa and braai area. Rooms all have TV and air-con.

Haus Blumers *(☎ 303887, Cnr Hage Geingob & School St, PO Box 1994)* Singles/ doubles B&B US$16/25. The rooms in this friendly place all have private bathrooms and most also have high ceilings, creating an illusion of space.

C'est Si Bon Lodge *(☎ 301240, fax 303208, e nsandman@iafrica.com.na, PO Box 2060, Schwimbadweb)* Singles/doubles US$48/63. Namibians and South Africans receive a 40% discount here. As the name would suggest, the ambience and the demeanour are very French. This incongruous hotel was designed with tour groups in mind, and is certainly the finest option in Otjiwarongo. The restaurant offers an especially varied menu, including soups, salads and sandwiches, and beef, seafood, pork and pasta dishes.

Hotel Bahnhof *(☎ 304801, fax 304803, e rectz@iway.na, Bahnhof St, PO Box 100)* Budget rooms US$20, singles/doubles with ceiling fan US$24/32, with air-con US$26/ 35. All rates include breakfast and MNET TV. This sparkling-clean hotel for business travellers is good value and is comfortable enough.

Hotel Hamburger Hof *(☎ 302520, fax 303607, Bahnhof St, PO Box 8)* Budget singles/doubles US$24/34, with TV & breakfast from US$35/49. The name of this long-standing town hotel may recall some sort of fast-food joint, but in fact it's just a nondescript place to lay your head at night. At lunch time it dishes up a varied lunch buffet for US$3.

Out of Town Staying outside Otjiwarongo is also an option.

Otjibamba Lodge *(☎ 303133, fax 304561, e bamba@iafrica.com.na, 3km south of Otjiwarongo, PO Box 134)* Single/double chalets B&B US$43/62. Facilities at this rel- atively low-key safari lodge include an a la carte restaurant, bar, pool and game farm.

Okonjima *(☎ 304563, fax 304565, e okonjima@mweb.com.na, w www.okonjima.com, PO Box 793, Otjiwarongo)* Single/double bungalows US$240/400. Rates include full board, walks, wildlife drives and other activities. Okonjima, the 'Place of Baboons', is technically a guest farm but more resembles a safari lodge. This place offers nature trails, a Bushman walk, hiking trails up to 10km, and the possibility of seeing over 300 bird species – but the big attraction is the cats. The owners' Africat Foundation sponsors a cheetah and leopard rehabilitation centre, where problem cats are taught not to ravage cattle, and also keeps orphaned or problem lions, cheetahs and other cats. It also has a warthog named Scratch and a house-trained caracal. Accommodation is in bungalows, but a remote tented camp should be open by the time you read this. Note that it's closed from 20 December to late January and that children under 12 aren't allowed. To reach it, turn west onto the D2515, 49km south of Otjiwarongo; follow this road for 15km and turn left onto the farm road for the last 10km.

Places to Eat

The hotels have bars and restaurants serving meals and snacks, and the crocodile farm also serves light meals. At several petrol stations along Hage Geingob St you'll find the usual range of takeaway facilities and shops selling meat pies and other snacks.

Kameeldoorn Garten *(School St)* Light lunches & dinners US$3-5. This small place on the outskirts offers a nice touch of simple sophistication.

Monali Pizzeria *(Hage Geingob St)* Mains & pizzas US$3-5. This central diner is upstairs along the main street.

Carstensen's *(☎ 302326, St George's St)* This excellent bakery and takeaway in the town centre is a long-standing Otjiwarongo institution.

Getting There & Away

Bus Otjiwarongo is on the Intercape Mainliner route between Windhoek (US$16, three hours) and Victoria Falls (US$47, 17 hours); it stops at Marina Toyota. Minibuses between Windhoek and the Owambo country pass through Otjiwarongo and stop at Engen petrol station. On the B1 into town from the south, watch west of the road for the twin Omatako peaks – Herero for 'Buttocks'.

The weekly Star Line bus leaves for Outjo (US$3, one hour) at 8am on Thursday, continuing to Khorixas (US$5, 4½ hours), Henties Bay (US$10.50, nine hours), Swakopmund (US$12, 12½ hours) and Walvis Bay (US$12.50, 13 hours). In the opposite direction, it leaves Walvis Bay at 1pm on Friday and arrives in Otjiwarongo at 12.15am. The 8am Wednesday bus to Okakarara (US$3, 1½ hours) passes within 21km of Waterberg Plateau Park.

Train Rail services between Windhoek or Walvis Bay and Tsumeb call at Otjiwarongo. For information, phone Trans-Namib (☎ 305200)

WATERBERG PLATEAU PARK

Waterberg Plateau Park *(admission US$3 per person plus US$3 per vehicle; open 8am-1pm & 2pm-sunset year-round)* takes in a 50km-long, 16km-wide Etjo sandstone plateau, looming 150m above the plain. Rainwater is absorbed by sandstone layers and percolates through the strata until it reaches the south-west tilting mudstone, forming an aquifer that emerges in springs at the cliff base. Around this sheer-sided 'lost world' is an abundance of freshwater springs, that support mosaic of trees and wildlife.

The park is also known as a repository for rare and threatened species, including sable and roan antelopes and both white and black rhinos. You may also see wild dogs, tsessebes, buffaloes, leopards, cheetahs and lesser bushbabies and over 200 bird species.

History

In 1873, a Rhenish mission station was established at Waterberg, but it was destroyed

NORTH CENTRAL NAMIBIA

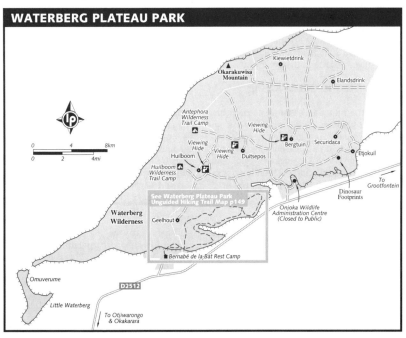

WATERBERG PLATEAU PARK

in 1880 during the Herero-Nama wars. In 1904, it was the site of the decisive Battle of the Waterberg between the German colonial forces and the Herero resistance. Due to superior weaponry and communications, the Germans prevailed and the remaining Herero were forced to flee eastward into the Kalahari. The final death blow was dealt by German soldiers, who were sent ahead to refuse the retreating Herero access to the region's few water holes.

On the weekend nearest 11 August, the local Herero, Scouts, MOTHs (Memorable Order of Tin Hats – a British colonial military fraternity), and the Alte Kamaraden (the German legion) commemorate the confrontation. The ceremony happens at the memorial in the cemetery near the warden's office. For attendees, sober dress is appropriate.

Information

The warden's office at the Bernabé de la Bat Rest Camp can help with tourist inquiries.

The useful booklet *Waterberg Flora: Footpaths In and Around the Camp* by Craven & Marais costs US$8 at the camp shop. Alternatively, see *Waterberg Plateau Park* by Ilme Schneider, sold in bookshops and rest camps around the country.

Bernabé de la Bat Walking Tracks

Around the pink sandstone rest camp are nine short walking tracks, including one up to the plateau rim at Mountain View. They're great for a pleasant day of easy walking, but watch for snakes, which sun themselves on rocks and even on the tracks themselves. No reservations are required for these walks.

Okarakuvisa Vultury

On the Okarakuvisa Mountain, on the plateau's northern edge, is Namibia's only Cape vulture. Cape vultures were nearly wiped out after insecticides were sprayed on surrounding farms in the 1950s, but in the early 1990s, the Ministry of Environment & Tourism (MET) attempted to increase their numbers by proffering a regular menu of kudu and gemsbok carcasses at a sort of

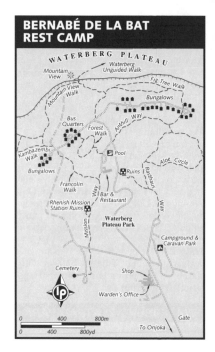

BERNABÉ DE LA BAT REST CAMP

'vulture restaurant'. That practice has now stopped, but you may still occasionally see the birds soaring above the plateau.

Unguided Hiking Trail

A four-day, 42km unguided hike around a figure-eight track begins at 9am every Wednesday from April to November. It costs US$12 per person and groups are limited to between three and 10 people. Hikers stay in basic shelters and don't need a tent, but must otherwise be self-sufficient. Hikes must be pre-booked through the NWR in Windhoek.

The first day begins at Mountain View and follows the escarpment for 13km to Otjozongombe shelter. The second day's walk to Otjomapenda shelter is just a three hour, 7km walk. The third day comprises an 8km route that loops back to Otjomapenda for the third night. The fourth and final day is a six hour, 14km return to Bernabé de la Bat. Both shelters have drinking water;

you'll need to drink 3 to 4L per day, especially in April, May, October and November.

Waterberg Wilderness Trail

Also from April to November, the four-day guided Waterberg Wilderness Trail operates every second, third and fourth Thursday of the month. The walks, which are led by armed guides, accommodate groups of six to eight people; they begin at 4pm on Thursdays from the Onjoka Wildlife Administration Centre and end early on Sunday afternoon. They cost US$27 per person and must be pre-booked through NWR in Windhoek. There's no set route and the itinerary is left to the whims of the guide. Accommodation is in simple huts, but participants must carry their own food and sleeping bags.

Organised Tours

Visitors may not explore the park in their own vehicles, but NWR operates morning and afternoon wildlife drives (US$7/3 per adult/child), which buzz around the plateau in open 4WD vehicles and stop to watch wildlife in strategically placed hides. Unfortunately, the drivers could use a few lessons in at least feigning enthusiasm.

Places to Stay & Eat

Bernabé de la Bat Rest Camp Camping US$13 for 2 people plus US$2 for each additional person, double 'tourisettes' US$40, 3-/5-bed self-catering bungalows US$42/44, 3-/4-bed self-catering bungalows US$52/70, 5-bed suite US$58. The three-bed bungalows are the best value, even with just one or two people, and include fans and braais.

The camp ***restaurant*** is open from 7am to 8.30am, noon to 1.30pm and 7pm to 9pm. The bar opens from noon to 2pm and 6pm to 10pm.

A shop and kiosk sell staples and snacks, and there's also a petrol station and a beautiful russet sandstone swimming pool that reflects the surrounding hills.

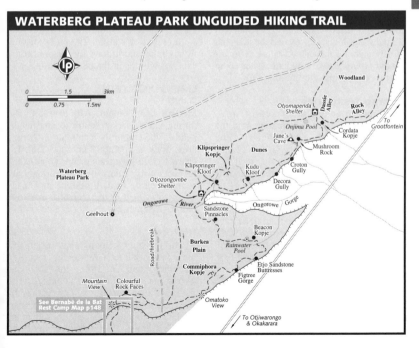

WATERBERG PLATEAU PARK UNGUIDED HIKING TRAIL

NORTH CENTRAL NAMIBIA

Getting There & Away

The nearest public transport is the 8am Wednesday bus from Otjiwarongo to Okakarara on the C22, which passes within 21km of Bernabé de la Bat. Taxis from Otjiwarongo start at around US$25. Note that bicycles and motorcycles aren't permitted in the park.

Those with a sturdy vehicle may want to leave or arrive on the particularly scenic D2512, which runs between Waterberg and Grootfontein.

OTAVI
☎ 067

Between Otjiwarongo and Tsumeb, the B1 passes Otavi, 'the Place of Water', near the mountains of the same name. The town was originally a German garrison with a natural spring used to irrigate the surrounding land to cultivate wheat. Otavi grew after 1906, when it became a copper-mining centre and was linked to Swakopmund by a narrow-gauge railway.

Otavi is now known as the site of the 'Otavi ape' discovery. In 1991, French and US palaeontologists uncovered the jawbone of a prehistoric ape-like creature *(Otavip-ithecus namibiensis)*, which may shed some light on the prehistoric 'missing link'.

Khorab Memorial

The Khorab Memorial, 2km north of Otavi, was erected in 1920 to commemorate the German troops who surrendered to the South African army under General Louis Botha on 9 July 1915. From the hotel, it's over the railway line and right along the signposted track.

Places to Stay & Eat

Lions Caravan Park Camping US$2 plus US$3/3.50/4 for 1/2/3 people and US$0.50 entry, 4-bed bungalow US$9 plus US$0.50 entry. This is a grassy place to pitch a tent, but the facilities are decaying.

Palmenecke Guest House (☎/fax 234199, 96 Hertzog Ave, PO Box 392) Singles/doubles B&B US$20/34. This is the best-appointed accommodation choice in Otavi; all rooms have showers, TV and air-con.

Otavi Gardens Hotel (☎ 234333, fax 234336, PO Box 11) Singles/doubles US$16/20. Breakfast costs an additional US$3 and foreigners pay an extra US$1.50. For meals, you can choose between the attached bar and restaurant or the petrol station takeaway.

Restcamp Zum Potjie (☎ 234300, fax 221964, [e] zumpot@tsu.namib.com, 8km from Otavi on the Tsumeb road, PO Box 202) Camping US$3 per person, single/double bungalows US$26/40. Set in a nice hilly area, this place offers a restaurant and basic accommodation. The bizarre name (pronounced 'tsoom-poykee') blends German and Afrikaans and means roughly 'in the pot', and yes, *potjie* meals (the stew cooked in the iron three-legged pot of the same name) are indeed available.

Getting There & Away

All minibuses between Windhoek and Tsumeb or Oshakati pass through Otavi. The Intercape Mainliner service between Windhoek (US$21, 4¼ hours) and Victoria Falls (US$42, 15¾ hours) stops at the Total 4-Ways petrol station. If you're driving through, be sure to look for the dromedary camels that inhabit the petrol station.

GROOTFONTEIN
☎ 067

Modern Grootfontein (Afrikaans for 'Big Spring') is a market centre located in the heart of the country's major cattle-farming area. With a distinctly colonial feel, it's characterised by an air of uprightness and respectability. Many of its buildings are constructed of local limestone and many streets are lined with jacaranda trees that bloom in September.

History

It was the town's eponymous spring that managed to attract Grootfontein's earliest travellers, and in 1885, the Dorsland (Afrikaans for 'Thirst Land') trekkers set up the short-lived Republic of Upingtonia. By 1887, the settlement was gone, but six years later, Grootfontein became the headquarters for the German South-West Africa Company, thanks to the area's mineral wealth. In 1896, the German Schutztruppe constructed a fort using local labour, and Grootfontein became a garrison town. For more historical information, see under individual sites of interest following.

Information

Grootfontein's marginally useful tourist office (☎ 243100) is at the end of the municipal building, just off Okavango Rd.

At the I-Cafe (☎ 243266) on Hidipo Hamutenya St, you'll pay US$3 per hour for email and Internet access.

Grootfontein Spring

The Herero knew this area as 'Otjiwanda tjongue', or 'Leopard's Crest', but the current name, Afrikaans for 'Big Spring', parallels the Nama name 'Gei-aus', which means the same thing. This reliable source of water has attracted both people and wildlife for thousands of years, and also became a halt for European hunters as early as the 1860s.

Later, the water attracted the area's first European settlers. In 1885, 40 families of Dorsland trekkers arrived from Angola to settle this land, which had been purchased by their leader, Will Jordan, from the Owambo chief Kambonde.

The spring and the adjacent Tree Park, which was planted by the South-West Africa Company, can be seen near the swimming pool at the east end of town.

German Fort & Museum

In 1896, a contingent of Schutztruppe soldiers was posted to Grootfontein and, using local labour, constructed a fort. It was enlarged several times in the early 20th century and, in 1922, a large limestone extension was added. Later, the fort served as a boarding school, but in 1968 it fell into disuse.

Only a last-minute public appeal saved the building from demolition, and in 1974 it was restored into the **municipal museum** *(admission free; open 4pm-6pm Tues-Fri, 9am-11am Wed)*. Displays outline the area's mineral wealth, early industries and colonial history, and there are collections of

> **Warning**
>
> Grootfontein has an ongoing security problem and if you're jostled in the street, it's probably safe to assume that a robbery attempt is under way. Don't walk around the centre with valuables and never leave anything in sight inside a parked vehicle.

minerals, domestic items, old cameras and typewriters, and a restored carpentry and blacksmith's shop. Outside opening hours, phone ☎ 242351 or ☎ 243584 to have the museum unlocked.

Cemetery

In the town cemetery, off Okavango Rd, you can search out the graves of several Schutztruppe soldiers who died in combat with local forces around the turn of the century. Naturally, the opposition was interred elsewhere.

Places to Stay

In Town Grootfontein has a few worthwhile accommodation options.

Oleander Municipal Caravan Park (☎ 243101) Camping US$4 plus US$1.50/1 per vehicle/person, self-catering singles/doubles US$44/52. The camping ground adjoins the municipal swimming pool. Security has improved, but it's still wise to watch your vehicle closely and keep any valuables inside your sleeping bag. The pool is open from 1 September to 30 April.

Die Kraal Camping Ground & Steak House (☎ 240300, 6km from Grootfontein on the Rundu road) Camping US$3 per person. This famed steak house provides a safer option for camping, but you'll need your own vehicle.

Meteor Hotel (☎ 242078, fax 243072, Okavango Rd, PO Box 346) Singles/doubles US$31/50, family room US$65, all with B&B. This is Grootfontein's town hotel, with the usual lack of character. However, the integrated bar can be fun and the dining room prepares decent meals. On Sundays, it does a US$6 lunch buffet from noon to 2pm and on Fridays, a US$6 pizza-bake.

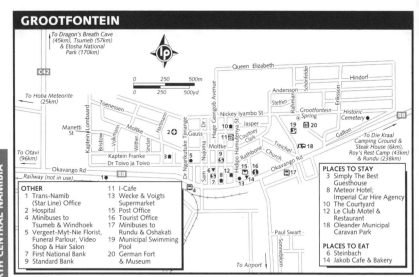

GROOTFONTEIN

To Dragon's Breath Cave
(45km), Tsumeb (57km)
& Etosha National
Park (170km)

Queen Elizabeth

Hindorf

Andersson

To Hoba Meteorite
(25km)

Steffen

Grootfontein
Spring

Historic
Cemetery ●

Nickey Iyambo St

Toenessen

Manetti
St

Jasper

To Die Kraal
Camping Ground &
Steak House (6km),
Roy's Rest Camp (43km)
& Rundu (238km)

To Otavi
(96km)

Kaptein Franke
Dr Toivo ja Toivo

Okavango Rd

Railway (not in use)

To Airport

To Airport

OTHER
1 Trans-Namib
   (Star Line) Office
2 Hospital
4 Minibuses to
   Tsumeb & Windhoek
5 Vergeet-Myt-Nie Florist,
   Funeral Parlour, Video
   Shop & Hair Salon
7 First National Bank
9 Standard Bank

11 I-Cafe
13 Wecke & Voigts
    Supermarket
15 Post Office
16 Tourist Office
17 Minibuses to
    Rundu & Oshakati
19 Municipal Swimming
    Pool
20 German Fort
    & Museum

PLACES TO STAY
3 Simply The Best
   Guesthouse
8 Meteor Hotel;
   Imperial Car Hire Agency
10 The Courtyard
12 Le Club Motel &
    Restaurant
18 Oleander Municipal
    Caravan Park

PLACES TO EAT
6 Steinbach
14 Jakob Cafe & Bakery

Le Club Motel & Restaurant *(☎ 242414, Hidipo Hamutenya St)* Singles/doubles US$23/34. The good-value rooms in this town motel have private bathrooms, DSTV and air-con.

The Courtyard *(☎ 240027, fax 240073, e courty@gfn.namib.com, 2 Gauss St, PO Box 1425)* Singles/doubles US$31/47. This place has a large swimming pool, air-con, cable TV, and enormous disabled-accessible rooms. Set dinners are available on request for US$5. Email and Internet access is available for US$3 per hour.

Simply the Best Guesthouse *(☎ 243315, fax 242431, 6 Wiegel St)* Singles/doubles US$13/20. The name seems a bit presumptuous, but the friendly owner, Mrs Brandt, likes to meet people and correspondingly, has opened her home to the travelling sort. Rates include TV, access to the pool, braai, and safe parking. If arriving during business hours, book in at Vergeet-Myt-Nie Florist, Funeral Parlour, Video Shop & Hair Salon *(☎ 242431)* on Dr Toivo ja Toivo St.

Out of Town Stay out of town for a bit of fresh air and some action adventure.

Gästefarm Dornhügel *(☎ 240439, 081-128 8820, fax 125 0126, e dornhuegel @iafrica.com.na, W www.natron.net/tour/dorn/huegel.htm, 24km off the D2844, PO Box 173, Grootfontein)*. Singles/doubles with half board US$77/134. This country game farm offers a rural atmosphere and wildlife drives on request.

Gästefarm Zur Aloé *(☎ 243916, PO Box 142)* Dorm beds US$11, singles/doubles US$20/27. This farm is 10km south-west of Grootfontein on the B8, toward Otavi. The highlight is a tour of the cave and underground lake. There's also bird-watching here and a water hole that attracts wildlife in the dry season.

Roy's Rest Camp *(☎/fax 240302, 1km off the Okavango road, opposite the Tsumkwe turn-off, e royscamp@iway.na, W www .triponline.net, PO Box 755)* Camping US$5 per person, singles/doubles US$31/44, 3-/4-bed bungalows US$59/64. Accommodation in this recommended place appears to jump straight from a fairy tale illustration – the handmade furnishings are all fabulously rustic, this also extends to the tamboti wood bar tables and chairs in the dining area. There's also a swimming pool and curio shop. Hiking and mountain biking possibilities include 3 and 5km trails, and there are tours of the working cattle ranch for a nominal charge. Breakfast/lunch/dinner here will set you back US$6/8/9.

Places to Eat

Die Kraal (☎ 240300, 6km on the Rundu road) Soup US$1.20; fish, schnitzel or kudu US$4; kebabs or ribs US$7; fillet steak US$6.50/9 for 250/500g; rump, sirloin and T-bone US$6.50 for 500g. Open 11am-11pm daily. Meat can't be ignored here in cattle country, and this steakhouse, 6km out on the Rundu road, specialises in just that. This place sizzles up Namibia's best – and most enormous steaks. Bookings are essential.

Le Club Motel & Restaurant (see Places to Stay) Breakfast US$2-3, starters US$2-3, burgers US$2, mains US$3.50-7. Open 6.45am-2.30am Mon-Fri, 8.30am-2pm & 5.30pm-11pm Sat, 9am-2pm & 6pm-9pm Sun. This restaurant/bar has a mind-boggling menu including pasta, chicken, seafood, beef, noodles and a vast array of other options; all items are available for takeaways.

Another option is the dining room at the *Meteor Hotel* (see Places to Stay). Takeaway meals are available at the *Shell petrol station* and the well-stocked *Wecke & Voigts* supermarket *(☎ 242061)*. There are also a couple of recommended bakeries: *Steinbach (☎ 242348)* and *Jakob Cafe & Bakery (☎ 242433)* serve up coffee, snacks and sweet treats.

Getting There & Away

Grootfontein is no longer on the passenger rail routes, but it is on the weekly Intercape Mainliner run between Windhoek (US$25, 6¼ hours) and Victoria Falls (US$39, 13¾ hours). It stops at the Maroela Motors petrol station on Okavango Rd.

Star Line (☎ 249 2201) runs buses to Tsumkwe (US$7, 6½ hours) at 11.30am Monday and Thursday, returning 10.15am Tuesday and Friday. Minibuses to and from Tsumeb, Windhoek, Rundu and Oshakati leave from the informal bus terminals on the main road at the appropriate end of town.

Getting Around

Grootfontein has a limited taxi service; Meteor Hotel is the Imperial Car Hire agency.

The Red Line

Between Grootfontein and Rundu, and Tsumeb and Ondangwa, the B8 and B1 cross the Red Line, the Animal Disease Control Checkpoint veterinary control fence separating the commercial cattle ranches of the south from the communal subsistence lands to the north. This fence bars the north-south movement of animals as a precaution against foot-and-mouth disease and rinderpest, and animals bred north of this line may not be sold to the south or exported to overseas markets.

As a result, the Red Line also marks the effective boundary between the First and Third Worlds. The landscape south of the line is characterised by a dry scrubby bushveld (open grassland) of vast ranches which are home only to cattle and a few scattered ranchers. However, north of the Animal Disease Control Checkpoint, travellers enter a landscape of dense bush, baobab trees, mopane scrub and small kraals, where people and animals wander along the road and the air is filled with smoke from cooking fires and bush-clearing operations.

AROUND GROOTFONTEIN
Hoba Meteorite

Near the Hoba Farm, 25km west of Grootfontein, the world's largest meteorite was discovered in 1920 by hunter Jacobus Brits. This cuboid bit of space debris is composed of 82% iron, 16% nickel and 0.8% cobalt, along with traces of other metals. No-one knows when it fell to earth (it's thought to have been around 80,000 years ago) but since it weighs in at around 54,000kg, it must have made a hell of a thump.

In 1955, after souvenir hunters began hacking off bits to take home, the site was declared a national monument, and a conservation project was launched with funds from the Rössing Foundation. There's now a visitors information board, a short nature trail and a shady picnic area. Admission is US$1.

From Grootfontein, follow the C42 toward Tsumeb. After 4km, turn west on the

D2859 and continue 18km to the Hoba Farm, then follow the 'Meteoriet' signs. There's no public transport, but taxis from Grootfontein cost around US$15.

Dragon's Breath Cave

If you're ticking off superlatives, how about this? Dragon's Breath Cave, on Harasib Farm, 46km from Grootfontein, holds the world's largest known underground lake. This fabulous two-hectare subterranean reservoir occupies an immense chamber 60m below the surface. Its waters are crystal clear and, with sufficient light, allow visibility for 100m. The name is derived from the spontaneous condensation caused by warm, moist outside air forcing its way into the cool chamber. At the time of writing, the cave was closed to the public and permission to explore it was granted only to professional caving expeditions. The ownership has recently changed and it may soon be set up to receive casual visitors.

TSUMEB

☎ 067

Tsumeb is situated at the apex of the Golden Triangle of roads linking it with Otavi and Grootfontein. The name is derived from the melding of the San word *tsoumsoub* (to dig in loose ground) and the Herero word *otjisume* (place of frogs). To fathom the latter derivation, however, requires some imagination. Tsumeb isn't really known for its frog population; it's just that the red, brown, green and grey streaks created by minerals looked like dried scum (in Afrikaans, *paddaslyk* or frog spawn) that had been scooped out of a water hole and splattered on the rocks. As a result, both the frogs and the digging equipment appear on the town crest.

The prosperity of this mining town is based on the presence of 184 known minerals, including 10 that are unique to this area. Its deposits of copper ore and a phenomenal range of other metals and minerals (lead, silver, germanium, cadmium and many others), brought to the surface in a volcanic pipe, as well as Africa's most productive lead mine (the world's 5th largest), give it the distinction of being a metallurgical and mineralogical wonder of the world.

Tsumeb specimens have found their way into museum collections around the globe, but the finest collection is displayed in the Smithsonian Natural History Museum in Washington, DC. You'll also see a respectable assembly of the region's mineralogical largesse and historical data in the town museum.

History

Prehistoric sites date Tsumeb's mining history back to the Iron Age. The first European to recognise its riches was Sir Francis Galton, who passed through in 1851, but it was over 40 years before others took serious interest. On 12 January 1893, Matthew Rogers, a British surveyor working for the South-West Africa Company of London, saw the extraordinarily colourful volcanic pipe. In his report he exclaimed: 'In the whole of my experience, I have never seen such a sight as was presented before my view at Tsumeb, and I doubt...that I shall ever see such another...'.

As a result, exploration began in earnest in 1900. Early on, the German company Otavi Minen und Eisenbahn Gesellschaft (OMEG) determined that the extent of the deposits merited a railway, and in November 1903 it signed a contract with the South-West Africa Company to construct the 560km narrow-gauge railway to the coast at Swakopmund. Despite the interruption caused by the German-Herero wars, construction of the railroad was completed in August 1906.

Mining operations commenced in 1907 and, after seven years, they were producing 75,000 tonnes of ore annually. WWI halted production, but it resumed in 1921, and by 1930 the annual output peaked at 236,000 tonnes. Operations were again interrupted by WWII and, after Germany lost the war, OMEG was put up for sale by the 'custodian of enemy property'. Tsumeb Corporation – a consortium of South African, US and British interests – was formed to purchase the operation at a cost of UK£1 million. A new flotation plant was built to separate zinc from copper and lead, and in 1948 production resumed. By the mid-1960s, the Tsumeb mining operation was recording a yield of over one million tonnes of ore every year.

Information

Travel North Namibia (☎ 220728, 081-124 6722, fax 220916, 🖅 travelnn@tsu.namib .com), 1551 Omeg Allee, PO Box 779, is the best, friendliest and most thorough tourist office in the country. Anita and Leon Pearson offer nationwide tourist information; accommodation and transport bookings; airline ticketing and charters; inexpensive car hire for Etosha trips; fax, email and Internet services; safe-storage facilities; and Etosha bookings – they really go the extra mile. They also sell original local arts and crafts.

Internet and email services are available from the Dot Com Café, on Omeg Allee, for US$1.50 per hour.

On hot days, you will probably want to have a dunk at Paradise Pool (☎ 081-245 3940). Admission is US$0.75/$0.50 per adult/child or pensioner. It's open 11am to 4.30pm daily.

For vehicle repairs, an honest and recommended mechanic is Mr Kalish, whose Motor and General Repairs shop is behind the Engen petrol station.

Tsumeb Mining Museum

Tsumeb's history is told in this museum *(Cnr Main St & 8th Rd; admission US$1.50; open 9am-noon & 3pm-6pm Mon-Fri, 3pm-6pm Sat)*, which is housed in the 1915 German private school. The building served two brief periods as a school and also did a stint as a hospital for German troops. In addition to outstanding mineral displays (you'll never have seen anything like psitticinite!), mining machinery, stuffed birds and Himba and Herero artefacts, it holds lots of militaria, including weapons recovered from Lake Otjikoto. This was part of a dump of military hardware, including German and South African field guns, cannons and vehicles, which was abandoned by German troops prior to their surrender to the South Africans in 1915.

Tsumeb Arts & Crafts Centre

Tsumeb Arts & Crafts Centre *(☎ 220257, 18 Main St; open 8.30am-1pm & 2.30pm-5.30pm Mon-Fri, 8.30am-1pm Sat)* markets Caprivian woodwork, San arts, Owambo basketry, karakul weavings, European-Namibian leatherwork and other traditional northern Namibian arts and crafts.

Grand Old Lady Mineshaft

Visitors can now see the Grand Old Lady mineshaft and the Glory Hole where Tsumeb's modern mining history began. Tours are no longer conducted, but the superstructure is there to see, rising above the northern end of town.

St Barbara's Church

Tsumeb's distinctive Roman Catholic church was consecrated in 1914 and dedicated to St Barbara, the patron saint of mineworkers. It contains some fine colonial murals and an odd tower, which makes it look less like a church than a municipal building in some small German town.

OMEG Minenbüro

Due to its soaring spire, the Otavi Minen und Eisenbahn Gesellschaft (OMEG) Minenbüro building on 1st St is frequently mistaken for a church – in fact, it looks more like a church than St Barbara's. It's probably Tsumeb's most imposing building – and few would ever guess that it dates back to 1907.

Tsumeb Cultural Centre

This complex *(☎/fax 220787, 1km on Grootfontein road, PO Box 1973; admission US$1.50/0.75 adult/child; open 8.30am-1pm Mon-Fri, 2.30pm-5.30pm Sat)* includes examples of housing styles, cultural demonstrations and artefacts from all major Namibian traditions.

Muramba Bushman Trails

Muramba Bushman Trails *(☎ 220659, 🖅 bushman@natron.net, PO Box 689)* is based on a large farm, 70km north-east of Tsumeb near Tsintsabis. Here, participants learn about the culture, traditions and pharmacopoeia of Namibia's first people.

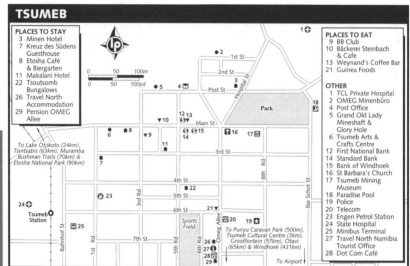

TSUMEB

PLACES TO STAY
3 Minen Hotel
7 Kreuz des Südens
    Guesthouse
8 Etosha Café
    & Biergarten
11 Makalani Hotel
22 Tsoutsomb
    Bungalows
26 Travel North
    Accommodation
29 Pension OMEG
    Allee

To Lake Otjikoto (24km),
Tsintsabis (63km), Muramba
Bushman Trails (70km) &
Etosha National Park (90km)

PLACES TO EAT
9 BB Club
10 Bäckerei Steinbach
    & Cafe
13 Weynad's Coffee Bar
21 Guinea Foods

OTHER
1 TCL Private Hospital
2 OMEG Minenbüro
4 Post Office
5 Grand Old Lady
    Mineshaft &
    Glory Hole
6 Tsumeb Arts &
    Crafts Centre
12 First National Bank
14 Standard Bank
15 Bank of Windhoek
16 St Barbara's Church
17 Tsumeb Mining
    Museum
18 Paradise Pool
19 Police
20 Telecom
23 Engen Petrol Station
24 State Hospital
25 Minibus Terminal
27 Travel North Namibia
    Tourist Office
28 Dot Com Café

To Punyu Caravan Park (500m),
Tsumeb Cultural Centre (3km),
Grootfontein (57km), Otavi
(65km) & Windhoek (431km)

To Airport

There are two unguided hiking trails through woodland and grassy ranchland. The Owner Reinhard Friederich and his Hai//kom (Heikum) San colleagues also hold guided morning walks in English or German (US$20, with lunch) on which participants can learn all about traditional lifestyles, bushcraft and the collecting of useful wild plants and herbs. There's also a small museum of implements and artefacts. Advance bookings are preferred. Overnight accommodation (US$14 per person) is available in either traditional beehive huts or thatched chalets.

To get there, follow the Tsintsabis road north of Tsumeb for 64km, then turn east on the D3016 and continue 6km to the farm.

Places to Stay

In Town The following have been ordered from cheap to more expensive.

Punyu Caravan Park (☎ 221056, fax 221464, Private Bag 2012) Tent/caravan sites US$4.50/6 plus US$1.75 per person and US$1.75 per vehicle, day visits to picnic sites US$4.50. Tsumeb's caravan park sits aside the lonely double-lane road just less than 1km from the town centre. It's

protected by an electrified fence, but you should still keep a close watch over your belongings.

Travel North Accommodation (☎ 220728, 081-124 6722, fax 220916, e travelnn@ tsu.namib.com, 1551 Omeg Allee) Dorm beds US$11, singles/doubles B&B US$16/ 24. This friendly lodge attached to the tourist office offers comfortable rooms, cooking facilities and a shady braai area. If you arrive after business hours, ring the bell on the gate.

Etosha Café & Biergarten (☎/fax 221207, 081-127 3855, Main St, PO Box 189) Rooms with shared bathroom US$11 per person. Karin Locher's well-loved cafe and beer garden also provides clean, inexpensive accommodation.

Kreuz des Südens Guesthouse (☎ 221005, fax 221067, 500-501 3rd St) Singles/doubles with shower US$15/23. Breakfast costs US$4. This small and recommended place has braai facilities.

Minen Hotel (☎ 221071, fax 221750, Cnr Post & Hospital Sts) Singles/doubles in the old section US$24/38, new section US$38/54. This hotel's greatest asset is probably its nice green setting, near the end of a lovely avenue of jacaranda trees. The rooms are set around a courtyard and have air-con. The a la carte restaurant operates only on weekends.

Pension OMEG Allee *(☎ 220631, fax 220821, 858 Omeg Allee, PO Box 284)* Singles/doubles B&B US$25/36. This clean and well-kept lodge reflects its German orientation. Limited cable TV is available.

Tsoutsomb Bungalows *(☎ 220404, fax 220592, 4th St, PO Box 133)* Self-catering self-contained 6-/8-bed bungalows US$38/ 51, or US$14 per person with 1 or 2 people. This place won't win any design awards, but if you have a large group, it's a convenient good-value option.

Makalani Hotel *(☎ 221051, fax 221575,* e *makalani@mweb.com.na,* w *www.makal anihotel.com, Cnr 3rd St & 4th Rd, PO Box 24)* Singles/doubles US$37/52. Now under new management, this friendly central hotel is an excellent choice. Rates include breakfast and rooms all have DSTV. The attached restaurant prepares good European-style lunches and dinners for US$9 and US$12. There are two bars to choose from: the lively Golden Nugget Bar and the more subdued Pierre's Pub.

Out of Town There are more possibilities out of the centre.

Tamboti Lodge *(☎/fax 222497, 081-129 4553,* e *tsmapt@iafrica.com.na, D3007, PO Box 780)* Camping US$5 plus US$2 per person, single/double bungalows or railway carriages US$36/46. Short wildlife drives cost US$2. This game farm 15km from Tsumeb provides a rural atmosphere, wildlife viewing and hiking within easy reach of town.

Auros Mountain Camp *(☎ 064-400933, 081-129 4969, fax 206907,* e *volkb@ iml-net.com.na,* w *www.natron.net/tour/auros /campe.html, Otavi Mountain Conservancy, PO Box 79, Swakopmund)* Three 2-bed A-frame chalets US$40 for 4 people plus US$10 for each additional person. This remote conservancy, high in the Auros Mountains, presents all sorts of wilderness activities: hiking (including a track up 2148m Umenaub), mountain biking, explo-

ration of the beautiful and well-decorated Leopard Cave (US$10 per group), and 4WD trails (US$20). Access is by 4WD only. Book directly or through Travel North Namibia in Tsumeb.

Guest Farm Ghaub *(☎ 240188, fax 231083,* w *www.namibsunhotels.com.na/ ghaub, PO Box 786, Grootfontein)* Singles/ doubles B&B US$40/60. This former mission station, founded in 1895, has been renovated as an historic accommodation option. Perhaps the most interesting feature of the mountainous property is the wonderful Ghaub Caverns (in fact, the entire area is riddled with limestone caverns), which have been declared a national monument. Guided cave tours cost US$4. To get there, go to Kombat between Grootfontein and Otavi, turn north on the D3863 and continue 34km to the T-junction. There, turn left and carry on 3km to Ghaub.

Places to Eat

Etosha Café & Biergarten (see Places to Stay for details) Breakfast US$2.50-4, lunch US$3-4. Open 7am-5pm Mon-Fri, 8am-1pm Sat. This friendly spot is great for coffee, a wonderful English or German breakfast, light lunches and afternoon drinks among the tropical flowers in the leafy beer garden.

BB Club *(☎ 221779, 3rd Rd)* Mains US$3-6. This popular bar and cafe, 'where friends meet', has an extensive menu, which includes Portuguese cuisine, seafood, steaks, pasta and pizza. It has billiard tables and on Fridays, there's a disco and party in the bar.

Small, quick places include ***Weynand's Coffee Bar*** *(Main St)*; ***Bäckerei Steinbach & Cafe***, serving light lunches, cappuccino and espresso; the locally popular ***JC Take-away Catering Restaurant***, which is open until 11pm nightly. There are also the various local petrol station takeaways for something really quick.

Getting There & Away

Bus The weekly Intercape Mainliner bus that runs between Windhoek (US$22, five hours) and Victoria Falls (US$40, 15 hours) stops at the Travel North Namibia tourist office. It arrives at 1am Friday northbound and 10.45am Monday southbound.

Minibuses travel frequently between Tsumeb, Grootfontein, Oshakati and Windhoek, from the petrol station on Bahnhof St.

Star Line connects Tsumeb with Oshakati (US$6, four hours) daily at 11.15am from Monday to Friday; services also go to Rundu (US$7, four hours).

Train Trains run three times weekly to and from Windhoek (US$6, 16 hours) and Walvis Bay (US$6, 17½ hours) – trains are split and combined at Kranzberg. For rail or Star Line bus information, contact Trans-Namib (☎ 220358).

Hitching As the main access for Etosha National Park, Tsumeb sees lots of hopeful hitchers looking for lifts to Namutoni. However, hitching can be slow, it's forbidden inside the park, and all visitors need reservations from NWR in Windhoek.

Getting Around

Imperial Car Hire (☎ 220728, fax 220916, e wdhcity@imperial.ih.co.za), 1551 Omeg Allee, PO Box 779, has special deals on Windhoek-Tsumeb transfers and special rates for trips into Etosha National Park. Rates start at US$47 per day (unlimited kilometres).

AROUND TSUMEB
Lake Otjikoto

In May 1851, explorers Charles Andersson and Francis Galton stumbled across the unusual Lake Otjikoto *(24km north-west of Tsumeb on the B1; admission US$1; open 8am-6.30pm summer, 8am-5.30pm winter)*. The name of the lake is Herero for 'Deep Hole', and its waters fill a limestone sinkhole measuring 100 by 150m. Galton measured the depth of the lake at 55m. Interestingly, Lake Otjikoto and nearby Lake Guinas are the only natural lakes in Namibia, and are also the only known habitats of the unusual mouth-breeding cichlid fish *(Pseudocrenilabrus philander)*. These psychedelic fish, which range from dark green to bright red, yellow and blue, are be-

lieved by biologists to eschew camouflage due to the absence of predators in this isolated environment. It's thought that these fish evolved from tilapia (bream) washed into the lake by ancient floods.

In 1915 the retreating German army dumped weaponry and ammunition into the lake to prevent it falling into South African hands. It's rumoured that they jettisoned five cannons, 10 cannon bases, three Gatling guns and between 300 and 400 wagonloads of ammunition. Some of this stuff was recovered and salvaged in 1916 at great cost and effort by the South African Army, the Tsumeb Corporation and the National Museum of Namibia. In 1970, divers discovered a Krupp ammunition wagon 41m below the surface; it's on display at the State Museum in Windhoek. In 1977 and 1983, two more ammunition carriers were salvaged and a cannon, captured from the South Africans early in the 20th century, has been restored and is now on display at the Tsumeb Mining Museum. Qualified divers can contact Theo Schoeman of the Windhoek Underwater Club (☎ 061-238320, 128 1945).

An enterprising local has fenced the lake and installed toilets and a curio shop. The lake itself is situated beyond a bizarre assemblage of clutter, but it's worth a stop, if only to read the sign on the curio shop.

Lake Guinas

South-west of Lake Otjikoto lies the geologically similar Lake Guinas, which is used to irrigate surrounding farmland. It's smaller than its counterpart but is also less touristy and twice as deep. It's also less accessible. Drive 27km north-west of Tsumeb on the B1 and turn south-west on the D3043. After 20km, turn south-east onto the D3031. The lake is 5km further along.

Etosha National Park

☎ 067

Etosha National Park is surely one of the world's greatest wildlife-viewing venues.

Its name, which means 'Great White Place of Dry Water', is taken from the vast white and greenish-coloured Etosha Pan. However, it's the surrounding bush and grasslands that provide habitat for Etosha's diverse wildlife. This vast park takes in more than 20,000 sq km and protects 114 mammal species, as well as 340 bird species, 16 reptiles and amphibians, one fish species and countless insects.

Geology

Etosha Pan is an immense, flat, saline desert covering over 5000 sq km that for a few days each year is converted by the rains into a shallow lagoon teeming with flamingoes and white pelicans. This prominent feature originated 12 million years ago as a vast shallow depression fed by the waters of the Kunene River. Over the aeons, climatic and tectonic changes lowered the water level and created a salt pan, which is fed in high rainfall years by in-flowing channels: either *oshanas* (dry river channels) or *omiramba* (fossil river valleys, which may flow underground). These include the oshanas Ekuma and Oshigambo in the north and the omuramba Owambo in the east.

History

The first Europeans in Etosha were traders and explorers John Andersson and Francis Galton, who arrived by wagon at Namutoni in 1851. They were followed in 1876 by an American trader, G McKeirnan, who observed: 'All the menageries in the world turned loose would not compare to the sight I saw that day'.

However, Etosha didn't attract the interest of tourists or conservationists until after the turn of the 20th century, when the governor of German South-West Africa, Dr F von Lindequist, became concerned about diminishing animal numbers and founded a 99,526 sq km reserve, which included Etosha Pan. At the time, the land was still unfenced and animals could follow their normal migration routes. In subsequent years, the park boundaries were altered a few times, and by 1970 Etosha had been reduced to its present 23,175 sq km.

Orientation & Information

Only the eastern two-thirds of Etosha is open to the general public; the western third is reserved exclusively for tour operators. Each of the three rest camps has an information centre, and the staff at either of the main gates can sell maps and provide basic information.

The park speed limit is set at 60km/h both to protect wildlife and keep down the dust. If any of your belongings won't tolerate a heavy dusting, pack them away in plastic. Car-cleaning services are available at any of the rest camps for a small fee.

Namutoni has a telephone and at Okaukuejo, you can book calls at the post office. There's no post office at Halali or Namutoni.

Want to see what's happening in Etosha any time of night or day? Log onto **W** www .africam.com and click on Namutoni, Halali or Okaukuejo, where Web cams trained on the water holes reveal the action every 30 seconds.

Visitors must check in at either Von Lindequist or Andersson Gates and purchase a permit, which costs US$4/0.20 per adult/child and US$3 per vehicle. The permits must then be presented at your reserved rest camp, where you pay any outstanding camping or accommodation fees (these are normally pre-paid through NWR in Windhoek). Note that pets and firearms are prohibited in Etosha National Park.

Those booked into the rest camps must show up before sunset and can only leave after sunrise; specific times are posted on the gates. Anyone returning later is locked out; if this happens, a blast on your car horn will send someone running to open the gate, but violators can expect a lecture on the evils of staying out late, a black mark on their park permit and perhaps even a fine.

All roads in the eastern section of Etosha are passable to 2WD vehicles, but wildlife viewing is best from the higher vantage point offered by a Land Rover, *bakkie* (pick-up truck) or minibus. The park road between Namutoni and Okaukuejo skirts Etosha Pan, providing great views of its vast spaces. Driving isn't permitted on the

ETOSHA NATIONAL PARK (EASTERN SECTION)

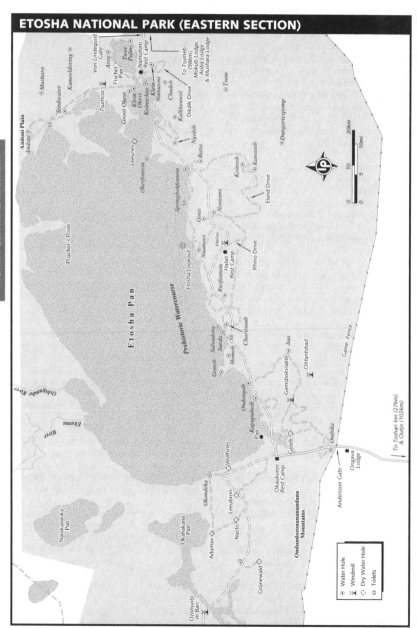

pan, but a network of gravel roads threads through the surrounding savannas and mopane woodland and even extends out to a viewing site, the Etosha Lookout, in the middle of the salt desert.

The best time for wildlife drives is at first light and late in the evening (but visitors aren't permitted outside the camps after dark). Each of the three rest camps have visitors registers, which describe any recent sightings in the vicinity.

Flora & Fauna

Etosha's most widespread vegetation type is mopane woodland, which fringes the pan and constitutes about 80% of the vegetation. The park also has umbrella-thorn acacias *(Acacia torilis)* and other trees that are favoured by browsing animals and from December to March, this sparse bush country bears a pleasant green hue.

Depending on the season, visitors may observe elephants, giraffes, Burchell's zebras, springboks, red hartebeests, blue wildebeests, gemsboks, elands, kudus, roans, ostriches, jackals, hyenas, lions, and even cheetahs and leopards. Among the endangered animal species are the black-faced impala and the black rhinoceros.

The park's wildlife density varies with the local ecology. As its name would suggest, Oliphantsbad (near Okaukuejo) is attractive to elephants, but for rhinos, you couldn't do better than the floodlit water hole at Okaukuejo. In general, the further east you go in the park, the more wildebeests, kudus and impalas join the springboks and gemsboks. The area around Namutoni, which averages 443mm of precipitation annually (compared with 412mm at Okaukuejo), is the best place to see the black-faced impala and the Damara dik-dik, Africa's smallest antelope. Etosha is also home to numerous smaller species, including both yellow and slender mongooses, honey badgers and leguaans.

In the dry winter season, wildlife clusters around water holes, while in the hot, wet summer months, animals disperse and spend the days sheltering in the bush. In the afternoon, even in the dry season, look care-

The Haunted Forest

The area dubbed the Haunted Forest, west of Okaukuejo, is so named for its bizarre moringa trees *(Moringa ovalifolia)*, which recall enormous pachypodia (elephant-foot trees) or the legendary boojum of Mexico's Baja California. San legend recounts that after God had found a home for all the plants and animals on earth, he discovered a bundle of leftover moringa trees. He flung them into the air and they fell to earth with their roots pointing skywards – and so they remain. Lately, this bizarre stand of bulbous remnants has suffered a good measure of elephant damage, but its unusual forms still merit attention and at least a few inspired photos.

fully for animals resting beneath the trees. Summer temperatures can reach 44°C, which isn't fun when you're confined in a vehicle, but this is the calving season and you may catch a glimpse of tiny zebra foals and fragile newborn springboks.

Birdlife is also profuse. Yellow-billed hornbills are common, and on the ground you should look for the huge kori bustard, which weighs 15kg and seldom flies. You may also observe ostriches, korhaans, marabous, white-backed vultures and many smaller species.

Places to Stay

Etosha is open to day visitors, but it's impossible to see much of the park in less than three days. Most visitors spend at least two nights at one of its three *rest camps* (Namutoni, Halali and Okaukuejo) that are spaced at 70km intervals. Each has its own character so it's worth visiting more than one.

Each camp is open year-round and has a restaurant, which is open 7am to 9am, noon to 2pm and 6pm to 10pm daily. There's a bar, shop, swimming pool, picnic sites, petrol station and kiosk. In March 1998 the *Namutoni restaurant* complex was destroyed by fire, but has been rebuilt. The restaurants serve meals from 7am to 8.30am, noon to 1.30pm and 6pm to 8.30pm. At other times, the kiosks are open.

In the Park At Namutoni, Halali and Okakuejo *camp sites* cost US$18 for two people plus US$2 for each additional person up to eight people; if you need a power point, you'll pay an additional US$0.80 per day. The camping ground at Namutoni Rest Camp supports quite a few nuisance jackals, some rabid, so keep your distance and pack edibles safely away in your vehicle. Bookings for all three camps must be made through the NWR in Windhoek.

Self-catering accommodation includes linen, towels, soap and kitchen facilities, but unless you're staying in luxury accommodation, you'll need to bring cooking equipment.

Okaukuejo Rest Camp Standard self-catering bungalows for 2/3/4 people US$31/42/45, luxury 4-bed bungalows US$51, 4-bed luxury suites US$92, double 'bus quarters' US$36. This camp (pronounced 'o-ka-**kui**-yo') is the site of the Etosha Research Station; the visitors centre outlines ongoing park research (one display identifies examples of animal droppings with their perpetrators). Okaukuejo's camping ground is a bit of a dust hole, but the self-catering accommodation may be the nicest in the park. The bungalows all have a kitchen, braai pit, and bathroom and toilet facilities. The 'bus quarters' rooms have a bathroom but no kitchen.

The floodlit water hole, with strategically placed viewing benches, is the best place in the park to see rhinos, particularly between 8pm and 10pm. For a preview, try **W** www.africam.co.za, which has a Web cam aimed at Okaukuejo's water hole. Another popular activity is the sunset photo frenzy from the top of Okaukuejo's landmark stone tower, which affords a view across the spaces to the distant Ondundozonananandana (Lost Shepherd Boy) Mountains; try saying that after three pints of Windhoek lager (or even before!).

Halali Rest Camp Self-catering luxury bungalows US$45/73 without/with satellite TV, 4-bed bungalows US$42, 4-bed economy bungalows US$38. Etosha's middle camp, Halali, nestles between several incongruous dolomite outcrops. The name is derived from a German term for the ritual horn-blowing to signal the end of a hunt, and a horn now serves as Halali's motif. The short Tsumasa hiking track leads up Tsumasa Kopje, the hill nearest the rest camp. A floodlit water hole extends wildlife viewing into the night, and allows observation of nocturnal creatures.

Namutoni Rest Camp 2-bed room with shared bathroom US$16, 2-bed economy rooms US$21-37, double chalets US$45, luxury flats/self-catering suites US$51/78. The most popular and best-kept of the camps is Namutoni, with its landmark whitewashed German fort. It originally served as an outpost for German troops, and in 1899 the German cavalry built a fort from which to control Owambo uprisings. In the battle of Namutoni, on 28 January 1904, seven German soldiers unsuccessfully tried to defend the fort against 500 Owambo warriors. Two years later, the damaged structure was renovated and pressed into service as a police station. In 1956, it was restored to its original specifications and two years later was opened as tourist accommodation.

The tower and ramparts provide a great view, and every evening, a crowd gathers to watch the sunset; arrive early to stake out a good vantage point. Each night, the flag is lowered and a ceremonial bugle call signals sundown and in the morning, a similar ritual drags you out of your bed or sleeping bag.

Beside the fort is a lovely freshwater limestone spring and the floodlit King Nehale water hole, which is filled with reedbeds and some extremely vociferous frogs. The viewing benches are nice for lunch or watching the pleasant riverbank scene, but unfortunately the spot attracts surprisingly few thirsty animals.

Outside the Park See the North Central Namibia map for locations of the following listings.

Mushara Lodge (☎ 229106, fax 229107, **e** mushara@iafrica.com.na, PO Box 1814, Tsumeb) Single/double lodges US$78/121. Lunch/dinner US$8/12. Wildlife drives are held from 7am to noon and 3pm to 6pm and cost US$43 per person. If you're looking for a pleasant option within ready access to Namutoni Rest Camp in Etosha National Park, this lodge is a good choice and the adjacent 2500-hectare concession offers varied wildlife viewing.

Mokuti Lodge (☎ 229084, fax 229091, e mokuti@mweb.com.na, w www.namib sunhotels.com.na/mokutilodge, 2km south of Von Lindequist Gate, PO Box 403, Tsumeb) Singles/doubles B&B from US$74/104, family rooms B&B US$114. This popular lodge offers an alternative to the national park rest camps and provides fly-in access to Etosha; Air Namibia and ComAv (see under Air in the Getting Around chapter) do scheduled flights. Mokuti doesn't pretend to be exclusive – it has over 100 rooms and offers pools, tennis courts, air-con and colour TV – but the low-profile buildings still create an illusion of intimacy. Wheelchair-accessible rooms are also available. Don't miss the attached reptile park and its resident snake collection – this alone is worth the cost of accommodation – which features residents captured around the lodge property (now that's a comforting thought). Here's your chance to see the deadly zebra snake, which is Namibia's most dangerous serpentine sort. The restaurant has a good reputation.

Aoba Lodge (☎ 229100, fax 229101, e aoba@tsu.namib.com, w www.natron .net.tour.etoaoba, PO Box 469, Tsumeb) Singles/doubles B&B US$80/120. Set evening meals cost an additional US$11. Situated on a 70 sq km private ranch, this lodge is well-known for its lion population. It caters for up to 20 people in well-appointed thatched bungalows. Etosha wildlife drives cost an additional US$75.

Ongava Lodge (☎ 061-274500, fax 239455, e info@nts.com.na, w www.wild erness-safaris.com, 8 Bismarck St, Windhoek, PO Box 6850, Windhoek) Singles/doubles US$352/532 July-Oct high season. There is a 10% discount in the low season; rates include meals and activities. This upmarket place (see the Etosha National Park (East Section) map) occupies its own wildlife reserve just outside Etosha's Andersson Gate. The double lodges afford wide vistas over the bush and there's also a rustic

tented camp, which offers more of a wilderness experience. All rates include wildlife-viewing; fly-in options are available through Wilderness Safaris Namibia (see Organised Tours in the Getting Around chapter).

Toshari Inn (☎/fax 333440, e toshari@ out.namib.com, w resafrica.net/ toshari-inn, 27km south of Andersson Gate, PO Box 164, Outjo) Singles/doubles B&B US$40/62. Lunch/dinner will set you back US$6/10. This modestly priced safari lodge offers hiking trails and bird-watching in a naturally prolific backdrop. Four of the rooms have self-catering facilities.

El Dorado Camping (☎ 333421) Camping US$6 per person, pre-erected double tents US$14. This low-key place along the highway between Outjo and Etosha offers an inexpensive alternative to safari lodges and national parks accommodation. It's nothing special, but it is convenient.

For meals in Etosha you're limited to the safari lodges (guests only) or the rest camp restaurants, kiosks, shops and bars.

Getting There & Away

Air Namibia (see Getting There & Away in the Windhoek chapter) travels four times a week between Eros airport in Windhoek and Mokuti airport. It costs US$85/138 one way/return.

The two main entry gates to Etosha are Von Lindequist (Namutoni), west of Tsumeb, and Andersson (Okaukuejo), north of Outjo. Tsumeb has the nearest commercial airport to Etosha, and is also the nearest bus and rail depot. From there, you'll have to either join a tour or hire a car as there is no scheduled public transport into the park. Imperial Car Rental has a branch office in Tsumeb (see the Tsumeb section), but book well in advance.

Hitching is prohibited inside Etosha, but hitchers may be able to find a lift from Tsumeb to Namutoni or Outjo to Okaukuejo. If you're lucky on this score, be sure to sort out your entry permits when you enter Etosha. Otherwise, your driver may have problems when trying to leave the park (it will appear that some of their original party have vanished!). Your best bet is to explain when you enter the park that you need separate entry permits for your own records.

Getting Around
Pedestrians, bicycles, motorcycles and hitching are prohibited in Etosha, and open bakkies must be screened off. Outside the rest camps, visitors must stay in their vehicles (except at toilet stops). Hitching is from Okaukuejo or Namutoni, but you may find lifts with maintenance people.

East of Windhoek

GOBABIS
☎ 062 • pop 11,000
Gobabis is situated on the Wit-Nossob River, 120km from the Botswana border at Buitepos. The name is Khoi-Khoi for the 'Place of Strife', but a slight misspelling (Goabbis) would render it 'Place of Elephants', which locals seem to prefer (despite its obvious shortage of elephants). The 970 farms of the surrounding Omaheke region cover 4.9 million hectares (an additional 3.5 million hectares belong to the Hereroland communal area) and provide over one-third of Namibia's beef. Gobabis is the main service centre in the region, and is likely to gain prominence as traffic increases on the Trans-Kalahari route between Windhoek and Botswana's capital, Gaborone.

Gobabis Green

It's said Gobabis once had a traffic light, but when it turned green, the cows ate it. That's not just any cows, but rather the purebred stock that makes up the Omaheke region's best: Red Poll, South Devon, Hereford, Sussex, Brown Swiss, Angus, Shorthorn, Simmenthaler, Santa Gertrudis and Brahman. While drought is definitely the norm in this semidesert country, the average rainfall of 200 to 300mm per year belies the fact that in a good rainy season, the vast landscapes of the Namibian Kalahari turn beautifully lush, green and cattle-friendly. And incidentally, the traffic light has somehow resurfaced.

Although Gobabis is the main service centre of the Namibian Kalahari, there isn't a lot to look at. The town's only historic building is the old military hospital, the **Lazarett**, which once served as a town museum. It's not officially open, but you can pick up a key at the library in the centre of town.

History
Gobabis came into existence in 1856, when a Rhenish mission station was established on the site. In 1865, an attempt by the head missionary to broker a peace agreement between the squabbling Damara and Khoi-Khoi resulted in his expulsion from the area and the temporary fall of the mission. Missionary work was reactivated in 1876, only to be shut down again by a renewal of hostilities. When they tired of fighting, the two groups turned and rebelled against the German occupation. Things got so out of hand that in 1895, Leutwein ordered German troops to quell the disturbances, resulting in the building of a fort that was later destroyed.

Information
For basic tourist information it's best to contact the Omaheke Tourist Information Centre (☎ 562270, Ⓔclowe@mweb.com.na, Ⓦ www.oma heketourism.com.na), PO Box 1622. It's beside the Spa Supermarket on the Buitepos road.

Organised Tours
Namibia Rural Development Project (☎ 061-237279, evenings 237479, Ⓔ nrdp@ iafrica.com.na, PO Box 24886, Windhoek) This company provides a glimpse of rural communities in eastern Namibia with three-day rural Omaheke tours (US$200), including visits to Harnas Wildlife Foundation & Guest Farm (see Places to Stay), Epukiro village and overnight at a Herero homestead. Departures are from Windhoek or Gobabis, and discounts are available to Southern African residents.

Places to Stay & Eat
In Town Gobabis has a number of accommodation options for visitors who want to explore the fascinating Omaheke Region.

Erni's B&B (☎ 565222, 081-244 4541) Singles/doubles US$24/28 with air-con, showers and MNET TV. The attached restaurant, bar and beer garden is probably Gobabis' finest eating establishment. Full/health breakfasts cost US$3.50/3, omelettes US$2-3, starters US$2, burgers or salads US$2 and mains US$5-7.

Onze Rust Guest House (☎ 562214, fax 565060, e onzerust@iafrica.com.na, W www .natron.net/tour/onzerust, 95 Rugby St) Rooms US$14 per person. The rooms have air-con, TV and a generally dark decor. Guests have access to the braai area. The four-bed room has a microwave and set meals (US$7) are available on request.

Gobabis Hotel (☎ 562568, fax 562641, Mark St) Singles/doubles B&B US$26/34. The swimming pool, bar, beer garden, restaurant and weekend disco at this business travellers hotel provide a good percentage of Gobabis' action.

Big 5 Central Hotel (☎ 562094, fax 564902, Voortrekker St) Camping US$6.50 per tent or caravan, rooms US$17 per person. This place has basic accommodation; the attached restaurant serves steak and seafood specials and the bar features pool tables and braai facilities.

Goba-Goba Lodge (☎ 564499, fax 564466, e jun@iafrica.com.na, PO Box 599) Singles/doubles B&B US$43/60. With lots of artwork and an excellent design, this friendly hotel, just outside the town centre, is Gobabis' nicest option. All rooms have air-con, DSTV and tasteful decor; set menu dinners are available on request.

Out of Town Head out of town for more space and more wildlife.

Xain Quaz (☎ 562688, 081-128 6682, fax 562824, e oostevel@mweb .com.na, PO Box 1282) Camping US$4 plus US$1.50 per person & US$1.50 per vehicle, pre-erected double tents US$11, double rooms US$20, 3-/4-bed bungalows US$23/40. This pleasant red-earth rest camp on a large ranch west of Gobabis has a pool, bar and wildlife-viewing trails.

Welkom Rest Camp (☎ 563584, fax 563762, PO Box 181) Camping US$3 per vehicle, US$3 per site and US$3 per person, 4-bed bungalows US$15 per person. This amenable rest camp is situated 18km from Gobabis, north of the highway that runs east of town.

Harnas Wildlife Foundation & Guest Farm (☎ 568788, fax 568738, e harnas@ mweb.com.na, W www.harnas.org or www .harnas.de, PO Box 548) Camp site US$21, 'Wendy' house (also called Doll's house) B&B US$57, Igloo Hut US$63 B&B. Day admission is US$7; wildlife drives/animal feedings cost US$11/16. Lunch/dinner costs US$9/12. This popular rural development project lets you see wildlife close-up, and provides a chance to cuddle baby cheetahs, leopards and lions – if they haven't already grown too big for that sort of thing. The idea is to return orphaned animals to the wild, but those who are sensitive to ecological issues may suspect conflicts of interest. To get there, turn north on the C22 past Gobabis and continue for 50km, then turn east on the D1668. After 42km, turn left at the Harnas gate and then 8km to the farm. Transfers are available from Windhoek.

Getting There & Away

Slow overnight trains run to and from Windhoek three times weekly. On Friday, the Thursday night train from Windhoek connects with a Star Line bus to Ghanzi in Botswana; it returns to Gobabis the next day.

BUITEPOS

Buitepos, a wide spot in the desert at the Namibia-Botswana border crossing, is little more than a petrol station and customs and immigration post.

Places to Stay & Eat

East Gate Service Station & Rest Camp (☎ 560405, fax 560406, e eastgate@namib net.com.na, Trans-Kalahari Hwy, PO Box 422, Gobabis) Camping US$3 per person, cabins US$7.50 per person, 4-bed bungalows US$32. This place, which sits on the Namibia-Botswana border, rises from the desert like a mirage, and is especially handy if you are hitching between Namibia and Botswana.

NORTH CENTRAL NAMIBIA

NORTH CENTRAL NAMIBIA

Kalahari Bush Breaks (☎ *568936, 082-552 1057,* e *kalaharibb@outdoorsa .co.za,* w *www.outdoorsa.co.za/kalaharibb/)* Camping US$1.50 per person, pre-erected double tents US$8.50, guesthouse US$34 per person with half board. This roadside rest camp on the Trans-Kalahari Hwy is 25km west of the border with Botswana, in a Kalahari setting. The three-level thatched guesthouse is beautiful, and there's plenty of wildlife, making it a great place to stop off between Windhoek and Botswana.

Getting There & Away

Star Line's Windhoek-Ghanzi bus stops at Buitepos. From Mamuno, just over the border in Botswana, buses leave for Ghanzi according to no set schedule, but travellers headed for Gaborone or Maun would fare better hitching.

Northern Namibia

Windhoek may be the capital, but Namibia's northern strip, with the country's highest population density, is its cultural heartland. Known as the 'Land of Rivers', this culturally varied region is bounded by the Kunene and Okavango Rivers along the Angolan border, and in the east by the Zambezi and the Kwando/Mashe/Linyanti/Chobe river systems.

North-eastern Namibia has the country's highest rainfall and is geographically distinct from the rest of the country. Most people live in small settlements on the plains of the Owambo region, or on or near the Okavango River, which flows eastwards and feeds Botswana's Okavango Delta.

The eastern part of the Otjozondjupa region, better known as Bushmanland (this South African designation just won't go away), is a wild and thinly populated piece of scrub, acacia forest and scattered San villages at the northern fringes of the Kalahari. This is one of Namibia's most fascinating areas, and to date remains little affected by tourism.

The Owambo Country

The regions of Omusati, Oshana, Ohangwena and most of Otjikoto – collectively known as the 'Four Os' – which make up the former district of Owamboland, comprise the homeland of the Owambo people, Namibia's largest population group. Most members of the eight Owambo clans pursue subsistence-agriculture lifestyles, growing their own crops and raising cattle and goats. Visitors will be impressed by the clean and well-kept nature of this rural area, which gives the overall impression of a healthy and prosperous African society.

The Owambo landscape is characterised by flat, sandy plains dotted with *makalani* palms, patches of savanna and mopane for-

Highlights

- Travel through the Owambo country, Namibia's most populous region.

- Relax at a riverside lodge along the Okavango River at Rundu.

- Join an expedition through the remote and wildlife-rich Khaudom Game Reserve.

- Overnight at one of the lodges on remote Mpalila Island and watch the wildlife and rapids.

- Stay at the wonderful Lianshulu Main Lodge or Lianshulu Bush Camp and explore the adjacent wetlands of Mudumu and Mamili National Parks.

- Visit the wilds of Bushmanland and learn about ancient San culture.

NORTHERN NAMIBIA

est. Its semidesert climate is characterised by cool nights and hot days; summer daytime temperatures can climb to over 40°C.

During the war for independence (see History in the Facts about Namibia chapter), Owamboland served as a base and primary support area for the South-West African People's Organization (Swapo). The villages of Uutapi (Ombalantu), Oshakati and Ondangwa were converted into bases and

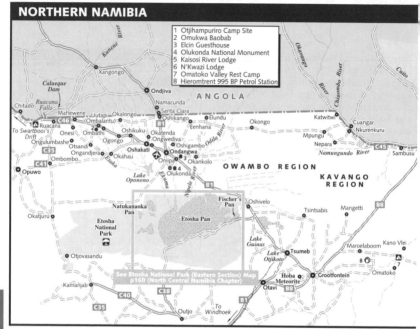

NORTHERN NAMIBIA

1 Otjihampuriro Camp Site
2 Omukwa Baobab
3 Elcin Guesthouse
4 Olukonda National Monument
5 Kaisosi River Lodge
6 N'Kwazi Lodge
7 Omatoko Valley Rest Camp
8 Hieromtrent 995 BP Petrol Station

supply centres for the occupying South African army. After the South Africans left, these new commercial centres attracted growing numbers of entrepreneurial people who set up small businesses. At the time of writing, the government is providing resources for housing projects, electricity lines, roads, irrigation, agriculture, health care, schools, telephone services and other projects.

Most Owambo people live in Oshana country, which is named for the web of *oshanas* (ephemeral, vegetated watercourses) of the Culevai drainage system. The oshanas, which originate in Angola, are filled during the occasional *efundja* (period of heavy rainfall). Because they're underlaid by solid rock, they hold underground water throughout the year. On the surface, however, once they flow into sandy soils, they spread out into shallow lakes or soak into the earth. Some *kraals* (fortified villages) and villages depend on bore holes, but the main water

supply runs through the Ogongo canal/aqueduct along the C46.

The Owambo country is well known for its high-quality basketry and canework, which is sold at roadside stalls or artisans' homes for very decent prices. Some of the nicest works include rounded baskets with lids, which come in every size up to 1m in diameter, and shallow woven plates and bowls. Designs are simple and graceful, usually incorporating a brown geometric pattern woven into the pale yellow reed.

Two useful publications are the *Tourism Map of the Ohangwena, Omusati, Oshana and Otjikoto Regions* (available at the Travel North Namibia office in Tsumeb – see Information under Tsumeb in the North Central Namibia chapter) and the phenomenal large-format book *A Profile of North Central Namibia*, by John Mendelsohn, Selma el Obeid and Carole Roberts. You can purchase it for US$20 at the Oshakati Bookshop.

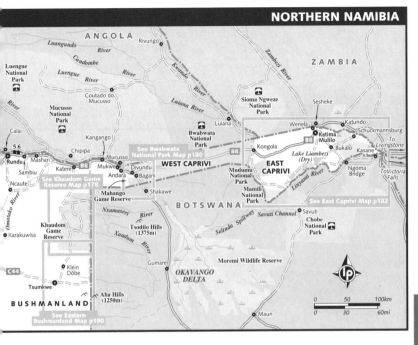

OSHAKATI
☎ 065

The Owambo capital, Oshakati, may be a friendly, bustling hive of activity, but the uninspiring commercial centre is little more than a strip of characterless development along the highway, which has recently become a dual carriageway punctuated by stop signs. The town's desultory nature is partially due to the fact that both it and Ondangwa served as South African Defence Force (SADF) bases during the liberation struggles from 1966–89, and were subjected to mortar and missile attacks.

Information
A good source of information is the Engen petrol station at the corner of the Ondangwa road and Sam Nujoma Rd. For changing money, the Bank of Namibia, Standard Bank, First National Bank and Bank of Windhoek have branches in the commercial centre.

For phone calls, go to Pick-a-Phone at the Yetu shopping centre or the Namibia Telecom office. Internet and email services are available at the Internet cafe Iway beside the Spar Supermarket; it's open 9am to 6.30pm Monday to Friday and 9am to 1pm Saturday.

You can buy Fuji and Agfa slide and print film at the Agfa Oshakati Photo Shop, with outlets on the main road and in the Game Centre. The Oshakati Bookshop offers used paperbacks, textbooks and a couple of reference titles. Oshoopala Bookshop in the Game Centre is notable for its total absence of books.

If you need a hospital and your health is important to you, avoid the government option and opt for the Onandjokwe Lutheran Hospital (☎ 240111) in Ondangwa or the Oshikuku Roman Catholic Hospital.

Things to See
While Oshakati lacks specific attractions, it's worth an hour or two wandering around

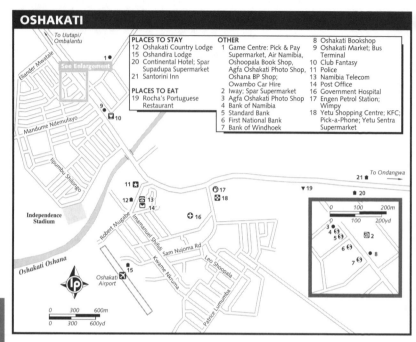

OSHAKATI

PLACES TO STAY
12 Oshakati Country Lodge
15 Oshandira Lodge
20 Continental Hotel; Spar
   Supadupa Supermarket
21 Santorini Inn

PLACES TO EAT
19 Rocha's Portuguese
   Restaurant

OTHER
1 Game Centre: Pick & Pay
  Supermarket, Air Namibia,
  Oshoopala Book Shop,
  Agfa Oshakati Photo Shop;
  Oshana BP Shop;
  Owambo Car Hire
2 Iway; Spar Supermarket
3 Agfa Oshakati Photo Shop
4 Bank of Namibia
5 Standard Bank
6 First National Bank
7 Bank of Windhoek
8 Oshakati Bookshop
9 Oshakati Market; Bus
  Terminal
10 Club Fantasy
11 Namibia Telecom
13 Namibia Telecom
14 Post Office
16 Government Hospital
17 Engen Petrol Station;
   Wimpy
18 Yetu Shopping Centre; KFC;
   Pick-a-Phone; Yetu Sentra
   Supermarket

the large covered market, which produces a range of mostly unpleasant smells. Here you'll find everything from clothing and baskets to mopane worms and glasses of freshly brewed *tambo* (millet beer). An odd monument – a dour fellow standing with a crashed plane – once graced the market but now only the plinth remains.

Places to Stay

Santorini Inn (☎/fax 220506, ℮ bookings@ santorini-inn.com, Ondangwa Rd, Private Bag 5569) Singles/doubles from US$44/54, chalets US$54/64.Want to feel like you've died and gone to Florida? Check out this two-star motel-style place, with a pool, bar, DSTV, restaurant, and a refrigeration shop, which ensures the air-con is working.

Oshandira Lodge (☎ 220443, fax 221 189, Oshakati Airport) Singles/doubles B&B US$35/47. This friendly place, where you're welcomed by huge stone Egyptian cats and a Horus statue, has been spruced up

with a pool, green lawns, restaurant, bar and sports TV.

Continental Hotel (☎ 220257, fax 221233, PO Box 6) Singles/doubles US$24/ 34 with air-con, US$18/24 without. From the outside, this could be a warehouse, but it's quite nice on the inside, with a bright patio, a la carte restaurant, bar and casino.

Oshakati Country Lodge (☎ 222380, fax 222384, ℮ countrylodge@osh.namib.com, PO Box 15200) Singles/doubles B&B US$53/72, family rooms B&B US$108. This hotel has posh and soulless accommodation for business travellers.

Places to Eat

Rocha's Portuguese Restaurant (☎ 221 800, Ondangwa Rd) Mains US$3-5. This is the place to head for simple Portuguese-style fare.

Oshana BP Shop (☎ 222952, Game Centre) Meat pies US$0.75, rotisserie chicken US$2.50. This petrol-station shop is open 24 hours a day for groceries and takeaways. It also bakes fresh bread daily.

Alternatively, you could try the dining rooms at the *Oshandira Lodge*, *Oshakati Country Lodge* or *Santorini Inn* (where the menu recommends the 'pig's trotters with sour cabbage, mashed potatoes and much more'). There's also a *KFC* in the Yetu shopping centre and a *Wimpy* in the Engen petrol station.

Self-caterers will find an ever-increasing number of supermarkets, which are open from Monday to Friday and on Saturday morning. On Sunday, the hours are shared by *Spar*, which is open from 8.30am to 2pm and *Pick & Pay*, open from 2pm to 6pm. There's also a *Spar Supadupa*, open until 10pm daily.

Entertainment
Oshakati enjoys a lively local entertainment scene, and lots of small clubs feature live bands.

Club Fantasy (☎ 220884, C46/Ondangwa road) This bar near the market is the most popular; it has a disco on Wednesday, Friday and Saturday.

Getting There & Away
Air Oshakati's airport is used for charters only; commercial flights use the airport in Ondangwa, 25km down the road.

Bus From the bus terminal at the market, minibuses frequently leave for Ondangwa; they also serve other towns on the Oshivelo-Ruacana route. Minibuses for Windhoek (US$9.50 – more on holidays, much to the dismay of locals) via Tsumeb set out when full, with the most departures on Sunday afternoons.

Namibia Contract Haulage bus (☎ 220 990), which runs between Windhoek and Oshakati (US$10), leaves from the bus terminal in Katutura at 7.30am and 5pm on Friday and departs from the market in Oshakati twice on Sunday. It's advisable to book a seat as early as possible.

Car & Motorcycle Car hire is available at Owambo Car Hire (☎ 222952, fax 222955,

[e] bdewet@iafrica.com.na), PO Box 15200, in the Game Centre.

The C46 and B1 through the Owambo region are tarred and in good condition, but off these routes, road maintenance is poor and 4WD is required in places, especially after rain. Petrol is available at Oshakati, Ondangwa, Oshikango and Uutapi (Ombalantu).

ONDANGWA
☎ 065

Ondangwa, the Owambo country's second-largest town, is a booming commercial centre known for its huge warehouses, which supply northern Namibia's more than 6000 *cuca* shops (small bush shops selling mainly beer). An especially interesting site is the open market, where on Monday and Friday, basket weavers bring their works for sale to the public and large-scale dealers.

To change money, check out the very pink First National Bank (which practically glows in the dark). If you need a vehicle mechanic, Dressel Haus garage has a good stock of parts.

Olukonda National Monument
Among the makalani palms and *mahango* (millet) fields at Olukonda village is a collection of historic Finnish mission buildings that now comprise the Olukonda National Monument (☎ 245668, fax 240472, [e] oluk onda.museum@elcin.org.na).

Nakambale House, the first mission house and northern Namibia's oldest structure, was built in the late 1870s by Finnish missionary Martti Rautanen (1845–1926), known locally as Nakambale. In 1889, Reverend Rautanen also built the area's first church. When a new church was constructed in 1972, the old building began to deteriorate and wasn't renovated until 1991, with the Finnish government contributing funds and expertise. Ask the attendant to let you have a look around; outside is the wagon that brought the first missionaries, and the churchyard accommodating the graves of Martti Rautanen, his family and the Owambo chief Ellifas.

The site also features a **museum** *(admission US$1; open 8am-1pm & 2pm-5pm*

What's Brewing in the Owambo Country?

Forget the Pig & Whistle, Hare & Hounds, King George & the Dragon or the Four Alls. The Owambo have their own pub culture, and the bars, nightclubs and bottle stores along the northern highways bear wonderfully colourful names. One bottle store is called Serious, another is the Fruit of Love and yet another is Fine to Fine. Perhaps the most honest is simply the unpretentious Botol Stor.

Then there are the bars: the Clinic Happy Bar, Hot Box, Daily Needs, Salon for Sure, Club Jet Style, Sorry to See, Let's Push, California City Style, Come Together Good Life, Happy Brothers & Sisters, Join Us, Hard Workers Bar, Every Day Bar, Bar We Like and USA No Money No Life. A few are more philosophical: The System, Just Another Life, The Agreement Centre, Take Time, Keep Trying No 1, Keep Trying No 2, Tenacity Centre and Try Again. There also seems to be a nautical theme emerging: Sea Point, Quay 4, Club LA Coast, Pelican, Friend Ship, Titanic, and Seven Seas Up & Down.

Some names, however, boggle the mind. Who, for example, named the Sign of Mr Hans, We Push & Pull, One Moo, No Wally Let's Support Bar, Let's Sweat for Tailor Bar, Club Say Father of Mustache, Let We Trust Uncle Simon, Three Sister in Beer Garden and Wet Come to Big Mama (hmmm…)? And given the choice, would you prefer to down a drop in the Peace Full Bar or the Water is Life, or choke down a foul brew in the Oshakati establishment known as Vile Waters?

Mon-Fri, 8am-1pm Sat, noon-5pm Sun), which reveals a wealth of fascinating Owambo history and culture. At the wonderful **Ndonga Homestead** *(admission US$1.50)*, you are able to tour a traditional Owambo kraal.

To get there, travel 8km east of Ondangwa, then from the Oniipa road junction, turn south and follow the D3606 for 5km.

Lake Oponono

Lost in a maze of routes and tracks 27km south of Ondangwa is Lake Oponono, a large wetland fed by the Culevai oshanas. After rains, it attracts an amazing variety of birdlife, including saddlebill storks, crowned cranes, flamingoes and pelicans.

Places to Stay & Eat

Ondangwa Rest Camp *(☎/fax 240351, e rest camp@osh.namib.com, behind the pink shopping centre, PO Box 643)* Camping US$5 per person. This camp, which surrounds a small lake, is a very nice option for campers. Amenities include fishing, swimming, shaded and grassy camp sites with electric lighting, clean ablutions and washing facilities, and there are wonderful frog songs at night. For snacks, there's a takeaway, and the attached **Oasis Restaurant & Beer Garden** does light lunches at noon and

meat- and fish-based a la carte meals in the evening.

Crest Lodge Pandu Ondangwa *(☎ 241 900, fax 241919, e ondangwa@crestanam ibia.com.na, W www.cresta-hospitality.com, PO Box 2827)* Singles/doubles US$53/64, suites US$132/138. Ondangwa's plush new hotel, which features bright rooms and tasteful artwork, is certainly the nicest in the Owambo region; discounts are available at weekends. For meals you can choose between the **Chatters Restaurant** and a wonderful little **takeaway** in the lobby.

Olukonda National Monument *(☎ 245 668, fax 240472, e olukonda.museum@ elcin.org.na, 5km along the D3606)* Camping US$5 per site plus US$2 per person, camping in traditional huts US$5.50/9.50 without/with bedding and breakfast, cottages US$7 per person. Here's your opportunity to sleep in a basic missionary cottage or a hut that would have been used historically by an Owambo chief or one of his wives. Breakfast is US$4 and traditional Owambo meals are US$4 (with advance booking).

Elcin Guesthouse *(☎ 248189, fax 240 472, Private Bag 2018, Oniipa)* Dorm beds in 2-/3-/7-bed rooms US$10/7.50/5.50. This place in Oniipa, 8km east of town, offers friendly, good-value accommodation as well as a takeaway shop.

For snacks, try **Tony's Takeaway** at the BP petrol station or the well-stocked **Qwik-Stop** at the Ondangwa Total petrol station.

Getting There & Away

Air Namibia flies to and from Windhoek's Eros Airport nine times weekly (US$89); three of these flights stop at Mokuti (Etosha National Park) and cost US$34.

All minibus services between Oshakati, Tsumeb and Windhoek stop at the BP petrol station in Ondangwa.

The Oshikango border crossing to Santa Clara in Angola, 60km north of Ondangwa, is open and carries frequent cross-border truck traffic. During the day, you may be able to hop across for a quick look around, but to stay overnight or travel further north, you'll need an Angolan visa that allows overland travel.

UUTAPI (OMBALANTU)

☎ 065

Dusty Uutapi, frequently called Ombalantu, forms one of Namibia's most typically African commercial towns, and makes a nice brief stop. This rapidly growing community now has a First National Bank, several petrol stations, the Remember the Unity of Africa supermarket and the Super Foods Takeaway.

The Omukwa Baobab

Uutapi's main attraction is its former SADF base, which is dominated by an enormous baobab tree. This tree, known locally as *Omukwa*, was once used to shelter cattle from invaders, and later was used as a turret from which to ambush invading tribes. It didn't work with the South African forces, however, who invaded and used the tree for everything from a chapel to a coffee shop (the sign outside reads 'Die Koffiekamer Koelte' or 'The Coffee Chamber Cult'), a post office, a storage shed and an interrogation chamber for prisoners of war. The site is now loosely described as the **Omusati Region Museum** *(1km on the D3612; admission free; open 24 hours)*, and includes a nearby bomb shelter and a lookout tower dating from the South African days.

Turn left at the police station 350m south of the Total petrol station and look for an obscure grassy track winding between desultory buildings towards the conspicuous baobab.

Ongulumbashe

Ongulumbashe (originally called Omugulugweembashe, meaning 'the Forest of Giraffes'), amid typically flat Owambo country scrubland, is the birthplace of modern Namibia. It was here on 26 August 1966 that the first shots of the war for Namibian independence were fired, and the People's Liberation Army of Namibia enjoyed its first victory over the South African troops who had been charged with rooting out and quelling potential guerrilla activities.

You will need permission to visit from the Swapo office in Uutapi. At the site, you can still see some reconstructed bunkers and the 'needle' monument marking the battle. An etching on the reverse side honours *pistolet-pulemyot shpagina* (PPSHA), the Russian-made automatic rifle that played a major role in the conflict. The event is commemorated yearly on 26 August.

From Uutapi (Ombalantu), turn south on the D3612. At the eastern end of the pleasant village of Otsandi (Tsandi), turn west down an unnumbered track and continue 20km to Ongulumbashe.

Ongandjera

Ongandjera, President Sam Nujoma's birthplace, has recently become an informal national shrine. The rose-coloured kraal that was his boyhood home is distinguished from its neighbours by a prominent Swapo flag hung in a tree. It's fine to look from a distance, but the kraal remains a private home and isn't open to the public.

Ongandjera lies on the D3612, 52km south-east of Uutapi (Ombalantu), just a few hundred metres outside the large village of Okahao. It's also accessible via the C41 from Oshakati.

Getting There & Away

Uutapi (Ombalantu) is on all minibus routes between Oshakati and Ruacana.

RUACANA

☎ 065

The Kunene River town of Ruacana takes its name from the Herero *orua hakahana* (the rapids). Here, the Kunene River splits into several channels before plunging over a dramatic escarpment and through a 2km-long gorge of its own making.

Tiny Ruacana was built as a company town to provide housing and services for workers on the 320-megawatt underground Ruacana hydroelectric project, which now supplies over half of Namibia's power. It has a more ordered feel than other Owambo population centres and, during the liberation struggles, it served as a base for the SADF.

In 1926, a German-Portuguese boundary dispute was settled when the upper Kunene was given to Angola. It was decided that below the falls the boundary would follow the main channel to the Atlantic Ocean.

Ruacana Falls

The dramatic 85m Ruacana Falls was once a natural wonder, but all that changed thanks to Angola's Calueque Dam, 20km upstream, and NamPower's Ruacana power plant. What little water makes it past the first barrage is collected by an intake weir, 1km above the falls, which ushers it into the hydroelectric plant to turn the turbines. On the rare occasions when there's a surfeit of water, Ruacana returns to its former glory as one of the most spectacular sights on the continent. In the wettest years (such as 2001), it's no exaggeration to say it rivals Victoria Falls.

To get there, turn north 15km west of Ruacana and follow the signs towards the border crossing. To visit the gorge, visitors must temporarily exit Namibia by signing the immigration register. From the Namibian border crossing, bear left (to the right lies the decrepit Angolan border crossing) to the end of the road. There you can look around the ruins of the old power station, which was destroyed by Namibian liberation forces; the buildings are pockmarked with scars from mortars and gunfire, providing a stark contrast to the otherwise peaceful scene.

Places to Stay & Eat

Otjihampuriro Camp Site (3km along the D3700) Camp sites US$3 per person, day visits US$1.50. Situated beside the Hippo Pools oxbow lagoon at the mouth of the Ruacana Gorge is this unappealing camping ground – the wrecked car poking out of the river adds a special touch. Lest prospective campers take one look and retreat, the aloof attendants collect fees at the entrance gate.

Oshea Guest House & Sunset Lodge (☎/fax 270092, evening 270034) Camping US$5 per person, rooms or bungalows with shared bathroom US$19 per person. This amenable guesthouse occupies an old Namibia Development Corporation house just off the Ruacana Loop. The rooms have fans and DSTV, and guests can use the braais (barbecues) and kitchen facilities. Meals are available on request. The camping and bungalow options are at the airy Sunset Lodge camping ground, across the Ruacana Loop from the guesthouse. When you phone, ask for Mrs Basingwaite.

NamPower Guesthouse (☎/fax 270031, Ruacana Loop) Singles/doubles US$25/42. This is the nicest accommodation in town, with a dining room and colourful tropical gardens, but it's open only to NamPower employees. Nonemployees with a reason to stay need permission from the main office in Windhoek (☎ 061-205 4111).

The corporate-sounding *Ruacana No 2 Supermarket* stocks basic supplies, but your best self-catering option is the *Mini-Market* at the BP petrol station.

Getting There & Away

Ruacana is near the junction of roads between Opuwo, the Owambo country and the rough 4WD route along the Kunen River to Swartbooi's Drift (see Swartbooi's Drift in the North-Western Namibia chapter). Note that mileage signs along the C46 confuse Ruacana town and the power plant, which are 15km apart; both are signposted 'Ruacana', so don't let them throw you too badly.

For westbound travellers, the 24-hour BP petrol station is the last before the Atlantic; it's also the terminal for afternoon minibuses to and from Oshakati and Ondangwa.

The Angolan border crossing is now open; however, while Namibians can cross readily, others need an Angolan visa that allows overland entry.

Kavango Region

The heavily wooded and gently rolling Kavango region is dominated by the Okavango River and its broad floodplains. There's little wildlife nowadays, but the water attracts millions of butterflies, many as yet unclassified, as well as a large crocodile population.

Throughout the region, people cultivate maize, sorghum, millet and green vegetables along the riverbanks, and supplement their diet with fish caught in woven funnel-shaped fish traps. The men also practise spearfishing from the riverbanks or from dugout canoes known as *watu* or *mekoro* (singular *mokoro*). The region is also home to the Mbarakweno San people, who remain largely subservient to local Mbukushu, Sambiyu and other Caprivi tribal groups, and whose services are 'inherited' within families.

In colonial days, Kavango was a focus of operations for German Roman Catholic missionaries, and the Church still sponsors missions, hospitals and clinics in Nyangana, Sambiu and Andara (which has an especially interesting statue of Christ). Several of the mission stations and hospitals along the Okavango River welcome travellers.

RUNDU & AROUND
☎ 066

Rundu occupies a lovely setting on the bluffs above the Okavango River. There's little of specific interest for tourists in this sultry tropical town, but it's a great spot to observe Rundu's African scene and its dominant Portuguese and Angolan cultures. The region also offers fine fishing, bird-watching and boating along the river.

Information
The Tourism Centre (☎/fax 256140, e ngandu@mweb.com), on the main road, distributes brochures, answers queries and organises accommodation and transport bookings,

including Intercape Mainliner tickets. It's open 8am to 5pm Monday to Friday and 8am to 1pm Saturday.

Internet and email access are available at the Olive Tree (☎ 255409) for US$3 per hour.

Rundu's well-stocked pharmacy is one of the best in northern Namibia.

Things to See
Most visitors will want to take a stroll around the large covered **market**, which is one of Africa's most sophisticated informal sales outlets. From July to September, don't miss the fresh papayas, sold straight from the trees. Alternatively, head for the **Khemo Open Market**, where you can shop for both African staples and Kavango handicrafts.

At Sambiu, east of Rundu, is a Roman Catholic **mission museum** *(☎ 251111, 30km along the Okavango River road; admission free; open by appointment)*, which exhibits crafts and woodcarvings from Angola and Kavango. Phone to arrange a visit.

Places to Stay
Ngandu Safari Lodge *(☎ 256723, fax 256726, e ngandu@mweb.com.na, W http://resafrica.net/ngandu-safari-lodge, Sarasungu Rd, PO Box 519)* Camping US$4/5.50 in tents/caravans, singles/doubles US$24/36, semiluxury rooms US$31/43, luxury rooms US$31/44, family rooms US$20 per person. The semiluxury rooms at this large and central lodge have a fridge and TV, while the luxury rooms have self-catering facilities and air-con. All rates include breakfast. This place also offers boat trips (US$14) and rents canoes (US$4 per hour) and quad-bikes (US$20 per hour).

Omashare River Lodge *(☎/fax 255753, fax 256111, Okavango River road)* Singles/doubles US$35/48 with fans, add US$3 for air-con. This locally popular place on the bluff is best known as a local casino.

Kavango River Lodge *(☎ 255244, fax 255013, e kavlodge@namib.com)* Singles/doubles US$38/51 B&B, family room US$74 B&B. This lodge, perched over the river, affords Rundu's best sunset view. The self-catering bungalows have air-con, TV

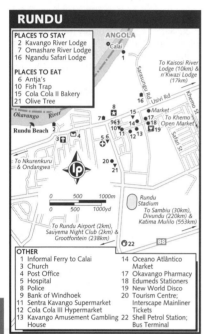

RUNDU

PLACES TO STAY
2 Kavango River Lodge
7 Omashare River Lodge
16 Ngandu Safari Lodge

PLACES TO EAT
6 Antja's
10 Fish Trap
15 Cola Cola II Bakery
21 Olive Tree

OTHER
1 Informal Ferry to Calai
3 Church
4 Post Office
5 Hospital
8 Police
9 Bank of Windhoek
11 Sentra Kavango Supermarket
12 Cola Cola III Hypermarket
13 Kavango Amusement Gambling House
14 Oceano Atlântico Market
17 Okavango Pharmacy
18 Edumeds Stationers
19 New World Disco
20 Tourism Centre; Interscape Mainliner Tickets
22 Shell Petrol Station; Bus Terminal

and breakfast supplies; ask for one with a veranda. Lunches/dinners cost US$6/8, guests may use the tennis courts, and boat trips/canoe hire cost US$11/6 per hour.

Kaisosi River Lodge (☎ 255265, fax 256566, 2km off Okavango River road) Camping US$5.50, single/double garden bungalows or 4-unit riverside chalets US$35/53. This pleasant riverside camp arranges raft cruises on the river for less than US$10 per person per hour. Lunch or dinner costs US$8 and transfers from the town/airport are US$8.50/14.

N'Kwazi Lodge (☎ 242070, 081-242 4897, fax 202058, e nkwazi@iafrica.com .na, 5km off Okavango River road, PO Box 245, Grootfontein) Camping US$4.50 per person, single/double bungalows B&B US$46/74. Valerie and Weynand Peypers' peaceful, beautiful and good-value riverside retreat offers great Afrikaner country-style meals and a warm friendly atmosphere; here guests are treated as family. Boat trips

on the river cost US$14 per hour for up to four people, sundowners are US$3 per person, water skiing is US$5.50, and local dance programs cost US$27 per show. Home-cooked lunches/dinners are available for US$7/10; transfers from town cost US$27 per group.

Places to Eat

Fish Trap (☎ 256702) Starters US$1.50-3, mains US$4-15. Open 9am-3pm & 6pm-midnight daily. If you want a surprise in Rundu, drop by this Portuguese-run restaurant, where the menu extends from such pure Portuguese wonders as *ameijoas a bulhão pato* (clams in butter, garlic and coriander leaf) and traditional Portuguese *bacalhau* (cod) concoctions to Angolan chicken *peri-peri* (chicken in a hot pepper sauce), Brazilian *feijoada* (meat stew with rice and beans), Spanish paella, African game meat, and a host of Italian pizza and pasta options. There's also *couvert* (Portuguese premeal snack bowl), soups and salads. It's truly a wonder in the wilderness.

Olive Tree (☎ 255409) Breakfast US$2.50, light meals US$1.50-2. Open 8am-5pm Mon-Sat. This is a nice informal spot for light meals, toasted sandwiches, sweets and coffee. It's also the local Internet cafe.

Antja's (☎ 256973, Hoof St) Breakfast US$2, salads US$0.50-1.50, fast food US$1-2. Open 7.30am-5pm Mon-Sat. This is a good option for breakfast, burgers, toasted sandwiches, pies, sweets and coffee (including espresso and cappuccino).

Croc Bits (Ngandu Safari Lodge, Sarasungu Rd) Mains US$3.50-7, weekend specials US$4.50. This restaurant, attached to the Ngandu Safari Lodge, offers good-value dining, with starters (including mushrooms and garlic snails), toasted sandwiches, burgers, and main dishes featuring chicken, fish and pork. On weekends, it offers steak and fish specials for US$4.50, including a free beer with your meal.

Self-caterers will find supplies at the several well-stocked supermarkets: the ***Sentra Kavango***, ***Oceano Atlântico*** and ***Cola Cola III Hypermarket***, all in the town centre.

You'll find baked goods at the ***Cola Cola II Bakery*** and a well-stocked shop at the Shell petrol station.

Entertainment

Sauyema Night Club *(Grootfontein road, Sauyema)* This popular and pleasantly integrated night spot features a tree sporting coloured lights in the suburb of Sauyema, south-west of town. On weekends, it rocks all night.

New World Disco *(☎ 255003, behind Edumeds stationers)* This sports bar attracts a mixed crowd with its wide-screen TV, pizza, beer and billiards. The disco is open nightly for dancing.

Kavango Amusement Gambling House Here you'll find gambling, light meals and disco dancing nightly.

Shopping

Thanks to their woodlands, Kavango people have developed woodcarving skills and produce Namibia's arguably finest woodwork. Animal figures, masks, wooden beer mugs, walking sticks and boxes are carved in the light *dolfhout* (wild teak) hardwood and make excellent souvenirs. The best carvings are elusive, but you'll find nice pieces at stands along the B8 towards Grootfontein. Some of the stands specialise in toy trucks, aeroplanes and helicopters. Others feature artistically woven rugs and variously sized earthen jars.

The San people also sell craft work – mainly bows, arrows, quivers and ostrich-eggshell necklaces – and can often be found near the Shell petrol station. For a casual tropical look, you could try a palm-leaf hat – a cross between a coolie and a Panama.

Getting There & Away

Bus & Minibus Intercape Mainliner's weekly buses between Windhoek (US$34, 9¼ hours) and Victoria Falls (US$34, 10¾ hours) pass Rundu's Shell petrol station at 5.15am Saturday northbound and 7.15pm Sunday southbound.

Star Line's twice-weekly services between Windhoek (US$9, 11 hours) and Katima Mulilo (US$10, seven hours) also call in at Rundu. Star Line runs a bus from Rundu to Tsumeb (US$7, four hours), via Grootfontein, at 8pm on Wednesday and Sunday. The bus from Grootfontein to Rundu (US$7, three hours) leaves at 7.30pm on Tuesday and Friday.

Minibuses from Windhoek, Grootfontein and Katima Mulilo stop at the Shell petrol station.

Car & Motorcycle Drivers travelling to and from Grootfontein should take special care due to the many pedestrians, animals and potholes that create road hazards. If you are heading east on the Golden Hwy, check locally to determine whether you must still connect with the military convoy that leaves Divundu, two hours from Rundu, at 9am and 3pm daily.

Ferry The rowboat ferry between Rundu and Calai in Angola, operates on demand from the riverbanks.

KHAUDOM GAME RESERVE

The wild and undeveloped 384,000-hectare Khaudom Game Reserve, which borders on Bushmanland, is like nowhere else in Africa. Meandering sand tracks lure you through pristine bush, where you may see roans, wild dogs, elephants, zebras and many other species in an unspoilt and untouristed setting. The park is crossed by a series of *omiramba* (fossil river valleys), which run parallel to the east-west-oriented Kalahari dunes. The birdlife is best in the wetter summer months, when poor roads will hamper visits; easiest access is in the dry winter season.

Places to Stay

Both Khaudom camps must be pre-booked through Namibia Wildlife Resorts (NWR) in Windhoek.

Khaudom Camp Camping US$12 for 2 people plus US$2 for each additional person up to 8 people, basic 4-bed huts US$14. This dune-top camp overlooks an ephemeral waterhole and provides a microcosm of the wider Kalahari.

Sikereti Camp Camping US$11 for 2 people plus US$2 for each additional person

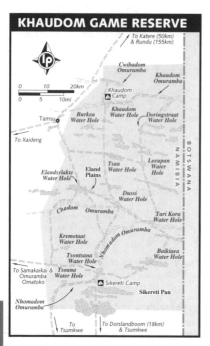

KHAUDOM GAME RESERVE

(Map labels:)
To Katere (50km) & Rundu (155km)

Cwibadom
Omuramba
Khaudom
Omuramba

Khaudom
Camp

0   10   20km
0   5   10mi

Khaudom
Water Hole   Doringstraat
Water Hole

Burkea
Water Hole

Tamsu

To Xaideng

BOTSWANA / NAMIBIA

Elandsvlakte
Water Hole

Eland
Plains

Tsau
Water Hole

Leeupan
Water
Hole

Dussi
Water Hole

Chadom   Omuramba

Tari Kora
Water Hole

Kremetaat
Water Hole

Khaudom Omuramba

Tsontsana
Water Hole

Baikiaea
Water Hole

To Samakaikai &
Omuramba
Omatoko

Tsoana
Water Hole

Sikereti Camp

Nhomadom
Omuramba

Sikereti Pan

To
Tsumkwe

To Dorslandboom (18km)
& Tsumkwe

---

up to 8 people, basic 4-bed huts US$14. Yes, the name means 'cigarette'. This wild camp, located in a grove of terminalia trees, is one of Africa's last undiscovered wonders, but full appreciation of this place requires sensitivity to its subtle charms. Hot showers are available, but you must light the donkey boiler yourself.

Getting There & Away

In the dry season, travelling on the deep sand roads is excruciating, and after rains, they deteriorate into mudslicks – but you're unlikely to regret the effort. NWR requires that parties travel in a convoy of at least two self-sufficient 4WDs and are equipped with food and water for at least three days. Caravans, trailers and motorcycles are prohibited.

From the north, take the sandy track from Katere on the B8 (signposted 'Khaudom'), 120km east of Rundu. After 45km, you'll reach the Cwibadom Omuramba, where you should turn east (left) into the park.

From the south, you can reach Sikereti Camp via Tsumkwe. From Tsumkwe, it's 20km to Groote Döbe and another 15km from there to the Dorslandboom turning (see the Eastern Bushmanland map later in this chapter). It's then 25km north to Sikereti Camp.

The Caprivi Strip

Namibia's spindly north-eastern appendage, the Caprivi Strip, is a largely unexceptional landscape typified by expanses of forest – mainly mopane and terminalia broadleaf. In fact, the land is so flat that the difference between the highest and lowest points in the Caprivi Strip, which measures nearly 500km in length, is a trifling 39m. Throughout the Caprivi are traces of the *shonas*, parallel dunes, which are remnants of a drier climate.

The Caprivi's original inhabitants were subsistence farmers who cultivated the banks of the Zambezi and Kwando Rivers. It has also long been home to substantial San populations, but none still follow their original nomadic hunter-gatherer lifestyles. Most inhabitants of the Caprivi are now situated along the Okavango, Zambezi and Kwando/Mashe/Linyanti/Chobe river systems.

Minor roads are in poor condition and apart from a handful of roadside cuca shops, there are no facilities along the Golden Hwy between Divundu and Kongola. Petrol is available only at Rundu, Divundu, Kongola, Linyanti and Katima Mulilo.

For many travellers, the Caprivi is the easiest access route between Victoria Falls, Botswana's Chobe National Park and the main body of Namibia. However, visitors with time, cash and patience will find such hidden gems as Mudumu and Mamili National Parks, the newly gazetted Bwabwata National Park, the Lizauli traditional village, the town of Katima Mulilo and a host of atmospheric safari lodges.

History

Until the late 19th century, the Caprivi area was known as Itenge and was ruled by Lozi (also called Barotse) kings. Although modern

Caprivians belong mainly to the Mafwe, Subia, Bayei and Mbukushu tribes, Lozi remains the regional language and is used as a medium of instruction in primary schools.

The Caprivi Strip's notably odd shape is a story in itself. In the late 19th century, the area was administered by the British Bechuanaland protectorate. In 1890, Germany laid claim to British-administered Zanzibar. Britain naturally objected and in July 1890, the Berlin Conference was called to settle the dispute. In the end, Queen Victoria acquired Zanzibar, and a strip along the eastern boundary of German South-West Africa was appended to Bechuanaland. Germany was granted the North Sea island of Helgoland and the strip, which was subsequently named the Caprivi Strip, after German chancellor General Count Georg Leo von Caprivi di Caprara di Montecuccoli.

Germany's motivation behind the swap was to acquire access to the Zambezi River, and to provide a link with Tanganyika and, ultimately, the Indian Ocean. Unfortunately, the British colonisation of Rhodesia stopped them well upstream of Victoria Falls, which proved a considerable barrier to navigation on the Zambezi.

The absorption of the Caprivi Strip into German South-West Africa didn't make world news, however, and it was nearly 20 years before some of its population discovered that they were under German control. In fact, not until October 1908 did the government dispatch an Imperial Resident, Herr Hauptmann Streitwolf, to oversee local administration.

The Lozi people reacted by rounding up all the cattle they could muster – including cattle belonging to rival tribes – and driving them out of the area. The cattle were eventually returned to their rightful owners, but most of the Lozi people chose to remain in Zambia and Angola rather than submit to German rule.

On 4 August 1914, Britain declared war on Germany and, just more than one month later, the German administrative seat at Schuckmannsburg was attacked by the British from their base at Sesheke and then seized by the police. An apocryphal tale

The Caprivi – Is it Safe?

At the time of writing Western Caprivi is considered a 'troubled' area, mainly due to past separatist tendencies (most recently in 1999) and spillover from the on-and-off civil war in Angola. It's estimated that at least 8000 Angolan refugees have fled across the border into Namibia and are now sheltering in the Caprivi region.

The well-publicised murder of a French family along the Golden Highway on 3 January 2000 was officially blamed on National Union for the Total Independence of Angola (Unita) rebels, but it has never been conclusively determined who was responsible for the deaths. In fact, most cross-border raids are inspired more by robbery than politics, and this may well have been the case in this tragic incident.

At the time of writing, drivers on the Golden Hwy between Divundu and Kongola must join the twice-daily Namibian Defence Force (NDF) convoy, which departs from either end at 9am and 3pm daily. It makes a toilet stop midway at the volatile Omega base.

Due to the presence of land mines, avoid walking into the bush along the highway and steer around piles of elephant dung on the road (in which guerrillas have been known to plant explosive devices). There's no call for paranoia, and it's likely that the convoy system will soon be abandoned, but those intending to travel along this route would be wise to keep informed.

Those hiring vehicles in Windhoek should ascertain in advance whether their insurance covers trips through this stretch.

NORTHERN NAMIBIA

recounts that German governor Von Frankenburg was entertaining the English resident administrator in Northern Rhodesia (now Zambia) when a servant presented a message from British authorities in Livingstone. After reading it, the British official declared his guest a prisoner of war, and thus, Schuckmannsburg fell into British hands. Whether the story is true or not, the seizure of Schuckmannsburg was the first Allied occupation of enemy territory of WWI.

During the British occupation, the Caprivi was again governed as part of Bechuanaland but it received little attention and was known as a lawless frontier area. When its administration was handed over to South Africa in 1935, the British moved their headquarters to Katima Mulilo, Seventh-Day Adventist missionaries set up a mission, and mercantile activities commenced. In 1939, the rather idiosyncratic magistrate, Major Lyle French W Trollope, was posted to Katima Mulilo and remained long enough to be regarded as local royalty.

BWABWATA NATIONAL PARK
☎ 066

Namibia's newest national park, gazetted in late 1999 (but not yet officially recognised by the Namibian government) includes the best of the former West Caprivi Game Reserve plus several adjacent ecologically significant areas. It takes in five main zones: the 20,500-hectare West Caprivi Triangle around Kongola, also known as the Kwando Core Area; the Mahango Game Reserve; the Popa Falls Rest Camp; the Buffalo Core Area, near Divundu (which lies astride the Okavango River opposite Mahango); and the best of the former West Caprivi Game Reserve. Although parts of the park lie west of the Okavango River and technically belong to the Kavango region, for the purpose of this book, we're including the entire area with the Caprivi Strip.

While private concessions handle their own bookings, all NWR accommodation in the park must be pre-booked through their office in Windhoek.

Divundu

Divundu, with two (nominally) 24-hour petrol stations and a relatively well-stocked supermarket, is merely a product of the road junction. The real population centres are the neighbouring villages of Mukwe, Andara and Bagani. On the road south is Popa Falls, Mahango Game Reserve and some lodges.

Mahango Game Reserve

This small but diverse 25,000-hectare park occupies a broad floodplain north of the

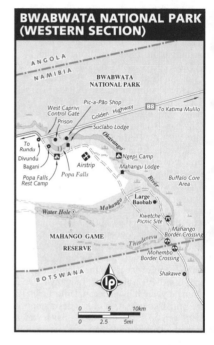

Botswana border and west of the Okavango River. In the dry season it attracts huge concentrations of thirsty elephants. Mahango is the only wildlife park in Namibia where visitors may walk on their own; winter is the best time to see wildlife and stay safely visible.

With a 2WD vehicle, you can either zip through on the Mahango transit route or follow the scenic loop drive past Kwetche picnic site, east of the main road. With 4WD, you can also explore the 20km Circular Drive loop, which follows the omiramba Thinderevu and Mahango to the best wildlife viewing. It's particularly nice to stop beside the river in the afternoon and watch the elephants swimming and drinking among hippos and crocodiles.

Transit traffic through Mahango doesn't require a permit, but to take either of the loop drives costs US$3 per vehicle plus US$3 per person. The same permit is valid for Popa Falls.

Popa Falls

Near Bagani, the Okavango River plunges down a broad series of cascades misleadingly known as Popa Falls *(day admission sunrise to sunset US$3 per person plus US$3 per vehicle)*. Admission to these falls is also valid for Mahango Game Reserve. The falls are nothing to get steamed up about, but periods of low water expose a drop of 4m. Bird-watchers will especially enjoy the variety and number of birds to be observed there.

West Caprivi Game Reserve

The Golden Hwy between Rundu and Katima Mulilo traverses the former West Caprivi Game Reserve. There are still a few elephants, but otherwise it serves mainly as a pantry for local hunters/poachers. Travellers using the NDF convoy along the Golden Hwy must pass through checkpoints at Divundu and Kongola; as long as the convoy is running, allow at least an hour at either end to check in and out.

West Caprivi Triangle

The West Caprivi Triangle, the wedge bounded by Angola on the north, Botswana on the south and the Kwando River on the east, is actually the Caprivi's richest wildlife area. However, hunting, bush clearing, burning and human settlement have created environmental stress. Access is via the road along the western bank of the Kwando River, near Kongola, but the best wildlife viewing is north of the main road, towards Angola. The area ranger station is at Susuwe, on the 4WD road north of Kongola.

Places to Stay & Eat

Western Section Following are the accommodation options in the western section of the park.

Popa Falls Rest Camp Camping US$12 for 2 people plus US$2 for each additional person, standard/luxury 4-bed huts US$26/ 28. A small on-site shop sells the essentials: tinned food, beer, candles and mosquito coils. A field kitchen is available for self-catering.

Ngepi Camp (☎ 259005, fax 259026, e neil@ngepi-experienceafrica.com, neil@

thepub.co.za, W www.ngepi-experienceafrica .com) Camping US$4 per person, tree huts US$27. The name is Mbukushu for 'How are You?', and folks who stay here are normally just fine. Tree huts are planned for 2002. Free pick-ups are available from Divundu at 5pm daily (book in advance). Organised activities include Mahango wildlife drives (US$25), canoe or mokoro trips (US$18), booze cruises (US$2), and mokoro trips in the Okavango Panhandle (US$85/115 for one/three days). It's 4km off the main road, but you need 4WD and in wet periods, it can be flooded, requiring a ferry to the camp.

Suclabo Lodge (☎ 259005, fax 259026, e marlon@ravemail.com.za, PO Box 874, Rundu) Camping B&B US$7 per person, single/double bungalows B&B US$74/96. This German-run lodge occupies a scenic bluff above the Okavango River. Boat trips are US$7 to US$9 and Mahango wildlife drives are US$20. The view is superb, but non-Germans may feel a bit out of place.

Mahangu Lodge (☎ 061-234342, fax 233872, e eden@mweb.com.na, PO Box 20080, Windhoek) Singles/doubles B&B US$80/131. This lodge, which occupies a lush setting within easy reach of the Bwabwata National Park, offers excellent bird-watching and organises fishing trips along the Okavango River. In the rainy season, it's surrounded by water and guests must be ferried from the parking area by boat. Dinner is included in the price.

Eastern Section At the eastern end of the park are several accommodation options. See also under Mudumu National Park, later in this section.

Nambwa Camp Site Camping US$11 per site. Nambwa, 14km south of Kongola, lacks facilities, but it's the only official camp in the park. Book and pick up a permit at the Susuwe ranger station, about 4km north of Kongola (4WD access only) on the west bank of the river. To reach the camp, follow the 4WD track south along the western bank of the Kwando River; a good place to visit while you're there is the wildlife-rich oxbow lagoon about 5km south of the camp.

NORTHERN NAMIBIA

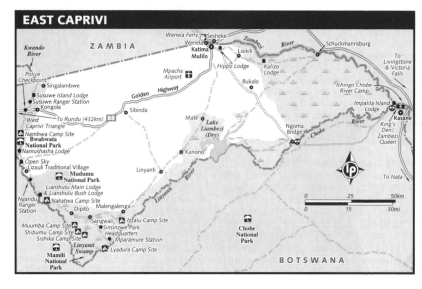

EAST CAPRIVI

Susuwe Island Lodge (☎ *27-11-706 7207, fax 463 8251, ℮ info@impalila.co.za, ᴡ www.islandsinafrica.com, PO Box 70378, Bryanston 2021, South Africa*) Single/ double chalets US$335/520 high season, US$254/312 mid-Jan–late Mar. All rates include activities and full board. This posh wilderness lodge, which is accessible only by 4WD, lies buried in a wildlife-rich area of savanna, woodland and wetland.

KATIMA MULILO
☎ 066

Sultry Katima Mulilo, Namibia's most remote outpost, sits out on a limb at the end of the Caprivi Strip. At 1200km from Windhoek, it's about as far from the capital as you can get in Namibia. This pleasant and very African town features lush vegetation and enormous trees, and was once known for the elephants that marched through. Nowadays, little wildlife remains, apart from the Zambezi hippos and crocodiles, but the river vegetation, the huge lush trees, and the tropical birds and monkeys make for pleasant walks along the riverbanks.

The Lozi name of this town means 'to Quench the Fire', probably in reference to the burning embers carried by travellers, which were extinguished by the Mbova rapids river crossing.

The Caprivi Cultural Festival is held annually in late September.

Along the Kongola road you'll pass informal stands selling the Caprivi's famous wood and soapstone elephant carvings.

Information
Your best source of information is Tutwa Tours (☎ 253048, ℮ tutwa@mweb.com.na), which runs day tours and transfers around the 'four-corners area' where Namibia, Zambia, Zimbabwe and Botswana meet.

From Monday to Friday during banking hours, the Bank of Windhoek, in the main square, changes cash and travellers cheques at an appropriately tropical pace.

The post office is open 8am to 1pm and 2pm to 5pm Monday to Friday.

Katima Mulilo's telephone code is in the process of changing from 0677 to 066; all numbers in this section take the 066 area code, unless otherwise noted.

For fax, email and Internet access, Cyber City (℮ cybercit@iafrica.com.na), in a hut near the market, charges US$0.25 per minute for Internet access and US$0.30 to send email.

A good honest place for vehicle repair is Katima Spares.

Caprivi Arts Centre

The Caprivi Arts Centre *(open 8am-5.30pm daily)*, run by the Caprivi Art & Cultural Association, is a good place to look for local curios and crafts, including elephant and hippo woodcarvings, baskets, bowls, kitchen implements, knives and traditional weapons. There's a good range and some of the work is remarkably original.

Places to Stay

Caprivi Traveller Guest House (☎ 252788) Dorm beds US$5, doubles US$14/16 with shared/private bathroom, caravans US$3.50/4 for 1/2 people. This clean and friendly backpackers lodge is the most economical accommodation in town. To get there, follow the Rundu road 1km from the centre, turn left onto the nameless gravel road and continue on for 400m; the guesthouse is on the left.

Hippo Lodge (☎/fax 253684, 6km along the Ngoma road) Camping US$3 per person, singles/doubles US$27/34. This very relaxed lodge with unmemorable service offers a wonderful sunset view over the Zambezi, and a riveting frog chorus after dark. At the time of writing there was no sign, but the cut-off is about 6km east of the centre on the Ngoma road; you'll have to pick your way along the rough 3km road to the lodge, which is just passable to 2WD vehicles.

Zambezi Lodge (☎/fax 253203, fax 253631, ℮ katima@iafrica.com.na, 2km along the Ngoma road, PO Box 98) Camping US$3 per person plus US$2 per vehicle, single/double self-catering bungalows US$51/71, family units US$95, all rates B&B. Amenities include a pool, restaurant, floating bar and nine-hole golf course (US$3.50 per player). This is the most up-market and central choice in town. At the attached restaurant, set lunches are US$5 and a la carte fish or beef dinners are US$8.50.

Mukusi Cabins (☎/fax 0677-3255, Engen petrol station, PO Box 1194) Budget rooms

KATIMA MULILO

PLACES TO STAY	OTHER
13 Mukusi Cabins; Engen Petrol Station	1 Police
18 Caprivi Traveller Guest House	3 Hospital
	4 Caprivi Arts Centre
PLACES TO EAT	6 Cyber City
2 Mad Dog McGee's	7 Market
5 Kamunu Centre; Chicken Inn	8 Caltex Petrol Station
9 Zambezi Takeaways; Shell Petrol Station	10 Katima Sports Complex
14 Coimbra Restaurant & Takeaways	11 Tutwa Tours
	12 Katima Spares
	15 Coimbra Supermarket & Takeaway
	16 Bank of Windhoek
	17 Post Office

US$14 per person, single/double cabins US$20/28, deluxe rooms US$30/37. This oasis-like lodge in the centre has everything from simple backpackers rooms with fan to small but comfortable air-con cabins. The lovely bar/restaurant dishes up a range of unexpected options – calamari, snails, kingclip etc – as well steak and chicken; breakfast is US$4 and main dishes cost US$6-8.

Kalizo Lodge (☎/fax 252802, ℮ kalizo@ mighty.co.za, 25km along the D3508, PO Box 1854, Ngweze) Camping US$6 per person, thatched reed chalets US$48 per person half board, US$94 per person full board, 4-bed self-catering chalets US$67. This place, 40km downstream, is known for its excellent fishing, bird-watching and river views. The full-board rate includes activities such as mokoro trips and quad-biking. It's accessible only by 4WD; turn north on the D3508, 15km east of Katima Mulilo, and continue 25km to the riverbank. Transfers from Katima Mulilo cost US$44.

Places to Eat

Mad Dog McGee's (☎ 0677-2021, One block off the Ngoma road) Mains US$3-6.

NORTHERN NAMIBIA

Also known as the SOS Club, this restaurant and bar, offering Katima Mulilo's most diverse menu, is a popular hangout for NGO staff, tourists and expats of all sorts. Specialities include pizzas, burgers, seafood, chicken and, of course, alcohol.

Coimbra (☎ *0677-3611, Off the main square)* Takeaways US$1.50-3, mains US$2-4. Near the square, the Coimbra specialises in Portuguese-African food and the lager goes down well on hot, sticky afternoons.

Chicken Inn *(Kamuna Centre)* Takeaways US$1.50-3. This chicken takeaway whips up fast, greasy chicken, chips and trimmings.

Tin Can Alley, in an enormous beer can outside the military base on the Ngoma road, is popular with local workers, and the *Zambezi Takeaway* at the Shell petrol station sells sandwiches, pies and chicken.

There are two supermarkets in the main square and there's a thriving open-air market near the Caprivi Arts Centre.

Getting There & Away

Air Katima Mulilo's airport is at the Mpacha NDF base, 18km south-west of town. Air Namibia has three flights weekly to and from Windhoek's Eros Airport (US$132). Charter flights to outlying lodges, such as Lianshulu, are available through ComAv (☎ 061-227512, fax 245612).

Bus & Minibus Minibuses stop at the Engen petrol station. Local buses between Katima Mulilo and Ngoma Bridge (US$3, 1½ hours) depart from the main square; they run according to no fixed schedule. Star Line buses leave Katima Mulilo for Rundu (US$10, seven hours) and Windhoek (US$21, 17 hours) twice weekly.

The weekly Intercape Mainliner buses between Windhoek (US$48, 16¼ hours) and Victoria Falls (US$16, 5¼ hours) stop at the Shell petrol station in Katima Mulilo; southbound, they pass at 1.15pm on Sunday and northbound, at 11.15am on Saturday.

Car & Motorcycle The tarred Golden Hwy between Katima Mulilo and Rundu opens up the Caprivi region to the rest of Namibia.

However, motorists must still join the free NDF convoy (9am and 3pm) between Kongola and Divundu (see the boxed text 'The Caprivi – Is it Safe?' earlier in this chapter).

Hitching The best places to wait for lifts on the Golden Hwy between Katima Mulilo and Rundu are the police checkpoints and petrol stations in Divundu and Kongola. Chances are that any eastbound/westbound vehicle from Rundu/Katima Mulilo will be doing the entire route.

To Botswana & Zambia The Wenela ferry (passengers free, US$12 for foreign-registered vehicles), 5km from Katima Mulilo, connects Wenela with the Zambian shore. Unofficial small boat ferries cost from US$0.50 to US$1.50, depending on your bargaining skills. In Wenela, you'll find taxis to Sesheke, from where buses leave for Livingstone (US$8, five hours) from 6am daily; the road is horrid.

With a private vehicle, the Ngoma Bridge border crossing enables you to access Chobe National Park, Kasane and Victoria Falls in just a couple of hours. If you stick to the Chobe National Park Transit Route, you're excused from paying Botswana park fees.

AROUND KATIMA MULILO
Schuckmannsburg

Schuckmannsburg, on the Zambezi 50km east of Katima Mulilo, was named after an early governor of German South-West Africa. It was founded in 1909 as the administrative capital of the Caprivi by Imperial Resident Herr Hauptmann Streitwolf and at the outbreak of WWI, it was the first enemy territory to be taken by the Allies (see History earlier in this section).

When South Africa took over Namibia in 1935, the administration moved to Katima Mulilo, and Schuckmannsburg languished; all that remains is a clinic, a police post and a handful of scattered huts. To reach Schuckmannsburg, follow the Ngoma Bridge road to Bukalo, 30km south-east of Katima Mulilo, and turn north-east on the D3509. From the junction, Schuckmannsburg is a rough 47km by 4WD.

Mpalila Island

Mpalila Island (also spelt Impalila), like a wedge driven between the Chobe and Zambezi Rivers, represents Namibia's outer limits at the 'four-corners meeting' of Zimbabwe, Botswana, Namibia and Zambia. The Kakumba sandbank actually reaches out and touches the mid-Zambezi point common to all four countries. In fact, on an area map, this international convergence resembles Michelangelo's *Creation of Adam* on the ceiling of the Sistine Chapel (really – check it out!).

Places to Stay This lovely island is home to several safari lodges that are within easy reach of Victoria Falls and Botswana's Chobe National Park; access in all cases is from Kasane, Botswana. The Kasane/Mpalila border crossing is open 7am to 12.30pm and 1.45pm to 5pm.

Impalila Island Lodge (☎/fax 27-11-706 7207, fax 463 8251, e info@impalila.co.za, w www.islandsinafrica.com, PO Box 70378, Bryanston 2021, South Africa) Singles/doubles US$335/520 high season, US$254/387 low season, 5-night packages US$1520/2340. Overlooking the impressive Mombova rapids, this lodge makes an excellent upmarket getaway. Rates include full board, wildlife walks, drives, cruises and boat transfers from the Impalila office (☎ 267-650795) in Kasane, Botswana. Air transfers to or from Victoria Falls/Susuwe Island Lodge (see Places to Stay & Eat under Bwabwata National Park earlier) cost US$110/130.

Ichingo Chobe River Lodge (☎ 267-650143, 713 02439, fax 650223, e ichingo@iafrica.com, w www.natron.net/ichingo, PO Box 55, Kasane, Botswana) Singles/doubles US$280/400 full board & activities. Also on Mpalila Island, guests can access this recently upgraded tented camp by boat from Kasane, Botswana, or by air charter to Mpalila Island's 1300m runway (a former SADF base). A five-passenger plane from Victoria Falls costs US$235, including a 'Flight of the Angels' over the falls en route. Activities include river cruises on the Chobe, mokoro trips, game drives in Botswana's Chobe National Park and fishing in the Chobe and Zambezi Rivers. You'd never guess you were in Namibia!

King's Den/Zambezi Queen (Botswana ☎/fax 267-650814, 716 30561, Namibia ☎ 066-253203, fax 253631, e katima@iafrica.com.na) Bungalows US$125 per person, *Zambezi Queen* riverboat cabins US$125 per person. This lodge, opposite Sedudu (Kasikile) Island, is affiliated with the Zambezi Lodge in Katima Mulilo. Rates include full board and transfers from Kasane, as well as bird-watching (450 species have been identified here), nature walks, village visits, fishing, and river cruises on the Chobe.

Lake Liambezi

As recently as 1958, Lake Liambezi was just a low-lying plain. However, in that year the water in the Zambezi rose to record levels and the backwash up the Chobe River poured over the higher ground between Ngoma Bridge and Katima Mulilo, in the process creating a new lake, which acted as a magnet for waterbirds.

In 1985, however, low rainfall restricted the backflow and the lake dried up and disappeared. For two years, fires ravaged the dry reeds and turned the lake into a blackened dust hole. It's thought that the catalyst of the process was the overhunting of hippos; without the hippos to flatten tracks through the reeds, river channels became choked with vegetation, which restricted inflow from the Chobe. During the high rainfall years of 2000 and 2001, the floodplains of the Chobe and Linyanti Rivers were transformed into vast expanses of shallow water, and it's possible that Lake Liambezi may once again re-emerge as a watery wonderland soon. Check locally on its current status.

Access is along tracks from the Ngoma Bridge road, best negotiated with 4WD.

MUDUMU NATIONAL PARK
☎ 061

This park once held Namibia's most stunning wildlife habitat and teemed with elephants, rhinos, giraffes, zebras, buffaloes, hippos, crocodiles, Cape clawless otters, waterbucks, elands, roans, wildebeests,

NORTHERN NAMIBIA

impalas, tsessebes, sables, lechwes, sitatungas and the rare puku, as well as predators such as lions, cheetahs, leopards, wild dogs and hyenas. By the late 1980s, however, the park had become a hunting concession gone mad. The wildlife was decimated by trophy hunters, while the native Caprivians, who believed that fires would ensure good rains, set the bush alight and turned it to scorched earth.

In 1989, in a last-ditch effort to rescue the area from total devastation, the Ministry of Environment & Tourism (MET) designated Mudumu and nearby Mamili as national parks. Under such protection, some of Mudumu's wildlife has begun to return, but it will take years of wise policy making and community awareness before it approaches its former glory.

Lizauli Traditional Village

As Mudumu's wildlife population increases, so does the number of conflicts between wildlife and humans: elephants raid crops, hippos injure people, and lions and crocodiles take cattle and other stock. The locals naturally question the motives of those who would protect wildlife at their expense. The environment falls victim to the bitterness of disgruntled communities for whom national parks, wildlife and tourism are a nuisance, and no-one wins.

In the hope of linking conservation, sustainable use of natural resources and local economic development, Grant Burton and Marie Holstensen of Lianshulu Lodge – along with MET, the private sector and the Linyanti Tribal Authority – helped the Lizauli community set up the Lizauli traditional village *(admission US$3; open 9am-5pm Mon-Sat)*.

Here, visitors can learn about traditional Caprivian lifestyles and gain insight into the local diet, fishing and farming methods, village politics, music, games, traditional medicine, basketry and tool-making and so

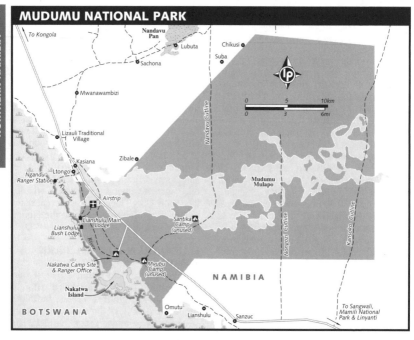

MUDUMU NATIONAL PARK

on. Mudumu game scouts are now recruited from Lizauli and other villages, and are given responsibility for community conservation and antipoaching education.

After the guided tour, visitors can shop for good-value local handicrafts without sales pressure (I picked up a hippo caller – an ingenious drum-like device used to prevent hippos raiding the crops!). Supporting this worthwhile effort is an effective way to improve the local economy and help restore some of Mudumu's former splendour. Lizauli is just off the D3511, about 30km south of Kongola.

Places to Stay

Nakatwa Camp Site (7km south-east of Lianshulu) Camping free. Mudumu's only camp site is little more than a dry spot to pitch a tent, overlooking extensive wetlands. It lacks facilities of any kind.

Lianshulu Main Lodge and *Lianshulu Bush Lodge* (☎ 254317, fax 254980, e lianshul@mweb.com.na, w www.namibiaweb.com/lianshulu, PO Box 90391, Windhoek) Singles/doubles US$300/400, US$81/110 if booked in Namibia, Main Lodge singles/doubles US$137/212, Bush Lodge US$450/660. These neighbouring lodges occupy a private concession inside the boundaries of Mudumu National Park, and they provide some of the country's most beautifully situated accommodation. Rates at the Bush Lodge include full board and activities. The Bush Lodge is dominated by an impressive bar and dining area overlooking the wetlands, and rates are all-inclusive. At Main Lodge, rates include half board; river cruises and wildlife drives cost US$13 each. With its cosy ambience, it offers a less formal experience than the Bush Lodge. At lunch time, leguaans (water monitors) beg for leftovers; at night-time, hippos emerge to graze and diners are serenaded by an enchanting wetland chorus of insects and the haunting 'tink-tink' of bell frogs. River cruises in the pontoon *Jacana* take you to nesting colonies of carmine bee-eaters; the area also supports over 400 other bird species and lots of wildlife, including elephants. To get there, follow the D3511 about 40km south of Kon-

gola and turn west on the signposted track. Air transfers from Windhoek/Katima Mulilo are US$137/20; car hire for visits to Victoria Falls is available to guests from US$59 per day.

Namushasha Lodge (☎/fax 240375, fax 256598, PO Box 6597, Windhoek) Singles/doubles US$70/115. Between Mudumu and Kongola on a bluff above the Kwando River, this place lies outside Mudumu National Park, and is accessible by boat or vehicle. It's popular with Namibian tourists and enjoys a faithful weekend clientele from Katima Mulilo.

Open Sky (☎/fax 253992, fax 221919, 26km along the D3511, PO Box 90538, Windhoek) Camping US$6 per person, US$12 for a pre-erected tent plus US$8 per person. This basic camp site, 26km south of Kongola, is situated on the banks of the Kwando. It's a terrific spot for bird-watching and is situated within striking distance of Mudumu. There is a bar and braai facilities available here.

MAMILI NATIONAL PARK

In years of good rains, wild and little-visited Mamili National Park becomes Namibia's equivalent of Botswana's Okavango Delta, a watery wonderland of wildlife-rich islands, river channels and delightful wetlands. The largely forested islands brim with sycamore figs, jackalberry, leadwood and sausage trees, and are fringed by reed and papyrus marshes and *vleis* (low, open landscapes). As with the Okavango Delta, the dry season is actually the period when the water levels are at their highest, so the best time to visit is between September and early November.

Although poaching has taken a toll, Mamili's wildlife (mainly semi-aquatic species such as hippos, crocodiles, pukus, red lechwes, sitatungas and otters) will still impress. You'll also see elephants, buffaloes, warthogs, giraffes and predators concentrated on Lupala and Nkasa Islands. However, Mamili's trump is its 430 bird species.

Accommodation is limited to five undeveloped wilderness camp sites: in the eastern area, *Lyadura* and *Nzalu*, and in the west, *Muumba*, *Shibumu* and *Sishika*.

NORTHERN NAMIBIA

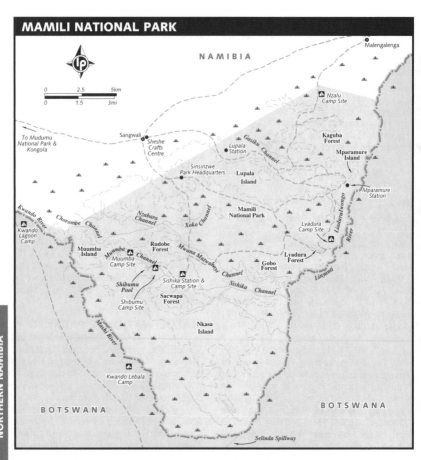

MAMILI NATIONAL PARK

Camping permits are available from MET in Katima Mulilo or NWR in Windhoek.

Access to the park is by 4WD track from Malengalenga, north-east of the park, or from Sangwali village, which is due north. At Sangwali, you may want to stop at the Sheshe Crafts Centre, which is a community project selling the work of local artisans.

Bushmanland

Thanks to increased interest in traditional Kalahari cultures, the eastern reaches of the Otjozondjupa region – better known as Bushmanland – are opening up to visitors. This lovely and remote area is the home of the Ju/hoansi San, who constitute a sub-group of the !Kung. Although Westerners may perceive the San as a self-sufficient hunter-gatherer society, it has been well over a decade since any Namibian groups have followed an entirely traditional lifestyle.

History

For thousands of years, the San pursued a traditional hunter-gatherer lifestyle in their harsh Kalahari home with little outside influence. In the 20th century, however, they – along with the rest of the world – saw plenty of changes.

From 1970, Bushmanland was established as a San homeland, but with Namibian independence in 1990, the San territory shrank from 33,300 sq km to 9700 sq km and 11 of their 15 bore holes were expropriated by other interests. As a result, the Ju/hoansi were left without sufficient land to maintain their traditional lifestyle. This forced many to abandon their n!oresi (homelands or 'lands where one's heart is') to work as farm labourers or migrate to Tsumkwe or other towns, where they met with Western influences. These shifts resulted in disease, prostitution, alcoholism, domestic violence, malnutrition and other social ills associated with poverty and dispossession.

During the war for Namibian independence, many remaining n!oresi were commandeered as South African military bases and 150 San men were attracted by high wages into the South African and territorial defence forces. They formed a Bushman battalion, known as Battalion 31, to fight the Swapo rebels in northern Namibia and Angola. As a result, the Western concept of a salaried wage was introduced into a non-cash economy. A peace-loving people, who had historically preferred to move on rather than face conflicts, were thus exposed to war and all its attendant horrors. Having said that, some of their ancestors had seen plenty of horrors, as the San were historically pressed into service as executioners in the kraals of Owambo chiefs.

In 1980, US film-maker John Marshall and his British colleague, Claire Marshall, arrived in Namibia. During the next 10 years they drilled bore holes, established 35 villages and formed the Ju/hoansi Bushmen Development Foundation, which encouraged San people to return to their traditional lands and begin farm dry-land crops and raise cattle. This fostered the creation of the Nyae Nyae Farmers' Cooperative Organisation to oversee production and assist in decisions that affect the farmers' interests.

Unfortunately, the foundation has recently suffered ideological conflicts among its expatriate staff. Points of contention include the introduction of cattle (an original cornerstone of the foundation) and tourism. Many purists feel that both are big trouble, while pragmatists believe both can better the lot of these forgotten people.

EASTERN BUSHMANLAND
☎ 064

The largely flat landscape of eastern Bushmanland is characterised by scrubby vegetation, but areas that receive more water, such as the meandering omiramba, also support baobabs and stands of camelthorn, red umbrella thorn and blackthorn acacia.

Despite official reassurances that cattle, agriculture and traditional gathering would be accommodated, attempts to create a game reserve in eastern Bushmanland have met with local resistance. However, even without official protection, the region supports a rich natural ecosystem. In the dry season, elephants, antelopes and other wildlife congregate around the *Panveld* (an area containing many phosphate-rich pans); when the rains come, they disperse to the west and north-west.

A note to visitors: This region of Namibia is one of the most fragile in Africa and tourism has been very limited. When visiting San villages, visitors are expected to trade for beadwork, walking sticks, ostrich-shell necklaces, bow and arrow sets, and so on. Prized items include T-shirts, shoes, trousers, baseball caps and other useful items. People will also ask for sugar and tobacco; you'll have to decide whether or not to encourage the use of these products and their attendant health risks. In any case, please trade fairly, avoid excessive 'payment' and help keep local dignity intact by resisting the urge to hand out gifts for nothing.

Information
Tourism in Eastern Bushmanland is regulated by the Nyae Nyae Conservancy (☎ 061-236327, fax 225997, e nndfn@ iafrica.com.na), with an office in Tsumkwe, which also collects fees and charges for activities from visitors. Admission is US$3 per visit, and you can arrange activities,

NORTHERN NAMIBIA

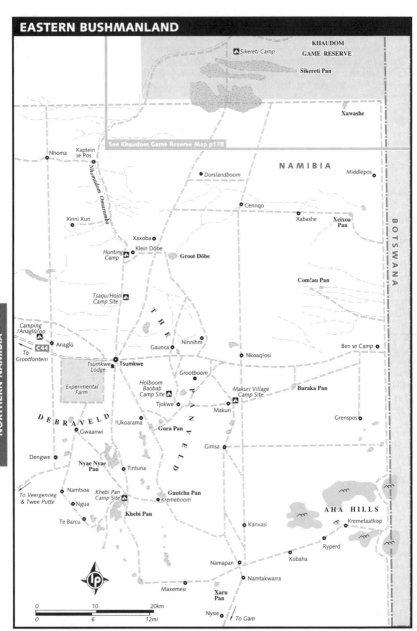

EASTERN BUSHMANLAND

NORTHERN NAMIBIA

KHAUDOM
GAME RESERVE

Sikereti Camp

Sikereti Pan

Xawashe

See Khaudom Game Reserve Map p178

Nhoma

Kaptein
se Pos

NAMIBIA

Middlepos

Dorslandboom

Cennqo

Xinni Xuri

Xabashe

Xeixoa
Pan

Xaxoba

Hunting
Camp

Klein Döbe

Groot Döbe

Com!au Pan

Tsaqu/Holo
Camp Site

THE

Camping
/Anaglú/oo

C44

Anaglú

Gaunca

Ninnihm

Nkoaqlosi

Ben se Camp

To
Grootfontein

Tsumkwe
Lodge

Tsumkwe

Grootboom

Holboom
Baobab
Camp Site

Experimental
Farm

Makuri Village
Camp Site

Baraka Pan

Tjokwe

P

Makuri

A

Grenspos

IUkoarama

N

DE BRAVELD

Gwaanwi

Gura Pan

V

E

Dengwe

Nyae Nyae
Pan

Tintuna

Gimsa

L

D

AHA HILLS

Namtsoa

Khebi Pan
Camp Site

Gautcha Pan

To Veergenoeg
& Twee Putte

Ngua

Kremeboom

Kremetaatkop

Te Barcu

Khebi Pan

Kanxasi

Ryperd

Namapan

Xobaha

Namtakwarra

Maxemesi

Xaru
Pan

0   10   20km

0   6   12mi

Nysie   To Gam

BOTSWANA

such as hunting with the San (US$7) and gathering wild foods (US$3.50). Fees are per guide, and you'll usually be offered three or four – don't accept more than five! In the evening, you can experience traditional music, dancing and clapping around the campfire, featuring as many as 15 performers, for US$30. Bookings should be made at Tsumkwe Lodge (see Places to Stay & Eat later in this section) before you head off into the bush. Ask for Arno Oosthuysen.

Tsumkwe

As the 'administrative capital' of the Bushmanland area, yellow-painted Tsumkwe is the only real settlement and service centre in this vast stretch of the Kalahari. Having said that, it's merely a wide spot in the sand and the town shop carries only a bare selection of supplies.

There's a telephone at the police station and you can pick up permits for Khaudom Game Reserve at the MET, 1km south of the Tsumkwe crossroads, but it's more reliable to book through NWR in Windhoek.

In town, the Reverend Piet Poggenpool exchanges food and clothing for arts and crafts produced by the rural San people, which makes eminent sense in a region where cash is practically useless – there's nothing to buy. The shop is an excellent place to look for San work, especially if you're not visiting the villages. From the Ministry of Regional and Local Government and Housing, turn east; it's the second house on the left.

Getting There & Away It's easy enough to reach Tsumkwe on the twice-weekly Star Line bus from Grootfontein (US$6.50, 6½ hours). It leaves Grootfontein at 11.30am Monday and Thursday and from Tsumkwe at 10.15am Tuesday and Friday.

The Tsumkwe road is negotiable by 2WD vehicles, but it's a long, tedious gravelled route that still gets rough in places. Petrol is available only sporadically at Tsumkwe Lodge (never on Sundays), which means that to travel east of the town and still make it back to Grootfontein will require carrying extra petrol. Note that the Hieromtrent 995

BP Station – 12km south of the C44 on the D2893, then 2km west on a ranch road – is no longer a reliable source of petrol.

The Panveld

Forming an arc east of Tsumkwe is a remote landscape of phosphate-rich pans. After the rains, the largest of these, Nyae Nyae, Khebi and Gautcha (all at the southern end of the arc), are transformed into superb wetlands. These ephemeral water sources attract itinerant water birds – including throngs of flamingoes – but they are also breeding sites for waterfowl: ducks, spurwing geese, cranes, crakes, egrets and herons. Other commonly observed birds include teals, sandpipers and reeves, as well as the rarer blacktailed godwit and the great snipe.

The Baobabs

The dry crusty landscape around Tsumkwe supports several large baobab trees, some of which have grown quite huge. The imaginatively named Grootboom (Big Tree) is one of the largest, with a circumference of over 30m. One tree with historical significance is the Dorslandboom, which was visited by the Dorsland (Thirst Land) trekkers who camped here on their trek to Angola in 1891 and carved their names into the tree. Another notable tree, the immense Holboom (Hollow Tree), dominates the bush near the village of Tjokwe.

Aha Hills

Up against the Botswana border, the flat landscape is broken only by the Aha Hills. Given the nearly featureless landscape that surrounds them, you may imagine that these low limestone outcrops were named when the first traveller uttered 'Aha, some hills'. In fact, it's a rendition of the sound made by the endemic barking gecko.

The region is pockmarked with unexplored caves and sinkholes, but don't attempt to enter them unless you have extensive caving experience. The hills are also accessible from the Botswana side. A border crossing, which will open up the entire region, is planned between Tsumkwe and Dobe, but as yet there's no way across.

NORTHERN NAMIBIA

Places to Stay & Eat

Tsumkwe Lodge *(☎ 203581 ask for ext 531, bookings ☎ 067-220060, fax 207497, 1km south of Tsumkwe crossroads, PO Box 1899, Tsumeb)* Camping US$3.50 per person, single/double bungalows US$42/62, US$64/ 107 full board. Here you'll find Bushmanland's most formal accommodation. It also rents Land Rovers and guides, and organises tours. Travel 1.5km south of the Tsumkwe crossroads, then turn right at the Ministry of Housing and then continue for 500m. Book through the lodge office in Tsumeb.

Nyae Nyae Conservancy Camp Sites Camping US$2.50 per person. The Nyae Nyae Conservancy (see Information, earlier in this section) has set up four official camp sites: the **Holboom Baobab** at Tjokwe, south-east of Tsumkwe; **Makuri**, a few kilometres east of that; **Tsaqu/Hojo**, north of Tsumkwe; and **Khebi Pan**, south of Tsumkwe, which is well out in the bush.

Camping/Anaglù/oo *(Anaglù Village)* Camping US$2 per person. This village has a nice little camp site with picnic areas, trash barrels, firewood, water, a toilet and showers. It lies 11km west of Tsumkwe on the C44, then 1km north.

Omatoko Valley Rest Camp *(Omatoko Crossing, C44)* Camping US$3/3.50 in tents/thatched shelters. The camp lies 11km south-west of the Kano Vlei veterinary gate at the D3306 junction. It's a scenic location, set deep in the Omatoko Omuramba and has solar power, a water pump, hot showers and a caretaker. Various activities are available, from bird-watching and horse riding to cultural tours and village visits.

There's a restaurant at Tsumkwe Lodge, and **Tsumkwe Winkel** sells limited groceries, but beyond that, you must be self-sufficient.

Getting Around

Most visitors swing through en route from central Namibia to the Caprivi Strip via Khaudom Game Reserve. There are no tarred roads and only the C44 is good gravel; other routes are little more than tracks, some very sandy. In remote areas, it's wise to travel in a convoy of two or more vehicles.

North-Western Namibia

For armchair travellers, Namibia is synonymous with the Skeleton Coast, a formidable desert coastline littered with shipwrecks and engulfed by icy breakers and sinister fog. As one moves inland, the dank fogs give way to the wondrous desert wilderness of Damaraland and the Kaokoveld (also known as the Kaokoland), where the predominant cultures include the hardy and enigmatic Damara and Himba peoples, and classic African wildlife has adapted to unimaginably harsh conditions.

Tourism and access to the region are both increasing, but there are no tarred roads; only major routes are maintained, and the most incredible landscapes lie astride rough 4WD tracks. Note that petrol is available only at Uis, Khorixas, Kamanjab, Palmwag, Sesfontein, Opuwo and Henties Bay.

Damaraland

In the northern Namib, dispersed springs and ephemeral rivers – the Hoanib, Uniab, Huab, Ugab, Omaruru etc – provide streaks of greenery and moisture for wildlife, people and livestock. Moving inland from the dunes and plains of the bleak Skeleton Coast, the terrain gradually rises through wild desert mountains toward the scrubby plateaus of central Namibia.

Damaraland, which occupies much of this transition zone, is named for the Damara people who make up much of its sparse population. Its broad spaces are one of Africa's last 'unofficial' wildlife areas, and you can still see zebras, giraffes, antelopes, elephants and even black rhinos ranging outside national parks or protected reserves. The region also features many natural attractions, including the Brandberg massif, which culminates in Namibia's highest peak – the 2573m Königstein. In addition, the Brandberg, Twyfelfontein and Spitzkoppe have some of Africa's finest prehistoric rock paintings and engravings.

Highlights

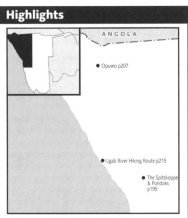

- Camp and climb at the Spitzkoppe, 'the Matterhorn of Africa'.
- Hike to the White Lady of the Brandberg.
- Look for ancient inspiration in the magnificent petroglyphs at Twyfelfontein.
- Take an adventurous 4WD expedition through the remote Kaokoveld.
- Travel through the Himba country to fabulous Epupa Falls.
- Hold your nose and visit the seal colonies at Cape Cross on the Skeleton Coast.

Unfortunately, without a private vehicle or patience with hitching, Damaraland's many natural wonders are reached only by organised safari. The good news is that many of the companies running safaris from Windhoek include the region in their itineraries (see Organised Tours in the Getting Around chapter for more information).

THE SPITZKOPPE
☎ 064

The 1728m-high Spitzkoppe *(D3716, Groot Spitzkoppe village; admission US$1.50 per person & US$0.80 per car; open sunrise-*

NORTH-WESTERN NAMIBIA

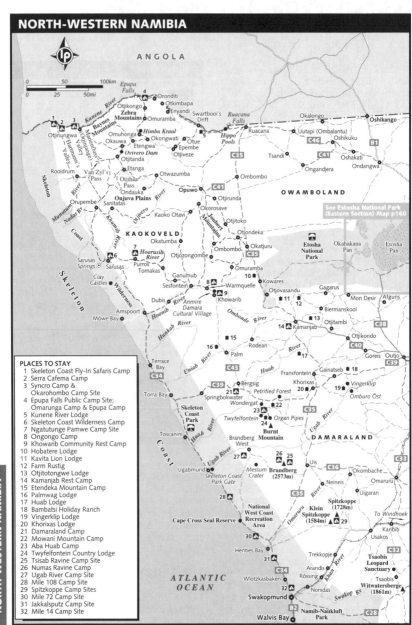

NORTH-WESTERN NAMIBIA

ANGOLA

OWAMBOLAND

See Estosha National Park
(Eastern Section) Map p160

KAOKOVELD

Etosha
National
Park

DAMARALAND

ATLANTIC
OCEAN

PLACES TO STAY
1 Skeleton Coast Fly-In Safaris Camp
2 Serra Cafema Camp
3 Syncro Camp &
  Okarohombo Camp Site
4 Epupa Falls Public Camp Site;
  Omarunga Camp & Epupa Camp
5 Kunene River Lodge
6 Skeleton Coast Wilderness Camp
7 Ngatutunge Pamwe Camp Site
8 Ongongo Camp
9 Khowarib Community Rest Camp
10 Hobatere Lodge
11 Kavita Lion Lodge
12 Farm Rustig
13 Otjitotongwe Lodge
14 Kamanjab Rest Camp
15 Etendeka Mountain Camp
16 Palmwag Lodge
17 Huab Lodge
18 Bambatsi Holiday Ranch
19 Vingerklip Lodge
20 Khorixas Lodge
21 Damaraland Camp
22 Mowani Mountain Camp
23 Aba Huab Camp
24 Twyfelfontein Country Lodge
25 Tsisab Ravine Camp Site
26 Numas Ravine Camp
27 Ugab River Camp Site
28 Mile 108 Camp Site
29 Spitzkoppe Camp Sites
30 Mile 72 Camp Site
31 Jakkalsputz Camp Site
32 Mile 14 Camp Site

sunset), one of Namibia's most recognisable landmarks, rises mirage-like above the dusty pro-Namib plains of southern Damaraland. Its dramatic shape has inspired its nickname as 'the Matterhorn of Africa', but similarities between this granite inselberg and the glaciated Swiss alp begin and end with its sharp peak. The Spitzkoppe is actually the remnant of an ancient volcano, formed in the same way as the nearby Brandberg and Erongo massifs. It was first climbed in 1946 and is now popular with both local and foreign rock climbers.

In 1986, the reserve surrounding the Spitzkoppe was transferred from the Damara Administration to the Ministry of Environment & Tourism (MET); it's currently protected as a MET conservation area and attended by the local community. Local guides charge around US$2.50 for a two- to three-hour tour.

The Pondoks

Immediately east of the Spitzkoppe rises the lower Pondok massif where, in 1896, the German South-West Africa Company established a farm and a dam to provide irrigation water. At the eastern end of this rocky jumble, a wire cable climbs the granite slopes to a vegetated hollow known as Bushman's Paradise, where an overhang shelters a vandalised panel of ancient rhino paintings; much of the damage is caused by a coat of shellac. (This site should not be confused with the Rhino Wall site on the Spitzkoppe itself.)

Places to Stay & Eat

***Camp sites** (☎ 530879, D3716, Gross Spitzkoppe village)* Camping US$3 per person plus US$0.80 per car, basic bungalows US$9.50/16 for 1/2 nights. This excellent community-based camping ground includes lovely camp sites, which are dotted around the base of the Spitzkoppe and surrounding outcrops. Most are set in magical rock hollows and provide a sense of real isolation. Facilities at the entrance include a reception office, ablutions blocks and braai stands. There's also a small stand selling local crafts and minerals, and a bar and restaurant are planned; for those without tents, simple bungalows are also available near the site entrance.

Proceeds from the site benefit the adjoining village of Groot Spitzkoppe. Water is

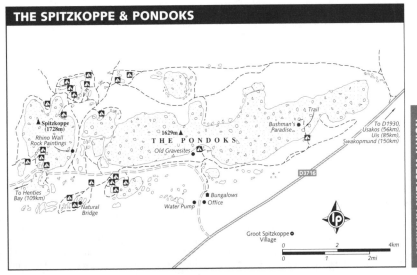

THE SPITZKOPPE & PONDOKS

Spitzkoppe (1728m)
Rhino Wall Rock Paintings
1629m ▲
THE PONDOKS
Old Gravesites
Bushman's Paradise
Trail
To D1930, Usakos (56km), Uis (85km), Swakopmund (150km)
D3716
To Henties Bay (109km)
Natural Bridge
Water Pump
■ Bungalows
● Office
Groot Spitzkoppe ● Village

0   2   4km
0   1   2mi

NORTH-WESTERN NAMIBIA

trucked in by tanker, but it's in short supply, so it's best to bring your own.

Getting There & Away

The nearest you'll get on public transport is the junction of the B2 (the Okahandja-Swakopmund road) and D1918, 30km away. Although several Swakopmund tour agencies run day trips, you'll regret not allowing more time to explore this incredible place.

Under normal dry conditions, a 2WD is sufficient to reach the mountain. Turn north-west off the B2 onto the D1918 toward Henties Bay, then after 1km, turn north on the D1930. After 27km (you actually pass the mountain), turn south-west on the D3716 until you reach Groot Spitzkoppe village. Here you turn west into the site.

THE BRANDBERG

The Brandberg (Fire Mountain), is named for the effect created by the setting sun on its western face, which causes this granite massif to resemble a burning slag heap glowing red. Its summit, Königstein, is Namibia's highest peak at 2573m.

For visitors, the Brandberg is best known for its rock paintings, and the late Harald Pager spent many years documenting the more than 8000 sites around the massif (three of his four volumes of work are now available in print, but only a few sites are readily accessible to the public). Technical rock climbers will also find plenty of joy, but the climb to the peak requires agility and patience to clamber over the huge boulders and rock faces that block the Tsisab and Numas Ravines.

Tsisab Ravine

The Brandberg's main attraction is the gallery of rock paintings located in the Tsisab (Leopard) Ravine. Its first European discoverer was the German surveyor Dr Reinhard Maack on a 1918 descent from Königstein.

From the car park, it's a well-marked 45-minute walk up a scenic track to Maack's Shelter, which contains the White Lady of the Brandberg (see the boxed text 'The White Lady of the Brandberg'); ignore any-

one claiming that a guide is compulsory. Along the way, watch for baboons, klipspringers and mountain zebras, and carry plenty of water. Further up the ravine are several other shelters and overhangs containing ancient paintings. As you climb higher, the terrain grows more difficult and, in places, the route becomes a harrowing scramble over house-sized boulders.

From Uis, head 15km north on the D2369 and turn west on the D2359, which leads 26km to the Tsisab car park. An attendant will guard your vehicle for a tip.

Numas Ravine

Numas Ravine, slicing through the western face of the Brandberg, is another treasure house of ancient paintings. Without a guide, however, your hunt for ancient art may wind up as more of a pleasant stroll through a dramatic ravine. Most people try to find the rock facing the southern bank of the riverbed, which bears paintings of a snake, a giraffe and an antelope. It lies about 30 minutes' walk up the ravine. After another half-hour, you'll reach an oasis-like freshwater spring and several more paintings in the immediate surroundings.

From the westward turning 14km south of Uis, follow the D2342 for 55km, where you'll see a rough track turning eastward. After about 10km, you'll reach a fork; the 4WD track on the right leads to the Numas Ravine car park.

Places to Stay

There are unofficial *camp sites* near the mouth of both the Numas and Tsisab Ravines, but neither has water or facilities. Camping is free, but an 'attendant' may ask for a 'donation'; you decide whether their services merit what is effectively a tip. Despite the barrel at the parking area, rubbish collection is very rare, so please burn your leftovers or carry them away.

MESSUM CRATER

One of Damaraland's most remote natural attractions is the highly mysterious-looking Messum Crater, two concentric circles of hills created by a collapsed volcano in the

The White Lady of the Brandberg

The best-known site at Tsisab Ravine, Maack's Shelter, contains the famous painting known as the White Lady of the Brandberg. The figure, which isn't necessarily a lady, stands about 40cm high. In one hand, it carries what appears to be a wine glass (South Africa's Sinnya Valley winery recognised this and uses the figure on its label) and in the other, a bow and several arrows. Its hair is straight and light-coloured – distinctly un-African – and the body is painted white from the chest down. It appears to be a central figure in a bizarre hunting procession, which includes several women, one of whom has skewered a small animal – an antelope with gemsbok horns and striped legs. Another figure, who may be a type of spiritual healer, is holding a bunch of carrots in his left hand, and in his right hand a stick with which he's prodding the white figure.

The first assessment of the painting was in 1948, when Abbé Henri Breuil speculated that the work had Egyptian or Cretan origins, based on similar ancient art he'd seen around the Mediterranean. However, this fanciful idea has now been discounted and it's generally accepted that the painting is of indigenous origin. The White Lady hasn't been reliably dated, but is generally thought to be around 16,000 years old.

Goboboseb Mountains. The crater measures more than 20km in diameter, creating a vast lost world, which visitors are likely to have to themselves. Note that camping is prohibited inside the crater. To avoid damage to formations and vegetation, drivers must stick to existing tracks.

Of its three main entrances, Messum is best accessed along the Messum River from the D2342 west of the Brandberg. Note that you must stick to the tracks at all times, especially if you choose either route involving the fragile lichen plains of the National West Coast Recreation Area. If you are driving in this area, you will require the relevant topographic sheets (available from the Office of the Surveyor General in Windhoek).

UIS
☎ 064

The company town of Uis (Khoi-Khoi for 'Bad Water') sprang up in 1958 when the South African Iscor corporation bought out the small-scale tin mining operations that had gone on since 1911. The mine closed in 1991 due to low world tin prices and although private operations still eke out a meagre living, Uis appears to be a ghost town in the making. Services include a convenience supermarket and a petrol station that's open from dawn to dusk Monday to Saturday.

Dâureb Craft & Brandberg Community Tourism Project (☎ 504030, PO Box 24) This group conducts guided tours to the Brandberg rock-art sites and introduces travellers to the Damara culture that prevails in the area. The craft outlet mostly sells items made from recycled mining materials. For information, contact Tertius !Oeamseb.

Places to Stay & Eat
Brandberg Rest Camp (☎ 504038, fax 504 037, e brandbrg@iml-net.com.na, Main road, PO Box 35) Camping US$4 per person, singles/doubles US$26/40, family rooms US$62. This camp, with an unobstructed view of Uis' tin-mine tailings, has a restaurant, mineral shop, swimming pool, tennis court and nine-hole golf course.

Haus Lizenstein (☎/fax 504052, e liz en@mweb.com.na) Camp sites US$6 per person, rooms per person B&B/half board US$31/40. This hospitable guesthouse offers clean, air-con rooms near the edge of town. Meals are available on request and it runs tours to the Brandberg (US$47, including breakfast in the Ugab riverbed) and mine tours (US$67).

KHORIXAS
☎ 067

As the administrative capital of Damaraland, the decrepit town of Khorixas might seem a good choice as a base for exploration, but there's little to detain visitors and most travellers stop only to refuel at the petrol station.

The bank opens only on weekday mornings. You may want to visit Khorixas Community Craft Centre, a self-help cooperative operated by the Save the Rhino Trust, which provides a retail outlet for local artists and artesans. There's also a tree nursery and a Craft Workshop & Education Centre, which is constructed from *dumpi* (375ml) beer bottles. In May, Khorixas further displays local artistry in an arts festival.

Places to Stay & Eat

Khorixas Lodge (☎ 331111, fax 331388, e khorixas@mweb.com.na, PO Box 2) Camping US$5/3 per adult/child, single/ double bungalows US$34/67, 4-bed family chalets US$56/98 for 1/2 people plus US$28 for each additional person, luxury 4-bed stone chalet US$160. This convenient place is 1km off the Torra Bay road, west of town. Amenities include a restaurant, braai area, swimming pool and general shop.

Apart from Khorixas Lodge, your only choices for food are the *Khorixas Bakery* and the petrol-station shop, which sells a limited selection of groceries.

Getting There & Away

The Star Line bus from Otjiwarongo (US$5, 4½ hours) to Walvis Bay (US$8, eight hours) passes the petrol station in Khorixas at 12.30pm on Thursday westbound, and at 9pm on Friday eastbound.

PETRIFIED FOREST

The Petrified Forest, 40km west of Khorixas, is an area of open *veld* (field) scattered

Lichen Fields

Neither plants nor animals, lichens actually consist of two components – an alga and a fungus – and perhaps provide nature's most perfect example of symbiosis between two living things. The fungus portion absorbs moisture from the air, while the alga contains chlorophyll, which produces sugar and starch to provide carbohydrate energy. Both algae and fungi are cryptogams, which means that they lack the sex organs necessary to produce flowers and seeds, and are therefore unable to reproduce as plants do.

Lichens come in many varieties. Perhaps the most familiar are the crustose varieties, which form orange, black, brown or pale green ring patterns on rocks, but there are also foliose lichen, which are free-standing. The gravel plains of the Namib support the world's most extensive fields of these foliose lichen, which provide stability for the loose soil in this land of little vegetation. These fields are composed mostly of stationary grey lichen *(Parmelia hypomelaena)* and free-standing black lichen *(Xanthomaculina convoluta)*, but there's also a rarer orange variety *(Teleschistes capensis)*, an especially bushy lichen which grows up to 10cm high.

By day, the lichen fields very much resemble thickets of dead shrivelled shrubs, but with the addition of water the magic appears. On nights of heavy fog, the dull grey and black fields uncurl and burst into blue, green and orange 'bloom'. It's the fungus component that provides the lichen's root system and physical rigidity, absorbs the water droplets and draws limited nutrients from the soil. At the first light of dawn, however, before the sun burns off the fog and sucks out the moisture, the alga kicks in with its contribution: using the water droplets, light and carbon dioxide to photosynthesise carbohydrates for both itself and the fungus.

Lichens are incredibly fragile and slow growing, and the slightest disturbance can crush them. Once that happens, it may take 40 or 50 years before any regeneration is apparent. Most of the damage is now caused by thoughtless off-road driving.

The best places to observe the Namib lichens are south-west of Messum Crater, in scattered areas along the salt road between Swakopmund and Terrace Bay, and near the start of the Welwitschia Drive, east of Swakopmund.

with petrified tree trunks up to 34m long and 6m in circumference, which are estimated to be around 260 million years old. The original trees belonged to an ancient group of cone-bearing plants that are known as *Gymnospermae*, which includes such modern plants as conifers, cycads and welwitschias (see the boxed text 'Welwitschias' in the Central Namib Desert chapter). Because of the lack of root or branch remnants, it's thought that the fossilied trunks were transported to the site in a flood.

About 50 individual trees are visible, some half buried in sandstone and many perfectly petrified in silica – complete with bark and tree rings. In 1950, after souvenir hunters had begun to take their toll, the site was declared a national monument and it's now strictly forbidden to carry off even a small scrap of petrified wood.

There's no admission fee, but guides are compulsory (tips are their only income); plan on US$1.25 per group for the 500m walking tour. At the entrance there's a large thatched picnic shelter and a small curio shop selling palm-ivory pendants, woodcarvings, local crystals and gems.

Getting There & Away
The Petrified Forest, signposted 'Versteende Woud', lies 40km west of Khorixas on the C39. En route from Khorixas, watch for the prominent sandstone formation known as 'the Ship', which is visible just south of the C39, 52km west of Khorixas.

VINGERKLIP
☎ 067
The 35m-high Vingerklip (Finger Rock), whch is also known as Kalk-Kegel (Limestone Pillar), rises above the Bertram farm, 75km east of Khorixas. It's an erosional remnant of a limestone plateau that was formed over 15 million years ago, and a large cave in its rubbly base makes it appear even more precariously balanced. It was first climbed in 1970 by American Tom Choate.

While the Vingerklip itself is the centrepiece, the entire valley presents a scene out of the Old West, and is in fact known as 'the Arizona of Namibia'.

Places to Stay
Bambatsi Holiday Ranch (☎ 313897, fax 313331, **e** bambatsi@natron.net, C39 at the D2743, PO Box 120, Outjo) Singles/doubles half board US$54/91. The ranch has nine rooms, pool, tennis court and mountain bikes for hire to explore the surrounding mopane-forested landscapes.

Vingerklip Lodge (☎ 290318, fax 290 319, **e** vingerkl@mweb.com.na, PO Box 443, Outjo) Singles/doubles half board US$84/120. This beautiful lodge enjoys a commanding setting; the panorama from the bar compares with the famous scenes of Monument Valley in old John Ford Westerns. Accommodation is in comfortable bungalows – you'll love the novel lounge chairs that overlook the fabulous view.

Getting There & Away
From Khorixas, follow the C39 east for 54km and turn south on the D2743. The Bertram farm is 21km south on this road and Vingerklip – which should be obvious at this stage – rises 1km west of the farm entrance.

TWYFELFONTEIN
☎ 067
The main attraction at Twyfelfontein (Doubtful Spring), at the head of the grassy Aba Huab Valley, is one of the most extensive galleries of rock art in Africa. The original name of this water source was /Ui-//Ais (Surrounded by Rocks), but in 1947 it was renamed by European settler Mr D Levin, who deemed its daily output of one cubic metre of water insufficient in this difficult environment.

Rock Engravings
However doubtful the water supply was, this perennial spring would historically have attracted bounteous wildlife and created a paradise for the hunters who eventually left their marks on the surrounding rocks.

Twyfelfontein's rock engravings *(D3214; admission US$1 per person plus US$1 per vehicle; open sunrise-sunset)*, otherwise known as petroglyphs, were made by cutting through the hard patina covering the local sandstone. In time, this skin reformed over the engravings, protecting them from erosion. Most of them date back at least 6000 years to the early Stone Age and are probably the work of ancient San hunters. From colour differentiation and weathering, researchers have identified at least six distinct phases, but some are clearly the work of copy-cat artists and probably date from the 19th century.

Animals, animal tracks and geometric designs are well represented but there are surprisingly few human figures. Many of the engravings depict animals that are no longer found in the area – elephants, rhinos, giraffes and lions – and an engraving of a sea lion indicates contact with the coast more than 100km away. Another portrays a lion with pawprints in place of feet and an oddly angular tail.

The former Twyfelfontein farm became a national monument in 1952 but it had no formal protection until 1986, when MET designated it a natural reserve. In the interim, many petroglyphs were damaged by vandals and some were removed altogether.

Twyfelfontein has over 2500 engravings but the loop trail leads past only the most striking sites. Guides are available (plan on US$1 as a tip), but the route is easy and if you want more time than the guide is prepared to allow, you can usually arrange to walk alone. Note that some guides get lazy and omit the first part of the tour, so make sure that the first stops include the spring, the pump and the claw-like Wave Rock.

Wondergat
Wondergat is an enormous sinkhole with daunting views into the subterranean world. Turn west off the D3254, 4km north of the D2612 junction. It's about 500m further on to Wondergat.

Burnt Mountain & Organ Pipes
South-east of Twyfelfontein rises a barren 12km-long volcanic ridge, at the foot of which lies the hill known as Burnt Mountain, an expanse of volcanic clinker that appears to have been literally exposed to fire. Virtually nothing grows in this eerie panorama of desolation, but over the road from the entrance is an incongruous quartz field, which glistens in the sun.

Burnt Mountain lies beside the D3254, 3km south of the Twyfelfontein turn-off. Over the road, you can follow an obvious path into a small gorge that contains a 100m stretch of unusual 4m-high dolerite (coarse-grained basalt) columns known as the Organ Pipes.

Places to Stay
Aba Huab Camp (D3254, Aba Huab river crossing, PO Box 131, Khorixas) Camping US$5 per person. This place describes itself as 'simple, rustic and natural' and has become a preferred stop for travellers. Camping is in tents or small thatched A-frame shelters. Hot showers, cold drinks and edible staples are available. It lies beside the Aba Huab riverbed, immediately north of the Twyfelfontein turn-off.

Twyfelfontein Country Lodge (☎ 697 021, fax 697023, e afrideca@mweb.com .na, 5km off the D3254, PO Box 6597, Windhoek) Single/double chalets B&B US$96/150. This architecturally monumental place sits embedded in the rock; the design, decor and furnishings are a must-see. On your way in, be sure not to miss the ancient rock engravings or the swimming pool with its incongruous desert waterfall. Lunch/ dinner (US$6/8) are served in the immense and airy elevated dining room.

Mowani Mountain Camp (☎ 061-232 009, fax 259430, e visions@namibianet .com, W www.namibianet.com/visions, 5km north of the D2612, PO Box 40788, Windhoek) Singles/doubles US$240/374. There's little to prepare you for this beautiful lodge. Hidden among a jumble of boulders, its domed buildings seem to disappear into the landscape and you don't see it until you're there. The main buildings all enjoy an ingenious natural air-conditioning system and the tented accommodation nestles out of sight amid the boulders. Every unit enjoys a stunning view. The rates include meals and drinks. Exclusive camp sites are also being established in a scenic valley away from the main lodge. Twyfelfontein tours (US$23 per person) and six-hour nature drives (US$47)

DAVID WALL

MANFRED GOTTSCHALK

PETER PTSCHELINZEW

Namibia boasts some fascinating architecture: Windhoek's Independence Ave **(top)** is home to colonial German buildings; Christuskirche **(bottom left)**, also in Windhoek, was the first church in Namibia built from marble; the historic train station at Swakopmund **(bottom right)**, built in 1901, is now a hotel.

MANFRED GOTTSCHALK

MANFRED GOTTSCHALK

ERIC WHEATER

MITCH REARDON

Namibia is home to people from many different tribal groups: a Herero couple on the road **(top)**; a Himba woman **(middle right)**; a San woman enjoys a quiet moment **(bottom right)**; and a San woman and child **(bottom left)**

are available, and hot-air ballooning will be available in the near future.

Getting There & Away

There's no public transport in the area and little traffic. Turn off the C39 73km west of Khorixas, turn south on the D3254 and continue 15km to a right turning signposted Twyfelfontein. It's 5km to the site.

KAMANJAB & AROUND

☎ 067

The unspectacular town of Kamanjab sits amid some lovely boulder-strewn countryside, and functions as a minor service centre for northern Damaraland and the southern Kaokoveld. Heading north, it has the last supplies and petrol before Sesfontein or Opuwo. The bank is open sporadically for foreign exchange.

The good gravel road north to Hobatere and Ruacana is open to 2WD vehicles. About 10km north of Hobatere, it crosses the Red Line, a veterinary cordon fence, where commercial ranching gives way to subsistence herding (see the boxed text 'The Red Line' in the North Central Namibia chapter). Here, the vegetation has suffered the ravages of millions of munching goats, and erosion has already begun to take its toll on the semidenuded landscape.

Rock Engravings

In the Peets Alberts Kopjes on Kamanjab farm, 10km along the Outjo road, there is a superior rock engraving site. Pick up the key at the Oase Guest House in town.

Places to Stay & Eat

In Town There are a few affordable places.

Kamanjab Rest Camp (☎ 330274, 081-128 7761, 3km along the Torra Bay road) Camping US$4.50 per person, chalets US$24 per person. This wooded camp, tucked away off the road, makes a friendly and comfortable stop; the area has prolific birdlife. The attached restaurant serves up three-course meals (most beef- and game-oriented) for around US$8.

Oase Guest House (☎/fax 330032) Singles/doubles B&B US$26/44. This wonder-fully friendly place in the heart of Kamanjab has comfortable rooms, a swimming pool and the only restaurant in town. It can also connect you with Jakaronga Himba-Safaris, which offers Kaokoland trips with overnight stays in Himba-style camp sites for US$118 per person per day.

Otherwise, meal options in Kamanjab are limited to the *supermarket*, *bakery* and *Impala Takeaway*, beside the Oase, which cooks up meat pies and other snacks.

Out of Town Kamanjab's scenic hinterlands support numerous interesting lodges.

Kavita Lion Lodge (☎ 330224, fax 330 269, e iti07537@mweb.com.na, PO Box 118) Camping US$7 per person, singles/doubles US$75/120. This lodge, run by friendly Uwe and Tammy Hoth, is situated on the borders of Etosha National Park and provides accommodation in pleasant bungalows. Here, injured or unruly lions find a home. In addition to guided wildlife walks and drives, it offers a lovely walking track and excursions into Etosha and the Kaokoveld. Some of the proceeds go to the Afri-Leo Foundation, which rescues problem lions from farming areas.

Otjitotongwe Lodge (☎/fax 330201, e otji totongwecheetahpark@hotmail.com, 24km on the C40, PO Box 60) Camping US$3.50 per person, bungalows half board US$54 per person. If you want to see cheetahs close up, this very popular camp site and bush bar is the place to go. Here, cheetah aficionados Tollie and Roeleen Nel keep tame cheetahs around their home and have set up a 40-hectare enclosure for wilder specimens, which they feed every afternoon. Whether or not you agree with the concept, for US$2 per person, you can join them on the circuit and score some wonderful photos. Their aim is to set some of their 'rescued' cheetahs free in Etosha National Park, but the government is currently opposed to the idea.

Farm Rustig (☎ 330250, fax 330037, e eden@mweb.com.na, D2695, PO Box 25) Camping US$5 per person, singles/doubles US$62/102. This 6000-hectare farm has rewarding wildlife viewing and offers good country cooking. Wildlife drives are

US$40 for up to eight people. There's also a hiking track to the Dolomite overlook. Turn north on the D2763 about 8km north-west of Kamanjab, and 14km later turn right on the D2695. The farm is situated 20km along this road.

Hobatere Lodge (☎ 061-253992, fax 221 919, e discoveraf@iafrica.com.na, w www .resafrica.net/hobatere-lodge/, 65km along the C35, PO Box 90538, Windhoek) Singles/ doubles full board US$76/140. The name of this private game lodge, over the park fence from Etosha's proposed Otjovasandu Camp, means 'You'll Find it Here' and – depending what 'it' is – that seems to hold a lot of

---

Euphorbia Euphoria

The several species of the prominent cactus-like genus euphorbia grow all over Southern Africa, from the highlands of Zimbabwe where they reach tree-size (Euphorbia ingens) to the gravel plains of Damaraland, Namibia, where there's a variety known as melkbos, or milkbush (Euphorbia damarana), after its milky sap. Although these and other euphorbias (including Euphorbia virosa) are poisonous to humans, they're regularly eaten by kudus, and for black rhinos they're a real treat. In fact, they've been dubbed 'black rhino's ice cream'.

Euphorbias have also been useful to humans. The ancient San boiled them down and used them in their rock paintings, and locals still use them for fishing. When placed in the water, their sticky sap clogs the gills of fish and suffocates them.

One variation – taxonomists can't decide whether it's related to other euphorbias – is the mysterious hoodia (Hoodia corrorii), which grows throughout Namibia's deserts. In periods of heavy rainfall, the hoodia erupts into foul-smelling purple blooms; the obnoxious odour recalls rotting meat and attracts flies, which drink its nectar and lay eggs in its flesh, then carry its pollen to other plants, thus propogating both species. Count yourself lucky if you manage to see it in bloom, but bear in mind that the smell could curdle your olfactory senses.

---

promise. This vast palette of stunning desert scenery has been compared to Kenya's Great Rift Valley, and it's a great habitat for mountain zebras, black-faced impalas and Damara dik-diks. Activities include wildlife drives and walks and forays into Etosha's western reaches. Follow the C35 north of Kamanjab for 65km and turn west at the Hobatere gate; from there, it's 15km to the lodge.

Huab Lodge (☎/fax 312923, e huab@ iafrica.com.na, w www.classicsafaricamps .com/huab.htm, PO Box 103) Bungalows full board US$154 per person. Huab Lodge enjoys a wonderful wildlife-rich setting amid dramatic granite kopjes (small hills) on the banks of the normally dry Huab River. Rates include drinks, wildlife walks and drives, laundry services, a swimming pool and a 40°C mineral hot spring. It's 55km from Kamanjab on the Khorixas road, then 35km west on the D2670.

Getting There & Away

There's no public transport and hitching is difficult, however, upmarket safari lodges can organise transfers, and several budget safari companies in Windhoek run Kaokoland trips that include the region.

PALMWAG

The Palmwag oasis lies amid stark red hills and plains in a surprisingly rich wildlife area, which is one of the last strongholds of the famous desert elephant. A super destination for day trips is the wildlife-rich Van Zylsgat Gorge on the Uniab River. Just to boggle your mind, consider the landscapes, which are covered with an evenly distributed layer of uniformly sized stones. How this came about is anyone's guess.

A great way to support initiative in this region of almost total unemployment is to buy a pendant made from !uinida or vegetable ivory, the nut of the makalani palm. Nuts are carved with animal designs, mounted on a thong and sold by local teenagers for less than US$2.

Places to Stay

Palmwag Lodge (☎ 064-404459, fax 404 664, e dassaf@iafrica.com.na, On the C43,

PO Box 339, Swakopmund) Camping US$7 per person, singles/doubles half board US$86/ 123. Operated by Desert Adventure Safaris, Palmwag nuzzles up to an anomalous green marsh. There are several excellent hiking routes and the human watering hole has a front-row view of its palm-fringed elephantine counterpart; even black rhinos drop by occasionally. Accommodation is in reed bungalows and guests can use the restaurant, bar and swimming pool. The reception issues permits (US$5 per vehicle and US$2.50 per person) to independently explore the concession; otherwise, join Desert Adventure Safaris on its three-hour drives to Aub Canyon and Van Zylsgat Gorge for US$19 per person.

Etendeka Mountain Camp (☎ *061-226 979, fax 226999,* e *logufa@mweb.com.na,* w *www.natron.net/tour/logufa, PO Box 21783, Windhoek)* Single/double self-contained tents US$207/307. Environmental experts Barbara and Dennis Liebenberg run this tented camp beneath the foothills of the truncated Grootberg Mountains. As a host of the Black Rhino Trust, this lodge actively supports the conservation of black rhinos. A highlight is the three-day, four-night hike, with overnight stops in trail camps. Drivers are met at the entrance at 3.30pm (April to September) or 4pm (October to March) and shuttled to the camp.

Damaraland Camp (☎ *061-274500, fax 239455,* e *info@nts.com.na,* w *www.wild erness-safaris.com, 13km on the C39 toward Springbowater)* Single/double tents US$280/ 387. Prices include full board and activities. Wilderness Safaris runs this solar-powered desert outpost with distant views of stark truncated hills (imagine visiting a Roadrunner cartoon!) and offers an oasis of luxury in a wild setting. The novel pool occupies a rocky gorge behind the camp. Activities include wildlife drives and walks, as well as guided hikes of up to a week. The camp is 13km down a rough track west of the Palmwag-Sesfontein road.

Getting There & Away

Palmwag is situated on the D3706, 157km from Khorixas and 105km from Sesfontein.

Coming from the south, you'll cross the Red Line at Palm, 1km south of the Palmwag Lodge. There's no public transport in this remote region.

SESFONTEIN
☎ 065

Dusty Sesfontein (Six Springs), Damaraland's most northerly outpost, is almost entirely encircled by the Kaokoveld. After a rinderpest outbreak in 1896, the German colonial government established a military post; a barracks was added in 1901 and four years later, a fort was constructed to control cattle disease, arms smuggling and poaching. This arrangement lasted until 1909 when the fort appeared to be redundant and was requisitioned by the police, who used it until the outbreak of WWI. In 1987, the fort was restored by the Damara Administration. After years of deterioration, it was converted into a comfortable lodge.

The town also has a Trek petrol station and several shops selling staples.

Things to See & Do

Sesfontein, which wouldn't seem out of place in the Algerian Sahara (think Tamanrasset!), is built around a petrol station and a German fort that has been converted into a lodge. Don't miss the historic **graveyard** or the views of the town and surrounding ranges from the shale and limestone hills behind the fort.

For adventurers who dream of uncharted territory, the spectacular and little-known **Otjitaimo Canyon** lurks about 10km north of the main road, along the western flanks of the north-south mountain range east of Sesfontein. To get here would involve a major expedition on foot, but if you're up for it, pick up the topographic sheets from the Office of the Surveyor General in Windhoek, pack lots of water (at least 4L per person per day) and expect unimaginable scenery and solitude.

The Herero village of **Warmquelle** (Warm Springs), which serves mainly as a district school, historically belongs to the Kaokoveld. The name derives from the warm springs on the Hoanib River, which seep out of the artesian system 1km east of the D3706; they were purchased in 1900 by Dr C Schletwein, as part of a vegetable farm that supplied the German troops at Sesfontein. In the early 1920s, the property was sold to the government as a reserve for the Topnaar Khoi-Khoi people, who no longer have much of a presence in the area. Visitors can still swim in the springs, but are certain to attract lots of attention.

In the Khowarib community, you can visit the friendly **Anmire Damara Cultural Village** *(admission US$2; open 9am-4pm Mon-Fri, 9am-1pm Sat & Sun Apr-Dec)*, with a collection of local huts, where local guides present Damara culture to visitors.

Organised Tours

Fort Sesfontein runs day tours to Himba and Damara villages, the Hoanib River, rock paintings, Ongongo and Khowarib. Half-day/full-day 4WD tours for up to four people cost US$120/214.

Places to Stay & Eat

Fort Sesfontein (☎ 275534, fax 275533, ⓔ fort6fontein@natron.net, ⓦ www.natron .net/tour/sesfontein/lodgee.htm, PO Box 4896, Windhoek) Camping US$7.50 per person, thatched huts US$8 per person, singles/doubles US$63/91, 4-bed family rooms US$230. The only original bit of the fort, now renovated as a rest camp, is the campers' bar and braai area. At the restaurant, breakfast/lunch/dinner will set you back US$8.50/8.50/18.

Ongongo Camp (6km along the Warmquelle road) Camping US$3 per person. Ongongo (Beautiful Little Place) is 6km up the Italian-built pipeline from Warmquelle and is run by the local community. It features the paradisiacal Blinkwater Falls and rock pool, created by a natural tufa formation and complete with native turtles. Bring a good sleeping bag and ground cover, and avoid camping below the falls whenever there's a chance of rain. Best of luck in finding someone to check you in; access requires a high-clearance vehicle.

Khowarib Community Rest Camp (5km along the Khowarib road) Camping/beehive huts US$3 per person. Khowarib occupies a bluff above the Hoanib River, 3km east of Khowarib on the D3706. Unfortunately, the floods of recent years have decimated the site, but it's attempting to regain its former appeal.

Getting There & Away

The road between Palmwag and Sesfontein is good gravel, and you'll only have problems if the Hoanib River is flowing. Unless it has been raining, the gravel road from Sesfontein to Opuwo is accessible to all vehicles, but there is one very steep hill that may prove impassable to trailers or wimpy vehicles. Petrol is available only in Sesfontein and Opuwo.

The Kaokoveld

Namibia's north-western corner, the Kaokoveld, is often described as Africa's last great wilderness. Even if that isn't exactly accurate, the area certainly is wild and represents Namibia at its most primeval. This vast repository of desert mountains and indigenous cultures is crossed only by untarred tracks and remains refreshingly short of tourist facilities. In this book, the terms Kaokoveld and Kaokoland are used interchangeably.

Even the Kaokoveld wildlife has adapted to the typically arid conditions. The desert elephant, of which only about 35 remain, has survived harsh conditions that would be devastating to other elephants. This adaptation, along with its especially long legs, has led leading taxonomists to consider it a subspecies of the African elephant *(Loxodonta africana)*. In addition to this, a few black rhinos remain, as well as gemsboks, kudus, springboks, ostriches, giraffes and mountain zebras.

Travelling in the Kaokoveld

Epupa Falls is now open to high-clearance 2WD vehicles, the Kamanjab-Opuwo road is open to all vehicles and the Sesfontein-Opuwo road accommodates anything that can handle one very steep hill. However, routes through the western Kaokoveld are all rugged 4WD tracks laid down by the South African Defence Force (SADF) during the bush war and they're maintained only by the wheels of passing vehicles.

Off the main tourist route from Sesfontein to Opuwo, Okongwati and Epupa Falls, there's little traffic and the scattered villages lack hotels, shops, showers, hospitals or vehicle spares or repairs. If that makes you uncomfortable, you may want to consider visiting the region with an established tour operator.

Those who are undaunted must make careful preparations. See Car & Motorcycle in the Getting Around chapter for detailed advice on safe driving in adverse conditions. For any trip off the Sesfontein-Opuwo road or the Ruacana-Opuwo-Epupa Falls route, you need a robust 4WD vehicle, plenty of time, and supplies to see you through the journey. This includes enough water for the entire trip. It's also useful to take a guide who knows the region and to travel in a convoy of at least two vehicles. Carry several spare tyres for each vehicle, a tyre iron, a good puncture repair kit and a range of vehicle spares, as well as twice as much petrol as the distances would suggest. For navigation, use a compass, or preferably a global positioning system (GPS), and the *Kaokoland-Kunene Region Tourist Map*, produced by Shell, as well as the relevant topographic sheets and Jan Joubert's 4WD guide (available from Cymot Greensport in Windhoek).

Poor conditions on some tracks may limit your progress to 5km/h, but after rains, streams and mud can stop a vehicle in its tracks. Allow a full day to travel between Opuwo and Epupa Falls, and several days each way from Opuwo to Hartmann's Valley and Otjinjange (Marienflüss). Note that Van Zyl's Pass may be crossed only from east to west. Alternative access is through the Rooidrum road junction north of Orupembe (via Otjihaa Pass).

OPUWO
☎ 065

Although it's the Kaokoveld 'capital', Opuwo is little more than a dusty collection

Language Basics

If you are travelling around the Kaokoveld and visiting villages, the following words of Otjiherero/Otjihimba may prove useful:

Hello/Good day.	*Moro.*
Good evening.	*Huenda.*
How are you?	*Muwepe nduka?* or *Kora?*
Fine, thanks.	*Nawa* or (more formally) *Ami mbiri nawa.*
Do you speak English/ Herero	*Ove uhungira otji Ingrissa/ Herero?*
Yes.	*Eee.*
No.	*Kako.*
How much would you like for this?	*Imbi mokasisa vingapi?*
Do you know the road to...?	*Motjiua ondjira ndjijenda...?*
Where is the...?	*...iripi?*
Goodbye.	*Kara nawa* (to one person) or *Karee nawa* (to many people).

of concrete commercial buildings ringed by traditional rondavels and Himba huts. In fact, in Herero, Opuwo means 'The End'.

Lots of Himba and Herero people from the bush gravitate to Opuwo's 'bright lights', and many tourists have passed this way. As a result, locals no longer appreciate having cameras waved in their faces (and who would?). The going rate for a 'people shot' is around US$0.50; please respect local wishes and either pay or put the camera away.

Most organised Kaokoveld safaris stop at small villages within a 20km radius of Opuwo.

Information
At the Kaoko Information Centre (☎ 273420, PO Box 217; open 8am-6pm daily), Kemuu Jakurama and KK Muhuka are happy to provide any guidance you may require. If you're off on a 4WD trip through the Kaokoveld,

Visiting a Fragile Environment

Camping in the Kaokoveld requires awareness of the environment and people. Avoid camping in shady and inviting riverbeds, as large animals often use them as thoroughfares, and even when there's not a cloud in the sky, flash floods can roar down them with alarming force. In the interests of the delicate landscape and flora, keep to obvious vehicle tracks; in this dry climate, damage caused by off-road driving may be visible for hundreds of years to come.

Because natural water sources are vital to local people, stock and wildlife, please don't use clear streams, springs or water holes for washing yourself or your gear. Similarly, avoid camping near springs or water holes lest you frighten the animals and inadvertently prevent them drinking.

You should ask permission before entering or camping near a settlement, particularly as you may inadvertently violate a sacred fire or cross a ritual burial line. Also, ask permission before taking photos. Most rural Himba people, especially those who've had little contact with tourists, will be willing models. Some, however, may ask for payment, generally in the form of sweets, tobacco, sugar, corn mielies or soft drinks. In the interest of protecting teeth that may never meet a dentist, it's probably best to stick with fruit or mielies.

Few visitors would want to see traditional Himba societies transformed into a Kaokoveld version of Disneyland, but as tourism increases and Western values encroach on the region, things will change. Along main routes, visitors may encounter traditionally dressed Himba people who wave down vehicles and ask for tips to model for photos. Naturally, whether you accept is up to you, but bear in mind that encouraging this trade draws people away from their herds and their seminomadic lifestyle and towards a cash economy that undermines long-standing values and community cooperation.

guides/translators are available for US$14 per person per day in your own vehicle. This is an especially good option if you want to make sensitive contact with remote Himba communities.

The post and telephone office is hidden behind the bakery; it's open from 8.30am to 4.30pm Monday to Friday and 8am to noon on Saturday.

For vehicle repairs, the BP station poses the least risk, but don't break down here if you can possibly avoid it. Note that Opuwo is your last opportunity to buy petrol before Kamanjab, Ruacana or Sesfontein.

Organised Tours

Ohakane Lodge (see Places to Stay following) runs half-day visits to Himba villages (US$57) and day trips to Epupa Falls (US$450) and offers Epupa Falls transfers (US$337 for up to five people). For all tours, book at least one week in advance.

Places to Stay

Ohakane Lodge (☎ *273031, fax 273025,* e *ohakane@iafrica.com.na, PO Box 8)*
Singles/doubles US$47/67. This lodge has air-con, nice chunky furniture and en suite facilities, and also features a swimming pool, bar and restaurant (guests only). In the evening it puts on a braai.

Power Safe Guesthouse (☎ 270137) Camping US$6, dorm beds US$10. This backpackers lodge has pleasantly cool dorms; camping is allowed on the green lawn. Guests may use the kitchen facilities. Turn at the BP petrol station then take the next right. Just past the old hospital, turn left. It's several houses down on the right, beside a mobile home.

Uniting Guest House (☎ 273400) Rooms B&B US$10 per person, doubles B&B US$12. This place is at the top of the hill past Power Safe Guesthouse. Turn right at the church; it's two houses down on the right. Guests can use the kitchen.

Opuwo Rest Camp (☎ 273043) Camping US$4, singles/doubles US$19/23. Occupying a natural amphitheatre, this place offers Opuwo's best camping. The easiest access is through the government housing project about 1km from town towards Sesfontein.

The signposted access along the road north normally requires a 4WD.

Places to Eat

Ohakane Lodge Coffee Shop (☎ 273031) Set lunches US$6. This coffee shop serves cakes, coffee and set lunches, including salad and cooked meats.

Oreness Restaurant Meals US$5. This French-owned restaurant, attached to the tourist office, is Opuwo's only real option for full meals.

At the *bakery* beside the BP petrol station you'll find doughnuts, pastries, yogurt, beer, bread and some of Namibia's best sausage rolls – but only in the morning before they sell out. Behind it is the *Madiba Fish & Chips*, which rarely has fish and chips, but you might find goat and chips. The only meals you'll get at the *Opuwo Recreation Club Restaurant* are liquid and alcoholic.

The best-stocked supermarket is the *Power Safe*; the *drankwinkel* (bottle store)

next door sells soft drinks and alcohol. *Opuwo Supermarket* beside the curio shop stocks only the basics.

Shopping

Curio Shop Open 8.30am-12.30pm & 2.30-5.30pm Mon-Fri, 8.30am-12.30pm Sat. Opuwo's brightly painted self-help curio shop sells local arts and crafts on consignment. You'll find all sorts of Himba adornments smeared with ochre: conch-shell pendants, wrist bands, chest pieces and even the headdresses worn by Himba brides. There's also a range of original jewellery, appliqued pillowslips, Himba and Herero dolls, drums and wooden carvings.

Getting There & Away

There's no public transport to Opuwo, but hitching is generally better from Ruacana than from the south.

SWARTBOOI'S DRIFT

☎ 065

From Ruacana, a rough 4WD track heads west along the Kunene River towards Swartbooi's Drift, where a **monument** commemorates the Dorsland trekkers who passed here en route to their future homesteads in Angola. The Namibia Blue Sodalite **mine**, 5km south of Swartbooi's Drift on the Otjiveze/Epembe road, describes its product as 'stone from the desert, blue like the sea'. Sodalites, which are coloured by volcanic intrusions, are used for tiles, wall decoration, ornamental columns and sculpture. You'll sometimes find sodalite along the road, but it's illegal to remove it from the company property.

Organised Tours

With a minimum of two participants, the *Kunene River Lodge* (see Places to Stay following) operates half- to five-day whitewater rafting trips on the Kunene River, from the class IV Ondarusu Rapids (upstream from Swartbooi's Drift) to Epupa Falls. For the popular one-day trip over the Ondarusu Rapids, including the raft, lunch and the services of a river guide trained by the South African Rivers Association (SARA) you'll

OPUWO

PLACES TO STAY
1 Opuwo Rest Camp
3 Uniting Guest House
4 Power Safe Guesthouse
10 Ohakane Lodge

PLACES TO EAT
13 Bakery
14 Madiba Fish & Chips
15 Oreness Restaurant; Kaoko Information Centre

OTHER
2 Church
5 Hospital
6 Curio Shop
7 Opuwo Supermarket
8 Opuwo Recreation Club Restaurant
9 BP Petrol Station
11 Drankwinkel
12 Power Safe Supermarket
16 School
17 Government Housing Project

To Okongwati Falls (111km) & Epupa Falls (175km)

To Etanga

0   100   200m
0   100   200yd

To Sesfontein (146km)

4WD Only

To Ruacana (140km) & Kamanjab (242km)

WARNING
Last fuel stop before Kamanjab, Ruacana & Sesfontein

NORTH-WESTERN NAMIBIA

pay US$40 per person. Additional days, which include meals and camping, cost around US$50 per person per day. The lodge also runs bird-watching excursions (US$14), booze cruises (US$14) and quad-bike trips (US$34).

Places to Stay
Kunene River Lodge (☎/fax 274300, 240 310, ℮ kunenerl@mweb.com.na, PO Box 643, Ondangwa) Camping US$4/1.50 per adult/child, pre-erected tents US$20/28, singles/doubles US$27/34. This friendly place 5km east of Swartbooi's Drift makes an idyllic riverside stop; camp sites are sheltered beneath towering riverside trees and the bungalows enjoy a pleasant garden setting. Guests can hire canoes (US$5.50 per outing), mountain bikes (US$5.50 per day) and fishing rods (US$4 per day). There are meals available at the adjoining restaurant and bar.

Getting There & Away
At Otjikeze/Epembe, 73km north-west of Opuwo, an eastward turning onto the D3701 leads 60km to Swartbooi's Drift. This is the easiest access route, and it's open to 2WD vehicles. The river road from Ruacana is extremely rough, but in dry conditions, it can be negotiated by high-clearance 2WD vehicle.

On the other hand, the 93km river road to Epupa Falls – along the lovely 'Namibian Riviera' – is extremely challenging even with 4WD and can take several days. It's much more pleasantly done on foot (see Getting There & Away under Epupa Falls later in this section).

OPUWO TO EPUPA FALLS
It's possible to drive from Opuwo to Epupa Falls with 2WD, but the route still requires high clearance and can be slow-going in places. Ramshackle Okongwati, 105km from Opuwo, has four shops selling basic supplies (the best is Ohange Store) and several bottle stores. Just beyond the village, the road crosses the Okongwati River; if it has been raining, 4WD is essential. Another 12km will take you to Omuhonga village,

where locals have established a traditional **Himba Kraal** (admission US$1.25) for the benefit of tourists. Avoid walking between the holy fire and the cattle kraal or the door of the main hut, as it is believed this will bring misfortune to the village. Further north, keep looking to the east of the road for the unusual Zebra Mountains – there's no question about the origin of the name!

EPUPA FALLS
At this dynamic spot, whose name means 'Falling Waters' in Herero, the Kunene River fans out and is ushered through a 500m-wide series of parallel channels, dropping a total of 60m over 1.5km. The greatest single drop – 37m – is commonly identified as *the* Epupa Falls. Here the river tumbles into a dark, narrow, rainbow-wrapped cleft. The river is in peak flow in April and May.

During periods of low water, the pools above the falls make fabulous natural Jacuzzis. You're safe from crocodiles in the eddies and rapids, but hang onto the rocks and keep away from the lip of the falls; once you're caught by the current, there's no way to prevent being swept over (as at least two people have learned too late). Swimming here isn't suitable for children.

There's excellent hiking along the river west of the falls and plenty of mountains to climb, affording panoramic views along the river and far into Angola.

Places to Stay, Eat & Drink
The **public camp site** on the river road has camping for US$5 per person. This enclosed camping ground, right at the falls, can get extremely crowded, but there are flush toilets and hot showers, which are maintained by the local community.

Omarunga Camp (☎/fax 067-330220, fax 061-257123, ℮ ermo@namibiaweb .com, Ⓦ www.namibiaweb.com/ermo, PO Box 27, Kamanjab) Camping US$5 per person, single/double tents US$58/96 half board. This German-run place belongs to Ermo Safaris and operates through a concession granted by the local chief. Activities include sunset hikes (US$8.50) and visits to a Himba village (US$31). Nonguests can pre-book breakfast/lunch/dinner (US$7.50/7.50/14).

Epupa Camp *(☎ 061-246427, fax 246 428,* [e] *travel@ntc.com.na, PO Box 90466, Windhoek)* Single/double tent accommodation US$144/214. This luxury camp, 800m upstream from the falls, was originally used by consultants for the abortive Epupa hydro project. The rates include meals and activities such as Himba visits, sundowner hikes, scenic river drives and trips to rock engravings.

Himba Bar, 400m upstream from the falls, is a little tin shack, which is *the* night spot at Epupa Falls. It's a great place to meet and party with the locals.

Getting There & Away

There's no public transport to Epupa Falls, but Ermo Safaris and the Namibia Travel Connection arrange air transfers for guests of Omarunga Camp and Epupa Camp.

The road from Okongwati is accessible to high-clearance 2WD vehicles, but it's still quite rough. The rugged 93km 4WD river route from Swartbooi's Drift may take several days, and it's far quicker to make the trip via Otjiveze/Epembe. Ohakane Lodge (see Places to Stay under Opuwo earlier) runs expensive transfers to Epupa Falls, but you must book a week in advance.

Keen hikers can manage the route along the 'Namibian Riviera' from Swartbooi's Drift to Epupa Falls (93km, five days) or from Ruacana to Epupa Falls (150km, eight days). You're never far from water, but there are lots of crocodiles and, even in the winter, the heat can be oppressive and draining. It's wise to go by the full moon, when you can beat the heat by walking at night. Carry extra supplies, since you may have to wait for lifts back.

THE NORTH-WEST CORNER

West of Epupa Falls is situated at the Kaokoveld of travellers' dreams: stark, rugged desert peaks, vast landscapes, sparse scrubby vegetation, drought-resistant wildlife and nomadic bands of Himba people and their tiny settlements of beehive huts. This region, which is contiguous with the Skeleton Coast Wilderness, has now been designated as the Kaokoland Conservation Area.

At the moment, the easiest way to visit this region is with an expensive fly-in safari or organised camping safari, but the cheapest way to do it is to hire a 4WD and set off on your own. If that's beyond your budget, you can wait around the petrol stations in Ruacana or Opuwo and talk with passing expeditions. If you're a cook, vehicle mechanic or doctor you have the best chances of convincing someone you're indispensable.

Routes

From Okongwati, the westward route through Etengwa leads to either Van Zyl's Pass or Otjihaa Pass. From Okauwa (with a landmark broken windmill) to the road fork at Otjitanda (which is a Himba chief's kraal), the way is extremely rough and slow-going – along the way, stop for a swim at beautiful Ovivero Dam. From Otjitanda, you must decide whether you're heading west over Van Zyl's Pass (which may only be traversed from east to west!) into Otjinjange (Marienflüss) and Hartmann's Valleys, or south over the equally beautiful but much easier Otjihaa Pass toward Orupembe.

You can also access Otjinjange (Marienflüss) and Hartmann's Valleys without crossing Van Zyl's Pass by turning north at the three-way junction in the middle of the Onjuva Plain, 12km north of Orupembe. At the T-junction in Rooidrum (Red Drum), you can decide which valley you want. Turn right for Otjinjange (Marienflüss) and left for Hartmann's. West of this junction, 17km from Rooidrum, you can also turn south along the fairly good route to Orupembe, Purros (provided that the Hoarusib River isn't flowing) and on to Sesfontein.

Alternatively, you can head west from Opuwo on the D3703, which leads 105km to Etanga; 19km beyond Etanga, you'll reach a road junction marked by a stone sign painted with white birds. At this point, you can turn north toward Otjitanda (27km away) or south toward Otjihaa Pass and Orupembe.

Flooding along the Hoarusib River in 2001 utterly destroyed the track between

Kaoko Otavi and Sanitatas, which was an alternative route between Opuwo and Orupembe. If it does re-open – which is unlikely in the near future – there's a village camp site at Onganga and at Kaoko Otavi there is the ruin of a church built by the Dorsland trekkers who were searching for their 'Beulah land' in the late 1870s. The ruin – little more than a heap of rubble – was declared a national monument in 1951.

Van Zyl's Pass

The beautiful but frightfully steep and challenging Van Zyl's Pass forms a dramatic transition between the Kaokoveld plateaus and the vast, grassy expanses of Marienflüss. This winding 13km stretch isn't suitable for trailers and may only be passed from east to west, which means you'll have to return either via Otjihaa Pass or through Purros (see Purros later).

Otjinjange & Hartmann's Valleys

Allow plenty of time to explore the wild and magical Otjinjange (better known as Marienflüss) and Hartmann's Valleys – broad sandy and grassy expanses descend gently to the Kunene River. Note that camping outside camp sites is prohibited at either valley.

There is one public camp site, as well as several camps run by safari operators.

Okarohombo Camp Site (Otjinungwa, Otjinjange Valley) Camping US$3.50 per person. The only public camp site is at the end of the road at the mouth of Otjinjange (Marienflüss); travellers must be self sufficient. There are only long-drop toilets and firewood is in very short supply.

There are three safari camps that are open only to clients of their respective operators: Desert Adventure Safaris' **Serra Cafema Camp** at the mouth of Hartmann's Valley, named for the striking mountain range across the Kunene River in Angola; Kaokohimba Safaris' **Syncro Camp**, in Marienflüss; and Skeleton Coast Fly-In Safaris' eponymous camp, in Hartmann's Valley. All three companies run upmarket safaris to the region (see Organised Tours in the Getting Around chapter for details).

Purros

Tiny Purros is situated on a broad sandy plain next to the Hoarusib River, 107km west of Sesfontein.

To foster sustainable tourism in the western Kaokoveld, the community maintains the **Ngatutunge Pamwe Camp Site**, 2km northeast of the village. Camping costs US$3 per person and visitors may join guided nature hikes, donkey-cart tours to Himba and Herero villages and wildlife drives to observe desert-adapted wildlife and learn about the natural pharmacopoeia. There are showers and flush toilets.

Along the beautiful 4WD route (under optimum conditions, it's passable to high-clearance 2WD) between Sesfontein and Purros, note the quartz plains, where bits of quartz mysteriously lay evenly distributed over the undulating surface. No-one has yet determined how this is possible.

When the Hoarusib isn't flowing, 4WD vehicles can continue west to Orupembe and either north into Otjinjange (Marienflüss) and Hartmann's Valleys or back over Otjihaa Pass to Okongwati.

The Skeleton Coast

The term Skeleton Coast is derived from the treacherous, fog-blanketed coast, which has long been a graveyard for unwary ships and their crews (see the boxed text 'Skeletons on the Coast'). Early Portuguese sailors called it As Areias do Inferno (the Sands of Hell), as once a ship washed ashore, the fate of the crew was sealed.

The term Skeleton Coast properly refers to the stretch of coastline between the mouths of the Ugab and Kunene Rivers, but is often used to describe Namibia's entire desert coast. For our purposes, it covers the National West Coast Recreation Area and the Skeleton Coast Park (including the Skeleton Coast Wilderness). These protected areas stretch from just north of Swakopmund to the Kunene River, taking in nearly two million hectares of dunes and gravel plains to form one of the world's most inhospitable waterless areas.

Skeletons on the Coast

Despite the many postcard images of rusting ships embedded in the hostile sands of the Skeleton Coast, the most famous shipwrecks have either long disappeared or remain remote and inaccessible to the average visitor. Little more than traces remain of the countless ships that must have been swept ashore on this barren coast during the sailing era. Of the more recent wrecks, few could be more remote than the *Dunedin Star*, which was deliberately run aground just south of the Angolan border after hitting some offshore rocks. The ship was en route from Britain around the Cape of Good Hope to the Middle East war zone, and it was carrying more than 100 passengers, a military crew and cargo.

Fifty of the passengers and crew were ferried ashore through heavy surf in a lifeboat. A wave slammed the *Dunedin Star* onto the beach and stranded the rest of the people on board. When help arrived two days later, getting the castaways off the beach proved an almost impossible task. Some people were hauled back onto the wreck by a line through the surf, and more were taken off the beach in another lifeboat (before it too was damaged by the surf). Meanwhile, one of the rescue ships had also been wrecked and a rescue aircraft, which managed to land on the beach, became bogged down in the sand. Eventually all the passengers were rescued; they were evacuated by an overland truck convoy which took two weeks of hard slog to cross 1000km of desert. Today, the *Dunedin Star* is little more than scattered wreckage.

Further south of the Skeleton Coast – and nearly as difficult to reach – are several more intact wrecks. The *Eduard Bohlen* ran aground south of Walvis Bay in 1909 while carrying equipment to the diamond fields in the far south. The shoreline has since changed so much that she now lies beached in a dune nearly 1km from the shore. On picturesque Spencer Bay, 200km further south and just north of the abandoned mining town of Saddle Hill, lay the dramatic wreck of the *Otavi*. This cargo ship was wrecked in 1945 and is mainly intact on Dolphin's Head (the highest point on the coast between Cape Town's Table Mountain and the Angolan border), although the bow has broken off. In 1972, Spencer Bay also claimed the Korean ship *Tong Taw*.

NATIONAL WEST COAST RECREATION AREA

The National West Coast Recreation Area, a 200km-long and 25km-wide strip from Swakopmund to the Ugab River, makes up the southern end of the Skeleton Coast. No permits are required and the C34 salt road from Swakopmund is passable with a 2WD.

It's extremely popular with sea anglers, who flock here from around Southern Africa to tackle such saltwater species as galjoens, steenbras, kabeljous and blacktails. Between Swakopmund and the Ugab River there are hundreds of concrete buildings, spaced at intervals of about 200m. These aren't coastal bunkers guarding against offshore attack, but merely toilet blocks for coastal anglers and campers.

On the roadsides, you may spot clusters of broad-leafed plants, which seems incongruous in such a desert. Chances are they're wild tobacco, which is native to the Americas. No-one knows how they arrived on this desolate coast, but it's speculated that the seeds were transported along with hay for the horses during the German–Khoi-Khoi wars. Botanists are currently removing the wild tobacco to learn what effect it has had on indigenous species.

For road access see Getting There & Away under Skeleton Coast Park later in this section.

Ugab River Camp Site

This lovely camp site, administered by the Save the Rhino Trust, lies just outside the Skeleton Coast Park. To get there, turn east onto the gravel road 67km north of Cape Cross; it's then 76km to this wild camp. This remote landscape is truly enigmatic and those who've visited have only glowing comments. It's the best place in Namibia to see the elusive black rhino, and you'll also find a range of hiking and exploring options.

Camp sites are US$3 per person; wildlife drives are US$14/11/8/7 per person with two/three/four/five people, and walking tours cost US$3 per person per hour. Carry all supplies for the length of your stay.

A Tern for the Worse

Around 90% of the world population of the tiny Damara tern (Sterna balaenarum), of which just 2000 breeding pairs remain, breed along the open shores and sandy bays of the Namib coast from South Africa to Angola. Adult Damara terns, which have a grey back and wings, a black head and white breast, measure just 22cm long and closely resemble swallows than they do other tern species, and are also considerably more agile. In their natural environment they feed offshore in small groups on shrimp and larval fishes.

Damara terns nest on gravelly flats well away from other more prominently marked birds lest they attract the attention of jackals, hyenas and other predators. They usually hatch only a single chick each year. However, because of their small size terns cannot carry food to predator-free islands to feed their chicks. Instead, they must remain near their food source.

When alarmed they try to divert the threat by flying off screaming; the nest and egg or chick are usually sufficiently well camouflaged to escape detection. However, if the breeding place is in any way disturbed, the parent tern abandons the nest and sacrifices the egg or chick to the elements. The following year, it seeks out a new nesting site, but more often than not, it discovers that potential alternatives are already overpopulated by other species, which it instinctively spurns.

Over the past few seasons, this has been a problem along the Namib coast, due mainly to the proliferation of off-road driving along the shoreline between Swakopmund and Terrace Bay. Over the past decade, the terns have failed to breed successfully and if the current situation continues, they may well be extinct within just a few years.

Henties Bay
☎ 064

At Henties Bay, 80km north of Swakopmund, the relatively reliable Omaruru River issues into the Atlantic (don't miss the novel golf course in the riverbed!). It was named for Hentie van der Merwe, who visited its spring in 1929. Because the river mouth creates a rich feeding ground for offshore fish, the village is a fishing resort that caters mainly to anglers from around Southern Africa. It consists mainly of holiday homes and refuelling and provisioning businesses for anglers headed up the coast.

Information A map of the best fishing spots is provided in the publication *Henties Bay – Beauty Beyond Description*, at the tourist office in Swakopmund.

The Bank of Windhoek is open Monday to Saturday and photo processing is available at the 3R Bookshop. Emergency services here include the police (☎ 500201) and ambulance (☎ 500020).

Organised Tours If you want to join the throngs and go ski-boat or surf angling, try *Avocet Fishing Tours* (☎/fax 500164, e avocet@iafrica.com.na, PO Box 480), which charges from US$59 per day, with tackle hire.

Places to Stay & Eat Henties Bay offers a modest selection of accommodation and eating options.

De Duine (☎ 500001, fax 500724, e afri deca@mweb.com.na, PO Box 1). Singles/doubles B&B with bathroom US$40/58. This very ordinary place is nevertheless the main accommodation option in Henties Bay. Despite the fact that it sits on the coast, not one room has a sea view – go figure that! Lunch and dinner are available for US$9 each. The front desk can organise fishing trips, scenic flights and tours to the Brandberg and Spitzkoppe.

Eagle Holiday Flats (☎ 500032, fax 500 299, e eaglesc@mweb.com.na, 175 Jakkasputz Rd, PO Box 20) 4-bed self-catering flats US$10 per person. This is the heart of Henties Bay action; attached is a bar, bakery, shop, bottle store and petrol station, as well as the Eagle Steak Ranch steakhouse, which rustles up beef-oriented meals.

Pirate's Cove Sports Bar & Pizza Bay (Jakkalsputz Rd) Pizzas US$4-7, mains US$6-7. This cubbyhole of a place, in the shopping centre on the main road through town, is an excellent choice. You can choose between pizza, calzone, meat and fish dishes, and a wonderful seafood platter. In the background, nonstop sports events play on TV.

Spitzkoppe Restaurant & Beer Garden (☎ 500394, Duine Rd) Mains US$3-6. This fine restaurant features Namibia's longest bar and some of its most bizarre pool tables (they're a must-see). It specialises in seafood (what else?) and the disco and slot machines will keep anyone busy until the wee hours.

Getting There & Away Henties Bay lies at the junction of the coastal salt road and the C35, which turns inland towards Damaraland. The Star Line bus between Otjiwarongo (US$11, nine hours) and Walvis Bay (US$2.50, 2½ hours) passes through Henties Bay at 5pm Thursday westbound and at 3.30pm Friday eastbound.

Cape Cross Seal Reserve

Cape Cross *(admission US$3 per person plus US$3 per vehicle; open 10am-5pm daily)* is known mainly as a breeding reserve for thousands of Cape fur seals (see the boxed text 'Cape Fur Seals' on the following page). In 1485, Portuguese explorer Diego Cão, the first European to set foot in Namibia, planted a 2m-high, 360kg *padrão* (a tribute to Portuguese king João II) at Cape Cross in honour of King John I of Portugal. In 1893, however, a German sailor, Captain Becker of the boat *Falke*, removed the cross and hauled it off to Germany. In 1894, Kaiser Wilhelm II ordered that a replica be made with the original inscriptions in Latin and Portuguese, as well as a commemorative inscription in German. There's also a second cross, made of dolerite, which was erected in 1980 on the site of Cão's original cross.

A pattern of concrete circles contains information on the area's history. It's laid out in the shape of the Southern Cross, the constellation that guided Diego Cão's original expedition.

A basic snack bar and toilets are available beside the seal slaughterhouse. No pets or motorcycles are permitted and visitors may not cross the barrier between the viewing area and the rocks where the colony lounges.

Places to Stay & Eat Along the salt road in the National West Coast Recreation Area are several bleak beach camp sites used mainly by sea anglers: *Myl 4 Caravan Park* (see under Swakopmund in the Central Namib Desert chapter), *Mile 14, Jakkalsputz, Mile 72* and *Mile 108*. Basic camp sites at Mile 14 or Jakkalsputz cost US$13 for two people plus US$2 for each additional person, including showers and drinking water, while Mile 72 and Mile 108 cost US$12 for two people plus US$2 for each additional person, without water. Mile 72 and Mile 108 each has a petrol station that is open until 6pm, and during Namibian school holidays they have kiosks selling snacks. At other times, you can buy fish from anglers along the beach, but it's wise to be self-sufficient.

SKELETON COAST PARK

At Ugabmund, 110km along the salt road north of Cape Cross, the salt road enters the Skeleton Coast Park; UK journalist Nigel Tisdall wrote of the gate in the *Daily Telegraph* 'If hell has a coat of arms, it probably looks like the entrance to Namibia's Skeleton Coast Park', and you're sure to agree with that assessment.

The zone south of the Hoanib River is open to individual travellers, but you need a permit, which costs US$3 per person and US$3 per vehicle. Accommodation is available only at Terrace Bay and Torra Bay (the latter is open only in December and January). To stay in either camp, you must pass the Ugabmund entrance before 3pm and/or Springbokwater before 5pm.

No day visits are allowed, but you can obtain a transit permit to pass between Ugabmund and Springbokwater for US$3

Cape Fur Seals

Cape Cross has the best-known breeding colony of Cape fur seals (Arctocephalus pusillus) along the Namib coast. This appealing species isn't a true seal at all, but an eared seal, which is actually a species of sea lion. Fur seals have a thick layer of short fur beneath the coarser guard hairs, which remain dry and trap air for insulation. This enables the animals to maintain an internal body temperature of 37°C and spend long periods in cold waters. At Cape Cross, a large colony of these seals takes advantage of the rich concentrations of fish in the cold Benguela Current.

Male Cape fur seals average less than 200kg, but during the breeding season they take on a particularly thick accumulation of blubber and balloon out to 360kg or sometimes more. Females are smaller, averaging 75kg, and give birth to a single, blue-eyed pup during late November or early December. About 90% of the colony's pups are born within just over a month.

Pups begin to suckle less than an hour after birth, but are soon left in communal nurseries while their mothers leave to forage for food. When the mothers return to the colony, they identify their own pup by a combination of scent and call.

The pups moult at the age of four to five months, turning from a dark grey to olive brown. Mortality rates in the colony are high, and up to a quarter of the pups fail to survive their first year, with the bulk of deaths occurring during the first week after birth. The main predators are the brown hyena (Hyaena brunnea) and black-backed jackal (Canis mesomelas), which account for 25% of pup deaths. Those that do survive may remain with their mothers for up to a year.

Cape fur seals eat about 8% of their body weight each day and the colonies along the western coast of Southern Africa annually consume more than a million tonnes of fish and other marine life (mainly shoaling fish such as pilchards, and cephalopods such as squid and octopuses). That's about 300,000 tonnes more than is taken by the fishing industries of Namibia and South Africa put together. Naturally, this has been a source of conflict between seals, anglers and commercial fishing enterprises.

The inevitable knee-jerk reaction to this has been artificial reduction of the seal population. Historically, the seal slaughter was a free-for-all, but in recent years, management programs have prevented the colony from growing. However, because marine predators other than seals also compete with humans for the same fish, a reduction in the seal population causes a proliferation of these predators and the number of fish available to the fishing industry still remains the same.

Still, the culling continues and every morning during the season – 1 April to 15 November – men take to the beach with butcher's knives to kill nearly 200 seals. Currently, the program is run by a private company, Sea Lion Products, which operates a slaughterhouse beside the snack bar. Here, the seals' genitals are removed for export to Asian markets (this lucrative market for aphrodisiacs is the major reason for the culls), the pelts are turned into high-quality skins for the European market, the meat goes to Taiwan and the rest is ground into a sort of protein sludge to be used as cattle feed. Sea Lion Products is understandably quite sensitive about its position here and although you're welcome to have a look around (if your stomach can take it), photography is forbidden.

per person and US$3 per vehicle. These are available through Namibia Wildlife Resorts (NWR) in Windhoek or Swakopmund, but can also be purchased at the gates. To transit the park you must pass the entry gate before 1pm and exit through the other before 3pm the same day. Transit permits aren't valid for Torra Bay or Terrace Bay, but in December and January, transit travellers may refuel in Torra Bay.

Ugab River Hiking Route

The 50km-long Ugab River guided hiking route is open to groups of between six and eight people on the second and fourth Tuesday of each month from April to October. Hikes start at 9am from Ugabmund and finish on Thursday afternoons. Most hikers stay Monday night at Mile 108 (40km south of Ugabmund), which allows you to arrive at Ugabmund in time for the hike. The hike costs US$27 per person and must be booked through NWR in Windhoek; hikers must provide and carry their own food and camping equipment. The route begins by crossing the coastal plain, then climbs into the hills and follows a double loop through lichen fields and past caves, natural springs and unusual geological formations. Watch for lions, hyenas, and gemsboks and other antelopes.

Torra Bay

Torra Bay is open only during December and January, to coincide with Namibian school holidays. In the backdrop rises a textbook field of barchan dunes, the southernmost extension of the incredible dunefield, which stretches all the way to the Curoca River in Angola.

There are *camp sites* costing US$13 for two people and US$2 for each additional person up to eight people. Petrol, water, firewood and basic supplies are available only when the camp is open. Campers may use the restaurant at Terrace Bay.

Terrace Bay

Terrace Bay, 49km north of Torra Bay, is more luxurious than its counterpart and is open year-round. As with all the Skeleton Coast sites, it caters mainly to surf anglers, but others will find interest in the sparse coastal vegetation and the line of lonely dunes to the north. Around the camp, you may spot black-backed jackals or brown hyenas.

At the *camp site*, single/double bungalows cost US$59/82 and the eight-bed self-catering luxury suite costs US$267 for up to eight people. All accommodation includes hot showers, half board and – of course – freezer space for the day's catch. The site has a restaurant, shop and petrol station.

Getting There & Away

The National West Coast Recreation Area and the southern half of the Skeleton Coast Park are accessed via the salt road from Swakopmund, which ends 70km north of Terrace Bay. Distances are measured in miles from Swakopmund. The park is also accessible via the C39 gravel road which runs between Khorixas and Torra Bay. Note that motorcycles are not permitted in the Skeleton Coast Park. Hitchhikers may be discouraged by the bleak landscape, cold sea winds, fog, sandstorms and sparse traffic.

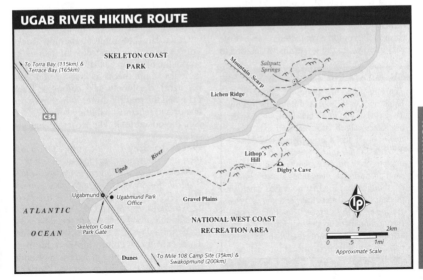

UGAB RIVER HIKING ROUTE

NORTH-WESTERN NAMIBIA

Skeleton Coast Wilderness

The Skeleton Coast Wilderness, between the Hoanib and Kunene Rivers, makes up the northern two-thirds of the Skeleton Coast Park. Here, seemingly endless stretches of foggy beach are punctuated by rusting shipwrecks and flanked by wandering dunes. Dolphins jump offshore and the beach rings with the cries of kelp gulls and gannets. It is amazing that this desolate landscape can support life, but 64 bird species have been counted, one-quarter of which are migratory waders from the northern hemisphere, including sandpipers, turnstones and plovers.

A single park ranger lives at Möwe Bay and radios daily weather reports to Swakopmund. This lonesome soul also maintains a small museum of shipwreck detritus and newspaper clippings recounting the stories of Skeleton Coast shipwreck survivors, which may be visited only by groups from the Skeleton Coast Wilderness Camp.

History In the early 1960s, Windhoek lawyer Louw Schoemann began bringing business clients to this region and became involved in a consortium to construct a harbour at Möwe Bay, at the southern end of the present-day Skeleton Coast Wilderness. However, in 1969 the South African government dropped the project, and in 1971 declared the region a protected reserve. Five years later, when the government decided to permit limited tourism, the concession was put up for bid and Schoemann's was the only tender. For the next 18 years, his company, Skeleton Coast Fly-In Safaris, led small group tours and practised ecotourism long before it became a buzzword. Sadly, Louw Schoemann passed away after losing the concession in 1993, but the family carried on with the business and continue to offer tours through the main Skeleton Coast Park, the Kunene region and areas further inland.

Currently, the concession is held by Wilderness Safaris Namibia, which continues to conserve this wonderful wilderness while still managing to provide unforgettable experiences.

Things to See & Do The wonders of this region defy description. Wilderness Safaris camp is situated a short distance from the lovely green oasis around **Sarusas Springs**, which is a perennial water source and has historically been a commercial source of amethyst-bearing geodes (cavities).

The **Clay Castles**, a series of fragile mud deposits along a tributary of the Hoarusib, were laid down in the dim and distant past, when the entire area lay beneath a vast lake. When the Hoarusib is flowing, it's bordered by off-putting deposits of quicksand.

Other sites of interest include **Rocky Point** and its excellent coastal fishing (a stay at the Skeleton Coast Wilderness Camp includes an afternoon fishing for your dinner here), the lonely **seal colony** at Cabo Frio, and the **roaring dunes**, which produce one of nature's most haunting sound effects (see the boxed text 'The Roaring Dunes').

Places to Stay If it's comfort you want, then the following place has the lot.

Skeleton Coast Wilderness Camp (☎ 061-274500, fax 239455, ⓔ info@nts.com.na, ⓦ www.wilderness-safaris.com, 8 Bismarck St, Windhoek, PO Box 6850, Windhoek) Singles/doubles for 4 days & 3 nights US$2304/4008, for 5 days & 4 nights US$2612/4424. This extremely comfortable Wilderness Safaris camp occupies a lovely spot amid the dunes, not far from Sarusas Springs.

The Roaring Dunes

The lonely barchan dunes of the northern Skeleton Coast hold a unique distinction: They roar. If you don't believe it, sit down on a lee face, dig in your feet and slide slowly down. If you feel a jarring vibration and hear a roar akin to a four-engine cargo plane flying low, don't bother looking up – it's just the sand producing its marvellous acoustic effect. It's thought that the roar is created when air pockets between electrically charged particles are forced to the surface. The effect is especially pronounced in the warmth of the late afternoon, when spaces between the sand particles are at their greatest.

Activities include viewing desert elephants along the Hoarusib, ocean fishing, dune climbing, hiking through the Clay Castles and appreciating the sparse local vegetation. There are only two weekly departures from Windhoek, so your entire stay will be with same group of people. Rates include accommodation, air transfers from Windhoek, meals, drinks and two activities per day.

Getting There & Away The Skeleton Coast Wilderness is closed to individual travellers and private vehicles may not enter the park. Access is limited to fly-in trips operated by Wilderness Safaris Namibia (see Places to Stay previous). The flights in and out travel one way over the Kaokoveld highlands and the other way along the Skeleton Coast (which is magnificent – plan on munching through at least two rolls of film).

Central Namib Desert

Unlike the lush Kalahari, the Namib Desert (often just known as the Namib) creates an impression of utter barrenness. Stretching more than 2000km along the coast from the mouth of South Africa's Oliphants River to San Nicolau in southern Angola, it defines the lonely coastline of south-western Africa. The Nama word 'Namib', which inspired the name of the entire country, rather prosaically means 'Vast Dry Plain'; but nowhere else on earth do such desolate landscapes reflect so many moods and characters. Around every bend is another grand vista and few visitors ever tire of the surprises.

The region's few watercourses slice through the gravel and sands, but only in years of good rain do they ever reach the sea. Inland, some flow regularly, but others contain water only during exceptionally rainy periods. Locally, though, these watercourses conduct sufficient subsurface moisture to sustain some greenery along their beds.

Much of the surface between Walvis Bay and Lüderitz is covered by enormous linear dunes, which roll back from the sea towards the inland gravel plains. In the north, the dunes stop at the Swakop River, where they give way to flat, arid gravel plains interrupted by isolated ranges and inselbergs.

Much of the Namib harbours ancient archaeological sites, providing evidence and artefacts of the hunting-and-gathering people who have lived here for around 750,000 years. The coastline is dotted with shell and fishbone middens from the people locals call *strandlopers* (beach walkers), who were probably early Khoi-Khoi or San people.

The Northern Reaches

KHOMAS HOCHLAND
☎ 062

From Windhoek, three mountain routes – the Bosua, Us and Gamsberg Passes – lead

Highlights

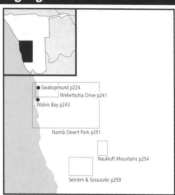

- See some of Africa's largest flocks of flamingoes in Walvis Bay lagoon.

- Spend a day sandboarding down the dunes at Swakopmund.

- Explore Namibia's German heritage in the architecture and sweet treats of Swakopmund.

- Hike the Waterkloof and Olive Trails – or take a longer hike – in the stunning Naukluft Mountains.

- Climb the dunes and watch the sunrise at the amazing oasis of Sossusvlei.

westwards through the Khomas Hochland, which forms a scenic transition zone between the high central plateau and the gravelly Namib Desert plains. All three are quite steep in places and are best travelled from east to west. Allow six to seven hours to drive any of them, and note that there's no petrol or services.

Bosua Pass Route

The northernmost of the three routes is Bosua Pass, which provides the shortest (but not the quickest) route between Windhoek

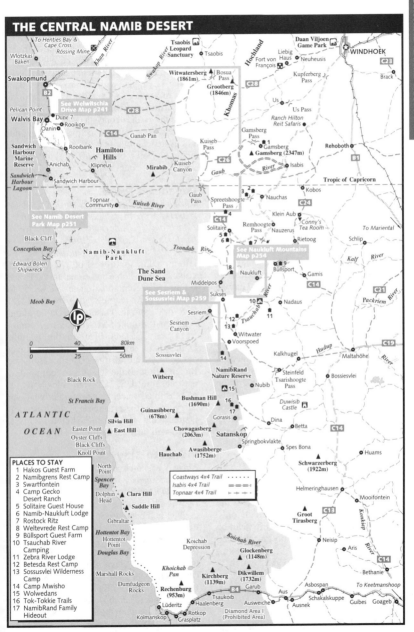

THE CENTRAL NAMIB DESERT

To Henties Bay & Cape Cross
Rössing Mine
Wlotzkas Baken
Swakopmund
B2
See Welwitschia Drive Map p241
C28
Pelican Point
Walvis Bay
Oanin
Rooikop
Dune 7
C14
Ganab Pan
Sandwich Harbour Marine Reserve
Rooibank
Hamilton Hills
Anichab
Klipneus
Sandwich Harbour
Sandwich Harbour Lagoon
Topnaar Community
See Namib Desert Park Map p251
Black Cliff
Conception Bay
Namib-Naukluft Park
Edward Bolen Shipwreck
Meob Bay
See Sesusvlei & Sossusvlei Map p259
Black Rock
ATLANTIC
OCEAN
St Francis Bay
Easter Point
East Hill
Silvia Hill
Black Cliffs
Knoll Point
North Point
Spencer Bay
Dolphin Head
Clara Hill
Saddle Hill
Gibraltar
Hottentot Bay
Hottentot Point
Douglas Bay
Marshall Rocks
Dumfudgeon Rocks
Khoichab Pan
Kirchberg (1139m)
Rechenburg (953m)
Lüderitz
Kolmanskop
Rotkop
Grasplatz

Khan River
Swakop River
Tsaobis Leopard Sanctuary
Tsaobis
Witwatersberg (1861m)
Bosua Pass
Grootberg (1846m)
C28
Khomas
Kuiseb Pass
C26
Mirabib
Kuiseb Canyon
Gaub
Kuiseb River
Gaub Pass
Spreetshoogte Pass
Nauchas
C14
Solitaire
Remhoogte Pass
Nauzerus
Rietoog
Klein Aub
Conny's Tea Room
Tsondab River
See Naukluft Mountains Map p254
The Sand Dune Sea
Middelpos
Naukluft
Büllsport
Gamis
C14
Sukses
Nadaus
Sesriem
Sesriem Canyon
Witwater
Voorspoed
Sossusvlei
NamibRand Nature Reserve
Nubib
Kalkhugel
Steinfeld
Tsarishoogte Pass
Bossiesvlei
Maltahöhe
Witberg
Bushman Hill (1690m)
Duwisib Castle
Guinasibberg (678m)
Gorasis
Dina
Betta
C14
Chowagasberg (2063m)
Satanskop
Springbokvlakte
Spes Bona
Huams
Awasibberg (1752m)
Hauchab
Schwarzerberg (1922m)
Groot Tirasberg
Helmeringhausen
Mooifontein
C13
Neisip
Aris
C14
Bethanie
Glockenberg (1148m)
Koichab River
Koichab Depression
Dikwillem (1732m)
Garub
Aus
Asbospan
Schakalskuppe
Guibes
Goageb
To Keetmanshoop
Tsaukoib
Haalenberg
Ausweiche
Ausnek
Diamond Area I (Prohibited Area)

Hochland
Liebig
Fort von François
Daan Viljoen Game Park
Neuheusis
WINDHOEK
C23
Kupferberg Pass
Brack
Us
Us Pass
Ranch Hilton Reit Safaris
Gamsberg Pass
Gamsberg
Gamsberg (2347m)
Isabis
Rehoboth
B1
Tropic of Capricorn
Kobos
C24
Schlip
To Mariental
Kalf River
Rietoog
Hudup
C19
Hudup River
Packriem River
C21
River

0 40 80km
0 25 50mi

Coastways 4x4 Trail ·········
Isabis 4x4 Trail = = =
Topnaar 4x4 Trail —+—+—

PLACES TO STAY
1 Hakos Guest Farm
2 Namibgrens Rest Camp
3 Swartfontein
4 Camp Gecko Desert Ranch
5 Solitaire Guest House
6 Namib-Naukluft Lodge
7 Rostock Ritz
8 Weltevrede Rest Camp
9 Büllsport Guest Farm
10 Tsauchab River Camping
11 Zebra River Lodge
12 Betesda Rest Camp
13 Sossusvlei Wilderness Camp
14 Camp Mwisho
15 Wolwedans
16 Tok-Tokkie Trails
17 NamibRand Family Hideout

and Swakopmund. It's one of Namibia's steepest routes, reaching a gradient of 1:5 or 20% slope as it descends onto the Namib plains; note that it isn't suitable for trailers. From Windhoek, take the C28 west past Daan Viljoen Game Park.

In the 17th and 18th centuries, indigenous people maintained small-scale smelting operations in the copper-producing area around the **Matchless Mine**, west of Daan Viljoen Game Park. In 1856, European colonists established the Walfisch Bay Mining Company but production lasted only until 1860, and except for a brief active period in 1902, it didn't open again until the 1960s. It was then run by the Tsumeb Corporation until it closed in 1983.

Along the road westwards, about 40km from Windhoek, it's worth stopping near Neuheusis to see the derelict two-storey mansion known as **Liebig Haus**, which was built in 1908 as the home and headquarters for the farm manager of an Anglo-German farming consortium. When it was occupied, this colonial dwelling was the picture of opulence, and even sported a lavish fountain in the salon. It's now dilapidated but may eventually be reincarnated as a hotel.

Near Karanab, 15km west of Neuheusis, are the ruins of **Fort von François** and its stables. It was named after Major Curt von François, who established a series of military posts to guard the road from Windhoek to Swakopmund. This one had an ignominious end as a drying-out station for German military alcoholics.

Us Pass Route

On the scenic Us Pass route, the D1982 follows the shortest distance between Windhoek and Walvis Bay. It isn't as steep as the Bosua Pass, reaching a gradient of only 1:10 or 10%, but the road condition can be poor, especially after rain. Follow the C26 south-west from Windhoek; after 38km, turn north-west on the D1982, which is signposted 'Walvis Bay via Us Pass'.

Gamsberg Pass Route

The gravel C36 from Windhoek to Walvis Bay drops off the edge of the Central Plateau at the Gamsberg Pass, which reaches an altitude of 2334m at the top of the Gamsberg Range. The name is a Khoisan and German construction meaning 'Obscured Range', after the flat-topped, 2347m Gamsberg Peak, which is capped with an erosion-resistant layer of sandstone. On clear days, it affords wonderful views across the Namib, but more often, the vista is concealed by dust.

The western side of the pass is steep, but not as treacherous as some would have you believe. Don't be put off or you'll miss some lovely countryside.

Organised Tours

Ranch Hilton Reit Safaris (☎ 061-217940, ☎ 081-127 0248, fax 256300, e info@reit safaris.com, reitsafari@iway.na, w www.re itsafari.com, Ranch Hilton, Gamsberg Pass, PO Box 20706, Windhoek) Ranch Hilton, 65km south-west of Windhoek, revolves around horse and camel tours. Horse riding and accommodation costs US$150 to US$225; with camels, they're US$275. Five-day Namib Desert or Damaraland rides cost from US$1575, six-day camel treks are US$1600/1750 in the Namib/Damaraland, and die-hard equestrians can opt for a beautiful nine-day ride from the Ranch Hilton to the sea at Swakopmund. It isn't cheap at US$2525, but rides book up months in advance. One group per year can carry on with a nine-day ride through Damaraland and up the Skeleton Coast, which will cost an additional US$3300.

Places to Stay

Farm Niedersachsen (☎ 572200, fax 572201, e niedersachsen@natron.net, w www.nat ron.net/tour/nieder/sachsend.ht, Us Pass, D1982, PO Box 3636, Windhoek) Singles/doubles half board US$54/91. This farm is on the Us Pass route (the D1982), 72km east of its junction with the C14. Although it's registered as a hunting farm, it also welcomes non-hunting guests. Have a look at one of the desert hideouts used by Henno Martin and Hermann Korn during WWII (see Kuiseb Canyon under Namib Desert Park later in this chapter for more on these two). It also organises desert 4WD excursions.

Kobo Kobo Hills Lodge (☎/fax 064-204711, PO Box 1616, Walvis Bay) Thatched cottages from US$120 per person with meals and activities. This lodge on Gert and Caroline Behrens' 8000-hectare ranch lies 8km east of the D1985, north of the Us Pass route (the D1982). The name means 'Black Eagle', and the farm has its own breeding pair of these birds, as well as lots of other feathered wildlife. The beautiful red granite peaks offer excellent hiking.

Hakos Guest Farm (☎ 572111, fax 256300, ⓔ hakos@mweb.com.na, ⓦ www .natron.net/tour/hakos, Gamsberg Pass, PO Box 5056, Windhoek) Camping US$5.50, singles/doubles B&B US$49/75. This scenic farm near the Gamsberg offers a range of activities, including a 4WD route (US$8 per day), wild hiking and a star-gazers' observatory (US$28 overnight). It also organises tours to the rugged Gamsberg (US$118 for up to six people).

SWAKOPMUND
☎ 064

With palm-lined streets, seaside promenades and fine hotels for all budgets, Swakopmund is Namibia's most popular holiday destination, and its pleasant summer climate and decent beaches attract surfers, anglers and beach lovers from all over Southern Africa.

For better or worse, Swakopmund feels overwhelmingly Teutonic – indeed, it has been described as more German than Germany. Lots of German-Namibians own holiday homes here, and the town draws throngs of overseas German-speaking tourists, who feel right at home with the town's pervasive *Gemütlichkeit*, a distinctively German appreciation of comfort and hospitality. With its many flower gardens, half-timbered houses and colonial-era structures, it seems that only the wind-blown sand and the palm trees distinguish Swakopmund from holiday towns along Germany's North Sea and Baltic coasts!

Swakopmund gets busy around the Namibian school holidays in December and January. Thanks to the mild temperatures and negligible rainfall, it enjoys a statistically superb climate (25°C in the summer and 15°C in the winter), but there's a bit of grit in the oyster. When an easterly wind blows, the town gets a good sandblasting, and the cold winter sea fogs often create an incessant drizzle and an unimaginably dreary atmosphere. However, this fog rolls up to 50km inland and provides life-sustaining moisture for desert plants, animals and 80 species of lichen.

History
Small bands of Nama people have occupied the Swakop River mouth from time immemorial, but the first permanent settlers were Germans who didn't arrive until early 1892. Because nearby Walvis Bay had been annexed by the British-controlled Cape Colony in 1878, Swakopmund remained German South-West Africa's only harbour, and as a result, it rose to greater prominence than its poor harbour conditions would have otherwise warranted. Early passengers were landed in small dories, but after the pier was constructed, they were winched over from the ships in basket-like cages (an example of these unusual contraptions is displayed in the Swakopmund Museum).

Construction began on the first building, the Alte Kaserne (Old Barracks), in September 1892. By the following year it housed 120 Schutztruppe soldiers and ordinary settlers arrived to put down roots. The first civilian homes were prefabricated in Germany and transported by ship and by 1909 Swakopmund had become a municipality.

The port eventually became the leading trade funnel for all of German South-West

Africa, and attracted government agencies and transport companies. During WWI, however, when South-West Africa was taken over by South Africa, the harbour was allowed to silt up (nearby Walvis Bay had a much better harbour) and Swakopmund transformed into a holiday resort. As a result, it's now generally more pleasant on the eye than the industrial-looking Walvis Bay.

Despite its climatic quirks, Swakopmund thrives from tourism. Another notable source of employment is the massive Rössing Corporation mine, which is east of town. It includes the world's largest opencast uranium mine.

Orientation

Since the publication of this book, Kaiser Wilhelm St has been renamed Sam Nujoma St. All references to Kaiser Wilhelm St should read Sam Nujoma St.

Information

Tourist Offices The Namib i Information Centre (☎/fax 404827, [e] swainfo@iafrica .com.na), Kaiser Wilhelm St, PO Box 829, is open 8am to 1pm and 2pm to 5pm Monday to Friday, and 9am to noon Saturday.

Also useful is the friendly Namibian Wildlife Resorts office (NWR; ☎ 204172, fax 402697), Woermannhaus, which is open 8am to 5pm; national park bookings and permits are available from 8am to 3.30pm Monday to Friday. This office books permits and camp sites for Namib-Naukluft Park. After hours and on weekends, pick up Namib-Naukluft entry permits from Hans Kriess Garage, at the corner of Kaiser Wilhelm and Breite Sts.

Money Swakopmund has branches of all major banks, which are open 9am to 3.30pm Monday to Friday and 8am to 11am Saturday. The Commercial Bank, upstairs from the Swakopmunder Buchhandlung on Kaiser Wilhelm St, is open for foreign-currency and travellers-cheque exchange from 7am to 5pm seven days a week.

Post & Communications The GPO, on Garnison St, has a public telephone for international calls and a fax office (☎ 402720).

For fax services, Photographic Enterprises (☎ 405872, fax 405874), Commercial Bank Arcade, 55 Kaiser Wilhelm St, charges US$0.50 per page, plus phone charges.

Email and Internet access is available through the Swakopmund Internet Café & Coffee Shop (☎ 464021), at the corner of Moltke and Kaiser Wilhelm Sts. It's open 7am to 10pm Monday to Saturday and 10am to 10pm Sunday. You'll also find email and Internet access at the Swakopmund Adventure Centre & I-café (see under Activities later); CompuCare & I-Café (☎ 463 775), at 12 Roon St; the Talk Shop Internet Cafe, Roon St; as well as The Alternative Space and Desert Sky Backpackers (see these last two under Places to Stay – Budget, later in this chapter).

Bookshops & Libraries CNA Bookshop on Roon St sells popular paperbacks and tourist publications.

For more serious German and English literature and novels, see the Swakopmunder Büchhandlung on Kaiser Wilhelm St.

Die Muschel Book & Artshop (☎/fax 402872), 10 Roon St, sells esoteric art and local history books.

Peter's Antiques, on Brücken St, has a room full of used books in English, German and Afrikaans for under US$1 per volume.

Researchers of Namibian and African topics can hole up in the Sam Cohen Library (☎ 402695), Kaiser Wilhelm St, open 9am to 1pm and 3pm to 5pm Monday to Friday, 10am to 12.30pm Saturday. It houses the town archives, the contents of which include newspapers dating from 1898, as well as 2000 titles on African topics.

Laundry The Laundryman (☎ 081-240 0423), Shop 5, 80 Brücken St, offers coin-operated laundry service from 8am to 9pm Monday to Friday, 8am to 5pm Saturday and 11.30am to 5pm Sunday.

Photography Photographic Enterprises (☎ 405872, fax 405874), Commercial Bank Arcade, 55 Kaiser Wilhelm St, provides good camera repairs and processing services. Highly lauded throughout Namibia, it's open 8am to 5.30pm Monday to Friday and 8am to 1pm Saturday.

Emergency For international-standard medical care try the Cottage Private Hospital in Tamariskia. For doctors' visits, see the recommended Drs Swiegers, Schikerling, Dantu and Biermann, all at Bismarck Medical Centre (☎ 405000). Swakopmund uses the following emergency numbers:

Cottage Private Hospital	☎ 412201, fax 412202
Fire Brigade	☎ 402411, after-hours pager 461503
Hospital/Ambulance	☎ 405731
Police	☎ 10111

Historical Buildings & Structures

Swakopmund brims with numerous historic examples of traditional German architecture. For further information on the town's colonial sites, pick up *Swakopmund – A Chronicle of the Town's People, Places and Progress*, which is sold at the museum and in local bookshops.

The Jetty In 1905 the need for a good cargo- and passenger-landing site led Swakopmund's founders to construct the original wooden pier. Over the years, however, it was battered by the high seas and damaged by woodworm, and in 1911 construction began on a 500m iron jetty. When the South African forces occupied Swakopmund, the port became redundant. The old wooden pier was removed in 1916 and the unfinished iron pier, still less than 300m long, was left to the elements. In 1985 it was closed for safety purposes, but a year later a public appeal raised 250,000 rand to restore the structure. It's now open to the general public, but is again suffering from neglect.

The Mole In 1899, architect FW Ortloff's seawall (better known as the Mole) was intended to enhance Swakopmund's poor harbour and create a mooring place for large cargo vessels. Unfortunately, Mr Ortloff was unfamiliar with the Benguela Current, which sweeps northwards along the coast, carrying with it a load of sand from the southern deserts. Within less than five years, the harbour entrance was choked off by a sand bank and two years later, the harbour itself had been invaded by sand to create what is now called Palm Beach. The Mole is currently used as a mooring for pleasure boats.

Lighthouse The lighthouse, an endearing Swakopmund landmark, was constructed in 1902. It was originally built 11m high, but an additional 10m was added in 1910.

Alte Kaserne German for 'Old Barracks', the Alte Kaserne *(Lazarett St)* is an imposing, fort-like building which was designed and built in 1906 by the railway company. It was used as a school and hostel for many years, and now serves as the HI hostel.

Marine Memorial Often known by its German name, Marine Denkmal, this memorial *(Garnison St)* was commissioned in 1907 by the Marine Infantry in Kiel, Germany, and was designed by Berlin sculptor AM Wolff. It commemorates the German First Marine Expedition Corps, which helped beat back the Herero uprisings of 1904. As a national historical monument, it will continue to stand, but one has to wonder how long it will be before the Herero erect a memorial of their own.

Kaiserliches Bezirksgericht (State House) This imposing building *(Strand St)* was designed by Carl Schmidt in 1901, constructed in 1902 and originally served as the District Magistrates' Court. It was extended in 1905 and again in 1945, when a tower was added. After WWI it was converted into the official holiday home of the territorial administrator. In keeping with that tradition, it's now the official Swakopmund residence of the executive president.

Altes Amtsgericht Designed by Otto Ertl, this gabled building *(Garnison St)* was constructed in 1908 as a private school.

SWAKOPMUND

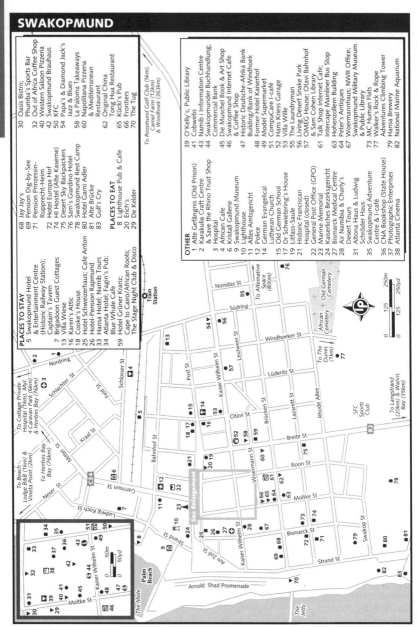

PLACES TO STAY
5 Swakopmund Hotel & Entertainment Centre (Historic Railway Station); Captain's Tavern
7 Brigadoon Guest Cottages
13 Villa Wiese
16 Karen's Attic
18 Cooke's House
25 Hotel Schweizerhaus; Cafe Anton
26 Hotel-Pension Rapmund
33 Hansa Hotel; Namib Tours
34 Atlanta Hotel; Fagin's Pub; Blue Whale Cafe
59 Hotel Grüner Kranz; Cape to Cairo/African Roots; The Stage Night Club & Disco

68 Jay Jay's
69 Pension Dig-by-See
71 Pension Prinzessin-Rupprecht-Heim
72 Hotel Europa Hof
74 HI Hostel (Alte Kaserne)
75 Desert Sky Backpackers
76 Sam's Giardino Hotel
78 Swakopmund Rest Camp
80 Hotel Garni Adler
81 Alte Brücke
83 Gull's Cry

PLACES TO EAT
8 Lighthouse Pub & Cafe
20 Erich's
29 De Kelder

30 Oasis Bistro; Phumba's Sports Bar
32 Out of Africa Coffee Shop
40 Western Saloon Pizzeria
42 Swakopmund Brauhaus
45 KFC
54 Papa's & Diamond Jack's Jazz & Blues
58 La Paloma Takeaways
60 Napolitana Pizzeria & Mediterranean Restaurant
62 Original China Tong Hua Restaurant
65 Kücki's Pub
66 Frontiers
70 The Tug

OTHER
1 Alte Gefängnis (Old Prison)
2 Karakulia Craft Centre
3 Hospital
4 African Cafe
6 Kristall Gallerie
9 Swakopmund Museum
10 Lighthouse
11 Altes Amtsgericht
12 Police
14 German Evangelical Lutheran Church
15 Old German School
17 Dr Schwietering's House
19 Litfass-Saule
21 Historic Franciscan Hospital (closed)
22 General Post Office (GPO)
23 Marine Memorial
24 Kaiserliches Bezirksgericht
27 Bismarck Medical Centre
28 Air Namibia & Charly's Desert Tours
31 Altona Haus & Ludwig Schröder Haus
35 Swakopmund Adventure Centre & I-cafe
36 CNA Bookshop (State House)
37 Photographic Enterprises
38 Atlanta Cinema

39 O'Kelly's; Public Library
41 Cobwebs
43 Namib i Information Centre
44 Swakopmunder Buchhandlung; Commercial Bank
45 Die Muschel Book & Art Shop
46 Swakopmund Internet Cafe & Coffee Shop
47 Historic Deutsche-Afrika Bank Building/Bank of Windhoek
48 Former Hotel Kaiserhof
49 Model Supermarket
51 CompuCare I-café
52 Hans Kriess Garage
53 Villa Wille
55 The Laundryman
56 Living Desert Snake Park
57 OMEG House; Otavi Bahnhof & Sam Cohen Library
61 Talk Shop Internet Cafe; Intercape Mainliner Bus Stop
63 Hohenzollern Building
64 Peter's Antiques
67 Woermannhaus; NWR Office; Swakopmund Military Museum & Public Library
73 MC Human Flats
77 Walker's Rock & Rope Adventures Climbing Tower
79 Hansa Brewery
82 National Marine Aquarium

To Rosmund Golf Club (5km), Camel Farm (12km) & Windhoek (363km)

Nonidas St
To Alternative Space (80km)
Südring
African Cemetery · Old German Cemetery
Windhoeker St
To The Dunes (1km)
Lüderitz St
Breite St
To Langstrand (20km) & Walvis Bay (35km)
Roon St
Moltke St
Bismarck St
Strand St

Train Station
Nordring
Schlosser St
Feld St
Kraal St
Leutwein St
Post St
Kaiser Wilhelm St
Otavi St
Brücken St
Lazarett St
Rhode Allee
Woermann St
SFC Sports Club

To Cottage Private Hospital (1km), Myl 4 Caravan Park (76km) & Henties Bay (76km)
To Beach & B&B (1km) & Vineta Point (2km)
To Henties Bay (76km)
Lodge B&B (76km)
Mittel St
Neser St
Bahnhof St
Garnison St
Ludwig Koch St
Strand St
Am Zoll St
Kaiser Wilhelm St
Kaiser Wilhelm St
Swakop St

See Enlargement

Palm Beach
Arnold Shad Promenade
The Mole
The Jetty

However, when the funds ran out, the government took over the project and requisitioned it as a magistrate's court. In the 1960s it functioned as a school dormitory, and now houses municipal offices. Just so no-one can doubt its identity, the words 'Altes Amtsgericht' (German for 'Old Magistrates' Court') are painted across the front.

Historic Railway Station (Bahnhof) The ornate and historical Bahnhof, built in 1901 as the terminal for the Kaiserliche Eisenbahn Verwaltung (German for 'Imperial Railway Authority') railway, connected Swakopmund with Windhoek. In 1910, when the railway closed down, the building assumed the role as main station for the narrow-gauge mine railway between Swakopmund and Otavi. It was declared a national monument in 1972 and now houses the Swakopmund Hotel & Entertainment Centre.

Franciscan Hospital The 1907 Franciscan hospital *(Post St)* was designed by colonial architect Otto Ertl. It was originally called the St Antonius Gebaude and functioned as a hospital until 1987.

Litfass-Saule In 1855 the Berlin printer Litfass came up with the notion of erecting advertising pillars on German street corners. For the citizens of early Swakopmund, they became a common source of information and advertising. The remaining example sits on the corner of Post and Breite Sts and now advertises Pepsi.

Hohenzollern Building The Baroque-style Hohenzollern Building *(Cnr Moltke & Brücken Sts)* has stood on this corner since 1906. It's fairly obvious that this imposing structure was originally intended as a hotel. Its rather outlandish decor is crowned by a fibreglass cast of Atlas supporting the world, which replaced the precarious cement version that graced the roof prior to renovations in 1988.

German Evangelical Lutheran Church In 1906 Dr Heinrich Vedder organised a Lutheran congregation. To accommodate the faithful, architect Otto Ertl designed the neo-Baroque Evangelical Lutheran Church *(Otavi St)*, which was constructed between 1910 and 1911. It was consecrated on 7 January 1912.

Old German School Opposite Lutheran Church is the 1913 German school. Its Baroque-style design is the result of a 1912 competition, which was won by budding German architect Emil Krause.

Deutsche-Afrika Bank Building This handsome neo-Classical building near the corner of Woermann and Moltke Sts has served as a bank since 1909, when it opened as the branch office of the Deutsche-Afrika Bank. It's now a functioning Bank of Windhoek branch.

Former Hotel Kaiserhof The former Hotel Kaiserhof *(Cnr Kaiser Wilhelm & Moltke Sts)* was built in 1905. It originally had two storeys but was destroyed in a fire nine years later and was rebuilt as a single-storey building.

Prinzessin Rupprecht Heim The single-storey Prinzessin Rupprecht Heim was constructed in 1902 and was first used as the *Lazarett* (military hospital). In 1914 it was transferred to the Bavarian Women's Red Cross, which named it for its patron, Princess Rupprecht, wife of the Bavarian crown prince. The idea was to expose convalescents to the healthy effects of the sea breeze. Until recently, one wing was used as a maternity ward (the tourist literature claims it was closed due to a storks' strike). It's now a private guesthouse.

Woermannhaus From the shore, the delightful German-style Woermannhaus stands out above surrounding buildings; you'd be forgiven for assuming it's the town hall. In fact, it was designed by Friedrich Höft and built in 1905 as the main offices of the Damara & Namaqua Trading Company but in 1909 it was taken over by the Woermann & Brock Trading Company, which supplied the current name. In the 1920s it was used as a school dormitory and later served as a merchant sailors hostel. It eventually fell into disrepair, but was declared a national monument and restored in 1976.

For years, the prominent Damara tower (formerly a water tower) provided a landmark for ships at sea and for traders arriving by ox wagon from the interior. It now affords a splendid panorama and houses the **Swakopmund Military Museum** *(admission US$1; open 10am-noon Mon, Tues, Thur-Sat & 3pm-6pm Mon-Thur)* and a gallery of historic paintings. Pay admission and pick up a key at the library.

Old German Homes The 1911 home of the early colonial builder Karl Hermann Wille, **Villa Wille** *(Cnr Otavi & Kaiser Wilhelm Sts)*, is a two-storey bungalow complete with an ornamental tower, which now houses Hotel Eberwein.

A block north is the 1910 home and surgery of Dr Schwietering *(Cnr Post & Otavi Sts)*, who was the town's doctor. The nice **colonial home** *(Post St)* next door, which houses the Cooke's House B&B, is also worth a look.

Along Bismarck St, south of Brücken St, is a line of simple and unimposing colonial homes and flats, including the **MC Human Flats**, which date back to 1902.

At the western end of Post St is the old **Lüdwig Schröder Haus**, constructed in 1903 for an employee of the Woermann Shipping Lines as an extension of the Woermann Lines headquarters. The next year, architect Friedrich Höft designed the **Altona Haus** around the corner on Moltke St. It would also serve as auxiliary company offices.

Alte Gefängnis (Old Prison) The impressive 1909 Alte Gefängnis was designed by architect Heinrich Bause, and if you didn't know it was a prison, you'd swear it was either an early East German train station or a health-spa hotel. In fact, the main building was used only for staff housing while the prisoners were relegated to less opulent quarters on one side. Note that it still serves as a prison and is considered a sensitive structure, so photography is not permitted.

OMEG Haus Thanks to the narrow-gauge railway to the coast, the colonial company Otavi Minen und Eisenbahn Gesellschaft (OMEG), which oversaw the rich Otavi and Tsumeb mines, also maintained an office in Swakopmund. Until 1910, OMEG Haus *(Kaiser Wilhelm St)* served as a warehouse. Next door is Otavi Bahnhof, the railway station for the narrow-gauge Tsumeb line; there are plans to turn it into a transport museum.

Living Desert Snake Park
The Living Desert Snake Park *(☎ 405100, 081-128 5100, 15 Kaiser Wilhelm St; admission US$1.50)* houses an array of serpentine sorts. The owner knows everything you'd ever want to know – or not know – about snakes, scorpions, spiders and other widely misunderstood creatures. She feeds them at 4pm daily.

National Marine Aquarium
The National Marine Aquarium *(Strand St; adult/child & pensioner US$1.50/0.75; open 10am-6pm Tues-Sat, 11am-5pm Sun, closed Mon except public holidays)*, on the waterfront, provides an excellent introduction to the cold offshore world in the South Atlantic. Most impressive is the tunnel through the largest aquarium, which allows close-up views of graceful rays, toothy sharks (you can literally count all the teeth!) and other little marine beasties found on Namibia's seafood platters. The fish are fed daily at 3pm, which makes an interesting spectacle.

Kristall Galerie
The appealing and architecturally astute Kristall Galerie *(☎ 406080, fax 406084, e gems@kristallgalerie.co.na, w www .kristallgalerie.com, Schlosser St; admission US$2.50; open 9am-5pm Mon-Sat)* features some of the planet's most incredible crystal formations, including the largest quartz crystal that has ever been found. The adjacent shop sells lovely mineral samples, crystal jewellery, and intriguing plates, cups and wine glasses that are carved from the local stone.

Beaches

Swakopmund is Namibia's main beach resort, but even in summer the water is never warmer than around 15°C. Swimming in the sea is best in the lee of the Mole sea wall. At the lagoon at the Swakop River mouth you can watch ducks, flamingoes, pelicans, cormorants, gulls, waders and other birds. North of town you can stroll along miles and miles of deserted beaches stretching towards the Skeleton Coast.

The best surfing is at Nordstrand or 'Thick Lip' near Vineta Point.

In Swakopmund, seaside amenities include a formal promenade, a pier, tropical gardens, minigolf and a heated swimming pool.

Dunes

A fascinating short hike will take you across the Swakop riverbed to the large dunefields south of town. The dune formations and unique vegetation are great for exploring and with a dune cart or a sheet of masonite, you can spend hours sledding down the slopes. The Alternative Space loans dune carts to its guests, and several tour companies offer sandboarding and quadbiking (see Activities later in this section). For more on dune types and dune communities see the special section 'The Namib Dunes'.

Swakopmund Museum

When ill winds blow, head for the Swakopmund Museum (☎ 402046, [e] museum@ mweb.com.na, Strand St; adults/students US$1.50/0.75; open 10am-12.30pm & 3pm-5.30pm daily), at the foot of the lighthouse, where you can hole up and learn about the town history. The museum occupies the site of the old harbour warehouse, which was destroyed in 1914 by a 'lucky' shot from a British warship.

Displays include exhibits on Namibia's history and ethnology, including information on local flora and fauna. Especially good is the display on the !nara melon (see the boxed text '!Nara Melons' in the later Walvis Bay section), a fruit which was vital to the early Khoi-Khoi people of the Namib region. It also harbours a reconstructed colonial home interior, Emil Kiewittand's apothecary shop and an informative display on the Rössing Mine. Military buffs will appreciate the stifling uniforms of the Camel Corps and the Shell furniture (so called because it was homemade from 1930s depression-era petrol and paraffin tins).

Hansa Brewery

Aficionados of the amber nectar will want to visit the Hansa Brewery (☎ 405021, 9 Rhode Allee; admission free), which is the source of Swakopmund's favourite drop. Free tours – with ample opportunity to sample the product – run on Tuesday and Thursday, but must be pre-booked.

Historical Cemeteries

It's worth having a quick wander past the historical cemeteries beside the Swakop River. The neatly manicured German cemetery dates from colonial times and the stones, which are maintained by the families, tell countless stories. The adjoining African cemetery makes an equally intriguing cultural statement, and has plenty of stories of its own.

Activities

Swakopmund aspires to become a dry version of Victoria Falls, and has made some progress in that direction with its sandboarding, quadbiking, parachuting and other adrenaline boosters.

Alter Action (☎/fax 402737, 081-128 2737, [e] alteraxn@iafrica.com.na) Sandboarding with this group is certain to increase your heart rate. For US$20/30 you can do lie-down/stand-up sandboarding (this is especially recommended for surfers and snowboarders), including the use of a new sandboard, gloves, goggles, transport to the dunes and enough sandboard polish to ensure an adrenaline high. The highlight is an 80km/h 'schuss' down a 120m sand mountain. Slogging up the dunes can be rather taxing work, so you need to be physically fit and healthy (which isn't a bad idea anyway).

Desert Explorers (☎ 408098, 081-129 2380, fax 405649, Atlanta Hotel, PO Box 456) This group runs ecologically sensitive **quadbiking tours** on the dunes, which include instruction, helmets, goggles and lunch for US$55 for two hours. Venues range from the Khan River and Swakop riverbed to the Moon Landscape and oasis of Goanikontes; a popular alternative to the longer tours is a simple sundowner on the dunes.

For more stomach-churning thrills, this group does **tandem skydives**. The rate of US$150 includes instruction and a jump from over 3000m, which gives divers a 30-second free fall and five to seven minutes 'on the chute'.

Tandem Adventures (☎ 081-124 2588) This group charges US$150 for a tandem parachute jump from 3300m.

Swakopmund Skydiving Club (☎ 402 841, 081-124 5167) This skydiving club offers static-line and tandem skydiving, as well as accredited courses.

Walker's Rock & Rope Adventures Climbing Tower (☎ 403122, ℮ walker@ iafrica.com.na, Swakopmund Football Club, Cnr Windhoeker St & Rhode Allee) Open 2.30pm-sunset Mon-Fri, 10am-sunset Sat & Sun. **Rock climbers** can practise here but it's soon to be moved to a more convenient spot and expanded. You can choose between beginning, intermediate and advanced routes, as well as abseiling. Instruction is available and staff will also help you prepare for a Spitzkoppe climb.

African Adventure Balloons (☎/fax 403455, 081-242 9481, ℮ flylow@mweb .com.na, PO Box 2238) This company offers sunrise and sunset **balloon rides** over the dunes. A half-/full-hour flight will cost US$127/180 per person, with a minimum of three people. (The same company also operates a flying fox, a thrilling cable slide at Rössing Mountain; for more information contact the Swakopmund Adventure Centre.)

Heino (☎ 081-127 9100) You can go **microlighting** with Heino, who charges US$50 for 40 minutes aloft.

Okakambe Trails (☎ 081-124 6626) This group runs 1½-hour **horseback trips** along the Swakop River to the Moon Landscape for US$42. It can also organise moonlight rides and rides along the beach and dunes.

Ocean Adventures (☎ 081-124 0208) These people will take you **fishing** for kabeljous, barbels, steenbras, galjoens, yellowtails and copper sharks. Boat fishing costs US$63 and rock and surf angling from the beach is US$72; rates include snacks, bait and equipment hire.

Henry's Fishing Safaris (☎ 404828, fax 463738, ℮ boatfish@iafrica.com.na, PO Box 520) This is another recommended company.

Rössmund Golf Club (☎ 405644, 5km east of Swakopmund, on the main road) Open daily. This par-72 18-hole course has equipment for hire.

Organised Tours

From Swakopmund, the only budget company running organised tours to Sossusvlei is *Crazy Kudu Safaris* (see Organised Tours in the Getting Around chapter). Several other operators offer sightseeing day tours and overnight trips.

Most of Swakopmund's day-touring companies charge the following for standard half-day and day tours: half-day options include Cape Cross (US$40), Rössing Mine gem tours (US$33) and Welwitschia Drive (US$27); see under Around Swakopmund later for details of these last two. Full-day trips run to the Spitzkoppe (US$46), the Kuiseb Delta and Walvis Bay Lagoon (US$52), the Namib Desert (US$40) and the Brandberg (US$50). Also popular are the sundowner tours on the dunes (US$11). The following operators offer local tours.

Charly's Desert Tours (☎ 404341, fax 404821, ℮ charlydt@mweb.com.na, 11 Kaiser Wilhelm St, PO Box 1400) This popular company does all the standard day tours.

Turnstone Tours (☎ 403123, fax 403290, ℮ turn@iafrica.com.na, ⓦ www.swk.na mib .com/turn) and *Namib Tours (☎/fax 404072, 081-128 6111, Roon St, Next to the Hansa Hotel, PO Box 1428)* do a number of standard day tours, plus longer excursions.

[Continued on page 233]

THE NAMIB DUNES

The Namib dunes, which take on mythical proportions in tourist literature and nature specials, stretch from the Orange to the Kuiseb Rivers in the south (this area is known as 'the dune sea') and from Torra Bay in Skeleton Coast Park to Angola's Curoca River in the north. They're composed of colourful quartz sand, and come in varying hues – from cream to orange and red and violet.

Unlike the ancient Kalahari dunes, those of the Namib are dynamic, shifting with the wind, which sculpts them into a variety of distinctive shapes. The top portion of the dune, which faces the direction of migration, is known as a slipface, where the sand spills from the crest and slips down. Various bits of plant and animal detritus also collect here and provide a meagre food source for dune-dwelling creatures, and it's here that most dune life is concentrated.

Parabolic Dunes

Along the eastern area of the dune sea – including around Sossusvlei – the dunes are classified as parabolic or multicyclic and are the result of variable wind patterns. These are the most stable dunes in the Namib and, therefore, are also the most vegetated.

Transverse Dunes

Near the coast south of Walvis Bay, the formations are known as transverse dunes, which are long narrow, linear dunes lying perpendicular to the prevailing south-westerly winds. Therefore, their slipfaces are oriented towards the north and north-east.

Seif Dunes

Around Homeb in the Namib Desert Park are the prominent linear or seif dunes (also known as linear dunes), which are enormous northwest-south-east-oriented sand ripples. With heights of up to 100m, they're spaced about 1km apart and show up plainly on satellite photographs. They're formed by seasonal winds; during the prevailing southerly winds of summer, the slipfaces lie on the north-eastern face. In the winter, the wind blows in the opposite direction and slipfaces build up on the south-western faces.

Star Dunes

In areas where individual dunes are exposed to winds from all directions, a formation known as a star dune appears. These dunes have multiple ridges and when seen from above may appear to have a star shape.

Barchan Dunes

Around the southern portion of the Skeleton Coast Park and south of Lüderitz, barchan dunes prevail. These are the most highly mobile dunes of all, and are created by unidirectional winds. As they shift, these dunes take on a crescent shape, with the horns of the crescent

Inset: The sand dunes of Namib-Naukluft Park are reputed to be among the world's highest. (Photo by David Else)

aimed in the direction of migration. It is barchan dunes that are slowly devouring the ghost town of Kolkmanskop near Lüderitz. These are the so-called 'roaring dunes' of the northern Skeleton Coast, named for the haunting roar created when air is pressed out from the interstices between the sand granules on the slipface. Therefore it's loudest in the warmth of the afternoon (see the boxed text 'The Roaring Dunes' in the North-Western Namibia chapter).

Hump Dunes

Considerably smaller than other dune types are hump dunes, which typically form in clusters on flat expanses near water sources. Sand builds up around vegetation – usually a tuft of grass – and is held in place by the roots of the plant, forming a sandy tussock. They rarely rise more than 2m to 3m above the surface.

The Dune Community

The Namib dunes may appear to be lifeless, but they actually support a complex ecosystem capable of extracting moisture from the frequent fogs. These are caused by condensation when cold, moist onshore winds, influenced mainly by the South Atlantic's Benguela Current, meet with the dry heat rising from the desert sands. They build up overnight, causing thick morning fogs that normally burn off during the heat of the afternoon. Underwater, the nitrogen-rich Benguela Current supports a rich soup of plankton, a dietary staple for fish, which in turn attracts birds and marine mammals to the coastline.

Nowhere else on earth does such diverse life exist in such harsh conditions, and it only manages here thanks to grass seed and bits of plant matter deposited by the wind and the moisture carried in by fog. On the gravel plains live ostriches, zebras, gemsboks, springboks, mongooses, ground squirrels and small numbers of other animals, such as black-backed jackals, bat-eared foxes, caracals, aardwolfs and brown hyenas. After good rains, seeds germinate and the seemingly barren gravel is transformed into a meadow of waist-high grass teeming with life.

The sand also shelters a diversity of small creatures and even a short walk on the dunes will reveal traces of this well-adapted community. By day, the surface temperatures may reach 70°C, but below, the spaces between sand particles are considerable, especially if you're a bug, and therefore, air circulates freely below the surface, providing a cool shelter. In the chill of a desert night, the sand retains some of the warmth absorbed during the day and provides a warm place to burrow. When alarmed, many creatures can also use the sand as an effective hiding place.

The best places to observe dune life are around Sossusvlei and on the dunes south of Homeb, on the Kuiseb River. Early in the morning, look at the tracks to see what has transpired during the night; it's easy to distinguish the trails of various dune-dwelling beetles, lizards, snakes, spiders and scorpions.

Much of the dune community is comprised of beetles, which are attracted by the vegetable material on the dune slipfaces; the Namib supports 200 species of the tenebrionid family alone. However, they're only visible when the dune surface is warm. At other times, they take shelter beneath the surface by 'swimming' into the sand.

Tenebrionid Beetle (Onomachris unguicularis) This fog-basking beetle, which is locally known as a toktokkie, has a particularly interesting way of drinking. By day, these beetles scuttle over the dunes in search of plant detritus, but at night, they bury themselves in the sand. They derive moisture by condensing fog on their bodies; on foggy mornings, toktokkies line up on the dunes, lower their heads, raise their posteriors in the air, and slide the water droplets down the carapace into the mouth. They can consume up to 40% of their body weight in water in a single morning.

Dancing Spider (Orchestrella longpipes) This large spider, known as 'the White Lady of the Namib' (doesn't the Latin name sound like a character in a children's novel?) constructs tunnels beneath the dune surface, where it shelters from heat and predators. These tunnels are prevented from collapsing by a lining of spider silk, which is laid down as they're excavated. This enormous spider can easily make a meal of creatures as large as a palmato gecko.

Golden Mole (Eremitalpa granti) The dunes are also home to this lovable yellowish-coloured carnivore that spends most of its day buried in the sand. It was first discovered in 1837, but wasn't again seen until 1963. The golden mole, which lacks both eyes and ears, doesn't burrow like other moles, but simply swims through the sand. Although it's rarely spotted – we know of only one Namibian who's ever seen one – you may want to look carefully around tufts of grass or hummocks for the large rounded snout, which may protrude above the surface. At night, it emerges and roams hundreds of metres over the dune faces foraging for beetle larvae and other insects.

Shovel-Snouted Lizard (Aporosaura anchitae) This lizard uses a unique method of regulating its body temperature while tearing across the scorching sand. It can tolerate body temperatures of up to 44°C, but surface temperatures on the dunes can climb as high as 70°C. To prevent overheating, the lizard does a 'thermal dance', raising its tail and two legs at a time off the hot surface of the sand. When threatened, the lizard submerges itself in the sand.

Palmato Gecko (Palmatogecko rangei) The exceptionally cute and unique palmato gecko is also known as the 'web-footed gecko', after its unusual feet, which act as scoops for burrowing in the sand. This translucent nocturnal lizard, which grows to 10cm in length, is coloured pinkish-brown on its back and has a white belly. The enormous eyes aid with its nocturnal hunting habits, and the gecko is often photographed using its long tongue to clear its eyes of dust and sand, or to drink from condensed fog droplets from the head and snout. Other gecko species present in the dunes include the barking gecko *(Ptenopus garrulus)* and the large-headed gecko *(Chondrodactylus anguilifer)*.

Namaqua Chameleon *(Chamaeleo namaquensis)* Another dune lizard, the bizarre and fearsome-looking Namaqua Chameleon, grows up to 25cm in length, and is identified by the unmistakable fringe of brownish bumps along its spine. When alarmed, it emits an ominous hiss and exposes its enormous yellow mouth and sticky tongue, which can spell the end for up to 200 large beetles every day. Like all chameleons, its cone-shaped eye sockets operate independently, allowing it to look in several directions at once.

Namib Sidewinding Adder *(Bitis peringueyi)* This small, buff-coloured snake is perfectly camouflaged on the dune surface. It grows to a length of just 25cm and navigates by gracefully moving sideways through the shifting sands. Because the eyes are on top of the head, the snake can bury itself almost completely in the sand and still see what's happening above the surface. When its unsuspecting prey happens along – normally a gecko or lizard – the adder uses its venom to immobilise the victim before devouring it. Although it is also poisonous to humans, the venom is so mild that it rarely causes more than an irritation.

Namib Sandsnakes *(Psammophis sp.)* The Namib's three species of sandsnakes are longer, slinkier and faster-moving than the adders, but hunt the same prey. These 1m-long back-fanged snakes grab the prey and chew on it until it's immobilised by venom, then swallow it whole. As with the adders, they're well camouflaged for life in the sand, coloured from off-white to pale grey. The back is marked with pale stripes or a pattern of dots.

Namib Skinks *(Typhlosaurus sp.)* Several varieties of skinks are commonly mistaken for snakes. Because they propel themselves by swimming in the sand, their limbs are either small and vestigial or missing altogether, and their eyes, ears and nostrils are tiny and therefore well-protected from sand particles. At the tip of their nose is a 'rostral scale', which acts as a bulldozer blade to clear the sand ahead and allow the skink to progress. Skinks spend most of their time burrowing beneath the surface, but at night, emerge on the dune slipfaces to forage. In the morning, you'll often see their telltale tracks.

MANFRED GOTTSCHALK

DAVID WALL

DAVID CIMINO

Desert winds are constantly shifting the sands of the Namib dunes. Star dunes **(top)** are exposed to winds from all directions, while transverse dunes **(bottom)** are formed by south-westerly winds. The dunes near the coast **(top right)** tower more than 300m over the underlying strata.

MANFRED GOTTSCHALK

PETER PTSCHELINZEW

JEAN-BERNARD CARILLET

When the sun rises over the desert horizon, the mercury starts to soar. By mid-afternoon, it's more than 40 degrees in the shade. There's no respite until dusk, and as the sun disappears, the temperature drops, often to below freezing.

[Continued from page 228]

Pleasure Flights *(☎/fax 404500,* e *red baron@iml-net.ocm.na,* w *www.pleasure flights.com.na, Kaiser Wilhelm St, PO Box 357)* This group offers 'flightseeing' over the colourful salt works, Sandwich Harbour, Welwitschia Drive, the Brandberg, the dunes, the Skeleton Coast and beyond. Sample prices include Sossusvlei (US$119), the Skeleton Coast (US$219) and the 'Forbidden Coast' south of Walvis Bay (US$78); rates are per person with at least five passengers.

Hata Angu Cultural Tours *(☎ 081-251 5916,* e *in_a_nut_shell@hotmail.com)* This company offers US$24 day tours that take you to Mondesa township to meet the guide, Paulus Shapala (founder of Youth Against Crime in Swakopmund). After a visit to the Damara chief, you visit a shebeen (local drinking establishment) to sample traditional Namibian food (including mopane worms and local libations). You'll then learn about Herero traditions from local women, stop by the Singles' Quarters and the market, and pass through the DRC (Democratic Republic of the Congo – a nickname for the TISA, or Temporary Informal Settlement Area), and see the pride that some of Namibia's poorest citizens take in their humble homes. There's also an evening tour, including a traditional Damara meal and a township shebeen crawl.

Special Events
Swakopmund stages several events that are German-oriented, including a **reitturnier** (gymkhana) in January and the **Swakopmund Karnival** in August (the colonial nature of this event may be a bit uncomfortable for outsiders).

Places to Stay
During the school holidays in December and January, Swakopmund accommodation books up well in advance, so be sure to book as early as possible.

Places to Stay – Budget
Myl 4 Caravan Park (☎ 461781, fax 462901, e *m4swakop@mweb.com.na,* w *www.trip online.net)* Camping US$3.50 per site plus US$1.50 per person, US$1.50 per vehicle (one-time charge) & US$1 for electricity, 6-bed bungalows US$40, 2-bed self-catering rooms US$12, 4-/6-bed self-catering flats US$26/40. This bleak beachfront camping ground, 6km north of town, is exposed to the wind, sand and drizzle and – despite the electric fence – security can be a problem. Having said that, it's one of the world's more unusual places to pitch a tent. Non-camping accommodation is wisely booked in advance.

Gull's Cry *(☎/fax 461591, 081-246 6774,* e *rdowning@iafrica.com.na, PO Box 1496)* Camp sites US$10 plus US$1.50 per person, US$1.75 for electricity (groups of 15 or more US$2 per person, with no site charge). This beachfront camping ground sits right on the sand, sheltered from the wind by lovely tamarisk trees. Facilities are basic and security can be a problem, but it's convenient to the centre. No pets are allowed.

The Alternative Space *(☎ 402713,* e *nam 00352@mweb.com.na, 46 Dr Alfons Weber St)* Dorm beds US$5. Travellers love the atmosphere here on the desert fringe, just a 10-minute walk from the dunes and 20 minutes from the centre. Highlights include the castle-like architecture, saturation artwork, its industrial-waste-recycling theme, a bizarre turret toilet, the free use of dune carts, and the always friendly welcome from Frenus, Sybille and Rafael. The catch is that only 'friends of Frenus' are welcome, but he's a great guy and makes friends easily. On Friday evenings the friends get together for a free fish braai (barbecue). Guests also have access to cooking facilities, email and Internet services and free town transfers.

Desert Sky Backpackers *(☎ 402339, 081-248 7771,* e *dsbackpackers@swak op.com,* w *www.swakop.com/dsb, 35 Laz-arett St, PO Box 2830)* Camping US$3 per person, dorm beds US$5.50, doubles US$19. At this comfortable and centrally located place, owner Quintin Lofty-Eaton offers everything backpackers come to expect from a well-appointed backpacker lodge: kitchen facilities, storage lockers, email and Internet access, and laundry services. Free coffee is available all day and if your focus in town is Fagin's Pub, it's within easy stumbling distance home.

Karen's Attic (☎ 404825, fax 402707, e kattic@iafrica.com.na, 37 Post St, PO Box 24) Dorm beds US$4.50, singles/doubles US$7/11. This quiet backpacker lodge is one of Namibia's plusher budget accommodation choices, with superior kitchen facilities and a comfortable TV lounge.

Swakopmund Rest Camp (☎ 402807, e swkmun@swk.namib.com, w www.swak opmund.restcamp.com, Roon St, Private Bag 5017) 4-bed A-frames US$35, 2-/4-bed 'fishermen's shacks' US$12/19, 4-bed flats US$26, 6-bed self-catering bungalows/flats US$40/47. This recently renovated camp is now quite smart and no longer merits its nickname, 'Stalag 13'. It's wise to pre-book for weekends and holidays. No animals or motorcycles are allowed.

HI Hostel (☎ 404164, Alte Kaserne, Lazarett St) Dorm beds US$4, doubles US$11. The ambience here is appropriately military, and mature adults may feel cramped. Kitchen and laundry facilities are available. Note the old German paintings that adorn the walls, including the crests of the German Federal States, which existed during the colonial era.

Jay Jay's (☎ 402909, Brücken St) Dorm beds US$3.50, singles/doubles without bathroom US$5/9, with bathroom US$6/11. This long-standing place is clean and well located, just half a block from the sea. Downstairs, it boasts a basic restaurant and lively bar.

Villa Wiese (☎ 407105, 081-243 9210, fax 406068, e villawiese@compuscan.co .za, Cnr Bahnhof & Windhoeker Sts, PO Box 2460) Dorm beds US$5, singles/doubles US$11/14. This friendly and funky backpacker place with a nice woody smell, housed in a historic mansion, caters mainly to overlanders. Kitchen facilities are available and the lounge television offers DSTV.

Hotel Grüner Kranz (☎ 402030, e swa koplodge@yahoo.com, 42 Breite St) Dorm beds US$5.50, singles/doubles with TV &

bathroom US$16/20. This hotel has recently been bought by the adrenaline activities squads and they're setting up a backpackers and overlander lodge. It offers Internet access, cooking facilities and laundry services, and also hosts the Stage Night Club & Disco (see Entertainment later).

Places to Stay – Mid-Range

Pension Dig-by-See (☎ 404130, fax 404 170, 4 Brücken St, e stelgodl@iafrica .com.na, PO Box 1580) Singles/doubles US$20/30, rooms for 3-4 people US$14 per person, all B&B. Also known as Digby's, this friendly spot near the sea is a longtime standard in Swakopmund. All rooms have a bath, shower, toilet and TV.

Pension Prinzessin-Rupprecht-Heim (☎ 402231, fax 402019, Lazarett St) Singles/ doubles with bathroom US$24/42, smaller singles with shared facilities US$24, family flats US$22 for 2 people plus US$14 per additional person. All rates include breakfast. This pension in the former colonial hospital has a lovely garden.

Hotel-Pension Rapmund (☎ 402035, fax 404524, e rapmund@iafrica.com.na, 6 Bismarck St, PO Box 425) Singles/doubles in the back US$26/39, with sea view US$28/42. This friendly B&B has grown considerably in recent years; it occupies an appealing spot overlooking the sea.

Atlanta Hotel (☎ 402360, 081-124 1919, fax 405649, e atlantah@iafrica .com.na, 6 Roon St, PO Box 456) Singles/doubles B&B US$31/38. This recently renovated hotel offers inexpensive but adequate central accommodation. All rooms have private bathroom and telephones.

Hotel Europa Hof (☎ 405061, fax 402391, e europa@iml-net.com.na, w www.nat ron.net/tour/europa/europad.htm, 39 Bismarck St, PO Box 1333) Singles/doubles/ triples US$47/69/82. This hotel resembles a Bavarian chalet, and simply overflows with European atmosphere, complete with colourful flower boxes, aloof service, marginal showers and European flags flying from the 1st-floor windows.

Hotel Garni Adler (☎ 405045, fax 404206, e adler@natron.net, w www.natron.net

/tour/adler/hoteld.htm, 3 Strand St, PO Box 1497) Standard singles/doubles US$48/70, with sea view US$48/74. This homely place resembles a modern house lost somewhere in German suburbia, but it does have a great sea view.

Hotel Schweizerhaus *(☎ 400331, fax 405 850,* e *schweizerhaus@mweb.com.na, 1 Bismarck St, PO Box 445)* Singles/doubles US$42/69, with sea view add US$6 per person. This beachside place has a good view of the lighthouse and is best known as the hotel attached to Cafe Anton.

Alte Brücke *(☎ 404918, fax 400153,* e *accomod@iml-net.com.na, PO Box 3360)* Camping US$7 per person (US$10 minimum), single/double self-catering chalets B&B US$36/53. Here at the river's mouth you can restrict your noise to sea sounds.

Brigadoon Guest Cottages *(☎ 406064, fax 464195,* e *brigadon@iafrica.com.na, 16 Ludwig Koch St, PO Box 1930)* Singles/ doubles B&B US$43/55. This wonderfully friendly B&B has three Victorian cottages in a garden setting opposite Palm Beach.

Cooke's House *(☎ 462837, 081-240 2088, fax 462839,* e *cooksb.b@mweb .com.na, Post St, PO Box 2628)* Singles/ doubles without bathroom US$20/30, with bathroom US$23/32. Rates include a German breakfast. This friendly B&B occupies a 1910 historic home in a quiet area of town. It's highly recommended.

Beach Lodge B&B *(☎ 400933, fax 400934,* e *volkb@iafrica.com.na,* w *www .natron.net/tour/belo/main.html, Stint St, PO Box 79)* Singles/doubles/triples B&B US$40/54/72. For self-catering, subtract US$2 per person. This remarkable boat-shaped place, which sits right on the beach sand, offers some of the most unusual architecture and best sea views in town. All rooms feature DSTV and both picture windows and huge port-holes affording views across the ocean expanses. If the beach is your bag, you can't beat it.

Places to Stay – Top End
Sam's Giardino Hotel *(☎ 403210, fax 403 500,* e *samsart@iafrica.com.na,* w *www .giardino.com.na, 89 Lazarett St, PO Box*

1401) Standard singles/doubles US$60/74, suites US$74-87, all B&B. Well-behaved pets stay free. This slice of Central Europe in the desert emphasises fine wine–tasting, cigar-smoking, and relaxing in the rose garden beside the fish pond. Its 'hospitality with a touch of heart' is a unique experience that shouldn't be missed.

Hansa Hotel *(☎ 400311, fax 402732,* e *hansa@iml-net.com.na, Roon St)* Singles/ doubles US$76/102. This place bills itself as 'luxury in the desert', and makes much of the fact that it has hosted the likes of Aristotle Onassis, Sir Laurens van der Post, Eartha Kitt, Oliver Reed and Ernest Borgnine. The individually decorated rooms are quite tasteful.

Swakopmund Hotel & Entertainment Centre *(☎ 400800, fax 400801,* e *shec@ iafrica.com.na, 2 Bahnhof St, PO Box 616)* Singles/doubles & family rooms B&B US$97/147. This four-star hotel in the historic train station includes the Mermaid Casino, a cinema, several restaurants, a large swimming pool and a conference centre (the management organises all sorts of activities for conference participants).

Places to Eat
As befits a seaside resort, Swakopmund's restaurants serve everything from takeaway fare right up to four-star gourmet meals.

Out of Africa Coffee Shop *(☎ 404752, 13 Post St)* Breakfast US$2.50, muffins US$1. Open Mon-Sat. At this locally popular place you'll find Namibia's finest coffee – espresso, cappuccino, latte and other specialities – served up in giant-sized French-style cups. Its motto is 'Life is too short to drink bad coffee', and it does something about it! It also makes enormous and indescribably delicious muffins – from cinnamon to blueberry – and truly memorable breakfasts. It's a great place to meet people you know – or people you want to know!

La Paloma Takeaways *(☎ 404700, Breite St)* Takeaways US$1.50-3. This established snack place does tasty and inexpensive takeaway food.

KFC *(☎ 405687, 13 Roon St)* Chicken takeaways US$1.50-4. Open 9am-10pm daily. This international standard serves up reliable, fast and fatty secret-recipe meals.

Kücki's Pub (☎ *402407, Moltke St*) Lunch US$2.50-5, dinner US$3-8, seafood platter US$15. Kücki's does Swakopmund's best pub meals; if your budget permits, don't miss the amazing seafood platter.

Cape to Cairo/African Roots (☎ *402030, 42 Breite St*) Starters US$2.50-3, beef dishes US$6-8, game US$6-9, fish US$5-9, seafood platter US$19 per person. Open 7pm-10.30pm daily. This popular restaurant at Hotel Grüner Kranz has a range of Namibian specialities and a good wine list; the menu features interesting African anecdotes.

Blue Whale Cafe (*Atlanta Hotel, Roon St*) Salads US$3-3.50, burgers US$3-4, fish or beef dinners US$4-4.50. This popular lunch spot offers sidewalk seating. Don't miss the especially creative lunch menu, which features healthy crepes and tempting sweets.

Lighthouse Pub & Cafe (☎ *400894, Main (Palm) Beach*) Mains US$3-6. This very busy place features all sorts of good-value seafood, including kabeljou, calamari, kingklip, lobster and a large seafood platter, as well as an appropriate view of the beach and crashing surf. Other specialities include burgers, pasta, steaks, ribs and pizzas.

Western Saloon Pizzeria (☎ *403925, fax 464176, 8 Moltke St*) Small pizzas US$2.50-4, large pizzas US$3-6. Open 4.30pm-11.30pm Mon-Fri, noon-2pm & 4.30pm-11.30pm Sat, 5pm-10.30pm Sun. This very popular cowboy-oriented place, with the theme 'Go Hard or Stay Home', is best known for its pizzas, but also serves up sandwiches and salads.

Papa's (☎ *404747, Shop-Rite Centre*) Pizzas US$3.50-7. The pizzas here are big and popular. Delivery (US$1) is available from 6.30pm to 9.30pm Tuesday to Sunday. On the last Friday of the month, Papa's stages a special Diamond Jack's jazz and blues evening.

Napolitana Pizzeria & Mediterranean Restaurant (☎ *402773, 33 Breite St*) Pasta from US$3, pizzas US$3.40-5, burgers US$3, steaks US$6, seafood US$5-20. Open 10am-2pm & 5.30pm-10pm daily. This superb and inexpensive place serves

up a range of meals and draught lager. The seafood platter (US$20) is a real treat. Pizza deliveries are available until 9.30pm for US$1.10 – even to Myl 4 Caravan Park.

Original China Tong Hua Restaurant (☎ *402081, Cnr Brücken & Roon Sts*) Mains US$2.50-5. This ethnic alternative specialises in Chinese cuisine and pizza.

Oasis Bistro (☎ *402333, 5 Moltke St*) Lunches US$2.50-5, dinners US$3-7. Open 8am-late. This place does excellent and imaginative breakfasts, lunches and dinners. The menu features salads, vegetarian specialities, crepes, gyros, game dishes, steaks and seafood specials. Try the savoury bacon, mushroom, tomato and cream cheese flapjack, or the honey, berry, nut and ice cream variety. Phumba Sports Bar, upstairs, is a popular local hangout (see Entertainment later).

Swakopmund Brauhaus (☎ *402214, 22 Kaiser Wilhelm St*) Mains US$3.50-8, vegetarian dishes US$4-5. Open 11.30am-2.30pm & 6pm-9.30pm Mon-Sat. This excellent restaurant and boutique brewery offers one of Swakopmund's most sought-after commodities (traditional German-style beer), as well as excellently prepared beef and seafood. German-oriented desserts range from US$1.50 to US$3.

Erich's (☎ *405141, 21 Post St*) Mains US$5-8. Open 8pm-11pm Mon-Sat. This upmarket place specialises in fish and steak dishes, and does a mean *Tiroler knödel-suppe* (Tyrolean dumpling soup).

The Tug (☎ *402356*) Mains US$4.50-10. This is an excellent upmarket choice for fresh fish. It's housed in the beached tugboat *Danie Hugo*, near the jetty, and makes a great seafood blow-out!

Captain's Tavern (☎ *400800, Swakopmund Hotel & Entertainment Centre*) Seafood starters US$3-5, mains US$5-7. This place serves up a boggling variety of wonderful seafood dishes. It also does steak and chicken, but they're definitely the second string.

De Kelder (☎ *402433, 10 Moltke St*) Mains US$5.50-7. Open lunch & dinner Tues-Sat. This is the place for steaks, seafood, pasta and ostrich stroganoff.

Cafe Anton (☎ 402419, Hotel Schweizer-haus) This pretentious spot serves up legendary (albeit skimpy) coffee, *apfelstrüdel* (apple strudel), *kugelhopf* (cake with nuts and raisins), *mohnkuchen* (poppyseed cake), *linzertorte* (cake flavoured with almond meal, lemon and spices and spread with jam) and other European delights. The outdoor seating is inviting for afternoon snacks in the sun.

Self-caterers can head for the well-stocked *Woermann & Brock* and *Model/ Pick & Pay* supermarkets.

Entertainment

Pubs, Discos & Clubs There's some good pubs and bars in Swakopmund.

O'Kelly's (☎ 407100, e soepie@iafrica .com.na, Roon St) Open 9pm-late daily. O'Kelly's emphasises local music, dancing and billiards; this is the place to go when you 'don't want to go home and you're too drunk to care'.

Phumba's Sports Bar (☎ 402333, 5 Moltke St) Open 8pm-late daily. This place above the Oasis Bistro is the local hang-out for rugger, footy and draught beer fanatics.

Fagin's Pub (☎ 402360, Roon St) This extremely popular, down-to-earth watering hole near the Atlanta Hotel is reminiscent of a US truckies' stop, complete with a jocular staff, a faithful clientele and evening videos of your day's adrenaline activities. When we visited it was *the* place to drink in Swakopmund.

The Stage Night Club & Disco (☎ 402 039) Open 9pm-6am Wed, Fri & Sat. Young locals love this dancing venue, upstairs in the Hotel Grüner Kranz (see Places to Stay – Budget earlier).

Captain's Tavern Pub (Swakopmund Hotel & Entertainment Centre) This is more highbrow than other Swakopmund nightspots, and sometimes has live music.

African Cafe (Schlosser St) For decadence accompanied by sports events, this is the place to go. It's open whenever the owner takes a notion, especially for rugby and Formula 1 racing.

Diamond Jack's Jazz & Blues Club This is a jazz-oriented venue located at Papa's pizzeria (see Places to Eat earlier) that operates on some Friday nights.

Cinemas Now that the historic Atlanta Cinema has closed, filmgoers are limited to the new *Atlanta Cinema (Cooperative Bank Arcade)*.

Shopping

Street stalls sell Zimbabwean crafts on the waterfront by the steps below Cafe Anton.

Save the Rhino Trust Shop (☎/fax 403829, e srtrhino@iafrica.com.na, 3 Knobloch St, PO Box 224) Open 8am-1pm & 2pm-5pm Mon-Fri, 8am-1pm Sat. This charitable organisation sponsors lots of local environmental projects, including the Save the Rhino camp site by the Ugab River. It also sells a host of worthwhile local arts and crafts.

Karakulia Craft Centre (☎ 461415, fax 461041, e kararugs@iafrica.com.na, w www.karakulia.com.na, 3 Knobloch St, PO Box 1258) This local carpet factory produces original and beautiful African rugs, carpets and wall-hangings in karakul wool and offers tours of the spinning, dyeing and weaving processes. It's open the same hours as the Save the Rhino Trust.

Cobwebs (☎ 404024, fax 464195, e brig adon@iafrica.com.na, 10 Moltke St, PO Box 1930) This arts shop sells African masks, crafts and other traditional artefacts.

Swakopmund Tannery (☎ 402633, fax 404205, 7 Leutwein St, PO Box 92) Open 8am-1pm & 2pm-5.30pm Mon-Fri, 8am-12.30pm Sat. Swakopmund is well known for its hard-wearing kudu leather *veldskoene* shoes, or 'Swakopmunders', which sell for US$18 to US$25. You'll also find handbags, sandals, belts and other leather goods at excellent prices.

Peter's Antiques (☎/fax 405624, 24 Moltke St) This place is an Ali Baba's cave of treasures, specialising in colonial relics, historic literature, West African art, politically incorrect German paraphernalia and genuine West African fetishes and other artefacts from around the continent. It's a place that travellers love to hate, but many succumb to its wonders.

Getting There & Away

Air Air Namibia (☎ 405123, fax 402196) flies between Windhoek's Eros Airport and Swakopmund (US$83) at least once daily.

Bus From the Talk Shop Internet Cafe in Roon St, the Intercape Mainliner departs four times weekly for Windhoek (US$13, 4¼ hours), with connections to and from South Africa. Minibuses between Swakopmund and Windhoek (US$8, three hours) stop at the Engen petrol station in Vineta township. Phone Eddie (☎ 081-242 0077) and request a pick-up from your accommodation.

The Star Line bus between Walvis Bay and Otjiwarongo passes through Swakopmund (see Getting There & Away under Walvis Bay). Private transfers to Walvis Bay for day tours are available through African Wanderer (☎ 462427) for US$12 per person return.

Train Overnight trains connect Windhoek with Swakopmund (US$7.50, 12½ hours) and Walvis Bay (US$1, 2½ hours) daily except Saturday. Thrice-weekly trains between Walvis Bay and Tsumeb (US$6, 17½ hours) pass through Swakopmund. Phone Trans-Namib (☎ 463538) for more information.

See the Getting Around chapter for information on the plush *Desert Express* 'rail cruise' to and from Windhoek.

Hitching Hitching isn't difficult between Swakopmund and Windhoek or Walvis Bay, but conditions can be rough if heading for Namib-Naukluft Park or the Skeleton Coast; hitchers risk heatstroke, sandblasting and hypothermia – sometimes in the same day.

Getting Around

Taxis run to and from the airport but otherwise, you can walk just about anywhere in town. For car-hire agencies, see under Car & Motorcycle in the Getting Around chapter.

AROUND SWAKOPMUND
☎ 064

Camel Farm

Want to play Lawrence of Arabia in the Namib Desert? Then visit the Camel Farm (☎ 400363; open 3pm-5pm), 15km east of Swakopmund on the B2. Camel rides cost US$10 for 40 minutes. To book rides and arrange transport from town, phone Ms Elke Elb.

Swakopmund Asparagus Farm

You surely never thought that asparagus could be a tourist attraction, but Swakopmund's delicious green gold grows in the wildest desert and makes for an interesting quick visit and taste test. Area farmers are also experimenting with olives. To reach Swakopmund Asparagus Farm (☎ 405134), take the Windhoek road 11km east of town and turn off at El Jada. It's 4km from there.

The *Martin Luther*

In the desert 4km east of Swakopmund languishes a lonely and forlorn little steam locomotive. In 1896 the 14,000kg engine was imported to Namibia from Halberstadt, Germany, by 1st Lieutenant Edmund Troost of the Imperial Schutztruppe. It was intended to replace the ox wagons that until that time carried freight between Swakopmund and the interior. Unfortunately, the loco exceeded Swakopmund's unloading capacity and had to be taken to Walvis Bay. Then its inauguration was delayed for four months while the good Lieutenant Troost dealt with the Nama-Herero wars. Meanwhile, the engineer who was contracted to reveal its secrets and put it in working order had returned to Germany at the expiration of his five-month contract.

Once the engine was running, it survived just a couple of short trips inland before grinding to a halt within sight of Swakopmund. When it became apparent that this particular technology wasn't making life any easier for anyone, it was abandoned where it stood and dubbed the *Martin Luther*, in reference to the great reformer's 1521 speech to the ecumenical body, the Diet of Reichstag, in Worms (Germany): 'Here I stand. May God help me, I cannot do otherwise.' The *Martin Luther* was restored in 1975 and declared a national monument, but is again suffering the ravages of nature.

Rössing Mine

Rössing Mine (☎ 402046), 55km east of Swakopmund, is the world's largest open-cast uranium mine. Uranium was first discovered in the 1920s by Peter Louw, but his attempts at development failed. In 1965 the concession was transferred to Rio Tinto Zinc and comprehensive surveys determined that the formation measured 3km long and 1km wide. Ore extraction came on line in 1970 but didn't reach capacity for another eight years. The current scale of operations is staggering: at full capacity the mine produces one million tonnes of ore per week.

Rössing (an affiliate of Rio Tinto Zinc), with 2500 employees, is currently the major player in Swakopmund's economy. The affiliated Rössing Foundation provides an educational and training centre in Arandis, north-east of the mine, as well as medical facilities and housing for its Swakopmund-based workers. It has promised that the eventual decommissioning of the site will entail a massive clean-up, but you may want to temper your enthusiasm about its environmental commitments until something is actually forthcoming.

Rössing Mine Tours (US$2), which last 4½ hours, leave from Swakopmund's Cafe Anton at 8am on the first and third Fridays of the month; proceeds go to the Swakopmund Museum (see under Swakopmund earlier in this chapter). Book at the museum by Thursday afternoon.

Trekkopje

The military cemetery at Trekkopje (see the North Central Namibia map) is about 112km east of Swakopmund and 1km north of the B2. In January 1915, after Swakopmund was occupied by South African forces, the Germans retreated and cut off supplies to the city by damaging the Otavi and State railway lines. However, the South Africans had already begun to replace the narrow-gauge track with a standard-gauge one, and at Trekkopje, their crew met German forces. When the Germans attacked their camp on 26 April 1915, the South Africans defended themselves with guns mounted on armoured vehicles and won easily. All fatalities of this battle are interred in the Trekkopje cemetery, which is immediately north of the railway line, near the old train station.

Welwitschia Drive

The Welwitschia Drive, which turns off the Bosua Pass route east of Swakopmund, lies inside the Namib-Naukluft Park, but is most often visited as a day trip from Swakopmund. At the NWR office or Namib I (see Information under Swakopmund earlier), you can pick up entry permits and leaflets with numbered references to 'beacons' or points of interest along the route. The drive takes about four hours.

A highlight is the fields of **grey and black lichen**. This form of desert life, which appears to be a small dead bush, was featured in the BBC production *The Private Life of Plants*. It was here that David Attenborough presented these delightful examples of plant-animal symbiosis (see the boxed text 'Lichen Fields' in the North-Western Namibia chapter), which burst into 'bloom' with the addition of fog droplets. If you're not visiting during a fog, sprinkle a few drops of water on them and watch the magic.

Another interesting stop is the **Baaiweg (Bay Rd)**, the ox-wagon track that was historically used to move supplies between the coast and central Namibia. The tracks remain visible because the lichen that were destroyed when it was built have grown back at a rate of only 1mm per year, and the ruts aren't yet obscured.

Farther east is the **Moon Landscape**, a vista across eroded hills and valleys carved by the Swakop River. Here you may want to take a quick 12km return side trip north to the farm and oasis of **Goanikontes**, which dates from 1848. It lies beside the Swakop River amid fabulous desert mountains and makes a nice picnic site. There are also several shady camp sites and basic bungalows are available for reasonable prices.

To the east along the main loop is further evidence of human impact in the form of a **camp site** used by South African troops for a few days in 1915. They were clearly *not* minimum-impact campers!

Welwitschias

Among Namibia's many botanical curiosities, the extraordinary *Welwitschia mirabilis*, which exists only on the gravel plains of the northern Namib Desert from the Kuiseb River to southern Angola, is probably the strangest of all. It was first noted in 1859, when Austrian botanist and medical doctor Friedrich Welwitsch stumbled upon a large specimen east of Swakopmund. He suggested it be named *tumboa*, which was one of the local names for the plant, but the discovery was considered to be so important that it was named after him instead. More recently, the Afrikaners have dubbed it *twee-blaarkanniedood* or 'two-leaf can't die', which is, more than anything else, a reference to its longevity.

Welwitschias reach their greatest concentrations on the Welwitschia Plains east of Swakopmund, near the confluence of the Khan and Swakop Rivers, where they're the dominant plant species. Although these plants are the ugly ducklings of the vegetable world, they've adapted well to their harsh habitat. It was once thought that the plant had a tap root down through clay pipes to access the water table 100m or more beneath the surface. In fact, the root is never more than 3m long and it's now generally accepted that, although the plant gets some water from underground sources, most of its moisture is derived from condensed fog. Pores in the leaves trap moisture and longer leaves actually water the plant's own roots by channelling droplets onto the surrounding sand.

Despite their dishevelled appearance, welwitschias actually have only two long and leathery leaves, which grow from opposite sides of the cork-like stem. Over the years, these leaves are darkened in the sun and torn by the wind into tattered strips, causing the plant to resemble a giant wilted lettuce.

Strangely, welwitschias are considered to be trees and are related to conifers, specifically pines, but they also share some characteristics of flowering plants and club mosses. Females bear the larger greenish-yellow to brown cones, which contain the plant's seeds, while the males have more cones, but they're smaller and salmon-coloured. They're a dioeceous species, meaning that male and female plants are distinct, but their exact method of pollination remains in question. It's thought that the large sticky pollen grains are carried by insects, specifically wasps.

Welwitschias have a slow rate of growth, and it's believed that the largest ones, whose tangled masses of leaf strips can measure up to 2m across, may have been growing for up to 2000 years! However, most mid-sized plants are less than 1000 years old. The plants don't even flower until they've been growing for at least 20 years. This longevity is probably only possible because they contain some compounds that are unpalatable to grazing animals, although black rhinos have been known to enjoy the odd plant.

The plants' most prominent inhabitant is the yellow and black pyrrhocorid bug (*Probergrothius sexpunctatis*), which lives by sucking sap from the plant. It's commonly called the push-me-pull-you bug, due to its almost continuous back-to-back mating.

DENNIS JONES

The welwitschia survives in areas with little to no rainfall.

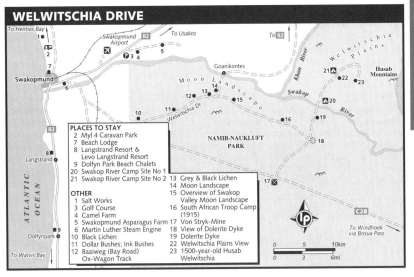

WELWITSCHIA DRIVE

PLACES TO STAY
2 Myl 4 Caravan Park
7 Beach Lodge
8 Langstrand Resort & Levo Langstrand Resort
9 Dolfyn Park Beach Chalets
20 Swakop River Camp Site No 1
21 Swakop River Camp Site No 2

OTHER
1 Salt Works
3 Golf Course
4 Camel Farm
5 Swakopmund Asparagus Farm
6 Martin Luther Steam Engine
10 Black Lichen
11 Dollar Bushes; Ink Bushes
12 Baaiweg (Bay Road) Ox-Wagon Track
13 Grey & Black Lichen
14 Moon Landscape
15 Overview of Swakop Valley Moon Landscape
16 South African Troop Camp (1915)
17 Von Stryk-Mine
18 View of Dolerite Dyke
19 Dolerite Dyke
22 Welwitschia Plains View
23 1500-year-old Husab Welwitschia

A few kilometres beyond the South African Troop Camp, the route turns north. Shortly thereafter, you'll approach a prominent black **dolerite dyke** splitting a ridgetop. This was created when molten igneous material forced its way up through a crack in the overlying granite and cooled.

Camping at the *Welwitschia Camp Sites* costs US$10 for two people plus US$2 for each additional person. These sites, near the Swakop River crossing on the Welwitschia Plains detour, are each available to one party of up to eight people. Book through NWR (see Information under Swapokmund earlier) in Windhoek or Swakopmund.

Salt Works
Originally, the site of the salt works (☎ 402611, 404015), north of Myl 4 Caravan Park, was one of many low salty depressions along the desert coast, but in 1933 the Klein family began extracting salt. When it ran out 20 years later, they excavated a series of shallow evaporation pans to concentrate and extract the minerals. Now, water is pumped into the pans directly from the sea and the onshore breeze provides an ideal catalyst for evaporation.

Water is moved through the several pans over a period of 12 to 18 months. The water-borne minerals are concentrated by evaporation and eventually crystals of sodium chloride and other salts develop. Thanks to the variety of algae in the mineral soup that's created at the various stages of desalination, each pond takes on a different brilliant colour: purple, red, orange, yellow and even greenish hues. From aloft, they take on the appearance of a colourful stained-glass window.

Thanks to the sheltered environment, the ponds provide a habitat for small fish, and for the flamingoes, avocets, sandpipers, teals, grebes, gulls, cormorants, terns and other endemic birds that feed on them. The Kleins have now registered the site as a private bird reserve, and they've also erected a large wooden platform – an artificial island – which is used by cormorants as a breeding site. After the breeding season, scrapers are sent onto the platform to collect the guano deposits.

Another peripheral enterprise is the **Richwater Oyster Company**, which was established in 1985 when 500,000 oysters were brought from the island of Guernsey in the

English Channel. The oyster farm occupies the first pan reached by the sea water.

The 1½-hour tours of the salt works and the oyster farm run from Monday to Friday; bookings are essential.

WALVIS BAY
☎ 064

Architecturally uninspiring Walvis Bay (pronounced '**vahl**-fis bay') is situated about 30km south of Swakopmund and has a sort of other-worldly charm, which may elude some visitors. Its superb natural harbour is created by the sandspit Pelican Point, which forms a natural breakwater and therefore creates the only decent port between Lüderitz and Luanda.

Until recently, Walvis Bay's claim to fame was a clutch of fish canneries. Now a busy port with 40,000 people, this modern city boasts a tanker berth, a dry dock and facilities to load and unload container ships. It also has a salt works and a fish-processing industry.

History
Portuguese navigator Bartolomeu Dias sailed into Walvis Bay in the *São Cristóvão* on 8 December 1487 and named it Bahia de Santa Maria da Conceição, but later, it came to be known as Bahia das Baleias, the 'Bay of Whales'. However, a lack of fresh water meant that this excellent natural harbour lay forgotten for the next 300 years.

From 1784, American whalers began operating in the area, calling it simply Whale Bay. Word got out that rich pickings were to be had and on 23 January 1793 the Dutch vessel *Meermin* arrived from the Cape to annex the bay and translate its name into Dutch: Walvisbaai. This sparked off a 200-year game of political football with the 1124 sq km enclave.

In 1795, when the Cape Colony was taken over by the British, Captain Alexander of the British fleet went north and claimed Walvis Bay for Britain. He hoped to ensure safe passage for vessels around the Cape.

Around the mid-1840s, Nama leader Jan Jonker Afrikaner constructed a trail to transport Matchless Mine copper to the port in

Walvis Bay. By 1878, after it was realised that Germany had its eye on Walvis Bay, the port was formally annexed by Britain and six years later, attached to the Cape Colony. In 1910 it became part of the Union of South Africa. When the Germans were defeated after WWI, South Africa was given the United Nations (UN) mandate to administer all of German South-West Africa and the Walvis Bay enclave was transferred to the mandate. This stood until 1977, when South Africa unilaterally decided to return it to the Cape Province. The UN wasn't impressed by this unauthorised act and insisted that the enclave be returned to the mandate immediately, but South Africa steadfastly refused to bow.

When Namibia achieved its independence in 1990, its new constitution included Walvis Bay as part of its territory, but the South Africans stubbornly held their grip. Given the strategic value of the natural harbour, plus the salt works (which produced 40,000 tonnes annually – 90% of South Africa's salt), the offshore guano platforms and the rich fishery, control over Walvis Bay became a matter of great importance for Namibia.

In 1992, after it had became apparent that white rule in South Africa was ending, the two countries agreed that South Africa would remove its border posts and that both countries would jointly administer the enclave. Finally, facing growing domestic troubles and its first democratic elections, South Africa gave in and at midnight on 28 February 1994 the South African flag was lowered for the last time, and the Namibian flag was raised.

Orientation
Walvis Bay is laid out in a grid pattern. Although some streets are now being renamed for South-West Africa People's Organization (Swapo) luminaries, the *streets* in Walvis Bay, from 1st to 15th, run north-east to south-west, while the *roads*, from 1st to 18th, run north-west to south-east. At times this does get confusing. North of town along the coast are the small holiday settlements of Dolfynpark and Langstrand.

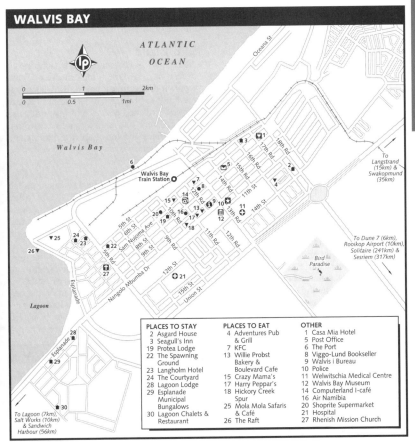

WALVIS BAY

ATLANTIC OCEAN

Oceana St

Walvis Bay

Walvis Bay Train Station

To Langstrand (15km) & Swakopmund (35km)

To Dune 7 (6km), Rooikop Airport (10km), Solitaire (241km) & Sesriem (317km)

Bird Paradise

Lagoon

Esplanade

Nangolo Mbumba Dr

Sam Nujoma Ave

To Lagoon (7km), Salt Works (10km) & Sandwich Harbour (56km)

PLACES TO STAY	PLACES TO EAT	OTHER
2 Asgard House	4 Adventures Pub	1 Casa Mia Hotel
3 Seagull's Inn	& Grill	5 Post Office
19 Protea Lodge	7 KFC	6 The Port
22 The Spawning	13 Willie Probst	8 Viggo-Lund Bookseller
Ground	Bakery &	9 Walvis i Bureau
23 Langholm Hotel	Boulevard Cafe	10 Police
24 The Courtyard	15 Crazy Mama's	11 Welwitschia Medical Centre
28 Lagoon Lodge	17 Harry Peppar's	12 Walvis Bay Museum
29 Esplanade	18 Hickory Creek	14 Computerland I-café
Municipal	Spur	16 Air Namibia
Bungalows	25 Mola Mola Safaris	20 Shoprite Supermarket
30 Lagoon Chalets &	& Café	21 Hospital
Restaurant	26 The Raft	27 Rhenish Mission Church

Information

Tourist Offices The very helpful Walvis i Bureau (☎ 209170, fax 209171), at 24 12th Rd, is open 9am to 5pm Monday to Friday and 9am to 1pm Saturday. Namib-Naukluft Park permits are available both here and at most Walvis Bay petrol stations.

Money Along the main street, Sam Nujoma Ave, are several banks, offering foreign exchange, and also a BOB automatic teller.

Post & Communications The post office on Sam Nujoma Ave provides public telephones and fax services. For email and Internet access, go to the Computerland I-café on Sam Nujoma Ave.

Bookshops The Viggo-Lund Bookseller on Sam Nujoma Ave is the only bookshop around, but don't expect much.

Laundry The Super Laundrette (☎ 209697), situated beside the CWB petrol station on Sam Nujoma Ave, is open from 8am to 8pm daily. Walvis Bay Laundry (☎ 202679), on 275 9th St, offers both laundry and dry-cleaning services.

CENTRAL NAMIB DESERT

Emergency Emergency services include the following:

Ambulance	☎ 205443
Fire Brigade	☎ 203117
Med-Rescue	☎ 200200
Police	☎ 10111
Welwitschia Hospital	☎ 207207

Walvis Bay Museum

The town museum *(Nangolo Mbumba Dr; admission free; open 9am-12.30pm & 3pm-4.30pm Mon-Fri)* is in the library. It concentrates on the history and maritime background of Walvis Bay, but also has archaeological exhibits, a mineral collection and natural history displays on the Namib Desert and the Atlantic Coast.

Rhenish Mission Church

Walvis Bay's oldest remaining building, the Rhenish Mission Church *(5th Rd)* was prefabricated in Hamburg, Germany, and reconstructed beside the harbour in 1880. Services were first held the following year. Because of machinery sprawl in the harbour area, it was relocated to its present site in the mid-20th century. It functioned as a church until 1966.

Bird Island

Along the Swakopmund road, 10km north of Walvis Bay, take a look at the offshore wooden platform known as Bird Island. It was built to provide a roost and nesting site for sea birds and a source of guano for use as fertiliser. The annual yield is around 1000 tonnes and the smell from the island is memorable.

The Railway

During the winter, rail services between Swakopmund and Walvis Bay are often plagued by windblown sand, which covers the tracks and undermines the track bed and sleepers. This isn't a new problem – 5km east of town on the C14, notice the embankment which has interred a section of narrow-gauge track from the last century. In front of the train station are the remains of the *Hope*, an old locomotive that once ran on the original narrow-gauge railway. Both were abandoned after the line was repeatedly buried beneath 10m sand drifts. The *Hope* is now a

---

Flamingoes

Flamingoes flock in large numbers to pools along the Namib Desert coast, particularly around Walvis Bay and Lüderitz. They're excellent fliers and have been known to migrate up to 500km overnight, following proliferations of algae and crustaceans not just along this barren coastline but all over Southern and Eastern Africa – including Etosha Pan, the Nata Delta on Botswana's Sua Pan, and the soda lakes of Kenya's Great Rift Valley.

Flamingoes have a complicated and sophisticated system for filtering the foodstuffs from highly alkaline – and toxic – soda lakes, seawater and brackish pans. The lesser flamingo filters algae and diatoms (microscopic organisms) from the water by sucking in and vigorously expelling water from its bill – which is held upside down in the water – several times per second. The minute particles are caught on fine hair-like protrusions which line the inside of the mandibles. The suction is created by the thick fleshy tongue, which rests in a groove in the lower mandible and pumps back and forth like a piston. It has been estimated that a million lesser flamingoes can consume over 180 tonnes of algae and diatoms daily.

While lesser flamingoes obtain food by filtration, the greater flamingo supplements its algae diet with small molluscs, crustaceans and other organic particles from the mud. When feeding, it will rotate in a circle stamping its feet, apparently to scare up a tasty potential meal.

The greater and lesser flamingoes are best distinguished by their colouration. Greater flamingoes are white to light pink, and their beaks are whitish with a black tip. Lesser flamingoes are a deeper pink – often reddish – colour, with dark-red beaks.

national monument and stands on 6th St in front of the train station.

The Port

With permission from the public relations officer of the Portnet (☎ 208320) or from the Railway Police, beside the train station at the end of 13th Rd, you can visit the fishing harbour and commercial port and see the heavy machinery that keeps Namibia's import-export business ticking. It's more interesting than it sounds. Take your passport.

Dune 7

In the bleak expanse just off the C14 7km by road from town, Dune 7 is popular with locals as a slope for sandboarding and skiing. The picnic site, which is now being engulfed by sand, has several shady palm trees tucked away in the lee of the dune. Water is sometimes available.

Nature Reserves

Three diverse wetland areas – the lagoon, the salt works and the Bird Paradise at the sewage works – together form Southern Africa's single most important coastal wetland for migratory birds. Up to 150,000 transient avian visitors stop by annually. Be sure to check out the birdlife information kiosk near the Esplanade Municipal Bungalows (see Places to Stay – Mid-Range later).

Lagoon The shallow and sheltered 45,000-hectare lagoon, south-west of town and west of the Kuiseb River mouth, attracts a range of coastal water birds and supports half the flamingo population of Southern Africa. You may also see chestnut banded plovers and curlew sandpipers, as well as other migrants and waders. It's also a permanent home of the rare Damara tern.

Salt Works South-west of the lagoon is the Walvis Bay salt works (☎ 202304). As with the one in Swakopmund, these pans concentrate salt from seawater with the aid of evaporation. The 3500-hectare salt-pan complex currently supplies over 90% of South Africa's salt. Phone to arrange the 1½-hour tour.

Bird Paradise Immediately east of town at the municipal sewage purification works is the nature sanctuary known as Bird Paradise, which consists of a series of shallow artificial pools, fringed by reeds. An observation tower and a short nature walk afford excellent bird-watching. It lies 500m east of town, off the C14 towards Rooikop airport.

Rooibank

Rooibank, at the south-eastern corner of the former Walvis Bay enclave, is named for a cluster of red granite outcrops on the northern bank of the Kuiseb River. This area is best known as the site of one of Namibia's few Topnaar Khoi-Khoi settlements. Notice the unusual vegetation, which includes the fleshy succulent dollar bush *(Zygophyllum stapffii)* and the !nara bush (see the boxed text '!Nara Melons'), a leafless plant that bears the spiky !nara melons, which are still a staple for the Topnaar Khoi-Khoi people.

To the east of Rooibank, 1.5km upstream towards **Scheppmansdorp**, is a marked 3km walking track which will take you along the sandy riverbed to some picturesque dunes. At Scheppmansdorp itself, a monument marks the site of the 1846 church built by the missionary Scheppman.

Organised Tours

The Spawning Ground (See Places to Stay – Budget) Wayne Hull here organises backpacker day tours. These take in the Walvis Bay Lagoon, Dune 7, and Bird Paradise (US$16); Pelican Point and the oyster farm (US$40); the Moon Landscape and Welwitschia Drive (US$38); Cape Cross (US$43, including fishing); and Sandwich Harbour (US$40).

Mola Mola Safaris (☎ 205511, fax 207593, e mola-mola@iafrica.com.na, w www.mola-mola.com.na, Cnr Esplanade & Atlantic St, PO Box 980) This group operates half-day seal and dolphin cruises (US$40), all-day Sandwich Harbour tours (US$91), shark-fishing (US$76) and angling at Henties Bay (US$300 per day for two people). Trips depart from its office at the yacht club.

Levo Tours (See Places to Stay – Mid-Range) Seal- and dolphin-watching tours

CENTRAL NAMIB DESERT

!Nara Melons

Historically, human existence in the Namib has been made possible by an unusual spiny plant, the !nara melon (*Acanthosicyos horrida*). It was first described taxonomically by the same Friedrich Welwitsch who gave his name to the welwitschia plant.

Although the !nara bush lives and grows in the desert – and lacks leaves to prevent water loss through transpiration – it is not a desert plant. Its moisture is taken from the groundwater table via a long tap root to derive moisture from underground sources and thereby monitors underground water tables: when the plants are healthy, so is the water supply! Its lack of leaves also protects it from grazing animals, although ostriches do nip off its tender growing shoots.

As with the welwitschia, the male and female sex organs in the !nara melon exist in separate plants. Male plants flower throughout the year, but it's the female plant that produces the 15cm melon each summer, providing a favourite meal for jackals, insects and humans. Indeed, it remains a primary food of the Topnaar Khoi-Khoi people and has also become a local commercial enterprise. Each year at harvest time, the Topnaar erect camps around the Kuiseb Delta to collect the fruits. Although melons can be eaten raw, most people prefer to dry them for later use, or prepare, package and ship them to urban markets.

with this outfit attached to Levo Langstrand Resort cost US$35; beach fishing or bottom-fishing for kabeljou and copper sharks is around US$60.

Eco-Marine Kayak Tours (☎/fax 203144, e jeannem@iafrica.com.na, w www.gateway-africa.com/kayak/index.html, PO Box 225) 3-/5-hour tours US$14/38. You can choose between paddles to shipwrecks, Pelican Point, Bird Island, seal- and dolphin-watching spots and the oyster farm.

Activities

At Langstrand, you can participate in a growing list of adrenaline activities, including sandboarding, quadbiking and parasailing. For more details, see Activities under Swakopmund, or visit the Swakopmund Adventure Centre (see earlier in this chapter).

Places to Stay – Budget

The Spawning Ground (☎ 205121, 081-127 7636, e spawning@iafrica.com.na, 55 6th St, PO Box 2934) Camping US$4.50 per person, dorm beds US$6. This must be Namibia's most oddly named accommodation, and no, it's not a brothel, but a very agreeable backpacker lodge. It adds a welcome bright splash of colour in an otherwise drab part of town. Note the chunky beds, which are made of salvaged wood from the old jetty.

Langstrand Resort (☎ 203134) Camping US$8 per site plus US$1 per person, 2-/4-bed bungalows US$27/39. This otherworldly place lies 15km north-east of town and looks like a desert mirage, especially in a fog or sandstorm. The restaurant has a good reputation; you can poke around tide pools and swim in the pool or from the jetty.

Places to Stay – Mid-Range

Levo Langstrand Resort (☎ 207555, 081-129 6270, e levo@namibnet.com, w www.levotours.com, Langstrand, PO Box 1860) 4-/6-bed self-catering units US$34/60. This comfortable place sits right on the beach at Langstrand, but oddly it doesn't take advantage of its potential sea views.

Seagull's Inn (☎ 202775, fax 202455, 215 Sam Nujoma Ave) Singles/doubles B&B US$17/27. This basic motel-style place is nothing special, but the prices are right.

Asgard House (☎ 209595, fax 209596, e asgard@iway.na, w www.gateway-africa.com/asgard, 72 17th Rd, PO Box 1300) Singles/doubles US$30/39. This is a homely little family-run guesthouse with a beautiful lounge, a garden and a frog pond (the frogs do their bit by eating the mosquitoes). It's friendly and recommended.

The Courtyard (☎ 206252, fax 207271, e courtyrd@iafrica.com.na, 16 3rd Rd, PO Box 3493) Doubles US$47. Guests of this spotlessly clean hotel have access to the pool, sauna, braai (barbecue) facilities and bright spacious garden.

Langholm Hotel (☎ 207666, fax 209430, e langholm@iafrica.com.na, W www.lang holm.com.na, 24 2nd St) Doubles B&B with TV US$47. This place is white, bright, airy and quiet.

Esplanade Municipal Bungalows (☎ 206145, fax 209714, e gkruger@walvis baycc.or.na, Esplanade, PO Box 86) 5-/7-bed self-catering bungalows US$34/40. This quiet complex of very large units between the dunes and the lagoon is near the sea wall, west of the town centre.

Lagoon Chalets & Restaurant (☎ 207151, fax 207469, e lagoonch@mweb.com.na, W www.lagoonchalets.com.na, Cnr 8th & 7th Rds, PO Box 2318) Camping US$11-14, 6-bed self-catering chalets US$32. The more-expensive camp sites have private cooking and washing facilities. This place is best known for its bar and seafood restaurant.

Dolfynpark Beach Chalets (☎ 204343, fax 209714, e gkruger@walvisbaycc.org .na, Dolphin Park) 4-bed self-catering chalets US$31. This beach lodge 12km north of town has a swimming pool and water park. You couldn't imagine a structure more alien to its setting than this. Kids will love the pool and 'hydro-slide'.

Protea Lodge (☎ 209560, fax 209565, e bay@iafrica.com.na, W www.proteahotels .com, Cnr Sam Nujoma Ave & 10th Rd, PO Box 30) Singles/doubles from US$46/52. This plush central place is the business traveller's hotel.

Lagoon Lodge (☎ 200850, fax 200851, e meiller@iafrica.com.na, W www.namib web.net/lagoonlodge, 2 Nangolo Mbumba Dr, PO Box 3964) Singles/doubles US$56/88. This very yellow French-run lodge enjoys a great setting beside the lagoon.

Places to Eat

Crazy Mama's (☎ 207364, Cnr Sam Nujoma Ave & 11th Rd) Pizzas US$3.50-5.50, mains US$3-6. Open for lunch & dinner Tues-Sun. This excellent choice features great service and atmosphere, the prices are right and it serves fabulous pizzas, salads and vegetarian options, among other things.

The Raft (☎ 204877, Esplanade) Mains US$5-10. Open for lunch & dinner daily. The wonderful and popular Raft, which sits on stilts offshore and looks more like a porcupine than a raft, serves indescribably fine fare; highly recommended are the hunters venison (ostrich and oryx stir-fry), the Greek salad and the vegetable skewer (kebab). You'll also have a great front-row view of the ducks, pelicans and flamingoes that inhabit the lagoon.

Harry Peppar's (☎ 203131, Cnr 11th Rd & Nangolo Mbumba Dr) Pizzas US$2.50-5. Open 11am-11pm daily. Harry comes up with all sorts of creative thick-crust pizzas. Delivery is free anywhere in town.

Mola-Mola Café (☎ 205511, Cnr Esplanade & Atlantic St) Coffee & snacks US$1-3. Open 10am-5pm daily. This cafe in the Mola-Mola Safaris office sells coffee, cakes and light meals.

Hickory Creek Spur (☎ 207991, 9th St) Mains US$3-6. Open 11am-2am daily. The ubiquitous South African chain specialising in steak has a recommended salad bar.

Adventures Pub & Grill (☎ 206803, 230 12th St) Pub meals US$3-4. Open 10am-very late daily. This laid-back place serves not only as a pub, but also a coffee shop and takeaway. You'll get traditional Namibian fare, as well as *potjies* (traditional stew cooked outdoors in a three-legged iron pot), braais and of course beer and pool tables. It's also a popular night spot.

Willie Probst Bakery & Boulevard Cafe (☎ 202744, Cnr 12th Rd & 9th St) Lunch US$2.50-6, takeaways US$1.50-3. Open for lunch & dinner Tues-Sun. This very bright place is always crowded at lunch hour; it specialises in stodgy German fare: pork, meatballs, schnitzel and the like.

Lagoon Restaurant (☎ 209412, Cnr 7th & 8th Rds) Starters US$2.50-3, mains US$4-10. Open noon-2.30pm & 6pm-10.30pm Mon-Sat, 5pm-10pm Sun. Here you'll find a large menu of mainly steak and fresh seafood. Book 24 hours in advance for fondue, potjie, seafood paella or game steaks.

KFC (☎ 206703, Sam Nujoma Ave) For fast food, you could head for the colonel's place.

Shoprite supermarket (Sam Nujoma Ave) This is the best self-catering option.

Entertainment

When the sun goes down, Walvis Bay rolls up its streets for the evening, and people seem too lethargic to care much. There are, however, a couple of things to do at night – and that's in addition to uncorking a bottle of booze or downing a six-pack of lager in one sitting.

Plaza Cinema (☎ 204027, Nangolo Mbumba Dr) The cinema shows films nightly; it also has a bar.

Adventures Pub & Grill (See Places to Eat) Open 10am-late daily. This popular travellers pub does meals. You can spend the evenings playing pool or darts; it also stages discos and live entertainment. Phone to see what's on.

Casa Mia Hotel (☎ 205975) This place has two bars: the Nautilus Bar and the more intimate Captain Simon's.

Getting There & Away

Air Air Namibia (☎ 203102) flies twice weekly between both of Windhoek's airports and Walvis Bay's Rooikop Airport (US$83), 10km south-east of town on the C14.

Bus Intercape Mainliner has four buses weekly between Windhoek and Walvis Bay (US$16, five hours), via Swakopmund. It stops at the Omega petrol station on the corner of Sam Nujoma Ave and 15th Rd. Minibuses run occasionally to Swakopmund and some continue to Windhoek.

Star Line's bus between Walvis Bay and Mariental, via Büllsport and Maltahöhe, operates only every second week. Its Friday bus to Otjiwarongo (US$13, 11 hours) passes through Swakopmund (US$1.75, one hour), Henties Bay (US$2.50, 2½ hours), Khorixas (US$8, eight hours) and Outjo (US$11.50, 9½ hours); it comes from Otjiwarongo on Thursdays. Book Star Line buses at the train station (☎ 208504).

Train The overnight rail service to Windhoek (US$10, 12 hours) leaves daily except Saturday at 7pm. On Tuesday, Thursday and Sunday northbound, it leaves for Tsumeb (US$12, 17½ hours) at 4.15pm, meeting a train from Windhoek at Kranzberg, where they add/exchange cars. For rail information, phone Trans-Namib (☎ 208504).

Getting Around

Minibus taxis operate around town, to the townships and to outlying areas, including the airport.

Namib-Naukluft Park

The present boundaries of Namib-Naukluft Park, one of the world's largest national parks, were established in 1978 by merging the Namib Desert Park and the Naukluft Mountain Zebra Park with parts of Diamond Area 1 and bits of surrounding government land. Today, it takes in over 23,000 sq km of desert and semidesert, including the diverse habitats of the Namib Desert Park between the Kuiseb and Swakop Rivers, the Naukluft (formerly the Naukluft Mountain Zebra Park), the high dunefield at Sossusvlei and the bird lagoon at Sandwich Harbour. (It also includes the Welwitschia Drive area, which is covered under Around Swakopmund, earlier in this chapter.)

The Namib Desert is one of the oldest and driest deserts in the world. As with the Atacama in northern Chile, it is the result of a cold current – in this case, the Benguela Current – sweeping north from Antarctica, which captures and condenses humid air that would otherwise be blown ashore. Its western strip is a sea of sand comprised mainly of apricot-coloured dunes interspersed with dry pans, of which Sossusvlei is the best known. This normally dusty pan is surrounded by 300m dunes, but on the rare occasions when the Tsauchab River flows, Sossusvlei fills with water and attracts gemsboks, springboks, ostriches and aquatic birds.

In the north, the dunes end abruptly at the Kuiseb River and the Namib takes on a different character: a landscape of endless grey-white gravel plains specked with isolated kopjes (small hills). It supports gemsboks, springboks and mountain zebras, as well as the bizarre welwitschia plants, whose only source of moisture is dew and fog. Historically, the region was also home to desert elephants and black rhinos, but these are now gone and attempts to reintroduce them have met with failure. The park's eastern extreme culminates in the dramatic Naukluft Massif, which is characterised by a high plateau bounded by gorges, caves and springs cut deeply from dolomite formations.

ORIENTATION & INFORMATION

Most of the main park roads are open to 2WD vehicles, but the minor roads are in poor condition and services are few. You don't need a permit to transit on the main routes – the C28, the C14, the D1982 or the D1998 – but to turn off onto minor roads, use picnic sites or visit sites of interest, you need a park permit. These cost US$3 per vehicle and US$3 per person (both fees are per day) at NWR offices in Windhoek or Swakopmund, at Sesriem, and at several after-hours petrol stations in Swakopmund and Walvis Bay.

Accommodation in the park is limited to a handful of exclusive Namib Desert Park camp sites and the camping grounds at Sesriem and Naukluft, but numerous private lodges and camping grounds are dotted around the park perimeter.

SANDWICH HARBOUR

Sandwich Harbour, 50km south of Walvis Bay, historically served as a commercial fishing and trading port, and indeed, the name may well be derived from an English whaler, the *Sandwich*, which operated in the mid-1780s. It's thought that the captain of this ship produced the first map of this coastline. (However, the name may also be a corruption of the German word *sandfische*, a type of shark often found here.)

Although it's now a total wilderness, Sandwich Harbour has historically hosted various enterprises, from fish processing and shark-oil extraction to sealing and guano collection. In the late 1800s the southern end of the lagoon even supported an extensive abattoir, which was set up by some enlightened soul who'd taken up the

Sandwiched Treasure

Local legend has it that over 200 years ago, a ship carrying a cargo of gold, precious stones and ivory intended as a gift from Lord Clive to the Moghul emperor was stranded at Sandwich Harbour en route to India. It's believed that the cargo, which, at the time, was valued at UK£6 million, lies somewhere beneath the towering dunes. However, not a trace of it has yet been found – and not for lack of searching.

notion of driving cattle over the dunes to the harbour for slaughter and export. All that remains of these efforts is an early- to mid-1900s hut used for guano collection, a rusting barge, a graveyard and some wooden beams from the abattoir.

The site is open 6am to 8pm daily; however, there are no facilities for visitors.

The Wetlands

Anichab, at the northern end of the reserve, lies 3.5km south of the angling concession car park. This area is characterised by a series of wetland pools filled from both the sea and the Anichab freshwater springs (created by water percolating through the dunefield from the Kuiseb River, 40km to the north). The name Anichab is derived from the Nama word for 'Spring Water' and under normal conditions, the Anichab springs reduce the salinity of the wetland area and make it amenable to salt-tolerant freshwater bird species. In the past, these reed-filled pools provided sustenance and nesting sites for an astonishing variety of waterbirds – 100 species in all and numbers up to 150,000.

Through the 1990s, however, the sand encroached on the southern part of the lagoon, causing the sandspit that protects the wetlands to recede. This in turn widened the area open to the sea, and the increased wave action built a beach along the eastern shore of the lagoon. With more sediment pouring in, the lagoon became shallower and saltier, and the northern sand spit sheltering the lagoon moved inland. This rendered it less appealing to the enormous flocks it once attracted, but that process now appears to have reversed – the lagoon is again growing and the birds are returning.

Topnaar 4WD Trail

The new 4WD trail that extends from Walvis Bay through the sand sea to Sandwich Harbour, Conception Bay and the fabulous *Edward Bolen* shipwreck creates a new level of challenge for 4WD enthusiasts. Only guided trips are available and while you can use a private vehicle, the very tough nature of the route lends itself to renting a Uri (a desert-adapted vehicle that is produced in Namibia). Currently, a six-day camping trip covering the entire route costs US$687 per person in your own vehicle and US$914 in a rented Uri. Other options that cover parts of the route start at US$327/540 in a private/rented vehicle.

Book tours through the Windhoek-based Tourist Junction (☎ 061-231246, fax 231703, ℮ info.tjunction@galileosa.co.za or info .riztours@galileosa.co.za, ⓦ www.tourist junction.com.na), PO Box 1591, Windhoek.

Getting There & Away

Several Swakopmund and Walvis Bay companies offer day trips to Sandwich Harbour (see Organised Tours under Swakopmund and Walvis Bay, earlier in this chapter).

Otherwise, you can take your own very sturdy high-clearance 4WD vehicle. Follow the left fork 5km south of Walvis Bay and when the road splits at the salt works, bear left again and continue across the marshy Kuiseb Delta. After 15km, you must show your park permit to enter the Namib-Naukluft Park.

For the final 20km into Sandwich Harbour you can either continue straight along the sandy beach (time your journey for low tide) or bear left past the control post and follow the tracks further inland. However, dune shifts may present tedious stretches of deep sand or alter the route entirely. Bring a shovel, tow rope and a couple of planks for unbogging.

For US$100, Mola-Mola Safaris in Walvis Bay will provide a day guide who will ride along and help you through this difficult route.

Vehicles aren't permitted beyond the car park at the southern limit of the angling concession, 3.5km north of MET's Anichab hut.

NAMIB DESERT PARK

The relatively accessible Namib Desert Park lies between the canyons of the Kuiseb River in the south and the Swakop River in the north. Although it does include a small area of linear dunes, it's characterised mostly by broad gravel plains punctuated by abrupt and imposing ranges of hills, many of which appear to have been moulded from chocolate or caramel.

Although this region doesn't support an abundance of large mammals, there is wildlife about. Along the road, you may see gemsboks, springboks and baboons, and dassies like to bask in the sun on the kopjes. The Kuiseb Canyon, on the Gamsberg Pass route between Windhoek and Walvis Bay, is also home to klipspringers and even leopards. Spotted hyenas are often heard at night and jackals make a good living from the herds of springboks on the plains.

For information on Welwitschia Drive, which is most often visited as a day trip from Swakopmund, see Around Swakopmund earlier in this chapter.

Kuiseb Canyon

The dramatic Kuiseb Canyon is on the Gamsberg Pass route west of the Khomas Hochland (see earlier in this chapter). For much of the year, the ephemeral Kuiseb River is no more than a broad sandy riverbed. It may flow for two or three weeks a year; it only gets as far as Gobabeb and seeps into the sand before reaching the sea. At Rooibank, drinking water for Walvis Bay is pumped from this subterranean supply.

It was here that geologists Henno Martin and Hermann Korn went into hiding for three years during WWII, as recounted in Martin's book *The Sheltering Desert*. The canyon's upper reaches are uninhabited, but where the valley broadens out, scattered Topnaar Khoi-Khoi villages occupy the north bank.

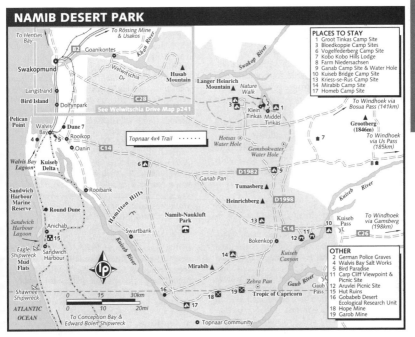

NAMIB DESERT PARK

PLACES TO STAY
1 Groot Tinkas Camp Site
3 Bloedkoppie Camp Sites
6 Vogelfederberg Camp Site
7 Kobo Kobo Hills Lodge
8 Farm Niedersachsen
9 Ganab Camp Site & Water Hole
10 Kuiseb Bridge Camp Site
13 Kriess-se-Rus Camp Site
14 Mirabib Camp Site
17 Homeb Camp Site

OTHER
2 German Police Graves
4 Walvis Bay Salt Works
5 Bird Paradise
11 Carp Cliff Viewpoint & Picnic Site
12 Aruvlei Picnic Site
15 Hut Ruins
16 Gobabeb Desert Ecological Research Unit
18 Hope Mine
19 Garob Mine

Gobabeb Desert Ecological Research Unit

Gobabeb, the 'Place of Figs', west of Homeb, is the site of the Desert Ecological Research Unit of the Desert Research Foundation of Namibia. This complex of laboratories, research facilities and a weather station was established in 1963 by South African researcher Dr Charles Koch and appropriately sits at the transition between the Namib's three ecosystems: the gravel plains, the sand dune sea and the Kuiseb Valley.

The centre isn't normally open to the public, but it does hold one or two 'open days' each year, which feature self-guided nature trails, lectures and field demonstrations, as well as educational demonstrations by the local Topnaar community. For specific dates contact the Director, Desert Ecological Research Unit, PO Box 1592, Swakopmund, or the Friends of Gobabeb Society, Desert Research Foundation, PO Box 37, Windhoek.

Hamilton Mountains

The range of limestone hills known as the Hamilton Mountains, south of Vogelfederberg, rises 600m above the surrounding desert plains. It provides lovely desert hikes and the fog-borne moisture supports an amazing range of succulents and other botanical wonders.

Isabis 4WD Trail

On Isabis and Hornkranz Farms, just outside the park, a remote 35km 4WD route cuts through the mountains and gorges surrounding the Isabis and Gaub Rivers. The route costs US$11 per vehicle plus US$4.50 per person and advance bookings are requisite; contact Joachim Cranz (☎ 061-228839), PO Box 9770, Windhoek.

It's also possible to hike through the 120m-deep Leopard Gorge or do a hair-raising mountain-bike ride (US$14) downhill from Gamsberg Pass; you need a minimum of six people.

Places to Stay

The Namib Desert Park has eight exclusive camps, some of which have multiple but widely spaced camp sites. Sites have tables, toilets and braais, but no washing facilities. Brackish water is available for cooking and washing but not drinking, so bring all you need. All sites must be pre-booked through NWR in Windhoek or Swakopmund.

Camping costs US$10 per site for two people plus US$2 for each additional person, up to a maximum of eight people. The camps may also be used as picnic sites with a park entry permit. Camping fees are payable when the park permit is issued.

Kuiseb Bridge Camp Site This shady double site, at the Kuiseb River crossing along the C14, is mainly just a convenient place to break up a trip between Windhoek and Walvis Bay. The location is scenic enough, but the dust and noise from passing vehicles makes it less appealing than other sites in the park. There are pleasant short walks into the canyon, but after rains, keep close tabs on the weather, as flash flooding is possible.

Kriess-se-Rus Camp Site This shaded site on the gravel plains, 107km east of Walvis Bay on the Gamsberg Pass route, lies amid camelthorn acacias beside a streambed. It's not the park's most scenic site, but makes a convenient stop between Windhoek and Walvis Bay.

Mirabib Camp Site With two very pleasant camp sites, Mirabib is comfortably placed beneath rock overhangs in a large granite inselberg. There's evidence that these shelters were used by nomadic peoples as many as 9000 years ago, and also by pastoralists in the 4th or 5th century.

Vogelfederberg Camp Site This small inselberg about 2km south of the C14 makes a convenient overnight camp within easy striking distance of Walvis Bay, 51km away, but it's more popular for picnics and short walks. Look for the intermittent pools on the top, which are home to *triops*, a species of brine shrimp whose eggs hatch only when the pools are filled with rainwater. The only shade is provided by a small overhang with two picnic tables and braai pits.

Bloedkoppie Camp Site The beautiful camp sites at the large inselberg Bloedkoppie, or 'Blood Hill', are among the most popular in the park. If you're coming from Swakopmund, they lie 15km north of the C28, along a signposted track. The northern sites are readily accessible to 2WD vehicles, but they often attract noisy yobs. The southern sites are quieter and more secluded, but can be reached only by 4WD. The surroundings offer pleasant walking, and at Klein Tinkas, 5km east of Bloedkoppie, you'll see the ruins of a colonial police station and the 1895 graves of two German police officers.

Groot Tinkas Camp Site This place, 15km east of Bloedkoppie, must be accessed with 4WD and rarely sees much traffic, so it's a good choice if you want seclusion. It enjoys a lovely setting beneath ebony trees and the surroundings are superb for nature walks. During rainy periods, the brackish water in the nearby dam attracts varied birdlife.

Ganab Camp Site & Water Hole The dusty and exposed site at Ganab (Nama for 'Camelthorn Acacias') sits beside a shallow streambed on the gravel plains. It's shaded by hardy acacia trees and a nearby windmill-powered bore hole provides water for antelopes, zebras, hyenas, aardwolfs, foxes and caracals.

Homeb Camp Site The scenic camp site at Homeb, with several individual sites, lies just upstream from the most accessible set of dunes in the Namib Desert Park. Residents of the nearby Topnaar Khoi-Khoi village dig wells in the riverbed to access water flowing beneath the surface. This hidden water also supports !nara melons, as well as a good stand of trees, including camelthorn acacia, ebony and figs, along the banks of the riverbed.

Swakop River The shady Swakop River camp sites lie – not surprisingly – beside the Swakop River, in the park's far northern reaches. The southern end is the nicest, with camelthorn, anaboom and tamarisk trees, while the northern end, beside a welwitschia plain, is flat and treeless. The only shade is beneath an odd sunken picnic site. The sites are accessible via Welwitschia Drive (see Around Swakopmund earlier in this chapter).

Getting There & Away

The only public transport through the Namib Desert Park is the Star Line bus, which runs every second week between Mariental and Walvis Bay. The westbound trip is on Monday and the eastbound on Tuesday.

KLEIN AUB
☎ 063

The village of Klein Aub, 94km west of Rehoboth on the C47, has a petrol station and *Conny's Tea Room* (☎ 525440), where there are light meals, snacks and coffee from 7am to 6pm daily.

NAUKLUFT MOUNTAINS
☎ 063

The Naukluft Mountains, which rise steeply from the gravel plains of the central Namib, is mainly a high-plateau area cut around the edges by a complex of steep gorges. Indeed, the park's name is German for 'Narrow Gorge'. The Tsondab, Tsams and Tsauchab Rivers all rise in the massif and the relative abundance of water creates an ideal habitat for mountain zebras, kudus, leopards, springboks and klipspringers.

History

In the early 1890s the Naukluft was the site of heated battle between the German colonial forces and the Witbooi Namas. The Nama resistance to German rule was led by the gifted military strategist Hendrik Witbooi, who refused to bow to colonial rule. In January 1893 a contingent of Schutztruppe soldiers under Major Curt von François was posted near Oniab, north of the Naukluft, and managed to force Witbooi and his followers to flee their settlement at Hoornkrans. Von François was transferred in March 1894 and replaced by Major Theodore Leutwein, who launched a campaign against the Nama forces in the Naukluft Mountains. At the end of that month, the German cavalryman Richard Kramers was killed in a skirmish near what is now the Hikers' Haven hut in the Naukluft Valley (his grave is still visible).

The Germans had estimated they could defeat the Nama within three days, but their unfamiliarity with the territory and lack of experience in guerrilla warfare slowed them down. In late August, they'd captured the Nama camp at Oniab, and Witbooi and his forces retreated into the mountains. The Germans chased the Nama across the plateau with their cannon and other firepower (portions of the old cannon route remain visible).

After heavy losses, Witbooi approached the Germans with a conditional surrender, which stipulated that he would accept German sovereignty over the country and permit them to set up a military post at Gibeon if he could retain his chieftaincy and the Nama could hang onto their lands and weapons. Leutwein accepted and the Battle of the Naukluft was over.

Hiking Routes

Most Naukluft visitors come to hike either the Waterkloof or Olive Trails. These hikes are open to day visitors, but most hikers want to camp at Koedoesrus, which must be pre-booked.

There are also four-day and eight-day loops, which have more restrictions attached. Thanks to stifling summer temperatures and potentially heavy rains, these two are only open from 1 March to the third Friday in October. Officially, you can only begin these hikes on the Tuesday, Thursday and Saturday of the first three weeks of each month. The price of US$13 per person includes accommodation at the Hikers' Haven hut on the night before and after the hike, as well as camping at trailside shelters and the Ubusis Canyon Hut. In addition, you'll have to pay US$3 per person per day and another US$3 per day for each vehicle you leave parked. Groups must comprise three to 12 people.

For general information on desert hiking, see the boxed text 'Desert Hiking' in the Facts for the Visitor chapter.

Waterkloof Trail This lovely 17km anticlockwise loop takes about seven hours to complete, and hikers must carry at least 2L of water per person.

The trail begins at the Koedoesrus Camp Site, 2km west of the park headquarters. It climbs the Naukluft River and past a frog-infested weir (don't miss the amazing reed tunnel!) and a series of pools, which offer cool and refreshing drinking and swimming. About 1km beyond the last pool, the trail turns west, away from the Naukluft River and up a kloof (ravine). From there to the halfway point, the route traverses increasingly open plateau.

Shortly after the halfway mark, the trail climbs steeply to a broad 1910m ridge, which is the highest point on the route. Here you'll have fabulous desert views before you begin a long, steep descent into the

NAUKLUFT MOUNTAINS

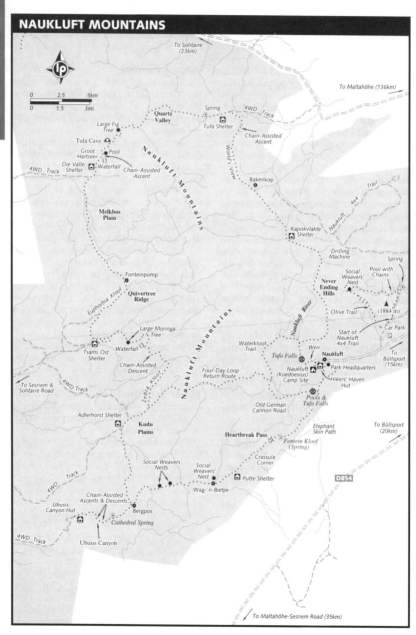

To Solitaire (23km)

To Maltahöhe (136km)

0   2.5   5km
0   1.5   3mi

Spring

Quartz Valley

4WD Track

Tufa Shelter

Chain-Assisted Ascent

Large Fig Tree

Tufa Cave

Naukluft Mountains

World's View

Groot Hartseer

Pool

Die Valle Shelter

Waterfall

4WD Track

Chain-Assisted Ascent

Bakenkop

Naukluft Trail

4x4 Trail

Melkbos Plain

Kapokvlakte Shelter

Drilling Machine

Spring

Fonteinpomp

Euphorbia Kloof

Quivertree Ridge

Social Weavers' Nest

Pool with Chains

Never Ending Hills

Naukluft River

Olive Trail

(1884 m)

Car Park

Large Moringa Tree

Naukluft Mountains

Start of Naukluft 4x4 Trail

Tsams Ost Shelter

Waterfall

Chain-Assisted Descent

Zebra Kloof

Waterkloof Trail

Weir

Tufa Falls

Naukluft

Park Headquarters

To Büllsport (15km)

Four-Day Loop Return Route

Naukluft (Koedoesrus) Camp Site

Hikers' Haven Hut

To Sesriem & Solitaire Road

4WD Track

Old German Cannon Road

Pools & Tufa Falls

Adlerhorst Shelter

Kudu Plains

Heartbreak Pass

Elephant Skin Path

To Büllsport (20km)

Fontein Kloof (Spring)

4WD Track

Social Weavers' Nests

Social Weavers' Nest

Crassula Corner

Putte Shelter

D854

Wag-'n-Bietjie

Chain-Assisted Ascents & Descents

Ubusis Canyon Hut

Bergpos

Cathedral Spring

4WD Track

Ubusis Canyon

To Maltahöhe-Sesriem Road (35km)

Gororosib Valley. Along the way, you'll pass several inviting pools full of reeds and tadpoles, and climb down an especially impressive waterfall before meeting up with the Naukluft River. Here, the route turns left and follows the 4WD track back to the park headquarters.

Olive Trail The 11km Olive Trail, named for the wild olives that grow alongside it, begins at the car park 4km north-east of the park headquarters. The walk runs clockwise around the triangular loop and takes four to five hours. Carry lunch and at least 2L of water per person.

The route begins with a steep climb onto the plateau, affording good views of the Naukluft Valley. It then turns sharply east and descends a constricted river valley, which becomes deeper and steeper and makes a couple of perfect U-turns before it reaches a point where hikers must traverse a canyon wall – past a pool – using anchored chains. In several places along this stretch, the dramatic geology presents an astonishing gallery of natural artwork. Near the end of the route, the trail strikes the Naukluft 4WD route and swings sharply south, where it makes a beeline back to the car park.

Four-Day & Eight-Day Loops The two big loops through the massif can be hiked in four and eight days. For many people the Naukluft is a magical place, but its charm is more subtle than that of Fish River Canyon in southern Namibia, for example. Some parts are undeniably spectacular – such as the Zebra Highway, Ubusis Canyon and Die Valle (look for the fantastic stallion profile on the rock beside the falls) but a couple of days involve walking in relatively open country or along some maddeningly rocky riverbeds.

The four-day 60km loop is actually just the first third of the eight-day 120km loop, combined with a 22km cross-country jaunt across the plateau back to park headquarters. It joins up with the Waterkloof Trail at its halfway point and follows it the rest of the way back to park headquarters. Alterna-

tively, you can finish the four-day route at Tsams Ost Shelter, mid-way through the eight-day loop, where a road leads out to the Sesriem-Solitaire Rd. However, you must pre-arrange to leave a vehicle there before setting off from park headquarters. Note that hikers may not begin from Tsams Ost without special permission from the rangers at Naukluft.

These straightforward hikes are marked by white footprints (except those sections that coincide with the Waterkloof Trail, which is marked with yellow footprints). Conditions are typically hot and dry, and water is reliably available only at overnight stops (at Putte, it's 400m from the shelter). Hikers must carry at least 4L of water per day. Eight-day hikers can lighten their packs by dropping off a re-supply cache of food and stove fuel at Tsams Ost Shelter prior to the hike.

To shorten the eight-day hike to seven days, it's possible to skip Ubusis Canyon by turning north at Bergpos and staying the second night at Adlerhorst; alternatively, very fit hikers combine the seventh and eighth days.

In four places – Ubusis Canyon, above Tsams Ost, Die Valle and just beyond Tufa Shelter – hikers must negotiate dry waterfalls, boulder-blocked kloofs and steep tufa formations with the aid of chains. Some people find this off-putting, so be sure you're up to it.

This area isn't big wildlife country, but throughout the route, you may see baboons, kudus, gemsboks, springboks and Hartmann's mountain zebras, and perhaps even leopards. However, the most dangerous creature you're likely to come across will be a black mamba or other poisonous snake, so watch where you plant your boots!

Naukluft 4WD Trail

Off-road enthusiasts can now exercise their machines on the new national park's 73km Naukluft 4WD Trail. It begins near the start of the Olive Trail and follows a loop near the north-eastern corner of the Naukluft area. The route costs US$27 per vehicle plus US$3 per person per day, including

Oshilulu Blues

Sitting on the veranda of the Cardboard Box Bar in Windhoek, downing a Windhoek Lager and watching one of those magical African sunsets, I had a chance meeting with a friend – a theologian and a religious man by nature – who had just returned from Oshakati in the Owambo country. We were both in a contemplative mood and we sat in silence watching the fading glow in the west. As the first stars appeared, I mustered my courage and asked my friend for his opinion on an experience I'd had the previous year. No one had yet heard the story and although I've now recounted it over many a campfire, at this point I was still hesitant about mentioning it lest my sanity be seriously questioned.

'At the time, I was living the nomadic life of a safari guide and had just fled with my group from the sandstorm-plagued Namib dunes and decamped in the relative calm of the Naukluft. Five hours and two punctures later, our tents were pitched at Koedoesrus, beneath ancient camelthorn acacia and the surrounding jagged peaks of the Naukluft Mountains.

After dinner, the clients retired to their tents and I lay down beside the glowing embers of the campfire, to fall asleep under an inky black sky dotted with the countless stars.

Some hours later, however, I was awakened by a rumble of thunder, and hastily pulled a tarpaulin over myself to keep off the impending rain. I tried to get back to sleep, but it wasn't long before the lightning was illuminating the peaks all around and I could hear the patter of rain on my improvised shelter. Before long, the issue turned from getting to sleep to simply keeping somewhat dry. As the storm increased in intensity, however, I realised it was a futile effort. Soon the rain was bucketing down in torrents and all I could do was try to ignore the damp seeping into my sleeping bag and calculate the odds of a lightning strike causing a camelthorn to crash down on top of me.

Suddenly, out of the corner of my eye, I saw movement in the bush. A jackal, I thought, hoping to scavenge food – certainly no human being in their right mind would be about on such a night. I quickly checked the clients' tents, reassuring myself that they were all safely zipped inside, keeping dry and attempting to ignore the tumult outside their canvas shelters.

---

accommodation in one of the four stone-walled A-frames at the 28km point. Facilities include shared toilets, showers and braais. Up to four vehicles/16 people are permitted at a time. Book through NWR in Windhoek.

Places to Stay & Eat

Naukluft (Koedoesrus) Camp Site Camping US$12 for 2 people plus US$2 for each additional person. This camp site, which is not open to day visitors, is pleasantly situated in a deep valley with hot showers. It books out quickly and the maximum stay is three nights. Firewood is sold at the park entrance ranger office.

There are also several accommodation options outside the park. For locations, see the Central Namib Desert map.

Büllsport Guest Farm (☎/fax 693371, e buellsport@natron.net, w www.natron.net /tour/buellspt/, Private Bag 1003, Maltahöhe) Singles/doubles with half board US$77/114. This scenic farm, owned by Ernst and Johanna Sauber, occupies a lovely, austere setting below the Naukluft Massif, and features a ruined colonial police station, the Bogenfels arch, and several resident mountain zebras. A highlight is the 4WD excursion up to the plateau (US$25) and hike back down the gorge, past several idyllic natural swimming pools. There's also a shop and petrol station.

Zebra River Lodge (☎ 693265, fax 693266, e marianne.rob@zebrariver.com, w www.zebrariver.com, 19km on the D850, PO Box 11742, Windhoek) Singles/doubles with full board US$72/120, self-catering cottage US$77. In a wonderful Tsaris Mountain setting is this friendly lodge that also provides some of the best home cooking in

Oshilulu Blues

But there was that movement again, and as I looked toward it, a bolt of lightning revealed a person who looked like a child, dressed in rags and carrying a large gnarled staff. Should I call out, I wondered? No, something wasn't right. As the figure moved closer, every lightning flash revealed more details.

With one bright flash, when the figure was no more than 10m away, I realised it wasn't a child, but a very old man, bent double and walking with a terrible limp. His face was partially covered with rags and he was shuffling forward, staring at the ground and leaning heavily on his staff. Then he slowly looked up at me, sitting there in the pouring rain, and it suddenly struck me that his skin was blue. Then I saw his eyes, which were a piercing, electric blue, glowing in the dark and staring my way with a fearsome, abject hatred. This creature appeared to be evil incarnate, and I froze, terrified, fixated on him until he turned slowly and limped off into the storm. As soon as he disappeared, the weather changed, and one of the most violent storms I've ever seen abated and retreated into a more peaceful night.

For a long while after, I sat there, wet and bewildered, then came to my senses and set about stoking up the fire. For the rest of the night, I sat there nervously, trying my best to dry off.'

The veranda was by now quiet and dark but for the dim light and a hum of voices from the bar. 'So what do you think of that?', I asked. As my friend reflected on my story, a young Herero woman, who'd been at the next table plaiting her friend's hair, approached us. She was clearly very nervous, and wouldn't stop looking at her feet. She kept muttering the word 'Oshilulu'.

'Oshilulu?', I asked. 'Yes', she explained, after some encouragement. Oshilulu is an evil spirit known throughout Southern Africa, by different names to different peoples. Some call him Tokoloshi, she told me, but he is always blue, and I was very fortunate indeed that nothing horrible had befallen me that stormy night.

To this day, whenever I see a storm brooding over Namibia's vast spaces, I wonder what sort of evil this fellow is cooking up – and whether I'll ever have the misfortune of seeing him again.

Sam McConnell, Windhoek

Namibia. The surrounding wonderland of desert mountains, plateaus, valleys and natural springs is accessible on a network of hiking trails and 4WD tracks (guided drives to the springs cost US$16). If you take it very slowly, the lodge road is accessible by 2WD vehicles; if it has been raining, the owners are happy to pick up booked guests at the gate 5km from the lodge.

Tsauchab River Camping (☎ *293416, fax 245286,* e *tsauchab@triponline.net, PO Box 221, Maltahöhe)* Camping US$4.50 per site plus US$5 per person, 4WD exclusive camp US$7 plus US$6 per person. If you're an avid hiker or just love excellent settings you're in for a treat. The shady named camp sites sit beside the Tsauchab riverbed – one occupies a huge hollow tree – and each has private ablutions, a sink and braai area. From the main site, an 11km day

hike climbs to the summit of Aloekop. Beside a spring 11km away from the main site is the 4WD exclusive site, which is the starting point for the wonderful 21km Mountain Zebra Hiking Trail. Meals are available on request and the farm shop sells bread, biscuits and home-made ginger beer.

Getting There & Away

The Naukluft is best reached via the C24 from Rehoboth and the D1206 from Rietoog; petrol is available at Büllsport and Rietoog. From Sesriem, 103km away, the nearest access is via the dip-ridden D854.

Star Line's Mariental–Walvis Bay bus passes Büllsport, but it's too infrequent to be of much use. Büllsport Guest Farm (see the preceding Places to Stay & Eat) does transfers from Windhoek (US$145 for up to four people).

SESRIEM & SOSSUSVLEI

☎ 063

Welcome to Namibia's number-one attraction, which seems to be the ultimate destination of every traveller in Namibia. If you visit Namibia and fail to reach Sossusvlei…well, it just wouldn't be normal!

The gateway to Sossusvlei is Sesriem; the name means 'Six Thongs', which was the number of joined leather ox-wagon thongs necessary to draw water from the bottom of the nearby gorge. Both Sesriem Canyon and Sossusvlei are open year-round between sunrise and sunset. If you want to witness the sunrise over Sossusvlei – as most people do – you must stay at Sesriem (the camping ground or Sossusvlei Lodge) or relatively nearby Kulala Desert Lodge. Otherwise, you can't pass the gate early enough to reach Sossusvlei before sunrise.

At Sesriem are the park headquarters, a small food shop and the Sossusvlei Lodge. All visitors headed for Sossusvlei must check in at the park office and secure a park entry permit (see National Parks in the Facts about Namibia chapter).

Serious sand dune buffs should also see the special section 'The Namib Dunes'.

Apart from the various lodges and the shop/restaurant 60km north-east of Sesriem at Solitaire, your only food option is the small shop at the Sesriem office, which sells little more than snacks and cold drinks.

Sesriem Canyon

The 1km-long, 30m-deep Sesriem Canyon, 4km south of the Sesriem headquarters, was carved by the Tsauchab River through the 15-million-year-old deposits of sand and gravel conglomerate. There are two pleasant walks: you can hike upstream to the brackish pool at its head or 2.5km downstream to its lower end. Note the natural sphinx-like formation on the northern flank near the canyon mouth.

Elim Dune

This oft-visited red dune, 5km from the Sesriem Camp Site, can be reached with 2WD vehicles, but also makes a pleasant morning or afternoon walk. It lies on the former Elim Farm, which is now included in the Namib-Naukluft Park.

Dune 45

The most accessible of the large red dunes along the Sossusvlei road is Dune 45, so called because it's 45km from Sesriem. It rises over 150m above the surrounding plains and is flanked by several scraggly and oft-photographed trees.

Sossusvlei

Sossusvlei, a large ephemeral pan, is set amid red sand dunes which tower up to 200m above the valley floor and more than 300m over the underlying strata. It rarely contains any water, but when the Tsauchab River has gathered enough volume and momentum to push beyond the thirsty plains to the sand sea (as it did in 1997 and 2001), it's transformed. The normally cracked dry mud gives way to an ethereal blue-green lake, surrounded by greenery and attended by aquatic birdlife, as well as the usual sand-loving gemsboks and ostriches.

If you experience a sense of *déjà vu* here, don't be surprised – Sossusvlei has appeared in many films and advertisements worldwide, and every story ever written about Namibia features a photo of it. This is the most accessible part of the 300km-long and 150km-wide sand sea that covers over 32,000 sq km of western Namibia and contains the world's highest, oldest and arguably most picturesque dunes. This sand probably originated in the Kalahari between three and five million years ago. It was washed down the Orange River and out to sea, where it was swept northwards with the Benguela Current to be deposited along the coast. The best way to get the measure of this sandy sprawl is to climb a dune, as most people do.

For more information on the Namib Dunes, see the special section in this chapter, which describes the dunes and their inhabitants.

At the end of the 65km 2WD road from Sesriem is the 2x4 Car Park, and only those with 4WD can drive the last 4km into the Sossusvlei Pan itself. Visitors with lesser

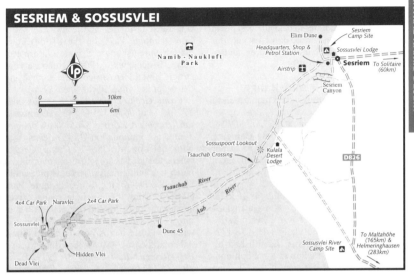

SESRIEM & SOSSUSVLEI

vehicles park at the 2x4 Car Park and walk or hitch the remaining distance, which takes about 1½ hours. Carry enough water for a hot sandy slog in the sun. The Sossus 4x4 Shuttle Service provides a shuttle service for US$3.50/5 one way/return but it isn't available for sunrise trips.

Hidden Vlei
The rewarding 4km return hike from the 2x4 Car Park to Hidden Vlei, an unearthly dry vlei (low, open landscape) amid lonely dunes, makes a rewarding excursion. The route is marked by white-painted posts. It's most intriguing in the afternoon, when you're unlikely to see another person.

Dead Vlei
The rugged 6km return walk from Sossusvlei to Dead Vlei is popular with those who think the former is becoming overly touristy. Despite the name, it's a lovely spot and is just as impressive as its more popular neighbour.

Organised Tours
Most Namib-Naukluft Park area lodges run day tours to Sossusvlei, and prices are gen-

erally proportional to the amount you're paying for accommodation (see Places to Stay).

Places to Stay – Budget
Sesriem Camp Site Camping US$19 for 2 people plus US$2 for each additional person, up to 8 people. Sesriem is the most convenient camp site for Sossusvlei. Sites must be booked at the NWR in Windhoek, but arrive before sunset or it'll reassign your site on a stand-by basis; anyone who was unable to book a site in Windhoek may get in on this nightly lottery.

Solitaire Guest House (☎ 061-240375, fax 256598, e afrideca@mweb.com.na, 65km north of Sesriem, Private Bag 1009, Maltahöhe) Camping US$4.50 per vehicle & US$3 per person, basic bungalows US$8 per person. This pleasant place, named for the dead tree that is its renowned motif, may have provided the inspiration for the film Baghdad Café, has featured in a Toyota Camry advert, and is the subject of the Dutch-language travelogue Solitaire. Although a plusher guest house will probably soon be built on the property, this warm, friendly spot in the desert remains a favourite with travellers, and everyone stops for one

CENTRAL NAMIB DESERT

reason or another (including petrol). At the shop, Moose continues to bake the best bread and apfelstrüdel in Africa (don't just take our word for it!), and the breakfasts are a fantastic way to wake yourself up.

Places to Stay – Mid-Range

See the Central Namib Desert map for all of the following.

Betesda Rest Camp (☎ 693253, D854, PO Box 9385, Eros, Windhoek) Camping US$3, self-catering bungalows US$27 per person. This friendly Christian-oriented place lies within easy reach of Sesriem. Meals are available on request.

Rostock Ritz (☎ 064-403622, fax 403623, e kuecki@mweb.com.na, w www.rostock ritzhomepage.com, PO Box 536, Swakopmund) Single/double chalets US$88/132. Discounts for Namibians. Established by the owner of Kücki's Pub in Swakopmund, this unusual camp lies east of the C14 just south of the C26 junction. Most interesting are the boulder-like domed chalets. Transport to hiking routes costs US$7.50; other activities include dune drives (US$27), visits to cave paintings (US$30), and Sossusvlei tours (US$54 to US$94, depending on the number of participants).

Namibgrens Rest Camp (☎ 062-572021, fax 061-222893, e rabie@namibnet.com, D1275, PO Box 21587, Windhoek) Camping US$4.50 per person, single/double rooms US$29/54. This beautiful game farm, known for its several wonderful hiking trails, occupies a scenic position on Namibia's steepest road, the Spreetshoogte Pass (in one place, there's a hair-raising 1:4 slope!). The hiking routes form a ragged cloverleaf; hikers accommodation (US$4.50 per day) is in basic huts where the loops cross. Hikers can fill their water bottles in bore holes along the way, while earth dams provide water for wildlife. Nonhikers can take the soft option and tour the farm by vehicle for US$11.

Swartfontein (☎ 062-572004, fax 061-226999, e orione2@iafrica.com.na or log ufa@mweb.com.na, w www.swartfontein .com, Spreetshoogte Pass, PO Box 32042, Pioneers Park, Windhoek) Singles/doubles

with half board US$67/107. This Italian-run guest farm lies at the top of 1850m Spreetshoogte Pass, on the 8100-hectare Namib-Spreetshoogte Private Nature Reserve. It occupies a 1900 farmhouse constructed by a German colonial soldier, but the decor is Italian all the way.

Camp Gecko Desert Ranch (☎/fax 062-572017, fax 061-251541, e geckonam@ iafrica.com.na, PO Box 3165, Swakopmund) Tented accommodation US$23 per person, with half board US$41. Camp Gecko, where the idea is to return an overgrazed ranch to a wilderness reserve, is pleasantly located west of the Spreetshoogte Pass (D1275). Activities include ranch drives and hiking trails. An odd but interesting feature is the Ongwe Animal Movie School, where wildlife learns how to act in films. All safaris cost US$0.50 per kilometre.

Weltevrede Rest Camp (☎ 293374, fax 293375, Private Bag 1009, Maltahöhe) Camping US$12 for 3 people plus US$4 for each additional person, bungalows full board US$60/107. Willie and Zanne Swarts' simple rest camp, 30km south of Solitaire, has shady camping and bungalow accommodation in a lonely desert setting. There's plenty of hiking available and guided trips run to the farm's rock paintings (US$3) and sundowners in the desert (US$11).

Places to Stay – Top End

Sossusvlei Lodge (☎ 293223, fax 293231, e sossusvl@iafrica.com.na, w www.moven pick-hotels.com, Sesriem, PO Box 6900, Ausspannplatz, Windhoek) Single/double bungalows B&B US$154/198. This curious place, which bears a strong resemblance to what happens when squabbling children topple a stack of coloured blocks, sits right at the Sesriem Camping Ground fence. People either love it or hate it, but it does make a statement.

Kulala Desert Lodge (☎ 293234, fax 293235, e kulala@mweb.com.na or info@ nts.com.na, w www.wilderness-safaris.com, 17km west of the D826, PO Box 6850, Windhoek) Singles/doubles US$155/244. This lovely Wilderness Safaris lodge is refreshingly unobtrusive and from a distance it resembles a Bedouin camp amid the dunes. Bungalows, which are built of adobe and canvas, all have private verandas. Because the owner Wilderness Safaris has a private entrance to Sossusvlei, guests can get in early to see the sunrise. Sossusvlei excursions cost US$64 per person.

Namib-Naukluft Lodge (☎ 061-263082, fax 215356, [e] afex@afex.com.na, [w] www .natron.net/afex, PO Box 22028, Windhoek) Singles/doubles with half board US$93/ 145. Set on a 13,000-hectare farm, this unusual-looking lodge occupies a boulder-strewn landscape about 20km south of Solitaire. Activities include sundowners beside the surrounding granite hills.

Sossusvlei Wilderness Camp (☎ 061-274501, fax 239455, [e] info@nts.com.na, D854, [w] www.wilderness-safaris.com, PO Box 6850, Windhoek) Singles/doubles with full board and activities US$300/532. This camp is situated on a mountainous 7000-hectare ranch about 40km south-east of Sesriem. Accommodation is in beautiful stone, timber and thatched bungalows nestled between rock kopjes for maximum privacy. Sossusvlei trips are included in the rates.

For more options, see NamibRand Nature Reserve following, and under Maltahöhe, in the Southern Namibia chapter.

Getting There & Away

Sesriem is reached via a signposted turn-off from Maltahöhe-Solitaire road (C14). You will find petrol at Solitaire, Sesriem and a bush BP station 93km south of Sesriem on the D826.

NAMIBRAND NATURE RESERVE

The large private NamibRand Nature Reserve, which abuts the Namib-Naukluft Park, was formed from a collection of private farms to eventually take in 200,000 hectares of dunes, desert grasslands and wild, isolated mountain ranges. It's currently the largest privately owned property in Southern Africa, but several concessionaires operate on the reserve, offering a range of experiences amid one of Namibia's most stunning and colourful landscapes.

A surprising amount of wildlife can be seen here, including large herds of gemsboks, springboks and zebras, as well as kudus, klipspringers, spotted hyenas, jackals, Cape and bat-eared foxes, and spotted hyenas. Less visible but still present are leopards and African wildcats.

Places to Stay

Wolwedans (☎ 061-230616, fax 220102, [e] nrs@iafrica.com.na, PO Box 5048, Windhoek) Singles/doubles Dunes Lodge US$254/387, Dune Camp US$160/254, Private Camp with self-catering US$158/ 220 or with full board US$347/520 (no activities). The architecturally lovely main lodge consists of raised wooden chalets in the dunes; canvas walls can be raised or lowered as necessary to keep out the wind-blown sand. It's enhanced by spectacular views and an elegant ambience. The Dune Camp is tented accommodation on raised wooden platforms, also with wonderful views, while the Private Camp is a canvas-walled bungalow. Activities include dune drives and game drives. The Dune Camp is open only from 1 March to 30 November and the Private Camp from 15 April to 15 October.

Tok-Tokkie Trails (☎ 264668 – ask for 5230, or 061-235454, Die Duine Farm, PO Box 162, Maltahöhe) US$106 per person per day. This unique company guides one- to four-day walking tours through the desert, dunes and mountains of NamibRand. The rate includes meals, equipment and a guide; camping is under the stars and bucket showers are available. A backup vehicle ensures that you carry only a day pack. There's also a small lodge at the farmhouse where you can stay before and after your walk.

Camp Mwisho (☎ 293233, fax 293241, [e] namibsky@mweb.com.na, PO Box 5197, Windhoek) Singles/doubles full board US$119/192. This tented camp beside red dunes is best known for its company Namib Sky, which offers balloon trips at dawn (US$246 per person) over the dune sea. They depart from either here or Sesriem and finish up with a champagne breakfast. It's accessible by 2WD vehicle.

NamibRand Family Hideout (☎ 061-223926, fax 232890, 🄴 ambruck@mweb.com.na, 🅆 www.members.mweb.com.na/nrfhideout, PO Box 9950, Windhoek) 10-bed self-catering farmhouse US$160. As its name suggests, this outpost in the south of the reserve is a secluded hideaway beside the dunes.

Sossusvlei Mountain Lodge (☎ 27-11-809 4300, 27-11-809 4514, 🄴 bookings@ccafrica.com, 🅆 www.ccafrica.com, Private Bag X27, Benmore 2010, South Africa) Rooms US$375 per person (no single supplement), with meals and activities. This amazing and elegant lodge melds so well with its environment that it becomes an integral part of the landscape. The chalets, built of the same stone that naturally surrounds them, all feature fireplaces, marble baths and covered patios. Of special interest is the observatory, with a high-powered telescope and local star charts. In fact, it made the *Condé Nast* hot list of best new hotels in the world. Bookings are through the Conservation Corporation Africa, in Johannesburg.

Southern Namibia

Southern Namibia takes in the vast expanses from Rehoboth south to the border with South Africa along the Orange River, east to the Botswana border and west to the Diamond Coast. It encompasses a range of environments, from the rich cattle country of Namaland and the semidesert of the Kalahari borders to the forbidden wilderness of the southern Namib and the sensational Fish River Canyon. Other major attractions include Hardap Dam Recreation Resort and Game Park, Duwisib Castle, the Kokerboom forests, Brukkaros crater, and the bizarre Bavarian-style town of Lüderitz, which positively brims with interesting colonial architecture.

The Central Plateau

Namibia's central plateau is characterised by wide open country, and the region's widely spaced and typically uninspiring towns function mainly as commercial market centres. This is Namibia's richest karakul sheep and cattle ranching area, and around the town of Mariental a growing range of citrus fruit and market vegetables is being cultivated under irrigation.

The region is bisected by Namibia's main north-south route, the B1, which stretches from Windhoek to the South African border. For most drivers, this excellent road is little more than a mesmerising broken white line stretching towards a receding horizon – a paradise for lead-foot drivers and cruise-control potatoes.

Most of the central plateau's attractions are situated off the main B1 route, and visitors with time and a vehicle will find plenty of intriguing and unspoilt possibilities along the way.

REHOBOTH
☎ 062

Rehoboth is the first town on the B1 south of Windhoek and is just a stone's throw north of

Highlights

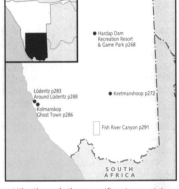

- Hardap Dam Recreation Resort & Game Park p268
- Lüderitz p283
- Around Lüderitz p288
- Kolmanskop Ghost Town p286
- Keetmanshoop p272
- Fish River Canyon p291
- SOUTH AFRICA

- Hike through the magnificent mountains and gaze across the broad spaces at Klein Aus Vista.

- Enjoy the dunes, wind and sea around the historic fishing town of Lüderitz.

- Rouse the spirits in the diamond-mining ghost town of Kolmanskop.

- Gaze into the Fish River Canyon or do a Fish River hike and then swim in the river's magical pools.

- Soak in the soothing hot waters at Ai-Ais.

- Canoe down the Orange River through spectacular canyon country.

the tropic of Capricorn. There's very little to lure visitors, but it's more lively than other Namibian towns south of the Red Line, and the streets are normally thronged with people and activity.

History
In the mid-19th century, the incumbent Nama peoples, who occupied the area around modern-day Rehoboth, were displaced by the Herero from the north. Rehoboth first developed around a Rhenish

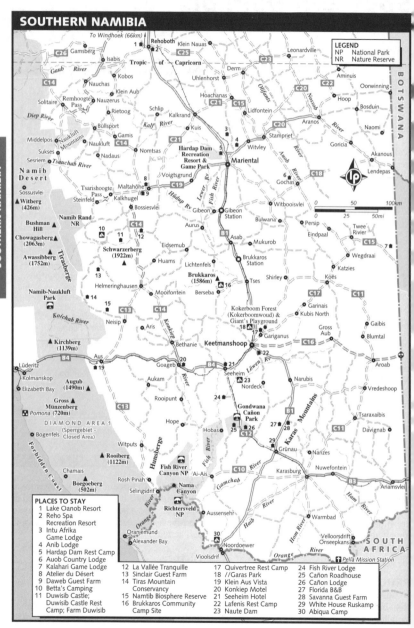

SOUTHERN NAMIBIA

PLACES TO STAY

1. Lake Oanob Resort
2. Reho Spa Recreation Resort
3. Intu Afrika Game Lodge
4. Anib Lodge
5. Hardap Dam Rest Camp
6. Auob Country Lodge
7. Kalahari Game Lodge
8. Atelier du Désert
9. Daweb Guest Farm
10. Betta's Camping
11. Duwisib Castle; Duwisib Castle Rest Camp; Farm Duwisib
12. La Vallée Tranquille
13. Sinclair Guest Farm
14. Tiras Mountain Conservancy
15. Namtib Biosphere Reserve
16. Brukkaros Community Camp Site
17. Quivertree Rest Camp
18. //Garas Park
19. Klein Aus Vista
20. Konkiep Motel
21. Seeheim Hotel
22. Lafenis Rest Camp
23. Naute Dam
24. Fish River Lodge
25. Cañon Roadhouse
26. Cañon Lodge
27. Florida B&B
28. Savanna Guest Farm
29. White House Ruskamp
30. Abiqua Camp

mission station founded in 1844 by the missionary Heinrich Kleinschmidt, who named it after a biblical site amidst wide open spaces. Kleinschmidt and his mission focused their attentions on the local Herero community, but were forced to relocate after an 1864 attack by Nama leader Jan Jonker Afrikaner. He and his family fled to the German mission at Otjimbingwe, where he died soon after.

The Rehoboth mission was revived in the early 1870s by the Basters, an ethnic group made up of mixed Khoi-Khoi and Afrikaner people, who had migrated north from the Cape under their leader Hermanus van Wyk. Their original plan had been to settle at the Orange River, but when the Cape government demanded proof of land ownership in the mid-1860s, they pushed north and set down stakes in Rehoboth. Permission to settle was given in exchange for an annual tribute of one horse to each of the Nama, Afrikaner and Herero groups.

The Rehoboth Basters remain proud of both their heritage and their name (Baster literally means 'bastards'). Never mind that the word is used as an insult elsewhere; to this independent, Western-oriented group, it emphasises a proud ancestry.

Rehoboth Museum
Housed in the 1903 residence of the settlement's first colonial postmaster, Rehoboth Museum (☎ 522954, Beside the post office; admission US$1.50; open 10am-noon & 2pm-4pm Mon-Fri, 10am-noon Sat) is dedicated to Rehoboth's natural and cultural history. An exhibition of photos taken from 1893 to 1896, feature the mission station, which was rebuilt by the Basters under Hermanus van Wyk. Outside is a garden of local plants and examples of historic homes and transport.

There's also an archaeological annexe at an Iron Age site, 10km from town, which can be visited by prior arrangement either by phoning or dropping by the museum.

Reho Spa
This spa (☎ 522774; admission US$1.50 plus US$1.50 to use the hot baths; open 7am-6pm daily), 1km south of the church, surrounds a thermal spring and is an elaborate spa complex complete with a 39°C thermal pool, bungalows and a camp site (see Places to Stay). The early Nama knew this place as *aris* (smoke), after the steam that rises from the hot spring. Note that the security here isn't optimum so watch your valuables.

Oanob Dam
The 2.7-sq-km Oanob Dam, 10km west of Rehoboth, was completed in 1990 to provide the district's water supply. A lookout offers an impressive view of the dam, and you'll find a picnic site and small exhibition outlining its history and construction. There are also several short walking tracks. Picnic sites cost US$8 and there's a bar and a camping ground (see Places to Stay).

Places to Stay & Eat
Reho Spa Recreation Resort (☎ 522774) Camping US$12 for two people plus US$2 for each additional person, 4-/5-/6-bed self-catering bungalows US$24/27/35. This spa resort, 1km south of the church, has a cafeteria, swimming pool and thermal bath (see the Reho Spa section); accommodation must be booked through Namibia Wildlife Resorts (NWR; see Tourist Offices under Information in the Windhoek chapter).

Lake Oanob Resort (☎ 522370, fax 524112, 6km on the D1237, ✉ oanob@ iafrica.com.na) Camping US$11 per site, 6-bed chalets for 2/4/5/6 people US$74/89/95/102, single/double rooms US$40/50. The beautiful stone-and-thatch self-catering bungalows, have balconies that overlook the water and provide all the comforts of home, including DSTV. It's a great place to relax and watch the herons on the incongruous blue lake.

Sigi's a la Carte Restaurant (☎ 522017) Mains US$2-4.50. On the main street of Rehoboth, this very basic place serves up standard beef and chicken dishes.

The only other place to eat is *Dolphin Fish and Chips* (☎ 522101). A good spot for quick snacks and groceries is the new *BP petrol station* on the B1.

Getting There & Away

Intercape Mainliner buses between Windhoek and South Africa stop at Rehoboth, as does the train between Windhoek and Keetmanshoop. Alternatively, minibuses to Rehoboth leave about every 20 minutes from the Rhino Park petrol station in Windhoek and cost US$2.

HOACHANAS

☎ 063

It's worth a short side trip to the tiny settlement of Hoachanas (on the C21, 33km east of Kalkrand on the B1) to visit **Farm Jena**. This is the home of the Anin Women's Project (the name is Nama for 'many birds'), where Nama women create lovely and colourful embroidered textiles – cotton and linen bedclothing, pillow slips, tablecloths and other items – for distribution to shops all over Namibia. Contact Anin (☎ 061-235509) in Windhoek to arrange a tour.

MARIENTAL

☎ 063

Mariental is a small administrative and commercial centre on the bus and rail lines between Windhoek and Keetmanshoop, and a popular petrol stop for drivers between Windhoek and South Africa. Thanks to large-scale irrigation from the Fish River and Hardap Dam, the area produces cotton, wheat, lucerne (alfalfa), maize, grapes, tomatoes and garden vegetables. It's also a centre for karakul and ostrich ranching.

Mariental is a convenient place to refuel or take an overnight break, but don't expect any action – this is one of the most lethargic and lifeless towns you'll ever see.

History

Mariental's original Nama name was *Zaragaebia* (Dusty). The current name, which means 'Maria's Valley', was taken from the farm belonging to the area's first white farmer, Hermann Brandt, who purchased the land from Nama chief Hendrik Witbooi in 1890 and named it in honour of his wife, Anna Marie Mahler.

From 1903 to 1907, colonial and Nama forces engaged in battle after battle, and quite a few civilians – nearly all Germans – died in guerrilla raids. After the railway was built through the town in 1912, Mariental residents petitioned for village status, but their hopes were dashed in 1915 when Germany gave in to the South African Defence Forces. It wasn't until the construction of Namibia's first Dutch Reformed church in 1920 that Mariental was granted official village status. The modern town remains a stronghold of the Nama people, who make up most of its population.

Information

Municipal Tourist Office (☎ 240347, ⓔ marmun@iafrica.com.na) is open 7am to noon and 1pm to 4pm Monday to Friday. It is friendly but it has the difficult task of luring bleary-eyed drivers off the open road for a look around Mariental. It's in the municipal office building, off Michael van Niekerk St, 1km from the centre of the town.

Places to Stay

Hotel Sandberg *(☎/fax 242291, fax 240738, Marie Brandt St)* Singles/doubles US$31/45. This hotel has been renovated but still receives mixed reviews from travellers. The attached pizzeria is quite popular.

Mariental Hotel *(☎ 242466, fax 242493, ⓔ mrlhotel@iafrica.com.na, Marie Brandt St, PO Box 619)* Singles/doubles US$36/48. A block down from the Sandberg, this is a more plush option, with a dining room.

Guglhupf Cafe *(☎ 240718, fax 242525, Park St, PO Box 671)* Singles/doubles US$20/34. This respectable little place makes a good inexpensive choice and it has a swimming pool and a nice little restaurant and cafe.

River Chalets *(☎ 240515, 081-128 2601, B1, PO Box 262)* Single/double self-catering chalets US$33/47. The bright and airy pastel chalets, which are far away from any river, are the town's most pleasant accommodation option.

The following accommodation options are located north of Mariental.

Intu Afrika Game Lodge *(☎ 061-248 741, fax 226535, ⓔ intu@iafrica.com.na, ⓦ www.namibiaweb.com.intuafrika, Onze*

Rust Game Ranch, PO Box 40047, Windhoek) Double tents B&B US$96, double rooms B&B with full board and activities US$320-460. This posh lodge, 62km from town, sits on a large game ranch amid red, vegetated Kalahari dunes. In 1996, a pair of anthropologists attempted to re-create a bit of the ancient Kalahari by bringing in about 40 !Kung San people to settle on the land. Activities include, hunting and gathering walks with the !Kung San people, learning about their traditions and purchasing their craftwork. However, there is some controversy regarding the ethics of using these people as a tourist attraction, especially considering the rates they charge here. It's best to use your own judgment.

Anib Lodge (☎ *240529, fax 240516,* ℮ *anib@natron.net,* ⓦ *www.naminfo.com /anib.htm, PO Box 800)* Singles/doubles US$101/158. This guest farm, 3km north of the C20 between Mariental and Stampriet, bills itself as 'your nest on the edge of the Kalahari'. Along with the secluded setting and comfortable accommodation (meals and activities included), it has a swimming pool and good bird-watching opportunities, and guests can borrow mountain bikes to explore the farm.

Places to Eat

Guglhupf Cafe (☎ *240718, Park St)* Breakfasts US$3.50-4, snacks US$2-3, mains US$3-7. This friendly place does breakfast, light lunches, and a range of pizzas, pastas, salads, as well as full steak, lamb and chicken dinners.

Wimpy (☎ *242138, B1 Highway)* Mains US$1-3. Open 24 hours. This fast-food chain is in the Engen petrol station complex.

Bambi's Takeaways (☎ *240767, Marie Brandt St)* Mains US$1-3. This typical takeaway place does a variety of burgers, toasties and schnitzel.

Getting There & Away

Bus The Intercape Mainliner bus between Windhoek and Cape Town in South Africa stops at the Engen petrol station in the centre of Mariental. Minibuses run several times daily between Windhoek and Keet-

manshoop, via Mariental. The Star Line bus between Mariental and Walvis Bay (US$11, 12 hours) runs every second week – westbound Monday and eastbound Tuesday.

Train The train between Windhoek (US$8, 6½ hours) and Keetmanshoop (US$7, 4½ hours) passes through Mariental southbound on Monday to Saturday and northbound on Sunday to Friday.

HARDAP DAM RECREATION RESORT & GAME PARK

Hardap Dam *(admission US$3 per vehicle plus US$3 per person; open sunrise-6pm daily)*, 15km north-west of Mariental, is a 25-sq-km dam attached to a 25,000-hectare wildlife park. Hardap is Nama for 'nipple', and it was named after the conical hills topped by the dolerite knobs dotting the area.

The idea of building a dam on the Fish River was first discussed in 1897 by German geologist Theodore Rehbock, but it was 63 years before the 39m dam wall was constructed to hold back a reservoir.

Things to See & Do

Most travellers come for the **blue lake**, which breaks up the arid plateau landscape and provides anglers with carp, barbel, mudfish and blue karpers. Admission entitles you to use the pool and the several picnic sites east of the lake. Between sunrise and sunset, you can walk anywhere in the reserve, but camping is allowed only at the rest camp. Note that swimming isn't permitted in the dam.

Hardap Dam **cruises** in a two-level sightseeing boat are offered by Oasis Ferries (☎ 243292).

The **visitor centre** (open sunrise-1pm & 2pm-sunset daily) sits perched on a crag overlooking the dam and the surrounding landscape of sparse vegetation and sombre colours. There's an information centre and an aquarium full of bored, anonymous fish from the lake. There is also a research establishment where the Ministry of Environment & Tourism (MET) studies the feasibility of fish breeding and commercial exploitation. Fishing licences are also available here.

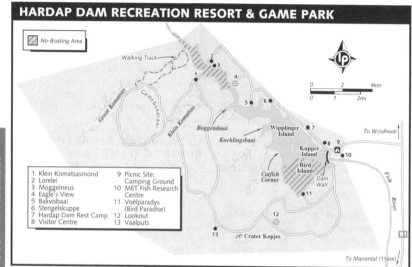

HARDAP DAM RECREATION RESORT & GAME PARK

No-Boating Area

Walking Track

Groot Komutsas
Gemsbokdraai
Klein Komutsas

Boggembaai
Kuchlingsbaai

Wipplinger Island
Kupper Island
Bird Island
Catfish Corner
Dam Wall

To Windhoek
Fish River
To Mariental (15km)

Crater Kopjes

1 Klein Komatsasmond
2 Lorelei
3 Moggelneus
4 Eagle's View
5 Bakvisbaai
6 Stengelskuppe
7 Hardap Dam Rest Camp
8 Visitor Centre
9 Picnic Site;
   Camping Ground
10 MET Fish Research
   Centre
11 Voëlparadys
   (Bird Paradise)
12 Lookout
13 Vaalputs

The 80km of gravel roads west of the dam lead through **game park**, which is home to antelopes, zebras, birds and small animals. There are few dangerous animals, so you may walk wherever you like. At the northern end is a 15km-loop walk with a shortcut across the middle, which makes it into a 9km loop. It's poorly marked so pay close attention.

The vegetation is a combination of flat shrub savanna plains with stands of camelthorn, wild green-hair trees and buffalo thorn. You're bound to see kudus, gemsboks, springboks, ostriches and mountain zebras, and possibly even an eland or red hartebeest. The rocky kopjes support dassies and klipspringers.

The reserve and reservoir areas provide a habitat for over 260 bird species, particularly water-loving birds: flamingoes, fish eagles, pelicans, spoonbills, Goliath herons, and many varieties of migrants and bush dwellers. However, you may wish to ignore the sign reading 'Voëlparadys' (Bird Paradise), which indicates a stand of dead camelthorn trees. A colony of white-breasted cormorants took up residence here immediately after the dam filled up in 1963, but when the water levels receded, the birds went off in search of a new paradise.

Places to Stay & Eat
Hardap Dam Rest Camp Camping US$13 for two people plus US$2 for each additional person, 12-bed dorm US$27 per person, bungalows US$27-65. This place includes a shop, restaurant, kiosk, swimming pool and petrol station. The restaurant and pool both enjoy wonderful cliff-top views over the lake. Bookings are through NWR in Windhoek.

Getting There & Away
There's no public transport to Hardap Dam, but the entrance is only 8km from the B1.

STAMPRIET & GOCHAS
☎ 063

Thanks to lush artesian springs, the small settlement of Stampriet enjoys ideal conditions for growing fruit and vegetables. The springs also attract an inordinate amount of birdlife to this otherwise desert area. At the **Gross Nabas farm**, about 25km south of Stampriet on the C15, a monument commemorates the German-Nama War fought from 2–4 January 1905, when colonial forces led by Lieutenant von Burgsdorff were defeated by Hendrik Witbooi's Nama resistance.

Gochas (Nama for 'many candle-thorn trees') is situated beside the Auob River, 53km south-east of Stampriet. A cemetery in the village bears the graves of numerous German soldiers killed in these and other turn-of-the-century battles with the Nama resistance. On the C18 south-west of the village, towards Witbooisvlei, are war memorials commemorating the battles on 3 and 5 January 1905, which took place on the **Haruchas Farm**, between the German troops of General Stuhlmann and the Nama led by Simon Kooper. To visit, you need to stop at the farm and ask for permission.

Places to Stay & Eat

Hotel Gochas (☎/fax 250098, PO Box 80) Singles/doubles US$19/37. This basic place is the only accommodation in the town. It has an equally basic restaurant, and of course, a bar.

Auob Country Lodge (☎ 250101, fax 250102, e auob@mweb.com.na, PO Box 17) Singles/doubles US$50/74. This simple but comfortable place occupies an 8000-hectare farm amid the red fossil Kalahari dunes. It's just 6km from Gochas.

Kalahari Game Lodge (☎ 6662 ask for 3112, fax 6662 ask for 3103, C15, PO Box 22, Koës) Doubles with half board US$187. This remote and beautiful 27,000-hectare property, 180km south-east of Gochas, abuts the South African border at the edge of the Kgalakgadi Trans-Frontier Park (formerly Kalahari Gemsbok National Park). Here, you're in the very heart of the Kalahari, and you'll see up to 200 bird species and all the signature mammals – including lions, gemsboks and meerkats – against a backdrop of brilliant red dunes. Wildlife drives cost US$20 per person.

Getting There & Away

Star Line has return buses from Mariental to Stampriet (US$2, 1½ hours) on Monday, Wednesday and Thursday. On Wednesday, it stops at Gochas (US$3.50, three hours).

Beware of Falling Rocks

In a single meteor shower sometime in the dim and distant past, more than 21 tonnes of 90% ferrous extraterrestrial boulders crashed to earth in southern Namibia. It's rare for so many meteorites to fall at once, and they are thought to have been remnants of an explosion in space, which were held together as they were drawn in by the earth's gravitational field.

Thus far, at least 77 meteorite chunks have been found within a 2500-sq-km area around Gibeon. The largest, which weighs 650kg, is housed in Cape Town Museum, while other bits have wound up as far away as Anchorage, Alaska. Between 1911 and 1913, soon after their discovery, 33 chunks were brought to Windhoek for safekeeping. Over the years, they've been displayed in Zoo Park and at Alte Feste in Windhoek, but have now found a home on Post Street Mall.

GIBEON
☎ 063

The former Rhenish mission station of Gibeon, 91km south of Mariental and 9km west of the B1, was founded by the missionary Knauer beside the Gorego-re-abes spring (Nama for 'where zebras drink') in 1863. It was named after the biblical character in the Old Testament book of Joshua.

In 1894, a German garrison was established in Gibeon on orders from Major Theodore Leutwein. While a fort was under construction, the troops were housed in the mission church. A kimberlite pipe was discovered here in the late 19th century, but brief attempts at diamond exploration were abandoned in the early 20th century.

As a result of the fierce battle on 27 April 1915, Gibeon's name will forever be associated with Germany's loss of southern Namibia to the South African Defence Forces. The results are visible in the graveyard beside the Gibeon train station, beyond the B1, 10km east of town.

These days, Gibeon is best known for the meteorites which grace Windhoek's Post Street Mall.

Getting There & Away

Star Line runs return buses from Mariental to Gibeon (US$2, two hours) on Wednesday and Friday.

BRUKKAROS

The 2km-wide crater of the extinct volcano Brukkaros (admission US$1.50 per person, payable at the community camp) is plainly visible from the B1 between Mariental and Keetmanshoop. The name combines the Afrikaans words *broek* (trousers) and *karos* (leather apron), in deference to Brukkaros' Nama name, Geitsigubeb, a traditional article of clothing worn by the Nama women.

History

Brukkaros was formed some 80 million years ago when a magma pipe came into contact with groundwater about 1km below the earth's surface. The super-heated water vaporised and expanded, causing the surface to swell into a bulge 10km across and 500m high. This created space for more magma to intrude, which in turn heated more water and caused further swelling. It reached the point where something had to give – and something did. The subsequent explosion caused the surface material and the water to collapse into the magma pipe, in turn setting off further explosions which ejected material from deep in the earth and then deposited it around the gaping crater, forming a rim.

Before too long, hot springs appeared in the crater, creating a lake and depositing quartz and other minerals. Over the following millions of years, erosion removed all the surrounding material, leaving the 650m erosion-resistant plug we see today.

Hiking

In the 1930s, a track was constructed to provide access to the Smithsonian Institute's sunspot-research post on the crater's western rim. This site was chosen for its abundance of sunshine and phenomenally clear air. From the modern car park (accessible by 4WD), it's a 3.5km hike to the crater's southern entrance. Along the way, watch for the remarkable crystal formations embedded in the rock. As you approach the crater entrance, the trail traverses the wall of the crater's outflow canyon, high above an intermittent waterfall.

From the crater entrance, you can either head for the kokerbooms and crystal fields on the crater floor or follow the route, which turns sharply left and climbs to an abandoned research station on the rim. You'll still see bits of rubbish left behind from when the station was abandoned. The walk takes about 2½ hours each way and as usual, be sure to carry plenty of water.

The Fickle Finger of Fate

The Mukurob, which was once a dramatically balanced stone pinnacle, collapsed on 8 December 1988 when seismic waves from the Armenian earthquake of 7 December reached Namibia. All that remains is a 1.5m-wide neck of rock on a pedestal, while bits of the 12m, 500-tonne rock-head lay scattered about.

The Mukurob was actually a remnant of the Weissrand sandstone formation, which was shot through with vertical intrusions of softer rock material. When that material eroded, most of the remaining sandstone blocks collapsed, but this one remained balanced there for at least 50,000 years.

Mukurob in Nama means 'look at the neck', which is probably a reference to the spindly pedestal where it once rested. Afrikaners called it the Vingerklip, or Finger Rock, and Anglo-Namibians knew it as the Finger of God. When the rock crashed down, white Namibians interpreted the event as a sign of divine discontent with the notion of Namibian independence. Blacks countered this notion with the speculation that God had in fact held up a single finger *until* the prospect of Namibian independence!

If you want to see the remnants, turn east from the B1 on to the D1066 about 2km south of the village of Asab; after 12km, turn right on to the D620 and continue along for 10km to the site.

Places to Stay

Brukkaros Community Camp Site Camping US$2 per person, stone bungalows US$8 per person. The clear night skies make camping at Brukkaros a truly magical experience. Water and washing facilities are available.

Getting There & Away

Brukkaros rises 35km west of Tses, on the B1. Follow the C98 west for 40km and then turn north on to the D3904 about 1km east of Berseba. It's then 8km to the car park.

BERSEBA

☎ 063

The tiny Nama settlement of Berseba dates back to 1850 and is now home to around 1800 people. This is as lonely and forlorn a place as you can imagine, but it's worth a brief side trip from Brukkaros to see the settlement's proud church, the graveyard and the corrugated-iron dome dwellings, which appear to be unique in Namibia. On Monday, Star Line operates a return bus from Keetmanshoop (US$2, two hours).

KEETMANSHOOP

☎ 063

Keetmanshoop, with 15,000 people, is the main crossroads of southern Namibia. It has more petrol stations per capita than any other town in Namibia, which perhaps hints at its main function for travellers.

History

The original Keetmanshoop was a Nama settlement evocatively called Nugaoes (Nama for 'black mud'), on the banks of the Swartmodder River (Afrikaans for 'black mud'). A mission station was established in April 1866 by Reverend Johann Schröder of the Rhenish Mission Society at the behest of the Nama people who had undergone a conversion to Christianity. When Reverend Schröder founded the town, it was named after German industrialist and philanthropist Johann Keetmann, who funded the mission.

Schröder's successor, Reverend Thomas Fenchel, constructed the first mission station and church, then stayed on for 33 years.

The church was swept away in the 1890 flood of black mud. Five years later, a new church was constructed and served the Christian community until 1930, when it was abandoned. Over the following years, it became a hang-out for squatters and suffered serious vandalism until 1960, when it was renovated. In 1978, it was declared a national monument and now houses the town museum.

Information

The helpful Southern Tourist Forum office (☎ 221266, fax 223813), in the municipal building, is open 7.30am to 12.30pm and 1.30pm to 4.30pm Monday to Friday and 9am to 11am Saturday.

Internet and email access are found at the Internet Cafe (☎ 225902) on 6th Ave for US$1.50 per hour. It's open 8am to 5pm Monday to Friday.

Keetmanshoop Museum

The museum *(Cnr Kaiser St & 7th Ave; open 7.30am-12.30pm & 2.30pm-4.30pm Mon-Fri)*, which is housed in the 1895 Rhenish mission church, outlines the history of Keetmanshoop displaying old photos, early farming implements, an old wagon and a model of a traditional Nama home. The garden outside contains a variety of interesting local plants. It welcomes donations.

Kaiserliches Postamt

Keetmanshoop has several fine examples of colonial architecture. The most prominent is the Kaiserliches Postamt *(Imperial Post Office; Cnr 5th Ave & Fenchel St)*. It was designed by architect Gottlieb Redecker and was built in 1910 for the newly established post and telegraph services. The prominent gable on the front once supported the telegraph mast and the remainder of the building housed postal officials, who made their deliveries by camel. It now houses the Southern Tourist Forum office.

Places to Stay

Municipal Camp & Caravan Park *(☎ 223 316, Cnr Kaiser St & 8th Ave)* Camping US$2 per vehicle plus US$3.50 per person.

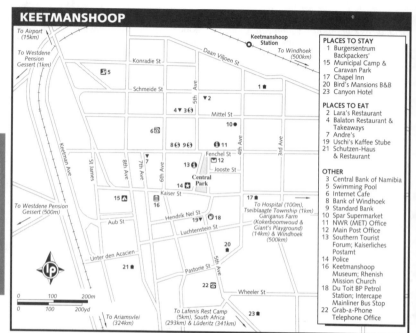

KEETMANSHOOP

PLACES TO STAY
1 Burgersentrum Backpackers'
15 Municipal Camp & Caravan Park
17 Chapel Inn
20 Bird's Mansions B&B
23 Canyon Hotel

PLACES TO EAT
2 Lara's Restaurant
4 Balaton Restaurant & Takeaways
7 Andre's
19 Uschi's Kaffee Stube
21 Schutzen-Haus & Restaurant

OTHER
3 Central Bank of Namibia
5 Swimming Pool
6 Internet Cafe
8 Bank of Windhoek
9 Standard Bank
10 Spar Supermarket
11 NWR (MET) Office
12 Main Post Office
13 Southern Tourist Forum; Kaiserliches Postamt
14 Police
16 Keetmanshoop Museum; Rhenish Mission Church
18 Du Toit BP Petrol Station; Intercape Mainliner Bus Stop
22 Grab-a-Phone Telephone Office

At this bougainvillea-decked place, the coin-operated laundry will probably be a welcome sight. The camp sites are now protected by razor wire. Showers cost an additional US$1.

Burgersentrum Backpackers' (☎ 223 454, 12 Schmeide St) Dorm beds US$7. This very simple place offers decent, cheap accommodation, but it's nothing special.

Westdene Pension Gessert (☎ 223892, 081-129 8242, e gesserts@iafrica .na, 148 13th Ave) Singles/doubles B&B US$26/38. This friendly and recommended place, 1km west of the town centre, is known for its truly amazing breakfasts.

Bird's Mansions (☎ 221711, e birdnest @iafrica.com.na, W birdnest.hyermart.net, 16 Pastorie St) Singles/doubles B&B US$27/44. Rooms at this good-value place have private bathroom, TV and phone. There's also a bar for guests.

Chapel Inn (☎/fax 223762, e frlodge@ iafrica.com.na, W www.resafrica.net/fish-river-lodge, 31A Kaiser St, PO Box 1840) Singles/doubles B&B US$22/35. This very friendly and recommended place, occupies a decommissioned church property, although the stone chapel occasionally holds services. The same owners run the Fish River Lodge (see later in this chapter) and can arrange transfers for US$47 per person (minimum two people). There are also tours to the Kokerboomwoud, which cost US$10.

Canyon Hotel (☎ 223361, fax 223714, 5th Ave, PO Box 950) Singles/doubles from US$44/68. This hotel is mainly used by business travellers and also by some tour groups.

Schutzen-Haus (☎ 223400, 8th Ave) Singles/doubles US$11/18. This is the local 'German Club' and has a popular restaurant, and clean, excellent-value accommodation with all rooms containing their own bath.

Lafenis Rest Camp (☎ 224316) Camping US$3.50 per site plus US$1.50 per person, 2-/4-bed self-catering bungalows US$38/

54. This plush camp, 5km south of the town, has horse riding and minigolf, as well as a laundry and a swimming pool.

Places to Eat

Lara's Restaurant (☎ 222233, Cnr 5th Ave & Schmeide St) Mains US$2-6. Open 11am-10pm daily. It may have strange decor and strange music, but the food is recommended.

Schutzen-Haus (☎ 223400, 8th Ave) Mains US$2-5. This German-style pub and restaurant is 200m south of the municipal camp site. The bar boasts an unusual L-shaped billiard table.

Andre's (☎ 222572, Fenchel St) Mains & pizzas US$3-5. Open for breakfast, lunch and dinner. This formerly fabulous restaurant has changed hands and now the results vary greatly.

Balaton Restaurant & Takeaways (☎ 222539, Mittel St) Mains US$3-5, takeaways US$1.50-3. Open for breakfast, lunch and dinner. This homely place specialises in Hungarian cuisine.

Uschi's Kaffee Stube (☎ 222445, Cnr 5th Ave & Hendrik Nel St) Pizzas US$2.50-5. Open 8am-7pm daily. This pizza place also serves breakfast, lunch, coffee, tea and afternoon snacks.

A couple of the petrol stations also have takeaways. For self-catering, your best option is *Spar Supermarket*, on the corner of 4th Ave and Mittel St.

Entertainment

Power House Bottle Store & Jupiter Disco (☎ 224693, 081-127 9666, Rose's Inn, Tseiblaagte) Afternoon/evening cover charge US$0.75/1. Keetmanshoop doesn't exactly rock around the clock, but what action there is focuses on the Power House & Jupiter. It's in the Tseiblaagte township, which is a high crime area, so don't attempt to walk there.

Swimming Pool (☎ 221271, Konradie St) US$0.20. Open 10am-7pm Mon-Fri. This pool is a refreshing option for a warm day in Namibia's sunniest town.

Getting There & Away

Bus Intercape Mainliner buses between Windhoek (US$24, five hours) and Cape Town (US$34, 13¾ hours) stop at Keetmanshoop's Du Toit BP petrol station. Southbound buses stop at 10pm on Sunday, Monday, Wednesday and Friday, and northbound buses at 12.45am on Monday, Wednesday, Friday and Saturday.

Minibuses connect Keetmanshoop with Windhoek a couple of times daily. Star Line (☎ 292202) has buses to Lüderitz (US$8, 4¾ hours), via Bethanie (US$7, 3½ hours) at 7.30am Monday to Saturday; from Lüderitz they leave at 12.30pm. Star Line also runs buses to Helmeringhausen (US$5.50, five hours) on Tuesday, Aroab (US$5, four hours) on Wednesday and Rosh Pinah (US$8.50, 7½ hours) on Tuesday and Thursday. Rosh Pinah buses continue to Oranjemund (US$11, 9½ hours), but you need Consolidated Diamond Mines (CDM) permission to enter the town.

Train Overnight trains run Sunday to Friday between Windhoek (US$9, 11 hours) and Keetmanshoop. On Wednesday and Saturday mornings, these trains continue to Upington in South Africa. For train information, phone Trans-Namib (☎ 292202).

Hitching It is fairly easy to hitch on the B1 between Keetmanshoop and Windhoek or Grünau, but there's less traffic between Keetmanshoop and Lüderitz. Hitchers to Fish River Canyon can best reach Ai-Ais via Grünau and Hobas via Seeheim.

AROUND KEETMANSHOOP
☎ 063

//Garas Park

The country north of Keetmanshoop is dotted with pockets of igneous intrusions, where intriguing heaps of dolerite boulders form fantasy landscapes enhanced by kokerboom trees.

//Garas Park (☎/fax 223217, e morkel@ namibnet.com, 22km north of town, PO Box 106; open 7am-7pm daily) is a private farm where the owners have laid out a series of nature drives and hiking tracks around a small camp site – all enhanced by lots of odd sculptures made from spare junk. Camping here costs US$3 plus US$1 per

car and US$1 per person. Day entry is US$1 per car and US$1 per person.

Kokerboom Forest & Giant's Playground

One of Namibia's largest stand of kokerbooms is at Kokerboomwoud, on the Gariganus Farm, 14km north-east of Gariganus.

Visitors can access the Giant's Playground, a bizarre natural rock garden a further 5km away. The odd, black 'building block' formations were created by igneous intrusions into overlying sediments around 170 million years ago. When the surrounding sediments eroded away, all that remained was the more resistant *ysterklip* or 'iron rock'.

Chapel Inn in Keetmanshoop runs day tours from the town for US$10 per person.

***Quivertree Rest Camp** (☎/fax 222835, e quiver@iafrica.com.na, PO Box 262)* Camping US$4 per person, 'igloo' bungalows US$20/30 singles/doubles. Quivertree offers the closest available accommodation to the Kokerboomwoud. Breakfast and dinner are available for US$3 and US$7.

Naute Dam

This large dam on the Löwen River is surrounded by low truncated hills. It attracts

---

Kokerbooms

Kokerbooms *(Aloe dichotoma)*, or quiver trees, are widespread throughout southern Namibia and north-western South Africa. They belong to the aloe family and can grow to heights of 8m. The name is derived from their lightweight branches, which were formerly used as quivers by the San hunters; they would remove the fibrous heart of the branch, leaving a strong, hollow tube.

The slow-growing kokerbooms occur mainly on rocky plains or slopes – they need rocks to anchor their shallow root systems – storing water in their succulent leaves, and fibrous trunk and branches. Water loss through transpiration is prevented by a waxy coating on the leaves and branches. In June and July, their yellow blooms appear, lending bright spots of colour to the desert.

---

large numbers of water birds and has been mooted as a new recreation area and wildlife reserve. On the northern shore is a lovely *picnic site* (US$1 per vehicle plus US$0.30 per person) and viewpoint. *Camping* (US$4 per person) is only available at a separate site on the southern shore.

To get to the dam, drive 30km west of Keetmanshoop on the B4 and turn south on the D545. The turn-off to the picnic site is about 25km down this road.

Seeheim

Heading south-west towards Lüderitz, you can take a break at the historic ***Seeheim Hotel** (☎/fax 250503, Seeheim rail halt, PO Box 1338)*. Camping US$7 per person, rooms without/with bathroom US$19/27 per person. This historic place is full of antique furniture and offers good value. The historic bar is particularly interesting – especially the beer-swilling shade-wearing baboon – and the restaurant is known for the best toasties in Namibia. It also does lunches and dinners, which are heavy on beef and game meat.

About 13km west of Seeheim (on the B4) is the Naiams farm, where a signpost indicates a 15-minute walk to the remains of a 1906 German fort. The fort was raised to prevent Nama attacks on German travellers and Lüderitz-bound freight.

GOAGEB
☎ 063

This apparently dying town has little to offer but petrol, which is very handy if you're heading to Lüderitz from Fish River Canyon. Otherwise, there's little to detain you but a sparsely stocked food shop and a bottle store that's fortunately locked up most of the time.

***Konkiep Motel** (☎ 283566, fax 283107, PO Box 98, Bethanie)* Rooms US$18 per person B&B. Situated beside Konkiep River, this place has simple cabins with a kitchen, pool and braai facilities. Ask for backpackers rates.

BETHANIE
☎ 063

One of Namibia's oldest settlements, Bethanie was first called Klipfontein (Afrikaans for 'rock spring'), but was later renamed Bethanien (this was eventually Anglicised to Bethanie), after the Jerusalem suburb. It was founded in 1814 by the London Missionary Society, but oddly enough, the first missionary, Reverend Heinrich Schmelen, wasn't English but German. London had experienced a staffing crisis and recruited missionaries trained in Berlin. After seven years, the mission was abandoned due to tribal squabbling, and although Schmelen attempted to revive it several times, he was thwarted by drought and in 1828 he left. After 12 years, Bethanie was handed over to the Rhenish Missionary Society.

Things to See

Schmelen's original 1814 mission station, Schmelenhaus, occupied a one-storey cottage. It was burned when he left Bethanie in 1828, but was rebuilt in 1842 by the first Rhenish missionary, Rev Hans Knudsen. The building now sits on the grounds of the Evangelical Lutheran Church and houses a **museum** full of old photos of the mission. If it's locked, a notice on the door will tell you where to pick up a key.

Other historical buildings include a **church**, built in 1859 by the missionary Hermann Kreft. It once had two towers, but they started to collapse and were removed. The church later served as a school, but is now dilapidated.

Also worth a look is the 1883 home of Captain Joseph Fredericks, the Nama chief who signed a treaty with the representatives of Adolf Lüderitz on 1 May 1883 for the transfer of Angra Pequena (Lüderitz). It was here in October the following year, that Captain Fredericks and the German Consul General, Dr Friedrich Nachtigal, signed a treaty of German protection over the entire territory.

Places to Stay & Eat

Bethanie Hotel (☎ 283071, Keetmanshoop St, PO Box 13) Singles/doubles US$22/35. This place continues to improve and it also has a dining room.

Bethanie Outfitters & Motors (☎ 283 007, Keetmanshoop St) Camping US$7,

singles/doubles US$15/19 B&B. You have to admit that it's enigmatically named!

Getting There & Away

The Bethanie turn-off is signposted on the B4, 140km west of Keetmanshoop. On Tuesday and Friday, a Star Line bus runs from Keetmanshoop (US$7, 3½ hours) to Bethanie at 7.30am and returns at 4pm. The daily Keetmanshoop-Lüderitz bus also stops at Bethanie.

DUWISIB CASTLE
☎ 063

Duwisib Castle *(D826; admission US$3 with guided tour; open 8am-1pm & 2pm-5pm daily)* is a curious baroque structure 70km south-west of Maltahöhe. It was built in 1909 by Baron Captain Hans-Heinrich von Wolf, who came from Dresden in Germany and was descended from Saxon nobility. After the German-Nama war, von Wolf went home and married Jayta Humphries, the step-daughter of the US consul in Dresden. Upon their return to German South-West Africa, the couple commissioned architect Willie Sander to design a home that would reflect von Wolf's commitment to the German military cause and closely resemble the Schutztruppe forts of Namutoni, Gibeon and Windhoek.

Although the stone for the castle was quarried nearby, much of the raw material was imported from Germany, and required 20 ox-wagons to transport it across the 330km of desert from Lüderitz. Artesans and masons were hired from as far away as Ireland, Denmark, Sweden and Italy. The result was a U-shaped castle with 22 rooms, suitably fortified and decorated with family portraits and military paraphernalia. Rather than windows, most rooms have embrasures, which emphasise von Wolf's apparent obsession with security.

In August 1914, the von Wolfs set sail for England in search of stud horses for their stables, but WWI broke out and their ship was diverted to Rio de Janeiro. Jayta (still a US citizen) found a passage on a Dutch ship to Holland, but von Wolf had to travel as a stowaway. Eventually, they both reached

Germany, where von Wolf rejoined the army. In 1916, however, he was killed at the Battle of the Somme in France. Jayta settled in Switzerland and in 1920, sold the castle to a Swedish family, who in turn sold it in 1937 to the Duwisib Pty Ltd.

Ownership of the Duwisib Castle and its surrounding 50 hectares were transferred to the state in the late 1970s. It was opened to the public in 1991 and now houses an impressive collection of 18th- and 19th-century antiques and armour.

Places to Stay

Duwisib Castle Rest Camp Camping US$12 for two people plus US$2 for each additional person. This very amenable camping ground occupies one corner of the castle grounds; pre-book through NWR in Windhoek. The adjoining kiosk sells snacks, coffee and cool drinks.

Farm Duwisib (☎/fax 223994, e nfy-elke@ mweb.com.na, D826) Doubles without/with full board US$50/86. This place, 300m from the castle, has self-catering rooms; meals are available on request. While you're there, look at the historic blacksmith shop up the hill.

Betta's Camping (☎ 0668 ask for 5603, fax 293168, e henri@iafrica.com.na, Cnr D826 & D407, PO Box 107, Maltahöhe) Camping US$4.50 per person. This relatively new camp site, 20km west of Duwisib Castle, is best known for its useful Caltex petrol station in the desert. Snacks are available here.

Getting There & Away

There isn't any public transport to Duwisib Castle. If you're coming from Helmeringhausen, head north on the C14 for 62km and turn north-west on to the D831. Continue for 27km, then turn west onto the D826 and travel a further 15km to the castle.

MALTAHÖHE
☎ 063

Without much to recommend it but an excellent little hotel, Maltahöhe provides an address for a very large swathe of southern Namibia, including lots of lodges, guest

farms and karakul ranches. The name, 'Malta's heights', honours Malta von Burgsdorff, who was the wife of Lieutenant von Burgsdorff. The lieutenant took over command of the Gibeon district following the German-Nama war.

The main sites of interest are the **historic graveyards**. The one just east of the town contains graves of Schutztruppe soldiers killed in the wars between the colonial forces and Nama leader Hendrik Witbooi. At the Nomtsas farm, 55km north, are the graves of the family and neighbours of Ernst Hermann, who were killed in 1904 by Hendrik Witbooi's rebels.

Places to Stay & Eat

Hotel Maltahöhe (☎ 293013, fax 293133, PO Box 20) Singles/doubles US$25/41. A couple of times this comfortable place has won Namibia's Best Country Hotel award. The restaurant and bar are open in the evening.

Atelier du Désert (☎/fax 293304, e bge nevincent@hotmail.com, PO Box 120) Singles/doubles US$27/39 B&B. This French-run guesthouse has five rooms and a nice little garden. Activities are available at the adjacent Swartkuppe farm. The rundown and unguarded *camp site* in the town should be used only in an emergency.

There are also several decent out-of-town options.

Daweb Guest Farm (☎/fax 293088, e da web@natron.net, w www.natron.net/tour /daweb, C14, PO Box 18) Camping US$4.50 per person, doubles with half board US$75. The name of this working cattle ranch, 2km south of Maltahöhe, is Nama for 'Tamarisk'. Rooms are in the lovely Cape Dutch–style farmhouse and guests can learn about Namibian cattle-ranching or participate in guided walking or 4WD expeditions in the surrounding countryside.

La Vallée Tranquille (☎/fax 293508, e tran quille@natron.net, w www.natron.net/tour/ tranquille/premier.html, C14, PO Box 70) Doubles US$102 with half board and activities. Set on a 13,000-hectare farm, 60km south of Maltahöhe, this French-run guesthouse provides a warm, friendly ambience.

Activities include hiking, donkey-cart rides and sundowners at a ruined fort.

Getting There & Away
Star Line's bus between Mariental and Walvis Bay passes through Maltahöhe every second week, and isn't much use to anyone. Travel in this region typically requires a private vehicle or a well-oiled thumb (and a good measure of patience).

HELMERINGHAUSEN
☎ 063
Tiny Helmeringhausen is little more than a homestead, hotel and petrol station, and has been the property of the Hester family since 1919.

Agricultural Museum
The village highlight is the idiosyncratic Agricultural Museum (☎ 283083, Main St; admission free; open on request), which was established in 1984 by the Helmeringhausen Farming Association. It may appear to be a pile of discarded junk, but on closer inspection, you'll find all sorts of interesting old furniture and farming implements – wagons, machinery and tools – collected from farms around the area, as well as an antique fire engine from Lüderitz. To visit pick up a key from the hotel next door.

Mooifontein
At the end of the 19th century, Mooifontein ('Beautiful Spring' – one of hundreds in Southern Africa), 21km south-east of the village, was the site of a German garrison. The current farmhouse is a rebuilt version of the original barracks, which was prefabricated in Germany in 1899 and transferred to this site beside the Konkiep River. You can also visit the semicircular cemetery for German soldiers who died during the German-Nama war between 1903 and 1907.

Places to Stay
Helmeringhausen Hotel (☎ 283083, fax 283 132, Main St, PO Box 21) Singles/doubles B&B US$38/42. At this friendly place the rooms are clean, the food is excellent, the beer is always cold and there's a well-

stocked cellar. However, even those who like game meat may feel uncomfortable being watched by all those accusing stuffed animal heads. On request, you may also partake in a tour to Mooifontein and nearby rock paintings.

Sinclair Guest Farm (☎ 226979, fax 226999, e logufa@mweb.com.na, 65km on the D407, PO Box 19) Singles/doubles with half board US$71/118. This two-star place was originally purchased from a Nama chief by two Scottish settlers in the 1870s to gain access to the historic copper mines and legend has it that the price was two wheelbarrows of brandy. Later, they set up a farm and sold it to the grandparents of the present owners. Guests can now enjoy organised walks, drives and excursions to the ancient copper workings 3km from the farmhouse.

Getting There & Away
On Tuesday, Star Line operates a return bus between Keetmanshoop (US$5.50, five hours) and Helmeringhausen, via Bethanie (US$3, three hours).

The South Coast

Namibia's southern coastal area includes the town of Lüderitz, which is rich in colonial architecture, the Sperrgebiet (the closed Diamond Area 1) and the southern end of the Namib-Naukluft Park.

AUS
☎ 063
Tranquil Aus is situated 125km east of Lüderitz on the B4. The curious name means 'out' in German, but is actually derived from a Khoi-Khoi word which means 'place of snakes'. After the Germans surrendered to the South African forces at Otavi on 9 July 1915, Aus became one of two internment camps for German military personnel. Military police and officers were sent to Okanjanje in the north and the noncommissioned officers went to Aus.

Before long, 1552 prisoners and 600 South African guards were housed in tents and exposed to poor conditions and extreme

SOUTHERN NAMIBIA

temperatures. These resourceful inmates, however, turned to brickmaking and constructed houses, then sold the excess bricks to the guards for 10 shillings per 1000. The houses weren't opulent – roofs were tiled with unrolled food tins – but they did provide protection from the elements. The prisoners also built several wood stoves, and eventually sank boreholes to provide water for the camp and built barracks for the guards.

After the Treaty of Versailles, the camp was dismantled and by May 1919, it was closed. Virtually nothing remains, but some attempt has been made to reconstruct one of the brick houses. The former camp is 4km east of the village, down a gravel road, then to the right; there's now a national plaque commemorating it.

If you understand Afrikaans, you may wish to seek out the book *Aus 1915–1919*, which contains a map and covers the historical background of the town. It's sold at the bookshop in Lüderitz.

Places to Stay & Eat

Bahnhof Hotel (*☎ 258091, Bahnhof St*) Singles/doubles US$24/27. Some people find that part of the appeal of rustic-looking Aus is this very friendly and quaint place. Rooms are musty but comfortable, and there's a perfectly acceptable bar and a restaurant.

Namib Garage (*☎/fax 258029, Bahnhof St, PO Box 29*) Camping US$3 per person, singles/doubles US$16/24. This enigmatically named place sells petrol and has a small grocery, takeaway and coffee shop as well as accommodation. Meals are available with advance booking.

Klein Aus Vista (*☎/fax 258021, [e] ausvista@ldz.namib.com, kleinaus@namibiaweb.com, PO Box 25*) Camping US$7 per vehicle plus US$2 per person, singles/doubles US$48/84, Geister Schlucht hut US$17 per person for up to six people plus US$13 for each additional person, Eagle's Nest hut singles/doubles US$38/62, Feral Horse Chalet 2/4 people US$34/56. The fabulous Klein Aus Vista, occupies a 10,000-hectare ranch along the Lüderitz

road, 3km west of Aus. Hikers will love the magical four-day hiking route, which traverses some of Namibia's most incredible landscapes. Meals are available at the main restaurant and bar, and accommodation is in rooms at the main lodge or in one of the two wonderful hiking huts: **Geister Schlucht** (Ghost Canyon) and **Eagle's Nest**. The former is a 10-bed dorm hut hidden in a Shangri-la-like valley surrounded by fabulous peaks; it's open to only one party at a time. The more opulent Eagle's Nest is built right into the rocks and enjoys a view over the vast Namib plains. It accommodates three parties at a time; in one of the rooms, 'The Cave', the bed is wedged between two enormous boulders. There's also the more pedestrian **Feral Horse Chalet** at the main lodge. All huts are equipped with a stove, fridge and hot showers. You can also rent mountain bikes, go horse riding (including multiday rides), and take guided tours to view the wild horses (see the boxed text 'Feral Desert Horses').

Namtib Biosphere Reserve (*☎/fax 061-233597, [e] namtib@iafrica.com.na, 12km off the D707, PO Box 19*) Singles/doubles US$52 per person, including meals and wildlife drive. Namtib Farm, in the desolate Tirasberge area north of Aus, has been listed as a biosphere reserve. Run by ecologically conscious owners, it's situated in a valley surrounded by mountains, with an ethereal view over the Namib plains. The simple rooms are adequate and it offers myriad opportunities for hikers. To get there, take the C13 north for 55km, then turn west on the D707 and continue for 48km until you reach the farm turn-off. From there, it's 12km east.

There are four beautiful Tiras mountain farms in the 125,000-hectare ***Tiras Mountain Conservancy*** (*☎ 0638 ask for 6522, fax 061-242535, [e] eco@iafrica.com.na, D707, PO Box 14, Helmeringhausen*). Each farm has its own unique character.

Getting There & Away

Star Line buses between Keetmanshoop and Lüderitz stop in Aus, and will also drop you off at Klein Aus Vista.

THE AUS-LÜDERITZ ROAD

If you've come as far as Aus, chances are you're heading for Lüderitz. Between Aus and the coast, the road crosses the desolate southern Namib, which is distinct from the flat gravel plains to the north; to the south is the prohibited Diamond Area 1. The pastel-coloured Awasib and Uri-Hauchab ranges rise from a greenish-grey plain through a mist of windblown sand and dust, the effect being both mesmerising and ethereal.

About 10km out of Aus, start watching out for feral desert horses (see the boxed text). About 20km west of Aus, turn north at the sign 'Feral Horses' and follow the track for 1.5km to Garub Pan. Here you'll find a hide and an artificial water hole,

which is pumped to provide water for the horses. The informative display has sadly faded due to the sun and windblown sand, but you may get something out of it.

When the wind blows – which is most of the time – the final 10km into Lüderitz may be blocked by a barchan dunefield that seems bent upon crossing the road. Conditions do get hazardous, especially if it's foggy, and the drifts pile quite high before road crews clean them off.

LÜDERITZ
☎ 063

Lüderitz is a surreal colonial relic huddling against the barren, windswept Namib Desert coast. Scarcely touched by the 21st

SOUTHERN NAMIBIA

Feral Desert Horses

On the desert plains west of Aus live some of the world's only wild desert-dwelling horses. The origin of these eccentric equines is unclear, however, several theories do abound. One theory suggests that the horses descended from German Schutztruppe cavalry horses abandoned during the South African invasion in 1915, while others claim they were brought in by Nama raiders moving north from beyond the Orange River. Yet another theory asserts that they descended from a load of shipwrecked horses en route from Europe to Australia. Still others maintain that the horses descended from the stud stock of Baron Captain Hans-Heinrich von Wolf, the original owner of the Duwisib Castle, who set off for Germany in search of more horses, but was killed in battle in France and never returned to Namibia.

These horses, whose bony and scruffy appearance belies their probable high-bred ancestry and apparent adaptation to the harsh conditions, are protected inside the Diamond Area 1. In years of good rain, they grow fat and their numbers increase. At present, the population fluctuates between 150 and 160, but there have never been more than 280 individual horses. Their only source of water is Garub Pan, which is fed by an artificial bore hole.

If not for the efforts of Consolidated Diamond Mines (CDM) security officer Jan Coetzer, the horses would probably have been wiped out long ago. He recognised that they were clearly horses of high breeding and managed to secure funding to install the bore hole at Garub Pan. At one stage, the Ministry of Environment & Tourism (MET) considered taming the horses for use on patrols in Etosha National Park, but nothing ever came of it. There have also been calls to exterminate the horses, by individuals citing possible damage to the desert environment and gemsbok herds. So far, however, the tourism value of the horses has swept aside all counter-arguments and in Europe, for instance, various wildlife organisations have organised fundraising drives for their benefit. So for the moment, at least, their future appears to be secure.

The horses may also be valuable for scientific purposes. The region where they live is so dry that the horses are relatively free of disease and parasites, and having been isolated for so long, they're unlikely to have any immunity to disease, making them ideal for immunity studies. In addition, as they urinate less and are smaller than their supposed ancestors, the horses are able to go without water for up to five days at a time. These adaptations may be valuable in helping scientists understand how animals cope with changing climatic conditions.

century, this remote town might recall a Bavarian *dorfchen* (small village), with its bakeries, coffee shops, *Jugendstil* (Art-Nouveau) architecture and a Lutheran church rising above the lesser buildings.

Here, the icy but clean South Atlantic supports seals, penguins and other marine life, and the desolate beaches are also home to flamingoes and ostriches. The picturesque port supports a fleet of crayfish (rock lobster) boats, which are active during the crayfish season from November to April. Other industries include the harvest of seaweed and seagrass, which are mainly exported to Japan, and experimental oyster, mussel and prawn farms.

History

Although artefacts have revealed that early Khoi-Khoi people passed through Lüderitz, it's unlikely that they lived permanently in such an inhospitable spot.

On 25 December 1487, Portuguese navigator Bartolomeu Dias and his three ships, sailed down the coast he called the Areias do Inferno (Sands of Hell) into Lüderitz Bay, which he named Angra das Voltas (Bay of the Turnabouts), because he could only enter the bay by tacking cautiously into the wind. (The bay later became known – somewhat less creatively – as Angra Pequena, or Little Bay.) Here Dias sheltered from the weather for five days, and in July 1488, he returned north from the Cape of Good Hope and, in keeping with Portuguese seafaring custom, he erected a stone cross near the bay entrance at Diaz Point.

Apart from a brief 1677 attempt by Cornelius Wobma of the Dutch East India Company to trade with the Nama, it was over 300 years before Europeans returned to Lüderitz. In 1793, faced with possible rival interests, the Dutch governor of the Cape sent Captain Duminy in his ship *Meermin* to annex Angra Pequena and its surrounding islands.

During the next half century, Dutch whalers operated in Lüderitz and the offshore islands became a rich source of guano. Between 1844 and 1848, hundreds of thousands of tonnes of guano were scraped off the most productive islands. Unfortunately,

the rich pickings attracted more guano collectors than the islands could support, leading to inevitable clashes. There are reports that initially, the various groups lobbed penguin eggs at each other to prevent perceived infringements of collection rights. When they graduated to firearms, a British warship was dispatched to restore order, and shortly thereafter, the British administration in the Cape sent Captain Alexander in his ship, the *Star*, to annex Angra Pequena and all guano islands for Britain's Cape Colony.

On 9 April 1883, Heinrich Vogelsang, under orders from Bremen merchant Adolf Lüderitz, entered into a treaty with Nama chief Joseph Fredericks. It granted Vogelsang the rights to any lands within an 8km radius of Angra Pequena in exchange for £100 sterling and 60 rifles; for a further £500 and another 60 rifles, he also purchased a 32km-wide coastal strip from the Orange River to the 26th parallel.

Later that year, Adolf Lüderitz made an appearance in Lüderitz, and on 24 April 1884, on Lüderitz' recommendation, the German chancellor Otto von Bismarck designated south-western Africa a protectorate of the German empire. In October 1886, on the verge of bankruptcy, Adolf Lüderitz sailed south to the Orange River in search of business prospects, but on the way back, he went missing at sea and was never seen again.

In 1904, during the German-Nama war, Lüderitz was used as a prisoner of war camp and two years later, the railway line was completed to Keetmanshoop. On 1 November 1909, after diamonds (see the boxed text 'Diamond Dementia in the Desert' later in this section) had brought growth and prosperity to this remote outpost, Lüderitz was officially granted town status.

Information

Tourist Offices The tourist office, run by Lüderitzbucht Safaris & Tours (☎ 202719), is currently the only place to buy visitor permits for Kolmanskop. It's open 7.30am to 12.30pm and 1.30pm to 5pm Monday to Friday, 8am to noon Saturday and 8.30am to 10am Sunday. It also sells curios, phonecards, film (including Fujichrome) and books; the inexpensive booklet *Stormcoast* provides an introduction to Lüderitz history.

The helpful NWR office (☎ 202752) is open from 7.30am to 1pm and 2pm to 4pm Monday to Friday.

Money Several major banks have branches on Bismarck St.

Post & Communications The post office on Bismarck St has public phones. For Internet access, Namibnet I-cafe (☎ 203084) is open from 9am to 1pm and 2pm to 5pm Monday to Friday and 9am to noon on Saturday. It costs US$2 for 30 minutes.

Bookshops The best place for books is the tourist office. Tailings Shop sells second-hand paperbacks, and the Kolmanskop Cafeteria in Kolmanskop has a selection of historic German novels and modern German pulp fiction.

Laundry You can clean up your act at Ann's Dry Cleaning & Laundry Service (☎ 203737).

Dangers & Annoyances Stay well clear of the Diamond Area 1 or Sperrgebiet (German for 'closed area'). The northern boundary is formed by the B4 and extends almost as far east as Aus. The Sperrgebiet boundary is patrolled by some fairly ruthless characters and trespassers will be prosecuted (or worse).

Felsenkirche

The prominent Evangelical Lutheran church, Felsenkirche *(Kirch St; admission free; open 6pm-7pm Mon-Sat Oct-Apr, 5pm-6pm Mon-Sat May-Sept)*, dominates Lüderitz from high on Diamond Hill. The town first petitioned for a church as early as 1906, and due to the German-Nama war, the railway and the discovery of diamonds, by 1909 the population was sufficient to bear the costs. It was designed by Albert Bause, who implemented the Victorian influences that he'd seen in the Cape. With the assistance from private donors in Germany, construction of

the church began in late 1911 and was completed the following year. The brilliant stained-glass panel situated over the altar was donated by Kaiser Wilhelm II and the Bible was a gift from his wife.

Happily, the opening hours coincide with the best time for viewing the extraordinary stained-glass work over the altar, which glows brilliantly in the late afternoon sun.

Lüderitz Museum

Lüderitz Museum *(☎ 202582, Diaz St; admission US$0.80; open 3.30pm-5pm Mon-Fri)* contains information on the town's history and includes displays on natural history, local indigenous groups, Bartolomeu Dias and the diamond-mining industry. Phone to arrange a visit outside standard opening hours.

Agate Bay

Agate Bay, just north of Lüderitz, is made of tailings from the diamond workings. There aren't many agates these days, but you'll find a fine sand partially consisting of tiny grey mica chips.

Colonial Architecture

Lüderitz is chock-a-block with colonial buildings and every view reveals something interesting. The curiously intriguing architecture, which mixes German Imperial and Jugendstil styles (check out the odd little Concert and Ball Hall), makes this bizarre little town appear even more other-worldly.

Goerke Haus Lieutenant Hans Goerke came to Swakopmund with the Schutztruppe in 1904 and was later posted to Lüderitz, where he served as a diamond company manager. His home *(Diamantberg St; admission US$1; open 2pm-3pm Mon-Fri, 4pm-5pm Sat)*, designed by architect Otto Ertl and constructed in 1910 on Diamond Hill, was one of the town's most extravagant.

Goerke left for Germany in 1912 and eight years later, his home was purchased by the newly formed CDM to house their chief engineer. When the CDM headquarters transferred to Oranjemund in 1944, the house was sold to the government and

SOUTHERN NAMIBIA

became occupied by the resident Lüderitz magistrate. In 1981, however, the magistrate was shifted to Keetmanshoop and the house so desperately needed repair that it was sold back to the CDM for a token sum of R10 on the condition that it be renovated.

The CDM did an admirable job, and now this amazing blend of Jugendstil elements and period furnishings is open to the public, except when the CDM has visitors.

Old Train Station Lüderitz's first train station (on the corner of Bahnhof & Bismarck Sts) was completed in 1907 – along with the railway line itself, but with the discovery of diamonds, the facilities became swamped and a new station was commissioned in 1912 to handle the increased traffic. The imposing but unused station that stands on the site today, was designed by state architect Lohse and took two years to complete.

Old Post Office The old post office *(Schinz St)* was originally designed by railway commissioner Oswald Reinhardt, but before the building was built his successor added a first floor and a tower. The building was completed in 1908 and it now houses the MET.

Activities

A rewarding activity is to dig for the lovely crystals of calcium sulphate and gypsum known as sand roses, which develop when moisture seeps into the sand and causes it to adhere and crystallise into flowery shapes. NWR issues digging permits that cost US$1.50 and are valid for a two-hour dig and up to three sand roses or a total weight of 1.5kg. Diggers must be accompanied by an MET official, and have to use their hands or other light tools to extract the sandroses. You may not use hard tools lest you damage other buried specimens.

Believe it or not, there's a golf course (at the time of writing, it was being re-located from the east of the town to a more secure site at Radford Bay). However, it isn't exactly green and there's no shortage of sand traps. The new clubhouse will probably be

open daily; check with the tourist office for the latest details.

Organised Tours

Coastways Tours Lüderitz (☎ 202362, fax 203220, e daggiecw@iafrica.com.na, PO Box 575) Coastway's three-day 4WD trail heads up the coast from Lüderitz through the old Diamond Area 2 to Saddle Hill and Spencer Bay (see the Central Namib Desert chapter map). Near Spencer Bay you can see the shipwrecks *Otavi*, a guano trader which ran aground in the 1940s; *United Trader*, which ran aground in the early 1970s carrying 700 tonnes of explosives – it was detonated in 1974 and debris rained down across a 5km radius; and the *Arkona*, which ran aground north of Spencer Bay. You'll have to drive over barren coastal dunes for much of the route so a good 4WD vehicle is essential. Trips cost US$45 per person per day and trips book up quickly so reserve a place well in advance.

Lüderitzbucht Safaris & Tours (☎ 202 719, fax 202863, e ludsaf@africaonline .com.na) Tours of the area are offered by this company, which runs the tourist office and organises Kolmanskop Tour Company trips and CDM permits for several areas of the Sperrgebiet: Kolmanskop, Elizabeth Bay, the Atlas Bay seal colony, the 55m Bogenfels Arch, Maerchental Valley and the ghost town of Pomona. For Kolmanskop, you must buy a CDM permit at least 30 minutes in advance and have your own transport (see Around Lüderitz); for other Sperrgebiet tours, which run with a minimum of four participants, permits must be issued at least a week in advance. Bring your passport.

Weather permitting, the schooner *Sedina (☎ 204030)* sails daily to the Cape fur seal sanctuary at Diaz Point. The two- to 2½-hour trip costs US$20. When the sea is calm enough, it also visits the jackass penguin sanctuary on Halifax Island. Be sure to take warm clothing.

Places to Stay

Shark Island Camping US$9 for 2 people plus US$2 for each additional person, stan-

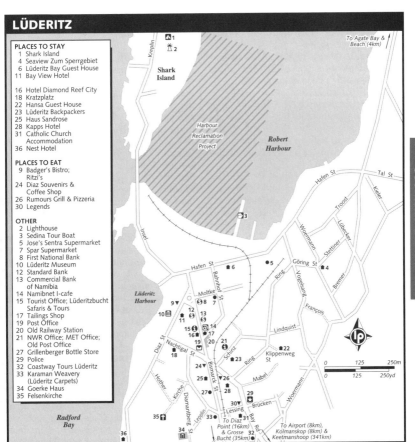

LÜDERITZ

PLACES TO STAY
1 Shark Island
4 Seaview Zum Sperrgebiet
6 Lüderitz Bay Guest House
11 Bay View Hotel

16 Hotel Diamond Reef City
18 Kratzplatz
22 Hansa Guest House
23 Lüderitz Backpackers
25 Haus Sandrose
28 Kapps Hotel
31 Catholic Church
   Accommodation
36 Nest Hotel

PLACES TO EAT
9 Badger's Bistro;
   Ritzi's
24 Diaz Souvenirs &
   Coffee Shop
26 Rumours Grill & Pizzeria
30 Legends

OTHER
2 Lighthouse
3 Sedina Tour Boat
5 Jose's Sentra Supermarket
7 Spar Supermarket
8 First National Bank
10 Lüderitz Museum
12 Standard Bank
13 Commercial Bank
   of Namibia
14 Namibnet I-cafe
15 Tourist Office; Lüderitzbucht
   Safaris & Tours
17 Tailings Shop
19 Post Office
20 Old Railway Station
21 NWR Office; MET Office;
   Old Post Office
27 Grillenberger Bottle Store
29 Police
32 Coastway Tours Lüderitz
33 Karaman Weavery
   (Lüderitz Carpets)
34 Goerke Haus
35 Felsenkirche

SOUTHERN NAMIBIA

---

dard/luxury bungalows US$37/64. Because of the recent harbour reclamation project, Shark Island is now an integral part of the mainland. It's situated by an aggravatingly windy camp site, which is connected to the town by a causeway. The centrepiece is a lighthouse that caps the central rock. Day entry will set you back US$1.50 per vehicle and US$1.50 per person. Book the bungalows through NWR (if space is available, bungalows and camp sites can also be booked at the entrance).

Lüderitz Backpackers (☎ 203632, fax 202000, e toya@ldz.namib.com, 7 Schinz St) Dorm beds US$7, doubles US$16. This place in an historic house offers all the usual backpacker amenities, including cooking facilities, a braai and good tourist information.

Catholic Church Accommodation (☎ 202 463, Bay Rd) Self-catering flats US$11 per person. This simple, but very good-value choice lets you cook your own meals. It's behind the Catholic Church off Bay Rd.

Haus Sandrose (☎ 202630, fax 202365, e sandrose@ldz.namib.com, clooser@afri caonline.com.na, 15 Bismarck St, PO Box 109) 2-/4-bed rooms US$34/67. This place has three very different rooms which are arranged around a sheltered garden; two of the units include self-catering facilities. Breakfast costs US$4.

Kratzplatz *(☎/fax 202458, 5 Nachtigal St)* Singles/doubles US$14/21. This little guesthouse offers good value.

Hansa Guest House *(☎/fax 203581,* e *stanley@ldz.namib.com, 5 Mabel St, PO Box 837)* Singles/doubles US$16/27. Occupying an historic home, this rustic guesthouse is situated high enough on the hill to provide wonderful sea views. Kitchen facilities are available.

Lüderitz Bay Guest House *(☎ 203019, Hafen St)* Singles/doubles with bathroom US$23/39. This German-style guesthouse overlooks the harbour and has well-appointed kitchen facilities.

Hotel Diamond Reef City *(☎ 203850, fax 203853,* e *fotofun@iafrica.com.na, Bismarck St, PO Box 1300)* Singles/doubles US$31/49. With a recommended restaurant and friendly reception, this rambling place is a good, comfortable choice right in the centre of Lüderitz. All rooms have high ceilings, private baths and cable TV, and some are quite oddly shaped.

Seaview Zum Sperrgebiet *(☎ 203411, fax 203414,* e *michaels@ldz.namib.com,* w *www.etosha.com/sea-view-hotel.htm, Cnr Woermann & Göring Sts)* Singles/doubles US$51/77, family rooms US$133. This imposing hotel boasts a glassed-in indoor swimming pool, a sauna, terraces and even an indoor banana tree. It's a natural favourite with German visitors, but the street name is probably ripe for changing.

Nest Hotel *(☎ 204000, fax 204001,* e *nest@ldz.namib.com,* w *www.natron .net/tour/nest-hotel/main.html, Diaz St, PO Box 690)* This bright place, on the rocky coast south of the centre, features seaview rooms, a sheltered pool and a sauna.

Bay View *(☎ 202288, fax 202402, Diaz St)* Singles/doubles US$30/51. This historic complex, owned by the Lüderitz family, has 30 cool and airy rooms, which open into shady courtyards; there's also a pool.

Kapps Hotel *(☎ 202345, fax 203555, Bay Rd)* Singles/doubles US$30/47. This is the town's oldest hotel but it has been recently renovated and retains only a hint of its historical ambience.

Places to Eat

If the sea has been bountiful, various hotels serve the catch of the day; specialities include crayfish, local oysters and kingklip. If the luck hasn't been running, you'll get frozen fish.

Diaz Souvenirs & Coffee Shop *(☎ 203 147, Cnr Bismarck St & Bay Rd)* Snacks from US$1, daily lunch specials US$3. Open 7.30am-6pm Mon-Fri, 7.30am-1pm & 3pm-6pm Sat, 8am-1pm & 3pm-6pm Sun. This bright place serves excellent toasties, light meals, coffee and cakes. On Sundays, the continental breakfast is US$3.50.

Badger's Bistro *(☎ 202855, Diaz St)* Lunch US$2.50-5, mains US$3-7, lobster US$15. Open 9am-midnight Mon-Fri, 9am-2pm & 6pm-midnight Sat. This is a great place for lunch, serving excellent burgers, toasted sandwiches, seafood specials, soup, salad and other light meals. In the evening, you can get beef and seafood, including lobster. It also has a popular bar attached where – unfortunately – the centrepiece is a noisy television.

Ritzi's Restaurant *(☎ 081-124 3353, Diaz St)* Mains US$6-10. Open 6pm-10pm Mon-Sat. This excellent seafood restaurant is always fully booked, so reservations are essential. Imaginative dishes are concocted from fish, lobster, venison and beef, but there's usually a vegetarian option. Enter through Badger's Bistro.

Rumours Grill & Pizzeria *(☎ 202655, Bay Rd)* Mains US$5-10, lobster from US$15. Open for lunch and dinner. This popular steak house at Kapp's Hotel, also serves up pizzas and other seafood. You can choose between the sports bar and the beer garden.

Legends *(☎ 203110, Bay Rd)* Mains US$5-10, lobster from US$15. Open 7pm Thur-Tues. This relatively elegant restaurant specialises in seafood – especially lobster – but you can also order beef and other mains.

For self-catering, there are ***Spar Supermarket*** and ***Jose's Sentra Supermarket***. The friendliest place to buy alcohol is ***Grillenberger Bottle Store***.

Entertainment
The best drinking spots are the sports bar at *Rumours* (☎ 202655) and the locally popular bar at *Badger's* (☎ 202855). Most of the hotels also have bars.

Shopping
Karaman Weavery (Lüderitz Carpets; ☎/fax 202272, ⓦ www.natron.net/luederitz-carpets/, 25 Bismarck St) Open 8am-1pm & 2pm-7pm Mon-Fri, Sat & Sun by arrangement. At this weavery, you will find local people handweaving high-quality rugs and garments in pastel desert colours, with Namibian flora and fauna the favoured designs. It accepts special orders and can post them worldwide.

Getting There & Away
Air Air Namibia travels four times a week between Windhoek and Lüderitz (US$105), continuing to Alexander Bay (Oranjemund). It also flies once weekly to and from Swakopmund (US$70) and twice weekly to and from Walvis Bay (US$70).

Bus The Star Line (☎ 312875) bus from Keetmanshoop (US$7, five hours) departs at 7.30am Monday to Saturday. It returns from Lüderitz at 12.30pm Sunday to Friday.

Car & Motorcycle Lüderitz and the scenery en route (see under The Aus-Lüderitz Road, earlier in this chapter) are worth the 300km trip from Keetmanshoop, via the tarred B4.

Getting Around
There's a limited taxi service between the airport and town centre. Car hire is available from J&A Trading & Shipping (☎ 202777).

AROUND LÜDERITZ
The Sperrgebiet
Sperrgebiet tours are booked through Lüderitzbucht Safaris & Tours, at the tourist office in Lüderitz (see the Organised Tours section earlier in this chapter). It organises CDM permits (adults/children aged six to 14 US$3.50/1.50) for Kolmanskop up to 30 minutes before a tour, but you must provide

your own transport to Kolmanskop. For other tours, you must secure the permit at least one week in advance through the Kolmanskop Tour Company (☎/fax 202445), including passport details for everyone in your group. It's open from 8.30am to 12.30pm Monday to Friday.

Kolmanskop A popular excursion from Lüderitz is the ghost town, Kolmanskop, which was named after an early Afrikaner trekker, Jani Kolman, whose ox-wagon became bogged in the sand there. Once the CDM headquarters (see the boxed text 'Diamond Dementia in the Desert'), Kolmanskop once boasted a casino, skittle alley and a theatre with fine acoustics. However, the slump in diamond sales after WWI and the discovery of richer pickings at Oranjemund ended its heyday and by 1956, the town was totally deserted. Some buildings have been restored, but many have been invaded by the dunes.

Tours in English and German are held at 9.30am and 10.45am Monday to Saturday, and at 10am Sundays and public holidays. Visitors must provide their own transport from town. To photograph Kolmanskop at other times of the day, you can purchase a special 'sunrise to sunset' permit for US$5.

After the tour, you can visit the museum, which contains relics and information on the

DAVID ELSE

The old ghost town of Kolmanskop has been abandoned since 1956.

SOUTHERN NAMIBIA

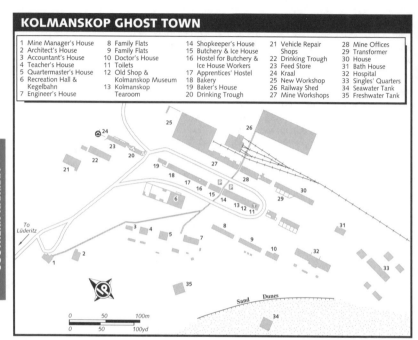

KOLMANSKOP GHOST TOWN

1 Mine Manager's House
2 Architect's House
3 Accountant's House
4 Teacher's House
5 Quartermaster's House
6 Recreation Hall & Kegelbahn
7 Engineer's House
8 Family Flats
9 Family Flats
10 Doctor's House
11 Toilets
12 Old Shop & Kolmanskop Museum
13 Kolmanskop Tearoom
14 Shopkeeper's House
15 Butchery & Ice House
16 Hostel for Butchery & Ice House Workers
17 Apprentices' Hostel
18 Bakery
19 Baker's House
20 Drinking Trough
21 Vehicle Repair Shops
22 Drinking Trough
23 Feed Store
24 Kraal
25 New Workshop
26 Railway Shed
27 Mine Workshops
28 Mine Offices
29 Transformer
30 House
31 Bath House
32 Hospital
33 Singles' Quarters
34 Seawater Tank
35 Freshwater Tank

history of Namibian diamond-mining. Check out the display on Oranjemund, the boom town to the south that supplanted Kolmanskop as the CDM headquarters and turned it into a ghost town.

The tearoom serves unimpressive cakes and chicory coffee until noon.

Elizabeth Bay In 1986, CDM again began prospecting in the northern Sperrgebiet and found bountiful diamond deposits around Elizabeth Bay, 30km south of Kolmanskop. The estimated 2.5 million carats weren't expected to last more than 10 years, but CDM installed a full-scale operation, and rather than duplicate their Lüderitz facilities here, they provided their workers with daily transport from the town. Half-day tours to Elizabeth Bay (US$27) also take in Kolmanskop and the Atlas Bay Cape fur seal colony.

Bogenfels One-third of the way down the Forbidden Coast between Lüderitz and

Oranjemund is the 55m natural sea arch known as Bogenfels (Bow Rock). Bogenfels has only been opened to tours (US$80) for a few years, which also take in the mining ghost town of Pomona, the Maerchental Valley, the Bogenfels ghost town and a large cave near the arch itself.

Lüderitz Peninsula

Radford Bay Radford Bay was named after David Radford, the first European to settle there in the 1860s. He lived from fishing and made a business of collecting shark liver oil. As there was no water, Radford survived by collecting the dews created by the heavy coastal fog. The **oyster farm** in Radford Bay wasn't offering tours at the time of research, but this may have changed. Ask at the Lüderitz tourist office for the latest information.

Sturmvogelbucht This picturesque and relatively calm bay has a lovely beach,

Diamond Dementia in the Desert

Although diamonds were discovered along the Orange River in South Africa from as early as 1866, and had also turned up among the guano workings on the offshore islands, it apparently didn't occur to anyone that the desert sands might also harbour a bit of crystal carbon.

In May 1908, however, railway worker Zacharias Lewala found a shiny stone along the railway line near Grasplatz and took it to his employer August Stauch, who knew exactly what it was. Stauch took immediate interest and to his elation, state geologist Dr Range confirmed that it was indeed a diamond. Stauch applied for a prospecting licence from the Deutsche Koloniale Gesellschaft and set up his own mining company, the Deutsche Diamanten Gesellschaft, to begin exploiting the presumed windfall.

This sparked off a frenzy, and hordes of prospectors descended upon Lüderitz with dreams of finding fabulous wealth buried in the sands. As a result, Lüderitz was soon rolling in dough, and service facilities sprang up to accommodate the growing population. In September 1908, after the diamond mania had escalated out of control and the German government intervened and established the Sperrgebiet. This 'closed area' extended from 26°S latitude southward to the Orange River mouth, and stretched inland for 100km. Independent prospecting was henceforth *verboten* and those who'd already staked their claims were forced to form mining companies.

In February 1909, a diamond board was created to broker all diamond sales and thereby control prices. However, after WWI, the world diamond market was so depressed that in 1920, Ernst Oppenheimer of the Anglo-American Corporation was able to purchase Stauch's company, along with eight other diamond-producing companies, and combine them to form the Consolidated Diamond Mines (CDM).

During WWI, Lüderitz had been occupied by South African forces and all residents of European descent were hauled off to POW camps in South Africa. They were later permitted to return, but by that time Lüderitz had been ransacked. After the war, Anglo-American's CDM (and all other diamond interests in South-West Africa) were amalgamated to form a new CDM, under the control of De Beers South Africa, which set up its headquarters at Kolmanskop. In 1928, however, rich diamond fields were discovered around the mouth of the Orange River and in 1944, CDM relocated to the purpose-built company town of Oranjemund. Kolmanskop's last inhabitants – including some transport staff and hospital personnel – finally left in 1956 and the dunes have been encroaching the town ever since.

In 1994, the small British-Canadian company Namibian Minerals Corporation (Namco) was awarded offshore diamond-mining concessions at Lüderitz and Hottentots Bay by the Namibian government. These areas were estimated to hold a total of 27 million carats at a value of US$4 billion. The diamonds are recovered by vacuuming the diamondiferous sands beneath the sea bed and they're currently doing quite well, but it remains to be seen whether Namco will affect De Beers' stranglehold on the market.

which is pleasant for a braai and is suitable for swimming, but the water temperature would be amenable only to a penguin or a polar bear. The rusty ruin there is the remains of a 1914 Norwegian whaling station, and the salty pan just inland attracts flamingoes and merits a quick stop.

Diaz Point At Diaz Point, 22km by road from Lüderitz, is a classic lighthouse and a replica of the cross erected in July 1488 by Portuguese navigator Bartolomeu Dias on his return from the Cape of Good Hope. Portions of the original have been dispersed as far as Lisbon, Berlin and Cape Town.

From the point, there's a view of a nearby seal colony and you can also see cormorants, flamingoes, wading birds and even the occasional pod of dolphins. Dress for windy and chilly weather.

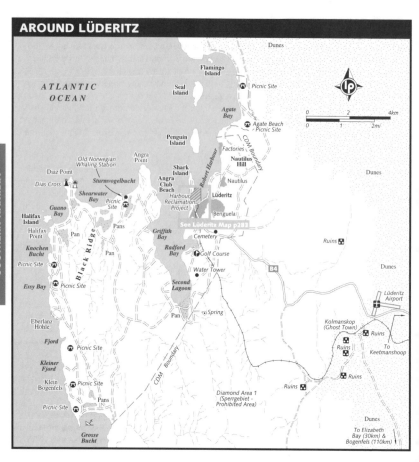

AROUND LÜDERITZ

ATLANTIC
OCEAN

Dunes

Flamingo
Island

Seal
Island

Picnic Site

Agate
Bay

Agate Beach
Picnic Site

Penguin
Island

CDM Boundary

Factories

Angra
Point

Old Norwegian
Whaling Station

Nautilus
Hill

Diaz Point

Shark
Island

Nautilus

Dias Cross

Sturmvogelbucht

Angra
Club
Beach

Robert Harbour

Lüderitz

Shearwater
Bay

Picnic
Site

Harbour
Reclamation
Project

Guano
Bay

Benguela

Halifax
Island

See Lüderitz Map p283

Halifax
Point

Pans

Griffith
Bay

Cemetery

Ruins

Pan

Black Ridge

Radford
Bay

Golf Course

Knochen
Bucht

Pan

Dunes

Picnic Site

Water Tower

B4

Essy Bay

Picnic Site

Second
Lagoon

Lüderitz
Airport

Pan

Spring

Eberlanz
Höhle

Kolmanskop
(Ghost Town)

Ruins

Fjord

Picnic Site

CDM Boundary

Ruins

To
Keetmanshoop

Kleiner
Fjord

Klein
Bogenfels

Picnic Site

Ruins

Pans

Ruins

Picnic Site

Diamond Area 1
(Sperrgebiet -
Prohibited Area)

Dunes

Grosse
Bucht

To Elizabeth
Bay (30km) &
Bogenfels (110km)

0   2   4km
0   1   2mi

Halifax Island This little island, just a
short distance offshore south of Diaz Point,
is the home of Namibia's best-known jackass penguin colony. With binoculars, you
can often see them gathering on the sandy
beach opposite the car park.

Grosse Bucht Grosse Bucht, the 'Big
Bay' at the southern end of Lüderitz Peninsula, is another wild and scenic beach. This
normally cold, windy spot is favoured by
flocks of flamingoes, which feed in the tidal
pools. It's also the site of a small but picturesque shipwreck on the beach. Just a few

kilometres up the coast is Klein Bogenfels,
a small rock arch beside the sea. When the
wind isn't blowing a gale, it makes a pleasant picnic spot.

ORANJEMUND
☎ 063

Oranjemund, at the mouth of the Orange
River, owes its existence to diamonds. So
great was its wealth, that in 1944 it supplanted Kolmanskop as the CDM headquarters. With a population of 8000, Oranjemund
is now an archetypal company town, with
100% employment, subsidised housing and

medical care for its workers and their families. Despite its desert location, CDM maintains a golf course and large areas of green parkland. In fact, CDM now accounts for 90% of the Namibian government's tax revenue, which explains why the company is still protected from land based competition and the Sperrgebiet continues to exist.

All Oranjemund visitors must have a permit from CDM and, as yet, there's no real tourism to the town. Applications for a permit must be made at least one month in advance of your intended visit and should be accompanied by a police affidavit stating that you've never been convicted of a serious crime. Normally, permits are issued only to those who have business in the town.

Security is so strict in Oranjemund that even broken equipment used in the mining operations may never leave the site, lest it be used to smuggle diamonds outside of the fence. Despite all this, a fair number of stolen diamonds manage to reach the illicit market. Thieves come up with some ingenious methods of smuggling diamonds over the security fence, including carrier pigeons, discarded rubbish and even tunnels.

Sperrgebiet Museum
If you have reason to visit Oranjemund, don't miss Sperrgebiet Museum (☎ 232183; admission free), which contains exhibits and relics from Sperrgebiet ghost towns, and background information on natural history – particularly fossils, diamonds and minerals.

Places to Stay
Stables Inn Lodge (☎ 232996, fax 232096, PO Box 405) Singles/doubles US$26/39. This is your main option in Oranjemund. It's only open to folks staying in the town on official business.

Getting There & Away
Oranjemund's airport is across the river in Alexander Bay, South Africa. The only road access to the town is also via Alexander Bay. Air Namibia has several weekly flights to and from Lüderitz, Walvis Bay, Swakopmund, Windhoek and Cape Town. Com-

---

Jackass Penguins

The jackass penguin or Cape penguin, which is common along the southern Namibian coast, lives in colonies on the many rocky offshore islets. Penguins' wings have evolved into flippers, which are used for rapid underwater locomotion, and their stocky appearance belies their ability to manoeuvre gracefully through the water. The skin is insulated against the cold water by a layer of air trapped beneath the feathers. Penguins also have supraorbital glands which excrete salts, allowing them to take their liquids from salt water.

Like Australia's fairy penguins, jackass penguins breed twice annually. They produce an average of three eggs per season, but egg mortality is fairly high. The penguins' main enemy is the Cape fur seal, which inhabits the same coastline.

---

pany transport is provided to and from the airport whenever a flight arrives or departs.

The Far South

Situated within the angle between South Africa's two most remote quarters, Namaqualand and the Kalahari, Namibia's bleak southern tip exudes a sense of isolation from whichever direction you approach it. Travelling along the highway, the seemingly endless desert plains stretch to the horizon in all directions. You can imagine how surprising it is to suddenly encounter the startling and spellbinding Fish River Canyon, which forms an enormous gash across the desert landscape.

GRÜNAU
☎ 063

For most travellers, Grünau is either the first petrol station north of the South African border or a place to await a lift to Ai-Ais, Fish River Canyon or points beyond. It's also a logical overnight stop for weary drivers between Cape Town and Windhoek, or for those arriving too late to reach the Fish River Canyon area lodges.

SOUTHERN NAMIBIA

SOUTHERN NAMIBIA

Places to Stay

Grünau Motors Rest Camp *(☎ 262026, fax 262017, B1, PO Box 3)* Camping US$8 for two people plus US$1.50 for each additional person, singles/doubles US$18/30. This 24-hour petrol station on the B1 has a shop, snack bar and takeaway place. It's also an Intercape Mainliner bus stop.

Grünau Hotel *(☎/fax 262001,* e *grunau 99@iafrica.com.na, PO Box 2)* Camping US$3 per site plus US$1.50 per person, backpacker accommodation US$8, singles/ doubles US$20/28. This hotel, 1km off the B1, has been greatly upgraded, but it still retains a bit of its anachronical ambience. It also has an acclaimed a la carte restaurant.

White House Ruskamp *(☎ 262061, 2km off the B3, PO Box 9)* Rooms US$12 per person. Dolf & Kinna de Wet's wonderful and popular B&B – yes, it is a white house – offers safe, quiet, self-catering accommodation. This renovated farmhouse, with several stunning architectural features, dates from 1912. Kitchen facilities are available, but they'll also provide set meals on request. To get there, head 11km towards Keetmanshoop on the B1 and turn west at the White House signpost; it's 4km off the road.

Florida B&B *(☎ 262061)* Rooms US$12 per person. This B&B, 1km off the B1, has pleasant self-catering bungalows 33km north of Grünau. Meals are available.

Savanna Guest Farm *(☎ 252070,* e *dis covaf@iafrica.com.na, B1, PO Box 14)* Singles/doubles US$28/40. Accommodation here is housed in an historic German garrison. The scenic 22,000-hectare farm is set near the foot of the scenic Karas Mountains, 40km north of Grünau, and there's lots of scope for exploration.

FISH RIVER CANYON NATIONAL PARK
☎ 063

Nowhere else in Africa will you find anything quite like Fish River Canyon. Fish River, which joins the Orange River 70km south of the canyon, has been gouging out this gorge for aeons, with stunning results. Although the typically breathless Namibian tourist literature claims that it's the world's second-largest canyon (after Arizona's Grand Canyon in the USA), it is in fact well down the list of the greatest gorges, but that makes it no less awe-inspiring. The chasm measures 160km in length and up to 27km in width, and the dramatic inner canyon reaches a depth of 550m.

The Fish River typically flows between March and April. Early in the tourist season, from April to June, it may diminish to a trickle and by mid-winter, to just a chain of remnant pools along the canyon floor.

The main access points are Hobas, near the northern end of the park, and Ai-Ais in the south. Both are administered by NWR, and all accommodation is best booked through the Windhoek office. Daily park permits cost US$3 per person and US$3 per vehicle, and are valid for both Hobas and Ai-Ais.

History
The early San people had a legend that the wildly twisting Fish River Canyon was gouged out by a frantically scrambling snake, Koutein Kooru, as he was pursued into the desert by hunters.

The geological story is only a bit different. Fish River Canyon is actually two canyons, one inside the other, which were formed in entirely different ways. It's thought that the original sedimentary layers of shale, sandstone and loose igneous material around Fish River Canyon were laid down nearly two billion years ago and were later metamorphosed by heat and pressure into more solid materials, such as gneiss. Just under a billion years ago, cracks in the formation admitted intrusions of igneous material, which cooled to form the dolerite dykes (these are now exposed in the inner canyon).

The surface sediments of the canyon then eroded into a basin and were covered by a shallow sea, which eventually filled with sediment – sandstone, conglomerate, quartzite, limestone and shale – washed down from surrounding exposed lands. Around 500 million years ago, a period of tectonic activity along crustal faults caused these layers to rift and to tilt at a 45° angle. These forces opened a wide gap in the earth's crust and formed a large canyon. This is what we now regard as the outer canyon, the bottom of which encompasses the first level of terraces that are visible approximately 170m below the east rim and 380m below the west rim. This newly created valley naturally became a watercourse (Fish River, oddly enough), that began eroding a meandering path along the valley floor and eventually gouged out what is now the 270m-deep inner canyon.

Hobas

The Hobas Information Centre, at the northern end of the park, is open from 7.30am to noon and 2pm to 5pm daily. It's also the check-in point for the five-day canyon hike. Packaged snacks and cool drinks are available here, but little else.

From Hobas, it's 10km on a gravel road to the Hikers' Viewpoint (the start of the hiking route), which has picnic tables, braai pits and toilets. Just around the corner is a good overview of the northern part of the canyon. The Main Viewpoint, a few kilometres south, has probably the best – and most photographed – overall canyon view. Both these vistas take in the sharp river bend known as Hell's Corner.

Places to Stay *Hobas Camp Site* Camping US$13 for two people plus US$2 for each additional person up to eight people. This pleasant and well-shaded camping ground near the park's northern end is situated about 10km from the main viewpoints. Facilities are clean, and there's also a kiosk and swimming pool, but no restaurant or petrol station.

Fish River Hiking Trail

The five-day hike from Hobas to Ai-Ais is Namibia's most popular long-distance walk – with good reason. The magical 85km route, which follows the sandy riverbed past a series of ephemeral pools (in May and June the river actually does flow), begins at Hikers' Viewpoint and ends at the hot spring resort of Ai-Ais.

Due to flash flooding and heat in the summer months, the route is open only from 15

FISH RIVER CANYON

To Grünau & Seeheim

To Ai-Ais

Sulphur Springs Trail

Table Mountain ▲

Short Cut

Short Cut

Kanebis River Track

Fish River

Emergency Exit

To Orange River

Ai-Ais

1 Hikers' Viewpoint
2 Hell's Corner
3 Main Viewpoint
4 Sunset Point
5 Dolerite Dyke
6 Rockies Point
7 Hobas Camp Site; Information Centre
8 The Edge
9 Dolerite Dyke
10 Sulphur Springs Viewpoint
11 Sulphur (Palm) Springs
12 South (Eagle's Rock) Viewpoint
13 Rock Pinnacle
14 Bushy Corner
15 Three Sisters Rocks
16 Kanebis Bend
17 Kooigoedhoogte Pass
18 Four Finger Rock
19 Thilo von Trotha's Grave
20 Refreshment Stand
21 Fool's Gold Corner
22 Kraal

SOUTHERN NAMIBIA

April to 15 September. Permits for groups of three to 40 people cost US$12 per person, plus US$3 per person for each day in the park and US$3 per day for each parked vehicle. You must also have a doctor's certificate of fitness; arrange your own transport and accommodation in Hobas and Ai-Ais; and sign an indemnity form releasing NWR from any responsibility.

Thanks to the typically warm, clear weather, you probably won't need a tent, but you must carry a sleeping bag and food. In Hobas, check on water availability in the canyon. In August and September, the last

15km of the walk can be completely dry and hikers will need several 2L water bottles to manage this hot, sandy stretch. Large plastic soft-drink bottles normally work just fine.

The Route From Hobas, it's 10km to Hikers' Viewpoint, which is the start of the trail. Hikers must find their own transport there. The steep and scenic section at the beginning takes you from the canyon rim to the river where you'll have a choice of fabulous sandy camp sites beside cool, green river pools.

Although the map in this book shows the route following the river quite closely, it's important to note that the best route changes from year to year. This is largely due to sand and vegetation deposited by the previous year's floods. In general, the easiest hiking will be along the inside of the river bends, where you're likely to find wildlife trails and dry, nonsandy terrain that's free of vegetation tangles, slippery stones or large boulders.

After an exhausting 13km hike through the rough sand and boulders along the east bank, the Sulphur Springs Viewpoint track joins the main route. If you're completely exhausted at this stage and simply can't handle the conditions, this route can be used as an emergency exit from the canyon. If it's any encouragement, however, the going does get easier as you move downstream, so why not head a further 2km downstream to Sulphur Springs, set up camp and see how you feel in the morning?

Sulphur Springs – more commonly called Palm Springs – is an excellent camp site with thermal sulphur pools (a touch of paradise) to soothe your aching muscles. The springs, which have a stable temperature of 57°C, gush up from the underworld at an amazing 30L per second and contain not only sulphur, but also chloride and fluoride.

Legend has it that during WWI, two German prisoners of war hid out at Sulphur Springs. One was apparently suffering from asthma and the other from skin cancer, but thanks to the spring's healing powers, both were cured. It's also said that the palm trees growing there sprang up from date pips discarded by

these two Germans. This site is also accessible on day walks down from the Sulphur Springs Viewpoint.

The next section of the hike consists mostly of deep sand, pebbles and gravel. The most direct route through the inside river bends requires hikers to cross the river several times. The Table Mountain formation lies 15km beyond Sulphur Springs and a further 15km on is the first short cut, which avoids an area of dense thorn scrub known as Bushy Corner. Around the next river bend, just upstream from the Three Sisters rock formation, is a longer short cut past Kanebis Bend up to Kooigoedhoogte Pass. At the top, you'll have a superb view of Four Finger Rock, an impressive rock tower consisting of four thick pinnacles that more closely resemble a cow's udder than fingers. If you see a sign reading 'Cold Drinks 7km', you're not hallucinating.

After descending to the river, you'll cross to the west bank and start climbing over yet another short cut (although you can also follow the river bend). At the southern end of this pass, on the west bank of the river, lies the grave of Lieutenant Thilo von Trotha, who was killed here after a 1905 confrontation between the Germans and the Nama.

The final 25km into Ai-Ais, which can be completed in one, long day, follows an easy, but sandy and rocky route. South of von Trotha's grave, the canyon widens out and becomes drier, with fewer bends and river pools are less frequent. At the end of winter, the final 15km are normally completely dry, so carry sufficient water. The lemonade and hot-dog stand advertised at Four Finger Rock is 5km south of von Trotha's grave. It's not 100% reliable, but when it's open, few hikers pass it by.

Day Walks Following the death of an ill-prepared hiker in 2001, NWR decided to prohibit day hikes into Fish River Canyon, despite the fact that over the years, thousands of people have done it without incident. During the cooler weather you may be able to get special permission at Hobas to hike down from Hikers' Viewpoint, but don't count on it.

Ai-Ais

The hot spring oasis of Ai-Ais (Nama for 'Scalding Hot') beneath the towering peaks at the southern end of Fish River Canyon National Park, is known for the thermal baths that originate beneath the river bed. Although the 60°C springs have probably been known to the San for thousands of years, the legend goes that they were 'discovered' by a nomadic Nama shepherd rounding up stray sheep. They're rich in chloride, fluoride and sulphur, and are reputedly salubrious for sufferers of rheumatism or nervous disorders. The hot water is piped to a series of baths and Jacuzzis, and an outdoor swimming pool.

A pleasant diversion is the short scramble to the peak which rises above the opposite bank (there's no trail). It affords a superb view of Ai-Ais and you'll even see the four pinnacles of Four Finger Rock rising far to the north. The return trip takes two hours.

In summer, there's a serious risk of flooding – Ai-Ais was destroyed by floods in both 1972 and 2000, and seriously damaged in 1988. Amenities include a shop, restaurant, petrol station, tennis courts, post office and, of course, a swimming pool, spa and mineral bath facilities (admission US$1.50 per session; open 9am-9pm daily).

Places to Stay & Eat The following place has something for everyone.

Ai-Ais Hot Springs Resort Camping US$13 for two people plus US$2 for each additional person up to eight people, 4-bed huts US$26, 2-/4-bed flats US$37/40, 2-bed 'luxury' flats US$43. Facilities here include washing blocks, braai pits and the use of resort facilities. All flats have private baths and basic self-catering facilities. Pre-book through NWR in Windhoek.

Restaurant Open 7am-9am, noon-2pm & 6pm-10pm daily. This typical NWR restaurant serves up palatable Namibian standards, focusing on beef, fish and chicken dishes. The attached shop sells basic groceries.

Getting There & Away

There's no public transport to either Hobas or Ai-Ais, but if you must hitch you should eventually be successful from mid-March to 31 October. Thanks to South African holiday traffic, the best-travelled route is to Ai-Ais via two turnings, one 36km north of Noordoewer and the other 30km south of Grünau. Once in Ai-Ais, plenty of holiday-makers head for the viewpoints around Hobas, thus facilitating hitching between Ai-Ais, Hobas and the beginning of the Hikers' Viewpoint trailhead.

AROUND FISH RIVER CANYON
☎ 063

Fish River Canyon National Park takes in only a portion of the canyon itself, and several sites and retreats outside the park provide more wonderful canyon experiences.

Fish River Lodge

The friendly Fish River Lodge, 60km north of Hobas, is situated on a ranch cradled in the confluence of the Löwen and Fish River Canyons amid some of the most amazing geology imaginable – don't just take our word for it! Highlights include the 4WD trip into the canyon to swim in the river pools, a 'garnet crawl', and seeing the bizarre petroglyphs in the rippled black dolerite.

From April to October, there's also the wonderful five-day, 85km Löwenfish hiking trail (US$43, including two nights accommodation at The Stable – see under Places to Stay). This hike takes in the Löwen Canyon and several days along Fish River Canyon, interrupted by several ascents to the plateau and descents down scenic kloofs. Camp sites (with no facilities) are situated at water sources along the way and the last night you can stay at the Koelkrans Camp (US$14 per person), with cooking facilities and hot showers. On the last day, hikers climb out of the canyon for the last time and follow a scenic route back to the lodge. Stages of the trip may be done as one- to four-day hikes.

There are three one-day sandy and rocky 4WD trails, which wander in and out of the canyon and cost from US$9 per vehicle and US$1.50 per person.

From Chapel Inn in Keetmanshoop, three-day backpackers trips cost US$120, including transport, full board and lodge accommodation, or US$70 with transport and self-catering accommodation in The Stable.

Camping at the Lodge *(☎ 266018, ☎/fax 223762, ⓔ frlodge@iafrica.com.na, ⓌⅣ www .resafrica.net/fish-river-lodge)* costs US$22 per vehicle and US$6 per person; dorm beds at The Stable are US$9 and singles/doubles B&B will set you back US$32/51. Lunch/ dinner is US$4.50/8. Pre-bookings at this place is essential.

Getting There & Away Transfers from Chapel Inn in Keetmanshoop are US$47 per person for a minimum of two people.

If you're driving to Fish River Lodge, head west from Keetmanshoop and turn south on the D545; after 33km, bear left at the junction. After a further 32km, you'll see the sign for Fish River Lodge on the right-hand side of the road. At this point, it's 22km west to the lodge. It's passable with a 2WD but in several places you'll have to take it very easy.

Gondwana Cañon Park

Founded in 1996, the 100,000-hectare Gondwana Cañon Park was created by amalgamating several former sheep farms and removing the fences to restore the wilderness country immediately north-east of Fish River Canyon National Park. Water holes have been established and wildlife is now returning to this wonderful, remote corner of Namibia. In the process, the park absorbed the former Augurabies-Steenbok Nature Reserve, which had been created earlier to protect not only steenboks, but also Hartmann's mountain zebras, gemsboks and klipspringers. Accommodation in the hikers hut here can be arranged through either the Cañon Lodge or Cañon Roadhouse.

Funding for the park is derived from a 5% bed levy at Cañon Lodge and Cañon Roadhouse. To book, contact Cañon Travel Centre *(☎ 061-230066, fax 251863, ⓔ nature .i@mweb.com.na, Ⓦ namibiaweb.com/can yon)*, PO Box 80205, Windhoek.

Cañon Lodge (☎ 266031) Singles/doubles US$80/117. This lodge, 7km from Hobas, is one of Namibia's most-interesting accom-

modation options. It consists of 26 red stone bungalows, which integrate perfectly into their boulder-strewn backdrop. This restaurant, decorated with historic farming implements, is housed in a restored 1908 farmhouse. Lunch/dinner here will set you back US$9/15.

Cañon Roadhouse (☎ 266029) Camping US$8 per site plus US$3 per person, singles /doubles US$54/86. This wonderfully unique place attempts to re-create a roadhouse out on the wildest stretches of Route 66 – at least as it exists in the collective imagination. Buffets are served on an antique motorcycle, the stunning window shades are made from used air filters, and the bar stools are air filters from heavy-duty vehicles and then there's the obligatory collection of number plates (where donations from your home country are gratefully accepted). Amenities include a swimming pool and an acclaimed a la carte *restaurant* with an imaginative menu: steak or game dishes with all the trimmings cost US$8, homemade pasta with salad is US$6, and there's a good wine list.

ORANGE RIVER
☎ 063

The Orange River has its headwaters in the Drakensberg Mountains of Natal, South Africa, and forms much of the boundary between Namibia and South Africa. It was named not for its muddy colour, but for Prince William V of Orange, who was the Dutch monarch in the late 1770s. The road from Noordoewer to Rosh Pinah makes a very nice desert adventure.

Noordoewer

Noordoewer, the main border crossing between Namibia and South Africa, sits astride the Orange River and is becoming a centre for viticulture, as well as canoeing and rafting adventures. If you want to change money here, head for the BP petrol station. The Bank of Windhoek is only open from 9am to 1pm Thursdays.

River Trips Several companies, backed up by riverside camps, offer laid-back canoeing and rafting trips on the Orange River between Noordoewer and Selingsdrif (spelt Sendelingsdrif on some maps). Part of the route follows the river boundary between Namibia's Fish River Canyon National Park and South Africa's Richtersveld National Park. Trips are normally done in stages and last from three to six days. The popular trips from Noordoewer to Aussenkehr aren't treacherous by any stretch – the white-water never exceeds class II – but they do provide access to some wonderfully wild canyon country.

Other possible stages include Aussenkehr to the Fish River mouth; Fish River mouth to Nama Canyon (this one has a few more serious rapids); and Nama Canyon to Selingsdrif. Felix Unite also does a five-day stage from Pella Mission to Goodhouse, further upstream. Generally, canoe trips are slightly more expensive than white-water rafting trips.

Amanzi Trails (☎ 27-21-559 1573, e amanzi .trails@new.co.za, W www.amanzitrails.co.za) This South African company does self-catered canoe trips from Noordoewer to Aussenkehr for US$68; this price includes canoes and guides only. Trips leave from Abiqua Camp, 13km off the Orange River Rd.

Felix Unite (☎ 297161, 082-495 8519, fax 297250, e carlosp@iafrica.com.na, bookings@ felix.co.za, W www.felixunite.com), PO Box 3, Noordoewer. Day trips in canoes cost US$11. The standard four-day trip from Noordoewer to Aussenkehr costs US$175, all inclusive, and a six-day trip from Noordoewer to the Fish River mouth is US$210. Felix also does special trips from Pella Mission to Goodhouse. The camp, at 13km on the Orange River Rd, is open only to overland trucks.

Rivers Incorporated (☎ 27-21-551 6659, 27-72-242 6822, e riversinc@mweb.co.za, W www .riversinc.co.za) From Noordoewer, one-/two-day rafting trips are US$20/ 54, with meals. It also does four-/six-day trips through the Richtersveld canyons for US$147/ 207 and three-day 'Gorge Adventures', including class V rapids and abseiling for US$127. Trips leave from Abiqua Camp.

River Rafters (☎ 27-21-712 5094, fax 27-21-712 5241, e rafters@mweb.co.za), PO Box 314, Bergvliet, 7964, Cape Town, South Africa. This company uses inflatable kayaks and has a put-in point and office just off the Orange River Rd, 11km from Noordoewer.

Places to Stay & Eat There are two places to keep in mind.

Camel Lodge (☎ 797171, fax 797143, B1, PO Box 1) Singles/doubles B&B US$26/34. This long-standing, motel-style place has been spruced up and now offers rooms with TV and air-con.

Abiqua Camp (☎ 297255, 13km on the Orange River Rd) Camping US$3.50 per person. This friendly and well-situated camp, sits on the riverbank opposite some interesting sedimentary formations. The Abiqua is the launch site for both the Amanzi Trails and Rivers Incorporated river trip operators. Meals are available on request and the site also has a small bar and shop; don't miss sampling the famous Orange Valley Cherry-Pep hot sauce, which is produced here. If there's no-one around when you arrive, go to the white house 500m back along the access road.

Rosh Pinah

The Israeli-sounding name of this remote mining village was bestowed by a German Jew, Moses Eli Kahan, who discovered copper here after WWI. With the drop in copper prices in the 1930s, the mining was abandoned, but in the late 1960s, the indefatigable Moses, now in his 80s, discovered veins of lead-zinc in the mountains. A South African zinc-mining firm still extracts up to 75,000 tonnes of ore annually.

There's no public hotel – only a company guesthouse – but you can camp outside town. To get to Rosh Pinah, take the C13 from Aus or tackle the rough but scenic 156km Orange River Road route from Noordoewer. Star Line buses link Keetmanshoop (US$8.50, 7¼ hours) with Rosh Pinah twice weekly; westbound buses leave at 8am on Thursday and Saturday and eastbound, buses leave at 9.15am on Monday and Friday.

KARASBURG
☎ 063
Although it's southern Namibia's third-largest town, Karasburg is not much more than a service centre along the main route between Namibia and Johannesburg. The name means 'Rocky Mountains', after the nearby

SOUTHERN NAMIBIA

Karas range; the Nama people, however, still call it by the Afrikaner name, Kalkfontein Suid ('Limestone Springs South'). Karasburg has a good supermarket, a bank, several petrol stations and accommodation.

Warmbad

The main site of interest is the mission, fort and spa village of Warmbad (German for 'warm bath'), 47km south of Karasburg. It was Namibia's first mission station, founded in 1805. The ruins of the old spa building have been restored as a national monument and a museum is planned for the portals and gatehouse of the old fort (now the police station). On Friday afternoons, Star Line runs a return bus between Karasburg and Warmbad (US$2, 45 minutes).

Places to Stay & Eat

Kalkfontein Hotel (☎/fax 270023, fax 270457, PO Box 207) Singles/doubles US$24/27. This meeting place in town has seen better days, but it retains a small-town charm. The rooms have air-con, and the hotel also has a restaurant and bar.

Pela Pela Guest House & Backpackers (☎ 270483, Opposite the post office) Dorm beds US$5.20, doubles/triples US$11/14. Believe it or not, Karasburg has a backpackers, and this good-value place is right in the centre of town.

Getting There & Away

Star Line's Monday and Thursday return bus travels between Karasburg and Noordoewer (US$4, 2¾ hours).

Wildlife Guide

WILDLIFE GUIDE

PRIMATES

Lesser bushbaby *Galago moholi*

Named for their plaintive wailing call – a conspicuous night sound of many African woodlands – bushbabies are actually primitive primates. They have small heads, large rounded ears, thick bushy tails and enormous eyes that are typical of nocturnal primates. The tiny lesser bushbaby is very light grey with yellowish colouring on its legs. Family groups of up to six or seven individuals hold small territories, but foraging is usually done alone. Tree sap and fruit are the mainstay of their diet, supplemented by insects. Bushbabies are fantastically agile in the trees, making rapid and spectacular leaps from branch to branch.

Size: Length 40cm, including a 20 to 25cm tail; weight 150 to 200g. **Distribution:** Woodland-savanna of the north-east. **Status:** Common but strictly nocturnal.

Vervet monkey *Cercopithecus aethiops*

The most common monkey of the woodland-savanna, the vervet is easily recognisable by its grizzled grey hair and black face fringed with white. The male has a distinctive bright blue scrotum, an important signal of status in the troop. Troops may number up to 30. The vervet monkey is diurnal and forages for fruits, seeds, leaves, flowers, invertebrates and the occasional lizard or nestling. It rapidly learns where easy pickings can be found around lodges and camp sites, but becomes a pest when it gets habituated to being fed. Most park authorities destroy such individuals, so please avoid feeding them.

Size: Up to 130cm long, including a 65cm tail; weight 3.5 to 8kg; male larger than female. **Distribution:** Woodland-savanna in far north-east; riverine woodlands around Orange River on the southern border and the Okavango and Kunene Rivers on the northern border. **Status:** Easy to see where it occurs.

Chacma baboon *Papio ursinus*

The doglike snout of the chacma baboon gives it a more aggressive appearance than most other primates, which have much more humanlike facial features. However, when you see the interactions within a troop, it's difficult not to make anthropomorphic comparisons. The chacma baboon lives in troops of up to 150, and there is no single dominant male. It is strictly diurnal and forages for grasses, fruits, insects and (occasionally) small vertebrates. The baboon is a notorious opportunist and may become a pest at camp sites, which it visits for hand-outs. Such individuals can be dangerous and are destroyed by park officials, so don't feed them.

Size: Shoulder height 75cm; length up to 160cm, including a 70cm tail; weight up to 45kg; male larger than female, and twice as heavy. **Distribution:** Throughout the country except the deserts along the east coast. **Status:** Common in many areas and active during the day.

CARNIVORES

Black-backed jackal *Canis mesomelas*

This jackal relies heavily on scavenging but is also an efficient hunter, taking insects, birds, rodents and even the occasional small antelope. It also frequents human settlements and takes domestic stock. It is persecuted by farmers, but is very resilient and can be readily seen on farms. Black-backed jackals form long-term pair bonds, and each pair occupies an area varying from 3 to 21.5 sq km. Litters contain one to six pups; they are often looked after by older siblings as well as by their parents. The less common side-striped jackal is grey in colour with a distinctive white-tipped tail.

JASON EDWARDS

Size: Shoulder height 35 to 50cm; length 95 to 120cm, including a 30 to 35cm tail; weight up to 12kg.
Distribution: Found throughout the country, except in the extreme north-east where they are replaced by the side-striped jackal. **Status:** Common and easily seen; active both night and day.

Bat-eared fox *Otocyon megalotis*

The huge ears of this little fox detect the faint sounds of invertebrates below ground before it unearths them in a burst of frantic digging. The bat-eared fox eats mainly insects, especially termites, but also wild fruit and small vertebrates. It is monogamous and is often seen in groups comprising a mated pair and offspring. Natural enemies include large birds of prey, spotted hyenas, caracals and larger cats. It will bravely attempt to rescue a family member caught by a predator by using distraction techniques and harassment, which extends to nipping larger enemies on the ankles.

ANDREW VAN SMEERDIJK

Size: Shoulder height 35cm; length 75 to 90cm, including a 30cm tail; weight 3 to 5kg. **Distribution:** Throughout the country, except the arid eastern coastal region. **Status:** Common, especially in national parks; mainly nocturnal but often seen in the late afternoon and early morning.

Wild dog *Lycaon pictus*

The wild dog's blotched black, yellow and white coat, and its large, round ears, make it unmistakable. It is highly sociable, living in packs of up to 40, though 12 to 20 is typical. Marvellous endurance hunters, the pack chases prey to the point of exhaustion, then cooperates to pull down the quarry. The wild dog is widely reviled for killing prey by eating it alive, but this is in fact probably as fast as any of the 'cleaner' methods used by carnivores. Mid-sized antelopes are its preferred prey, but it can kill large buffaloes. Wild dogs require enormous areas of habitat and are one of the most endangered large carnivores in Africa.

ANDREW VAN SMEERDIJK

Size: Shoulder height 65 to 80cm; length 100 to 150cm, including a 35cm tail; weight 20 to 35kg.
Distribution: Occurs only in the parks of the Caprivi area, and Etosha and Khaudom National Parks.
Status: Highly threatened, with numbers declining severely from a naturally low density.

Spotted hyena *Crocuta crocuta*

Widely reviled as a scavenger, the spotted hyena is actually a highly efficient predator with a fascinating social system. Females are larger than and dominant to males and have male physical characteristics, the most remarkable of which is an erectile clitoris (which renders the sexes virtually indistinguishable). Clans, which can contain dozens of individuals, are led by females. The spotted hyena is massively built and appears distinctly canine, but is more closely related to cats than to dogs. It can reach speeds of up to 60km/h and a pack can easily dispatch adult wildebeests and zebras. Lions are its main natural enemy.

Size: Shoulder height 85cm; length 120 to 180cm, including a 30cm tail; weight 55 to 80kg. **Distribution:** Occurs in the north and, except for the coastal strip, the central west. **Status:** Common where there is suitable food; mainly nocturnal but also seen during the day.

Lion *Panthera leo*

The lion spends much of the night hunting, patrolling territories and playing. It lives in prides of up to about 30, the core comprising four to 12 related females, which remain in the pride for life. Males form coalitions and defend the female groups from foreign males. The lion is strictly territorial, defending ranges of between 50 to 400 sq km. Young males are ousted from the pride at the age of two or three, entering a period of nomadism that ends at around five years old, when they are able to take over their own pride. Lions hunt virtually anything, but wildebeests, zebras and buffaloes are the mainstay of their diet.

Size: Shoulder height 120cm; length 250 to 300cm, including 100cm tail; weight up to 260kg (male), 180kg (female). **Distribution:** Found only in the far north. **Status:** Relatively common where it occurs; mainly nocturnal but easy to see during the day.

Cheetah *Acinonyx jubatus*

The world's fastest land mammal, the cheetah can reach speeds of at least 105km/h but becomes exhausted after a few hundred metres and therefore usually stalks prey to within 60m before unleashing its tremendous acceleration. The cheetah preys on antelopes weighing up to 60kg, as well as hares and young wildebeests and zebras. Litters may be as large as nine, but in open savanna habitats most cubs are killed by other predators, particularly lions. Young cheetahs disperse from the mother when aged around 18 months. The males form coalitions; females remain solitary for life.

Size: Shoulder height 85cm; length 180 to 220cm, including a 70cm tail; weight up to 65kg. **Distribution:** Widely but thinly distributed throughout the country, except for the far south and the western coastal region. **Status:** Uncommon, with individuals moving over large areas; active by day.

UNGULATES (HOOFED ANIMALS)

African elephant *Loxodonta africana*

The African elephant usually lives in small family groups of between 10 and 20, which frequently congregate in much larger herds at a common water hole or food resource. Its society is matriarchal and herds are dominated by old females. Bulls live alone or in bachelor groups, joining the herds when females are in season. A cow may mate with many bulls during her oestrus. An adult's average daily food intake is about 250kg of grass, leaves, bark and other vegetation. An elephant's life span is about 60 to 70 years, though some individuals may reach 100 or more.

DENNIS JONES

Size: Shoulder height up to 4m (male), 3.5m (female); weight 5 to 6.5 tonnes (male), 3 to 3.5 tonnes (female). **Distribution:** Restricted to parts of the north. **Status:** Common in some parks.

Rhinoceroses White rhinoceroses *Ceratotherium simum;* Black rhinoceros *Diceros bicornis* (pictured)

Poaching for horns has made the rhino Africa's most endangered large animal. White rhinos are not white; their name is a corruption of 'wide (lipped) rhino'. White rhinos are grazers (using their broad mouths to crop short grass) and prefer open plains; black (hook-lipped) rhinos are browsers (grasping vegetation off bushes with their pointed upper lips) and live in scrubby country. White rhinos are generally docile; black rhinos are prone to charging when alarmed – their eyesight is extremely poor and they've been known to charge trains or elephant carcasses.

JASON EDWARDS

Size: White – shoulder height 180cm, weight 2000 to 2300kg, front horn to 160cm; black – shoulder height 160cm, weight 800 to 1100kg, front horn to 120cm. **Distribution:** White rhinos have been reintroduced to the Waterberg Plateau Park; black rhinos occur in the north-west. **Status:** Endangered and difficult to see.

Zebras Burchell's zebra *Equus burchellii* (pictured); Hartmann's mountain zebra *Equus zebra hartmannae*

Burchell's zebra has shadow lines between its black stripes; the mountain zebra lacks shadows and has a gridiron pattern above its tail. Zebras are grazers but occasionally browse on leaves and scrub. The social system centres on small groups of related mares over which stallions fight fiercely. Stallions may hold a harem for as long as 15 years, but they often lose single mares to younger males, which gradually build up their own harems. Zebras are preyed upon by all the large carnivores, with lions being their main predators.

DAVID WALL

Size: Shoulder height 140 to 160cm; weight 250 to 390kg; females of both species are slightly smaller. **Distribution:** Burchell's occurs on the grassy plains of the north; Hartmann's in the mountainous areas of the eastern half of the country. **Status:** Burchell's is common and easy to see, Hartmann's much less so.

Hippopotamus *Hippopotamus amphibius*

The hippo is found close to fresh water, spending most of the day submerged and emerging at night to graze on land. It can consume about 40kg of vegetable matter each evening. It lives in large herds, tolerating close contact in the water but foraging alone when on land. Adult bulls aggressively defend territories against each other and most males bear the scars of conflicts (often a convenient method of sexing hippos). Cows with calves are aggressive towards other individuals. The hippo is extremely dangerous on land and kills many people each year, usually when someone inadvertently blocks the animal's retreat to the water.

Size: Shoulder height 150cm; weight 1000 to 2000kg; male larger than female. **Distribution:** Restricted to the Caprivi region and the Okavango and Kunene River systems. **Status:** Common in major water courses.

Giraffe *Giraffa camelopardalis*

The name 'giraffe' is derived from the Arabic word *zarafah* (the one who walks quickly). Both sexes have 'horns' – these are actually short projections of skin-covered bone. Despite the giraffe's incredibly long neck, it still has only seven cervical vertebrae – the same number as all mammals, including humans. The giraffe browses on trees, exploiting a zone of foliage inaccessible to all other herbivores except elephants. Juveniles are prone to predation and a lion will even take down fully grown adults. The giraffe is at its most vulnerable at water holes and always appears hesitant when drinking.

Size: Height 3.5 to 4.5m (female), 4 to 5.2m (male); weight 700 to 1000kg (female); 900 to 1400kg (male). **Distribution:** Found throughout the country's northern-most quarter. **Status:** Common where it occurs and easy to see.

Greater kudu *Tragelaphus strepsiceros*

The greater kudu is Africa's second-tallest antelope and the males carry massive spiralling horns much sought after by trophy hunters. It is light grey in colour with between six and 10 white stripes down the sides and a white chevron between the eyes. The kudu lives in small herds comprising females and their young, periodically joined by the normally solitary males during the breeding season. It is primarily a browser and can eat a variety of leaves, but finds its preferred diet in woodland-savanna with fairly dense bush cover. Strong jumpers, it readily clears barriers more than 2m high.

Size: Shoulder height up to 150cm; weight 200 to 300kg (male), 120 to 220kg (female); horns up to 180cm long. **Distribution:** Throughout the country, except for the far west and extreme south. **Status:** Common.

Eland *Taurotragus oryx*

Africa's largest antelope, the eland is massive. Both sexes have horns averaging about 65cm long, which spiral at the base and sweep straight back. The male has a distinctive hairy tuft on the head, and stouter horns than the female. The eland prefers savanna scrub, feeding on grass and leaves in the early morning and from late afternoon into the night. It normally drinks daily, but can go for over a month without water. It usually lives in groups of around six to 12, generally comprising several females and one male. Larger aggregations (up to 1000) sometimes form at 'flushes' of new grass.

Size: Shoulder height 150 to 180cm (male), 125 to 150cm (female); weight 450 to 950kg (male), 300 to 500kg (female); horns up to 100cm long. **Distribution:** Drier parts of the north-east. **Status:** Naturally low density but relatively common in their habitat and easy to see.

African buffalo *Syncerus caffer*

The African buffalo is the only native wild cow of Africa. Both sexes have distinctive curving horns that broaden at the base and meet over the forehead in a massive 'boss'; those of the female are usually smaller. It has a fairly wide habitat tolerance but requires areas with abundant grass, water and cover. The African buffalo is gregarious and may form herds numbering thousands. Group composition is fluid and smaller herds often break away, sometimes rejoining the original herd later. Although it is generally docile, the buffalo can be very dangerous and should be treated with caution.

Size: Shoulder height 160cm; weight 400 to 900kg; horns up to 125 cm long; female somewhat smaller than male. **Distribution:** Found only in the parks in the Caprivi area and in Khaudom Game Reserve. **Status:** Common and can be approachable where they are protected.

Gemsbok *Oryx gazella*

The gemsbok can tolerate arid areas uninhabitable to most antelopes. It can survive without drinking (obtaining enough water from its food) and tolerates extreme heat. As a means of conserving water, gemsbok can let their body temperature climb to levels that would kill most mammals. A solid, powerful animal with long, straight horns present in both sexes, it is well equipped to defend itself and sometimes kills attacking lions. Herds usually contain five to 40 individuals but aggregations of several hundred can occur. The gemsbok is principally a grazer, but also browses on thorny shrubs unpalatable to many species.

Size: Shoulder height 120cm; weight 180 to 240kg; horns up to 120cm long; males more solid with thicker horns. **Distribution:** Found throughout the country, except for the extreme south. **Status:** Common where it occurs, but often shy, fleeing from humans.

Blue wildebeest *Connochaetes taurinus*

The blue wildebeest is gregarious, forming herds up to tens of thousands strong in some parts of Africa, often in association with zebras and other herbivores. In Southern Africa, numbers are much reduced and huge herds are a rarity. Males are territorial and attempt to herd groups of females into their territory. The wildebeest is a grazer, and moves constantly in search of good pasture and water. Because it prefers to drink daily and can survive only five days without water, the wildebeest will migrate large distances to find it. During the rainy season it grazes haphazardly, but in the dry season it congregates around water holes.

Size: Shoulder height 140cm; weight 140 to 230kg (females), 200 to 300kg (males); horns up to 85cm long; male larger than female. **Distribution:** Occurs only in the far north-east. **Status:** Very common where it occurs.

Impala *Aepyceros melampus*

Often dismissed because it is so abundant, the impala is a unique antelope with no close relatives. Males have long, lyre-shaped horns averaging 75cm in length. It is gregarious, forming herds of up to 100 or so. Males defend females during oestrus, but outside the breeding season males congregate in bachelor groups. The impala is known for its speed and ability to leap – it can spring as far as 10m in one bound, or 3m into the air. The most widespread impala in Namibia is a distinct subspecies, the black-faced impala, found only in north-western Namibia and parts of Angola.

Size: Shoulder height 90cm; weight 40 to 70kg; horns up to 80cm long; male larger than female. **Distribution:** The black-faced impala is found in part of the north-west, the eastern subspecies occurs in the Caprivi region. **Status:** Both common where they occur.

Springbok *Antidorcas marsupialis*

The springbok is one of the fastest antelopes (reaching speeds up to 88km/h) and has a distinctive stiff-legged, arched-backed bounding gait called 'pronking', which is commonly displayed when it sees predators. When pronking, it raises a white crest along the back (normally hidden within a skin fold) and the white hairs of the rump. It is extremely common in arid areas, usually in herds (whose social structure varies considerably) of up to 100. It can survive without drinking, but may move large distances to find new grazing, sometimes congregating in herds of thousands when doing so. Both sexes have ridged, lyre-shaped horns.

Size: Shoulder height 75cm; weight 25 to 55kg; horns up to 50cm long; male larger than female. **Distribution:** Found throughout the country, except for the wetter parts of the north and north-east, and the country's most arid areas in the extreme west. **Status:** Common and easy to see.

Excursion to Victoria Falls

Along with Egypt's Pyramids of Giza, Mali's Dogon villages, the Namib dunes and South Africa's Table Mountain, Victoria Falls is one of Africa's great contributions to world tourism. It lies at a crossroads, of sorts: The convergence of four countries – Zimbabwe, Zambia, Botswana and Namibia – and the confluence of two of the continent's greatest river systems, the Zambezi and the Kwando-Mashi-Linyanti-Chobe.

The waterfall itself can only be described as spectacular – in fact, a dream come true for its millions of past visitors – as well as Kodak, Fuji and Agfa. Over an incredible 1.7km-wide precipice, an average of 550,000 cubic metres of water per minute plummets 90 to 107m into the Zambezi gorges, but during the March to May flood stage, that may increase to more than 10 times the dry-season volume.

As with several other world-class waterfalls, Victoria Falls is shared by two countries. Historically, Livingstone in Zambia was the destination of choice, but political strife during the Kaunda presidency transferred attention to the Zimbabwean shore. During the 1990s, the small town of Victoria Falls was transformed, adopting a distinctly circus-like atmosphere, with kitsch curio shops, pseudo-traditional dance shows, reptile parks, bungee jumping, white-water rafting, microlighting, canoeing, muzak zebra- striped tour buses, marimba revues, buzzing low-flying aircraft, casino hotels, golf courses, touts and con artists.

Zimbabwe's political strife has returned the spotlight to Zambia. Once fallen, the shabby town of Livingstone is booming, and on the Zambian side, foreigners can visit the falls for a fraction of the Zimbabwean price.

Zimbabwe

international access code ☎ 263

The town of Victoria Falls has so far been saved from the worst of the political and

Highlights

- Gaze in amazement at Victoria Falls from the Zimbabwean side... .

- Keep gazing – but closer up – from the Zambian side.

- Time your visit to coincide with the full moon and see the enigmatic lunar rainbow over Victoria Falls.

- Check out Zambia's historical scene at the Livingstone Museum in Livingstone.

- Try bungee jumping, microlighting, canoeing, white-water rafting or another adrenaline activity from either side of the falls.

economic turmoil that is affecting other parts of Zimbabwe, but tourist numbers have dropped off significantly and political instability could arrive eventually.

VISAS & DOCUMENTS

Visas (for a maximum of 90 days) are available at the Zimbabwe border, and only citizens of Ireland, the UK, Canada and Sweden are exempt. Everyone else pays US$30/45 for a single/double-entry visa. Multiple-entry visas (US$55) are difficult

Zim or Zam?

For many, the big question is: Do I visit Victoria Falls from Zimbabwe or Zambia? The answer is easy: see both sides.

The Zimbabwean side affords a broad, overall view of the falls, and also allows you to drop into the gorge at Cataract View, where you'll see the best rainbows. From the Zambian side, you can saunter right up to the falling water and gaze down the face of the falls, or get right out into the spray at the dramatic Knife Edge. Inexpensive accommodation on the Zimbabwean side is within walking distance of the falls, while the Zambian options are mainly in Livingstone, which is a taxi ride away.

Whichever side, entry tickets are for one visit only, and there are no visitor facilities inside the falls parks on either side. Before you go, spend some time thinking about water and the things it can damage – then leave those things behind or pack them well in plastic – and be sure not to wear anything that will create a public scandal if it gets wet!

country	unit		Zimbabwean dollars
Australia	A$1	=	Z$31.43
Botswana	P1	=	Z$10.64
Canada	C$1	=	Z$38.56
Euro zone	€1	=	Z$54.46
Namibia	N$1	=	Z$7.35
New Zealand	NZ$1	=	Z$25.82
South Africa	R1	=	Z$7.35
UK	UK£1	=	Z$83.21
USA	US$1	=	Z$56.92
Zambia	ZK100	=	Z$1.70

Cash advances (in Zimbabwe dollars) with Visa and MasterCard are possible with no commission at the Barclays and Standard Chartered banks. Note that changing money on the street is illegal and the street money changers can be relied upon to rip you off 100% of the time – rather than any agreed number of Zimbabwe dollars, your foreign currency will buy you a newspaper, Zambian kwacha or some other similarly less-valuable substance; alternatively, the street money changer will report you to the police and you'll have to pay a bribe to avoid further difficulties. Having said that, everyone in Zimbabwe is desperate for hard currency, and informal currency exchange in shops or with established businesspeople is generally in the best interest of everyone involved and doesn't have to be dangerous.

All food, drinks, public transport and minor items must be purchased with Zimbabwe dollars; most budget and mid-range hotels and agencies selling tours and adventure activities quote their rates in US dollars but accept both Zimbabwe dollars (with some reluctance) and US dollars (with glee). Top-end hotels and air fares must be paid in US dollars. Payment in cash (in any currency) for major expenses (eg, rafting trips, hotels and air fares) requires an additional 15% tax. However, payment by foreign currency travellers cheque or credit card avoids the tax. Prices listed here include taxes.

to obtain and must be organised through Zimbabwean embassies.

If you're planning to stay overnight in Zambia and then return to Zimbabwe, be sure to apply for a double-entry visa. For day trips (ie, for white-water rafting or microlighting), you're allowed to leave Zimbabwe and return on a single-entry visa. For more information, see the boxed text 'Over the Bridge & into Zambia' later in this chapter.

MONEY

Given Zimbabwe's political turmoil – and the ongoing destruction of its two main sources of foreign exchange (agriculture and tourism) – the Zimbabwe dollar continues to spiral downward and the illegal currency black market grows. At major bureaus de change, you'll generally fare a little better than at banks, but daily rates can fluctuate by as much as 10%. The following table represents official bank rates at the time of going to print:

VICTORIA FALLS NATIONAL PARK
☎ 113

The entrance to Victoria Falls National Park (☎ 2204, admission US$20/10 per foreign

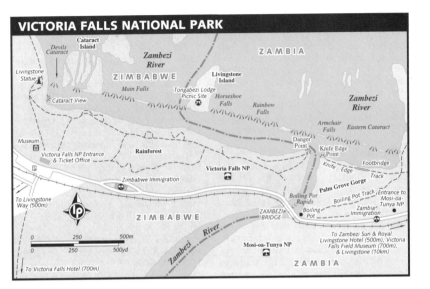

VICTORIA FALLS NATIONAL PARK

adult/child; open 6.30am-6pm daily) lies within easy walking distance of Victoria Falls town and features a network of tracks, which follow the canyon rim to some spectacular viewpoints. One of the most dramatic is **Cataract View**, at the bottom of a steep stairway into the gorge. The impressive **Danger Point** viewpoint features slippery and unfenced drop-offs into the great abyss; a short walk away is a view of the **Zambezi Bridge**, which attracts locals interested in watching mad foreigners diving off, attached only to long rubber bands.

For two days before and after the full moon, you can also visit from 7pm to 8pm to see the renowned lunar rainbow (US$30).

VICTORIA FALLS

The town of Vic Falls (as it's often called) is a tourist trap with little remaining that depicts its history. It has no ambience, but the modern facilities suit many visitors and it is very close to the falls.

Information

The Victoria Falls Publicity Association (☎ 4202), on Parkway, distributes brochures and sells the outdated *Victoria Falls Map*

(US$1). It's fine for general information but don't expect much and you won't be disappointed. It's open from 8am to 5pm daily. The Zimbabwe Tourism Authority office (☎ 4376), Adam Stander Dr, provides very basic information on the whole country.

Barclays and Standard Chartered banks are just off Livingstone Way, and bureaus de change are dotted along Parkway and in Soper's Arcade. Touts may offer up to Z$100 for US$1, but don't even think about it; the point is to somehow rip you off.

The post office is just off Livingstone Way. Long-distance calls can be made from travel agencies and the Internet centre upstairs in Soper's Arcade. Gold Print, behind Hunters Bar on Parkway, offers Internet access for US$1.40/3.50 per 15/60 minutes, and Vic Falls Cybercafe in Soper's Arcade charges US$1.40/6.50.

Backpackers Bazaar (☎ 5828, e back pack@africaonline.co.zw), just off Parkway, is the best place for independent travel advice and bookings for budget travellers.

Gold Print and The Zambezi Print Shop in Soper's Arcade sell print and slide film and develop prints (but not slide film) for US$5.75/8 per 24/36 exposures.

Dangers & Annoyances

Victoria Falls attracts lots of inexperienced travellers, and therefore presents a ripe harvest for determined touts, scumbag con artists and bogus money changers. While these objectionable characters are normally more of a nuisance than a danger, it's wise to be wary of scams, leave your valuables somewhere safe, avoid leaving anything inside your vehicle, and use taxis after dark.

Falls Craft Village

The touristy Falls Craft Village (Traditional Living in Zimbabwe; ☎ 4309, e craftvil@ telcovic.co.zw; admission US$6; open 8.30am-4.30pm Mon-Sat, 8.30am-12.30pm Sun) presents a mock-up of traditional Zimbabwean life, with ethnic huts and craftspeople. Admission includes an informative booklet that describes what you're seeing. From 6.30pm to 8pm there's the Magic of Africa traditional dance show, which costs US$12 per person.

Zambezi Wildlife Sanctuary & Crocodile Ranch

This long-standing sanctuary (☎ 4604, e ilal azws@africaonline.co.zw; admission US$3; open 6am-6pm daily) boasts over 5000 crocodiles, as well as caged lions and leopards. Entry includes a guided tour; phone in advance to find out the feeding times for the crocs and cats. It's a pleasant two-hour walk from town, but a spate of muggings suggest that it's better to use a taxi (US$4) or a guided tour (US$18 per person).

Places to Stay – Budget

Municipal Camp & Caravan Park (☎ 4311, Livingstone Way) Camping US$3, dorm beds US$4.50, single/double chalets with fridge US$7.50/9.30, 4-bed self-catering cottages US$12.50. This government-run complex badly needs security measures and other renovations, but it's still popular with overland companies.

Club Shoestring (☎ 011-800731, 12 West Dr) Camping US$4, dorm beds US$9, doubles with bathroom US$20. This is a good, social option for backpackers. Unfortunately, the camp site isn't terribly private.

Guests have access to the kitchen, bar and a 'chill-out' veranda.

Pat's Place (☎ 5893, 209 West Dr) Dorm beds U$3, doubles US$10. This quiet, friendly and secure place has only a few beds, so book or arrive early. There's a small pool and kitchen facilities and breakfast is available for US$2.

Victoria Falls Backpackers Lodge (☎ 22 09, e matopo@telcovic.co.zw, 357 Gibson Rd) Camping US$5, rooms, bungalows or A-frames US$10 per person. This quiet, leafy and welcoming place features a swimming pool, kitchen facilities and a friendly ambience. The gregarious owner, Gareth McDonald, also offers inexpensive transfers (US$10 per person) to Kazungula, on the Botswana border.

Settlers Retreat (☎ 011-216351, 224 Reynard Rd) Camping US$5, dorm beds US$8, doubles US$14. This new place is clean, quiet and homely, and has nicely furnished rooms with fans and shared bath. Guests have access to a TV lounge and swimming pool. Breakfast is available here for US$3.

Places to Stay – Mid-Range

Villa Victoria (☎ 4386, e villavic@tel covic.co.zw, 165 Courtney Selous Cres) Singles/doubles with fan and bathroom US$30/40, doubles with shared bathroom US$20. The large, clean and well-furnished rooms inside the house are reasonable value, but the tiny cottages are not worthwhile if you're travelling as a single. It has kitchen facilities, a TV lounge and swimming pool.

APG Lodge (☎ 3440, fax 2349, Nyathi Rd) Doubles with bathroom, air-con & fan B&B US$50. This bright place is one of several similar places along, or just off, Mopane St in the leafy western suburbs. The lovingly furnished rooms are sparkling and it's ideal for a moderate splurge and/or lengthy stay. There are kitchen facilities, a TV lounge and splash pool. Look for the signs off Mopane St.

The Sprayview Hotel (☎ 4344, e spray view@africaonline.co.zw, Livingstone Way) Singles/doubles B&B US$55/80. This motel

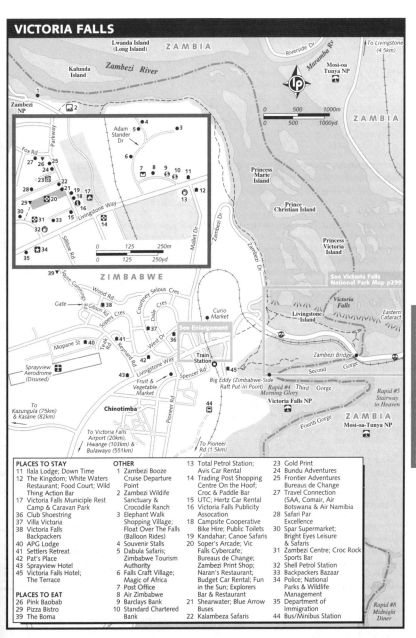

VICTORIA FALLS

PLACES TO STAY
11 Ilala Lodge; Down Time
12 The Kingdom; White Waters
    Restaurant; Food Court; Wild
    Thing Action Bar
17 Victoria Falls Municipe Rest
    Camp & Caravan Park
36 Club Shoestring
37 Villa Victoria
38 Victoria Falls
    Backpackers
40 APG Lodge
41 Settlers Retreat
42 Pat's Place
43 Sprayview Hotel
45 Victoria Falls Hotel;
    The Terrace

PLACES TO EAT
26 Pink Baobab
29 Pizza Bistro
39 The Boma

OTHER
1 Zambezi Booze
  Cruise Departure
  Point
2 Zambezi Wildlife
  Sanctuary &
  Crocodile Ranch
3 Elephant Walk
  Shopping Village;
  Float Over The Falls
  (Balloon Rides)
4 Souvenir Stalls
5 Dabula Safaris;
  Zimbabwe Tourism
  Authority
6 Falls Craft Village;
  Magic of Africa
7 Post Office
8 Air Zimbabwe
9 Barclays Bank
10 Standard Chartered
   Bank

13 Total Petrol Station;
   Avis Car Rental
14 Trading Post Shopping
   Centre On the Hoof;
   Croc & Paddle Bar
15 UTC; Hertz Car Rental
16 Victoria Falls Publicity
   Assocation
18 Campsite Cooperative
   Bike Hire; Public Toilets
19 Kandahar; Canoe Safaris
20 Soper's Arcade; Vic
   Falls Cybercafe;
   Bureaus de Change;
   Zambezi Print Shop;
   Naran's Restaurant;
   Budget Car Rental; Fun
   in the Sun; Explorers
   Bar & Restaurant
21 Shearwater; Blue Arrow
   Buses
22 Kalambeza Safaris

23 Gold Print
24 Bundu Adventures
25 Frontier Adventures
   Bureaus de Change
27 Travel Connection
   (SAA, Comair, Air
   Botswana & Air Namibia
28 Safari Par
   Excellence
30 Spar Supermarket;
   Bright Eyes Leisure
   & Safaris
31 Zambezi Centre; Croc Rock
   Sports Bar
32 Shell Petrol Station
33 Backpackers Bazaar
34 Police; National
   Parks & Wildlife
   Management
35 Department of
   Immigration
44 Bus/Minibus Station

complex has large and well-furnished rooms; the swimming pool and playground are ideal for families.

Places to Stay – Top End

The Kingdom (☎ 4289, e reservations@ kingdom.zimsun.co.zw, Cnr Mallet Dr & Livingstone Way) Doubles B&B US$228. This oddity – a bizarre cross between Great Zimbabwe, Sun City and Las Vegas – redefines bad taste in Victoria Falls (and we all thought the heap of egg cartons cum prison fortress known as Elephant Hills was an eyesore…). In fact, here you can see firsthand how low both tourism and architecture can sink. Southern African residents pay about 25% of the foreigners rate.

Victoria Falls Hotel (☎ 4751, e reservations@tvfh.zimsun.co.zw, Mallet Dr) Singles/doubles US$347/396. Even if you can't afford it, drop by to stroll through the gardens and soak up the colonial elegance.

Walking on Vic Falls' Wild Side

Companies in Victoria Falls (Zimbabwe) and Livingstone (Zambia) offer a staggering array of activities, and some travellers have so much fun bungee jumping and/or rafting that they forget to visit the falls!

All activities listed here can be undertaken from either town for the same cost. Prices normally include transfers to/from your hotel, national park entrance fees and visas for Zimbabwe if coming from Zambia (or vice versa). Some meals may also be included.

Those with a lot of stamina may want to consider a whirlwind combination, involving several activities for a discounted price. For example, in the low season, you may be able to do canoeing or rafting, plus a wildlife drive and an evening booze cruise for as little as US$80.

Adventure Companies

Most activities can be booked at any travel agency in Victoria Falls or Livingstone but it is often much better to book directly through the company offering the trip.

Victoria Falls, Zimbabwe

Bundu Adventures (☎ 011-210946) Parkway
Dabula Safaris (☎ 4453, e dabula@africaonline.co.zw) Adam Stander Dr
Frontier Adventures (☎ 3587, fax 5809) Parkway
Kalambeza Safaris (☎ 5938, e kalambeza@pci.co.zw) Parkway
Kandahar (☎ 3589, e adrift@africaonline@co.zw) Parkway
Safari Par Excellence (☎ 2054, e reservations@safpar.co.zw, w www.itech.co.za/safpar) The Mall
Shearwater (☎ 4471, e shearadv@shearwater.co.za) Soper's Arcade. Shearwater also acts as a major booking agency

Livingstone, Zambia

Abseil Africa (☎ 323454, e abseil@zamnet.zm) near Livingstone Adventure Centre, Mosi-oa-Tunya Rd
Bundu Adventures (☎ 324407, e zambezi@zamnet.zm, w www.bundu-adventures.com) 1st Stop Booking Shop, Mosi-oa-Tunya Rd
Bwaato Adventures (☎ 324227, e bwaato@zamnet.zm) New Fairmount hotel
Livingstone Safaris (☎ 322267, e gecko@zamnet.zm) based at Gecko's Guesthouse, off Mosi-oa-Tunya Rd
Makora Quest (☎ 324253, e quest@zamnet.zm) Livingstone Adventure Centre, Mosi-oa-Tunya Rd
Serious Fun (☎ 323912, e seriousfun@zamnet.zm, w www.riversurfing.com) Livingstone Adventure Centre, Mosi-oa-Tunya Rd
Taonga Safaris (☎ 324081, e taonga@zamnet.zm) Zigzag Coffee House, Mosi-oa-Tunya Rd
Wild Side Tours & Safaris (☎ 323726, e wild@zamnet.zm, w www.zambiatourism.com/wildside) Mosi-oa-Tunya Rd

Ilala Lodge (☎ 4737, e *ilalazws@afri caonline.co.zw, Livingstone Way)* Singles/ doubles B&B US$143/230. This well-located hotel offers charming, luxurious and convenient accommodation.

Places to Eat

All hotels offer good-value buffet breakfasts and other meals, but the renowned buffet breakfast at Victoria Falls Hotel is open to hotel guests only.

Naran's (Soper's Arcade) Breakfast US$1-2, sandwiches US$1-1.70, curry US$2. Open 8.30am-5pm Mon-Sat. This Indian-run eatery is great for drinks, snacks, lunch and breakfast. Not surprisingly, the speciality is curry.

On the Hoof (☎ 2250, *Trading Post Shopping Centre, Livingstone Way)* Mains US$2.30-3. Closed evenings. This is the best of several upmarket steak restaurants. The eclectic choice includes pumba pudding

---

Walking on Vic Falls' Wild Side

Activities

All prices are per person.

Abseiling (Book at Abseil Africa) Livingstone. Conducted at Batoka Gorge (Zambia); cost US$95 per day, including breakfast, lunch and drinks.

Balloon Flight (The Vic Falls Balloon Company ☎ 2172, e francis@balloons.co.zw) Vic Falls. The unmissable balloon is actually tied to a cable, so it doesn't actually 'float over the falls', but the views are spectacular; US$25 for 15 minutes.

Booze Cruises (Kalambeza Safaris, Dabula Safaris and Safari Par Excellence) in Vic Falls; (Bwaato Adventures includes traditional music, Taonga Safaris and Wild Side Tours & Safaris) in Livingstone. These are great fun even if you don't see much wildlife; the Zambezi River seems crowded with other boats. 'Breakfast cruises' cost about US$30, 'lunch cruises' (with food and drinks) about US$25, sunset 'booze cruises' (snacks and drinks) are US$15 to US$18, and 'dinner cruises' (meal and drinks) about US$30.

Bungee Jumping (Africa Extreme ☎ 324156, e extreme@zamnet.zm; Vic Falls Bungi ☎ 324231, e bridge@zamnet.zm) Livingstone. Why not jump 111m off Victoria Falls Bridge with a rubber band around your ankles? US$90 per jump.

Canoeing (Bundu Adventures, Kandahar and Safari Par Excellence) Vic Falls; (Bundu Adventures and Makora Quest) Livingstone. More sedate than rafting, but still loads of fun; US$70/85 for half/full day, and overnight trips available.

Flight (Southern Cross Aviation ☎ 4618, e dabula@africaonline.co.zw; United Air Services ☎ 4220, e uasvfall@telcovic.co.zw) Vic Falls; (Del-Air ☎ 320058, fax 323095) Livingstone. Fixed-wing flights cost US$55/80 for 25/40 minutes. The longer flight also goes over Zambezi National Park.

Helicopter (Zambezi Helicopter Company ☎ 3569, e reservations@helicopters.co.zw) Vic Falls; (Del-Air, see Flight above) Livingstone. Costs about US$75/140 for 15/30 minutes.

Jet Boat (Jet Extreme ☎ 321375, e jtx@zamnet.zm) Livingstone. Popular with adrenaline junkies, this costs US$60 for 45 minutes.

Microlight (Bush Birds Flying Safaris ☎ 2210, e ulazim@samara.co.zw) Vic Falls; (Batoka Sky ☎ 320 058, e reservations@batokasky.com) Livingstone. These are quieter, and get closer to the falls, than planes and helicopters; US$75/100/170 for 15/30/55 minutes.

Rafting (Shearwater, Bundu Adventures, Safari Par Excellence and Frontier Adventures) Vic Falls; (Bundu Adventures) Livingstone. The Zambezi rapids are among the world's wildest (and safest) but which rapids are rafted depends on water levels; US$55/85 for half/full day, including meals.

Riverboard (Bundu Adventures, Shearwater, Frontier Adventures and Safari Par Excellence) Vic Falls; (Bundu Adventures) Livingstone. What about lying on a boogie board and careering down the rapids? US$85/95 for half/full day, including meals and drinks.

Wildlife Drives & Safaris (Dabula Safaris, Bundu Adventures and Safari Par Excellence) Vic Falls; (Bundu Adventures, Wild Side Tours & Safaris, Bwaato Adventures, Livingstone Safaris and Makora Quest) Livingstone. 'Half-day' (three-hour) drives around Mosi-oa-Tunya National Park (Zambia) from US$30 to US$45, full-day trips to Chobe National Park (Botswana) about US$105, and Hwange National Park (Zimbabwe) about US$165.

EXCURSION TO VICTORIA FALLS

(warthog steak roll), ostrich burger, and crocodile – all with chips and salad. It's good value and you can also enjoy a brew from the adjacent Croc & Paddle.

Pink Baobab (☎ 4455, Fox Rd) Breakfast US$2-3, lunch US$2.50-4. Closed evenings. The garden setting here offers plenty of shade and umbrellas, but it's a bit pricey and the servings aren't terribly generous. It also sells books and maps.

Pizza Bistro (☎ 4396, Soper's Arcade) Breakfast US$2.70, pasta US$3, single pizzas US$3, crepes US$2.50. This popular place near Explorers Bar features charming decor and friendly service. However, the pizzas are unremarkable, so you may want to stick with the pasta.

The Boma (☎ 3238, e *saflodge@saf lodge.co.zw, Squire Cummings Rd)* Dinner & show US$18. This popular buffet serves up warthog and mopane worms (complete with a certificate verifying your temerity), but the less adventurous can choose from less esoteric options. Dinners are accompanied by local song and dance; bookings are essential.

Spar Supermarket (Courtney Selous Cres) is the town's biggest and best food store; it also has a bakery.

Entertainment

Croc Rock Sports Bar (Zambezi Centre) On most evenings, this rather downmarket bar serves as a popular nightclub, and on the weekend it features well-attended live music performances.

Explorers Bar & Restaurant (☎ 4468, Soper's Arcade) Known far and wide, Explorers is the main venue for hard-drinking expatriates, overland truck drivers, white-water raft jockeys and their assorted fans. Regulars love the sports performances on the big screen TV, as well as the pick-up opportunities.

Wild Thing Action Bar (The Kingdom Hotel) Adrenaline-pumped bungee jumpers and rafters flock to this place to watch videos of their experience. Not surprisingly, the prices are nearly as high as some of the clientele.

Down Time (Ilala Lodge) Same story, different companies.

Shopping

Much of Adam Stander Dr is a tourist trap full of souvenir shops selling tacky mass-produced and overpriced goods. A better option is the *curio market* at the end of the street or *Fun In The Sun* in Soper's Arcade. Alternatively, try the classier *Trading Post Shopping Centre* on Livingstone Way or *Elephant Walk Shopping Village*, off Adam Stander Dr.

Getting There & Away

Air Air Namibia flies between Windhoek and Victoria Falls three times weekly from US$276 return, plus a Namibian departure tax of US$12.

Air Zimbabwe (☎ 4316), just off Livingstone Way, has daily flights from Vic Falls to Harare (US$179/359 one way/return), often via Hwange (US$109/226) and Kariba (US$129/257). Special half-price fares are often available.

The agency for South African Airways (SAA), Comair, Air Botswana and Air Namibia is Travel Connection (☎ 2053), Flame Lily Court, beside Pink Baobab cafe.

The international departure tax (US$20) must be paid when you check in.

Bus The grubby local bus/minibus terminal is in Chinotimba township, which is a risky 15-minute walk or a US$1.40 taxi ride from the centre. Minibuses to Hwange (US$4, one hour) leave when full and several buses depart each morning for Bulawayo (US$9, six to seven hours).

The reliable Blue Arrow leaves the Shearwater office, on Parkway, at 9am on Wednesday, Friday and Sunday for Bulawayo (US$21, four hours), via Hwange (US$8.50, 1½ hours). Book seats through Shearwater.

The weekly Intercape Mainliner travels between Windhoek and Victoria Falls (US$56), departing Windhoek at 8pm Friday and arriving in Victoria Falls at 4pm Saturday. In the other direction, it leaves Vic Falls at 9am Sunday and arrives in Windhoek at 3.30am Monday. Although it passes through Botswana en route, travellers may not disembark in Kasane.

Train There are trains departing from Victoria Falls in Zimbabwe for Bulawayo at 6.30am daily (US$11/8.20/4.50 for 1st/2nd/economy class), via Hwange (US$3.70/2.75/1.50). Unfortunately, diesel shortages mean that the train is more often than not cancelled. For updated information, contact the reservation counter (☎ 4391), which is open from 2am to 6.15pm Monday to Friday and 4.30pm to 6.15pm Saturday and Sunday.

Getting Around
To/From the Airport UTC (☎ 4225) on Parkway charges US$5 per person, while most hotels and agencies charge US$10. Taxis start at US$20, but only with hard bargaining.

Car Rental Most major international car rental companies – ie, Hertz (☎ 4297), Avis (☎ 4532) and Budget (☎ 2243) – are represented. Rates start at US$27 per day plus US$0.35 per kilometre, plus petrol and insurance. The best option is Bright Eyes Leisure & Safaris (☎ 3268, ⓔ briteyes@africaonline.co.zw), above Spar Supermarket, which charges US$17 per day plus US$0.16 per kilometre, petrol and insurance. All companies allow cars to be driven into Zambia, Botswana and Namibia, but advise them in advance so they can arrange the necessary paperwork (note that entry into Zambia requires purchasing expensive, and virtually worthless, insurance; police checks are made at Muramba). Foreigners can use their home licence to rent a vehicle.

Over the Bridge & Into Zambia

From Victoria Falls, Zimbabwe, you can walk or take a taxi (US$3) to the Zimbabwean immigration post and then continue 1.3km on foot over the spectacular Zambezi Bridge. Alternatively, you can take a rickshaw (about US$1). Just upstream, you'll have a view of the falls, and the water forcing its way through the narrow gap in the cliffs to swirl around the Boiling Pot Whirlpool. From the Zambian immigration post, it's just a short walk to the park on the Zambian side of the falls, where you'll pay US$10 for good close-up views of the falls.

Just past the bridge is the Zambian border crossing, and 100m beyond it, the entrance to Mosi-oa-Tunya National Park. Minibuses (US$0.60) and share taxis (US$1 per person) leave when full to Livingstone, about 11km away. Mugging is common along this route, so it may be unwise to walk or ride a bicycle. Drivers should also take care if stopping at the viewpoint where the road runs very close to the falls – people have been jumped here, as well.

Taxis (US$3.50), minibuses (US$0.60) and share taxis (US$1.50 to US$2 per person) leave when full to Livingstone, about 7km away. Mugging is common along this route also, so it may be unwise to walk or ride a bicycle.

Most travel agencies and hotels in Vic Falls and Livingstone charge about US$25 for minibus transfers between the two towns. See Places to Stay – Budget under Livingstone for information on better-value transfers between Vic Falls and Livingstone.

If you're just crossing for the day, advise the Zimbabwean officials before leaving the country so you won't need to buy a new visa when you return later in the day. Similarly, Zambian officials charge only US$10 for day visas – this is mainly for participants in adrenaline activities 'north of the border'. If you're staying overnight or spending more time in Zambia, you can avoid visa fees by pre-booking accommodation or activities 48 hours in advance (see Visas & Documents in the Zambia section, later in this chapter).

There are no official foreign exchange facilities at either border crossing, but money changers hang around at both border posts and national park entrance gates. (If you're just crossing for the day, you won't need Zambian kwacha, as everything can be paid for in US dollars. If you're staying longer, you're better off changing in Livingstone, anyway.) Both immigration posts are open from 6am to 10pm daily.

EXCURSION TO VICTORIA FALLS

Bicycle Campsite Cooperative Bike Hire on Parkway charges US$1/3.50/5 per hour/half day/full day (minimum of two hours). Other informal bicycle hire places are found along Adam Stander Dr. If you decide to take a rented bicycle into Zambia, make sure you take a receipt to show the immigration authorities.

Local Transport You can walk anywhere in Vic Falls. You'll find taxis around the immigration posts or the Spar Supermarket. Fares are around US$0.70 per kilometre.

Zambia

international access code ☎ 260
Victoria Falls is shared by Zimbabwe and Zambia, which are divided by the Zambezi River. On the Zambian side, you'll have less-manicured surroundings and close-up views of the mesmerising waters as they plunge over the falls.

VISAS & DOCUMENTS

Zambian visas (maximum of 90 days), available at major borders, are free for citizens of Australia, Ireland, Canada and South Africa. British travellers pay a whopping US$65/80 for single/double entry visas and others pay US$25/40. Multiple-entry visas (US$80) are issued only at Zambian embassies.

For those who require them, visas for one-day activities in Zambia are normally organised by the safari company or agency and will set you back US$10. If you want more time, you can get a visa fee waiver by pre-booking some aspect of your trip with a Zambian company – a hotel, lodge, hostel, safari company or travel agency. The company will 'introduce' you to the country and put your name on a daily 'manifest'; however, you must book 48 hours in advance.

MONEY

Bureaus de change and banks change major currencies (plus Botswana pula and Zimbabwe dollars). Barclays Bank charges 1.5% commission for travellers cheques,

and 2% commission for credit card cash advances (in Zambian kwacha only). Standard Chartered Bank charges about the same commissions and has ATMs for Visa. The following are official bank rates.

country	unit		Zambian kwacha
Australia	A$1	=	ZK1497
Botswana	P1	=	ZK511
Canada	C$1	=	ZK1830
Euro zone	€1	=	ZK1685
South Africa	R1	=	ZK378
UK	UK£1	=	ZK4126
USA	US$1	=	ZK3040
Zimbabwe	Z$1	=	ZK33

Zambia's 17.5% VAT has been excluded from accommodation in Livingstone (only) until further notice. Using a credit card to pay for anything attracts a surcharge of around 5%.

Public transport, food, drinks and other minor items must be paid in Zambian kwacha. Most hotels, tours and activities quote their prices in US dollars and kwacha; you can choose which one you use. All international and domestic air fares must be paid in US dollars.

MOSI-OA-TUNYA NATIONAL PARK
☎ 03
Most of the Zambian side of Victoria Falls, and sections of the Zambezi riverbank, both upstream and downstream of the falls, is included within Mosi-oa-Tunya National Park (which also includes a separate game park with impressive wildlife). The entrance to the falls is adjacent to the Zambian immigration post.

Victoria Falls

This national park *(admission US$3; open 6am-6pm daily)*, with its rather grandiose name, is a collection of walking tracks leading to various falls viewpoints.

The entrance fee can be paid in US dollars or any regional currency, except Zimbabwe dollars.

Don't miss the **Eastern Cataract walk**, which is guaranteed to soak you to the bone; it leads across a harrowing footbridge to the Knife Edge Point. Alternatively, follow the steep track down to the roiling whirlpool known as the Boiling Pot.

Victoria Falls Field Museum (☎ 321396), inside the park about 700m east of the entrance to the national park, explains the cultural and geological history of the falls. Park entry tickets include museum admission. It was under reconstruction at the time of writing.

Beside the museum is a small snack bar, and close by, a collection of curio stalls, selling mainly woodcarvings and other souvenirs, where the prices (and salespeople) are very competitive.

Mosi-oa-Tunya Game Park

Officially called the Zoological Park but commonly known as the Mosi-oa-Tunya Game Park, this delightful reserve (admission US$3 per person, US$3.50 per vehicle; open 6am-6pm daily) contains Zambia's only rhinos (five of them, to be exact), and also harbours herds of buffaloes, wildebeests, zebras, warthogs, giraffes and elephants. The entrance to the park is near the airfield and the 'booze cruise' jetty, at the end of the road that branches off the main road between Livingstone and the Zimbabwe border. The only way to get around is by private vehicle or participate in an organised wildlife drive (these are available from Livingstone).

LIVINGSTONE
☎ 03

Zambia's shabby but historic and booming tourist capital is a major attraction in Southern Africa, as well as a worthy alternative base for visits to Victoria Falls.

Information

The marginally helpful Tourist Centre (☎ 321 404, e zntbliv@zamnet.zm, Mosi-oa-Tunya Rd) distributes a few free brochures and sells postcards and souvenirs. It's open from 8am to 1pm and 2pm to 5pm Monday to Friday and 8am to 1pm Saturday. However, your best options for reliable information are the backpackers lodges.

Banks and bureaus de change are located on Mosi-oa-Tunya Rd (the main road); changing money with informal street money changers is illegal and risky.

The post office is along the main road, and you can make local and international calls at the Zamtel Call Centre next door. To dial Livingstone from Victoria Falls (Zimbabwe), simply dial 8 and the local number. For email and Internet access, the best place is Cyber Post at the Livingstone Adventure Centre; also good is Zulu Net at African Gifts. Both charge US$6 per hour.

Film is available at the Shoprite supermarket. Photo Express, in Liso House on the main road, charges US$5.75/8 to develop 24/36 print (only) film.

Livingstone Museum

Livingstone Museum (☎ 323566, e livmus@ zamnet.zm, Mosi-oa-Tunya Rd; admission US$3; open 9am-4.30pm daily) houses an interesting collection of archaeological and anthropological relics, including a copy of a Neanderthal skull estimated at over 100,000-years-old. The original, which is known as the Broken Hill Man (formerly Rhodesian Man and Kabwe Man), was uncovered near Kabwe (north of Lusaka), during the colonial era and is now displayed in the UK. There are also examples of ritual artefacts and Tonga material crafts, an African village mock-up, a collection of David Livingstone paraphernalia and a display of Africa maps dating back to 1690.

Mukuni Village

At Mukuni Village (☎ 320601; admission US$3; open daylight hours), 18km southwest of Livingstone, visitors can gain an insight into the traditional life and food of the Leya people. Chief Mukuni, who lives here, is the grandson of the historic Chief Mukuni who met David Livingstone when he passed through over a century ago. The entrance fee – actually a donation – funds community projects, such as boreholes, water tanks, and a clinic. After visiting the site, you'll be invited to peruse the local crafts sales area, where the pressure can get a bit intense; if you don't feel comfortable with the tactics, move on and make it known that visitors normally prefer a less aggressive approach.

Taxis from town cost around US$5 per person.

Places to Stay – Budget

Budget places in Livingstone offer transfers from Zimbabwe; for around US$10/20 for a dorm bed/private room, they'll pick you up from the border, include one night's accommodation and arrange a free Zambian visa (usually valid for 14 days, but often renewable). This can be arranged directly or through Backpackers Bazaar on the Zimbabwe side. You'll normally need to book at least 48 hours in advance.

Fawlty Towers (☎ *323432,* e *ahorizon@ zamnet.zm, Mosi-oa-Tunya Rd)* Camping US$3 per person, dorm beds US$10, doubles with fan and shared/private bath US$20/30. This place continues to be popular; the pleasant garden doubles as the camp site and the rooms are nothing special. All rooms have mosquito nets and there is a nice pool, TV lounge and kitchen facilities.

Gecko's Guesthouse (☎ *322267,* e *gec ko@zamnet.zm, Limulunga Rd)* Camping US$2 per person, dorm beds US$6, singles/ doubles with shared bathroom US$13/20. This popular but quiet place attracts more subdued travellers. It's not especially central, but does offer a small pool, kitchen, convivial bar and limited meals.

Jolly Boys Backpackers (☎ *324229,* e *jboys@ zamnet.zm, Mokambo Rd)* Camping US$3, dorm beds US$6. This very laidback place continues to be a popular option, with a kitchen, activities desk, pool table, excellent swimming pool and bar. The dorms may be crowded and noisy – and the camp site is wedged between the car park and bar – but it's still good value. Breakfast costs US$1. It's likely that in 2002, the entire place will be shifting to a larger site near the museum and the current site will become a more upmarket guesthouse.

Maramba River Lodge (☎/*fax 324189,* e *maramba@zamnet.zm)* Camping US$5, doubles US$30, tent accommodation US$10 per person. This very relaxed place situated next to the Maramba River is known for the

elephants that meander harmlessly through the site.

Papagayo (☎ *320237,* e *papagayo@ zamnet.zm, Mwela St)* Camping US$3 per person, dorm beds US$6, rooms US$15 per person. New on the scene, this converted house offers vast rooms (double, twin or family), plus a simple dorm with bunk beds. There's a garden, swimming pool, squash court, kitchen, bar, meals, laundry facilities and friendly French-speaking management.

Jungle Junction (☎ *324127,* e *jungle@ zamnet.zm, 21 Obote Way)* Small huts US$75/120/125/150 for one/two/three/four nights, medium huts US$85/120/155/190, large huts US$95/140/185/230; if you're alone, add US$5/10/15 for small/medium/ large huts; in all cases, your fifth night is free. Rates include all meals, transfers from/ to Livingstone and mokoro canoeing trips during your stay. This incredible spot at Katombora rapids, 60km upstream from Livingstone, will never be forgotten. Access alone is priceless – you couldn't pay for the experience…just take our word for it! Alternatively, you can visit the affiliated ***Bovu Island***, which is patterned after a traditional local village. Camping is US$6 per person or US$35/60/100 for one week/two weeks/one month; return transfers from Livingstone are US$20 per person. Bookings are handled through the same office as Jungle Junction.

Places to Stay – Mid-Range

Living Inn (☎ *324203, John Hunt Way)* Doubles with fan/air-con US$20/25. This friendly place has quite a few rooms arranged around a tiny courtyard. It's central and good value, but the rooms are musty and could stand renovations.

Ngolide Lodge (☎ *321091,* e *ngolide@ zamnet.zm, Mosi-oa-Tunya Rd)* Singles/ doubles US$28/37. Although a little inconvenient, this place is certainly recommended for its good service, and the comfortable and nicely furnished (but smallish) rooms. Rooms come with fan, TV, kettle and bathroom.

New Fairmount (☎ *320726,* e *nfhc@ zamnet.zm, Mosi-oa-Tunya Rd)* Singles/

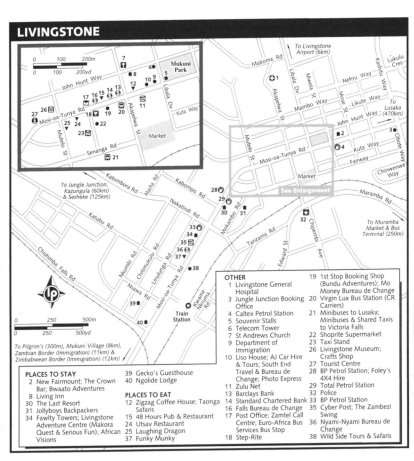

LIVINGSTONE

PLACES TO STAY
2 New Fairmount; The Crown Bar; Bwaato Adventures
8 Living Inn
30 The Last Resort
31 Jollyboys Backpackers
34 Fawlty Towers; Livingstone Adventure Centre (Makora Quest & Serious Fun); African Visions
39 Gecko's Guesthouse
40 Ngolide Lodge

PLACES TO EAT
12 Zigzag Coffee House; Taonga Safaris
15 48 Hours Pub & Restaurant
24 Utsav Restaurant
25 Laughing Dragon
37 Funky Munky

OTHER
1 Livingstone General Hospital
3 Jungle Junction Booking Office
4 Caltex Petrol Station
5 Souvenir Stalls
6 Telecom Tower
7 St Andrews Church
9 Department of Immigration
10 Liso House; AJ Car Hire & Tours; South End Travel & Bureau de Change; Photo Express
11 Zulu Net
13 Barclays Bank
14 Standard Chartered Bank
16 Falls Bureau de Change
17 Post Office; Zamtel Call Centre; Euro-Africa Bus Services Bus Stop
18 Step-Rite
19 1st Stop Booking Shop (Bundu Adventures); Mo Money Bureau de Change
20 Virgin Lux Bus Station (CR Carriers)
21 Minibuses to Lusaka; Minibuses & Shared Taxis to Victoria Falls
22 Shoprite Supermarket
23 Taxi Stand
26 Livingstone Museum; Crafts Shop
27 Tourist Centre
28 BP Petrol Station; Foley's 4X4 Hire
29 Total Petrol Station
32 Police
33 BP Petrol Station
35 Cyber Post; The Zambezi Swing
36 Nyami-Nyami Bureau de Change
38 Wild Side Tours & Safaris

doubles B&B US$26/31. The rooms, with bathroom and TV, are quiet and well furnished, but overpriced – the whole place is caught up in a 1960s time warp.

Places to Stay – Top End

Zambezi Sun & Royal Livingstone Hotel (e *intresv@sunint.co.za*) The only hotels on the Zambia side of Victoria Falls are the Zambezi Sun and the Royal Livingstone Hotel, both part of the South African Sun International chain. Both of these, along with 'The Falls' shopping and casino complex, occupy a 'resort area' inside the Mosi-

oa-Tunya National Park. The Zambezi Sun bills itself as a three-star hotel, and is large and unashamedly colourful with brazen over-the-top designs influenced by a medley of African images from classic Ndebele to contemporary Morrocan kasbah.

The opulent Royal Livingstone Hotel bills itself as five-star, and features colonial decor in the lounge, foyer and dining area. These brand new places were completed in mid-2001, and rates have yet to be fixed; if you're interested in staying there, it's best to book through a local travel agency, as special deals may be available.

Places to Eat

Zigzag Coffee House (☎ 324081, Mosi-oa-Tunya Rd) Breakfast US$2, coffee US$1.50, pizzas US$2, pancakes US$1. This is the best place for coffee, milkshakes, smoothies and cakes, and a small choice of snacks and light meals. It's relaxing to hang out here on the comfy chairs inside or sit under the umbrellas on the footpath. The window is a treasure trove of local information.

Funky Munky (☎ 320120, Mosi-oa-Tunya Rd) Small/large pizzas US$2.40/3, salads US$1.65, sandwiches from US$1.20. Open to 7.30pm daily. The service is friendly at this recommended place, and the choice of tasty burgers, pizzas, sandwiches and so on, is impressive.

Hippo's (behind Fawlty Towers, off Mosi-oa-Tunya Rd) This popular open-air restaurant-bar serves snacks and meals during the day, and a very good value buffet dinner every evening (US$5).

Pilgrim's (☎ 322692, Mosi-oa-Tunya Rd) Breakfast US$2.75-4, lunch US$2.75-4.50. Open 7am-5pm daily. Part of a plant nursery about 300m down the road from the Ngolide Lodge, Pilgrims is worth a walk or minibus/taxi trip. It specialises in morning and afternoon teas.

48 Hours Pub & Restaurant (Mosi-oa-Tunya Rd) Sandwiches US$1.70, burgers US$3.40, mains from US$4. Open 8.30am-late. During the day the outdoor seating is popular and the inside restaurant is quiet, although it offers a decent range of meals for good prices. In the evening, the restaurant morphs into a bar, and is a good place to drink if you're after a local ambience.

Laughing Dragon (☎ 097-846919, Mutelo St) Starters US$2.75, soups US$1.75, veg/meat dishes US$2.75/5. There is nothing fancy about Livingstone's only authentic Chinese restaurant, but it's good value especially if you choose a rice or noodle dish (about US$3.35).

Utsav Restaurant (☎ 322259, Mosi-oa-Tunya Rd) Mains US$3.50-4.50. Also known as 'Exciting Biting', this cosy and authentic Indian restaurant – complete with Hindi music – is worth a visit. Budget travellers can eat heartily with the 'backpacker special' (US$4), which includes rice, salad, two curries, naan and a soft drink (soda).

Self-caterers are best served by the *Shoprite supermarket* (just off Mosi-oa-Tunya Rd), which also has a bakery.

Entertainment

Step-Rite (off Mosi-oa-Tunya Rd) Admission US$0.50. This cheap outdoor bar serves drinks during the day and at night is a disco-cum-nightclub with live music most evenings. Some lowlifes hang around here at night so take a taxi home.

The Crown Bar (New Fairmount hotel) The Crown tries hard, with pool tables, international sports on TV and a disco (entry about US$1) most weekends, but (like the hotel) it seems to be living in the 1960s.

Hippo's (behind Fawlty Towers, off Mosi-oa-Tunya Rd) This is probably the most popular bar in town for tourists, travellers, and off-duty raft guides, with reasonable prices and good music.

Shopping

For quality souvenirs, go to *African Visions* (Mosi-oa-Tunya Rd) near Livingstone Adventure Centre. *The Crafts Shop* (Livingstone Museum) offers a large range of local handicrafts at good prices. *Zulu Net* (Mosi-oa-Tunya Rd) has a small but impressive array of batik fabrics and carvings at excellent prices. The *souvenir stalls* in the southwestern corner of Mukuni Park (prepare to negotiate) are a hassle-free place to browse.

Getting There & Away

Air Thanks to Zambia's booming tourism (Zimbabwe's loss is Zambia's gain...), Livingstone has two airports; the main one, 6km north of the town centre, was being upgraded to accommodate international flights. The 'old' airfield, nearer Victoria Falls, is the take-off site for helicopter and microlight flights.

Zambia Airways (☎ 097-794430, e roan hq@zamnet.zm) operates flights between Lusaka and Livingstone on Friday and Sunday (US$130/260, one way/return). Nationwide airlines (e livingstone@nationwide .co.za) plans to introduce a weekly flight

EXCURSION TO VICTORIA FALLS

to/from Johannesburg (Jo'burg) for about US$250 return. As neither airline currently has an office in Livingstone, contact South End Travel (☎ 320773, fax 322128), Liso House, Mosi-oa-Tunya Rd, for bookings.

Bus From the minibus terminal on Senanga Rd, just off Mosi-oa-Tunya Rd, minibuses leave when full for Lusaka (US$9, 6½ hours), via Choma (US$5, 2½ hours). Minibuses (US$0.60) and shared taxis (US$1) to Victoria Falls (on the Zambian side), and the Zambian immigration post, leave from the same spot.

At least one bus leaves daily for Sesheke (US$8, four to five hours), opposite Katima Mulilo, Namibia. The first one leaves anytime after 6am from the Maramba market bus station; cross the railway line, turn left past the police station and continue about 1km. (Note that this market sells just about anything imaginable, and is a great place to visit in its own right.) If you arrange it the day before, this bus will also call in at Jolly Boys, so you won't have to traipse out to Maramba. Some buses continue from Sesheke to the Namibian border at the Wenela ferry, which will save you a 4km walk or an expensive taxi ride.

Virgin Lux (also called CR Carriers) offers fast and comfortable buses four times a day to Lusaka (US$12.50, 5½ hours), via Choma (US$6.50, two hours), from along Mosi-oa-Tunya Rd. From the post office, the Euro-Africa Bus Services runs one daily Lusaka bus (fares are the same).

Train The *Zambezi Express* departs Livingstone for Lusaka (US$13/10.50/7.65/6 in sleeper/1st-class/standard/economy class, 15 hours) on Sunday, Tuesday and Thursday evening, and leaves Lusaka on Monday,

Wednesday and Friday evening. Schedules change often, so it's wise to phone the station (☎ 321001) for the latest info. The sleeper and 1st-class fares include bedding.

Getting Around
To/From the Airport The international airport, 6km from central Livingstone, is accessible by taxi (US$3).

Car Rental AJ Car Hire & Tours (☎ 322 090, ⓔ ajcarhire@zamnet.zm), Liso House, Mosi-oa-Tunya Rd, charges U$65 per day, plus petrol and insurance, for a Toyota Corolla. Livingstone 4x4 Hire (☎ 320888, fax 320887, ⓔ 4x4hire@zamnet.zm, ⓦ 222 .4x4hireafrica.com), Foley's Garage & BP Station, Mosi-oa-Tunya Rd, offers a four to five passenger Land Rover for US$75 per day (including unlimited kilometres and insurance), plus petrol, for local trips. The rates for longer trips start at US$120 per day (with unlimited kilometres and insurance), plus petrol.

Zambian rental vehicles can normally be driven into Zimbabwe (but not Botswana or Namibia); inform the hire company before leaving Zambia.

Taxi Taxis between Livingstone and the Zimbabwean border cost US$3.50, while share taxis charge from US$1.50 to US$2 per person.

Bicycle Most budget accommodation options rent mountain bikes to guests for about US$6/9 for a half/full day. This is a great way to get around – including trips over the border to Zimbabwe – but carry the receipt with you. See also the warning in the boxed text 'Over the Bridge & Into Zambia' earlier.

Language

BANTU & KHOISAN LANGUAGES

As a first language, most Namibians speak either a Bantu language – which would include Owambo, Herero and Caprivian languages – or a Khoisan language, which may be Khoi-Khoi (Nama), Damara, or a San dialect.

The Bantu language group includes eight dialects of Owambo; the official Owambo dialects are Kwanyama and Ndonga. In the Caprivi, the most widely spoken language is Lozi (or Rotsi), which originated in Barotseland in Zambia. Herero people (not surprisingly) speak Herero, a rolling melodious language, rich in colourful-sounding words.

Khoisan dialects are characterised by 'click' elements which make them difficult to learn, and only a few foreigners ever get the hang of them. Clicks are made by compressing the tongue against different parts of the mouth to produce different sounds.

Many native Khoisan speakers also speak at least one Bantu and one European language, normally Afrikaans. The language of the Damara people, who are actually of Bantu origin, is also a Khoisan dialect.

EUROPEAN LANGUAGES

The new constitution drawn up at the time of Namibian independence designated English as the official language. Although that may seem odd when, at the time, English was the native tongue of only about 2% of the population, it was decided that with English, all ethnic groups would be at equal disadvantage. Furthermore, it was recognised that adopting the language of international business would appeal to both tourists and investors.

On the other hand Afrikaans is also widely used, and although often dismissed as the language of apartheid, it's the first language of nearly 150,000 Namibians of diverse ethnic backgrounds, so it's unlikely to disappear any time soon. Most Namibian coloureds and Rehoboth Basters speak Afrikaans as a first language and only in the Caprivi is English actually preferred over Afrikaans as a lingua franca.

German is also widely spoken, but is the first language of only about 2% of people. In the far north, around Rundu and Katima Mulilo, you'll also hear a lot of Portuguese.

Afrikaans

Afrikaans pronunciation is comparatively straightforward. Its Germanic roots are evident in the characteristic guttural emphasis and the rolled 'r'. The following pronunciation guide includes sounds most likely to trouble native English speakers.

a	as the 'u' in 'pup'
e	as in 'ten'
i	as the 'e' in 'angel'
o	as the 'o' in fort, or 'oy' in 'boy'
u	as the 'e' in 'angel', but with lips pouted
r	rolled, as in Italian 'primo'
aai	as the 'y' in 'why'
ae	like 'ah'
ee	as in 'deer'
ei	as the 'ay' in 'play'
oe	as the 'oo' in 'loot'
oë	as the 'oe' in 'doer'
ooi	as the 'oy' in 'boy' preceded by 'w'
oei	as the 'ooey' in 'phooey', preceded by 'w'
ui	as the 'ay' in 'hay''
tj	as the 'ch' in 'chunk'

Greetings & Civilities

Hello.	*Hallo.*
Good morning.	*Goeiemôre.*
Good afternoon.	*Goeiemiddag.*
Good evening.	*Goeienaand.*
Good night.	*Goeienag.*
Please.	*Asseblief.*
Thank you.	*Dankie.*
How are you?	*Hoegaandit?*
Well, thank you.	*Goed dankie.*
Pardon.	*Ekskuus.*

Useful Words & Phrases

Yes.	*Ja.*
No.	*Nee.*
Maybe.	*Miskien.*
Sure.	*Sekerlik.*
What?	*Wat?*
How?	*Hoe?*
How many/much?	*Hoeveel?*
When?	*Wanneer?*
Where?	*Waar?*
Do you speak English/ Afrikaans?	*Praat u Engels/ Afrikaans?*
I only understand a little Afrikaans.	*Ek verstaan net 'n bietjie Afrikaans.*

Getting Around

travel	*reis*
arrival	*aankoms*
departure	*vertrek*
to	*na*
from	*van*
ticket	*kaartjie*
single	*enkel*
return	*retoer*

Around Town

art gallery	*kunsgalery*
avenue	*laan*
building	*gebou*
church	*kerk*
city centre	*middestad*
city	*stad*
enquiries	*navrae*
information	*inligting*

Signs – Afrikaans

Ingang	**Entrance**
Uitgang	**Exit**
Kamers Beskikbaar	**Rooms Available**
Vol/Geen Kamers Geskikbaar	**Full/No Vacancies**
Inligting	**Information**
Oop	**Open**
Toe/Gesluit	**Closed**
Polisie Stasie	**Police Station**
Toilet	**Toilets**
Man	**Men**
Vrou	**Women**

left	*links*
office	*kantoor*
on the corner	*op die hoek*
pharmacy/chemist	*apteek*
right	*regs*
road	*pad*
rooms	*kamers*
station	*stasie*
street	*straat*
tourist bureau	*toeristeburo*
town	*stad*

In the Country

bay	*baai*
beach	*strand*
caravan park	*woonwapark/ karavaanpark*
field/plain	*veld*
game reserve	*wildtuin*
hiking trail (short)	*wandelpad*
hiking trail (long)	*staproete*
marsh	*vlei*
mountain	*berg*
point	*punt*
river	*rivier*

Food & Drinks

beer	*bier*
bread	*brood*
cheese	*kaas*
cup of coffee	*koppie koffie*
dried and salted meat	*biltong*
farm sausage	*boerewors*
fish	*vis*
fruit	*vrugte*
glass of milk	*glas melk*
meat	*vleis*
vegetables	*groente*
wine	*wyn*

Time & Days

today	*vandag*
tomorrow	*mere*
yesterday	*gister*
daily	*daagliks*
public holiday	*openbare vakansiedag*
am	*vm*
pm	*nm*

Emergencies – Afrikaans

Help!	*Help!*
Call a doctor!	*Roep 'n doktor!*
Call the police!	*Roep die polisie!*
I'm lost.	*Ek is veloorer.*

Monday	*Maandag* (abbr *Ma*)
Tuesday	*Dinsdag (Di)*
Wednesday	*Woensdag (Wo)*
Thursday	*Donderdag (Do)*
Friday	*Vrydag (Vr)*
Saturday	*Saterdag (Sa)*
Sunday	*Sondag (So)*

Numbers

1	*een*
2	*twee*
3	*drie*
4	*vier*
5	*vyf*
6	*ses*
7	*sewe*
8	*agt*
9	*nege*
10	*tien*
11	*elf*
12	*twaalf*
13	*dertien*
14	*veertien*
15	*vyftien*
20	*twintig*
21	*een en twintig*
30	*dertig*
40	*veertig*
50	*vyftig*
60	*sestig*
70	*sewentig*
80	*tagtig*
90	*negentig*
100	*honderd*
1000	*duisend*

German

Owing to the country's colonial legacy, many Namibians speak German as a first or second language. It serves as the lingua franca in Swakopmund and is also widely used in Windhoek and Lüderitz.

Greetings & Civilities

Good day.	*Guten Tag.*
Goodbye.	*Auf Wiedersehen.*
Yes.	*Ja.*
No.	*Nein.*
Please.	*Bitte.*
Thank you.	*Danke.*
You're welcome.	*Bitte sehr/Bitte schön.*
Sorry. (excuse me, forgive me)	*Entschuldigung.*
Do you speak English?	*Sprechen Sie Englisch?*
How much is it?	*Wieviel kostet es?*

Getting Around

Where is the ...?	*Wo ist die ...?*
Go straight ahead.	*Gehen Sie geradeaus.*
Turn left.	*Biegen Sie links ab.*
Turn right.	*Biegen Sie rechts ab.*
near/far	*nahe/weit*
left luggage lockers	*Schliessfächer*
timetable	*Fahrplan*
bus stop	*Bushaltestelle*
train station	*Bahnhof (Bf)*

Around Town

a bank	*eine Bank*
the ... embassy	*die ... Botschaft*
the market	*der Markt*
the newsagent	*der Zeitungshändler*
the pharmacy	*die Apotheke*
the post office	*das Postamt*
the tourist office	*das Verkehrsamt*
What time does it open/close?	*Um wieviel Uhr macht es auf/zu?*

Time, Days & Numbers

What time is it?	*Wie spät ist es?*
today	*heute*
tomorrow	*morgen*
yesterday	*gestern*
in the morning	*morgens*
in the afternoon	*nachmittags*

Monday	*Montag*
Tuesday	*Dienstag*
Wednesday	*Mittwoch*
Thursday	*Donnerstag*
Friday	*Freitag*
Saturday	*Samstag/Sonnabend*
Sunday	*Sonntag*

0	null
1	eins
2	zwei/zwo
3	drei
4	vier
5	fünf
6	sechs
7	sieben
8	acht
9	neun
10	zehn
11	elf
12	zwölf
13	dreizehn
100	hundert
1000	tausend

| one million | eine Million |

Owambo

Owambo (Oshiwambo) – and specifically the Kwanyama dialect – is the first language of more Namibians than any other and also the language of the ruling SWAPO party. As a result, it's spoken as a second or third language by many non-Owambo Namibians of both Bantu and Khoisan origin.

Greetings & Civilities

Good morning.	Wa lalapo.
Good evening.	Wa tokelwapo.
How are you?	Owu li po ngiini?
I'm fine.	Ondi li nawa.
Yes.	Eeno.
No.	Aawe.
Please.	Ombili.
Thank you.	Tangi.
Do you speak English?	Oho popi Oshiingilisa?
How much is this?	Ingapi tashi kotha?
Excuse me.	Ombili manga.
I'm sorry.	Onde shi panda.

Getting Around

Where is the ...?	Openi pu na ...?
here	mpaka
there	hwii
near	popepi
far	kokule
this way	no onkondo
that way	ondjila
Turn right.	Uka kohulyo.
Turn left.	Uka kolumoho.
I'm lost.	Ombili, onda puka.
Can you please help me?	Eto vuluwu pukulule ndje?

Time, Days & Numbers

yesterday	ohela
today	nena
tomorrow	ongula

Monday	Omaandaha
Tuesday	Etiyali
Wednesday	Etitatu
Thursday	Etine
Friday	Etitano
Saturday	Olyomakaya
Sunday	Osoondaha

1	yimwe
2	mbali
3	ndatu
4	ne
5	ntano
6	hamano
7	heyali
8	hetatu
9	omugoyi
10	omulongo

Herero/Himba

The Herero and Himba languages are quite similar, and will be especially useful when travelling around remote areas of north central Namibia and especially the Kaokoveld, where Afrikaans remains a lingua franca and few people speak English.

Greetings & Civilities

Hello.	Tjike.
Good morning.	Wa penduka.
Good afternoon.	Wa uhara.

Good evening.	*Wa tokerua.*
Good night.	*Ongurova ombua.*
Yes.	*Ii.*
No.	*Kako.*
Please.	*Arikana.*
Thank you.	*Okuhepa.*
How are you?	*Kora?*
Well, thank you.	*Mbiri naua, okuhepa.*
Pardon.	*Makuvi.*

What?	*Onguae?*
How?	*Vi?*
How many?	*Vi ngapi?*
When?	*Rune?*
Where?	*Pi?*

Do you speak ...?	*U hungira ...?*
Afrikaans	*Otjimburu*
English	*Otjingirisa*
Herero	*Otjiherero*
Himba	*Otjihimba*
Owambo	*Otjiwambo*

Getting Around

travel	*ouyenda*
arrival	*omeero*
departure	*omairo*
to	*ko*
from	*okuza*
single (one way)	*ourike*
return	*omakotokero*
ticket	*okatekete*

In the Country

caravan park	*omasuviro uo zo karavana*
game reserve	*orumbo ro vipuka*
hiking trail (short)	*okaira komakaendro uo pehi (okasupi)*
hiking trail (long)	*okaira ko makaendero uo pehi (okare)*
marsh	*eheke*
mountain	*ondundu*
point	*onde*
river (channel)	*omuramba*

Time, Days & Numbers

today	*ndinondi*
tomorrow	*muhuka*
yesterday	*erero*

Emergencies – Herero/Himba

Help!	*Vatera!*
Call a doctor!	*Isana onganga!*
Call the police!	*Isana oporise!*
I'm lost.	*Ami mba pandjara.*

Monday	*Omandaha*
Tuesday	*Oritjaveri*
Wednesday	*Oritjatatu*
Thursday	*Oritjaine*
Friday	*Oritjatano*
Saturday	*Oroviungura*
Sunday	*Osondaha*

1	*iimue*
2	*imbari*
3	*indatu*
4	*iine*
5	*indano*
6	*hamboumue*
7	*hambomabari*
8	*hambondatu*
9	*imuvyu*
10	*omurongo*

Damara/Nama

The very similar dialects of the Damara and Nama peoples, whose traditional lands take in most of Namibia's wildest desert regions, belong to the Khoisan group of languages.

As with the San dialects (see following), they feature several 'click' elements, which are created by slapping the tongue against the teeth, palate or side of the mouth. These are normally represented by exclamation points, !, single or double slashes, / and // and a vertical line crossed by two horizontal lines, ‡.

Greetings & Civilities

Hello.	*!Gâi tses.*
Good morning	*!Gâi-//oas.*
Good evening	*!Gâi-!oes.*
Good bye.	*!Gâise hâre.*
(to a person staying)	
Good bye.	*!Gâise !gûre.*
(to a person leaving)	
Yes.	*I.*
No.	*Hâ-â.*

Please.	*Toxoba.*
Thank you.	*Aio.*
Excuse me.	*‡Anba tere.*
Sorry/Pardon.	*Mati.*
How are you?	*Matisa?*
I am well.	*!Gâi a.*
Do you speak English?	*Engelsa !khoa idu ra?*
What is your name?	*Mati du /onhâ?*
My name is ...	*Ti /ons ge a ...*

Useful Words & Phrases

Where is the ...?	*Mapa...hâ?*
Go straight.	*‡Khanuse ire.*
Turn left.	*//Are /khab ai ire.*
Turn right.	*//Am /khab ai ire.*
far	*!nu a*
near	*/gu a*
What time is it?	*Mati ko /laexa i?*
today	*nets*
tomorrow	*//ari*
I'd like ...	*Tage ra ‡khaba ...*
How much?	*Mati ko?*
market	*‡kharugu*
shop	*!khaib*
small	*‡khariro*
large	*kai*

Animals

baboon	*//arub*
dog	*arib*
elephant	*‡khoab*
giraffe	*!naib*
goat	*piri*
horse	*hab*
hyaena	*‡khira*
leopard	*/garub*
lion	*xami*
monkey	*/norab*
rabbit	*!oâs*
rhino	*!nabas*
warthog	*gairib*
zebra	*!goreb*

Numbers

1	*/gui*
2	*/gam*
3	*!nona*
4	*haka*
5	*kore*

6	*!nani*
7	*hû*
8	*//khaisa*
9	*khoese*
10	*disi*
50	*koro disi*
100	*/oa disi*
1000	*/gui /oa disi*

!Kung San

The click-ridden languages of Namibia's several San groups are surely among the world's most difficult for outsiders to learn. Perhaps the most useful dialect is that of the !Kung people, who in Namibia are concentrated in Eastern Bushmanland.

In normal speech, the language features four different clicks (lateral, palatal, dental and labial), which in Namibia are usually represented by **//**, **‡**, **/**, and **!**, respectively. However, a host of other orthographies are in use around the region, and clicks may be represented as 'nx', 'ny', 'c', 'q', 'x', '!x', '!q', 'k', 'zh', and so on. To simplify matters, in the very rudimentary phrase list that follows, all clicks are represented by '!k' (locals will usually forgive you for ignoring the clicks and using a 'k' sound instead).

Greetings & Civilities

Hello.	*!Kao.*
Good morning.	*Tuwa.*
Good-bye, go well.	*!King se !kau.*
How are you? (to m/f)	*!Ka tseya/tsiya?*
Thank you (very much).	*(!Kin)!Ka.*
What is your name? (to m/f)	*!Kang ya tsedia/ tsidia?*
My name is ... (m/f)	*!Kang ya tse/tsi ...*

Lozi

Lozi is the most common Caprivian dialect, and is spoken through much of the Caprivi region, especially around Katima Mulilo.

Greetings & Civilities

Hello. *Eeni, sha.* (to anybody)
Lumela. (to a peer)
Mu lumeleng' sha.
(to one or more persons of higher social standing)

Goodbye. *Siala foo/Siala hande/ Siala sinde.* (to a peer)
Musiale foo/ Musiale hande/Musiale sinde. (to more than one peer or one or more persons of higher social standing)

Good morning *U zuhile.* (to a peer)
Mu zuhile. (to more than one peer or one or more persons of higher social standing)

Good afternoon/ *Ki manzibuana.* (to evening.* anybody)
U tozi. (to a peer)
Mu tozi. (to one or more persons of higher social standing)

Good night. *Ki busihu.* (to anybody)

Please. *Sha.* (only used to people of higher social standing)

Thank you. *N'itumezi.*
Excuse me. *Ni swalele.* (informal)
Mu ni swalele. (polite)
Thank you very *N'i tumezi hahulu.* much.

Useful Words & Phrases

Yes. *Ee.* (to a peer)
Eeni. (to more than one peer or one or more persons of higher social standing

Add *sha* at the end to mean sir or madam.

No. *Awa.* (to a peer or peers)
Batili. (to one or more persons of higher social standing)

Do you speak *Wa bulela sikwa?* (to English? peers)
W'a utwa sikwa? (to more than one peer or one or more persons of higher standing)
Mw'a bulela sikwa?
Mw'a utwa sikwa?

I don't understand. *Ha ni utwi.*

What is your name? *Libizo la hao ki wena mang'?* (to peer)
Libizo la mina ki mina bo mang'? (to a person of higher social standing)

What is this? *Se king'?*
What is that? *S'ale king'/Ki sika (far away) mang's'ale?*
Where? *Kai?*
Here. *Fa/Kafa/Kwanu*
(Over) there. *F'ale/Kw'ale*
Why? *Ka baka lang'/Kauli?*
How much? *Ki bukai?*
enough/finish *Ku felile*

Time & Numbers

What time is it? *Ki nako mang'?*
today *kachenu*
tomorrow *kamuso kakusasasa* (early morning) or *ka mamiso*
tomorrow *kamuso*
yesterday *mabani*

1	*il'ingw'i*
2	*z'e peli* or *bubeli*
3	*z'e t'alu* or *bulalu*
4	*z'e ne* or *bune*
5	*z'e keta-lizoho*
6	*z'e keta-lizoho ka ka li kang'wi*
7	*supile*
10	*lishumi*
20	*mashumi a mabeli*
1000	*likiti*

Setswana

The language of the Tswana people is pronounced more or less as it's written. Two exceptions are **g**, which is pronounced as English 'h' or, more accurately, as a strongly aspirated 'g', and **th**, which is pronounced as a slightly aspirated 't'.

Greetings & Civilities

Hello.	*Dumêla mma/rra.*
(to woman/man)	
Hello.	*Dumêlang.*
(to group)	
Hello!	*Ko ko!*
(announcing your arrival outside a yard or house)	
Goodbye.	*Tsamaya sentle.*
(to person leaving)	
Goodbye.	*Sala sentle.*
(to person staying)	
Yes.	*Ee.*
No.	*Nnyaa.*
Please.	*Tsweetswee.*
Thank you.	*Kea leboga.*
Excuse me/Sorry.	*Intshwarele.*
Pardon me.	*Ke kopa tsela.*
	(lit: 'I want road.')
OK/No problem.	*Go siame*
Do you speak English?	*A o bua Sekgoa?*
Does anyone speak English?	*A go na le o o bua Sekgoa?*
I understand.	*Ke a tlhaloganya.*
I don't understand.	*Ga ke tlhaloganye.*
How much is it?	*Ke bokae?*

Getting Around

Which way is ...?	*Tsela ... e kae?*
Can you show me on the map ...?	*A o mpotshe mo mepeng?*
Is it far?	*A go kgala?*
Go straight ahead.	*Thlamalala.*
Turn left.	*Chikela mo molemong.*
Turn right.	*Chikela mo mojeng.*
near	*gaufi*
far	*kgakala*

Time, Days & Numbers

What time is it?	*Ke nako mang?*
today	*gompieno*
tomorrow	*ka moso*
tonight	*bosigong jono*
yesterday	*maabane*
next week	*beke e e tlang*
afternoon	*tshogololo*
night	*bosigo*

Monday	*mosupologo*
Tuesday	*labobedi*
Wednesday	*laboraro*
Thursday	*labone*
Friday	*latlhano*
Saturday	*matlhatso*
Sunday	*tshipi*

0	*lefela*
1	*bongwe*
2	*bobedi*
3	*borara*
4	*bone*
5	*botlhano*
6	*borataro*
7	*bosupa*
8	*borobabobedi*
9	*boroba bongwe*
10	*lesome*
20	*masome a mabedi*
30	*masome a mararo*
40	*masome a mane*
50	*masome a matlhano*
60	*masome amarataro*
70	*masome a supa*
80	*masome a a robang bobedi*
90	*masome a a robang bongwe*
100	*lekgolo*
1000	*sekete*

one million	*sedikadike*

Emergencies – Setswana

Help!	*Nthusa!*
Call a doctor.	*Bitsa ngaka.*
Call the police.	*Bitsa mapodisi.*
Leave me alone!	*Ntlhogela!*
I'm lost.	*Ke la tlhegile.*

Glossary

Although English is widely spoken in Namibia, native speakers from Australasia, North America and the UK will notice that many words have developed different meanings locally. There are also a number of unusual terms that have been borrowed from Afrikaans, Portuguese or indigenous languages.

In African English, repetition for emphasis is common: something that burnt you would be 'hot hot'; fields after the rains would be 'wet wet'; a crowded minibus with no more room is 'full full', and so on.

ablutions block – camping ground building with toilets, showers and a washing-up area; also known as an amenities block.

ANC – African National Congress; ruling party in South Africa

apartheid – literally 'separate development of the races'; a political system in which people are officially segregated according to their race

ATV – all-terrain vehicle

bakkie – utility or pick-up truck; pronounced 'bucky'

barchan dunes – migrating crescent-shaped sand dunes

Basarwa – *Batswana* name for the San people

Batswana – the citizens of Botswana

bilharzia – disease caused by blood flukes (parasitic flatworms) that are transmitted by freshwater snails

biltong – a normally delicious dried meat that can be anything from beef to kudu or ostrich

boerewors – Afrikaner farmer's sausage

boomslang – dangerous 2m-long snake that likes to hang out in trees

braai – barbecue; a Southern African institution that usually features loads of meat grilled on a special stand (called a *braaivleis*)

bushveld – flat grassy plain covered in thorn scrub

cassper – South African National Defence Forces *(SANDF)* armoured vehicle

CDM – Consolidated Diamond Mines

chilli bites – spicy *biltong*, seasoned with *peri-peri*

cuca shops – small bush shops of northern Namibia; named for an Angolan beer that was once sold there

dagga – marijuana; pronounced 'dakha'

dam – what other English-speakers would call a reservoir

dam wall – what other English-speakers would call a dam

dolfhout – wild teak

donkey boiler – This sounds cruel but it actually has nothing to do with donkeys; it's a water tank positioned over fire and used to heat water for showers or other purposes.

drankwinkel – literally 'drink shop', an off-licence or bottle store

drift – river ford

DTA – Democratic Turnhalle Alliance

dumpi – a 375ml bottle of beer

Dutchman – term of abuse for an Afrikaner man

efundja – period of heavy rainfall in northern Namibia

eh – all-purpose ending to sentences, even very short ones, such as 'Thanks, eh'. (Canadians, you're not alone!)

ekipa – traditional medallion historically worn by Owambo women as a sign of wealth and status

eumbo – immaculate Owambo *kraal*; very much like a small village enclosed within a pale fence

euphorbia – several species of cactus-like succulents

4WD – four-wheel drive, locally known as 4x4 (four-by-four); similarly, 2WD is known as 2x4 (two-by-four)

game – applies to all large, wild four-footed creatures

Gemütlichkeit – a distinctively German atmosphere of comfort and hospitality
GPS – global positioning system; device that identifies local latitude and longitude coordinates by taking readings from satellites
GRN – Government of the Republic of Namibia, hence the green GRN number plates

IMF – International Monetary Fund
inselberg – isolated range or hill typical of the pro-Namib and Damaraland plains
Izzit? – rhetorical question that most closely translates as 'Really' and is used without regard to gender, person or number of subjects. Therefore, it could mean 'Is it?', 'Are you?', 'Is he?', 'Are they?', 'Is she?', 'Are we?' etc. Also, 'How izzit?', for 'How's it going?'.

jesse – dense, thorny scrub, normally impenetrable to humans
jol – party, both verb and noun
jugendstil – German Art-Nouveau architecture prevalent in Swakopmund and parts of Windhoek and Lüderitz
just now – refers to some time in the future but implies a certain degree of imminence; it could be half an hour from now or two days from now

karakul – variety of Central-Asian sheep that is known for its high-grade wool and pelts
Khoisan – language grouping taking in all Southern African indigenous languages, including *San* and Khoi-Khoi (or *Nama*), as well as the language of the Damara (a Bantu people who speak a Khoi-Khoi dialect)
kimberlite pipe – geological term for a type of igneous intrusion, in which extreme heat and pressure have turned coal into diamonds
kloof – ravine or small valley
koeksesters – small, gooey Afrikaner doughnuts, dripping in honey or sugar syrup
kokerboom – quiver tree; grows mainly in southern Namibia
konditorei – German pastry shop; found in larger Namibian towns

kopje – pronounced 'koppie'; a small hill, often just a pile of boulders on an otherwise flat plain
kraal – Afrikaans version of the Portuguese word '*curral*'; either an enclosure for livestock, a fortified village of mud huts, or an Owambo homestead

lapa – circular area with a firepit, used for socialising
lekker – pronounced 'lakker'; anything that's good, nice or tasty
location – Namibian and South African name for *township*

mahango – millet; a staple of the Owambo diet and used for brewing a favourite alcoholic beverage
makalani – see *vegetable ivory*
make a plan – to sort things out; this saying can refer to anything from working out a complicated procedure to skirting around bureaucracy
marimba – African xylophone, made from strips of resonant wood with various-sized gourds for sound boxes
mealie pap – Afrikaans name for maize-meal porridge; a staple food for most Namibians
MET – Namibia's Ministry of Environment & Tourism
miombo – dry open woodland, comprised mostly of acacia and/or mopane or similar *bushveld* vegetation
mokoro – dugout canoe propelled by a poler who stands in the stern; plural *mekoro*
mopane worms – the caterpillar of the moth Gonimbrasiabelina, these lovely larval delicacies are available in mopane trees and Namibian markets
morgen – unit of land measurement used by early Boer farmers, equal to about 1.25 hectares

Nacobta – Namibian Community-Based Tourism Association group, which organises community-based amenities for tourists, such as rest camps and tours of traditional areas.
Nama – popular name for Namibians of Khoi-Khoi, Topnaar or Baster heritage

!nara – type of melon that grows in the Namib Desert; a dietary staple of the Topnaar Khoi-Khoi people

nartjie – tasty local tangerine; pronounced 'narkie'

NDF – Namibian Defence Forces, the Namibian military

NGO – nongovernmental organisation

n!oresi – traditional San lands; literally 'lands where one's heart is'

now now – definitely not now, but sometime sooner than *just now*

NWR – Namibian Wildlife Resorts; semi-private overseer of visitor facilities in Namibia's national parks

nxum – the 'life force' of the San people's tradition

omaeru – soured milk; a dietary staple of the Herero people

omuramba – fossil river channel, normally between long, vegetated sand dunes; plural *omiramba*

omulilo gwoshilongo – 'sacred fire' that serves as a shrine in each Owambo *eumbo*; a log of mopane that is kept burning around the clock

oshana – dry river channel in northern Namibia and north-western Botswana

oshikundu – tasty alcoholic beverage made from *mahango*; popular throughout traditional areas of northern Namibia

padrão – tribute to a royal patron, erected by early Portuguese navigators along the African coast

pan – dry flat area of grassland or salt deposits, often a seasonal lake bed

panveld – area containing many pans

participation safari – an inexpensive safari in which clients pitch their own tents, pack the vehicle and share cooking duties

Peace Corps – USA volunteer organisation

peg – milepost

peri-peri – very hot pepper sauce of Portuguese/Angolan origin

photographic safari – safari in which participants carry cameras rather than guns

plus-minus – meaning 'about', eg, 'The bus will come in plus-minus 10 minutes.'

potjie – pronounced 'poy-kee', a three-legged pot used to make stew over an open fire. The word also refers to the stew itself, as well as a gathering in which a potjie forms the main dish.

pronking – four-legged leaping, as done by some antelope (particularly springboks), apparently for the sheer fun of it

robot – not R2-D2, it's just a traffic light

rondavel – a round hut, which is often thatched

rooibos – literally 'red bush' in Afrikaans; an insipid herbal tea that reputedly has therapeutic qualities

RSA – Republic of South Africa

rubber duck – inflatable boat

rusks – solid bits of biscuit-like bread made edible by immersion in tea or coffee

San – language-based name for indigenous people of Bushman heritage

SANDF – South African National Defence Force

seif dunes – prominent linear sand dunes, as found in the Central Namib Desert

self-catering – term applied at lodges and rest camps where guests cook their own meals

shandy – refreshing mixed drink comprising lemonade, soda water and angostura bitters over ice; in one variation, the 'sneaky puff adder', vodka replaces the soda water

shebeen – illegal drinking establishment-cum-brothel

shongololo – ubiquitous giant millipede

Sperrgebiet – 'closed area'; alluvial diamond region of south-western Namibia

strandlopers – literally 'beach walkers'; term used to describe the ancient inhabitants of the Central Namib Desert, who may have been ancestors of the San or Nama peoples

Swapo – South-West Africa People's Organization; Namibia's liberation army and the ruling political party

tackies – trainers, sneakers, tennis shoes, gym shoes etc

toasties – a Namibian term for toasted sandwiches

toktokkie – Afrikaans for the fog-basking *tenebrionid* beetle, *Onomachris unguicularis*

township – indigenous suburb; generally a high-density black residential area

toxic sludge – disgusting mixed drink comprised of tequila or vodka combined with brandy or schnapps and hot cherry jelly (that's jello, for those in the USA). To drink one is a badge of honour; fortunately, it hasn't spread outside of Southern Africa.

trypanosomiasis – sleeping sickness; disease transmitted by the bite of the tsetse fly

tsama – bitter desert melon historically eaten by the San people; it's also eaten by livestock

Unesco – United Nations Education, Scientific and Cultural Organisation

Unita – União pela Independência Total de Angola; National Union for the Total Independence of Angola

Uri – desert-adapted vehicle that is produced in Namibia

UTC – Universal Time Co-ordinate (formerly GMT); the time at the prime meridian at Greenwich, UK

van der Merwe – archetypal Boer country bumpkin who is the butt of jokes throughout Southern Africa

vegetable ivory – fruit of the *makalani* palm *(Hyphaene petersiana)*; hard white nut used for carvings and known in Herero as *ozonduka*, and in Damara as *!uinida*

veld – open grassland, normally in plateau regions

veldskoens – comfortable bush shoes of soft leather, similar to moccasins; sometimes called *vellies*

vetkoek – literally 'fat cake'; an Afrikaner doughnut

vlei – pronounced 'flay'; any low open landscape, sometimes marshy

VSO – Volunteer Service Overseas

wag 'n bietjie – literally 'wait-a-bit'; Afrikaans for the buffalo thorn tree

watu – Kavango dugout canoe, used on rivers and in the wetlands of north-eastern Namibia

welwitschia – cone-bearing shrub *(Welwitschia mirabilis)* native to the northern Namib plains

Thanks

Many thanks to all the travellers who wrote to us with helpful hints, useful advice and interesting anecdotes:

Martin Abel, Robert Ablett, Ben Ackland, Marc Adams, Giancarlo Albis, Sandy Aldridge, Guy Alexander, Julie Alexander, Miguel Alvim Gonzalez, Sam Amssoms, J Anderson, Tarek Andres, Michelle Anesbury, Leigh Anne Walton, Mike Appleton, Keira Armstrong, Mike Arron, Lisa Arthur, Malcolm Arthur, Ally Asselman, Jeremy & Laurie Baig, Jamie Baldwin, Claire Barnes, Tiffany Barry, Richard Bartlett, Liz Bayley, Claudine Beers, Jerry Bell, Bennett, Mario Biagioni, Gavin Biggs, Annemarie Binns, Steve Bolnick, H Book, Ruth Borden, Jason Borthwick, Greg Bos, Chantal Boulle, Bob & Anne Bown, Lucienne Braam, Andrew Bracken, Bob & Sally Brennand, Carolyn Brewer, Annemarie Britz, Alastair Brodie, David Brokensha, Ian Broughton, S & A Broughton, Stephanie Brownbridge, Alex Brownlie, N K Bryant, Cristiano Burmester, Rev R Butler, Kristen J Cadman, Markella Callimassia, Hayley Cameron, Iain Cameron, Jamie Cara-Southey, Tim Care, Bryony Carne, Richard Carr, Monica & Miguel Casviner, Yvonne Chaddendale, Francois Chassing, David Chiapasco, Davide Chiapasco, Mike Clark, Jeanette Clayton, Mike Clyne, Matthew Coghlan, Ilan Cohen, Juan Colmenar Rueda, Laurel Colton, Andrea Condiescu, Barb Connellan, Robin Connolly, Tristan Cooper, Phillipe Cornelis, Brenda & Barry Cottle, Elizabeth & John Cox, Dr Donald Cramer, Wendy Crawford, Andrew Cripps, Jody Culham, Jennifer Cullins, Uwe Danapel, Gareth Dart, Claas Daun, Robert de Beaugrande, Walter De Boeck, Hilary Dean-Hughes, Rob Delacour, Richard Desomme, C Dieffenbacher, K van Dorenmalen, Tamsen Douglass Love, Ben Druss, Rick Duchscher, Annemiek Duijvesteijn, Wendy Easen, Rob Edmiston, Gerd & Birgit Eggert, Magnus Eriksen, Joanne Everall, Tanja & Steven Faber, Bernard Farjounel, Carol Faulkes, Enid Fidler, Joey & Dianne Field, Victor Fiorillo, Cathy Fischer, Julie Fisher, Pat Fitzgerald, Olivia Flynn, Marjolyn Fohhe, Robert Foitzik, Carla Foolen, Yannick Fortin, Majorie Foster, Stephen Foster, Stephane Foucaud, Brian Freestone, Ingmar Frei, Isobel Frisken, Tanja Frohlich, Fern Fromey, Dengue Fver, Carolina Galt, Majolijn & von Oliver Garczynski, Colin Gardiner, Beverly Garland, Rob Garner, Christine Gascoyne, Dr Ruth Gasser, Matthew Gavin MD, Malcolm & Penny Gee, Marco Giangualano, Peter Ginn, Ulrich Gisser, Richard & Vanessa Good, Belinda & Richard Gordon, Rinda Gordon, Michael Graf, Will Graham, Kevin Green, Stefan Grosse, Peter G Gubbins, Doug & Martha Guerrant, Jeff Gunn, Luke Haas, Sally Hagen, Walter Hager, Andrew Halliday, Mark Harding, Andrea Harold, Robin Hartle, Charles Hartwig, Ruth Harvey, Sue Haskins, Marten Hasselbom, Phillip & Patricia Haupt, Michael Hauser, Ruth Hayward, Ted Hearn, Angela Heidrich, Melanie Hempel, Mark Hemsley, Joan Henderson, Lutz Hensel, Sarah Hilding, Richard Hipstroff, Joan Hoff, William Hofmeyr, M Hofstetter, Milena Holcova, M J Holden, Jenny Holman, Peter Holmes, Christine Holtschoppen, Yael Hoogland, Roaxanne Hosford, James Howson, Mat Hrubey, F C Hubbard, Rachel Hunter, Corey Innes, Gustaaf Isebaert, Tom Ivancic, Mette Jacobsgaard, Bridgett James, Lenka Janecek, M Janink-Wegeneeys, Leanne & Derek Janzen, Tim Jenkins, Peter Johnson, Peta Jones, Simon & Helen Jones, Bo Jonsson, Jacqui Kadey, Steffi Kahl, Dirk Kascher, Leanne Kaufman, Eileen Kawola, Kathleen & John Kay, Peter Kelly, Christoph Kessel, Philip Kestelman, Maren Kirchoff, Maria Klambauer, Amy Klinke, Petter Konig, Ans Koot, Vera Kotz, Geeske & Ewan Kouwenhoven, Anne Kristiansen, George & Gary Kroese, Fred Krueger, Steffi Kubenka, Joachim Kuhnapfel, Philippe Kulig, Anne Kusttenhill-Lowe, Wiebke Laasch, Eileen Lacey, A R Lalloo, Elizabeth Lamond, Chris Lanyon, Bob Larcher, Sally & George Larson, Fabrizio Lazzeri, Rebecca Lee, Felix C Leung, Mrs & Mrs M Levy, Cameron Lindsay, Matt Link, Bob Lipske, Michele Lischi, Lawrie Little, Andrea Lobbecke, Paolo Lolli, E Lotz, Harris Lucas, Sarah Lunn, Iain Mackay, Michael Magee, Gabrielle Malnati, Andrew Maltman, Algars Manor, Steve Marcus, P D & S Y Markham, Helen

Marsh, Sally & David Martin, Anna Maspero, Lucy Masterson, Paul Matthys, L Mazel, Louis Mazel, Errol McCullough, Trevor McDonald, Charles McFeely, E E McKinney, J F McLaren, Monica McLean, Heather McNeice, Colin McVey, Enrico Meeuwsen, Arjen van de Merve, Johanna Meter, Maria & Lorenzo Micheletta, Daniela Migliorati, Edith Millan, David Miller, Paul Miller, Simon Miller-Cranko, Greg Minns, Heather Mitchell, Steve Mitchell, Amanda Mohabir, Alison Momeyer, Val & Paul de Montille, Jess Moore, Rosa Ma Moratonas Daunis, Cynara Mori, Larry Moulton, Eric & Michelle Mueller, Birgit Muhr, Christo Muller, Elaine & Russell Murdoch, Dan Nadel, Zohar Navou, Berhard Niebaum, Jurgen Nijs, Teresa Nolan, Boerma Nooiji, Mark Nowak, Charlotte Nutt, Anna Nylund, Felicitas Ochotta, Heilke Ohlenbusch, Anja Onderwater, Brad Ottens, O B Oussoren, Paul Parke, Owen Parnell, Wendy Parnell, J M & M H Parton, Agnes Peeters, David Pennels, Diane Perdon, Nina Persson, Jeffrey Pestrak, Corinna Peters, Sue Phillip, Ges Pierrot, Monica & Vittorio Pietri, Janet & Guy Pinneo, Ryan Pittman, Linda Poel, Reijco van de Pol, Nancy Pole-Wilhite, Huibert Poot, Nash Prebtani, J Prince, Michael V Prollius, Harold Prow, Peter Puemans, Peter Puttemans, Philippe Quix, Charles Radcliffe, Jeff Randall, Pat Rapley, P A Reavley, Tom Renders, Geoff Renner, Graham Richards, Yvonne Richards, Matthew Richardson, Richard A Riegels, Matthias Ripp, Kevin Roach, Brittany Rogers, John Rolph, Kerstin Rosen, Florian Roser, Norberto Rosetti, Valerie Ross, Sandy Roth, Marian Rothman, Andrea Russell, Dr Cameron Ryan, Donncha & Karen Ryder, M Sabatier, Will Sam, Ellie Sandercock, Andreas Sandler, Barbara Sawyer, Maja Schaap, Don Schenck, Jens M Scherpe, Lisa Schipper, Frank Schmidt, Reinhard Schmidt, Maja Schmitt, Sebastian Schmitz, Frederic Schneider, Wade & Fran Schroeder, Holger Schulze, Sebastian Schwertner, Dr P R Scott, Shetal Shah, Trish Shalloe, Julie Sheard, Burley & Irene Shepard, Latham Shinder, Andrew Silk, Tom Silverside, Katie Sim, Oliver Simon, Heidi Simons, Rowena & Barry Simpson, Kristian Skjerning-Kyed, Chris Smaje, Terry Smit, Craig Smith, D Smith, Mary Smith, Matthew Smith, Peter & Anne Smith, Russell Smith, T J Smith, Joost & Conny Snoep, Luis Spain, E Spanjaard, Tim Spicer, Marilyn Staib, Pascal Stauble, Annick Stenman, Colin Stevenson, Helen Steward, Tracy Stewart, Willemke Stilma, Elise Stray, Amy Sumner, David Swabey, M F Tang, Lynette Tapper, Ruth Taylor, David & Evonne Templeton, Bas Tensen, Theo Theune, Huw Thomas, N Thompson, David Thomson, Oliver Thornton, Gerald Tieleboerger, Kerry Tiley, Jessima Timberlake, Matt Todd, Sally Tong, Alex & Becca Tostevin, Dominic Turnbull, Pauline Ubels, Dave Unger, Johann Vaatz, Will van Baars, Floris van Eijk, Marieke van Schaik, Andrew Van Smeerdijk, Inge van Spran, Vera Vandervelde, Jan Venema, Nico Verloop, J D R Vernon, Jose Verweij-Hoogendijk, Family Vesentini, Trine Viken Sumstad, Tomaz Vizintin, Arlinde Vletter, Martin von Knorre, Dr Alexander J de Voogt, Tracey & Mike Vopni, Martin & Margaret Wakalin, B J Wakefield, E & D Wakefreed, Charles Wale, Jane & Graham Walker, A C Ward, H Weenen-Swaan, Wolfgang Wegener, Suzanne Wehl, Ulli Weinreich, Janie M West, Clare White, Welby Whiting, Marc van der Wielen, Sally Wilde, Edward Willem Spiegel, Adrian Williams, Barbara & Grant Williams, Samantha Williamson, David Willis, John Wilmut, Alexander Winter, Keith Wood, Mark Worthington, Ulf Wortmann, Melanie Wright, Zhou Yu, Pat Veldhuijzen van Zanten, Barry Zeve, David & Paula Zilbart, Daniella Zipkin

Lonely Planet Guides by Region

onely Planet is known worldwide for publishing practical, reliable and no-nonsense travel information in our guides and on our Web site. The Lonely Planet list covers just about every accessible part of the world. Currently there are 16 series: Travel guides, Shoestring guides, Condensed guides, Phrasebooks, Read This First, Healthy Travel, Walking guides, Cycling guides, Watching Wildlife guides, Pisces Diving & Snorkeling guides, City Maps, Road Atlases, Out to Eat, World Food, Journeys travel literature and Pictorials.

AFRICA Africa on a shoestring • Botswana • Cairo • Cairo City Map • Cape Town • Cape Town City Map • East Africa • Egypt • Egyptian Arabic phrasebook • Ethiopia, Eritrea & Djibouti • Ethiopian Amharic phrasebook • The Gambia & Senegal • Healthy Travel Africa • Kenya • Malawi • Morocco • Moroccan Arabic phrasebook • Mozambique • Namibia • Read This First: Africa • South Africa, Lesotho & Swaziland • Southern Africa • Southern Africa Road Atlas • Swahili phrasebook • Tanzania, Zanzibar & Pemba • Trekking in East Africa • Tunisia • Watching Wildlife East Africa • Watching Wildlife Southern Africa • West Africa • World Food Morocco • Zambia • Zimbabwe, Botswana & Namibia
Travel Literature: Mali Blues: Traveling to an African Beat • The Rainbird: A Central African Journey • Songs to an African Sunset: A Zimbabwean Story

AUSTRALIA & THE PACIFIC Aboriginal Australia & the Torres Strait Islands •Auckland • Australia • Australian phrasebook • Australia Road Atlas • Cycling Australia • Cycling New Zealand • Fiji • Fijian phrasebook • Healthy Travel Australia, NZ & the Pacific • Islands of Australia's Great Barrier Reef • Melbourne • Melbourne City Map • Micronesia • New Caledonia • New South Wales • New Zealand • Northern Territory • Outback Australia • Out to Eat – Melbourne • Out to Eat – Sydney • Papua New Guinea • Pidgin phrasebook • Queensland • Rarotonga & the Cook Islands • Samoa • Solomon Islands • South Australia • South Pacific • South Pacific phrasebook • Sydney • Sydney City Map • Sydney Condensed • Tahiti & French Polynesia • Tasmania • Tonga • Tramping in New Zealand • Vanuatu • Victoria • Walking in Australia • Watching Wildlife Australia • Western Australia
Travel Literature: Islands in the Clouds: Travels in the Highlands of New Guinea • Kiwi Tracks: A New Zealand Journey • Sean & David's Long Drive

CENTRAL AMERICA & THE CARIBBEAN Bahamas, Turks & Caicos • Baja California • Belize, Guatemala & Yucatán • Bermuda • Central America on a shoestring • Costa Rica • Costa Rica Spanish phrasebook • Cuba • Cycling Cuba • Dominican Republic & Haiti • Eastern Caribbean • Guatemala • Havana • Healthy Travel Central & South America • Jamaica • Mexico • Mexico City • Panama • Puerto Rico • Read This First: Central & South America • Virgin Islands • World Food Caribbean • World Food Mexico • Yucatán
Travel Literature: Green Dreams: Travels in Central America

EUROPE Amsterdam • Amsterdam City Map • Amsterdam Condensed • Andalucía • Athens • Austria • Baltic States phrasebook • Barcelona • Barcelona City Map • Belgium & Luxembourg • Berlin • Berlin City Map • Britain • British phrasebook • Brussels, Bruges & Antwerp • Brussels City Map • Budapest • Budapest City Map • Canary Islands • Catalunya & the Costa Brava • Central Europe • Central Europe phrasebook • Copenhagen • Corfu & the Ionians • Corsica • Crete • Crete Condensed • Croatia • Cycling Britain • Cycling France • Cyprus • Czech & Slovak Republics • Czech phrasebook • Denmark • Dublin • Dublin City Map • Dublin Condensed • Eastern Europe • Eastern Europe phrasebook • Edinburgh • Edinburgh City Map • England • Estonia, Latvia & Lithuania • Europe on a shoestring • Europe phrasebook • Finland • Florence • Florence City Map • France • Frankfurt City Map • Frankfurt Condensed • French phrasebook • Georgia, Armenia & Azerbaijan • Germany • German phrasebook • Greece • Greek Islands • Greek phrasebook • Hungary • Iceland, Greenland & the Faroe Islands • Ireland • Italian phrasebook • Italy • Kraków • Lisbon • The Loire • London • London City Map • London Condensed • Madrid • Madrid City Map • Malta • Mediterranean Europe • Milan, Turin & Genoa • Moscow • Munich • Netherlands • Normandy • Norway • Out to Eat – London • Out to Eat – Paris • Paris • Paris City Map • Paris Condensed • Poland • Polish phrasebook • Portugal • Portuguese phrasebook • Prague • Prague City Map • Provence & the Côte d'Azur • Read This First: Europe • Rhodes & the Dodecanese • Romania & Moldova • Rome • Rome City Map • Rome Condensed • Russia, Ukraine & Belarus • Russian phrasebook • Scandinavian & Baltic Europe • Scandinavian phrasebook • Scotland • Sicily • Slovenia • South-West France • Spain • Spanish phrasebook • Stockholm • St Petersburg • St Petersburg City Map • Sweden • Switzerland • Tuscany • Ukrainian phrasebook • Venice • Vienna • Wales • Walking in Britain • Walking in France • Walking in Ireland • Walking in Italy • Walking in Scotland • Walking in Spain • Walking in Switzerland • Western Europe • World Food France • World Food Greece • World Food Ireland • World Food Italy • World Food Spain **Travel Literature:** After Yugoslavia • Love and War in the Apennines • The Olive Grove: Travels in Greece • On the Shores of the Mediterranean • Round Ireland in Low Gear • A Small Place in Italy

Lonely Planet Mail Order

L onely Planet products are distributed worldwide. They are also available by mail order from Lonely Planet, so if you have difficulty finding a title please write to us. North and South American residents should write to 150 Linden St, Oakland, CA 94607, USA; European and African residents should write to 10a Spring Place, London NW5 3BH, UK; and residents of other countries to Locked Bag 1, Footscray, Victoria 3011, Australia.

INDIAN SUBCONTINENT & THE INDIAN OCEAN Bangladesh • Bengali phrasebook • Bhutan • Delhi • Goa • Healthy Travel Asia & India • Hindi & Urdu phrasebook • India • India & Bangladesh City Map • Indian Himalaya • Karakoram Highway • Kathmandu City Map • Kerala • Madagascar • Maldives • Mauritius, Réunion & Seychelles • Mumbai (Bombay) • Nepal • Nepali phrasebook • North India • Pakistan • Rajasthan • Read This First: Asia & India • South India • Sri Lanka • Sri Lanka phrasebook • Tibet • Tibetan phrasebook • Trekking in the Indian Himalaya • Trekking in the Karakoram & Hindukush • Trekking in the Nepal Himalaya • World Food India **Travel Literature:** The Age of Kali: Indian Travels and Encounters • Hello Goodnight: A Life of Goa • In Rajasthan • Maverick in Madagascar • A Season in Heaven: True Tales from the Road to Kathmandu • Shopping for Buddhas • A Short Walk in the Hindu Kush • Slowly Down the Ganges

MIDDLE EAST & CENTRAL ASIA Bahrain, Kuwait & Qatar • Central Asia • Central Asia phrasebook • Dubai • Farsi (Persian) phrasebook • Hebrew phrasebook • Iran • Israel & the Palestinian Territories • Istanbul • Istanbul City Map • Istanbul to Cairo • Istanbul to Kathmandu • Jerusalem • Jerusalem City Map • Jordan • Lebanon • Middle East • Oman & the United Arab Emirates • Syria • Turkey • Turkish phrasebook • World Food Turkey • Yemen **Travel Literature:** Black on Black: Iran Revisited • Breaking Ranks: Turbulent Travels in the Promised Land • The Gates of Damascus • Kingdom of the Film Stars: Journey into Jordan

NORTH AMERICA Alaska • Boston • Boston City Map • Boston Condensed • British Columbia • California & Nevada • California Condensed • Canada • Chicago • Chicago City Map • Chicago Condensed • Florida • Georgia & the Carolinas • Great Lakes • Hawaii • Hiking in Alaska • Hiking in the USA • Honolulu & Oahu City Map • Las Vegas • Los Angeles • Los Angeles City Map • Louisiana & the Deep South • Miami • Miami City Map • Montreal • New England • New Orleans • New Orleans City Map • New York City • New York City City Map • New York City Condensed • New York, New Jersey & Pennsylvania • Oahu • Out to Eat – San Francisco • Pacific Northwest • Rocky Mountains • San Diego & Tijuana • San Francisco • San Francisco City Map • Seattle • Seattle City Map • Southwest • Texas • Toronto • USA • USA phrasebook • Vancouver • Vancouver City Map • Virginia & the Capital Region • Washington, DC • Washington, DC City Map • World Food New Orleans **Travel Literature:** Caught Inside: A Surfer's Year on the California Coast • Drive Thru America

NORTH-EAST ASIA Beijing • Beijing City Map • Cantonese phrasebook • China • Hiking in Japan • Hong Kong & Macau • Hong Kong City Map • Hong Kong Condensed • Japan • Japanese phrasebook • Korea • Korean phrasebook • Kyoto • Mandarin phrasebook • Mongolia • Mongolian phrasebook • Seoul • Shanghai • South-West China • Taiwan • Tokyo • Tokyo Condensed • World Food Hong Kong • World Food Japan **Travel Literature:** In Xanadu: A Quest • Lost Japan

SOUTH AMERICA Argentina, Uruguay & Paraguay • Bolivia • Brazil • Brazilian phrasebook • Buenos Aires • Buenos Aires City Map • Chile & Easter Island • Colombia • Ecuador & the Galapagos Islands • Healthy Travel Central & South America • Latin American Spanish phrasebook • Peru • Quechua phrasebook • Read This First: Central & South America • Rio de Janeiro • Rio de Janeiro City Map • Santiago de Chile • South America on a shoestring • Trekking in the Patagonian Andes • Venezuela **Travel Literature:** Full Circle: A South American Journey

SOUTH-EAST ASIA Bali & Lombok • Bangkok • Bangkok City Map • Burmese phrasebook • Cambodia • Cycling Vietnam, Laos & Cambodia • East Timor phrasebook • Hanoi • Healthy Travel Asia & India • Hill Tribes phrasebook • Ho Chi Minh City (Saigon) • Indonesia • Indonesian phrasebook • Indonesia's Eastern Islands • Java • Lao phrasebook • Laos • Malay phrasebook • Malaysia, Singapore & Brunei • Myanmar (Burma) • Philippines • Pilipino (Tagalog) phrasebook • Read This First: Asia & India • Singapore • Singapore City Map • South-East Asia on a shoestring • South-East Asia phrasebook • Thailand • Thailand's Islands & Beaches • Thailand, Vietnam, Laos & Cambodia Road Atlas • Thai phrasebook • Vietnam • Vietnamese phrasebook • World Food Indonesia • World Food Thailand • World Food Vietnam

ALSO AVAILABLE: Antarctica • The Arctic • The Blue Man: Tales of Travel, Love and Coffee • Brief Encounters: Stories of Love, Sex & Travel • Buddhist Stupas in Asia: The Shape of Perfection • Chasing Rickshaws • The Last Grain Race • Lonely Planet ... On the Edge: Adventurous Escapades from Around the World • Lonely Planet Unpacked • Lonely Planet Unpacked Again • Not the Only Planet: Science Fiction Travel Stories • Ports of Call: A Journey by Sea • Sacred India • Travel Photography: A Guide to Taking Better Pictures • Travel with Children • Tuvalu: Portrait of an Island Nation

LONELY PLANET

You already know that Lonely Planet produces more than this one guidebook, but you might not be aware of the other products we have on this region. Here is a selection of titles that you may want to check out as well:

South Africa, Lesotho & Swaziland
ISBN 1 86450 322 X

Southern Africa
ISBN 0 86442 662 3

Botswana
ISBN 1 74059 041 4

East Africa
ISBN 0 86442 676 3

Cape Town
ISBN 0 86442 759 X

Zambia
ISBN 1 74059 045 7

Africa on a shoestring
ISBN 0 86442 663 1

Read This First: Africa
ISBN 1 86450 066 2

Watching Wildlife Southern Africa
ISBN 1 86450 035 2

Cape Town City Map
ISBN 1 86450 076 X

Southern Africa Road Atlas
ISBN 1 86450 101 4

Healthy Travel Africa
ISBN 1 86450 050 6

Zimbabwe
ISBN 1 74059 043 0

Available wherever books are sold

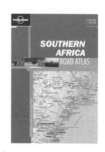

Index

Abbreviations

Text

Boxed Text

MAP LEGEND

CITY ROUTES

Freeway	Freeway
Highway	Primary Road
Road	Secondary Road
Street	Street
Lane	Lane
	On/Off Ramp

	Unsealed Road
	One Way Street
	Pedestrian Street
	Stepped Street
	Tunnel
	Footbridge

REGIONAL ROUTES

	Tollway, Freeway
	Primary Road
	Secondary Road
	Unsealed Road

BOUNDARIES

	International
	State
	Disputed
	Fortified Wall

TRANSPORT ROUTES & STATIONS

	Train
	Ferry
	Walking Trail

	Walking Tour
	Path
	Pier or Jetty

HYDROGRAPHY

	River; Creek
	Rapids
	Waterfalls
	Spring/Watering Hole
	Dry Watering Hole

	Lake
	Dry Lake
	Salt Lake
	Swamp
	Windmill/Bore

AREA FEATURES

	Building
	Park, Gardens

	Market
	Sports Ground

	Beach
	Cemetery

	Campus
	Rock

POPULATION SYMBOLS

CAPITAL	National Capital
CAPITAL	State Capital

CITY	City
Town	Town

Village	Village
	Urban Area

MAP SYMBOLS

	Airfield; Airport		Embassy/Consulate		Mine		Pub or Bar
	Bank		Golf Course		Monument		Ruins
	Bird Sanctuary		Hospital		Mountain		Shelter
	Border Crossing		Information		Museum		Shipwreck
	Bus Station/Stop		Internet Cafe		National Park		Shopping Centre
	Camping Area		Kraal		Parking		Stately Home
	Caravan Park		Lookout		Petrol		Taxi Rank
	Cave		Place to Eat		Picnic Area		Telephone
	Church		Place to Stay		Police Station		Tourist Information
	Cinema		Point of Interest		Post Office		Wildlife Sanctuary; Game Reserve

Note: not all symbols displayed above appear in this book

LONELY PLANET OFFICES

Australia
Locked Bag 1, Footscray, Victoria 3011
☎ 03 8379 8000   fax 03 8379 8111
email: talk2us@lonelyplanet.com.au

USA
150 Linden St, Oakland, CA 94607
☎ 510 893 8555   TOLL FREE: 800 275 8555
fax 510 893 8572
email: info@lonelyplanet.com

UK
10a Spring Place, London NW5 3BH
☎ 020 7428 4800   fax 020 7428 4828
email: go@lonelyplanet.co.uk

France
1 rue du Dahomey, 75011 Paris
☎ 01 55 25 33 00   fax 01 55 25 33 01
email: bip@lonelyplanet.fr
www.lonelyplanet.fr

World Wide Web: www.lonelyplanet.com or AOL keyword: lp
Lonely Planet Images: lpi@lonelyplanet.com.au